GIMP 2.6

USER GUIDE

GIMP 2.6

USER GUIDE

*The online documentation for the
GNU Image Manipulation Program.
Now in printed form!*

Waking Lion Press

ISBN 978-1-4341-0331-4

The manual itself is available online here:
http://docs.gimp.org/en/

Published by Waking Lion Press, an imprint of the Editorium:
www.wakinglionpress.com
Neither of these has any affiliation with Gimp or the GNU Project.
Waking Lion Press™ and the Editorium™ are trademarks of the Editorium, LLC, West Valley City, UT, 84128

GNU Image Manipulation Program

User Manual

Copyright © 2002, 2003, 2004, 2005, 2006, 2007 The GIMP Documentation Team

COLLABORATORS

	TITLE :		REFERENCE :
	GNU Image Manipulation Program		

ACTION	NAME	DATE	SIGNATURE
WRITTEN BY		July 26, 2007	

REVISION HISTORY

NUMBER	DATE	DESCRIPTION	NAME
$Revision: 1985 $	2007-07-15		romanofski

Contents

Preface

User Manual Authors and Contributors

Content Writers William Skaggs, Ćedric Gémy, Julien Hardelin, Raymond Ostertag, Mel Boyce, Daniel Egger, Róman Joost, Oliver Ellis

Graphics, Stylesheets Jakub Steiner, Róman Joost, Daniel Egger

Build System, Technical Contributions Sven Neumann, Michael Natterer, Henrik Brix Andersen, Daniel Egger, Thomas Schraitle, Chris Hübsch, Axel Wernicke

Project Maintenance Róman Joost, Daniel Egger

Part I

Getting started

Chapter 1

Introduction

1.1 Welcome to the GIMP

The GIMP is a multiplatform photo manipulation tool. GIMP is an acronym for GNU Image Manipulation Program. The GIMP is suitable for a variety of image manipulation tasks, including photo retouching, image composition, and image construction.

It has many capabilities. It can be used as a simple paint program, an expert quality photo retouching program, an online batch processing system, a mass production image renderer, an image format converter, etc.

GIMP is expandable and extensible. It is designed to be augmented with plug-ins and extensions to do just about anything. The advanced scripting interface allows everything from the simplest task to the most complex image manipulation procedures to be easily scripted.

One of The GIMP's strengths is its free availability from many sources for many operating systems. Most GNU/Linux distributions include The GIMP as a standard application. The GIMP is also available for other operating systems such as Microsoft Windows or Apple's Mac OS X (Darwin). The GIMP is a Free Software application covered by the General Public License (GPL license). The GPL provides users with the freedom to access and alter the source code that makes up computer programs.

1.1.1 Authors

The first version of the GIMP was written by Peter Mattis and Spencer Kimball. Many other developers have contributed more recently, and thousands have provided support and testing. GIMP releases are currently being orchestrated by Sven Neumann and Mitch Natterer and many other people called the GIMP-Team.

1.1.2 The GIMP-Help system

The GIMP Documentation Team and other users have provided you with the information necessary to understand how to use The GIMP. The User Manual is an important part of this help. The current version is on the web site of the Documenation Team in HTML format. The HTML version is also available as context sensitive help (if you installed it) while using GIMP by pressing the **F1** key. Help on specific menu items can be accessed by pressing the **F1** key while the mouse pointer is focused on the menu item. Read on to begin your GIMP journey.

1.1.3 Features and Capabilities

The following list is a short overview of some of the features and capabilities which GIMP offers you:

- A full suite of painting tools including brushes, a pencil, an airbrush, cloning, etc.

- Tile-based memory management, so image size is limited only by available disk space

- Sub-pixel sampling for all paint tools for high-quality anti-aliasing

- Full Alpha channel support for working with transparency

- Layers and channels

- A procedural database for calling internal GIMP functions from external programs, such as Script-Fu

- Advanced scripting capabilities

- Multiple undo/redo (limited only by disk space)

- Transformation tools including rotate, scale, shear and flip

- File formats supported include GIF, JPEG, PNG, XPM, TIFF, TGA, MPEG, PS, PDF, PCX, BMP and many others

- Selection tools including rectangle, ellipse, free, fuzzy, bezier and intelligent

- Plug-ins that allow for the easy addition of new file formats and new effect filters

1.2   What's New in GIMP?

GIMP 1.0 evolved gradually into the very stable and widely used 1.2 release. Three years later, as the GIMP development came closer to the next stable release, they decided that the level of fundamental change to the inner workings of the program justified calling the new stable version 2.0. GIMP 2.0.0 was released on March 23, 2004. For GIMP 2.2, the developers aimed at a short cycle, adding a number of important features that did not require instability-inducing low level changes. GIMP 2.2.0 was released on December 19, 2004. This section briefly describes the new features that were added in GIMP 2.2, as well as the features that were introduced in GIMP 2.0. If you are interested in the history of GIMP you are welcome to read Appendix A.

Here is a brief summary of some of the most important new features introduced in GIMP 2.2. There are many other smaller changes that long-time users will notice and appreciate (or complain about!). There are also important changes at the level of plug-in programming and script-fu creating that are not covered here.

1.2.1   Interoperability and Standards Support

- You can drag-and-drop or copy-and-paste image data from the GIMP to any application which supports image/png drops (currently Abiword and Kword at least) and image/xml+svg drops (Inkscape supports this one). So you can copy-and-paste curves into the GIMP from Inkscape, and then drag a selection into Abiword to include it inline in your document.

- Patterns can now be any supported GtkPixbuf format, including png, jpeg, xbm and others.

- GIMP can load gradients from SVG files, and palettes from ACT and RIFF files.

- Drag-and-drop support has been extended. You can now drop files and URIs onto an image window, where they will be opened in the existing image as new layers.

Note
Please note, that Drag and Drop will not work for Apple Mac OS X between GIMP and the finder. This is due to a lack of functionality on Apples X11.app

1.2.2   Shortcut Editor

You can now edit your shortcuts in a dedicated dialog, as well as continue to use the little-known dynamic shortcuts feature (which has been there since 1.2).

1.2.3   Plug-in Previews

We have provided a standard preview widget for plug-in authors which greatly reduces the amount of code required to support previews. David Odin has integrated this widget into all the current filters, so that now many more filters in the GIMP include a preview which updates in real time, and the various previews behave much more consistently.

1.2.4   Real-Time Previews of Transform Operations

The transform tools (shear, scale, perspective and rotate) can now show a real-time preview of the result of the operation when the tool is in 'Traditional' mode. Previously, only a transforming grid was shown.

1.2.5   GNOME Human Interface Guide Conformance

A lot of work has been done on making the GIMP's interface simpler and more usable for newcomers. Most dialogs now follows the GNOME HIG to the best of our knowledge. In addition, dialogs have separated out or removed many 'Advanced' options, and replaced them with sane defaults or hidden them in an expander.

1.2.6   GTK+ 2.4 Migration

- Menus use the GtkUIManager to generate menu structure dynamically from XML data files.

- A completely revamped File Chooser is used everywhere in the GIMP for opening or saving files. The best thing about it is that it lets you create a set of 'bookmarks', making it possible to navigate quickly and easily to commonly used directories.

- GIMP now supports fancy ARGB cursors when they are available on the system.

1.2.7   Basic Vector Support

Using the GFig plug-in, the GIMP now supports the basic functionality of vector layers. The GFig plug-in supports a number of vector graphics features such as gradient fills, Bezier curves and curve stroking. It is also the easiest way to create regular or irregular polygons in the GIMP. In the GIMP 2.2, you can create GFig layers, and re-edit these layers in GFig afterwards. This level of vector support is still quite primitive, however, in comparison to dedicated vector-graphics programs such as Inkscape.

1.2.8   Also . . .

There are many other smaller user-visible features. A rapid-fire list of some of those features is below.

- It is now possible to run the GIMP in batch mode without an X server.

- We have a GIMP binary (GIMP-console) which is not linked to GTK+ at all.

- Improved interface for extended input devices

- Editable toolbox: You can now decide which tools should be shown in the Toolbox, and their order. In particular, you can add any or all of the Color Tools to the Toolbox if you wish to.

- Histogram overlays R, G and B histograms on the Value histogram, and calculates the histogram only for the contents of the selection.

- Shortcuts are now shared across all GIMP windows.

Chapter 2

Fire up the GIMP

2.1 Running GIMP

Most often, you start GIMP either by clicking on an icon (if your system is set up to provide you with one), or by typing **gimp** on a command line. If you have multiple versions of the GIMP installed, you may need to type **gimp-2.2** to get the latest version. You can, if you want, give a list of image files on the command line after the program name, and they will automatically be opened by GIMP as it starts. It is also possible, though, to open files from within GIMP once it is running.

In most operating systems, you can set things up so that various types of image files are 'associated' with GIMP, and cause it to start automatically when icons for them are double-clicked.

 Tip If you want to cause a certain file type to automatically open in GIMP, you should associate it with 'gimp-remote' ('gimp-win-remote' under Windows) rather than with 'gimp'. The gimp-remote program is an auxiliary that comes with gimp. If gimp is not already running on the system when gimp-remote is executed, it is started and the image given as argument to gimp-remote is loaded. If gimp is already running, though, the image is simply loaded into the already-running program.

2.1.1 Known Platforms

The GIMP is the most widely supported image manipulation available today. The platforms that The GIMP is known to work on include:

GNU/Linux, Apple Mac OS X (Darwin), Microsoft Windows 95, 98, Me, XP, NT4, 2000, OpenBSD, NetBSD, FreeBSD, Solaris, SunOS, AIX, HP-UX, Tru64, Digital UNIX, OSF/1, IRIX, OS/2 and BeOS.

The GIMP can easily be ported to other operating systems because of its source code availability.

2.1.2 Language

All being well, GIMP detects the system language. This may fail on some machines and you may want use another language. It is possible to change the language:

Linux *In LINUX*: in console mode, type LANGUAGE=en gimp or LANG=en gimp replacing en by fr, de, ... according to the language you want. Background: By using LANGUAGE=en you're setting an environment variable for the executed program gimp here.

Windows XP Control Panel/System/ Advanced/"Environment" button/ In "System Variables" area: "Add" button: Enter LANG for Name and fr or de... for Value. Watch out! You have to click on three successive "OK" to validate your choice.

If you often change language, you can create a batch file. Open NotePad. Type the following commands (for french for instance):

```
set lang=fr
cd c:\Program Files\GIMP-2.0\bin
GIMP-2.2.exe
```

Save this file as GIMP-FR.BAT (or another name, but always with a .BAT extension. Create shortcut and drag it to your desktop.

Windows ME Start/Programs/ Accessories/System Tools/System Informations/Tools/System Configuration Utility/"Environment" tab/"New" button: Enter LANG for Name and fr or de... for Value.

Windows 95/Windows 98 *Under Window 95 and Windows 98*, add the line `set lang=en` in the 'C:\autoexec.bat' file.

Apple Mac OS X Go to System Preferences, click on the International icon, and in the Language tab, the desired language should be the first in the list.

2.1.3 Command Line Arguments

Ordinarily you don't need to give any arguments when starting GIMP, but here is a list of some that may at one time or anther be useful. This is not a complete list; on Unix systems you can get a complete list by running `man gimp` in a terminal window.

-h, --help Display a list of all commandline options.

-v, --version Print the version of GIMP being used, and exit.

--verbose Show detailed startup messages.

-d, --no-data Do not load patterns, gradients, palettes, or brushes. Often useful in non-interactive situations where startup time is to be minimized.

--display *display* Use the designated X display (does not apply to GIMP on Microsoft Windows).

-s, --no-splash Do not show the splash screen while starting.

--session *name* Use a different `sessionrc` for this GIMP session. The given session name is appended to the default `sessionrc` filename.

-g, --gimprc *gimprc* Use an alternative `gimprc` instead of the default one. The `gimprc` file contains a record of your preferences. Useful in cases where plugins paths or machine specs may be different.

-c, --console-messages Do not popup dialog boxes on errors or warnings. Print the messages on the console instead.

-b, --batch *commands* Execute the set of commands non-interactively. The set of commands is typically in the form of a script that can be executed by one of the GIMP scripting extensions. When commands is –, the commands are read from standard input.

2.2 Starting GIMP the first time

The first time you run GIMP, it goes through a series of steps to set up options and directories. This process creates a subdirectory of your home directory called `.gimp-2.2`. All of the information about the choices you make here goes into that directory. If you later remove that directory, or rename it as something like `.gimp-2.2.bak`, then the next time you start GIMP, it will go through the whole setup sequence again, creating a new `.gimp-2.2` directory. You can exploit this if you want to explore the effect of different choices without destroying your existing installation, or if you have screwed things up so badly that your existing installation needs to be nuked.

For the most part, setting up GIMP is very easy, and you can just accept the defaults at each step, and possibly adjust things later using the Preferences dialog. The main thing you might want to give a little thought to at the start is the amount of memory to allocate for GIMP's tile cache.

Here is a walk-through of the setup process:

1. Since this window mentions the GNU General Public License you know it is truly a Welcome dialog you are entering into. Also, note the 'Continue' button. GIMP does not even ask that you agree to it, merely whether you want to continue. Feel free to press the continue button.

Figure 2.1: Welcome

The Welcome screen

2. The purpose of this screen is only to make the user aware of the GIMP personal settings directory, subdirectories and files creation process, before it begins. You just have to have a look and click to proceed.

Figure 2.2: Personal GIMP Directory

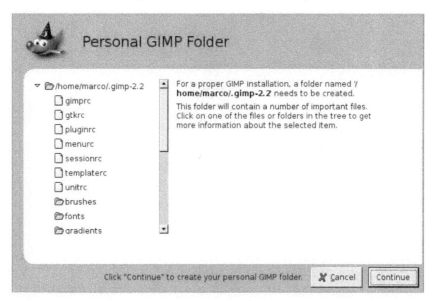

The Personal Directory screen

3. This window shows you the files that GIMP will create. It will have some complaints if you told it to install some place that it don't have permission to be. There is a scroll bar to see all the things GIMP has created for you.

Figure 2.3: User Installation Log

The User Installation Log screen.

4. Setting your memory usage is not an easy thing. So much depends on what your needs are for the GIMP and what hardware you have to work with. You have two options at this point. Go with the default value the developers have set here, or determine the best value. A brief tile-cache explanation. might help you determine this value. The tile-cache information might also be helpful to you if you are encountering memory problems when using the GIMP.

On a Unix system, /tmp might be a good place for the swap.

Figure 2.4: GIMP Performance Tuning

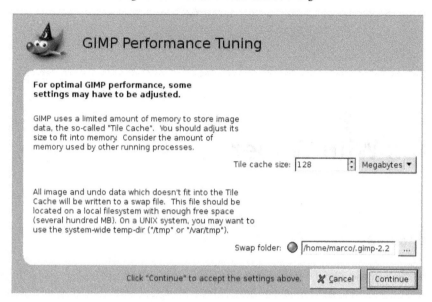

The User Performance Tuning screen

Finally . . . So now you have GIMP installed and configured, and are ready to go. Just a couple of suggestions before you start, though: First, when you run GIMP, by default it shows a "tip" each time it starts up. These tips tell you things that are very useful but not easy to learn by experimenting, so they are worth paying attention to. If you find it too distracting to look at them each time you start, you can disable them; but please go through them when you have the chance: for your convenience, you can read them at any time using the menu command Help → Tips. Second, if at some point you are trying to do something, and GIMP seems to have suddenly stopped functioning, the section Getting Unstuck may help you out. Happy Gimping!

Chapter 3

First Steps With Wilber

3.1 Basic Concepts

This section is intended to give you a brief introduction to the basic concepts and terminology you will need to understand in order to make sense of the rest of the documentation. Everything here is explained in much greater depth elsewhere. With a few exceptions, we have avoided cluttering this section with a lot of links and cross-references: everything mentioned here is so high-level that you should easily be able to locate it in the index.

Images Images are the basic entities that GIMP works with. Roughly speaking, an 'image' corresponds to a single file, such as a TIFF or JPEG file. You can also think of an image as corresponding to a single display window, but this is not quite correct: it is possible to have multiple windows all displaying the same image. It is not possible to have a single window display more than one image, though, or for an image to have no window displaying it.

A GIMP image may be quite a complicated thing. Instead of thinking of it as something like a sheet of paper with a picture on it, you should think of it as more like a book, whose pages are called 'layers' In addition to a stack of layers, a GIMP image may contain a selection mask, a set of channels, and a set of paths. In fact, GIMP provides a mechanism for attaching arbitrary pieces of data to an image, as which are called 'parasites'

In GIMP, it is possible to have many images open at the same time. If they are large, each image may use many megabytes of memory, but GIMP uses a sophisticated tile-based memory management system that allows it to handle even very large images gracefully. There are, however, limits, and it is usually beneficial when working with images to put as much memory into your system as possible.

Layers If an image is like a book, then a layer is like a page within the book. The simplest images only contain a single layer, and can be treated like single sheets of paper, but sophisticated GIMP users often deal with images containing many layers, even dozens of them. Layers need not be opaque, and they need not cover the entire extent of an image, so when you look at an image's display, you may see more than just the top layer: you may see elements of many layers.

Channels In GIMP Channels are the smallest units of subdivision in the stack of layers from which the image is constructed. Every Channel in a layer has exactly the same size as the layer it belongs to and consequently consists of the same pixels. Every pixel can be regarded as a container which can be filled with a value ranging from 0 to 255. The exact meaning of this value depends on the type of channel, e.g. in the RGB color model the value in the R-channel means the amount of red which is added to the colour of the different pixels, in the selection channel the value denotes how strong the pixels are selected and in the alpha channel the values denote how transparent the corresponding pixels are.

Selections Often when you do something to an image, you only want a part of it to be affected. The 'selection' mechanism makes this possible. Each image has its own selection, which you normally see as a moving dashed line separating the selected parts from the unselected parts (the so-called 'marching ants'). Actually this is a bit misleading: selection in GIMP is really graded, not all-or-nothing, and really the selection is represented by a full-fledged grayscale channel. The dashed line that you normally see is simply a contour line at the 50%-selected level. At any time, though, you can visualize the selection channel in all its glorious detail by toggling the QuickMask button.

A large component of learning how to use GIMP effectively is acquiring the art of making good selections—selections that contain exactly what you need and nothing more. Because selection-handling is so centrally important, GIMP gives you a large number of tools for doing it: an assortment of selection-making tools, a menu of selection operations, and the ability to switch to Quick Mask mode, in which you can treat the selection channel as though it were a color channel, thereby 'painting the selection'

Undoing When you make mistakes, you can undo them. Nearly everything you can do to an image is undoable. In fact, you can usually undo a substantial number of the most recent things you did, if you decide that they were misguided. GIMP makes this possible by keeping a history of your actions. This history consumes memory, though, so undoability is not infinite. Some actions use very little undo memory, so that you can do dozens of them before the earliest ones are deleted from this history; other types of actions require massive amounts of undo memory. You can configure the amount of memory GIMP allows for the undo history of each image, but in any situation, you should always be able to undo at least your 2-3 most recent actions. (The most important action that is not undoable is closing an image. For this reason, GIMP asks you to confirm that you really want to close the image if you have made any changes to it.)

Plug-ins Many, probably most, of the things you do to an image in GIMP are done by the GIMP application itself. However, GIMP also makes extensive use of 'plug-ins' which are external programs that interact very closely with GIMP, and are capable of manipulating images and other GIMP objects in very sophisticated ways. Many important plug-ins come packaged together with GIMP, but there are also many available by other means. In fact, the ability to write plug-ins (and scripts) is the easiest way for people not on the GIMP development team to add new capabilities to GIMP.

All of the commands in the Filters menu, and a substantial number of commands in other menus, are actually implemented by plug-ins.

Scripts In addition to plug-ins, which are programs written in the C language, GIMP can also make use of scripts. The largest number of existing scripts are written in a language called Script-Fu, which is special to GIMP (for those who care, it is a dialect of the Lisp-like language called Scheme). It is also possible to write GIMP scripts in Python or Perl. These languages are more flexible and powerful than Script-Fu; their disadvantage is that they depend on software that does not automatically come packaged with GIMP, so they are not guaranteed to work correctly in every GIMP installation.

3.2 Main Windows

Figure 3.1: The screenshot illustrates the standard windows of GIMP

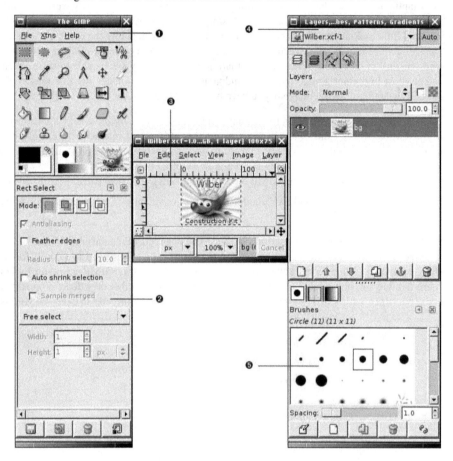

The screenshot above shows the most basic arrangement of GIMP windows that can be used effectively. Three windows are shown:

① *The Main Toolbox:* This is the heart of the GIMP. It contains the highest level menu, plus a set of icon buttons that can be used to select tools, and more.

② *Tool options:* Docked below the main Toolbox is a Tool Options dialog, showing options for the currently selected tool (in this case, the Rectangle Select tool).

③ *An image window:* Each image open in GIMP is displayed in a separate window. Many images can be open at the same time: the limit is set only by the amount of system resources. It is possible to run GIMP without having any images open, but there are not very many useful things to do then.

④ *Layers Dialog:* This dialog window shows the layer structure of the currently active image, and allows it to be manipulated in a variety of ways. It is possible to do a few very basic things without using the Layers dialog, but even moderately sophisticated GIMP users find it indispensible to have the Layers dialog available at all times.

⑤ *Brushs/Patterns/Gradients:* The docked dialog below the layer dialog shows the dialogs for managing brushes, patterns and gradients.

This is a minimal setup. There are over a dozen other types of dialogs used by GIMP for various purposes, but users typically create them when they are needed and close them when they are not. Knowledgeable users generally keep the Toolbox (with Tool Options) and Layers dialog around at all times. The Toolbox is essential to many GIMP operations; in fact, if you close it, GIMP will exit. (You are asked to confirm that you want to do this, though.) The Tool Options are actually a separate dialog, shown docked to the Main Toolbox in the screenshot. Knowledgeable users almost always have them set up this way: it is very difficult to use tools effectively without being able to see how their options are set. The Layers dialog comes into play whenever you work with an image that has multiple layers: once you advance beyond the very most basic stages of GIMP expertise, this means *almost always*. And finally, of course, the necessity of having images displayed in order to work with them is perhaps obvious.

Note

 If your GIMP layout gets trashed, fortunately the arrangement shown in the screenshot is pretty easy to recover. In the File menu from the Main Toolbox, selecting File → Dialogs → Create New Dock → Layers, Channels, and Paths will give you a Layers dialog just like the one shown. In the same menu, selecting File → Dialogs → Tool Options gives you a new Tool Options dialog, which you can then dock below the Main Toolbox. (The section on Dialogs and Docking explains how to dock dialogs.) There is no need to be able to create a new Main Toolbox, because you cannot get rid of the one you have without causing GIMP to exit.

Unlike some other programs, GIMP does not give you the option of putting everything—controls and image displays—all into a single comprehensive window. GIMP developers have always felt that this is a poor way of working, because it forces the program to perform a wide range of functions that are much better done by a dedicated window manager. Not only would this waste a lot of programmer time, it is almost impossible to do in a way that works correctly across all of the operating systems GIMP is intended to run on.

Earlier versions of GIMP (up to GIMP 1.2.5) were very profligate with dialogs: advanced users often had half a dozen or more dialogs open at once, scattered all over the screen and very difficult to keep track of. GIMP 2.0 is much better in this respect, because it allows dialogs to be docked together in a flexible way. (The Layers dialog in the screenshot actually contains four dialogs, represented by tabs: Layers, Channels, Paths, and Undo.) The system takes a little while to learn, but once you learn it, we hope that you will like it.

The following sections will walk you through the components of each of the windows shown in the screenshot, explaining what they are and how they work. Once you have read them, plus the section describing the basic structure of GIMP images, you should have learned enough to use GIMP for a wide variety of basic image manipulations. You can then look through the rest of the manual at your leisure (or just experiment) to learn the almost limitless number of more subtle and specialized things that are possible. Have fun!

3.2.1 The Main Toolbox

Figure 3.2: Screenshot of the Toolbox

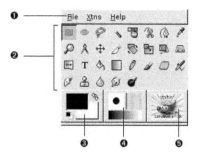

The Main Toolbox is the heart of the GIMP. It is the only part of the application that you cannot duplicate or close. Here is a quick tour of what you will find there.

Tip
In the Toolbox, as in most parts of GIMP, moving the mouse on top of something and letting it rest for a moment will usually bring up a "tooltip" message that may help you understand what the thing is or what you can do with it. Also, in many cases you can press the **F1** key to get help about the thing that is underneath the mouse.

① *Toolbox Menu:* This menu is special: it contains some commands that cannot be found in the menus that are attached to images. (Also some that can.) These include commands for setting preferences, creating certain types of dialogs, etc. The contents are described systematically in the Toolbox Menu section.

② *Tool icons:* These icons are buttons which activate tools for a wide variety of purposes: selecting parts of images, painting on them, transforming them, etc. The Toolbox Introduction section gives an overview of how to work with tools, and each tool is described systematically in the Tools chapter.

③ *Foreground/Background colors:* The color areas here show you GIMP's current foreground and background colors, which come into play in many operations. Clicking on either one of them brings up a color selector dialog that allow you to change to a different color. Clicking on the double-headed arrow swaps the two colors, and clicking on the small symbol in the lower left corner resets them to black and white.

④ *Brush/Pattern/Gradient* The symbols here show you GIMP's current selections for: the Paintbrush, used by all tools that allow you to paint on the image ("painting" includes operations like erasing and smudging, by the way); for the Pattern, which is used in filling selected areas of an image; and for the Gradient, which comes into play whenever an operation requires a smoothly varying range of colors. Clicking on any of these symbols brings up a dialog window that allows you to change it.

⑤ *Active Image:* (This is a new feature in GIMP 2.2) In GIMP, you can work with many images at once, but at any given moment, one of them is the 'active image'. Here you find a small iconic representation of the active image. Clicking on it brings up a dialog with a list of all the currently open images, allowing you to make a different one active if you want to. (Clicking on the window where the image is displayed will accomplish the same thing, though.)

 Note
The "Active Image" preview is disabled by default. If you want it, you can enable it in the Toolbox Preferences tab.

 Note
At every start, GIMP selects a tool (the brush), a color, a brush and a pattern by default, always the same. If you want GIMP to select the last tool, color, brush and pattern you used when quitting your previous session, check the "Set input device settings on exit" in Preferences/Input Devices.

3.2.2   Image Window

Figure 3.3: A screenshot of the image window illustrating the important components

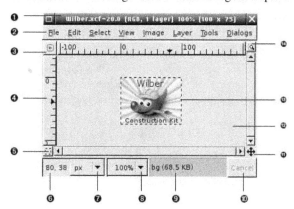

In GIMP, each image that you have open is displayed in its own separate window. (In some cases, multiple windows may all display the same image, but this is unusual.) We will begin with a brief description of the components that are present by default in an ordinary image window. Some of these, in fact, can be made to disappear using commands in the View menu; but you will probably find that you don't want to do that.

- *Title Bar:* At the top of the image window you will probably see a emphasis bar, showing the name of the image and some basic information about it. The emphasis bar is actually provided by the windowing system, not by GIMP itself, so its appearance may vary with different operating systems, window managers, and/or themes. In the Preferences dialog you can customize the information that appears here, if you want to.

- *Image Menu:* Directly below the emphasis bar appears the Image Menu (unless it has been suppressed). This menu gives you access to nearly every operation you can perform on an image. (There are some 'global' actions that can only be accessed via the Toolbox menu.) You can also get the Image Menu by right-clicking inside the image [1] , or by left-clicking on the little 'arrow' symbol in the upper left corner, if for some reason you find one of these more convenient. More: most menu operations can also be activated from the keyboard, using Alt plus an 'accelerator' key underlined in the menu emphasis. More: you can define your own custom shortcuts for menu actions, if you enable Use Dynamic Keyboard Shortcuts in the Preferences dialog.

- *Menu Button:* Clicking on this little button gives you the Image Menu, except in a column instead of a row. Mnemonics users who don't want the menu bar visible can acces to this menu by pressing the Shift-F10 key.

- *Ruler:* In the default layout, rulers are shown above and to the left of the image, indicating coordinates within the image. You can control what type of coordinates are shown if you want to. By default, pixels are used, but you can change to other units, using the Units setting described below.

  One of the most important uses of rulers is to create *guides*. If you click on a ruler and drag into the image display, a guideline will be created, which you can use to help you position things accurately. Guides can be moved by clicking on them and dragging, or deleted by dragging them out of the image display.

- *QuickMask Toggle:* At the lower left corner of the image display is a small button that toggles on or off the Quick Mask, which is an alternate, and often extremely useful, way of viewing the selected area within the image. For more details see QuickMask.

- *Pointer Coordinates:* In the lower left corner of the window is a rectangular area used to show the current pointer coordinates (that is, the mouse location, if you are using a mouse), whenever the pointer is within the image boundaries. The units are the same as for the rulers.

---

[1] Users with an Apple Macintosh and a one button mouse can use Ctrl-mousebutton instead.

⑦ *Units menu:* (This feature is new in GIMP 2.2; it does not appear in GIMP 2.0). By default, the units used for the rulers and several other purposes are pixels. You can change to inches, cm, or several other possibilities using this menu. (If you do, note that the setting of 'Dot for dot' in the View menu affects how the display is scaled: see Dot for Dot for more information.

⑧ *Zoom button:* (This feature is new in GIMP 2.2; it does not appear in GIMP 2.0). There are a number of ways to zoom the image in or out, but this menu is perhaps the simplest.

⑨ *Status Area:* The Status Area appears below the image display. Most of the time, by default, it shows which part of the image is currently active, and the amount of system memory that the image is consuming. You can customize the information that appears here, by changing your Preferences. When you perform time-consuming operations, the status area changes temporarily to show what operation is being performed, and its state of progress.

Note
Note that the amount of memory consumed by the image is quite different from the image file size. For instance, a 69.7Kb .PNG image will occupy 246Kb in memory when displayed. Two reasons for that. First, image is reconstituted from the compressed .PNG file. Then, GIMP keeps a copy of the image in memory to be used by the Undo command.

⑩ *Cancel Button:* At the lower right corner of the window appears the Cancel button. If you start a complex, time-consuming operation (most commonly a plug-in), and then decide, while it is being computed, that you didn't really want to do it after all, this button will cancel it immediately.

Note
There are a few plug-ins that respond badly to being canceled, possibly leaving corrupted pieces of images behind.

⑪ *Navigation control:* This is a small cross-shaped button at the lower right corner of the image display. Clicking on it, and holding the left mouse button down, brings up a window showing a miniature view of the image (Navigation Preview), with the displayed area outlined. You can pan to a different part of the image by moving the mouse while keeping the button depressed. For large images of which only a small part is displayed, the navigation window is often the most convenient way of getting to the part of the image you are looking for. (See Navigation Dialog for other ways to access the Navigation Window). (If your mouse has a middle-button, click-drag with it to span across the image).

⑫ *Inactive Padding Area:* This padding area seperates the active image display and the inactive padding area, so you're able to distinguish between them. You cannot apply any Filters or Operations in generall on the inactive area.

⑬ *Image Display:* The most important part of the image window is, of course, the image display or canvas. It occupies the central area of the window, surrounded by a yellow dotted line showing the image boundary, against a neutral gray background. You can change the zoom level of the image display in a variety of ways, including the Zoom setting described below.

⑭ *Image Window Resize Toggle:* If this button is pressed, the image itself will be resized if the image window is resized.

3.2.3 Dialogs and Docking

3.2.3.1 Docking Bars

In GIMP 2.0 and 2.2, you have a lot of flexibility about the arrangement of dialog windows on your screen. Instead of placing each dialog in its own window, you can group them together using docks. A "dock" is a container window that can hold a collection of persistent dialogs, such as the Tool Options dialog, Brushes dialog, Palette dialog, etc. Docks cannot, however, hold image windows: each image always has its own separate window. They also can't hold non-persistent dialogs, such as the Preferences dialog or the New Image dialog.

Figure 3.4: A dock, with docking bars highlighted

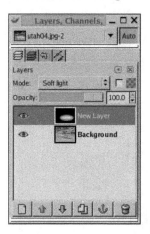

Each dock has a set of *docking bars*, as highlighted in the adjoining figure. These are thin gray bars, very unobtrusive and easy not to notice: most people don't realize that they exist until they are specifically pointed out.

3.2.3.2   Docking Drag Handles

Each dockable dialog has a *drag handle area*, as highlighted in the figure on the right. You can recognize this by the fact that the cursor changes to a hand shape when the pointer is over the drag handle area. To dock a dialog, you simply click on its drag handle area, and drag it onto one of the docking bars in a dock: the dialog will be added to the aimed window. If you drag it onto the aimed window itself, then it will be added as a tab.

Figure 3.5: A dialog in a dock, with the drag handle area highlighted.

This screenshot shows the area that allows to take a dialog off the dock.

You can drag more than one dialog onto the same docking bar. If you do, they will turn into tabs, represented by iconic symbols at the top. Clicking on the tab handle will bring a tab to the front, so that you can interact with it.

3.2.3.3   Image Menu

Some docks contain an *Image Menu*: a menu listing all of the images open in GIMP, and displaying the name of the image whose information is shown in the dock. You can use the Image Menu to select a different image (don't confuse this menu for the Image

Menu that is the Menu of the active image on your screen). If the Auto button is depressed, then the menu always shows the name of GIMP's currently active image, that is, the image you are currently working on.

Figure 3.6: A dock with an Image Menu highlighted

By default, a 'Layers, Channels, and Paths' dock shows an Image Menu at the top, and other types of docks do not. You can always add or remove an Image Menu, however, using the "Show Image Menu" toggle in the Tab menu, as described below. (Exception: you cannot add an Image Menu to the dock that contains the Toolbox.)

3.2.3.4   Tab Menu

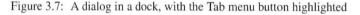

Figure 3.7: A dialog in a dock, with the Tab menu button highlighted

In each dialog, you can access a special menu of tab-related operations by pressing the Tab Menu button, as highlighted in the figure on the right. Exactly which commands are shown in the menu varies a bit from dialog to dialog, but they always include operations for creating new tabs, or closing or detaching tabs.

Figure 3.8: Tab menu from the Layers dialog

The Tab menu gives you access to the following commands:

Context Menu At the top of each Tab menu is an entry that opens into the dialog's context menu, which contains operations specific to that particular type of dialog. For example, the context menu for the Patterns dialog contains a set of operations for manipulating patterns.

Add Tab This entry opens into a submenu allowing you to add a large variety of dockable dialogs as new tabs.

Figure 3.9: 'Add tab' sub-menu

Close Tab This entry closes the dialog. Closing the last dialog in a dock causes the dock itself to close. Choosing this menu entry has the same effect as pressing the "Close Tab" button.

Detach Tab This entry detaches the dialog from the dock, creating a new dock with the detached dialog as its only member. It has the same effect as dragging the tab out of the dock and releasing it at a random location.

Preview Size

Figure 3.10: Preview Size submenu of a Tab menu El submenú "Tamaño de la vista previa".

Many, but not all, dialogs have Tab menus containing a Preview Size option, which opens into a submenu giving a list of sizes for the items in the dialog (cp. Figure 3.10). For example, the Brushes dialog shows pictures of all available brushes: the Preview Size determines how large the pictures are. The default is Medium.

Tab Style

Figure 3.11: Tab Style submenu of a Tab menu

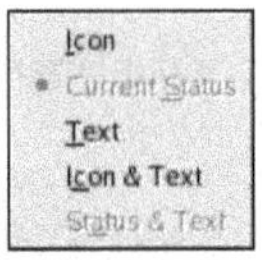

This entry is available when multiple dialogs are in the same dock: it opens into a submenu allowing you to choose how the tabs at the top will appear (cp. Figure 3.11). There are five choices, not all of which will be available for all types of dialogs:

Icon This choice gives you an icon representing the dialog type.

Current Status This choice is only available for dialogs that allow you to select something, such as a brush, a pattern, a gradient, etc. It gives you a tab showing a representation of the item currently selected.

Text This choice gives you a tab showing the dialog type in text.

Icon and Text This choice gives you wider tabs, containing both an icon and the type of dialog in text.

Status and Text This choice, where available, shows the item currently selected, as well as the type of dialog.

View as List; View as Grid These entries are shown in dialogs that allow you to select an item from a set: brushes, patterns, fonts, etc. You can choose whether to view the items as a vertical list, with the name of each beside it, or as a grid, with representations of the items but no names. Each has its advantages: viewing as a list gives you more information, but viewing as a grid allows you to see many more possibilities at once. The default for this varies across dialogs: for brushes and patterns, the default is a grid; for most other things, the default is a list.

Show Image Menu This is a toggle. If it is checked, then an Image Menu is shown at the top of the dock. It is not available for dialogs docked below the Toolbox. Dont confuse this menu for the Image Menu, that is the menu of the active image on your screen.

Auto Follow Active Image If this option is checked, the related dialog will be that of the current image and will change if you select another image. For example, if you have two images and the Histogram dialog on your screen (and this option checked in this dialog), then the histogram of the activated image will be displayed.

3.3 Undoing

Almost anything you do to an image in GIMP can be undone. You can undo the most recent action by choosing Edit → Undo from the image menu, but this is done so frequently that you really should memorize the keyboard shortcut, Ctrl-Z.

Undoing can itself be undone. After having undone an action, you can *redo* it by choosing Edit → Redo from the image menu, or use the keyboard shortcut, Ctrl-Y. It is often helpful to judge the effect of an action by repeatedly undoing and redoing it. This is usually very quick, and does not consume any extra resources or alter the undo history, so there is never any harm in it.

Caution

If you undo one or more actions and then operate on the image in any way except by using Undo or Redo, it will no longer be possible to redo those actions: they are lost forever. The solution to this, if it creates a problem for you, is to duplicate the image and then operate on the copy. (*Not* the original, because the undo/redo history is not copied when you duplicate an image.)

If you often find yourself undoing and redoing many steps at a time, it may be more convenient to work with the Undo History dialog, a dockable dialog that shows you a small sketch of each point in the Undo History, allowing you to go back or forward to that point by clicking.

Undo is performed on an image-specific basis: the "Undo History" is one of the components of an image. GIMP allocates a certain amount of memory to each image for this purpose. You can customize your Preferences to increase or decrease the amount, using the Environment page of the Preferences dialog. There are two important variables: the *minimal number of undo levels*, which GIMP will maintain regardless of how much memory they consume, and the *maximum undo memory*, beyond which GIMP will begin to delete the oldest items from the Undo History.

Note

Even though the Undo History is a component of an image, it is not saved when you save the image using GIMP's native XCF format, which preserves every other image property. When the image is reopened, it will have an empty Undo History.

The implementation of Undo by GIMP is rather sophisticated. Many operations require very little Undo memory (e.g., changing visibility of a layer), so you can perform long sequences of them before they drop out of the Undo History. Some operations (changing layer visibility is again an example) are *compressed*, so that doing them several times in a row produces only a single point in the Undo History. However, there are other operations that may consume a lot of undo memory. Most filters are examples of this: because they are implemented by plug-ins, the GIMP core has no really efficient way of knowing what they have changed, so it has no way to implement Undo except by memorizing the entire contents of the affected layer before and after the operation. You might only be able to perform a few such operations before they drop out of the Undo History.

3.3.1 Things That Cannot be Undone

Most actions that alter an image can be undone. Actions that do not alter the image generally cannot be. This includes operations such as saving the image to a file, duplicating the image, copying part of the image to the clipboard, etc. It also includes most actions that affect the image display without altering the underlying image data. The most important example is zooming. There are, however, exceptions: toggling QuickMask on or off can be undone, even though it does not alter the image data.

There are a few important actions that do alter an image but cannot be undone:

Closing the image The Undo History is a component of the image, so when the image is closed and all of its resources are freed, the Undo History goes along. Because of this, unless the image has not been modified since the last time it was saved, GIMP always asks you to confirm that you really want to close it. (You can disable this in the Environment page of the Preferences dialog; if you do, you are assuming responsibility for thinking about what you are doing.)

Reverting the image 'Reverting' means reloading the image from file. GIMP actually implements this by closing the image and creating a new image, so the Undo History is lost as a consequence. Because of this, if the image is unclean, GIMP always asks you to confirm that you really want to revert the image.

'Pieces' of actions Some tools require you to perform a complex series of manipulations before they take effect, but only allow you to undo the whole thing rather than the individual elements. For example, the Intelligent Scissors require you to create a closed path by clicking at multiple points in the image, and then clicking inside the path to create a selection. You cannot undo the individual clicks: undoing after you are finished takes you all the way back to the starting point. For another example, when you are working with the Text tool, you cannot undo individual letters, font changes, etc.: undoing after you are finished removes the newly created text layer.

Filters, and other actions performed by plugins or scripts, can be undone just like actions implemented by the GIMP core, but this requires them to make correct use of GIMP's Undo functions. If the code is not correct, a plugin can potentially corrupt the Undo History, so that not only the plugin but also previous actions can no longer properly be undone. The plugins and scripts distributed with GIMP are all believed to be set up correctly, but obviously no guarantees can be given for plugins you obtain from other sources. Also, even if the code is correct, canceling a plugin while it is running can sometimes leave the Undo History corrupted, so it is best to avoid this unless you have accidentally done something whose consequences are going to be very harmful.

3.4 GIMPLite Quickies

This tutorial is based on text and images Copyright © 2004 Carol Spears. The original tutorial can be found in the internet [TUT02].

3.4.1 Intention

So, you have The GIMP installed on your computer, you need to make a quick change to an image for some project, but don't want to learn about computer graphics right now in order to get the image changed. Totally understandable. The GIMP is a powerful image manipulator with many options and tools. However, it is quick and somewhat intuitive (after a time) for the small jobs as well. Hopefully, these quickies will help you with your quick problem and help you to stay friends with The GIMP and ready for its more complex tools and methods later, when you have the time and inspiration.

A couple of words about the images used here. The came from APOD [APOD01], Astronomy Picture of the Day. The screenshots were taken on my desktop which is sporting this APOD [APOD02] image.

All you should need to know to start here is how to find your image and open it. (File → Open from the toolbox menu).

3.4.2 Change the Size of an Image (Scale)

Problem: you have a huge image and you want to put it nicely for viewing on a web page. The GIMP is a quick solution. Our example image is this beauty m51_hallas_big.jpg from APOD [APOD03].

Figure 3.12: Example Image for Scaling

The first thing that you might notice is that The GIMP opens the image at a logical size for viewing. So, if your image is really big (like the sample image) it will display it zoomed out until it fits nicely. You can tell if The GIMP has done this by the percentage number in the title bar. Just because it looks right in this 'View' doesn't mean anything.

The other thing to look at in the titlebar is the mode. If it says RGB in the title bar, you are fine. If it says Indexed or grayscale there, you should read the Section 3.4.6.

Figure 3.13: GIMP Used for Image Scaling

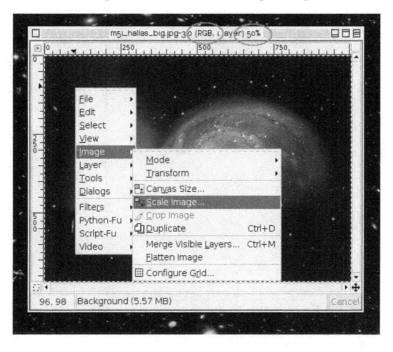

Image entry in the menu and the sub menu from the screenshot should reveal itself. Click on Scale Image.... When ever you click an option from the menu that has ... behind it, expect another dialog. This time, you should get the Scale Image Dialog.

Figure 3.14: Dialog for Image Scaling in Pixels

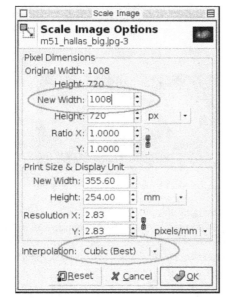

If you have a desired width, put it in the dialog at the top where it says New Width. If you don't have such a number in mind, you can steal the width of The GIMP's default image size, which is 256 pixels. This is demonstrated in the figure above.

Figure 3.15: Dialog for Image Scaling in Inches

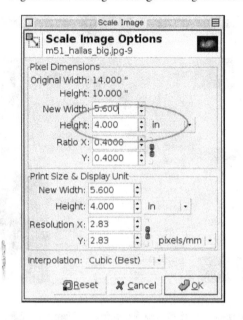

Perhaps you want your image to look more like a 4x6 inch photo on most image rendering web browsers. Simply switch the units to 'inches' and put 4 inches in the height box (opting for smaller than 4x6 rather than bigger). You can see this dialog above.

Let The GIMP choose the other dimension length for you. Meaning, it will take more image knowledge to change both width and height and have it look correct. So only change one and let The GIMP change the rest. To change the other length see Section 3.4.4.

3.4.3 Make JPEGs Smaller

Figure 3.16: Example Image for JPEG Saving

You can make your jpegs smaller without changing the pixel width of the image. Actually you can change the weight of the image a lot. I used an(other) image from APOD [APOD04]. The original image is huge (3000 pixels wide) so I also made a smaller (pixel width) image available. To prepare this image for the web, you should first reduce the image to a better width and height for web viewing as described in the Section 3.4.2. Right click on the properly scaled image and follow the menus File → Save As... at the image window. The Save Dialog will pop up.

I generally type the filename I want into the text box, but the Extension drop menu can tell you the available file formats (depending on the libraries you have installed and the conditions of the image you are trying to save). If The GIMP complains right now, or if 'JPEG' is grayed out in the Extensions menu you should just cancel out of everything and step through the Section 3.4.6.

In the JPEG Save Dialog, you can opt for The GIMP defaults which reduce the size quite a bit, without hurting the visual quality in a way that I can detect. This would be the safest and quickest thing to do.

Figure 3.17: Dialog for Image Saving as JPEG

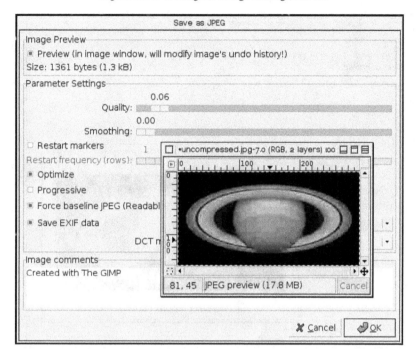

If you would like to make it smaller still, make sure that the 'Preview' toggle is on and then watch the image area and change the compression level by moving the 'Quality' slider down. You can see the quality of the image changing, especially towards the leftmost end of the slider. Above is a screenshot of me doing this very thing. As you can see, very small is also very bad. I have a screenshot of me setting the Quality slider to a more acceptable level below.

Figure 3.18: Dialog for Image Saving as JPEG

Save as JPEG

Image Preview
☐ Preview (in image window, will modify image's undo history!)
Size: unknown

Parameter Settings

0.42

Quality: ▓▓▓▓▓▓▓▓▓▓▓▓▓▓▓▓▓▓

0.00

Smoothing: ▓

☐ Restart markers

lordofrings_hst_med.jpg-1.0 (RGB, 1 layer) 25%

Restart frequency (rows)

☑ Optimize
☐ Progressive
☑ Force baseline JPEG (F
☑ Save EXIF data

Image comments
Created with The GIMP

Background (8.63 MB)   Cancel

✗ Cancel   ↵ OK

I have not been showing the actual jpegs I created so that we could end this quickie with a race.

Figure 3.19: Example for High JPEG Compression

(a) *Quality: 0.06; Size: 1361 Bytes*   (b) *Quality: 0.42; Size: 3549 Bytes*

Figure 3.20: Example for Moderate JPEG Compression

(a) *Quality: 0.85 (GIMPs default); Size: 6837 Bytes*   (b) *Quality: 1.00; Size: 20,971 Bytes*

3.4.4 Crop An Image

Figure 3.21: Example Image for Cropping

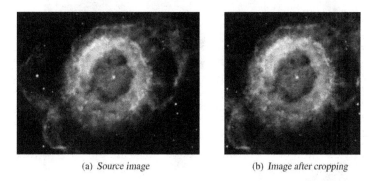

(a) *Source image*   (b) *Image after cropping*

Many reasons to need to crop an image. Making rectangles square, or making squares into rectangles. Cutting alot of useless background to bring out the subject better. etc. To get to the crop tool, you can either push the button on the toolbox or right click on the image and follow the menu Tools → Transform Tools → Crop and Resize in the image window. This will change the cursor and allow you to click and drag a rectangular shape. The button in the toolbox is the nicest way to get to any of the tools. I have chosen one of the huge and beautiful APOD images [APOD05].

Figure 3.22: Select a Region to Crop

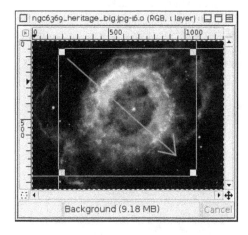

I always click on the approximate upper left corner and drag to the lower right corner. You don't need to worry about being accurate on this first swipe with the crop tool, since a little dialog will pop up and you can make a better choice for your new borders there.

Figure 3.23: Dialog for Cropping

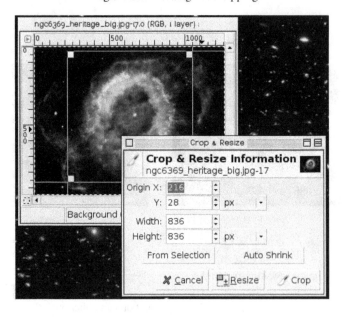

After completeing the click and drag motion, a little 'Crop and Resize Information Dialog' (shown above also) pops up, telling you information about the borders that were defined in the click and drag. We will have to change all of the numbers. If you would like to make this rectangular image square, you should find the width and height from the Get Image Information Quickie (see Section 3.4.5. Use the smallest of the two lengths to determine the size of the square. In my 300 x 225 pixel image, the largest square I can get is 225 x 225 pixels, and I will need to make sure the Y origin is 0. At that point, I use the image and the squares to get the best part of the image for the area. The upper right and lower left crop squares will move the marked area. The other two (upper left and lower right) will change the dimensions of the marked area, so be careful. I have a screenshot of this, right after I fixed the width and height and the Y origin, but before the final positoning. The arrows show the move points. I decided that the image looked the best with the X Origin at 42.

3.4.5 Find Info About Your Image

Figure 3.24: Example Image for Finding Info

This window will tell you the pixel lengths. Right click on the image and follow View → Info Window... from the image window. I got another image from APOD [APOD06]. It is pretty big. (Not as big as Saturn though) You can see in the dialog below, it is 2241 x 1548 pixels.

Figure 3.25: Dialog for Image Info

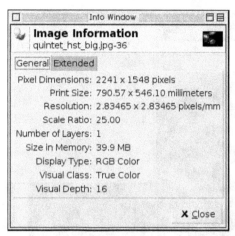

If you are just making a square out of a rectangle, like in the Section 3.4.4, you need only to open the dialog and find the lesser length and use that as described. Since this is very little information, and definately not enough to fill the space between the menu thumbnail and the dialog screenshot in my layout, I thought I would run through some calculator exercises that might help you to meet your image needs.

Figure 3.26: Scale Problem

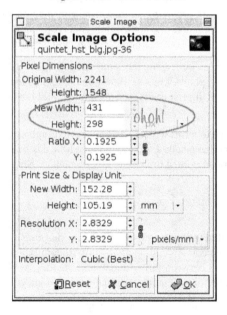

It is nice to have images appear on a browser window as a photo would. Photos online appear to be 4x6 inches when scaled to 288x432 pixels (72 dpi for many monitors). There is a problem, however, if you try to scale this image. The ratio of width to length of the original does not match the ratio of the photo. So, to make the scaled image the correct size crop 10 pixels from the height. For the sample image, it was best to crop 10 pixels off from the top. The final image should 'appear' as a 6x4 inch photo on most monitors.

Figure 3.27: Problem Solved by Cropping

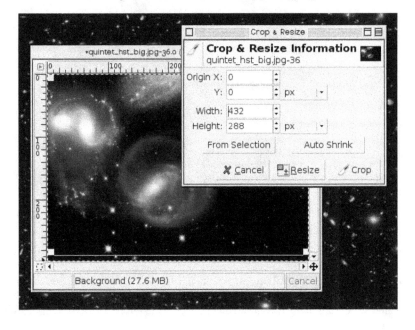

There will be problems whenever mixing scanned photos with digital photos and also with scanned negatives. Modern film developing machines automatically crop one half of an inch off from each image -- the rumor is that the photo printing machines match a certain style of camera view. If you are preparing an image to be printed on a machine like this; or if you are planning on a gallery where the images are from different sources, some intelligent cropping to fit the best size for the medium you have chosen will be a plus. If this is confusing; please blame the photo printing industry and not The GIMP.

You can change the Resolution of your image as well, using the same methods as we used in the Scale, although, in my somewhat limited use, the issue is more about how many pixels. Let's say you want to get this image printed at the photo lab. 300 pixels for every inch is preferred. This original image will print easily as a 7 x 5 photo. 2241px/300ppi = 7.47 in. Get out your calculator for the short side. 1548/300 = _.

There is another brutal fact you should come to terms with if you are new to graphics and computers. Just because it looks good on the screen doesn't mean that it will print that nicely. I tried to emulate how this image would appear printed at 300dpi. Sorry. There are some options, for instance my friend printed images and then scanned them back in. Terrible business!

3.4.6 Change the Mode

As with anything else, images come in different kinds and serve different purposes. Sometimes, a small size is important (for web sites) and at other times, retaining a high colour depth in all its glory (a family portrait) is what you want. GIMP can handle all of this, and more, primarily by converting between three fundamental modes, as seen in this menu. In order to switch your image to one of these modes, you open it and follow that menu and click the mode you want.

RGB - This is the default mode, used for high quality rich colour images. This is also the mode to do most of your image work with including scaling, cropping and even flipping as it gives the computer more information to work with. This extra information also makes RGB Mode the largest to store as a result.

A little bit of detail if you are interested. Each pixel or point when in this mode consists of three different components. R->Red, G->Green, B->Blue. Each of these in turn can have an intensity value of 0-255. So, at every pixel, what you see is an additive combination of these three components. All these combinations result in a way to represent millions of colours.

As an example to practice with images have been provided in various sizes and formats. Indexed images of different sizes: from a very old APOD a small gif and a larger gif of the same image from a later APOD. Also the same image in RGB as provided by Earth Observatory a smaller version and a huge version.

Indexed - This is the mode usually used when file size is of concern, or when you are working with images with few colours. It involves using a fixed number of colours, 256 or less, at each point to represent the colour at that point. The defaults to attempting to figure out an "optimum palette" to best represent your image. Try it, you can undo it if you don't like the results, or use a custom palette or more colours.

Figure 3.28: Dialog 'Change to Indexed Colors'

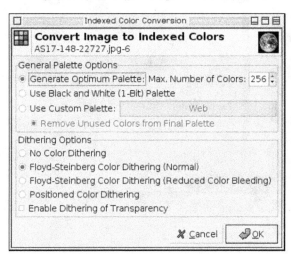

As you might expect, since the information needed to represent the colour at each pixel is less, the file size is a lot smaller. However, sometimes, there will be options in the various menus that seem to have been "greyed" out for no apparent reason. This usually means the filter or option cannot be applied when your image is in its current mode. Changing the mode to RGB as outlined above should solve this issue. If that doesn't work either, perhaps the option you're trying requires your layer to have the ability to be transparent. This can be done just as easily via (Image)->Layer->Transparency->Add Alpha Channel.

Figure 3.29: Add Alpha Channel

Grayscale - In case you want to convert your brilliant colour image to something that's black and white (with a lot of shades of grey), this is one of the easiest ways in which to do it. Some photos do look a lot fancier when displayed in grayscale. Again, if you're interested in some detail, this is achieved by taking the RGB values at the pixels in your image, and suitably weighted averaging them to get an intensity at that point.

There is no need to convert an image to a specific mode before saving it in your favourite format, as the GIMP is smart enough to export.

3.4.7 Flip An Image

Figure 3.30: Example Image to Flip

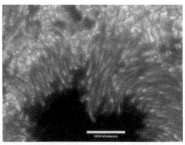

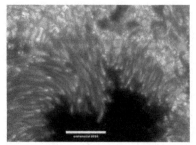

(a) *Source image* (b) *Flipped image*

When you need the person in the photo looking in the other direction, or you need the top of the image to be the bottom. Mirroring

the image (sort of). Right click on the image and follow the menus Tools → Transform Tools → Flip, or use the [button] button on the toolbox.

Using another APOD image [APOD07] I demonstrated all of the flips on this image. You might get bored before it is over ....

The tool used as is (the default) will simply flip the image at its vertical axis.

3.5 How to Draw Straight Lines

This tutorial is based on Text and images Copyright © 2002 Seth Burgess. The original tutorial can be found in the internet [TUT01].

3.5.1 Intention

Figure 3.31: Example of straight drawn lines

This tutorial shows you how you can do straight lines with the GIMP, using a feature called the Shift Key. Straight lines are a convenient way to make things that aren't so terribly affected by the imprecision of a mouse or tablet, and to take advantage of the power of a computer to make things look neat and orderly. This tutorial doesn't use Straight Lines for complex tasks; its intended to show how you can use it to create quick and easy line effects.

1. PREPARATIONS

Figure 3.32: Introducing the **Shift**-key

(a)   (b)

The invention called the typewriter introduced the **Shift** Key. You generally have 2 of them on your keyboard. They look something like the picture on the left. They are located on the left and right sides of your keyboard. The other invention, called the Mouse, was invented by Douglas C. Engelbart in 1970. These come in different varieties, but always have at least one button located on them. They are located on your desk, or sometimes on a mouse pad.

2. CREATING A BLANK DRAWABLE

Figure 3.33: New image

First, create a new image. Any size will do. You can do so by selecting File+New from the menu in the toolbox window.

3. CHOOSE A TOOL

Figure 3.34: Paint tools in the toolbox

Then click on the paintbrush. Any of the red-highlighted tools on the above toolbox can do lines.

4. CREATE A STARTING POINT

Figure 3.35: Starting point

After you click the paintbrush tool, you can click the image. A single dot will appear on the screen. The size of this dot represents the current brush size, which you can change in the Brush Dialog (see Section 13.3.2). Now, lets start drawing a line. Hold down the **Shift** button, and keep it down.

5. DRAWING THE LINE

Figure 3.36: Drawing the line

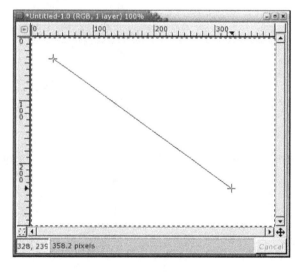

After you have a starting point, and have held down the **Shift** Key, you'll see a line like above if you're running GIMP version 1.2.x or later. Press the first button on the Mouse (the leftmost one usually) and then let it go. During that whole 'click' of the Mouse button, you need to keep the **Shift** Key held down.

3.5.2 Final

See how the line is drawn on top of the preview? This is a powerful feature of the Paint Brush. You can use it with any of the tools shown in step 3, or even draw more lines at the end of this one. Our last step is to let go of the **Shift** key. And there you have it. Some more examples are shown below. Questions? Comments? Let us know. Happy GIMPing!

3.5.2.1 Examples

Figure 3.37: Examples I

(a) *This one I turned on gradient in the Paint Brush Tool.*   (b) *This one I used the Clone tool, and set the source to "Maple Leaves" pattern.*

Figure 3.38: Examples II

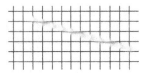 

(a) *This one I rendered a grid, and then used the Smudge Tool with a low spacing and a slightly larger brush.*   (b) *This one I rendered a plasma cloud, and used the Erase Tool with a square brush.*

Figure 3.39: Example III

This one I used the Dodge tool on the top and left of a blue box, then used the burn tool on the right and bottom.

Chapter 4

Getting Unstuck

4.1 Getting Unstuck

4.1.1 Stuck!

All right, okay: you're stuck. You're trying to use one of the tools on an image, and nothing is happening, and nothing you try makes any difference. Your fists are starting to clench, and your face is starting to feel warm. Are you going to have to kill the program, and lose all your work? This sucks!

Well, hold on a second. This happens pretty frequently, even to people who've used the GIMP for a long time, but generally the cause is not so hard to figure out (and fix) if you know what to look at. Lets be calm, and go through a checklist that will probably get you GIMPing happily again.

4.1.2 Common Causes of GIMP Non-Responsiveness

There is a floating selection

Figure 4.1: Layers dialog showing a floating selection.

How to tell: If there is a floating selection, many actions are impossible until it is anchored. To check, look at the Layers dialog (making sure it's set to the image you're working on) and see whether the top layer is called 'Floating Selection'.

How to solve: Either anchor the floating selection, or convert it into an ordinary (non-floating) layer. If you need help on how to do this, see Floating Selections.

The selection is hidden

Figure 4.2: Unstuck show selection menu

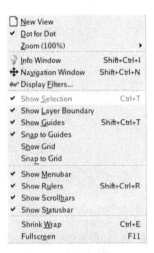

In the View menu, make sure that "Show Selection" is checked.

How to tell: If this is the problem, merely reading this will already have made you realize it, probably, but to explain in any case: sometimes the flickering line that outlines the selection is annoying because it makes it hard to see important details of the image, so GIMP gives you the option of hiding the selection, by unchecking Show Selection in the View menu. It is easy to forget that you have done this, though.

How to fix: If this hasn't rung any bells, it isn't the problem, and if it has, you probably know how to fix it, because it doesn't happen unless you explicitly tell it to; but anyway: just go to the View menu for the image and, if Show Selection is unchecked, click on it..

You are acting outside of the selection

Figure 4.3: Unstuck select all

Click All in the Select menu to make sure that everything is selected.

How to fix: If doing this has destroyed a selection that you wanted to keep, hit Ctrl-Z (undo) a couple of times to restore it, and then we'll figure out what the problem is. There are a couple of possibilities. If you couldn't see any selection, there may have been a very tiny one, or even one that contained no pixels. If this was the case, it surely is not a selection that you wanted to keep, so why have you gotten this far in the first place? If you can see a selection but thought you were inside it, it might be inverted from what you think. The easiest way to tell is to hit the Quick Mask button: the selected area will be clear and the unselected area will be masked. If this was the problem, then you can solve it by toggling Quick Mask off and choosing Invert in the Select menu.

The active drawable is not visible

Figure 4.4: Unstuck layer invisibility

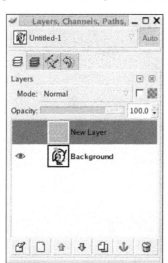

Layers dialog with visibility off for the active layer.

How to tell: The Layers dialog gives you ability to toggle the visibility of each layer on or off. Look at the Layers dialog, and see whether the layer you are trying to act on is active (i.e., darkened) and has an eye symbol to the left of it. If not, this is your problem.

How to fix: If your intended target layer is not active, click on it in the Layers dialog to activate it. (If none of the layers there is active, the active drawable might be a channel -- you can look at the Channels tab in the Layers dialog to see. This does not change the solution, though.) If the eye symbol does not appear, click in the Layers dialog at the left edge to toggle it: this should make the layer visible. See the Help section for the Layers Dialog if you need more help.

The active drawable is transparent

Figure 4.5: Unstuck layer transparency

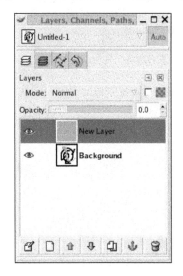

Layers dialog with opacity set to zero for the active layer.

How to fix: Move the slider.

You are trying to act outside the layer How to tell: In GIMP, layers don't need to have the same dimensions as the image: they can be larger or smaller. If you try to paint outside the borders of a layer, nothing happens. To see if this is happening, look for a black-and-yellow dashed rectangle that does not enclose the area you're trying to draw at.

How to fix: You need to enlarge the layer. There are two commands at the bottom of the Layer menu that will let you do this: Layer to Image Size, which sets the layer bounds to match the image borders; and Layer Boundary Size, which brings up a dialog that allows you to set the layer dimensions to whatever you please.

The image is in indexed color mode. How to tell: GIMP can handle three different color modes: RGB(A), Indexed and Grayscale. The indexed colormode uses a colormap, where all used colors on the image are indexed. The color picker in GIMP however, let you choose RGB colors. That means, if you try to paint with a different color than it is indexed in the colormap, you end up in very undetermined results (e.g. it paints with the wrong color or you can't paint).

How to fix: Always use the RGB Color mode to paint on images. You can verify and select another color mode from the Mode menuitem in the Image menu.

Part II

How do I Become a GIMP Wizard?

Chapter 5

Getting Images Into GIMP

This chapter is about getting images into GIMP. It explains how to create new images, how to load images from files, how to scan them and how to make screenshots.

But in the first place we want to introduce you to the general structure of images in GIMP.

5.1 Image Types

It is tempting to think of an *image* as something that corresponds with a single display window, or to a single file such as a JPEG file, but really a GIMP image is a rather complicated structure, containing a stack of layers plus several other types of objects: a selection mask, a set of channels, a set of paths, an "undo" history, etc. In this section we are going to take a detailed look at all of the components of an image, and the things you can do with them.

The most basic property of an image is its *mode*. There are three possible modes: RGB, grayscale, and indexed. RGB stands for Red-Green-Blue, and indicates that each point in the image is represented by a 'red' level, a 'green' level, and a 'blue' level. Because every humanly distinguishable color can be represented as a combination of red, green, and blue, RGB images are full-color. Each color channel has 256 possible intensity levels. More details in Color Models

In a grayscale image, each point is represented by a brightness value, ranging from 0 (black) to 255 (white), with intermediate values representing different levels of gray.

Figure 5.1: Components of the RGB and CMY Color Model

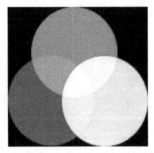 

(a) *In the RGB Color Model, mixing Red, Green and Blue gives White. That's what happens on your screen.*

(b) *In the CMY(K) color model, mixing Cyan, Magenta and Yellow gives Black. That's what happen's when you print on a white paper. The printer will actually use the black cartridge for economical reasons and better color rendering.*

Essentially the difference between a grayscale image and an RGB image is the number of 'color channels': a grayscale image has one; an RGB image has three. An RGB image can be thought of as three superimposed grayscale images, one colored red, one green, and one blue.

Actually, both RGB and grayscale images have one additional color channel, called the *alpha* channel, representing opacity. When the alpha value at a given location in a given layer is zero, the layer is completely transparent, and the color at that location is determined by what lies underneath. When alpha is maximal, the layer is opaque, and the color is determined by the color of the layer. Intermediate alpha values correspond to varying degrees of translucency: the color at the location is a proportional mixture of color from the layer and color from underneath.

Figure 5.2: Example of an image in RGB and Grayscale mode

(a) *An image in RGB mode, with the channels corresponding to Red, Green and Blue.*

(b) *An image in Grayscale mode, with the channel corresponding to Luminosity.*

In GIMP, every color channel, including the alpha channel, has a range of possible values from 0 to 255; in computing terminology, a depth of 8 bits. Some digital cameras can produce image files with a depth of 16 bits per color channel. GIMP cannot load such a file without losing resolution. In most cases the effects are too subtle to be detected by the human eye, but in some cases, mainly where there are large areas with slowly varying color gradients, the difference may be perceptible.

Figure 5.3: Example of an image with alpha channel

(a) *Red channel* (b) *Green channel* (c) *Blue channel* (d) *The Alpha channel shows the image area which is transparent.* (e) *A color image in RGB mode with an Alpha channel.*

The third type, *indexed* images, is a bit more complicated to understand. In an indexed image, only a limited set of discrete colors are used, usually 256 or less. These colors form the 'colormap' of the image, and each point in the image is assigned a color from the colormap. Indexed images have the advantage that they can be represented inside a computer in a way which consumes relatively little memory, and back in the dark ages (say, ten years ago), they were very commonly used. As time goes on, they are used less and less, but they are still important enough to be worth supporting in GIMP. (Also, there are a few important kinds of image manipulation that are easier to implement with indexed images than with continuous-color RGB images.)

Some very commonly used types of files (including GIF and PNG) produce indexed images when they are opened in GIMP. Many of GIMP's tools don't work very well on indexed images–and many filters don't work at all–because of the limited number of colors available. Because of this, it is usually best to convert an image to RGB mode before working on it. If necessary, you can convert it back to indexed mode when you are ready to save it

GIMP makes it easy to convert from one image type to another, using the Mode command in the Image menu. Some types of conversions, of course (RGB to grayscale or indexed, for example) lose information that cannot be regained by converting back in the other direction.

Note

If you are trying to use a filter on an image, and it appears grayed out in the menu, usually the cause is that the image (or, more specifically, the layer) you are working on is the wrong type. Many filters can't be used on indexed images. Some can be used only on RGB images, or only on grayscale images. Some also require the presence or absence of an alpha channel. Usually the fix is to convert the image to a different type, most commonly RGB.

5.2 Creating new Files

You can create new files in GIMP by using the following menuitem: File → New. This opens the Create a new image dialog, where you can modify the initial width and height of the file or using the standard values. More information about this dialog can be found in Section 14.5.2.

5.3 Opening Files

There are several ways of opening an existing image in GIMP:

5.3.1 Open File

The most obvious is to open it using a menu, by choosing File → Open from either the Toolbox menu or an image menu. This brings up a File Chooser dialog, allowing you to navigate to the file and click on its name. This method works well if you know the name of the file you want to open, and where it is located. It is not so convenient if you want to find the file on the basis of a thumbnail.

Note

When you open a file, using the File menu or any other method, GIMP needs to determine what type of file it is. Unless there is no alternative, GIMP does not simply rely on the extension (such as ".jpg") to determine the file type, because extensions are not reliable: they vary from system to system; any file can be renamed to have any extension; and there are many reasons why a file name might lack an extension. Instead, GIMP first tries to recognize a file by examining its contents: most of the commonly used graphics file formats have "magic headers" that permit them to be recognized. Only if the magic yields no result does GIMP resort to using the extension.

Figure 5.4: The 'File Open' dialog.

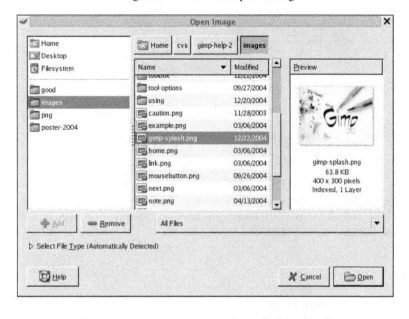

GIMP 2.2 introduced a new File Chooser that provides several features to help you navigate quickly to the file you are looking for. Perhaps the most important is the ability to create 'bookmarks' for folders that you use often. Your list of bookmarks appears on the left side of the dialog. The ones at the top ('Home', 'Desktop', etc) come automatically; the others you create using the 'Add' button at the bottom of the list. Double-clicking on a bookmark takes you straight to that directory.

At the center of the dialog appears a listing of the contents of the selected directory. Subdirectories are shown at the top of the list, files below them. By default all files in the directory are listed, but you can restrict the listing to image files of a specific type using the File Type selection menu that appears beneath the directory listing.

When you click on a file entry in the listing, if it is an image file, a preview will appear on the right side of the dialog, along with some basic information about the properties of the image. Note that previews are cached when they are generated, and there are some things you can do that may cause a preview to be incorrect. If you suspect that this may be happening, you can force a new preview to be generated by holding down the Ctrl key and clicking in the Preview area.

One thing that strikes many people when they first see the File Open dialog is that there is no way to enter the name of the file using the keyboard. Actually this can be done, but the feature is a bit hidden: if you type Ctrl-L with the dialog focused, an "Open Location" dialog pops up, with a space to type the file name. This dialog is described in more detail below.

Note

 In the great majority of cases, if you select a file name from the list, and click the 'Open' button in the lower right corner or the dialog, GIMP will automatically determine the file type for you. On rare occasions, mainly if the file type is unusual and the name lacks a meaningful extension, this may fail. If this happens, you can tell GIMP specifically what type of file it is by expanding the 'Select File Typ' option at the bottom of the dialog, and choosing an entry from the list that appears. More commonly, though, if GIMP fails to open an image file, it is either corrupt or not in a supported format.

5.3.2 Open Location

If instead of a file name, you have a URI (i.e., a web address) for the image, you can open it using the menu, by choosing File → Open Location from either the Toolbox menu or an image menu. This brings up a small dialog that allows you to enter (or paste) the URI.

Figure 5.5: The 'Open Location' dialog.

The Open Location dialog.

5.3.3 Open Recent

If the image is one that you previously created using GIMP, perhaps the easiest way to open it is from the menu, using File → Open Recent. This gives you a scrollable list of the images you have most recently worked on in, with icons beside them. You need only select the one you want, and it will be opened.

5.3.4 File Browser

If you have associated the file type of the image with GIMP, either when you installed GIMP or later, then you can navigate to the file using a file manager (such as Nautilus in Linux, or Windows Explorer in Windows), and once you have found it, double-click on the icon. If things are set up properly, this will cause the image to open in GIMP.

5.3.5 Drag and Drop

Alternatively, once you have found the file, you can click on its icon and drag it into the GIMP Toolbox. (If instead you drag it into an existing GIMP image, it will be added to that image as a new layer or set of layers).

For many applications, you can click on a displayed image (a full image, not just a thumbnail) and drag it into the GIMP toolbox.

5.3.6 Copy and Paste

For some applications, if the application gives you a way of copying the image to the clipboard (the **Print Screen** key lets you copy the screen into the clipboard), you can then open the image in GIMP by choosing File → Acquire → Paste as New from the Toolbox menu. Support for this is somewhat variable, however, so your best bet is to try it and see whether it works.

5.3.7 Image Browser

In Linux, you might want to take a look at a program called gThumb, an image-management application that in several ways nicely complements GIMP. In gThumb, you can cause an image to open in GIMP either by right-clicking on the icon and selecting GIMP from among the list of options, or by dragging the icon into the GIMP Toolbox. See the gThumb home page [GTHUMB] for more information. Other similar applications are : GQview [GQVIEW], XnView [XNVIEW].

Chapter 6

Getting images out of GIMP

6.1 Files

The GIMP is capable of reading and writing a large variety of graphics file formats. With the exception of GIMP's native XCF file type, file handling is done by Plugins. Thus, it is relatively easy to extend GIMP to new file types when the need arises.

Not all file types are equally good for all purposes. This part of the documentation should help you understand the advantages and disadvantages of each type.

6.1.1 Saving Images

When you are finished working with an image, you will want to save the results. (In fact, it is often a good idea to save at intermediate stages too: GIMP is a pretty robust program, but we have heard rumors, possibly apocryphal, that it may have been known on rare and mysterious occasions to crash.) Most of the file formats that GIMP can open, can also be used for saving. There is one file format that is special, though: XCF is GIMP's native format, and is useful because it stores *everything* about an image (well, almost everything; it does not store 'undo' information). Thus, the XCF format is especially suitable for saving intermediate results, and for saving images to be re-opened later in GIMP. XCF files are not readable by most other programs that display images, so once you have finished, you will probably also want to save the image in a more widely used format, such as JPEG, PNG, TIFF, etc.

6.1.2 Saving Files

There are several commands for saving images. A list, and information on how to use them, can be found in the section covering the File menu.

GIMP allows you to save the images you create in a wide variety of formats. It is important to realize that the only format capable of saving *all* of the information in an image, including layers, transparency, etc., is GIMP's native XCF format. Every other format preserves some image properties and loses others. When you save an image, GIMP tries to let you know about this, but basically it is up to you to understand the capabilities of the format you choose.

Figure 6.1: Example of an Export dialog

As stated above, there is no file format, with the exception of GIMP's native XCF format, that is capable of storing all the data in a GIMP image. When you ask to save an image in a format that will not completely represent it, GIMP notifies you of this, tells you what kind of information will be lost, and asks you whether you would like to 'export' the image in a form that the file type can handle. Exporting an image does not modify the image itself, so you do not lose anything by doing this. See Export file.

Note
When you close an image (possibly by quitting GIMP), you are warned if the image is "dirty"; that is, if it has been changed without subsequently being saved. Saving an image in any file format will cause the image to be considered "not dirty", even if the file format does not represent all of the information from the image.

6.1.2.1 Saving as GIF

Figure 6.2: The GIF Save dialog

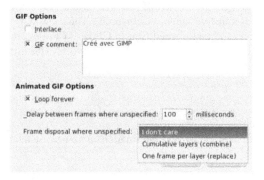

GIF Options

Interlace Interlace : when this option is checked, the image will be displayed progressively on the Web page. It was interesting when computers and modems were slow, as it allowed to stop loading an image of no interest.

GIF comment GIF comment: beware of do not insert characters outsite the ASCII range, because of the GIF format supports 7-bits ASCII texts only, that GIMP can't provide. If you insert inadvertitely a non-ASCII char, the option will be automatically disabled.

Animated GIF Options

Loop forever Loop forever : when this option is checked the animation will start playing again repeatedly until you stop it.

Delay between frames if unspecified Delay between frames if unspecified : you can set the delay, in milliseconds, between frames if it has not been set before. In this case, you can modify every delay in the Layer Dialog.

Frame disposal when unspecified Frame disposal when unspecified : If this has not been set before, you can set how frames will be superimposed. You can select among three options :

- I don't care : you can use this option if all your layers are opaque. Layers will overwrite what is beneath.
- Cumulative Layers (combine) : previous frames will not be deleted when a new one is displayed.
- One frame per layer (replace) : previous frames will be deleted before displaying a new frame.

6.1.2.2 Saving as JPEG

JPEG files usually have an extension .jpg, .JPG, or .jpeg. It is a very widely used format, because it compresses images very efficiently, while minimizing the loss of image quality. No other format comes close to achieving the same level of compression. It does not, however, support transparency or multiple layers. For this reason, saving images as JPEG often requires them to be exported from GIMP.

Figure 6.3: The JPEG Save dialog

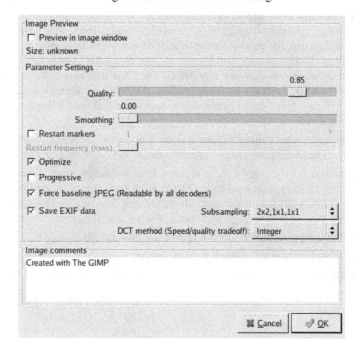

The JPEG algorithm is quite complex, and involves a bewildering number of options, whose meaning is beyond the scope of this documentation. Unless you are a JPEG expert, the Quality parameter is probably the only one you will need to adjust.

 Caution

After you save an image as a JPEG file, the image is no longer considered 'dirty' by GIMP, so unless you make further changes to it, you will not receive any warning if you close it. Because JPEG is lossy and does not support transparency or multiple layers, some of the information in the image might then be lost. If you want to save all of the information in an image, use GIMP's native XCF format.

Quality When you save a file in JPEG format, a dialog is displayed that allows you to set the Quality level, which ranges from 0 to 100. Values above 95 are generally not useful, though. The default quality of 85 usually produces excellent results, but in many cases it is possible to set the quality substantially lower without noticably degrading the image. You can test the effect of different quality settings by checking Show Preview in image window in the JPEG dialog. Checking this option causes each change in quality (or any other JPEG parameter) to be shown in the image display. (This does not alter the image, though: it reverts back to its original state when the JPEG dialog is closed.)

Advanced settings Some information about the advanced settings:

Optimize If you enable this option, the optimization of entropy encoding parameters will be used.

Smoothing By using this option, you can smooth the image when saving.

Progressive With this option enabled the compression of the image will be inserted progressively in the file. This is done with the intent to give a progressive refinement of the image appearance during the slow connection web downloads, similar and with the same purpose of the corresponding option present in the GIF images too.

Force baseline JPEG Force creation of a baseline JPEG (non-baseline JPEGs can't be read by all decoders)

Subsampling Human eye is not sensitive in the same way all over color spectrum. Compression can use this to consider as identical slightly different colors. Three methods are available :

- 2x2, 1x1, 1x1 : important compression; suits images with weak borders but tends to denature colors.
- 1x1, 1x1, 1x1 : preserves borders and contrasting colors, but compression is less.
- 1x1, 1x1, 1x1 (4:2:2) : between other both.

Save EXIF data JPEG files from many digital cameras contain extra information, called EXIF data, which specifies camera settings and other information concerning the circumstances under which the image was created. GIMP's ability to handle EXIF data depends on whether the 'libexif' library is available on your system; it is not automatically packaged with GIMP. If GIMP was built with libexif support, then EXIF data is preserved if you open a JPEG file, work with the resulting image, and then save it as JPEG. The EXIF data is not altered in any way when you do this (which means that some of its fields are no longer valid). If GIMP was not built with EXIF support, this does not prevent files with EXIF data from being opened, but it does mean that the EXIF data will not be present when the resulting image is later saved.

DCT Method DCT is 'discrete cosine transform', and it is the first step in the JPEG algorithm going from the spatial to the frequency domain. The choices are 'float', 'integer' (the default), and 'fast integer'.

- float : The float method is very slightly more accurate than the integer method, but is much slower unless your machine has very fast floating-point hardware. Also note that the results of the floating-point method may vary slightly across machines, while the integer methods should give the same results everywhere.
- integer (the default): This method is faster than 'float', but not as accurate.
- fast integer : The fast integer method is much less accurate than the other two.

Save Preview This option lets you save a thumbnail with the image.

Image comments In this text box, you can enter a comment which will be saved with the image.

6.1.2.3 Saving as PNG

Figure 6.4: The 'Save as PNG' dialog

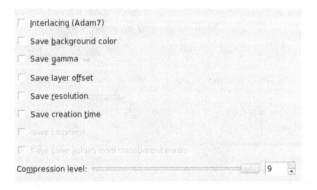

Interlacing Interlacing: When this option is checked, the image is progressively displayed on a Web page. So, slow computer users can stop downloading if they are not interested.

Save background color Save background color: If your image has many transparency levels, the Internet browsers which recognize only two levels, will use the background color of your Toolbox instead. But Internet Explorer does not use these informations.

Save gamma Save gamma: informations about your monitor will be saved, so that the image will be displayed in the same way on other computers, provided that the display program supports these informations, what is rarely the case.

Save layer offset Save layer offset: No interest. Images with layers are flattenned before saving to PNG and layer offset is taken in account.

Save Resolution Save Resolution: Save the image resolution, in dpi (dot per inch).

Save creation time Save creation time: That will be the date of last saving.

Save comment Save comment: you can read this comment in the Info-window.

Save color values from transparent pixels With this option is checked, the color values are saved even if the pixels are completely transparent.

Compression level Compression level: Since compression is not lossy, the only reason to use a compression level less than 9 would be a too long time to compress file on a slow computer. Nothing to fear from decompression: it is as quick whatever the compression level.

Save defaults Save defaults: If you click on this button, your settings will be saved and can be used by other savings by clicking on the Load defaults.

Note

Since PNG format supports indexed images, you have better reduce the number of colors before saving if you want to have the lightest file for the Web. See Section 14.9.6.

Computers work on 8 bits blocks named 'Byte'. A byte allows 256 colors. Reducing the number of colors below 256 is not useful: a byte will be used anyway and the file size will not be less. More, this 'PNG8' format, like GIF, uses only one bit for transparency; only two transparency levels are possible, transparent or opaque.

If you want PNG transparency to be fully displayed by Internet Explorer, you can use the AlphaImageLoader DirectX filter in the code of your Web page. See Microsoft Knowledge Base [MSKB-294714]. Please note, that this should not be necessary for InternetExplorer 7 and above.

6.1.2.4 Saving as TIFF

Figure 6.5: The TIFF Save dialog

Compression This option give you the opportunity to choose the compression method that is appropriate for your image:

- None : fast method, but resulting in a big file.
- LZW : The image will be compressed using the 'Lempel-Ziv-Welch' algorithm, a lossless compression technique. This is an old method, still efficient and fast. More informations at [WKPD-LZW].
- Pack Bits : PackBits is a fast, simple compression scheme for run-length encoding of data. Apple introduced the PackBits format with the release of MacPaint on the Macintosh computer. A PackBits data stream consists of packets of one byte of header followed by data. (Source: [WKPD-PACKBITS])
- Deflate
- JPEG

Save color values from transparent pixels With this option the color values are saved even if the pixels are completely transparent.

Comment In this text box, you can enter a comment which will be associated with the image.

6.2 Preparing your Images for the Web

One of the most common purposes GIMP is used for is to prepare images for adding them to a web site. This means that images should look as nice as possible while keeping the file size as small as possible. This little step-by-step guide will tell you how to achieve a smaller file size with minimal degradation of image quality.

6.2.1 Images with an Optimal Size/Quality Ratio

An optimal image for the web depends upon the image type and the file format you have to use. If you want to put a photograph with a lot of colors online, you have to use JPEG as your primary file format. If your image contains fewer colors, that is, if it is not a photograph, but is more a drawing you created (such as a button or a screenshot), you would be better off using PNG format. We will guide you through the process of doing this.

1. First, open the image as usual. I have opened our Wilber as an example image.

Figure 6.6: The Wilber image opened in RGBA mode.

2. The image is now in RGB mode, with an additional Alpha channel (RGBA). There is usually no need to have an alpha channel for your web image. You can remove the alpha channel by flattening the image.

   If you open a photograph, you probably won't have to remove the alpha channel, because a photograph doesn't usually have one, so the file is already opened in RGB mode.

 Note
If the image has a soft transition into the transparent areas, you cannot remove the alpha channel, since the information which would be used for fading out will not be saved in the file. If you would like to save an image with transparent areas which do not have a soft transition, (similar to GIF), you can remove the alpha channel.

---

3. After you have flattened the image, you are able to save the image in PNG format for your web site.

Note
You can save your image in PNG format with the default settings, but using maximum compression. Doing this will have no negative affects on the quality of the picture, as it would have with JPEG format. If your image is a photograph with lots of colors, you would be better off saving it as jpeg. The main thing is to find the best tradeoff between quality and compression. You can find more information about this topic in "JPEG".

6.2.2 Reducing the File Size Even More

If you want to reduce the size of your image a bit more, you could convert your image to Indexed mode. That means that all of the colors will be reduced to only 256 values. Converting images with smooth color transitions or gradients to indexed mode will often give poor results, because it will turn the smooth gradients into a series of bands. This method is also not recommended for photographs because it will make the image look coarse and grainy.

Figure 6.7: The indexed image

An indexed image can look a bit grainy. The left image is Wilber in its original size, the right one is zoomed in by 300 percent.

1. Use the command described in Section 14.9.3 to convert your RGB image to indexed mode.

2. After you have converted the image to indexed mode, you are once again able to save your image in PNG format.

6.2.3 Saving Images with Transparency

There are two different approaches used by graphic file formats for supporting transparent image areas: simple binary transparency and alpha transparency. Simple binary transparency is supported in GIF format. Here, one color from the indexed color palette is marked as the transparent color. Alpha transparency is supported in PNG format. Here, the transparency information is stored in a separate channel, the Alpha channel.

Note
There is usually no need to save images in GIF format any more, because PNG supports all the features of GIF and offers additional features (e.g., alpha transparency). Nevertheless, this format is still used for animations.

1. First of all, we will use the same image as in the previous tutorials, Wilber the GIMP mascot.

Figure 6.8: The Wilber Image Opened in RGBA Mode.

2. To save an image with alpha transparency, you must have an alpha channel. To check if the image has an alpha channel, go to the channel dialog and verify that an entry for 'Alpha' exists, besides Red, Green and Blue. If this is not the case, add a new alpha channel from the layers menu.

3. You can now remove the background layer to get a completely transparent background, or create a gradient from color to transparency. You are only limited by your imagination. To demonstrate the cabilities of alpha transparency, we'll make a soft glow in the background around our Wilber.

4. After you're done with your image, you can save it in PNG format.

Figure 6.9: Mid-Tone Checks in the background layer represent the transparent region of the saved image while you are working on it in GIMP.

Chapter 7

Painting with GIMP

7.1 The Selection

Often when you operate on an image, you only want part of it to be affected. In GIMP, you make this happen by *selecting* that part. Each image has a *selection* associated with it. Most, but not all, GIMP operations act only on the selected portions of the image.

Figure 7.1: How would you isolate the tree?

There are many, many situations where creating just the right selection is the key to getting the result you want, and often it is not very easy to do. For example, in the above image, suppose I want to cut the tree out from its background, and paste it into a different image. In order to do this, I need to create a selection that contains the tree and nothing but the tree. It is difficult because the tree has a very complex shape, and in several spots is hard to distinguish from the objects behind it.

Figure 7.2: Selection shown as usual with dashed line

Now here is a very important point, and it is crucial to understand this. Ordinarily when you create a selection, you see it as a dashed line enclosing a portion of the image. The idea you could get from this is that the selection is a sort of container, with the selected parts of the image inside, and the unselected parts outside. This concept of the selection is okay for many purposes, but it is not really correct.

Actually the selection is implemented as a *channel*. In terms of its internal structure, it is identical to the red, green, blue, and alpha channels of an image. Thus, the selection has a value defined at each pixel of the image, ranging between 0 (unselected) and 255 (fully selected). The advantage of this approach is that it allows some pixels to be *partially selected*, by giving them intermediate values between 0 and 255. As you will see, there are many situations where it is desirable to have smooth transitions between selected and unselected regions.

What, then, is the dashed line that appears when you create a selection?

It is a *contour line*, dividing areas that are more than half selected from areas that are less than half selected.

Figure 7.3: Same selection in QuickMask mode

You should always bear in mind, when looking at the dashed line that represents the selection, that it only tells you part of the story. If you want to see the selection in complete detail, the easiest way is to click the QuickMask button in the lower left corner of the image window. This causes the selection to be shown as a translucent overlay atop the image. Selected areas are unaffected; unselected areas are reddened. The more completely selected an area is, the less red it appears.

QuickMask mode, and its uses, are described in detail below. Meanwhile, if you are following this discussion by trying things out in GIMP, you should know that many operations work differently in QuickMask mode, so go ahead and toggle it off again for now (by clicking the QuickMask button once more).

Figure 7.4: Same selection in QuickMask mode after feathering

7.1.1 Feathering

With the default settings, the basic selection tools, such as the Rectangle Select tool, create sharp selections. Pixels inside the dashed line are fully selected, and pixels outside completely unselected. You can verify this by toggling QuickMask: you see a clear rectangle with sharp edges, surrounded by uniform red. In the Tool Options, however, is a checkbox called 'Feather edges'. If you enable this, the tool will instead create graduated selections. The feather radius, which you can adjust, determines the distance over which the transition occurs.

If you are following along, try this out with the Rectangle Select tool, and then toggle QuickMask. You will now see that the clear rectangle has a fuzzy edge.

Feathering is particularly useful when you are cutting and pasting, in helping the pasted object to blend smoothly and unobtrusively with its surroundings.

Actually, it is possible to feather a selection at any time, even if it was originally created as a sharp selection. You can do this from the image menu, by choosing Select → Feather. This brings up a dialog that allows you to set the feather radius. You can do the opposite--sharpen a graduated selection into an all-or-nothing selection--by choosing Select → Sharpen.

Note

For technically oriented readers: feathering works by applying a Gaussian blur to the selection channel, with the specified blurring radius.

7.1.2   Making a Selection Partially Transparent

You can set layer opacity, but you cannot do that directly for a selection. It is quite useful to make the image of a glass transparent. You can achieve this by using these methods:

- For simple selections, use the Eraser tool with the wanted opacity.

- For complex selections: use the command Selection → Floating to create a floating selection. This creates a new layer called 'Floating Selection'. Activate it and use the opacity slider to get the wanted opacity. Then anchor the selection: outside the selection, the mouse pointer comes with an anchor icon. When you click, the floating selection disappears from the Layer Dialog and the selection is at the right place and partially transparent (anchoring works this way only if a selection tool is activated : you can also use the command in the context menu that you get by right clicking on the selected layer in the layer dialog).

  And, if you use this function frequently: Ctrl-C to copy the selection, Ctrl-V to paste it, creating so a floating selection, adapt the opacity then make Layer/New Layer that pastes the floating selection into the new layer. You can also create a shortcut for the New Layer command to use keys only.

- Another way: Layer → Mask → Layer mask to add a layer mask to the layer with the selection, initializing it with the selection. Then use a brush with the wanted opacity to paint the selection with black, i-e paint it with transparency. Then Layer/Mask/Apply Layer Mask. See Section 13.2.1.3.

- If you want to **make transparent the solid background of an image**, add an Alpha channel and select the background by using the Magic Wand. Then, with the Color Picker tool, select the background color which becomes the foreground color in Toolbox. Use Fill tool with this color on the selection, in the 'Color Erase' mode. This method erases pixels which have this color; other pixels are partially erased and their color is changed.

  The simplest method is the Edit → Erase command, which gives complete transparency and doesn't allow to enjoy the Opacity setting of the Fill tool.

7.2 Creating and Using Selections

7.2.1 Moving a Selection

Figure 7.5: Moving the Selection Reveals the Background Layer

After creating a rectangular, elliptic or free selection, or when you are using the Magic wand, the default mouse pointer is the moving cross. Click-and-drag then allows you to move the selection and its contents, while the initial position remains empty.

If you only want to move the selection border and not its contents, then press the **Alt** key and click-and-drag the selection.

Note

Sometimes the **Alt** key is used by the window manager and you move the image window instead of the selection. If this is the case, you have two possibilities:

1. Select the move tool and change the 'Affect' option.

2. Try to use the Alt-Shift or Alt-Ctrl keys to move the selection.

Moving a selection without emptying its initial position is more complicated: while pressing the **Ctrl** key, move the mouse pointer a little bit, then also press the **Alt** key, then click-and-drag the selection. This can be done more easily by using the Move tool in Selection mode.

Moving a selection automatically creates a floating layer (floating selection). See Floating selection. The mouse pointer then looks like an anchor when it is outside of the selection. This means that the selection will be permanently anchored at the place you choose when you click the mouse button.

As soon as this floating selection is created in the Layer dialog (and you can create it with Selection/Float), you can use the keyboard arrow keys to move the selection horizontally or vertically.

7.2.2   Creating a Free Selection

Figure 7.6: Using the Free Selection Tool

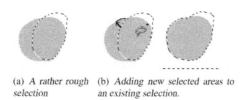

(a) *A rather rough*   (b) *Adding new selected areas to*
selection   *an existing selection.*

When using the lasso to select an object, some parts of the object and its proximity may be incorrectly either selected or not selected. You can correct these defects by pressing the **Shift** or **Ctrl** keys while using the lasso. Here is how to do it: While pressing **Shift**, draw the new border with the lasso and close the selection, including a part of the first selection. As soon as you release the mouse button, both selections are added together. You could subtract the extra part of the first selection in a similar way by pressing **Ctrl**.

 Note

To correct selection defects precisely, use the Quick Mask.

7.3   QuickMask

Figure 7.7: Image with QuickMask enabled

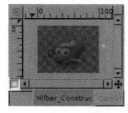

The selection tools sometimes show their limits when they have to be used for creating a complex selection. In these cases, using the QuickMask can make things much easier. Simply put, the QuickMask allows you to paint a selection instead of just tracing its outline.

7.3.1   Overview

Normally when you create a selection in GIMP, you see it represented by the "marching ants" that trace along its outline. But really there may be a lot more to a selection than the marching ants show you: in GIMP a selection is actually a full-fledged grayscale channel, covering the image, with pixel values ranging from 0 (unselected) to 255 (fully selected). The marching ants are drawn along a contour of half-selected pixels. Thus, what the marching ants show you as either inside or outside the boundary is really just a slice through a continuum.

The QuickMask is GIMP's way of showing you the full structure of the selection. Activating it also gives you the ability to interact with the selection in new, and substantially more powerful, ways. To activate the QuickMask, click on the small red-outlined button at the lower left of the image window. The button is a toggle, so clicking it again will return you to normal marching-ant mode. You can also activate the QuickMask by selecting in the image window menu Select → Toggle QuickMask, or by using the Shift-Q shortcut.

Activating the QuickMask shows you the selection as though it were a translucent screen overlying the image, whose transparency at each pixel indicates the degree to which that pixel is selected. By default the mask is shown in red, but you can change this if another mask color would be more convenient. The less a pixel is selected, the more it is obscured by the mask. Fully selected pixels are shown completely clear.

When you are in QuickMask mode, many image manipulations act on the selection channel rather than the image itself. This includes, in particular, paint tools. Painting with white causes the painted pixels to be selected; painting with black causes them to be unselected. You can use any of the paint tools, as well as the bucket fill and gradient fill tools, in this way. Advanced users of the GIMP learn that 'painting the selection' is the easiest and most effective way to delicately manipulate it.

Tip
To save the selection done by the Quickmask to a new channel; Make sure that there is a selection and that Quickmask is not active in the image window. Select in the image menu Select/Save to Channel. This will create a new channel in the channel dialog called SelectionMask 1.

Tip
When QuickMask is active, Cut and Paste act on the selection rather than the image. You can sometimes make use of this as the most convenient way of transferring a selection from one image to another.

You can learn more on Quickmask and Selection masks in the section dedicated to the channel dialog.

7.3.2 Properties

There are two QuickMask properties you can change by right-clicking on the QuickMask button.

- Normally the QuickMask shows unselected areas 'fogged over ' and selected areas 'in clear', but you can reverse this by choosing 'Mask Selected Areas' instead of the default 'Mask Unselected Areas'.

- By choosing 'Configure Color and Opacity', you can bring up a dialog that allows you to set these to values other than the defaults, which are red at 50% opacity.

7.4 Using the Quickmask

1. Open an image or begin a new document;

2. Activate the Quickmask using the left-bottom button in the image window. If a selection is present the mask is initialized with the content of the selection;

3. Choose any drawing tool. Paint on the Quick Mask using black color to remove selected areas and white color to add selected areas. You can use grey colors to get partially selected areas.

   You can also use selection tools and fill these selections with the Bucket Fill tool. This does not destroy the Qmask selections!

4. Toggle off the Quickmask using the left-bottom button in the image window: the selection will be displayed with its marching ants.

7.5 Paths

Paths are curves (known as Bézier-curves). In GIMP it's very easy to learn and to use them. To understand their concepts and mechanism you can go to the glossary Bézier-curve or to Wikipedia http://en.wikipedia.org/wiki/Bézier_curve. It is a very powerful tool to design sophisticated forms. To use it in GIMP you must operate by two successive ways: 1st Create the path and 2nd Stroke path.

According to the terminology used in GIMP, 'Stroke path' means here to apply a specific style to the path (color, width, pattern...).

Paths are used for two main purposes:

- A closed path can be converted into a selection.

- An open or closed path can be *stroked*, that is, painted on the image, in a variety of ways.

Figure 7.8: Illustration of four different path creating.

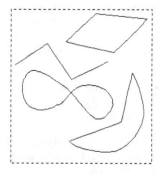

Four examples of GIMP paths: one closed and polygonal; one open and polygonal; one closed and curved; one with a mixture of straight and curved segments.

7.5.1 Path Creating

At this step you can design a skeleton of wished form; this skeleton will be modified later by various ways. To do this you can go to Paths. A short example will be useful to understand the creating process.

- In menu click Tools → Path in image window

- or on the relevant icon in toolbox

- or use hotkey **B**

Your pointer changes into a pen feature with a curve beginning; if you click in the image you print a point (white inner circle whith a black border); moving mouse and right-clicking again you create automatically a second point linked to previous one. You can carry on as often as you wish it to design a polyline, but to learn you need two points only. Now if you approach pointer close to segment ranging between the two points, the little '+' close to pointer changes into a cross (for moving). Now press down right button moving pointer to any side.

Then two events occur: one is a bending of the segment to moving direction and this bending is proportional with displacement, and the second reveals at the two curve ends two segments ended with squares (named handles). If you drop prompt on these squares this one changes into a pointing finger. Now if you are pressing down right button and are moving your mouse you can see consequence on the curve feature. By this mean you can change starting curve orientation as well as its 'lenghthening' on modified side.

Figure 7.9: Appearance of a path while it is being manipulated using the Path tool.

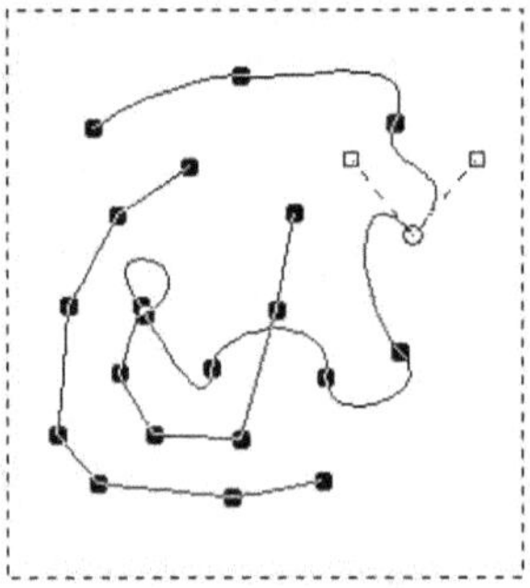

Black squares are anchor points, the open circle is the selected anchor, and the two open squares are its handles. Note that this path has two components.

Paths can be created and manipulated using the Path tool. Paths, like layers and channels, are components of an image. When an image is saved in GIMP's native XCF file format, any paths it has are saved along with it. The list of paths in an image can be viewed and operated on using the Paths dialog. If you want to move a path from one image to another, you can do so by copying and pasting using the popup menu in the Paths dialog, or by dragging an icon from the Paths dialog into the destination image's window.

GIMP paths belong to a mathematical type called 'Bezier paths'. What this means in practical terms is that they are defined by *anchors* and *handles*. 'Anchors' are points the path goes through. 'Handles' define the direction of a path when it enters or leaves an anchor point: each anchor point has two handles attached to it.

Paths can be very complex. If you create them by hand using the Path tool, unless you are obsessive they probably won't contain more than a few dozen anchor points (often many fewer); but if you create them by transforming a selection into a path, or by transforming text into a path, the result can easily contain hundreds of anchor points, or even thousands.

A path may contain multiple *components*. A 'component' is a part of a path whose anchor points are all connected to each other by path segments. The ability to have multiple components in paths allows you to convert them into selections having multiple disconnected parts.

Each component of a path can be either *open* or *closed*: 'closed' means that the last anchor point is connected to the first anchor point. If you transform a path into a selection, any open components are automatically converted into closed components by connecting the last anchor point to the first anchor point with a straight line.

Path segments can be either straight or curved. A path all of whose segments are straight is called 'polygonal'. When you create a path segment, it starts out straight, because the handles for the anchor points are initially placed directly on top of the anchor points, yielding handles of zero length, which produce straight-line segments. You can make a segment curved by dragging a handle away from one of the anchor points.

One nice thing about paths is that they are very light in terms of resource consumption, especially in comparison with images. Representing a path in RAM only requires storing the coordinates of its anchors and handles: 1K of memory is enough to hold quite a complex path, but not enough to hold even a 20x20 pixel RGB layer. Therefore, it is quite possible to have literally hundreds of paths in an image without putting any significant stress of your system. (How much stress managing them would put on *you* is, of course, another question.) Even a path with thousands of segments consumes minimal resources in comparison to a typical layer or channel.

7.5.2 Paths and Selections

GIMP lets you transform the selection for an image into a path; it also lets you transform paths into selections. For information about the selection and how it works, see the Selection section.

When you transform a selection into a path, the path closely follows the 'marching ants'. Now, the selection is a two-dimensional entity, but a path is a one-dimensional entity, so there is no way to transform the selection into a path without losing information. In fact, any information about partially selected areas (i.e., feathering) will be lost when the selection is turned into a path. If the path is transformed back into a selection, the result is an all-or-none selection, similar to what would be obtained by executing "Sharpen" from the Select menu.

7.5.3 Transforming Paths

Each of the Transform tools (Rotate, Scale, Perspective, etc) can be set to act specifically on paths, using the 'Affect:' option in the tool's Tool Options dialog. This gives you a powerful set of methods for altering the shapes of paths without affecting other elements of the image.

By default a Transform tool, when it is set to affect paths, only acts on a single path: the *active path* for the image, which is shown highlighted in the Paths dialog. You can make a transformation affect more than one path, and possibly other things as well, using the 'transform lock' buttons in the Paths dialog. Not only paths, but also layers and channels, can be transform-locked. If you transform one element that is transform-locked, all others will be transformed in the same way. So, for example, if you want to scale a layer and a path by the same amount, click the transform-lock buttons so that 'chain' symbols appear next to the layer in the Layers dialog, and the path in the Paths dialog; then use the Scale tool on either the layer or the path, and the other will automatically follow.

7.5.4 Stroking a Path

Figure 7.10: The four paths from the top illustration, each stroked in a different way.

Paths do not alter the appearance of the image pixel data unless they are *stroked*, using Edit → Stroke Path from the image menu or the Paths dialog right-click menu, or the 'Stroke Path' button in the Tool Options dialog for the Path tool.

Choosing 'Stroke Path' by any of these means brings up a dialog that allows you to control the way the stroking is done. You can choose from a wide variety of line styles, or you can stroke with any of the Paint tools, including unusual ones such as the Clone tool, Smudge tool, Eraser, etc.

Figure 7.11: The Stroke Path dialog.

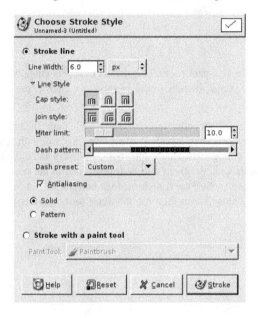

You can further increase the range of stroking effects by stroking a path multiple times, or by using lines or brushes of different widths. The possibilities for getting interesting effects in this way are almost unlimited.

7.5.5 Paths and Text

Figure 7.12: Text converted to a path

(a) *Text converted to a path and then transformed using the Perspective tool.*

(b) *The path shown above, stroked with a fuzzy brush and then gradient-mapped using the Gradient Map filter with the Yellow Contrast gradient.*

A text item created using the Text tool can be transformed into a path using the Create path from text button in the Tool Options for the Text tool. This can be useful for several purposes, including:

- Stroking the path, which gives you many possibilities for fancy text.

- More importantly, transforming the text. Converting text into a path, then transforming the path, and finally either stroking the path or converting it to a selection and filling it, often leads to much higher-quality results than rendering the text as a layer and transforming the pixel data.

7.5.6 Paths and SVG files

SVG, standing for 'Scalable Vector Graphics', is an increasingly popular file format for *vector graphics*, in which graphical elements are represented in a resolution-independent format, in contrast to *raster graphics*; in which graphical elements are represented as arrays of pixels. GIMP is mainly a raster graphics program, but paths are vector entities.

Fortunately, paths are represented in SVG files in almost exactly the same way they are represented in GIMP. (Actually fortune has nothing to do with it: GIMP's path handling was rewritten for GIMP 2.0 with SVG paths in mind.) This compatibility makes it possible to store GIMP paths as SVG files without losing any information. You can access this capability in the Paths dialog.

It also means that GIMP can create paths from SVG files saved in other programs, such as Inkscape or Sodipodi, two popular open-source vector graphics applications. This is nice because those programs have much more powerful path-manipulation tools than GIMP does. You can import a path from an SVG file using the Paths dialog.

The SVG format handles many other graphical elements than just paths: among other things, it handles figures such as squares, rectangles, circles, ellipses, regular polygons, etc. GIMP 2.0 cannot do anything with these entities, but GIMP 2.2 can load them as paths.

Note
Creating paths is not the only thing GIMP can do with SVG files. It can also open SVG files as GIMP images, in the usual way.

7.6 Brushes

Figure 7.13: Brush strokes example

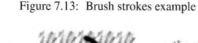

A number of examples of brushstrokes painted using different brushes from the set supplied with GIMP. All were painted using the Paintbrush tool.

A *brush* is a pixmap or set of pixmaps used for painting. GIMP includes a set of 10 "paint tools", which not only perform operations that you would think of as painting, but also operations such as erasing, copying, smudging, lightening or darkening, etc. All of the paint tools, except the ink tool, use the same set of brushes. The brush pixmaps represent the marks that are made by single "touches" of the brush to the image. A brush stroke, usually made by moving the pointer across the image with the mouse button held down, produces a series of marks spaced along the trajectory, in a way specified by the characteristics of the brush and the paint tool being used.

Brushes can be selected by clicking on an icon in the Brushes dialog. GIMP's *current brush* is shown in the Brush/Pattern/Gradient area of the Toolbox. Clicking on the brush symbol there is one way of activating the Brushes dialog.

When you install GIMP, it comes presupplied with a number of basic brushes, plus a few bizarre ones that serve mainly to give you examples of what is possible (i. e., the "green pepper" brush in the illustration). You can also create new brushes, or download them and install them so that GIMP will recognize them.

GIMP can use several different types of brushes. All of them, however, are used in the same way, and for most purposes you don't need to be aware of the differences when you paint with them. Here are the available types of brushes:

Ordinary brushes Most of the brushes supplied with GIMP fall into this category. They are represented in the Brushes dialog by grayscale pixmaps. When you paint using them, the current foreground color (as shown in the Color Area of the Toolbox) is substituted for black, and the pixmap shown in the brushes dialog represents the mark that the brush makes on the image.

To create such a brush: Create a small image in gray levels using zoom. Save it with the .gbr extension. Click on Refresh button in the Brush Dialog to get it in preview without it being necessary to restart GIMP.

Color brushes Brushes in this category are represented by colored images in the Brushes dialog. They can be a text. When you paint with them, the colors are used as shown; the current foreground color does not come into play. Otherwise they work the same way as ordinary brushes.

To create such a brush: Create a small RGBA image. For this, open New Image, select RGB for image type and Transparent for fill type. Draw your image and save it first to .xcf file to keep its properties. Then save it to *.gbr* format. Click on *Refresh* button in Brush Dialog to get your brush without it being necessary to restart Gimp.

 Tip
You can transform a selection to a brush by using the command: Script-Fu → Selection → To Brush.

Image hoses / Image pipes Brushes in this category can make more than one kind of mark on an image. They are indicated by small red triangles at th lower right corner of the brush symbol in the Brushes dialog. They are sometimes called "animated brushes" because the marks change as you trace out a brushstroke. In principle, image hose brushes can be very sophisticated, especially if you use a tablet, changing shape as a function of pressure, angle, etc. These possibilities have never really been exploited, however; and the ones supplied with GIMP are relatively simple (but still quite useful).

You will find an example on how to create such brushes in Animated brushes

Parametric brushes These are brushes created using the Brush Editor, which allows you to generate a wide variety of brush shapes by using a simple graphical interface. A nice feature of parametric brushes is that they are *resizable*. In GIMP 2.2, it is possible, using the Preferences dialog, to make key presses or mouse wheel rotations cause the current brush to become larger or smaller, if it is a parametric brush.

One category that GIMP does not have is full-fledged *procedural* brushes: brushes whose marks are calculated procedurally, instead of being taken from a fixed pixmap. (Actually this is not quite correct: the Ink tool uses a procedural brush, but it is the only one available in GIMP.) A more extensive implementation of procedural brushes is a goal of future development for GIMP.

In addition to the brush pixmap, each GIMP brush has one other important property: the brush *Spacing*. This represents the distance between consecutive brush-marks when a continuous brushstroke is painted. Each brush has an assigned default value for this, which can be modified using the Brushes dialog.

7.7 Adding New Brushes

To add a new brush, after either creating or downloading it, you need to save it in a format GIMP can use. The brush file needs to be placed in the GIMP's brush search path, so that GIMP is able to index and display it in the Brushes dialog. You can hit the Refresh button, which reindexes the brush directory. GIMP uses three file formats for brushes:

GBR The .gbr ("gimp *b*rush") format is used for ordinary and color brushes. You can convert many other types of images, including many brushes used by other programs, into GIMP brushes by opening them in GIMP and saving them with file names ending in .gbr. This brings up a dialog box in which you can set the default Spacing for the brush. A more complete description of the GBR file format can be found in the file gbr.txt in the devel-docs directory of the GIMP source distribution.

GIH The .gih ("*gimp image hose*") format is used for animated brushes. These brushes are constructed from images containing multiple layers: each layer may contain multiple brush-shapes, arranged in a grid. When you save an image as a .gih file, a dialog comes up that allows you to describe the format of the brush. Look at The GIH dialog box for more information about the dialog. The GIH format is rather complicated: a complete description can be found in the file gih.txt in the devel-docs directory of the GIMP source distribution.

VBR The .vbr format is used for parametric brushes, i. e., brushes created using the Brush Editor. There is really no other meaningful way of obtaining files in this format.

To make a brush available, place it in one of the folders in GIMP's brush search path. By default, the brush search path includes two folders, the system brushes folder, which you should not use or alter, and the brushes folder inside your personal GIMP directory. You can add new folders to the brush search path using the Brush Folders page of the Preferences dialog. Any GBR, GIH, or VBR file included in a folder in the brush search path will show up in the Brushes dialog the next time you start GIMP, or as soon as you press the Refresh button in the Brushes dialog.

Note

When you create a new parametric brush using the Brush Editor, it is automatically saved in your personal brushes folder.

There are a number of web sites with downloadable collections of GIMP brushes. Rather than supplying a list of links that will soon be out of date, the best advice is to do a search with your favorite search engine for 'GIMP brushes'. There are also many collections of brushes for other programs with painting functionality. Some can be converted easily into GIMP brushes, some require special conversion utilities, and some cannot be converted at all. Most fancy procedural brush types fall into the last category. If you need to know, look around on the web, and if you don't find anything, look for an expert to ask.

7.8 The GIH Dialog Box

When your new animated brush is created, it is displayed within the image window and you would like save it into a gih format. You select File → Save as... menu, name your work with the gih extension in the new window relevant field and as soon as you pressed the Save button, the following window is displayed:

Figure 7.14: The dialog to describe the animated brush.

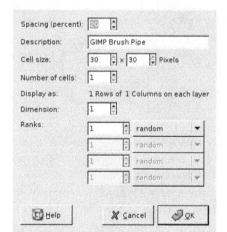

This dialog box shows up, if you save an image as GIMP image hose

This dialog box has several options not easy to understand. They allow you to determine the way your brush is animated.

Spacing (Percent) "Spacing" is the distance between consecutive brush marks when you trace out a brushstroke with the pointer. You must consider drawing with a brush, whatever the paint tool, like stamping. If Spacing is low, stamps will be very close and stroke look continuous. If spacing is high, stamps will be separated: that's interesting with a color brush (like "green pepper" for instance). Value varies from 1 to 200 and this percentage refers to brush "diameter": 100% is one diameter.

Description It's the brush name that will appear at the top of Brush Dialog (grid mode) when the brush is selected.

Cell Size That's size of cells you will cut up in layers... Default is one cell per layer and size is that of the layer. Then there is only one brush aspect per layer.

We could have only one big layer and cut up in it the cells that will be used for the different aspects of the animated brush.

For instance, we want a 100x100 pixels brush with 8 different aspects. We can take these 8 aspects from a 400x200 pixels layer, or from a 300x300 pixels layer but with one cell unused.

Number of cells That's the number of cells (one cell per aspect) that will be cut in every layer. Default is the number of layers as there is only one layer per aspect.

Display as: This tells how cells have been arranged in layers. If, for example, you have placed height cells at the rate of two cells per layer on four layers, GIMP will display: "1 rows of 2 columns on each layer".

Dimension, Ranks, Selection There things are getting complicated! Explanations are necessary to understand how to arrange cell and layers.

GIMP starts retrieving cells from each layer and stacks them into a FIFO stack (First In First Out: the first in is at the top of the stack and so can be first out). In our example 4 layers with 2 cells in each, we'll have, from top to bottom: first cell of first layer, second cell of first layer, first cell of second layer, second cell of second layer..., second cell of fourth layer. With one cell per layer or with several cells per layer, result is the same. You can see this stack in the Layer Dialog of the resulting .gih image file.

Then GIMP creates a computer array from this stack with the Dimensions you have set. You can use four dimensions.

In computer science an array has a "myarray(x,y,z)" form for a 3 dimensions array (3D). It's easy to imagine a 2D array: on a paper it's an array with rows and columns

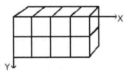

With a 3d array we don't talk rows and columns but Dimensions and Ranks. The first dimension is along x axis, the second dimension along y axis, the third along z axis. Each dimension has ranks of cells.

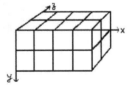

To fill up this array, GIMP starts retrieving cells from the top of stack. The way it fills the array reminds that of an odometer: right rank digits turn first and, when they reach their maximum, left rank digits start running. If you have some memories of Basic programming you will have, with an array(4,2,2), the following succession: (1,1,1),(1,1,2),(1,2,1),(1,2,2),(2,1,1),(2,1,2),(2,2, (4,2,2). We will see this later in an example.

Besides the rank number that you can give to each dimension, you can also give them a Selection mode. You have several modes that will be applied when drawing:

- *Incremental* : GIMP selects a rank from the concerned dimension according to the order ranks have in that dimension

- *Random* : GIMP selects a rank at random from the concerned dimension.

- *Angular* : GIMP selects a rank in the concerned dimension according to the moving angle of the brush.

  The first rank is for the direction 0, upwards. The other ranks are affected, counter clockwise, to an angle whose value is 360/number of ranks. So, with 4 ranks in the concerned dimension, the angle will move 90 counterclockwise for each direction change: second rank will be affected to 270 (-90) (leftwards), third rank to 180 (downwards) and fourth rank to 90 (rightwards).

- *Speed, Pressure, x tilt* and *y tilt* are options for sophisticated drawing tablets.

EXAMPLES

A one dimension image pipe Well! What is all this useful for? We'll see that gradually with examples. You can actually place in each dimension cases that will give your brush a particular action.

Let us start with a 1D brush which will allow us to study selection modes action. We can imagine it like this:

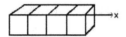

Follow these steps:

1. Open a new 30x30 pixels image, RGB with Transparent fill type. Using the Text tool create 4 layers "1", "2", "3", "4". Delete the "background" layer.

2. Save this image first with .xcf extension to keep its properties then save it as .gih.

3. The Save As Dialog is opened: select a destination for your image. OK. The GIH dialog is opened: Choose Spacing 100, give a name in Description box, 30x30 for Cell Size, 1 dimension, 1 rank and choose "Incremental" in Selection box. OK.

4. You may have difficulties to save directly in the GIMP Brush directory. In that case, save the .gih file manually into the /usr/share/gimp/gimp 2.0/brushes directory. Then come back into the Toolbox, clic on the brush icon to open the Brush Dialog then click on "Refresh". Your new brush appears in the Brush window. Select it. Select pencil tool for instance and click and hold with it on a new image

   $$2\ 3\ 4\ 1\ 2\ 3\ 4\ 1\ 2\ 3$$

   You see 1, 2, 3, 4 digits following one another in order.

5. Take your .xcf image file back and save it as .gih setting Selection to "Random": digits will be displayed at random order:

   $$1\ 3\ 2\ 1\ 4\ 3\ 4\ 2\ 3\ 4\ 4$$

6. Now select "Angular" Selection:

$$\begin{array}{ccc} 2 & 2 & \\ & & 3 \\ & 3 & \\ 4\ 4\ 4 & & 3 \end{array}$$

A 3 dimensions image hose We are now going to create a 3D animated brush: its orientation will vary according to brush direction, it will alternate Left/Right hands regularly and its color will vary at random between black and blue.

The first question we have to answer to is the number of images that is necessary. We reserve the first dimension (x) to the brush direction (4 directions). The second dimension (y) is for Left/Right alternation and the third dimension (z) for color variation. Such a brush is represented in a 3D array "myarray(4,2,2)":

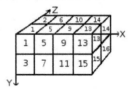

There are 4 ranks in first dimension (x), 2 ranks in second dimension (y) and 2 ranks in third dimension (z). We see that there are 4x2x2 = 16 cells. We need 16 images.

1. *Creating images of dimension 1 (x)*: Open a new 30x30 pixels image, RGB with Transparent Fill Type. Using the zoom draw a left hand with fingers upwards. Save it as handL0k.xcf (hand Left O Black).

   Open the Layer Dialog. Double click on the layer to open the Layer Attributes Dialog and rename it to handL0k.

   Duplicate the layer. Let visible only the duplicated layer, select it and apply a 90 rotation (Layer/Transform/ 90 rotation counter-clockwise). Rename it to handL-90k.

   Repeat the same operations to create handL180k and handL90k.

2. *Creating images of dimension 2 (y)*: This dimension in our example has two ranks, one for left hand and the other for right hand. The left hand rank exists yet. We shall build right hand images by flipping it horisontally.

   Duplicate the handL0k layer. Let it visible only and select it. Rename it to handR0K. Apply Layer/Transform/Flip Horizontally.

   Repeat the same operation on the other left hand layers to create their right hand equivalent.

   Re-order layers to have a counter-clockwise rotation from top to bottom, alternating Left and Right: handL0k, handR0k, handL-90k, handR-90k, ..., handR90k.

3. *Creating images of dimension 3 (z)*: The third dimension has two ranks, one for black color and the other for blue color. The first rank, black, exists yet. We well see that images of dimension 3 will be a copy, in blue, of the images of dimension 2. So we will have our 16 images. But a row of 16 layers is not easy to manage: we will use layers with two images.

   Select the handL0k layer and let it visible only. Using Image/Canvas Size change canvas size to 60x30 pixels.

   Duplicate hand0k layer. On the copy, fill the hand with blue using Bucket Fill tool.

   Now, select the Move tool. Double click on it to accede to its properties: check "Move the Current Layer" option. Move the blue hand into the right part of the layer precisely with the help of Zoom.

   Make sure only handL0k and its blue copy are visible. Right click on the Layer Dialog: Apply the "Merge Visible Layers" command with the option "Expand as Necessary". You get a 60x30 pixels layer with the black hand on the left and the blue hand on the right. Rename it to "handL0".

   Repeat the same operations on the other layers.

4. *Set layers in order*: Layers must be set in order so that GIMP can find the required image at some point of using the brush. Our layers are yet in order but we must understand more generally how to have them in order. There are two ways to imagine this setting in order. The first method is mathematical: GIMP divides the 16 layers first by 4; that gives 4 groups of 4 layers for the first dimension. Each group represents a direction of the brush. Then, it divides each group by 2; that gives 8 groups of 2 layers for the second dimension: each group represents a L/R alternation. Then another division by 2 for the third dimension to represent a color at random between black and blue.

   The other method is visual, by using the array representation. Correlation between two methods is represented in next image:

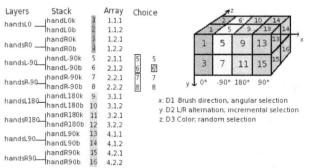

   How will GIMP read this array?: GIMP starts with the first dimension which is programmed for 'angular', for instance -90. In this -90 rank, in yellow, in the second dimension, it selects a L/R alternation, in an 'incremental' way. Then, in the third dimension, in a random way, it chooses a color. Finely, our layers must be in the following order:

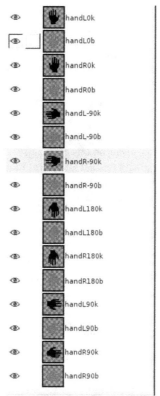

5. Voilà. Your brush is ready. Save it as .xcf first then as .gih with the following parameters: Spacing:100 Description:Hands Cell Size: 30x30 Number of cells:16 Dimensions: 3

   • Dimension 1: 4 ranks Selection: Angular
   • Dimension 2: 2 ranks Selection: Incremental
   • Dimension 3: 2 ranks Selection: Random

   Place your .gih file into GIMP brush directory and refresh the brush box. You can now use your brush.

Figure 7.15: Here is the result by stroking an elliptical selection with the brush:

This brush alternates right hand and left hand regularly, black and blue color at random, according to four brush directions.

7.9 Creating a Brush with Variable Size

You can create a brush with a size which will vary by rotating the mouse wheel or by using the keyboard arrow keys.

1. Start with opening the Brush dialog by double_clicking on the Brush area in Toolbox, or by going through File → Dialogs → Brushes.

2. Click on the New Brush button to open the Brush Editor dialog. Name your brush at once, 'Dynamic' for instance. Your brush will appear in the Brush Dialog with a blue corner.

3. Now, go to File → Preferences → Input Controllers.

   - Check the Enable this controller box.

   - Scroll through the Events list and select Scroll up (Shift). Avoid Scroll up (Ctrl) because **Ctrl** is yet used by tools to turn to the Color Picker mode.

   - Click on the Edit button to open a window that allows you to assign an action to the selected event. If an action is assigned to the event yet, the window opens on this event; else, click on the small triangular button close to the Context item to drop the list down. Scroll through this list and select the context-brush-radius-increase item. (You could choose context-brush-radius-increase-skip). Click on OK.

   - Do the same way to assign the 'context-brush-radius-decrease' action to the 'Scroll down (Shift)' event to decrease the brush size.

4. Save your brush by clicking on the Save button in the Brush Editor.

Now, if you have selected your Dynamic brush, when you work with a tool that has a 'Brush' option while pressing the **Shift** key, the brush size will vary by using the mouse wheel. This change will be visible in real time in the brush area of the Toolbox and in the Brush Dialog.

By enabling the 'Main Keyboard' tab, you can, in the same way, assign an action to the events of the keyboard arrow keys.

 Note

Actions are not removed from the window when you delete the brush. You have to delete them manually by clicking on the Delete button after selecting them.

7.10 Gradients

Figure 7.16: Some examples of GIMP gradients.

Gradients from top to bottom: FG to BG (RGB); Full saturation spectrum; Nauseating headache; Browns; Four bars

A *gradient* is a set of colors arranged in a linear order. The most basic use of gradients is by the Blend tool, sometimes known as the 'gradient tool' or 'gradient fill tool': it works by filling the selection with colors from a gradient. You have many options to choose from for controlling the way the gradient colors are arranged within the selection. There are also other important ways to use gradients, including:

Painting with a gradient Each of GIMP's basic painting tools allows you the option of using colors from a gradient. This enables you to create brushstrokes that change color from one end to the other.

The Gradient Map filter This filter allows you to 'colorize' a grayscale image, by replacing each shade of gray with the corresponding color from a gradient. See Section 15.3.8 for more information.

When you install GIMP, it comes presupplied with a large number of interesting gradients, and you can add new ones that you create or download from other sources. You can access the full set of available gradients using the Gradients dialog, a dockable dialog that you can either activate when you need it, or keep around as a tab in a dock. The 'current gradient', used in most gradient-related operations, is shown in the Brush/Pattern/Gradient area of the Toolbox. Clicking on the gradient symbol in the Toolbox is an alternative way of bringing up the Gradients dialog.

Figure 7.17: Gradient usage

Four ways of using the Tropical Colors gradient: a linear gradient fill, a shaped gradient fill, a stroke painted using colors from a gradient, and a stroke painted with a fuzzy brush then colored using the Gradient Map filter.

A few useful things to know about GIMP's gradients:

- The first four gradients in the list are special: they use the Foreground and Background colors from the Toolbox Color Area, instead of being fixed. FG to BG (RGB) is the RGB representation of the gradient from the Foreground color to the Background color in Toolbox. FG to BG (HSV counter-clockwise) represents the hue succession in Color Circle from the selected hue to 360. FG to BG (HSV clockwise represents the hue succession in Color Circle from the selected hue to 0. With FG to transparent , the selected hue becomes more and more transparent. You can modify these colors by using the Color Selector. Thus, by altering the foreground and background colors, you can make these gradients transition smoothly between any two colors you want.

- Gradients can involve not just color changes, but also changes in opacity. Some of the gradients are completely opaque; others include transparent or translucent parts. When you fill or paint with a non-opaque gradient, the existing contents of the layer will show through behind it.

- You can create new *custom* gradients, using the Gradient Editor. You cannot modify the gradients that are supplied with GIMP, but you can duplicate them or create new ones, and then edit those.

The gradients that are supplied with GIMP are stored in a system `gradients` folder. By default, gradients that you create are stored in a folder called `gradients` in your personal GIMP directory. Any gradient files (ending with the extension `.ggr`) found in one of these folders, will automatically be loaded when you start GIMP. You can add more directories to the gradient search path, if you want to, in the Gradients tab of the Data Folders pages of the Preferences dialog.

New in GIMP 2.2 is the ability to load gradient files in SVG format, used by many vector graphics programs. To make GIMP load an SVG gradient file, all you need to do is place it in the `gradients` folder of your personal GIMP directory, or any other folder in your gradient search path.

 Tip
You can find a large number of interesting SVG gradients on the web, in particular at OpenClipArt Gradients [OPENCLIPART-GRADIENT]. You won't be able to see what these gradients look like unless your browser supports SVG, but that won't prevent you from downloading them.

7.11 Patterns

A *pattern* is an image, usually small, used for filling regions by *tiling*, that is, by placing copies of the pattern side by side like ceramic tiles. A pattern is said to be *tileable* if copies of it can be adjoined left-edge-to-right-edge and top-edge-to-bottom-edge without creating obvious seams. Not all useful patterns are tileable, but tileable patterns are nicest for many purposes. (A *texture*, by the way, is the same thing as a pattern.)

Figure 7.18: Pattern usage

Three ways of using the Leopard pattern: bucket-filling a selection, painting with the Clone tool, and stroking an elliptical selection with the pattern.

In GIMP there are three main uses for patterns:

- With the Bucket Fill tool, you can choose to fill a region with a pattern instead of a solid color.

- With the Clone tool, you can paint using a pattern, with a wide variety of paintbrush shapes.

- When you *stroke* a path or selection, you can do it with a pattern instead of a solid color. You can also use the Clone tool as your choice if you stroke the selection using a painting tool.

 Tip
Note: Patterns do not need to be opaque. If you fill or paint using a pattern with translucent or transparent areas, then the previous contents of the area will show through from behind it. This is one of many ways of doing 'overlays' in GIMP.

When you install GIMP, it comes presupplied with a few dozen patterns, which seem to have been chosen more or less randomly. You can also add new patterns, either ones you create yourself, or ones you download from the vast number available online.

GIMP's *current pattern*, used in most pattern-related operations, is shown in the Brush/Pattern/Gradient area of the Toolbox. Clicking on the pattern symbol brings up the Patterns dialog, which allows you to select a different pattern. You can also access the Patterns dialog by menu, or dock it so that it is present continuously.

To add a new pattern to the collection, so that it shows up in the Patterns dialog, you need to save it in a format GIMP can use, in a folder included in GIMP's pattern search path. There are several file formats you can use for patterns:

PAT The `.pat` format is used only by GIMP, so you will not find patterns in this format unless they were created specifically for GIMP. You can, however, convert any image into a `.pat` file by opening it in GIMP and then saving it using a file name ending in `.pat`.

PNG, JPEG, BMP, GIF, TIFF New in GIMP 2.2 is the ability to use `.png`, `.jpg`, `.bmp`, `.gif`, or `.tiff` files as patterns.

To make a pattern available, you place it in one of the folders in GIMP's pattern search path. By default, the pattern search path includes two folders, the system `patterns` folder, which you should not use or alter, and the `patterns` folder inside your personal GIMP directory. You can add new folders to the pattern search path using the Pattern Folders page of the Preferences dialog. Any PAT file (or, in GIMP 2.2, any of the other acceptable formats) included in a folder in the pattern search path will show up in the Patterns dialog the next time you start GIMP.

There are countless ways of creating interesting patterns in GIMP, using the wide variety of available tools and filters -- particularly the rendering filters. You can find tutorials for this in many locations, including the GIMP home page [GIMP]. Some of the filters have options that allow you to make their results tileable. Also, see Section 15.2.7, this filter allows you to blend the edges of an image in order to make it more smoothly tileable.

Figure 7.19: Pattern script examples

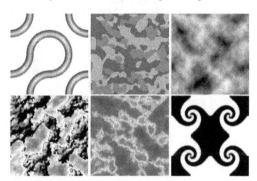

Examples of patterns created using six of the Pattern script-fu's that come with GIMP. Default settings were used for everything except size. (From left to right: 3D Truchet; Camouflage; Flatland; Land; Render Map; Swirly)

Also of interest are a set of pattern-generating scripts that come with GIMP: you can find them in the Toolbox menu, under Xtns → Script-Fu → Patterns. Each of the scripts creates a new image filled with a particular type of pattern: a dialog pops up that allows you to set parameters controlling the details of the appearance. Some of these patterns are most useful for cutting and pasting; others serve best as bumpmaps.

7.12   Palettes

A *palette* is a set of discrete colors. In GIMP, palettes are used mainly for two purposes:

- They allow you to paint with a selected set of colors, in the same way an oil painter works with colors from a limited number of tubes.

- They form the colormaps of indexed images. An indexed image can use a maximum of 256 different colors, but these can be any colors. The colormap of an indexed image is called an "indexed palette" in GIMP.

Actually neither of these functions fall very much into the mainstream of GIMP usage: it is possible to do rather sophisticated things in GIMP without ever dealing with palettes. Still, they are something that an advanced user should understand, and even a less advanced user may need to think about them in some situations, as for example when working with GIF files.

Figure 7.20: The Palettes dialog

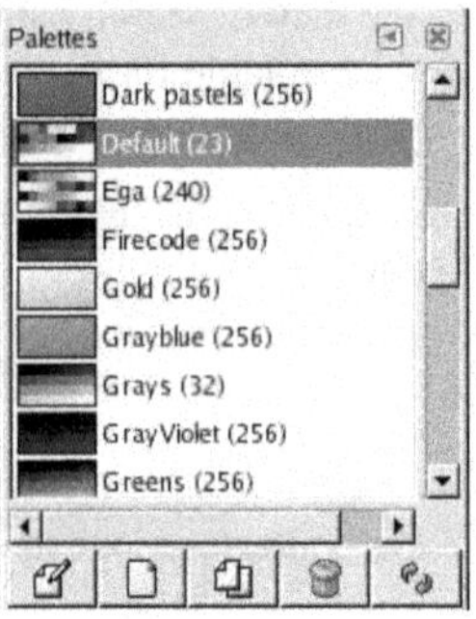

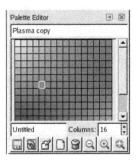

When you install GIMP, it comes supplied with several dozen predefined palettes, and you can also create new ones. Some of the predefined palettes are commonly useful, such as the 'Web' palette, which contains the set of colors considered 'web safe'; many of the palettes seem to have been chosen more or less whimsically. You can access all of the available palettes using the Palettes dialog. This is also the starting point if you want to create a new palette.

Figure 7.21: The Palette Editor El editor de paletas

Double-clicking on a palette in the Palettes dialog brings up the Palette Editor, showing the colors from the palette you clicked on. You can use this to paint with the palette: clicking on a color sets GIMP's foreground to that color, as shown in the Color Area of the Toolbox. Holding down the **Ctrl** key while clicking, on the other hand, sets GIMP's background color to the color you click on.

You can also, as the name implies, use the Palette Editor to change the colors in a palette, so long as it is a palette that you have created yourself. You cannot edit the palettes that are supplied with GIMP; however you can duplicate them and then edit the copies.

When you create palettes using the Palette Editor, they are automatically saved as soon as you exit GIMP, in the palettes folder of your personal GIMP directory. Any palette files in this directory, or in the system palettes directory created when GIMP is installed, are automatically loaded and shown in the Palettes dialog the next time you start GIMP. You can also add other folders to the palette search path using the Palette Folders page of the Preferences dialog.

GIMP palettes are stored using a special file format, in files with the extension .gpl. It is a very simple format, and they are ASCII files, so if you happen to obtain palettes from another source, and would like to use them in GIMP, it probably won't be very hard to convert them: just take a look at any .gpl and you will see what to do.

7.12.1 Colormap

Confusingly, GIMP makes use of two types of palettes. The more noticeable are the type shown in the Palettes dialog: palettes that exist independently of any image. The second type, *indexed palettes*, form the colormaps of indexed images. Each indexed image has its own private indexed palette, defining the set of colors available in the image: the maximum number of colors allowed in an indexed palette is 256. These palettes are called 'indexed' because each color is associated with an index number. (Actually, the colors in ordinary palettes are numbered as well, but the numbers have no functional significance.)

Figure 7.22: The Colormap dialog

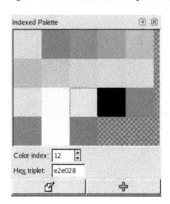

The colormap of an indexed image is shown in the Indexed Palette dialog, which should not be confused with the Palettes dialog. The Palettes dialog shows a list of all of the palettes available; the Colormap dialog shows the colormap of the currently active image, if it is an indexed image - otherwise it shows nothing.

You can, however, create an ordinary palette from the colors in an indexed image---actually from the colors in any image. To do this, choose Import Palette from the right-click popup menu in the Palettes dialog: this pops up a dialog that gives you several options, including the option to import the palette from an image. (You can also import any of GIMP's gradients as a palette.) This possibility becomes important if you want to create a set of indexed images that all use the same set of colors.

When you convert an image into indexed mode, a major part of the process is the creation of an indexed palette for the image. How this happens is described in detail in Section 14.9.6. Briefly, you have several methods to choose from, one of which is to use a specified palette from the Palettes dialog.

Thus, to sum up the foregoing, ordinary palettes can be turned into indexed palettes when you convert an image into indexed mode; indexed palettes can be turned into ordinary palettes by importing them into the Palettes dialog.

7.13 Drawing Simple Objects

In this section, you will learn how to create simple objects in GIMP. It's pretty easy once you figure out how to do it. GIMP provides a huge set of Tools and Shortcuts which most new users get lost in.

7.13.1 Drawing a Straight Line

Let's begin by painting a straight line. The easiest way to create a straight line is by using your favorite painting tool, the mouse and the keyboard.

Figure 7.23: The dialog shows a new image, filled with a white background.

1.

Create a new image. Select your favorite painting tool or use the pencil, if in doubt. Select a foreground color, but be sure that the foreground and background colors are different.

Figure 7.24: The dialog shows a new image, with the first dot which indicates the start of the straight line. The dot has a black foreground color.

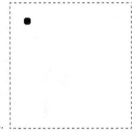

Create a starting point by clicking on the image display area with the left mouse button. Your canvas should look similar to Figure 7.23.

Figure 7.25: The screenshot shows the helpline, which indicates how the finished line will look.

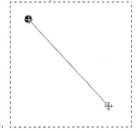

Now, hold down the **Shift** button on your keyboard and move the mouse away from the starting point you created. You'll see a thin line indicating how the line will look.

Figure 7.26: The line created appears in the image window after drawing the second point (or end point), while the **Shift** key is still pressed.

If you're satisfied with the direction and length of the line, click the left mouse button again to finish the line. The GIMP displays a straight line now. If the line doesn't appear, check the foreground and background colors and be sure that you kept the **Shift** key pressed while painting. You can keep creating lines by continuing to hold the **Shift** key and creating additional end points.

7.13.2   Creating a Basic Shape

1. Drawing shapes is not the main purpose for using GIMP. However, you may create shapes by either painting them using the technique described in Figure 7.23 or by using the selection tools. Of course, there are various other ways to paint a

shape, but we'll stick to the easiest ones here. So, create a new image and check that the foreground and background colors are different.

Figure 7.27: The screenshot shows how a rectangular selection is created. Press and hold the left mouse button while you move the mouse in the direction of the red arrow.

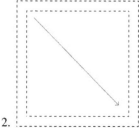

2.

Basic shapes like rectangles or ellipses, can be created using the selection tools. This tutorial uses a rectangular selection as an example. So, choose the rectangular selection tool and create a new selection: press and hold the left mouse button while you move the mouse to another position in the image (illustrated in figure Figure 7.27). The selection is created when you release the mouse button. For more information about key modifiers see selection tools.

Figure 7.28: The screenshot shows a rectangular selection filled with the foreground color.

3.

After creating the selection, you can either create a filled or an outlined shape with the foreground color of your choice. If you go for the first option, choose a foreground color and fill the selection with the bucket fill tool. If you choose the latter option, create an outline by using theStroke selection menu item from the Edit menu. If you're satisfied with the result, remove the selection.

Chapter 8

Combining Images

8.1 Introduction to Layers

A good way to visualize a GIMP image is as a stack of transparencies: in GIMP terminology, each individual transparency is called a *layer*. There is no limit, in principle, to the number of layers an image can have: only the amount of memory available on the system. It is not uncommon for advanced users to work with images containing dozens of layers.

The organization of layers in an image is shown by the Layers dialog, which is the second most important type of dialog window in GIMP, after the Main Toolbox. The appearance of the Layers dialog is shown in the adjoining illustration. How it works is described in detail in the Layers Dialog section, but we will touch on some aspects of it here, in relation to the layer properties that they display.

Each open image has at any time a single *active drawable*. A 'drawable' is a GIMP concept that includes layers, but also several other types of things, such as channels, layer masks, and the selection mask. (Basically, a 'drawable' is anything that can be drawn on with painting tools). If a layer is currently active, it is shown highlighted in the Layers dialog, and its name is shown in the status area of the image window. If not, you can activate it by clicking on it. If none of the layers are highlighted, it means the active drawable is something other than a layer.

In the menubar above an image window, you can find a menu called Layer, containing a number of commands that affect the active layer of the image. The same menu can be accessed by right-clicking in the Layers dialog.

8.1.1 Layer Properties

Each layer in an image has a number of important attributes:

Name Every layer has a name. This is assigned automatically when the layer is created, but you can change it. You can change the name of a layer either by double-clicking on it in the Layers dialog, or by right-clicking there and then selecting the top entry in the menu that appears, Edit Layer Attributes.

Presence or absence of an alpha channel As explained in the previous section, an alpha channel encodes information about how transparent a layer is at each pixel. It is visible in the Channel Dialog: white is complete opacity, black is complete transparency and grey levels are partial transparencies.

The background layer is particular. If you have just created a new image, it has still only one layer which is a background layer. If the image has been created with an opaque Fill type, this one layer has no Alpha channel. If you add a new layer, even with an opaque Fill type, an Alpha channel is automatically created, which applies to all layers apart from the background layer. To get a background layer with transparency, either you create your new image with a transparent Fill type, or you use the Add an Alpha Channel.

Every layer other than the bottom layer of an image must have an alpha channel. For the bottom layer, it is optional. Many operations cannot be performed on layers that lack an alpha channel. Moving the layer to a different position in the layer stack is one obvious example (since only bottom layers are allowed not to have an alpha channel), but any operation involving transparency would also be included. You can add an alpha channel to a layer that lacks one using the menu command Layer → Transparency → Add Alpha Channel, or by right-clicking in the Layers dialog and selecting Add Alpha Channel from the popup menu that appears.

Example for Alpha channel

Figure 8.1: Alpha channel example: Basic image

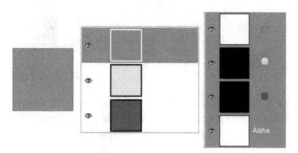

This image has three layers painted with pure 100% opaque Red, Green, and Blue. In the Channel Dialog, you can see that an alpha Channel has been added. It is white because the image is not transparent since there is at least one 100% opaque layer. The current layer is the red one : since it is painted with pure red, there is no green and no blue and the corresponding channels are black.

Figure 8.2: Alpha channel example: One layer transparent

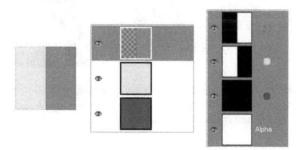

The left part of the first layer has been made transparent (Rectangular selection, Edit/Clear). The second layer, green, is visible. The Alpha channel is still white, since there is an opaque layer in this part of the image.

Figure 8.3: Alpha channel example: Two layers transparent

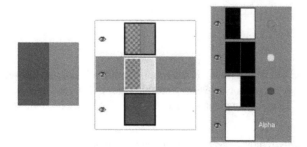

The left part of the second layer has been made transparent. The third layer, blue, is visible through the first and second layers. The Alpha channel is still white, since there is an opaque layer in this part of the image.

Figure 8.4: Alpha channel example: Three layers transparent

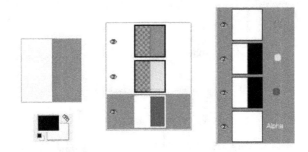

The left part of the third layer has been made transparent. The Alpha channel is still white and the left part of the layer is white, opaque! The background layer has no Alpha channel. In this case, the Clear command works like the Eraser and uses the Background color of Toolbox.

Figure 8.5: Alpha channel example: Alpha channel added to the Background

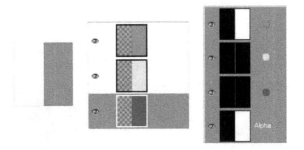

We used the LayerTransparencyAdd Alpha Channel command, which is active on the Background layer only. Now, the left part of the image is fully transparent and has the color of the page the image is lying on. The left part of the Alpha Channel thumbnail is black (transparent) in the Channel Dialog.

Layer type The layer type is determined by the image type (see previous section) and the presence or absence of an alpha channel. These are the possible layer types:

- RGB
- RGBA
- Gray
- GrayA
- Indexed
- IndexedA

The main reason this matters is that most filters (in the Filters menu) only accept a subset of layer types, and appear grayed out in the menu if the active layer does not have an acceptable type. Often you can rectify this either by changing the mode of the image or by adding or removing an alpha channel.

Visibility It is possible to temporarily remove a layer from an image, without destroying it, by clicking on the symbol in the Layers dialog. This is called 'toggling the visibility' of the layer. Most operations on an image treat toggled-off layers as if they did not exist. When you work with images containing many layers, with varying opacity, you often can get a better picture of the contents of the layer you want to work on by hiding some of the other layers.

Tip
If you *Shift*-click on the eye symbol, this will cause all layers *except* the one you click on to be hidden.

Linkage to other layers If you click between the eye icon and the layer thumbnail, you get a chain icon ( ), which enables you to group layers for operations on multiple layers (for example with the Move tool or a transform tool).

Size In GIMP, the boundaries of a layer do not necessarily match the boundaries of the image that contains it. When you create text, for example, each text item goes into its own separate layer, and the layer is precisely sized to contain the text and nothing more. Also, when you create a new layer using cut-and-paste, the new layer is sized just large enough to contain the pasted item. In the image window, the boundaries of the currently active layer are shown outlined with a black-and-yellow dashed line.

The main reason why this matters is that you cannot do anything to a layer outside of its boundaries: you can't act on what doesn't exist. If this causes you problems, you can alter the dimensions of the layer using any of several commands that you can find near the bottom of the Layer menu.

 Note
The amount of memory that a layer consumes is determined by its dimensions, not its contents. So, if you are working with large images or images that contain many layers, it might pay off to trim layers to the minimum possible size.

Opacity The opacity of a layer determines the extent to which it lets colors from layers beneath it in the stack show through. Opacity ranges from 0 to 100, with 0 meaning complete transparency, and 100 meaning complete opacity.

Mode The Mode of a layer determines how colors from the layer are combined with colors from the underlying layers to produce a visible result. This is a sufficiently complex, and sufficiently important, concept to deserve a section of its own, which follows. See Section 8.2.

Layer mask In addition to the alpha channel, there is another way to control the transparency of a layer: by adding a *layer mask*, which is an extra grayscale drawable associated with the layer. A layer does not have a layer mask by default: it must be added specifically. Layer masks, and how to work with them, are described much more extensively in the Layer Mask section.

'Keep transparency' setting In the upper right corner of the Layers dialog appears a small checkbox that controls the 'keep transparency' setting for the layer. If this is checked, then the alpha channel for the layer is locked, and no manipulation has any effect on it. In particular, nothing that you do to a transparent part of the layer will have any effect.

8.2 Layer Modes

GIMP has twenty-one layer modes. Layer modes are also sometimes called 'blending modes'. Selecting a layer mode changes the appearance of the layer or image, based on the layer or layers beneath it. If there is only one layer, the layer mode has no effect. There must therefore be at least two layers in the image to be able to use layer modes.

You can set the layer mode in the Mode menu in the Layers dialog. GIMP uses the layer mode to determine how to combine each pixel in the top layer with the pixel in the same location in the layer below it.

 Note
There is a drop-down list in the Toolbox options box which contains modes that affect the painting tools in a similar way to the layer modes. You can use all of the same modes for painting that are available for layers, and there are two additional modes just for the painting tools, which are described here at the end of the list of layer modes.

Layer modes permit complex color changes in the image. They are often used with a new layer which acts as a kind of mask. For example, if you put a solid white layer over an image and set the layer mode of the new layer to 'Saturation', the underlying visible layers will appear in shades of gray.

Figure 8.6: Images (masks) for layer mode examples

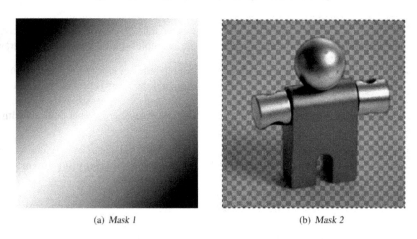

(a) *Mask 1*   (b) *Mask 2*

Figure 8.7: Images (backgrounds) for layer mode examples

(a) *Key fob*   (b) *Ducks*

In the descriptions of the layer modes below, the equations are also shown. This is for those who are curious about the mathematics of the layer modes. You do not need to understand the equations in order to use the layer modes effectively, however.

The equations are in a shorthand notation. For example, the equation

$E = M + I$

EQUATION 8.1: Example

means, ' For each pixel in the upper (*M*ask)and lower (*I*mage) layer, add each of the corresponding color components together to form the *E* resulting pixel's. color. ' Pixel color components must always be between 0 and 255. Unless the description below says otherwise, a negative color component is set to 0 and a color component larger than 255 is set to 255.

The examples below show the effects of each of the modes. The image on the left is the normal state and the image on the right shows the results of the layer mode.

Since the results of each mode vary greatly depending upon the colors on the layers, these images can only give you a general idea of how the modes work. You are encouraged to try them out yourself. You might start with two similar layers, where one is a copy of the other, but slightly modified (by being blurred, moved, rotated, scaled, color-inverted, etc.) and seeing what happens with the layer modes.

Normal

Figure 8.8: Example for layer mode 'Normal'

(a) Both images are blended into eachother with the same intensity.

(b) With 100% opacity only the upper layer is shown when blending with Normal.

Normal mode is the default layer mode. The layer on top covers the layers below it. If you want to see anything below the top layer when you use this mode, the layer must have some transparent areas.

The equation is:

$$E = M$$

EQUATION 8.2: Equation for layer mode Normal

Dissolve

Figure 8.9: Example for layer mode 'Dissolve'

(a) Both images are blended into eachother with the same intensity.

(b) With 100% opacity only the upper layer is shown when blending with dissolve.

Dissolve mode dissolves the upper layer into the layer beneath it by drawing a random pattern of pixels in areas of partial transparency. It is useful as a layer mode, but it is also often useful as a painting mode.

This is especially visible along the edges within an image. It is easiest to see in an enlarged screenshot. The image on the left illustrates 'Normal' layer mode (enlarged) and the image on the right shows the same two layers in 'Dissolve' mode, where it can be clearly seen how the pixels are dispersed.

Multiply

Figure 8.10: Example for layer mode 'Multiply'

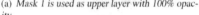

(a) *Mask 1 is used as upper layer with 100% opacity.*   (b) *Mask 2 is used as upper layer with 100% opacity.*

Multiply mode multiplies the pixel values of the upper layer with those of the layer below it and then divides the result by 255. The result is usually a darker image. If either layer is white, the resulting image is the same as the other layer (1 * I = I). If either layer is black, the resulting image is completely black (0 * I = 0).

The equation is:

$$E = \tfrac{1}{255}(M * I)$$

EQUATION 8.3: Equation for layer mode Multiply

The mode is commutative; the order of the two layers doesn't matter.

Divide

Figure 8.11: Example for layer mode 'Divide'

(a) *Mask 1 is used as upper layer with 100% opacity.* (b) *Mask 2 is used as upper layer with 100% opacity.*

Divide mode multiplies each pixel value in the lower layer by 256 and then divides that by the corresponding pixel value of the upper layer plus one. (Adding one to the denominator avoids dividing by zero.) The resulting image is often lighter, and sometimes looks 'burned out'.

The equation is:

$$E = 256 \frac{I}{M+1}$$

EQUATION 8.4: Equation for layer mode Divide

Screen

Figure 8.12: Example for layer mode 'Screen'

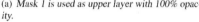

(a) *Mask 1 is used as upper layer with 100% opacity.* (b) *Mask 2 is used as upper layer with 100% opacity.*

Screen mode inverts the values of each of the visible pixels in the two layers of the image. (That is, it subtracts each of them from 255.) Then it multiplies them together, inverts this value again and divides by 255. The resulting image is usually brighter, and sometimes 'washed out' in appearance. The exceptions to this are a black layer, which does not change the other layer, and a white layer, which results in a white image. Darker colors in the image appear to be more transparent.

The equation is:

$$E = 1 - \frac{(255-M)*(255-I)}{255}$$

EQUATION 8.5: Equation for layer mode Screen

The mode is commutative; the order of the two layers doesn't matter.

Overlay

Figure 8.13: Example for layer mode 'Overlay'

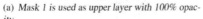

(a) *Mask 1 is used as upper layer with 100% opacity.*   (b) *Mask 2 is used as upper layer with 100% opacity.*

Overlay mode inverts the pixel value of the lower layer, multiplies it by two times the pixel value of the upper layer, adds that to the original pixel value of the lower layer, divides by 255, and then multiplies by the pixel value of the original lower layer and divides by 255 again. It darkens the image, but not as much as with 'Multiply' mode.

The equation is: [1]

$$E = \frac{1I}{255} * (I + \frac{2M}{255} * (255 - I))$$

EQUATION 8.6: Equation for layer mode Overlay

Dodge

---

[1]

The equation is the *theoretical* equation. Due to Bug #162395 , the actual equation is equivalent to Soft light. It is difficult to fix this bug without changing the appearance of existing images.

Figure 8.14: Example for layer mode 'Dodge'

(a) *Mask 1 is used as upper layer with 100% opacity.*   (b) *Mask 2 is used as upper layer with 100% opacity.*

Dodge mode multiplies the pixel value of the lower layer by 256, then divides that by the inverse of the pixel value of the top layer. The resulting image is usually lighter, but some colors may be inverted.

In photography, dodging is a technique used in a darkroom to increase the exposure in particular areas of the image. This brings out details in the shadows. When used for this purpose, dodge may work best on Grayscale images and with a painting tool, rather than as a layer mode.

The equation is:

$$E = \frac{I*256}{(255-M)+1}$$

EQUATION 8.7: Equation for layer mode Dodge

Burn

Figure 8.15: Example for layer mode 'Burn'

(a) *Mask 1 is used as upper layer with 100% opacity.*   (b) *Mask 2 is used as upper layer with 100% opacity.*

Burn mode inverts the pixel value of the lower layer, multiplies it by 256, divides that by one plus the pixel value of the upper layer, then inverts the result. It tends to make the image darker, somewhat similar to 'Multiply' mode.

In photography, burning is a technique used in a darkroom to decrease the exposure in particular areas of the image. This brings out details in the highlights. When used for this purpose, burn may work best on Grayscale images and with a painting tool, rather than as a layer mode.

The equation is:

$$E = 255 - \frac{(255 - I) * 256}{M + 1}$$

EQUATION 8.8: Equation for layer mode Burn

Hard light

Figure 8.16: Example for layer mode 'Hard light'

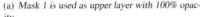

(a) *Mask 1 is used as upper layer with 100% opacity.* (b) *Mask 2 is used as upper layer with 100% opacity.*

Hard light mode is rather complicated because the equation consists of two parts, one for darker colors and one for brighter colors. If the pixel color of the upper layer is greater than 128, the layers are combined according to the first formula shown below. Otherwise, the pixel values of the upper and lower layers are multiplied together and multiplied by two, then divided by 256. You might use this mode to combine two photographs and obtain bright colors and sharp edges.

The equation is complex and different according to the value >128 or $\leq$128 :

$$M > 128 : E = 255 - \frac{(255 - I) * (255 - (2 * (M - 128)))}{256}$$

EQUATION 8.9: Equation for layer mode Hard light, M > 128

$$M \leq 128 : E = \frac{I * M * 2}{256}$$

EQUATION 8.10: Equation for layer mode Hard light, M $\leq$ 128

Soft light

Figure 8.17: Example for layer mode 'Soft light'

(a) *Mask 1 is used as upper layer with 100% opacity.*

(b) *Mask 2 is used as upper layer with 100% opacity.*

Soft light is not related to 'Hard light' in anything but the name, but it does tend to make the edges softer and the colors not so bright. It is similar to 'Overlay' mode. In some versions of GIMP, 'Overlay' mode and 'Soft light' mode are identical.

The equation is complicated. It needs Rs, the result of Screen mode :

$$R_s = \frac{255 - ((255 - I) * (255 - M))}{256}$$

EQUATION 8.11: Equation for layer mode Screen

$$E = \frac{((255 - I) * M * I) + (I * R_s)}{255}$$

EQUATION 8.12: Equation for layer mode Soft light

Grain extract

Figure 8.18: Example for layer mode 'Grain extract'

(a) *Mask 1 is used as upper layer with 100% opacity.*

(b) *Mask 2 is used as upper layer with 100% opacity.*

Grain extract mode is supposed to extract the 'film grain' from a layer to produce a new layer that is pure grain, but it can also be useful for giving images an embossed appearance. It subtracts the pixel value of the upper layer from that of the lower layer and adds 128.

The equation is:

$$E = I - M + 128$$

EQUATION 8.13: Equation for layer mode Grain extract

Grain merge

Figure 8.19: Example for layer mode 'Grain merge'

(a) *Mask 1 is used as upper layer with 100% opacity.*   (b) *Mask 2 is used as upper layer with 100% opacity.*

Grain merge mode merges a grain layer (possibly one created from the 'Grain extract' mode) into the current layer, leaving a grainy version of the original layer. It does just the opposite of 'Grain extract'. It adds the pixel values of the upper and lower layers together and subtracts 128.

The equation is:

$$E = I + M - 128$$

EQUATION 8.14: Equation for layer mode Grain merge

Difference

Figure 8.20: Example for layer mode 'Difference'

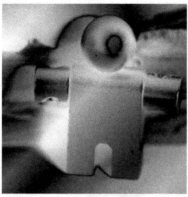

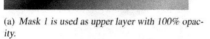

(a) *Mask 1 is used as upper layer with 100% opacity.*   (b) *Mask 2 is used as upper layer with 100% opacity.*

Difference mode subtracts the pixel value of the upper layer from that of the lower layer and then takes the absolute value of the result. No matter what the original two layers look like, the result looks rather odd. You can use it to invert elements of an image.

The equation is:

$$E = |I - M|$$

EQUATION 8.15: Equation for layer mode Difference

The mode is commutative; the order of the two layers doesn't matter.

Addition

Figure 8.21: Example for layer mode 'Addition'

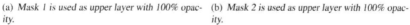

(a) *Mask 1 is used as upper layer with 100% opacity.*   (b) *Mask 2 is used as upper layer with 100% opacity.*

Addition mode is very simple. The pixel values of the upper and lower layers are added to each other. The resulting image is usually lighter. The equation can result in color values greater than 255, so some of the light colors may be set to the maximum value of 255.

The equation is:

$$E = min((M+I), 255)$$

EQUATION 8.16: Equation for layer mode Addition

The mode is commutative; the order of the two layers doesn't matter.

Subtract

Figure 8.22: Example for layer mode 'Subtract'

(a) *Mask 1 is used as upper layer with 100% opacity.*

(b) *Mask 2 is used as upper layer with 100% opacity.*

Subtract mode subtracts the pixel values of the upper layer from the pixel values of the lower layer. The resulting image is normally darker. You might get a lot of black or near-black in the resulting image. The equation can result in negative color values, so some of the dark colors may be set to the minimum value of 0.

The equation is:

$$E = max((I-M), 0)$$

EQUATION 8.17: Equation for layer mode Subtraction

Darken only

Figure 8.23: Example for layer mode 'Darken only'

(a) *Mask 1 is used as upper layer with 100% opacity.*

(b) *Mask 2 is used as upper layer with 100% opacity.*

Darken only mode compares each component of each pixel in the upper layer with the corresponding one in the lower layer and uses the smaller value in the resulting image. Completely white layers have no effect on the final image and completely black layers result in a black image.

The equation is:

$$E = min(M, I)$$

EQUATION 8.18: Equation for layer mode Darken only

The mode is commutative; the order of the two layers doesn't matter.

Lighten only

Figure 8.24: Example for layer mode 'Lighten only'

(a) *Mask 1 is used as upper layer with 100% opacity.*

(b) *Mask 2 is used as upper layer with 100% opacity.*

Lighten only mode compares each component of each pixel in the upper layer with the corresponding one in the lower layer and uses the larger value in the resulting image. Completely black layers have no effect on the final image and completely white layers result in a white image.

The equation is:

$$E = max(M, I)$$

EQUATION 8.19: Equation for layer mode Lighten only

The mode is commutative; the order of the two layers doesn't matter.

Hue

Figure 8.25: Example for layer mode 'Hue'

(a) *Mask 1 is used as upper layer with 100% opacity.* (b) *Mask 2 is used as upper layer with 100% opacity.*

Hue mode uses the hue of the upper layer and the saturation and value of the lower layer to form the resulting image. However, if the saturation of the upper layer is zero, the hue is taken from the lower layer, too.

Saturation

Figure 8.26: Example for layer mode 'Saturation'

(a) *Mask 1 is used as upper layer with 100% opacity.* (b) *Mask 2 is used as upper layer with 100% opacity.*

Saturation mode uses the saturation of the upper layer and the hue and value of the lower layer to form the resulting image.

Color

Figure 8.27: Example for layer mode 'Color'

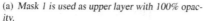

(a) *Mask 1 is used as upper layer with 100% opacity.* (b) *Mask 2 is used as upper layer with 100% opacity.*

Color mode uses the hue and saturation of the upper layer and the value of the lower layer to form the resulting image.

Value

Figure 8.28: Example for layer mode 'Value'

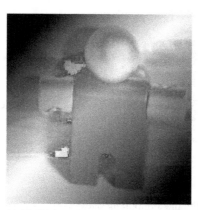 

(a) *Mask 1 is used as upper layer with 100% opacity.* (b) *Mask 2 is used as upper layer with 100% opacity.*

Value mode uses the value of the upper layer and the saturation and hue of the lower layer to form the resulting image. You can use this mode to reveal details in dark and light areas of an image without changing the saturation.

Each layer in an image can have a different layer mode. (Of course, the layer mode of the bottom layer of an image has no effect.) The effects of these layer modes are cumulative. The image shown below has three layers. The top layer consists of Wilber surrounded by transparency and has a layer mode of 'Difference'. The second layer is solid light blue and has a layer mode of 'Addition'. The bottom layer is filled with the 'Red Cubes' pattern.

Figure 8.29: Multi layer example

GIMP also has similar modes which are used for the painting tools. These are the same twenty-one modes as the layer modes, plus an additional two modes which are specific to the painting tools. You can set these modes from the Mode menu in the Tools option dialog. In the equations shown above, the layer you are painting on is the 'lower layer' and the pixels painted by the tool are the 'upper layer'. Naturally, you do not need more than one layer in the image to use these modes, since they only operate on the current layer and the selected painting tool. The two additional painting modes are described here.

Behind

The Behind mode is only available from the Toolbox options, not as a layer mode from the Layers dialog. When you paint with a tool in 'Behind' mode, it paints *behind* objects that are already painted on the layer. That means that this mode only makes sense when you are painting on a layer that has transparent areas, otherwise you wouldn't be able to see any difference in the resulting image.

In the example image, Wilber is on the top layer, surrounded by transparency. The lower layer is solid light blue. The Bucket Fill tool was used, with an Affect mode of 'Selection', and the entire layer was selected. A pattern was used to paint with the Bucket Fill tool.

Color Erase

The Color Erase mode is only available from the Toolbox options, not as a layer mode from the Layers dialog. When you paint with a tool in 'Color Erase' mode, it finds areas in the layer which have the current painting color and erases them, turning those areas transparent. The layer must have an alpha channel (so that transparency is allowed) for an effect to be seen.

In the example image, the color of the Bucket Fill tool was white, so white parts of Wilber were erased and the blue background shows through.

8.3 Creating New Layers

There are several ways to create new layers in an image. Here are the most important ones:

- Selecting Layer → New Layer in the image menu. This brings up a dialog that allows you to set the basic properties of the new layer; see the New Layer dialog section for help with it.

- Selecting Layer → Duplicate Layer in the image menu. This creates a new layer, that is a perfect copy of the currently active layer, just above the active layer.

- When you 'cut' or 'copy' something, and then paste it using Ctrl-V or Edit → Paste, the result is a 'floating selection', which is a sort of temporary layer. Before you can do anything else, you either have to anchor the floating selection to an existing layer, or convert it into a normal layer. If you do the latter, the new layer will be sized just large enough to contain the pasted material.

8.4 Text and Fonts

Figure 8.30: Example of a text item

Example of a text item, showing the boundary of the text layer. (Font: Utopia Bold)

One of the greatest improvements of GIMP 2.0 over GIMP 1.2 is in the handling of text. In GIMP 2.0 and 2.2, each text item goes in a separate Text layer, and you can come back later to the layer and edit the text in it. You can also move the text around in the image, or change the font, or the font size. You can use any font available on your system. You can control justification, indentation, and line spacing.

Actually, you can operate on a text layer in the same ways as any other layer, but doing so often means giving up the ability to edit the text without losing the results of your work.

Figure 8.31: GIMP text editor

To understand some of the idiosyncrasies of text handling, it may help for you to realize that a text layer contains more information than the pixel data that you see: it also contains a representation of the text in a text-editor format. You can see this in the text-editor window that pops up while you are using the Text tool. Every time you alter the text, the image layer is redrawn to reflect your changes.

Now suppose you create a text layer, and then operate on it in some way that does not involve the Text tool: rotate it, for example. Suppose you then come back and try to edit it using the Text tool. As soon as you edit the text, the Text tool will redraw the layer, wiping out the results of the operations you performed in the meantime.

Because this danger is not obvious, the Text tool tries to protect you from it. If you operate on a text layer, and then later try to edit the text, a message pops up, warning you that your alterations will be undone, and giving you three options: (1) edit the text anyway; (2) cancel; (3) create a new text layer with the same text as the existing layer, leaving the existing layer unchanged.

8.5 Text

8.5.1 Embellishing Text

Figure 8.32: Fancy text

Four fancy text items created using logo scripts: alien neon, bovination, frosty, and chalk. Default settings were used for everything except font size.

There are many things you can do to vary the appearance of text beyond just rendering it with different fonts or different colors. By converting a text item to a selection or a path, you can fill it, stroke the outlines, transform it, or generallly apply the whole panoply of GIMP tools to get interesting effects. As a demonstration of some of the possibilities, try out the "logo" scripts in the Toolbox menu, at Xtns → Script-Fu → Logos. Each of these scripts allows you to enter some text, and then creates a new image showing a logo constructed out of that text. If you would like to modify one of these scripts, or construct a logo script of your own, the Using Script-Fu and Script-Fu Tutorial sections should help you get started. Of course, you don't need Script-Fu to create these sorts of effects, only to automate them.

8.5.2 Adding Fonts

For the most authoritative and up-to-date information on fonts in GIMP, consult the 'Fonts in GIMP 2.0' page [GIMP-FONTS] at the GIMP web site. This section attempts to give you a helpful overview.

GIMP uses the FreeType 2 font engine to render fonts, and a system called Fontconfig to manage them. GIMP will let you use any font in Fontconfig's font path; it will also let you use any font it finds in GIMP's font search path, which is set on the Font Folders page of the Preferences dialog. By default, the font search path includes a system GIMP-fonts folder (which you should not alter, even though it is actually empty), and a `fonts` folder inside your personal GIMP directory. You can add new folders to the font search path if it is more convenient for you.

FreeType 2 is a very powerful and flexible system. By default, it supports the following font file formats:

- TrueType fonts (and collections)
- Type 1 fonts
- CID-keyed Type 1 fonts
- CFF fonts
- OpenType fonts (both TrueType and CFF variants)
- SFNT-based bitmap fonts
- X11 PCF fonts

- Windows FNT fonts

- BDF fonts (including anti-aliased ones)

- PFR fonts

- Type42 fonts (limited support)

You can also add modules to support other types of font files. See FREETYPE 2 [FREETYPE] for more information.

Linux On a Linux system, if the Fontconfig utility is set up as usual, all you need to do to add a new font is to place the file in the directory ~/.fonts. This will make the font available not only to GIMP, but to any other program that uses Fontconfig. If for some reason you want the font to be available to GIMP only, you can place it in the fonts subdirectory of your personal GIMP directory, or some other location in your font search path. Doing either will cause the font to show up the next time you start GIMP. If you want to use it in an already running GIMP, press the *Refresh* button in the Fonts dialog.

Windows The easiest way to install a font is to drag the file onto the Fonts directory and let the shell do its magic. Unless you've done something creative, it's probably in its default location of C:\windows\fonts or C:\winnt\fonts. Sometimes double-clicking on a font will install it as well as display it; sometimes it only displays it. This method will make the font available not only to GIMP, but also to other Windows applications.

To install a Type 1 file, you need both the .pfb and .pfm files. Drag the one that gets an icon into the fonts folder. The other one doesn't strictly need to be in the same directory when you drag the file, since it uses some kind of search algorithm to find it if it's not, but in any case putting it in the same directory does no harm.

In principle, GIMP can use any type of font on Windows that FreeType can handle; however, for fonts that Windows can't handle natively, you should install them by placing the font files in the fonts folder of your personal GIMP directory, or some other location in your font search path. The support Windows has varies by version. All that GIMP runs on support at least TrueType, Windows FON, and Windows FNT. Windows 2000 and later support Type 1 and OpenType. Windows ME supports OpenType and possibly Type 1 (but the most widely used Windows GIMP installer does not officially support Windows ME, although it may work anyway).

Note
GIMP uses Fontconfig to manage fonts on Windows as well as Linux. The instructions above work because Fontconfig by default uses the Windows fonts directory, i. e., the same fonts that Windows uses itself. If for some reason your Fontconfig is set up differently, you will have to figure out where to put fonts so that GIMP can find them: in any case, the fonts folder of your personal GIMP directory should work.

8.5.3   Font Problems

Problems with fonts have probably been responsible for more GIMP 2 bug reports than any other single cause, although they have become much less frequent in the most recent releases in the 2.0 series. In most cases they have been caused by malformed font files giving trouble to Fontconfig. If you experience crashes at startup when GIMP scans your font directories, the best solution is to upgrade to a version of Fontconfig newer than 2.2.0. As a quick workaround you can start gimp with the --no-fonts command-line option, but then you will not be able to use the text tool.

Another known problem is that Pango 1.2 cannot load fonts that don't provide an Unicode character mapping. (Pango is the text layout library used by GIMP.) A lot of symbol fonts fall into this category. On some systems, using such a font can cause GIMP to crash. Updating to Pango 1.4 will fix this problem and makes symbol fonts available in GIMP.

A frequent source of confusion occurs on Windows systems, when GIMP encounters a malformed font file and generates an error message: this causes a console window to pop up so that you can see the message. *Do not close that console window. It is harmless, and closing it will shut down GIMP.* When this happens, it often seems to users that GIMP has crashed. It hasn't: closing the console window causes Windows to shut GIMP down. Unfortunately, this annoying situation is caused by an interaction between Windows and the libraries that GIMP links to: it cannot be fixed within GIMP. All you need to do, though, if this happens, is minimize the console window and ignore it.

Chapter 9

Enhancing Photographs

9.1 Working with Digital Camera Photos

9.1.1 Introduction

One of the most common uses of the GIMP is to fix digital camera images that for some reason are less than perfect. Maybe the image is overexposed or underexposed; maybe rotated a bit; maybe out of focus: these are all common problems for which GIMP has good tools. The purpose of this chapter is to give you an overview of those tools and the situations in which they are useful. You will not find detailed tutorials here: in most cases it is easier to learn how to use the tools by experimenting with them than by reading about them. (Also, each tool is described more thoroughly in the Help section devoted to it.) You will also not find anything in this chapter about the multitude of "special effects" that you can apply to an image using GIMP. You should be familiar with basic GIMP concepts before reading this chapter, but you certainly don't need to be an expert–if you are, you probably know most of this anyway. And don't hesitate to experiment: GIMP's powerful "undo" system allows you to recover from almost any mistake with a simple Ctrl-Z.

Most commonly the things that you want to do to clean up an imperfect photo are of four types: improving the composition; improving the colors; improving the sharpness; and removing artifacts or other undesirable elements of the image.

9.1.2 Improving Composition

9.1.2.1 Rotating an Image

It is easy, when taking a picture, to hold the camera not quite perfectly vertical, resulting in a picture where things are tilted at an angle. In GIMP, the way to fix this is to use the Rotate tool. Activate this by clicking its icon in the Toolbox, or by pressing the 'R' key capitalized) while inside the image. Make sure the Tool Options are visible, and at the top, make sure for 'Affect:' that the left button ('Transform Layer') is selected. If you then click the mouse inside the image and drag it, you will see a grid appear that rotates as you drag. When the grid looks right, click rotate or press the enter key, and the image will be rotated.

Now as a matter of fact, it isn't so easy to get things right by this method: you often find that things are better but not quite perfect. One solution is to rotate a bit more, but there is a disadvantage to that approach. Each time you rotate an image, because the rotated pixels don't line up precisely with the original pixels, the image inevitably gets blurred a little bit. For a single rotation, the amount of blurring is quite small, but two rotations cause twice as much blurring as one, and there is no reason to blur things more than you have to. A better alternative is to undo the rotation and then do another, adjusting the angle.

Fortunately, GIMP provides another way of doing it that is considerably easier to use: in the Rotate Tool Options, for the Transform Direction you can select "Backward (Corrective)". When you do this, instead of rotating the grid to compensate for the error, you can rotate it to *line up* with the error. If this seems confusing, try it and you will see that it is quite straightforward.

Note

Note: New in GIMP 2.2 is the option to preview the results of transformations, instead of just seeing a grid. This makes it easier to get things right on the first try.

After you have rotated an image, there will be unpleasant triangular "holes" at the corners. One way to fix them is to create a background that fills the holes with some unobtrusive or neutral color, but usually a better solution is to crop the image. The greater the rotation, the more cropping is required, so it is best to get the camera aligned as well as possible when you take the picture in the first place.

9.1.2.2 Cropping

When you take a picture with a digital camera, you have some control over what gets included in the image but often not as much as you would like: the result is images that could benefit from trimming. Beyond this, it is often possible to enhance the impact of an image by trimming it so that the most important elements are placed at key points. A rule of thumb, not always to be followed but good to keep in mind, is the 'rule of thirds', which says that maximum impact is obtained by placing the center of interest one-third of the way across the image, both widthwise and heightwise.

To crop an image, activate the Crop tool in the Toolbox, or by pressing the 'C' key (capitalized) while inside the image. With the tool active, clicking and dragging in the image will sweep out a crop rectangle. It will also pop up a dialog that allows you to adjust the dimensions of the crop region if they aren't quite right. When everything is perfect, hit the Crop button in the dialog.

9.1.3 Improving Colors

9.1.3.1 Automated Tools

In spite of sophisticated exposure-control systems, pictures taken with digital cameras often come out over- or under-exposed, or with color casts due to imperfections in lighting. GIMP gives you a variety of tools to correct colors in an image, ranging to automated tools that run with a simple button-click to highly sophisticated tools that give you many parameters of control. We will start with the simplest first.

GIMP gives you five automated color correction tools. Unfortunately they don't usually give you quite the results you are looking for, but they only take a moment to try out, and if nothing else they often give you an idea of some of the possibilities inherent in the image. Except for "Auto Levels", you can find them in the Layer menu, by following the menu path Layer → Colors → Auto in the image menu.

Here they are, with a few words about each:

Normalize This tool (it is really a plug-in) is useful for underexposed images: it adjusts the whole image uniformly until the brightest point is right at the saturation limit, and the darkest point is black. The downside is that the amount of brightening is determined entirely by the lightest and darkest points in the image, so even one single white pixel and/or one single black pixel will make normalization ineffective.

Equalize This is a very powerful adjustment that tries to spread the colors in the image evenly across the range of possible intensities. In some cases the effect is amazing, bringing out contrasts that are very difficult to get in any other way; but more commonly, it just makes the image look weird. Oh well, it only takes a moment to try.

Color Enhance Help me, what exactly does this do? Obviously it makes some things more saturated.

Stretch Contrast This is like 'Normalize', except that it operates on the red, green, and blue channels independently. It often has the useful effect of reducing color casts.

Auto Levels This is done by activating the Levels tool (Tools → Color Tools → Levels in the image menu), clicking on the image to bring up the tool dialog, and then pressing the Auto button near the center of the dialog. You will see a preview of the result; you must press Okay for it to take effect. Pressing Cancel instead will cause your image to revert to its previous state.

If you can find a point in the image that ought to be perfect white, and a second point that ought to be perfect black, then you can use the Levels tool to do a semi-automatic adjustment that will often do a good job of fixing both brightness and colors throughout the image. First, bring up the Levels tool as previously described. Now, look down near the bottom of the Layers dialog for three buttons with symbols on them that look like eye-droppers (at least, that is what they are supposed to look like). The one on the left, if you mouse over it, shows its function to be 'Pick Black Point'. Click on this, then click on a point in the image that ought to be black–really truly perfectly black, not just sort of dark–and watch the image change. Next, click on the rightmost of the three buttons ('Pick White Point'), and then click a point in the image that ought to be white, and once more watch the image change. If you are happy with the result, click the Okay button otherwise Cancel.

Those are the automated color adjustments: if you find that none of them quite does the job for you, it is time to try one of the interactive color tools. All of these, except one, can be accessed via Tools->Color Tools in the image menu. After you select a color tool, click on the image (anywhere) to activate it and bring up its dialog.

9.1.3.2 Exposure Problems

The simplest tool to use is the Brightness/Contrast tool. It is also the least powerful, but in many cases it does everything you need. This tool is often useful for images that are overexposed or underexposed; it is not useful for correcting color casts. The tool gives you two sliders to adjust, for 'Brightness' and 'Contrast'. If you have the option 'Preview' checked (and almost certainly you should),you will see any adjustments you make reflected in the image. When you are happy with the results, press Okay and they will take effect. If you can't get results that you are happy with, press Cancel and the image will revert to its previous state.

A more sophisticated, and only slightly more difficult, way of correcting exposure problems is to use the Levels tool. The dialog for this tool looks very complicated, but for the basic usage we have in mind here, the only part you need to deal with is the 'Input Levels' area, specifically the three triangular sliders that appear below the histogram. We refer you to the Levels Tool Help for instructions; but actually the easiest way to learn how to use it is to experiment by moving the three sliders around, and watching how the image is affected. (Make sure that 'Preview' is checked at the bottom of the dialog.)

A very powerful way of correcting exposure problems is to use the *Curves* tool. This tool allows you to click and drag control points on a curve, in order to create a function mapping input brightness levels to output brightness levels. The Curves tool can replicate any effect you can achieve with Brightness/Contrast or the Levels tool, so it is more powerful than either of them. Once again, we refer you to the Curves Tool Help for detailed instructions, but the easiest way to learn how to use it is by experimenting.

The most powerful approach to adjusting brightness and contrast across an image, for more expert GIMP users, is to create a new layer above the one you are working on, and then in the Layers dialog set the Mode for the upper layer to 'Multiply'. The new layer then serves as a 'gain control' layer for the layer below it, with white yielding maximum gain and black yielding a gain of zero. Thus, by painting on the new layer, you can selectively adjust the gain for each area of the image, giving you very fine control. You should try to paint only with smooth gradients, because sudden changes in gain will give rise to spurious edges in the result. Paint only using shades of gray, not colors, unless you want to produce color shifts in the image.

Actually, 'Multiply' is not the only mode that is useful for gain control. In fact, 'Multiply' mode can only darken parts of an image, never lighten them, so it is only useful where some parts of an image are overexposed. Using 'Divide' mode has the opposite effect: it can brighten areas of an image but not darken them. Here is a trick that is often useful for bringing out the maximum amount of detail across all areas of an image:

1. Duplicate the layer (producing a new layer above it).

2. Desaturate the new layer.

3. Apply a Gaussian blur to the result, with a large radius (100 or more).

4. Set Mode in the Layers dialog to Divide.

5. Control the amount of correction by adjusting opacity in the Layers dialog, or by using Brightness/Contrast, Levels, or Curves tools on the new layer.

6. When you are happy with the result, you can use Merge Down to combine the control layer and the original layer into a single layer.

In addition to 'Multiply' and 'Divide', you may every so often get useful effects with other layer combination modes, such as 'Dodge', 'Burn', or 'Soft Light'. It is all too easy, though, once you start playing with these things, to look away from the computer for a moment and suddenly find that you have just spent an hour twiddling parameters. Be warned: the more options you have, the harder it is to make a decision.

9.1.3.3 Adjusting Hue and Saturation

In our experience, if your image has a color cast---too much red, too much blue, etc---the easiest way to correct it is to use the Levels tool, adjusting levels individually on the red, green, and blue channels. If this doesn't work for you, it might be worth your while to try the Color Balance tool or the Curves tool, but these are much more difficult to use effectively. (They are very good for creating certain types of special effects, though.)

Sometimes it is hard to tell whether you have adjusted colors adequately. A good, objective technique is to find a point in the image that you know should be either white or a shade of gray. Activate the Color Picker tool (the eyedropper symbol in the Toolbox), and click on the aforesaid point: this brings up the Color Picker dialog. If the colors are correctly adjusted, then the red, green, and blue components of the reported color should all be equal; if not, then you should see what sort of adjustment you need to make. This technique, when well used, allows even color-blind people to color-correct an image.

If your image is washed out---which can easily happen when you take pictures in bright light---try the Hue/Saturation tool, which gives you three sliders to manipulate, for Hue, Lightness, and Saturation. Raising the saturation will probably make the image look better. In same cases it is useful to adjust the lightness at the same time. ('Lightness' here is similar to 'Brightness' in the Brightness/Contrast tool, except that they are formed from different combinations of the red, green, and blue channels.) The Hue/Saturation tool gives you the option of adjusting restricted subranges of colors (using the buttons at the top of the dialog), but if you want to get natural-looking colors, in most cases you should avoid doing this.

Tip
Even if an image does not seemed washed out, often you can increase its impact by pushing up the saturation a bit. Veterans of the film era sometimes call this trick 'Fujifying', after Fujichrome film, which is notorious for producing highly saturated prints.

When you take pictures in low light conditions, in some cases you have the opposite problem: too much saturation. In this case too the Hue/Saturation tool is a good one to use, only by reducing the saturation instead of increasing it.

9.1.4 Adjusting Sharpness

9.1.4.1 Unblurring

If the focus on the camera is not set perfectly, or the camera is moving when the picture is taken, the result is a blurred image. If there is a lot of blurring, you probably won't be able to do much about it with any technique, but if there is only a moderate amount, you should be able to improve the image.

The most generally useful technique for sharpening a fuzzy image is called the Unsharp Mask. In spite of the rather confusing name, which derives from its origins as a technique used by film developers, its result is to make the image sharper, not 'unsharp'. It is a plug-in, and you can access it as Filters->Enhance->Unsharp Mask in the image menu. There are two parameters, 'Radius' and 'Amount'. The default values often work pretty well, so you should try them first. Increasing either the radius or the amount increases the strength of the effect. Don't get carried away, though: if you make the unsharp mask too strong, it will amplify noise in the image and also give rise to visible artifacts where there are sharp edges.

Tip
Sometimes using Unsharp Mask can cause color distortion where there are strong contrasts in an image. When this happens, you can often get better results by decomposing the image into separate Hue-Saturation-Value (HSV) layers, and running Unsharp Mask on the Value layer only, then recomposing. This works because the human eye has much finer resolution for brightness than for color. See the sections on Decompose and Compose for more information.

Next to "Unsharp Mask" in the Filters menu is another filter called Sharpen, which does similar things. It is a little easier to use but not nearly as effective: our recommendation is that you ignore it and go straight to Unsharp Mask.

In some situations, you may be able to get useful results by selectively sharpening specific parts of an image using the Blur or Sharpen tool from the Toolbox, in "Sharpen" mode. This allows you to increase the sharpness in areas by painting over them with any paintbrush. You should be restrained about this, though, or the results will not look very natural: sharpening increases the apparent sharpness of edges in the image, but also amplifies noise.

9.1.4.2 Reducing Graininess

When you take pictures in low-light conditions or with a very fast exposure time, the camera does not get enough data to make good estimates of the true color at each pixel, and consequently the resulting image looks grainy. You can 'smooth out' the graininess by blurring the image, but then you will also lose sharpness. There are a couple of approaches that may give better results. Probably the best, if the graininess is not too bad, is to use the filter called Selective Blur, setting the blurring radius to 1 or 2 pixels. The other approach is to use the Despeckle filter. This has a nice preview, so you can play with the settings and try to find some that give good results. When graininess is really bad, though, it is often very difficult to fix by anything except heroic measures (i.e., retouching with paint tools).

9.1.4.3 Softening

Every so often you have the opposite problem: an image is *too* crisp. The solution is to blur it a bit: fortunately blurring an image is much easier than sharpening it. Since you probably don't want to blur it very much, the simplest method is to use the 'Blur' plug-in, accessed via Filters->Blur->Blur from the image menu. This will soften the focus of the image a little bit. If you want more softening, just repeat until you get the result you desire.

9.1.5 Removing Unwanted Objects from an Image

There are two kinds of objects you might want to remove from an image: first, artifacts caused by junk such as dust or hair on the lens; second, things that were really present but impair the quality of the image, such as a telephone wire running across the edge of a beautiful mountain landscape.

9.1.5.1 Despeckling

A good tool for removing dust and other types of lens grunge is the Despeckle filter, accessed as Filters->Enhance->Despeckle from the image menu. Very important: to use this filter effectively, you must begin by making a small selection containing the artifact and a small area around it. The selection must be small enough so that the artifact pixels are statistically distinguishable from the other pixels inside the selection. If you try to run despeckle on the whole image, you will hardly ever get anything useful. Once you have created a reasonable selection, activate Despeckle, and watch the preview as you adjust the parameters. If you are lucky, you will be able to find a setting that removes the junk while minimally affecting the area around it. The more the junk stands out from the area around it, the better your results are likely to be. If it isn't working for you, it might be worthwhile to cancel the filter, create a different selection, and then try again.

If you have more than one artifact in the image, it is necessary to use Despeckle on each individually.

9.1.5.2 Garbage Removal

The most useful method for removing unwanted 'clutter' from an image is the Clone tool, which allows you to paint over one part of an image using pixel data taken from another part (or even from a different image). The trick to using the clone tool effectively is to be able to find a different part of the image that can be used to 'copy over' the unwanted part: if the area surrounding the unwanted object is very different from the rest of the image, you won't have much luck. For example, if you have a lovely beach scene, with a nasty human walking across the beach who you would like to teleport away, you will probably be able to find an empty part of the beach that looks similar to the part he is walking across, and use it to clone over him. It is quite astonishing how natural the results can look when this technique works well.

Consult the Clone Tool Help for more detailed instructions. Cloning is as much an art as a science, and the more you practice at it, the better you will get. At first it may seem impossible to produce anything except ugly blotches, but persistence will pay off.

In some cases you may be able to get good results by simply cutting out the offending object from the image, and then using a plug-in called 'Resynthesizer' to fill in the void. This plug-in is not included with the main GIMP distribution, but it can be obtained from the author's web site [PLUGIN-RESYNTH]. As with many things, your mileage may vary.

9.1.5.3 Removing Red-eye

When you take a flash picture of somebody who is looking directly toward the camera, the iris of the eye can bounce the light of the flash back toward the camera in such a way as to make the eye appear bright red: this effect is called 'red eye', and looks very bizarre. Many modern cameras have special flash modes that minimize red-eye, but they only work if you use them, and even then they don't always work perfectly. Interestingly, the same effect occurs with animals, but the eyes may show up as other colors, such as green.

GIMP does not include a special tool for removing red-eye, but it isn't all that hard to do. Basically the idea is to zoom the area around the eye so that it is nice and large and easy to work with; then make a selection of the red part of the eye and a bit of the area around it; feather the selection so that you don't create sharp-looking edges; and finally desaturate the red channel inside the selection using one of the color tools---Levels, Curves, or Hue/Saturation. It takes a little practice the first few times, but once you have the technique mastered, you should be able to quickly and easily create quite a natural looking eye color.

If you would like a more automated approach, you can try downloading a recently created redeye plug-in [PLUGIN-REDEYE] from the GIMP Plug-in Registry. We have not received any feedback so far about how well it works. It comes in source code form, so you will need to be able compile it in order to use it. (See Installing New Plug-ins for information on how to do this.)

9.1.6 Saving Your Results

9.1.6.1 Files

What file format should you use to save the results of your work, and should you resize it? The answers depend on what you intend to use the image for.

- If you intend to open the image in GIMP again for further work, you should save it in GIMP's native XCF format (i. e., name it something.xcf), because this is the only format that guarantees that none of the information in the image is lost.

- If you intend to print the image on paper, you should avoid shrinking the image, except by cropping it. The reason is that printers are capable of achieving much higher dot resolutions than video monitors---600 to 1400 dots per inch for typical printers, as compared to 72 to 100 dots per inch for monitors. A 3000 x 5000 image looks huge on a monitor, but it only comes to about 5 inches by 8 inches on paper at 600 dpi. There is usually no good reason to *expand* the image either: you can't increase the true resolution that way, and it can always be scaled up at the time it is printed. As for the file format, it will usually be fine to use JPEG at a quality level of 75 to 85. In rare cases, where there are large swaths of nearly uniform color, you may need to set the quality level even higher or use a lossless format such as TIFF instead.

- If you intend to display the image on screen or project it with a video projector, bear in mind that the highest screen resolution for most commonly available systems is 1600 x 1200, so there is nothing to gain by keeping the image larger than that. For this purpose, the JPEG format is almost always a good choice.

- If you want to put the image on a web page or send it by email, it is a good idea to make every effort to keep the file size as small as possible. First, scale the image down to the smallest size that makes it possible to see the relevant details (bear in mind that other people may be using different sized monitors and/or different monitor resolution settings). Second, save the image as a JPEG file. In the JPEG save dialog, check the option to 'Preview in image window' , and then adjust the Quality slider to the lowest level that gives you acceptable image quality. (You will see in the image the effects of each change.) Make sure that the image is zoomed at 1:1 while you do this, so you are not misled by the effects of zooming.

See the File Formats section for more information.

9.1.6.2 Printing Your Photos

As in most softwares, in GIMP, printing needs to go to main menu File → Print. However it is very usefull to keep in mind some elementary concepts to prevent some unpleasant surprises when looking at result, or to cure them if that occurs. You always must remember:

- that image displayed on the screen is in RGB mode and printing will be in CMYK mode; consequently color feature you'll get on printed sheet will not be exactly what you was waiting for. That depends on the used corresponding chart. For the curious ones some adding explanations can be got through a click on these usefull Wikipedia links:

  ICC Profile [WKPD-ICC]

  CMYK [WKPD-CMYK]

  Gamut [WKPD-GAMUT]

- that a screen resolution is roughly within a range from 75 up to 100 dpi; a printer resolution is about 10x higher (or more) than a screen one; printed image size depends on avalaible pixels and resolution; so actual printed size doesn't correspond inevitably to what is displayed on screen nor avalaible sheet size.

Consequently, before any printing it is relevant to go to: Image → Print size and choose here your convenient output size in 'print size' box adjusting either sizes or resolution; you can see that the both values are linked without possibility to dissociate them. You can see too that you can dissociate x and y resolution but it is risky! Probably this possibility is open because printers are built with different x vs. y resolutions. Nevertheless if you unlinked them you can be very surprised! You can try this in special effects.

Last recommandation: think of checking your margins as well as centering. It would be a pity if a too much large margin cuts off some part of your image or if an inapropriate centering damages your work espacially if you use a special photo paper.

9.1.6.3 EXIF Data

Modern digital cameras, when you take a picture, add information to the data file about the camera settings and the circumstances under which the picture was taken. This data is included in JPEG or TIFF files in a structured format called EXIF. For JPEG files, GIMP is capable of maintaining EXIF data, if it is built appropriately: it depends on a library called 'libexif', which may not be available on all systems. If GIMP is built with EXIF support enabled, then loading a JPEG file with EXIF data, and resaving the resulting image in JPEG format, will cause the EXIF data to be preserved unchanged. This is not, strictly speaking, the right way for an image editor to handle EXIF data, but it is better than simply removing it, which is what earlier versions of GIMP did.

If you would like to see the contents of the EXIF data, you can download from the registry an Exif Browser plug-in [PLUGIN-EXIF]. If you are able to build and install it on your system, you can access it as Filters->Generic->Exif Browser from the image menu. (See Installing New Plug-ins for help.)

Chapter 10

Pimp my GIMP

10.1 Grids and Guides

You will probably have it happen many times that you need to place something in an image very precisely, and find that it is not easy to do using a mouse. Often you can get better results by using the arrow keys on the keyboard (which move the affected object one pixel at a time, or 25 pixels if you hold down the **Shift** key), but GIMP also provides you with two other aids to make positioning easier: grids and guides.

Figure 10.1: Image used for examples below

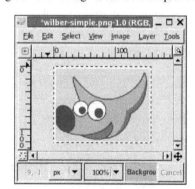

10.1.1 The Image Grid

Figure 10.2: Image with default grid

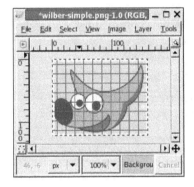

Each image has a grid. It is always present, but by default it is not visible until you activate it by toggling View → Show Grid in the image menu. If you want grids to be present more often than not, you can change the default behavior by checking "Show grid" in the Image Window Appearance page of the Preferences dialog. (Note that there are separate settings for Normal Mode and Fullscreen Mode.)

The default grid appearance, set up when you install GIMP, consists of plus-shaped black crosshairs at the grid line intersections, with grid lines spaced every 10 pixels both vertically and horizontally. You can customize the default grid using the Default Image Grid page of the Preferences dialog. If you only want to change the grid appearance for the current image, you can do so by choosing Image → Configure Grid from the image menu: this brings up the Configure Grid dialog.

Figure 10.3: A different grid style

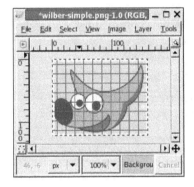

Not only can a grid be helpful for judging distances and spatial relationships, it can also permit you to align things exactly with the grid, if you toggle View → Snap to Grid in the image menu: this causes the pointer to "warp" perfectly to any grid line located within a certain distance. You can customize the snap distance threshold by setting "Snap distance" in the Tool Options page of the Preferences dialog, but most people seem to be happy with the default value of 8 pixels. (Note that it is perfectly possible to snap to the grid even if the grid is not visible. It isn't easy to imagine why you might want to do this, though.)

10.1.2 Guides

Figure 10.4: Image with four guides

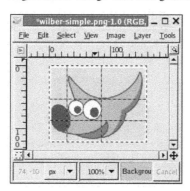

In addition to the image grid, GIMP also gives you a more flexible type of positioning aid: *guides*. These are horizontal or vertical lines that you create by clicking on one of the rulers and dragging into the image. You can create as many guides as you like, positioned whereever you like. To move a guide after you have created it, activate the Move tool in the Toolbox (or press the **M** key), you can then click and drag a guide. To delete a guide, simply drag it outside the image. Holding down the Shift key, you can move everything but a guide, using the guides as an effective alignment aid.

As with the grid, you can cause the pointer to snap to nearby guides, by toggling View → Snap to Guides in the image menu. If you have a number of guides and they are making it difficult for you to judge the image properly, you can hide them by toggling View → Show Guides. It is suggested that you only do this momentarily, otherwise you may get confused the next time you try to create a guide and don't see anything happening.

If it makes things easier for you, you can change the default behavior for guides in the Image Window Appearance page of the Preferences dialog. Disabling "Show guides" is probably a bad idea, though, for the reason just given.

Note
Another use for guides: the Guillotine plugin can use guides to slice an image into a set of sub-images.

Note
See also Guides in Glossary.

10.2 Rendering a Grid

How can you create a grid that is actually part of the image? You can't do this using the image grid: that is only an aid, and is only visible on the monitor or in a screenshot. You can, however, use the Grid plugin to render a grid very similar to the image grid. (Actually, the plugin has substantially more options.)

See also Grid and Guides.

10.3 How to Set Your Tile Cache

During the data processing and manipulation of pictures, GIMP becomes in the need of much main memory. The more is available the better is. GIMP uses the operating system memory available resources as effectively as possible, striving to mantain the work on the pictures fast and comfortable for the user. That Data memory, during the treatment, is organized in buffered blocks of graphic data, wich could exists in two different form of data memory: in the slow not removable disk or in the fast main RAM memory. GIMP uses preferibly the last one but, when it is scarse, the first is accessed for the remaining data. These chunks of graphic data are commonly referred as "tiles" and the entire system si called "tile cache".

A low value for tile cache means that GIMP sends data to the disk very quickly, not making real use of the available RAM, and making the disks work for no real reason. Too high a value for tile cache, and other applications start to have less system resources, forcing them to use swap space, which also makes the disks work too hard; some of them may even terminate or start to malfunction due lack of RAM.

How do you choose a number for the Tile Cache size? Here are some tips to help you decide what value to use, as well as a few tricks:

- The easiest method is to just forget about this and hope the default works. This was a usable method when computers had little RAM, and most people just tried to make small images with GIMP while running one or two other applications at the same time. If you want something easy and only use GIMP to make screenshots and logos, this is probably the best solution.

- If you have a modern computer with plenty of memory–say, 512 MB or more–setting the Tile Cache to half of your RAM will probably give good performance for GIMP in most situations without depriving other applications. Probably even 3/4 of your RAM would be fine.

- Ask someone to do it for you, which in the case of a computer serving multiple users at the same time can be a good idea: that way the administrator and other users do not get mad at you for abusing the machine, nor do you get a badly underperfoming GIMP. If it is your machine and only serves a single user at a given time, this could mean money, or drinks, as price for the service.

- Start changing the value a bit each time and check that it goes faster and faster with each increase, but the system does not complain about lack of memory. Be forewarned that sometimes lack of memory shows up suddenly with some applications being killed to make space for the others.

- Do some simple math and calculate a viable value. Maybe you will have to tune it later, but maybe you have to tune it anyway with the other previous methods. At least you know what is happening and can get the best from your computer.

Let's suppose you prefer the last option, and want to get a good value to start with. First, you need to get some data about your computer. This data is the amount of RAM installed in your system, the operating system's swap space available, and a general idea about the speed of the disks that store the operating system's swap and the directory used for GIMP's swap. You do not need to do disk tests, nor check the RPM of the disks, the thing is to see which one seems clearly faster or slower, or whether all are similar. You can change GIMP's swap directory in the Folders page of the Preferences dialog.

The next thing to do is to see how much resources you require for other apps you want to run at the same time than GIMP. So start all your tools and do some work with them, except GIMP of course, and check the usage. You can use applications like free or top, depending in what OS and what environment you use. The numbers you want is the memory left, including file cache. Modern Unix keeps a very small area free, in order to be able to keep large file and buffer caches. Linux's *free* command does the maths for you: check the column that says 'free', and the line '-/+ buffers/cache'. Note down also the free swap.

Now time for decisions and a bit of simple math. Basically the concept is to decide if you want to base all Tile Cache in RAM, or RAM plus operating system swap:

1. Do you change applications a lot? Or keep working in GIMP for a long time? If you spend a lot of time in GIMP, you can consider free RAM plus free swap as available; if not, you need to go to the following steps. (If you're feeling unsure about it, check the following steps.) If you are sure you switch apps every few minutes, only count the free RAM and just go to the final decision; no more things to check.

2. Does the operating system swap live in the same physical disk as GIMP swap? If so, add RAM and swap. Otherwise go to the next step.

3. Is the disk that holds the OS swap faster or the same speed as the disk that holds the GIMP swap? If slower, take only the free RAM; if faster or similar, add free RAM and swap.

4. You now have a number, be it just the free RAM or the free RAM plus the free OS swap. Reduce it a bit, to be on the safe side, and that is the Tile Cache you could use as a good start.

As you can see, all is about checking the free resources, and decide if the OS swap is worth using or will cause more problems than help.

There are some reasons you want to adjust this value, though. The basic one is changes in your computer usage pattern, or changing hardware. That could mean your assumptions about how you use your computer, or the speed of it, are no longer valid. That would require a reevaluation of the previous steps, which can drive you to a similar value or a completly new value.

Another reason to change the value is because it seems that GIMP runs too slowly, while changing to other applications is fast: this means that GIMP could use more memory without impairing the other applications. On the other hand, if you get complaints from other applications about not having enough memory, then it may benefit you to not let GIMP hog so much of it.

If you decided to use only RAM and GIMP runs slowly, you could try increasing the value a bit, but never to use also all the free swap. If the case is the contrary, using both RAM and swap, and you have problems about lack of resources, then you should decrease the amount of RAM available to GIMP.

Another trick is to put the Swap Dir on a very fast disk, or on a different disk than the one where most of your files reside. Spreading the operating system swap file over multiple disks is also a good way to speed things up, in general. And of course, you might have to buy more RAM or stop using lots of programs at the same time: you can not expect to edit a poster on a computer with 16MB and be fast.

You can also check what memory requirements your images have. The larger the images, and the number of undos, the more resources you need. This is another way to choose a number, but it is only good if you always work with the same kind of images, and thus the real requirements do not vary. It is also helpful to know if you will require more RAM and/or disk space.

10.4   Creating Shortcuts to Menu Functions

Many functions which are accessible via the image menu have a default keyboard shortcut. You may want to create a new shortcut for a command that you use a lot and doesn't have one or, more rarely, edit an existing shortcut. There are two methods for doing this.

1. First, you have to activate this capability by checking the Use dynamic keyboard shortcuts option in the Interface item of the Preferences menu. This option is usually not checked, to prevent accidental key presses from creating an unwanted shortcut.

2. While you're doing that, also check the Save keyboard shortcuts on exit option so that your shortcut will be saved.

3. To create a keyboard shortcut, simply place the mouse pointer on a command in the menu: it will then be highlighted. Be careful that the mouse pointer doesn't move and type a sequence of three keys, keeping the keys pressed. You will see this sequence appear on the right of the command.

4. It is best to use the Ctrl-Alt-Key sequence for your custom shortcuts.

Figure 10.5: Configure Keyboard Shortcuts

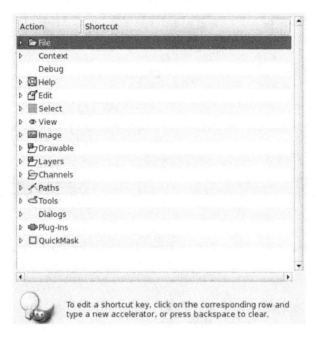

1. You get to this Editor by clicking on Configure keyboard shortcuts in the 'Interface' item of the Preferences menu.

2. As shown in this dialog, you can select the command you want to create a shortcut for, in the 'Action' area. Then you type your key sequence as above. In principle, the Space bar should clear a shortcut. (In practice, it clears it, but doesn't delete it.)

3. This shortcut editor also allows you to *control the tool parameter settings* with the keyboard. At the top of this dialog, you can find a Context menu that takes you to the tool parameters. To make your work easier, tool types are marked with small icons.

 Note
Custom Keyboard shortcuts are stored in one of Gimp's hidden directory (/home/[username]/.gimp-2. 2/menurc) under Linux, and C:\Documents~and~Settings\[Username]\.gimp-2.2\menurc under Windows XP. It is a simple text file that you can transport from one computer to another.

10.5 Dialogs and Docking

10.5.1 Creating Docking Dialogs

You can dock several windows into a same window. You can do this in more than one way, particularly by using the File → Dialogs menu from the Main Toolbox, or by using the Add command in the Tab menu from any dialog. As a convenience, there are also three pre-built docks you can create using the File → Dialogs → Create New Dock menu path from the Main Toolbox:

Layers, Channels and Paths This gives you a dock containing:

- The Channels dialog
- The Layers dialog

- The Paths dialog
- The Undo dialog

Brushes, Patterns and Gradients This gives you a dock containing:

- The Brushes dialog
- The Patterns dialog
- The Gradients dialog
- The Palettes dialog
- The Fonts dialog

Misc. Stuff This gives you a dock containing:

- The Buffers dialog
- The Images dialog
- The Document History dialog
- The Image Templates dialog

Tip

Just because you have a lot of flexibility does not mean that all choices are equally good. There are at least two things we recommend:

1. Keep the Tool Options dialog docked directly beneath the Main Toolbox at all times.

2. Keep the Layers dialog around at all times, in a separate dock from the Main Toolbox, with an Image Menu above it. (Use 'Show Image Menu' in the dialog Tab menu to display the Image menu if you have somehow lost it.)

Note

See also Dialogs and Docking

10.5.2 Removing Tabs

Figure 10.6: A dialog in a dock, with the 'Close Tab' button highlighted

If you want to remove a dialog from a dock, there are two ways you can do it. First, if you click on the drag handle area and drag the dialog away, releasing it someplace other than a docking bar, it will form a new dock in its own right. Second, clicking on the 'Close Tab' button (highlighted in the figure to the right) will close the frontmost dialog.

10.6   Customize Splash-Screen

Open your file browser and check the option 'Show Hidden Files'.

Under Linux, go to /home/user_name/.gimp-2.2. Under Windows, go to c:\Documents and Settings\user_name\.gimp-2.2\.

If the 'splashes' directory doesn't exist, create it.

Copy your image(s) into this 'splashes' directory. On start, GIMP will read this directory and choose one of the images at random.

Chapter 11

Scripting

11.1 Plugins

11.1.1 Introduction

One of the nicest things about GIMP is how easily its functionality can be extended, by using plugins. GIMP plugins are external programs that run under the control of the main GIMP application and interact with it very closely. Plugins can manipulate images in almost any way that users can. Their advantage is that it is much easier to add a capability to GIMP by writing a small plugin than by modifying the huge mass of complex code that makes up the GIMP core. Many valuable plugins have C source code that only comes to 100-200 lines or so.

Several dozen plugins are included in the main GIMP distribution, and installed automatically along with GIMP. Most of them can be accessed through the Filters menu (in fact, everything in that menu is a plugin), but a number are located in other menus. In many cases you can use one without ever realizing that it is a plugin: for example, the "Normalize" function for automatic color correction is actually a plugin, although there is nothing about the way it works that would tell you this.

In addition to the plugins included with GIMP , many more are available on the net. A large number can be found at the GIMP Plugin Registry [GIMP-REGISTRY], a web site whose purpose is to provide a central repository for plugins. Creators of plugins can upload them there; users in search of plugins for a specific purpose can search the site in a variety of ways.

Anybody in the world can write a GIMP plugin and make it available over the web, either via the Registry or a personal web site, and many very valuable plugins can be obtained in this way some are described elsewhere in the User's Manual. With this freedom from constraint comes a certain degree of risk, though: the fact that anybody can do it means that there is no effective quality control. The plugins distributed with GIMP have all been tested and tuned by the developers, but many that you can download were just hacked together in a few hours and then tossed to the winds. Some plugin creators just don't care about robustness, and even for those who do, their ability to test on a variety of systems in a variety of situations is often quite limited. Basically, when you download a plugin, you are getting something for free, and sometimes you get exactly what you pay for. This is not said in an attempt to discourage you, just to make sure you understand reality.

 Warning
Plugins, being full-fledged executable programs, can do any of the things that any other program can do, including install back-doors on your system or otherwise compromise its security. Don't install a plugin unless it comes from a trusted source.

These caveats apply as much to the Plugin Registry as to any other source of plugins. The Registry is available to any plugin creator who wants to use it: there is no systematic oversight. Obviously if the maintainers became aware that something evil was there, they would remove it. (That hasn't happened yet.) There is, however, for GIMP and its plugins the same warranty as for any other free software: namely, none.

Caution

Plugins have been a feature of GIMP for many versions. However, plugins written for one version of GIMP can hardly ever be used successfully with other versions. They need to be ported: sometimes this is easy, sometimes not. Many plugins are already available in several versions. Bottom line: before trying to install a plugin, make sure that it is written for your version of GIMP.

11.1.2 Using Plugins

For the most part you can use a plugin like any other GIMP tool, without needing to be aware that it is a plugin. But there are a few things about plugins that are useful to understand.

One is that plugins are generally not as robust as the GIMP core. When GIMP crashes, it is considered a very serious thing: it can cost the user a lot of trouble and headache. When a plugin crashes, the consequences are usually not so serious. In most cases you can just continuing working without worrying about it.

Note

Because plugins are separate programs, they communicate with the GIMP core in a special way: The GIMP developers call it 'talking over a wire'. When a plugin crashes, the communication breaks down, and you will see an error message about a 'wire read error'.

Tip

When a plugin crashes, GIMP gives you a very ominous-looking message telling you that the plugin may have left GIMP in a corrupted state, and you should consider saving your images and exiting. Strictly speaking, this is quite correct, because plugins have the power to alter almost anything in GIMP, but for practical purposes, experience has shown that corruption is actually quite rare, and many users just continue working and don't worry about it. Our advice is that you simply think about how much trouble it would cause you if something went wrong, and weigh it against the odds.

Because of the way plugins communicate with GIMP, they do not have any mechanism for being informed about changes you make to an image after the plugin has been started. If you start a plugin, and then alter the image using some other tool, the plugin will often crash, and when it doesn't will usually give a bogus result. You should avoid running more than one plugin at a time on an image, and avoid doing anything to the image until the plugin has finished working on it. If you ignore this advice, not only will you probably screw up the image, you will probably screw up the undo system as well, so that you won't even be able to recover from your foolishness.

11.1.3 Installing New Plugins

The plugins that are distributed with GIMP don't require any special installation. Plugins that you download yourself do. There are several scenarios, depending on what OS you are using and how the plugin is structured. In Linux it is usually pretty easy to install a new plugin; in Windows, it is either easy or very hard. In any case, the two are best considered separately.

11.1.3.1 Linux

Most plugins fall into two categories: small ones whose source code is distributed as a single .c file, and larger ones whose source code is distributed as a directory containing multiple files including a Makefile.

For a simple one-file plugin, call it borker.c, installing it is just a matter of running the command **gimptool-2.0 --install borker.c**. This command compiles the plugin and installs it in your personal plugin directory, ~/gimp-2.2/plugins unless you have changed it. This will cause it to be loaded automatically the next time you start GIMP. You don't need to be root to do these things; in fact, you shouldn't be. If the plugin fails to compile, well, be creative.

Once you have installed the plugin, how do you activate it? The menu path is determined by the plugin itself, so to answer this you need to either look at the documentation for the plugin (if there is any), or launch the Plugin Description dialog (from

Xtns/Plugins Details) search the plug-in by its name and look ot the Tree view tab. If you still don't find, finally explore the menus or look at the source code in the Register section -- whichever is easiest.

For more complex plugins, organized as a directory with multiple files, there ought to be a file inside called either INSTALL or README, with instructions. If not, the best advice is to toss the plugin in the trash and spend your time on something else: any code written with so little concern for the user is likely to be frustrating in myriad ways.

Some plugins (specifically those based on the GIMP Plugin Template) are designed to be installed in the main system GIMP directory, rather than your home directory. For these, you will need to be root to perform the final stage of installation (when issuing the **make install** command).

If you install in your personal plugin directory a plugin that has the same name as one in the system plugin directory, only one can be loaded, and it will be the one in your home directory. You will receive messages telling you this each time you start GIMP. This is probably a situation best avoided.

11.1.3.2 Windows

Windows is a much more problematic environment for building software than Linux. Every decent Linux distribution comes fully supplied with tools for compiling software, and they are all very similar in the way they work, but Windows does not come with such tools. It is possible to set up a good software-building environment in Windows, but it requires either a substantial amount of money or a substantial amount of effort and knowledge.

What this means in relation to GIMP plugins is the following: either you have an environment in which you can build software, or you don't. If you don't, then your best hope is to find a precompiled version of the plugin somewhere (or persuade somebody to compile it for you), in which case you simply need to put it into your personal plugin directory. If you do have an environment in which you can build software (which for present purposes means an environment in which you build GIMP), then you no doubt already know quite a bit about these things, and just need to follow the Linux instructions.

If you would like to set up a build environment, and are ready for the heroism involved, you can find a reasonably recent description of how to go about it in the GIMP Wiki, at HowToCompileGimp/MicrosoftWindows [GIMP-WIKI01]. Since it is a Wiki, anybody is free to edit it, so please keep it up to date by adding advice based on your own experiences.

11.1.3.3 Apple Mac OS X

How you install plugins on OS X mostly depends on how you installed the GIMP itself. If you were one of the brave and installed GIMP through one of the package managers like fink [DARWINORTS] or darwinports, [FINK] the plugin installation works exactly the way it is described for the Linux platform already. The only difference is, that a couple of plugins might be even available in the repository of you package manager, so give it a try.

If you on the other hand are one of the Users that preferred to grab a prebuild GIMP package like GIMP.app, you most probably want to stick to that prebuild stuff. So you can try to get a prebuild version of the plugin of you dreams from the author of the plugin, but I'd not want to bet on this. Building your own binaries unfortunately involves installing GIMP through one of the package managers mentioned above.

11.1.4 Writing Plugins

If you want to learn how to write a plugin, you can find plenty of help at the GIMP Developers web site [GIMP-DEV-PLUGIN]. GIMP is a complex program, but the development team has made strenuous efforts to flatten the learning curve for plugin writing: there are good instructions and examples, and the main library that plugins use to interface with GIMP (called 'libgimp') has a well-documented API. Good programmers, learning by modifying existing plugins, are often able to accomplish interesting things after just a couple of days of work.

11.2 Using Script-Fu Scripts

11.2.1 Script-Fu?

Script-Fu is what the Windows world would call "macros" But Script-Fu is more powerful than that. Script-Fu is based on an interpreting language called Scheme, and works by using querying functions to the GIMP database. You can do all kinds of things with Script-Fu, but an ordinary GIMP user will probably use it for automating things that:

- You want to do frequently.

- Are really complicated to do, and hard to remember.

Remember that you can do a whole lot with Script-Fu. The scripts that come with GIMP can be quite useful, but they can also serve as models for learning Script-Fu, or at least as a framework and source of modification when you make your own script. Read the Script-Fu Tutorial in the next section if you want to learn more about how to make scripts.

We will describe some of the most useful scripts in this chapter, but we won't cover them all. There are simply too many scripts. Some of the scripts are also very simple and you will probably not need any documentation to be able to use them.

Script-Fu (a dialect of Scheme) isn't the only scripting language available for GIMP. But Script-Fu is the only scripting language that is installed by default. Other available scripting extensions are Perl and Tcl. You can download and install both extensions at the GIMP Plugin Registry [GIMP-REGISTRY].

11.2.2 Installing Script-Fus

One of the great things about Script-Fu is that you can share your script with all your GIMP friends. There are many scripts that come with GIMP by default, but there are also vast quantities of scripts that are available for download all around the Internet.

1. If you have downloaded a script, copy or move it to your scripts directory. It can be found in the Preferences: FoldersScripts.

2. Do a refresh by using Exts → Script-Fu → Refresh Scripts from the toolbox. The script will now appear in one of your menus. If you don't find it, look for it under the root file menu filters. If it doesn't appear at all, something was wrong with the script (e.g. it contains syntax errors).

11.2.3 Do's and Don'ts

A common error when you are dealing with Script-Fus is that you simply bring them up and press the OK button. When nothing happens, you probably think that the script is broken or buggy, but there is most likely nothing wrong with it.

11.2.4 Different Kinds Of Script-Fus

There are two kinds of Script-Fus -- standalone scripts and image-dependent scripts. You will find the standalone variants under Xtns → Script-Fu → *Type of Script* in the main toolbox menu, and the image-dependent scripts are placed under Script-Fu → *Type of Script* in the image menu.

11.2.5 Standalone Scripts

We will not try to describe every script in depth. Most Script-Fus are very easy to understand and use. At the time of this writing, the following types are installed by default:

- Patterns

- Web page themes

- Logos

- Buttons

- Utils

- Make Brush

- Misc.

Patterns You will find all kinds of pattern-generating scripts here. Generally, they are quite useful because you can add many arguments to your own patterns.

We'll take a look at the Land script. In this script you have to set the image/pattern size, and specify what levels of random to use for your land creation. The colors used to generate the land map are taken from the currently selected gradient in the gradient editor. You must also supply values for the level of detail, land and sea height/depth and the scale. Scale refers to the scale of your map, just as in an ordinary road map, 1:10 will be typed as 10.

Web Page Themes Here is clearly a practical use for scripts. By creating a script for making custom text, logos, buttons arrows, etc., for your web site, you will give them all the same style and shape. You will also be saving a lot of time, because you don't have to create every logo, text or button by hand.

You will find the GIMP.org theme under the Web page theme submenu. If you want to create your own theme, this script will serve as an excellent template that you can modify to create a theme for your web site.

Most of the scripts are quite self-explanatory, but here are some hints:

- Leave all strange characters like ' and " intact.
- Make sure that the pattern specified in the script exists.
- Padding refers to the amount of space around your text.
- A high value for bevel width gives the illusion of a higher button.
- If you type TRUE for "Press", the button will look pushed down.
- Choose transparency if you don't want a solid background. If you choose a solid background, make sure it is the same color as the web page background.

Logos Here you will find all kinds of logo-generating scripts. This is nice, but use it with care, as people might recognize your logo as being made by a known GIMP script. You should rather regard it as a base that you can modify to fit your needs. The dialog for making a logo is more or less the same for all such scripts:

1. In the Text String field, type your logo name, like Frozenriver.
2. In the Font Size text field, type the size of your logo in pixels.
3. In the Font text field, type the name of the font that you want to use for your logo.
4. To choose the color of your logo, just click on the color button. This brings up a color dialog.
5. If you look at the current command field, you can watch the script run.

Make Buttons Under this headline you'll find a script that makes beveled buttons. The script has a dozen parameters or so, and most of them are similar to those in the logo scripts. You can experiment with different settings to come up with a button you like.

Utils Under Utils you will find a small but nice script: the Fontmap script, which makes an image of your fonts. You will have to type the names of the fonts you want displayed in the Fonts text field.

The Custom gradient script creates an image of the current custom gradient in the gradient editor. This can be useful if you want to pick colors from a gradient as in a palette.

Misc. Under Misc. you'll find scripts that can be quite useful, but aren't suitable for the other submenus. An example is the Sphere script. You will have to set the radius in pixels to determine the sphere size. The lighting angle is where at the sphere you point the spotlight. This value also has an impact on the sphere shadow. If you don't want a shadow, you just have remove the tick on the "shadow" checkbox. The last thing you have to select is background color, and the color of your sphere.

Make Brush This script lets you make your own custom rectangular/circular brushes, with or without feathered (blurred) edges. The script will automatically store your brush in your personal brush directory. You just have to press refresh in the Brush Selection dialog to use your newly created brush.

11.2.6   Image-Dependent Scripts

These are scripts that perform operations on an existing image. In many ways they are like the plug-ins in the Filters menu. The following script groups are installed by default:

- Alchemy

- Alpha to logo

- Animators

- Decor

- Render

- Selection

- Shadow

- Stencil Ops

- Utils

Stencil Ops Here, you'll find two scripts: Carve-It and Chrome-It, which can render some truly nice artistic effects on grayscale images.

Drop Shadow Drop Shadow will cast a shadow behind your selected object. It has three important parameters. X and Y offset determine where the shadow will be placed in relation to the selected object. Offset is measured in pixels. High values make the shadow look like it's far away, and low values will make it look closer to the object. The blur value is also important, because a shadow that is cast far from the object has a higher blur level.

Perspective Shadow Perspective Shadow has a very important parameter: the perspective angle. If this angle is set to 0 or 180, there will be no shadow, because the script assumes that the object has no thickness. This also means that this script looks fine in certain angles, but unnatural in others. The other parameters are quite self-explanatory. You'll get more blur if the horizon is far away, and the shadow length is the length in relation to the selected object.

11.3   A Script-Fu Tutorial

In this training course, we'll introduce you to the fundamentals of Scheme necessary to use Script-Fu, and then build a handy script that you can add to your toolbox of scripts. The script prompts the user for some text, then creates a new image sized perfectly to the text. We will then enhance the script to allow for a buffer of space around the text. We will conclude with a few suggestions for ways to ramp up your knowledge of Script-Fu.

Note
This section as adapted from a tutorial written for the GIMP 1 User Manual by Mike Terry.

11.3.1   Getting Acquainted With Scheme

11.3.1.1   Let's Start Scheme'ing

The first thing to learn is that:

Every statement in Scheme is surrounded by parentheses ().

The second thing you need to know is that:

The function name/operator is always the first item in the parentheses, and the rest of the items are parameters to the function.

El nombre de función/operadores, siempre, lo primero en los paréntesis, y el resto son parámetros de la función.

However, not everything enclosed in parentheses is a function -- they can also be items in a list -- but we'll get to that later. This notation is referred to as prefix notation, because the function prefixes everything else. If you're familiar with postfix notation, or own a calculator that uses Reverse Polish Notation (such as most HP calculators), you should have no problem adapting to formulating expressions in Scheme.

The third thing to understand is that:

Mathematical operators are also considered functions, and thus are listed first when writing mathematical expressions.

This follows logically from the prefix notation that we just mentioned.

11.3.1.2 Examples Of Prefix, Infix, And Postfix Notations

Here are some quick examples illustrating the differences between *prefix*, *infix*, and *postfix* notations. We'll add a 1 and 3 together:

- Prefix notation: + 1 3 (the way Scheme will want it)
- Infix notation: 1 + 3 (the way we "normally" write it)
- Postfix notation: 1 3 + (the way many HP calculators will want it)

11.3.1.3 Practicing In Scheme

Now, let's practice what we have just learned. Start up GIMP, if you have not already done so, and choose Xtns → Script-Fu → Console. This will start up the Script-Fu Console window, which allows us to work interactively in Scheme. In a matter of moments, the Script-Fu Console will appear:

11.3.1.4 The Script-Fu Console Window

At the bottom of this window is an entry-field entitled Current Command. Here, we can test out simple Scheme commands interactively. Let's start out easy, and add some numbers:

```
(+ 3 5)
```

Typing this in and hitting **Enter** yields the expected answer of 8 in the center window.

Now, what if we wanted to add more than one number? The '+' function can take two or more arguments, so this is not a problem:

```
(+ 3 5 6)
```

This also yields the expected answer of 14.

So far, so good -- we type in a Scheme statement and it's executed immediately in the Script-Fu Console window. Now for a word of caution....

11.3.1.5 Watch Out For Extra Parentheses

If you're like me, you're used to being able to use extra parentheses whenever you want to -- like when you're typing a complex mathematical equation and you want to separate the parts by parentheses to make it clearer when you read it. In Scheme, you have to be careful and not insert these extra parentheses incorrectly. For example, say we wanted to add 3 to the result of adding 5 and 6 together:

```
3 + (5 + 6) + 7 = ?
```

Knowing that the + operator can take a list of numbers to add, you might be tempted to convert the above to the following:

```
(+ 3 (5 6) 7)
```

However, this is incorrect -- remember, every statement in Scheme starts and ends with parens, so the Scheme interpreter will think that you're trying to call a function named '5' in the second group of parens, rather than summing those numbers before adding them to 3.

The correct way to write the above statement would be:

```
(+ 3 (+ 5 6) 7)
```

11.3.1.6 Make Sure You Have The Proper Spacing, Too

If you are familiar with other programming languages, like C/C++, Perl or Java, you know that you don't need white space around mathematical operators to properly form an expression:

```
3+5, 3 +5, 3+ 5
```

These are all accepted by C/C++, Perl and Java compilers. However, the same is not true for Scheme. You must have a space after a mathematical operator (or any other function name or operator) in Scheme for it to be correctly interpreted by the Scheme interpreter.

Practice a bit with simple mathematical equations in the Script-Fu Console until you're totally comfortable with these initial concepts.

11.3.2   Variables And Functions

Now that we know that every Scheme statement is enclosed in parentheses, and that the function name/operator is listed first, we need to know how to create and use variables, and how to create and use functions. We'll start with the variables.

11.3.2.1 Declaring Variables

Although there are a couple of different methods for declaring variables, the preferred method is to use the let* construct. If you're familiar with other programming languages, this construct is equivalent to defining a list of local variables and a scope in which they're active. As an example, to declare two variables, a and b, initialized to 1 and 2, respectively, you'd write:

```
(let*
    (
        (a 1)
        (b 2)
    )
    (+ a b)
)
```

or, as one line:

```
(let* ( (a 1) (b 2) ) (+ a b) )
```

Note
You'll have to put all of this on one line if you're using the console window. In general, however, you'll want to adopt a similar practice of indentation to help make your scripts more readable. We'll talk a bit more about this in the section on White Space.

This declares two local variables, a and b, initializes them, then prints the sum of the two variables.

11.3.2.2 What Is A Local Variable?

You'll notice that we wrote the summation (+ a b) within the parens of the let* expression, not after it.

This is because the let* statement defines an area in your script in which the declared variables are usable; if you type the (+ a b) statement after the (let* ...) statement, you'll get an error, because the declared variables are only valid within the context of the let* statement; they are what programmers call local variables.

11.3.2.3 The General Syntax Of let*

The general form of a let* statement is:

```
(let* ( variables )
   expressions )
```

where variables are declared within parens, e.g., (a 2), and expressions are any valid Scheme expressions. Remember that the variables declared here are only valid within the let* statement -- they're local variables.

11.3.2.4 White Space

Previously, we mentioned the fact that you'll probably want to use indentation to help clarify and organize your scripts. This is a good policy to adopt, and is not a problem in Scheme -- white space is ignored by the Scheme interpreter, and can thus be liberally applied to help clarify and organize the code within a script. However, if you're working in Script-Fu's Console window, you'll have to enter an entire expression on one line; that is, everything between the opening and closing parens of an expression must come on one line in the Script-Fu Console window.

11.3.2.5 Assigning A New Value To A Variable

Once you've initialized a variable, you might need to change its value later on in the script. Use the set! statement to change the variable's value:

```
(let* ( (theNum 10) ) (set! theNum (+ theNum \
   theNum)) )
```

Try to guess what the above statement will do, then go ahead and enter it in the Script-Fu Console window.

 Note

The '\' indicates that there is no line break. Ignore it (don't type it in your Script-Fu console and don't hit Enter), just continue with the next line.

11.3.2.6 Functions

Now that you've got the hang of variables, let's get to work with some functions. You declare a function with the following syntax:

```
(define
   (
      name
      param-list
   )
   expressions
)
```

where *name* is the name assigned to this function, *param-list* is a space-delimited list of parameter names, and *expressions* is a series of expressions that the function executes when it's called. For example:

```
(define (AddXY inX inY) (+ inX inY) )
```

AddXY is the function's name and inX and inY are the variables. This function takes its two parameters and adds them together.

If you've programmed in other imperative languages (like C/C++, Java, Pascal, etc.), you might notice that a couple of things are absent in this function definition when compared to other programming languages.

- First, notice that the parameters don't have any "types" (that is, we didn't declare them as strings, or integers, etc.). Scheme is a type-less language. This is handy and allows for quicker script writing.

- Second, notice that we don't need to worry about how to "return" the result of our function -- the last statement is the value "returned" when calling this function. Type the function into the console, then try something like:

```
(AddXY (AddXY 5 6) 4)
```

11.3.3   Lists, Lists And More Lists

We've trained you in variables and functions, and now enter the murky swamps of Scheme's lists.

11.3.3.1   Defining A List

Before we talk more about lists, it is necessary that you know the difference between atomic values and lists.

You've already seen atomic values when we initialized variables in the previous lesson. An atomic value is a single value. So, for example, we can assign the variable "x" the single value of 8 in the following statement:

```
(let* ( (x 8) ) x)
```

(We added the expression x at the end to print out the value assigned to x-- normally you won't need to do this. Notice how let* operates just like a function: The value of the last statement is the value returned.)

A variable may also refer to a list of values, rather than a single value. To assign the variable x the list of values 1, 3, 5, we'd type:

```
(let* ( (x '(1 3 5))) x)
```

Try typing both statements into the Script-Fu Console and notice how it replies. When you type the first statement in, it simply replies with the result:

```
8
```

However, when you type in the other statement, it replies with the following result:

```
(1 3 5)
```

When it replies with the value 8 it is informing you that x contains the atomic value 8. However, when it replies with (1 3 5), it is then informing you that x contains not a single value, but a list of values. Notice that there are no commas in our declaration or assignment of the list, nor in the printed result.

The syntax to define a list is:

```
'(a b c)
```

where a, b, and c are literals. We use the apostrophe (') to indicate that what follows in the parentheses is a list of literal values, rather than a function or expression.

An empty list can be defined as such:

```
'()
```

or simply:

```
()
```

Lists can contain atomic values, as well as other lists:

```
(let*
  (
      (x
        '("The GIMP" (1 2 3) ("is" ("great" () ) ) )
      )
  )
  x
)
```

Notice that after the first apostrophe, you no longer need to use an apostrophe when defining the inner lists. Go ahead and copy the statement into the Script-Fu Console and see what it returns.

You should notice that the result returned is not a list of single, atomic values; rather, it is a list of a literal (`"The GIMP"`), the list (`1 2 3`), etc.

11.3.3.2   How To Think Of Lists

It's useful to think of lists as composed of a 'head' and a 'tail'. The head is the first element of the list, the tail the rest of the list. You'll see why this is important when we discuss how to add to lists and how to access elements in the list.

11.3.3.3   Creating Lists Through Concatenation (The Cons Function)

One of the more common functions you'll encounter is the cons function. It takes a value and prepends it to its second argument, a list. From the previous section, I suggested that you think of a list as being composed of an element (the head) and the remainder of the list (the tail). This is exactly how cons functions -- it adds an element to the head of a list. Thus, you could create a list as follows:

```
(cons 1 '(2 3 4) )
```

The result is the list (`1 2 3 4`).

You could also create a list with one element:

También, podrías crear una lista con un elemento:

```
(cons 1 () )
```

You can use previously declared variables in place of any literals, as you would expect.

11.3.3.4   Defining A List Using The `list` Function

To define a list composed of literals or previously declared variables, use the list function:

```
(list 5 4 3 a b c)
```

This will compose and return a list containing the values held by the variables a, b and c. For example:

```
(let* (
          (a 1)
          (b 2)
          (c 3)
       )
       (list 5 4 3 a b c)
)
```

This code creates the list (`5 4 3 1 2 3`).

11.3.3.5 Accessing Values In A List

To access the values in a list, use the functions `car` and `cdr`, which return the first element of the list and the rest of the list, respectively. These functions break the list down into the head::tail construct I mentioned earlier.

11.3.3.6 The `car` Function

`car` returns the first element of the list (the head of the list). The list needs to be non-null. Thus, the following returns the first element of the list:

```
(car '("first" 2 "third"))
```

which is:

```
"first"
```

11.3.3.7 The `cdr` function

`cdr` returns the rest of the list after the first element (the tail of the list). If there is only one element in the list, it returns an empty list.

```
(cdr '("first" 2 "third"))
```

returns:

```
(2 "third")
```

whereas the following:

```
(cdr '("one and only"))
```

returns:

```
()
```

11.3.3.8 Accessing Other Elements In A List

OK, great, we can get the first element in a list, as well as the rest of the list, but how do we access the second, third or other elements of a list? There exist several "convenience" functions to access, for example, the head of the head of the tail of a list (`caadr`), the tail of the tail of a list (`cddr`), etc.

The basic naming convention is easy: The a's and d's represent the heads and tails of lists, so

```
(car (cdr (car x) ) )
```

could be written as:

se podría escribir como:

```
(cadar x)
```

To view a full list of the list functions, refer to the Appendix, which lists the available functions for the version of Scheme used by Script-Fu.

To get some practice with list-accessing functions, try typing in the following (except all on one line if you're using the console); use different variations of car and cdr to access the different elements of the list:

```
(let* (
      (x '( (1 2 (3 4 5) 6)  7  8  (9 10) )
      )
   )
   ; place your car/cdr code here
)
```

Try accessing the number 3 in the list using only two function calls. If you can do that, you're on your way to becoming a Script-Fu Master!

Note

In Scheme, a semicolon (";") marks a comment. It, and anything that follows it on the same line, are ignored by the script interpreter, so you can use this to add comments to jog your memory when you look at the script later.

11.3.4 Your First Script-Fu Script

Do you not need to stop and catch your breath? No? Well then, let's proceed with your fourth lesson -- your first Script-Fu Script.

11.3.4.1 Creating A Text Box Script

One of the most common operations I perform in GIMP is creating a box with some text in it for a web page, a logo or whatever. However, you never quite know how big to make the initial image when you start out. You don't know how much space the text will fill with the font and font size you want.

The Script-Fu Master (and student) will quickly realize that this problem can easily be solved and automated with Script-Fu.

We will, therefore, create a script, called Text Box, which creates an image correctly sized to fit snugly around a line of text the user inputs. We'll also let the user choose the font, font size and text color.

11.3.4.2 Editing And Storing Your Scripts

Up until now, we've been working in the Script-Fu Console. Now, however, we're going to switch to editing script text files.

Where you place your scripts is a matter of preference -- if you have access to GIMP's default script directory, you can place your scripts there. However, I prefer keeping my personal scripts in my own script directory, to keep them separate from the factory-installed scripts.

In the .gimp-2.2 directory that GIMP made off of your home directory, you should find a directory called scripts. GIMP will automatically look in your .gimp-2.2 directory for a scripts directory, and add the scripts in this directory to the Script-Fu database. You should place your personal scripts here.

11.3.4.3 The Bare Essentials

Every Script-Fu script defines at least one function, which is the script's main function. This is where you do the work.

Every script must also register with the procedural database, so you can access it within GIMP.

We'll define the main function first:

```
(define (script-fu-text-box inText inFont inFontSize inTextColor))
```

Here, we've defined a new function called script-fu-text-box that takes four parameters, which will later correspond to some text, a font, the font size, and the text's color. The function is currently empty and thus does nothing. So far, so good -- nothing new, nothing fancy.

11.3.4.4 Naming Conventions

Scheme's naming conventions seem to prefer lowercase letters with hyphens, which I've followed in the naming of the function. However, I've departed from the convention with the parameters. I like more descriptive names for my parameters and variables, and thus add the "in" prefix to the parameters so I can quickly see that they're values passed into the script, rather than created within it. I use the prefix "the" for variables defined within the script.

It's GIMP convention to name your script functions script-fu-abc, because then when they're listed in the procedural database, they'll all show up under script-fu when you're listing the functions. This also helps distinguish them from plug-ins.

11.3.4.5 Registering The Function

Now, let's register the function with GIMP. This is done by calling the function `script-fu-register`. When GIMP reads in a script, it will execute this function, which registers the script with the procedural database. You can place this function call wherever you wish in your script, but I usually place it at the end, after all my other code.

Here's the listing for registering this function (I will explain all its parameters in a minute):

```
(script-fu-register
  "script-fu-text-box"                           ;func name
  "Text Box"                                     ;menu label
  "Creates a simple text box, sized to fit\
    around the user's choice of text,\
    font, font size, and color."                 ;description
  "Michael Terry"                                ;author
  "copyright 1997, Michael Terry"                ;copyright notice
  "October 27, 1997"                             ;date created
  ""                        ;image type that the script works on
  SF-STRING     "Text:"        "Text Box"   ;a string variable
  SF-FONT       "Font:"        "Charter"    ;a font variable
  SF-ADJUSTMENT "Font size"    '(50 1 1000 1 10 0 1)
                                            ;a spin-button
  SF-COLOR      "Color:"       '(0 0 0)     ;color variable
)
(script-fu-menu-register "script-fu-text-box" "<Toolbox>/Xtns/Script-Fu/Text")
```

If you save these functions in a text file with a .scm suffix in your script directory, then choose Xtns → Script-Fu → Refresh Scripts, this new script will appear as Xtns → Script-Fu → Text → Text Box.

If you invoke this new script, it won't do anything, of course, but you can view the prompts you created when registering the script (more information about what we did is covered next).

Finally, if you invoke the Procedure Browser (Xtns → Procedure Browser), you'll notice that our script now appears in the database.

11.3.4.6 Steps For Registering The Script

To register our script with GIMP, we call the function script-fu-register, fill in the seven required parameters and add our script's own parameters, along with a description and default value for each parameter.

THE REQUIRED PARAMETERS

- The **name** of the function we defined. This is the function called when our script is invoked (the entry-point into our script). This is necessary because we may define additional functions within the same file, and GIMP needs to know which of these functions to call. In our example, we only defined one function, text-box, which we registered.

- The **location** in the menu where the script will be inserted. The exact location of the script is specified like a path in Unix, with the root of the path being either toolbox or right-click.

  If your script does not operate on an existing image (and thus creates a new image, like our Text Box script will), you'll want to insert it in the toolbox menu -- this is the menu in GIMP's main window (where all the tools are located: the selection tools, magnifying glass, etc.).

If your script is intended to work on an image being edited, you'll want to insert it in the menu that appears when you right-click on an open image. The rest of the path points to the menu lists, menus and sub-menus. Thus, we registered our Text Box script in the Text menu of the Script-Fu menu of the Xtns menu of the toolbox (Xtns → Script-Fu → Text → Text Box).

If you notice, the Text sub-menu in the Script-Fu menu wasn't there when we began -- GIMP automatically creates any menus not already existing.

- A **description** of your script, to be displayed in the Procedure Browser.

- **Your name** (the author of the script).

- **Copyright** information.

- The **date** the script was made, or the last revision of the script.

- The **types** of images the script works on. This may be any of the following: RGB, RGBA, GRAY, GRAYA, INDEXED, INDEXEDA. Or it may be none at all -- in our case, we're creating an image, and thus don't need to define the type of image on which we work.

11.3.4.7 Registering The Script's Parameters

Once we have listed the required parameters, we then need to list the parameters that correspond to the parameters our script needs. When we list these params, we give hints as to what their types are. This is for the dialog which pops up when the user selects our script. We also provide a default value.

This section of the registration process has the following format:

Param Type	Description	Example
SF-VALUE	Accepts numbers and strings. Note that quotes must be escaped for default text, so better use SF-STRING.	42
SF-STRING	Accepts strings.	"Some text"
SF-COLOR	Indicates that a color is requested in this parameter.	'(0 102 255)
SF-TOGGLE	A checkbox is displayed, to get a Boolean value.	TRUE or FALSE
SF-IMAGE	If your script operates on an open image, this should be the first parameter after the required parameters. GIMP will pass in a reference to the image in this parameter.	3
SF-DRAWABLE	If your script operates on an open image, this should be the second parameter after the SF-IMAGE param. It refers to the active layer. GIMP will pass in a reference to the active layer in this parameter.	17

11.3.5 Giving Our Script Some Guts

Let us continue with our training and add some functionality to our script.

11.3.5.1 Creating A New Image

In the previous lesson, we created an empty function and registered it with GIMP. In this lesson, we want to provide functionality to our script -- we want to create a new image, add the user's text to it and resize the image to fit the text exactly.

Once you know how to set variables, define functions and access list members, the rest is all downhill -- all you need to do is familiarize yourself with the functions available in GIMP's procedural database and call those functions directly. So fire up the

DB Browser and let's get cookin'!

Let's begin by making a new image. We'll create a new variable, `theImage`, set to the result of calling GIMP's built-in function `gimp-image-new`.

As you can see from the DB Browser, the function `gimp-image-new` takes three parameters -- the image's width, height and the type of image. Because we'll later resize the image to fit the text, we'll make a 10x10 RGB image. We'll store the image's width and sizes in some variables, too, as we'll refer to and manipulate them later in the script.

```
(define (script-fu-text-box inText inFont inFontSize inTextColor)
(let*
       (
        ; define our local variables
        ; create a new image:
        (theImageWidth  10)
        (theImageHeight 10)
        (theImage (car
                       (gimp-image-new
                        theImageWidth
                        theImageHeight
                        RGB
                        )
                   )
        )
        (theText)        ;a declaration for the text
                         ;we create later
```

Note: We used the value RGB to specify that the image is an RGB image. We could have also used 0, but RGB is more descriptive when we glance at the code.

You should also notice that we took the head of the result of the function call. This may seem strange, because the database explicitly tells us that it returns only one value -- the ID of the newly created image. However, all GIMP functions return a list, even if there is only one element in the list, so we need to get the head of the list.

11.3.5.2   Adding A New Layer To The Image

Now that we have an image, we need to add a layer to it. We'll call the `gimp-layer-new` function to create the layer, passing in the ID of the image we just created. (From now on, instead of listing the complete function, we'll only list the lines we're adding to it. You can see the complete script here.) Because we've declared all of the local variables we'll use, we'll also close the parentheses marking the end of our variable declarations:

```
;create a new layer for the image:
   (theLayer
           (car
                (gimp-layer-new
                 theImage
                 theImageWidth
                 theImageHeight
                 RGB-IMAGE
                 "layer 1"
                 100
                 NORMAL
                 )
            )
    )
) ;end of our local variables
```

Once we have the new layer, we need to add it to the image:

```
(gimp-image-add-layer theImage theLayer 0)
```

Now, just for fun, let's see the fruits of our labors up until this point, and add this line to show the new, empty image:

```
        (gimp-display-new theImage)
```

Save your work, select Xtns → Script-Fu → Refresh Scripts, run the script and a new image should pop up. It will probably contain garbage (random colors), because we haven't erased it. We'll get to that in a second.

11.3.5.3   Adding The Text

Go ahead and remove the line to display the image (or comment it out with a ; as the first character of the line).

Before we add text to the image, we need to set the background and foreground colors so that the text appears in the color the user specified. We'll use the gimp-context-set-back/foreground functions:

```
        (gimp-context-set-background ' (255 255 255) )
        (gimp-context-set-foreground inTextColor)
```

With the colors properly set, let's now clean out the garbage currently in the image by filling the drawable with the background color:

```
        (gimp-drawable-fill theLayer BACKGROUND-FILL)
```

With the image cleared, we're ready to add some text:

```
        (set! theText
                    (car
                        (gimp-text-fontname
                        theImage theLayer
                        0 0
                        inText
                        0
                        TRUE
                        inFontSize PIXELS
                        "Sans")
                    )
        )
```

Although a long function call, it's fairly straightforward if you go over the parameters while looking at the function's entry in the DB Browser. Basically, we're creating a new text layer and assigning it to the variable theText.

Now that we have the text, we can grab its width and height and resize the image and the image's layer to the text's size:

```
        (set! theImageWidth   (car (gimp-drawable-width  theText) ) )
        (set! theImageHeight  (car (gimp-drawable-height theText) ) )
        (gimp-image-resize theImage theImageWidth theImageHeight 0 0)
        (gimp-layer-resize theLayer theImageWidth theImageHeight 0 0)
```

If you're like me, you're probably wondering what a drawable is when compared to a layer. The difference between the two is that a drawable is anything that can be drawn into, including layers but also channels, layer masks, the selection, etc; a layer is a more specific version of a drawable. In most cases, the distinction is not important.

With the image ready to go, we can now re-add our display line:

```
        (gimp-display-new theImage)
```

Save your work, refresh the database and give your first script a run!

11.3.5.4 Clearing The Dirty Flag

If you try to close the image created without first saving the file, GIMP will ask you if you want to save your work before you close the image. It asks this because the image is marked as dirty, or unsaved. In the case of our script, this is a nuisance for the times when we simply give it a test run and don't add or change anything in the resulting image -- that is, our work is easily reproducible in such a simple script, so it makes sense to get rid of this dirty flag.

To do this, we can clear the dirty flag after displaying the image:

```
(gimp-image-clean-all theImage)
```

This will set dirty count to 0, making it appear to be a "clean" image.

Whether to add this line or not is a matter of personal taste. I use it in scripts that produce new images, where the results are trivial, as in this case. If your script is very complicated, or if it works on an existing image, you will probably not want to use this function.

11.3.6   Extending The Text Box Script

11.3.6.1   Handling Undo Correctly

When creating a script, you want to give your users the ability to undo their actions, should they make a mistake. This is easily accomplished by calling the functions `gimp-undo-push-group-start` and `gimp-undo-push-group-end` around the code that manipulates the image. You can think of them as matched statements that let GIMP know when to start and stop recording manipulations on the image, so that those manipulations can later be undone.

If you are creating a new image entirely, it doesn't make sense to use these functions because you're not changing an existing image. However, when you are changing an existing image, you most surely want to use these functions.

Undoing a script works nearly flawlessly when using these functions.

11.3.6.2   Extending The Script A Little More

Now that we have a very handy-dandy script to create text boxes, let's add two features to it:

- Currently, the image is resized to fit exactly around the text -- there's no room for anything, like drop shadows or special effects (even though many scripts will automatically resize the image as necessary). Let's add a buffer around the text, and even let the user specify how much buffer to add as a percentage of the size of the resultant text.

- This script could easily be used in other scripts that work with text. Let's extend it so that it returns the image and the layers, so other scripts can call this script and use the image and layers we create.

11.3.6.3   Modifying The Parameters And The Registration Function

To let the user specify the amount of buffer, we'll add a parameter to our function and the registration function:

```
(define (script-fu-text-box inTest inFont inFontSize inTextColor inBufferAmount)
(let*
       (
          ; define our local variables
          ; create a new image:
          (theImageWidth  10)
          (theImageHeight 10)
          (theImage (car
                       (gimp-image-new
                        theImageWidth
                        theImageHeight
                        RGB
```

```
                        )
                    )
                )
            (theText)            ;a declaration for the text
                                 ;we create later
            (theBuffer)          ;added
            (theLayer
                    (car
                        (gimp-layer-new
                        theImage
                        theImageWidth
                        theImageHeight
                        RGB-IMAGE
                        "layer 1"
                        100
                        NORMAL
                        )
                    )
                )
            ) ;end of our local variables
        [Code here]
    )
```

```
(script-fu-register
  "script-fu-text-box"                      ;func name
  "Text Box"                                ;menu label
  "Creates a simple text box, sized to fit\
    around the user's choice of text,\
    font, font size, and color."           ;description
  "Michael Terry"                          ;author
  "copyright 1997, Michael Terry"          ;copyright notice
  "October 27, 1997"                       ;date created
  ""                      ;image type that the script works on
  SF-STRING       "Text:"         "Text Box" ;a string variable
  SF-FONT         "Font:"         "Charter"  ;a font variable
  SF-ADJUSTMENT   "Font size"     '(50 1 1000 1 10 0 1)
                                             ;a spin-button
  SF-COLOR        "Color:"        '(0 0 0)   ;color variable
  SF-ADJUSTMENT   "Buffer amount" '(35 0 100 1 10 1 0)
                                             ;a slider
)
(script-fu-menu-register "script-fu-text-box" "<Toolbox>/Xtns/Script-Fu/Text")
```

11.3.6.4 Adding The New Code

We're going to add code in two places: right before we resize the image, and at the end of the script (to return the new image, the layer and the text).

After we get the text's height and width, we need to resize these values based on the buffer amount specified by the user. We won't do any error checking to make sure it's in the range of 0-100% because it's not life-threatening, and because there's no reason why the user can't enter a value like "200" as the percent of buffer to add.

```
(set! theBuffer (* theImageHeight (/ inBufferAmount 100) ) )
(set! theImageHeight (+ theImageHeight theBuffer theBuffer) )
(set! theImageWidth  (+ theImageWidth  theBuffer theBuffer) )
```

All we're doing here is setting the buffer based on the height of the text, and adding it twice to both the height and width of our new image. (We add it twice to both dimensions because the buffer needs to be added to both sides of the text.)

Now that we have resized the image to allow for a buffer, we need to center the text within the image. This is done by moving it to the (x, y) coordinates of (theBuffer, theBuffer). I added this line after resizing the layer and the image:

```
        (gimp-layer-set-offsets theText theBuffer theBuffer)
```

Go ahead and save your script, and try it out after refreshing the database.

All that is left to do is return our image, the layer, and the text layer. After displaying the image, we add this line:

```
        (list theImage theLayer theText)
```

This is the last line of the function, making this list available to other scripts that want to use it.

To use our new text box script in another script, we could write something like the following:

```
        (set! theResult (script-fu-text-box
                            "Some text"
                            "Charter" "30"
                            '(0 0 0)
                            "35"
                            )
        )
        (gimp-image-flatten (car theResult))
```

Congratulations, you are on your way to your Black Belt of Script-Fu!

Part III

Function Reference

Chapter 12

Toolbox

12.1 The Toolbox

The GIMP provides a comprehensive toolbox in order to quickly perform basic tasks such as making selections or drawing paths. The many tools contained within The GIMP's toolbox are discussed in detail here.

The GIMP has a diverse assortment of tools that let you perform a large variety of tasks. The tools can be thought of as falling into five categories: *Selection tools*, which specify or modify the portion of the image that will be affected by subsequent actions; *Paint tools*, which alter the colors in some part of the image; *Transform tools*, which alter the geometry of the image; *Color tools*, which alter the distribution of colors across the entire image; and *Other tools*, which don't fall into the other four categories.

(In case you're curious, in GIMP lingo a "tool" is a way of acting on an image that requires access to its display, either to let you indicate what you want to do by moving the pointer around inside the display, or to show you interactively the results of changes that you have made. But if you want to think of a tool as a saw, and an image as a piece of wood, it probably won't do you a great deal of harm.)

Most tools can be activated by clicking on an icon in the Toolbox. Some, however (namely, the Color tools), are accessible only via the menus, either as *Tools->Color Tools* or as *Layer->Colors*. Every tool, in fact, can be activated from the *Tools* menu; also, every tool can be activated from the keyboard using an accelerator key.

In the default setup, created when GIMP is first installed, not all tools show icons in the Toolbox: the Color tools are omitted. You can customize the set of tools that are shown in the Toolbox using the Tools dialog. There are two reasons you might want to do this: first, if you only rarely use a tool, it might be easier to find the tools you want if the distracting icon is removed; second, if you use the Color tools a lot, you might find it convenient to have icons for them easily available. In any case, regardless of the Toolbox, you can always access any tool at any time using the Tools menu from an image menubar.

The shape of the cursor changes when it is inside an image, to one that indicates which tool is active.

12.1.1 Tool Options

Figure 12.1: Tool Options dialog for the Rectangle Select tool.

If you have things set up like most people do, activating a tool causes its Tool Options dialog to appear below the Toolbox. If you don't have things set up this way, you probably should: it is very difficult to use tools effectively without being able to manipulate their options.

Tip
The Tool Options appear beneath the Toolbox in the default setup. If you lose it somehow, you can get it back by creating a new Tool Options dialog using File → Dialogs → Tool Options and then docking it below the Toolbox. See the section on Dialogs and Docking if you need help.

Each tool has its own specific set of options. The choices you make for them are kept throughout the session, until you change them. In fact, the tool options are maintained from session to session. The persistence of tool options across sessions can sometimes be an annoying nuisance: a tool behaves very strangely, and you can't figure out why until you remember that you were using some unusual option the last time you worked with it, two weeks ago.

At the bottom of the Tool Options dialog appear four buttons:

Save Options to This button allows you to save the settings for the current tool, so that you can restore them later. It brings up a small dialog allowing you to give a name to the array of saved options. When you Restore options, only saved sets for the active tool are shown, so you need not worry about including the name of the tool when you assign a name here.

Restore Options This button allows you to restore a previously saved set of options for the active tool. If no option-sets have ever been saved for the active tool, the button will be insensitive. Otherwise, clicking it will bring up a menu showing the names of all saved option sets: choosing a menu entry will apply those settings.

Delete Options This button allows you to delete a previously saved set of options for the active tool. If no option-sets have ever been saved for the active tool, the button will be insensitive. Otherwise, clicking it will bring up a menu showing the names of all saved option sets: choosing a menu entry will delete those settings.

Reset Options This button resets the options for the active tool to their default values.

12.2 Selection Tools

12.2.1 Common Features

Selection tools are designed to select regions from images or layers so you can work on them without affecting the unselected areas. Each tool has its own individual properties, but the selection tools also share a number of options and features in common.

These common features are described here; the variations are explained in the following sections for each tool specifically. If you need help with what a 'selection' is in GIMP, and how it works, see Selection.

There are six selection tools:

- Rectangle Select

- Ellipse Select

- Free Select (the Lasso)

- Select Contiguous Regions (the Magic Wand)

- Select by Color

- Select Shapes from Image (Intelligent Scissors)

In some ways the Path tool can also be thought of as a selection tool: any closed path can be converted into a selection. It also can do a great deal more, though, and does not share the same set of options with the other selection tools.

12.2.1.1 Key modifiers (Defaults)

The behavior of selection tools is modified if you hold down the **Ctrl**, **Shift**, and/or **Alt** keys while you use them.

Note
Advanced users find the modifier keys very valuable, but novice users often find them confusing. Fortunately, it is possible for most purposes to use the Mode buttons (described below) instead of modifier keys.

Ctrl When creating a selection, holding down the **Ctrl** key can have two different actions according to the way you use it:

- If you hold down the key *before clicking* to start the selection, this selection will be in *Subtraction* mode as long as you press the key.

- If you hold down the **Ctrl** key *after clicking* to start the selection, the effect will depend on the tool you are using.

Alt Holding **Alt** will allow movement of the current selection (only its frame, not its content). If the whole image is moved instead of the selection only, try Shift-Alt. Note that the **Alt** key is sometimes intercepted by the windowing system (meaning that GIMP never knows that it was pressed), so this may not work for everybody.

Shift When creating a selection, holding down the **Shift** key can have two different actions according to the way you use it:

- If you hold down the key *before clicking* to start the selection, this selection will be in *Addition* mode as long as you press the key.

- If you hold down the **Shift** key *after clicking* to start the selection, the effect will depend on the tool you are using: for example, the selection will be a square with the Rectangle Select tool.

Ctrl-Shift Using Ctrl-Shift together can do a variety of things, depending on which tool is used. Common to all selection tools is that the selection mode will be switched to intersection, so that after the operation is finished, the selection will consist of the intersection of the region traced out with the pre-existing selection. It is an exercise for the reader to play with the various combinations available when performing selections while holding Ctrl-Shift and releasing either both or either prior to releasing the mouse button.

Space bar Pressing the **Space Bar** while using a selection tool transforms this tool into Move tool as long as you press the bar.

12.2.1.2 Options

Here we describe the tool options that apply to all selection tools: options that apply only to some tools, or that affect each tool differently, are described in the sections devoted to the individual tools. The current settings for these options can be seen in the Tool Options dialog, which you should always have visible when you are using tools. (Most users keep it docked directly below the Toolbox.) To make the interface consistent, the same options are presented for all selection tools, even though some of them don't have any effect for some of the tools.

Mode This determines the way that the selection you create is combined with any pre-existing selection. Note that the functions performed by these buttons can be duplicated using modifier keys, as described above. For the most part, advanced users use the modifier keys; novice users find the mode buttons easier.

Replace mode will cause any existing selection to be destroyed or replaced when the new selection is created.

Add mode will cause the new selection to be added to any existing selection regions.

Subtract mode will remove the new selection area from any existing selection regions.

Intersection mode will make a new selection from the area where the existing selection region and the new selection region overlap.

Antialiasing This option only affects a few of the selection tools: it causes the boundary of the selection to be drawn more smoothly.

Feather Edges This options allows the boundary of the selection to be blurred, so that points near the boundary are only partially selected. For further information regarding feathering, see the glossary entry Feathering.

12.2.1.3 Additional information

Note
When moving a selection beyond the boundaries of the image canvas, the selection will be cropped to the image area. Selections can exist on the visible canvas only. Selection movements and changes are, however, kept in the undo buffer should you need to repair an error.

12.2.2 Rectangle Selection Tool

Figure 12.2: Rectangle Select icon in the Toolbox

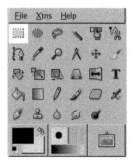

The Rectangle Selection tool is designed to select rectangular regions of an image: it is the most basic of the selection tools, but very commonly used. For information on selections and how they are used in GIMP see Selections; for information on features common to all selection tools see Selection Tools.

This tool is also used for rendering a rectangle on an image. To render a filled rectangle, create a rectangular selection, and then fill it using the Bucket Fill tool. To create a rectangular outline, the simplest and most flexible approach is to create a rectangular selection and then stroke it.

If you want to round the edges of a rectangular selection, the easiest method is using Select → Rounded Rectangle from the image menu.

12.2.2.1 How to Activate

You can access to the Selection Tool in different ways:

- From the image menu bar Tools → Selection Tools → Rect Select;

- By clicking on the tool icon in the ToolBox,

- By using the keyboard shortcut **R**.

12.2.2.2 Key modifiers

 Note

See Selection Tools for help with modifier keys that affect all these tools in the same way. Only effects that are specific to the Rectangle Select tool are explained here.

- **Ctrl**: Pressing the Ctrl key after starting your selection, and holding it down until you are finished, causes your starting point to be used as the center of the selected rectangle, instead of a corner. Note that if you press the Ctrl key *before* starting to make the selection, the resulting selection will be subtracted from the existing selection.

- **Shift**: Pressing the Shift key after starting your selection, and holding it down until you are finished, constrains the selection to be square. Note that if you press the Shift key *before* starting to make the selection, the resulting selection will be added to the existing selection.

- Ctrl-Shift: Pressing both keys after starting your selection combines the two effects, giving you a square selection centered on your starting point. Note that pressing these keys before starting your selection intersects the resulting selection with the existing one and the pointer change shape accordingly.

12.2.2.3 Tool Options

Figure 12.3: Tool Options for the Rectangle Select tool

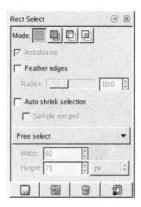

 Note

See Selection Tools for help with options that are common to all these tools. Only options that are specific to the Rectangle Select tool are explained here.

Antialiasing This option performs no function for this tool and is present to unify the user interface between the various selection types.

Auto Shrink Selection The Auto Shrink Selection checkbox will make your next selection automatically shrink to the nearest rectangular shape available on the image layer. The algorithm for finding the best rectangle to shrink to is 'intelligent', which in this case means that it sometimes does surprisingly sophisticated things, and sometimes does surprisingly strange things. In any case, if the region that you want to select has a solid-colored surround, auto-shrinking will always pick it out correctly. Note that the resulting selection does not need to have the same shape as the one you sweep out.

If Sample Merged is also enabled, then Auto Shrink will use the pixel information from the visible display of the image, rather than just from the active layer. For further information regarding Sample Merge, see the glossary entry Sample Merge.

Size Constraints

Figure 12.4: Size Constraint Option Menu for the Rectangle Select tool

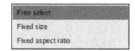

This menu allows you the option of constraining the shape of the rectangle in three different ways.

- **Free Select** This option places no constraint on the rectangle.
- **Fixed Size** This will allow you to manually specify a size for the selection using the Width, Height, and Unit controls.
- **Fixed Aspect Ratio** This option allows you to resize the selection while keeping the aspect ratio fixed according to the two numbers entered in the Width and Height controls.

12.2.3 Ellipse Selection Tool

Figure 12.5: Ellipse Select icon in the Toolbox

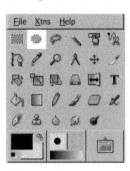

The Ellipse Selection tool is designed to select circular and elliptical regions from an image, with high-quality anti-aliasing if you want it. For information on selections and how they are used in GIMP see Selections; for information on features common to all selection tools see Selection Tools.

This tool is also used for rendering a circle or ellipse on an image. To render a filled ellipse, create an elliptical selection, and then fill it using the Bucket Fill tool. To create an elliptical outline, the simplest and most flexible approach is to create an elliptical selection and then stroke it. However, the quality of anti-aliasing with this approach is rather crude. A higher quality outline can be obtained by creating two elliptical selections with different sizes, subtracting the inner one from the outer one; however this is not always easy to get right. The command Selection → Border... makes it easy.

12.2.3.1 How to Activate

The Ellipse Selection Tool can be activated from an image menu as Tools → Selection Tools → Ellipse Select; from the Toolbox by clicking on the tool icon ; or from the keyboard using the shortcut **e**.

12.2.3.2 Key modifiers

 Note
See Selection Tools for help with modifier keys that affect all these tools in the same way. Only effects that are specific to the Ellipse Select tool are explained here.

- **Ctrl**: Pressing the Ctrl key after starting your selection, and holding it down until you are finished, causes your starting point to be used as the center of the selected ellipse, instead of a corner of the rectangle that may contain it. Note that if you press the Ctrl key *before* starting to make the selection, the resulting selection will be subtracted from the existing selection.

- **Shift**: Pressing the Shift key after starting your selection, and holding it down until you are finished, constrains the selection to be a circle. Note that if you press the Shift key *before* starting to make the selection, the resulting selection will be added to the existing selection.

- Ctrl-Shift: Pressing both keys combines the two effects, giving you a circular selection centered on your starting point.

12.2.3.3 Options

Figure 12.6: Tool Options for the Ellipse Select tool

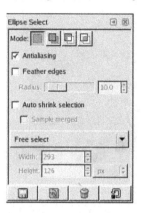

Note

See Selection Tools for help with options that are common to all these tools. Only options that are specific to the Ellipse Select tool are described here.

You can access to the Ellipse Selection options by double-clicking on the icon.

Antialiasing Checking this option will make the edge of the selection appear smoother, by partially selecting pixels that the edge passes through. The idea of antialiasing is discussed in more detail under the glossary entry Antialiasing. You will probably find that you get more satisfactory results by using it, in most cases. The main situation where you might want not to use it is in cutting and pasting, where partial selection can sometimes create strange color fringes.

Auto Shrink Selection The Auto Shrink Selection checkbox will make your next selection automatically shrink to the nearest elliptical shape available on the image layer. The algorithm for finding the best ellipse to shrink to is "intelligent", which in this case means that it sometimes does surprisingly sophisticated things, and sometimes does surprisingly strange things. In any case, if the region that you want to select has a solid-colored surround, auto-shrinking will always pick it out correctly. Note that the resulting elliptical selection does not need to have the same shape as the one you sweep out.

If Sample Merged is also enabled, then the Auto Shrink will use the pixel information from all the layers of the image. For further information regarding Sample Merge, see the glossary entry Sample Merged.

Size Constraints

Figure 12.7: Size Constraint Option Menu for the Ellipse Select tool

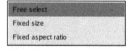

This menu allows you the option of constraining the shape of the ellipse in three different ways.

- **Free Select** This option places no constraint on the ellipse.
- **Fixed Size** This will allow you to manually specify a size for the selection using the Width, Height, and Unit controls.
- **Fixed Aspect Ratio** This option allows you to resize the selection while keeping the aspect ratio fixed according to the two numbers entered in the Width and Height controls.

12.2.4   Free Selection Tool (Lasso)

Figure 12.8: Free Selection icon in the Toolbox

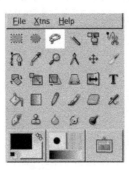

The Free Selection tool, or Lasso, lets you create a selection by drawing it free-hand with the pointer, while holding down the left mouse button (or, for a stylus, pressing it against the tablet). When you release the mouse button, the selection is closed by connecting the current pointer location to the start location with a straight line. You can go outside the edge of the image display and come back in if you want to. The Lasso is often a good tool to use for 'roughing in' a selection; it is not so good for precise definition. Experienced users find that it is often convenient to begin with the lasso tool, but then switch to QuickMask mode for detail work.

For information on selections and how they are used in GIMP see Selections. For information on features common to all selection tools see Selection Tools.

Note

The Free Selection tool is much easier to use with a tablet than with a mouse.

12.2.4.1   How to Activate

The Lasso Tool can be activated from an image menu as Tools → Selection Tools → Free Select; from the Toolbox by clicking

on the tool icon   ; or from the keyboard using the shortcut **f**.

12.2.4.2   Key modifiers

The Free Select tool does not have any special key modifiers, only the ones that affect all selection tools in the same way. See Selection Tools for help with these.

12.2.4.3 Options

Figure 12.9: Tool Options for the Lasso tool

The Free Select tool has no special tool options, only the ones that affect all selection tools in the same way. See Selection Tools for help with these.

You can find the lasso options by double-clicking on the icon in the Toolbox.

12.2.5 Fuzzy selection (Magic wand)

Figure 12.10: Magic Wand tool icon in the Toolbox

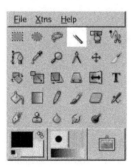

The Fuzzy Select (Magic Wand) tool is designed to select areas of the current layer or image based on color similarity. It starts selecting when you click at a spot in the image, and expands outward like water flooding low-lying areas, selecting contiguous pixels whose colors are similar to the starting pixel. You can control the threshold of similarity by dragging the mouse downward or to the right: the farther you drag it, the larger the selected region. And you can reduce the selection by dragging upwards or to the left.

When using this tool, it is very important to pick the right starting point. If you select the wrong spot, you might get something very different from what you want, or even the opposite.

The Wand is a good tool for selecting objects with sharp edges. It is fun to use, so beginners often start out using it a lot. You will probably find, however, that the more you use it, the more frustrated you become with the difficulty of selecting exactly what you what, no more, no less. Perhaps the most frustrating aspect is that after you have released the mouse button, you can't make small adjustments to the threshold: you have to start over again from scratch. More experienced users find that the Path and Color Select tools are often more efficient, and use the Wand less. Still, it is useful for selecting an area within a contour, or touching up imperfect selections. It often works very well for selecting a solid-colored (or nearly solid-colored) background area.

Note that as the selected area expands outward from the center, it does not only propagate to pixels that touch each other: it is capable of jumping over small gaps. The distance it can jump over is set in the Tool Options page of the Preferences dialog: the "Default threshold" for Finding Contiguous Regions. By raising or lowering this value, you can make the Magic Wand either more or less aggressive. (Filling with the Bucket Fill and Blend tools will also be affected.)

12.2.5.1 How to Activate

The Magic Wand Tool can be activated from an image menu as Tools → Selection Tools → Fuzzy Select; from the Toolbox by clicking on the tool icon ; or from the keyboard using the shortcut **z**. ("Z" stands for "Zauber", the German word for Magic.)

12.2.5.2 Key modifiers (Defaults)

The Fuzzy Select tool does not have any special key modifiers, only the ones that affect all selection tools in the same way. See Selection Tools for help with these.

12.2.5.3 Options

Figure 12.11: Tool Options for the Magic Wand tool

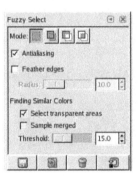

> **Note**
> See Selection Tools for help with options that are common to all these tools. Only options that are specific to the Magic Wand tool are explained here.

Finding Similar Colors These options affect the way the Magic Wand expands the selection out from the initial point.

> **Select Transparent Areas** This option gives the Magic Wand the ability to select areas that are completely transparent. If this option is not checked, transparent areas will never be included in the selection.

> **Sample Merged** This option becomes relevant when you have several layers in your image, and the active layer is either semi-transparent or is set to another Layer Mode than Normal. If this is the case, the colors present in the layer will be different from the colors in the composite image. If the 'Sample Merged' option is unchecked, the wand will only react to the color in the active layer when it creates a selection. If it is checked it will react to the composite color of all visible layers. For further information, see the glossary entry Sample Merged.

> **Threshold** This slider determines the range of colors that will be selected at the moment you click the pointer on the initial point, before dragging it: the higher the threshold, the larger the resulting selection. After the first button-press, dragging the pointer downward or to the right will increase the size of the selection; dragging upward or to the left will decrease it. Thus, you have the same set of possibilities regardless of the Threshold setting: what differs is the amount of dragging you have to do to get the result you want.

12.2.6   Select By Color Tool

Figure 12.12: Select by Color tool icon in the Toolbox

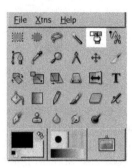

The Select by Color tool is designed to select areas of an image based on color similarity. It works a lot like the Fuzzy Select tool ('Magic Wand'). The main difference between them is that the Magic Wand selects *contiguous* regions, with all parts connected to the starting point by paths containing no large gaps; while the Select by Color tool selects all pixels that are sufficiently similar in color to the pixel you click on, regardless of where they are located. Also, clicking and dragging in the image has no effect on the Select by Color tool.

12.2.6.1   How to Activate

The Select By Color Tool can be activated from an image menu as Tools → Selection Tools → Select by Color; from the Toolbox

by clicking on the tool icon  ; or from the keyboard using the shortcut Shift -Ctrl-C

12.2.6.2   Key modifiers (Defaults)

The select by color tool does not have any special key modifiers, only the ones that affect all selection tools in the same way. See Selection Tools for help with these.

12.2.6.3   Options

Figure 12.13: Tool Options for the Select by Color tool

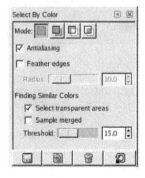

Note
See Section 12.2.1 for help with options that are common to all these tools. Only options that are specific to the Select by Color tool are explained here. Note that they are the same options as the Magic Wand tool has.

You can find the Magic Wand options by double-clicking on the icon in the Toolbox.

Finding Similar Colors These options affect the way the Select by Color tool expands the selection out from the initial point.

- **Select Transparent Areas** This option gives the Select by Color tool the ability to select areas that are completely transparent. If this option is not checked, transparent areas will never be included in the selection.

- **Sample Merged** This option becomes relevant when you have several layers in your image, and the active layer is either semi-transparent or is set to another Layer Mode than Normal. If this is the case, the colors present in the layer will be different from the colors in the composite image. If the "Sample Merged" option is unchecked, the Select by Color tool will only react to the color in the active layer when it creates a selection. If it is checked it will react to the composite color of all visible layers. For further information, see the glossary entry Sample Merged.

- **Threshold** This slider determines the range of colors that will be selected: the higher the threshold, the larger the resulting selection.

 Note
Regarding moving selection, this tool doesn't work like others: when selection by color is created, you can move it only if you select another selection tool...

12.2.7 Scissors Tool

Figure 12.14: Intelligent Scissors tool icon in the Toolbox.

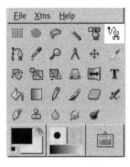

The Intelligent Scissors tool is an interesting piece of equipment: it has some features in common with the Lasso, some features in common with the Path tool, and some features all its own. It is useful when you are trying to select a region defined by strong color-changes at the edges. To use the Scissors, you click to create a set of "control nodes" at the edges of the region you are trying to select. The tool produces a continuous curve passing through these control nodes, following any high-contrast edges it can find. If you are lucky, the path that the tool finds will correspond to the contour you are trying to select.

Each time you left-click with the mouse, you create a new control point, which is connected to the last control point by a curve that tries to follow edges in the image. To finish, click on the first point (the cursor changes to indicate when you are in the right spot). You can adjust the curve by dragging the control nodes, or by clicking to create new control nodes. When you are satisfied, click anywhere inside the curve to convert it into a selection.

Warning

Be sure not to click inside the curve until you are completely done adjusting it. Once you have converted it into a selection, undoing takes you back to zero, and you will have to to start constructing the curve again from scratch if you need to change it. Also be sure not to switch to a different tool, or again all of your carefully created control nodes will be lost. (But you still can transform your selection into a path and work it with the Path tool.)

Unfortunately, there seem to be some problems with the edge-following logic for this tool, with the result that the selections it creates tend to be pretty crude in a lot of cases. A good way to clean them up is to switch to QuickMask mode, and use paint tools to paint in the problematic parts. On the whole, most people find the Path tool to be more useful than the Scissors, because, even though it does not have the intelligent edge-finding capability, the paths it produces persist until you delete them, and can be altered at any time.

12.2.7.1 How to Activate

The Intelligent Scissors can be activated from an image menu as Tools → Selection Tools → Intelligent Scissors; from the

Toolbox by clicking on the tool icon  ; or from the keyboard using the shortcut **i**.

12.2.7.2 Key modifiers (Defaults)

The Scissor tool does not have any special key modifiers, only the ones that affect all selection tools in the same way. See Selection Tools for help with these.

12.2.7.3 Options

Figure 12.15: Tool Options for the Intelligent Scissors

 Note

See Selection Tools for help with options that are common to all these tools. Only options that are specific to the Intelligent Scissors tool are explained here.

Show Interactive Boundary If this option is enabled, dragging a control node during placement will indicate the path that will be taken by the selection boundary. If it is not enabled, the node will be shown connected to the previous node by a straight line while you are dragging it around, and you won't see the resulting path until you release the pointer button. On slow systems, if your control nodes are far apart, this may give a bit of a speed-up.

12.3 Brush Tools

12.3.1 Common Features

Figure 12.16: The Brush tools

The GIMP Toolbox includes nine "brush tools", all grouped together at the bottom (in the default arrangement). The feature they all have in common is that all of them are used by moving the pointer across the image display, creating brushstrokes. Four of them – the Pencil, Paintbrush, Airbrush, and Ink tools – behave like the intuitive notion of "painting" with a brush. The others use a brush to modify an image in some way rather than paint on it: the Eraser erases; the Clone tool copies from a pattern or image; the Convolve tool blurs or sharpens; the Dodge/Burn tool lightens or darkens; and the Smudge tool smears.

The advantages of using GIMP with a tablet instead of a mouse probably show up more clearly for brush tools than anywhere else: the gain in fine control is invaluable. These tools also have special 'Pressure sensitivity' options that are only usable with a tablet.

In addition to the more common 'hands-on' method, it is possible to apply brush tools in an automated way, by creating a selection or path and then 'stroking' it. You can choose to stroke with any of the brush tools, including nonstandard ones such as the Eraser, Smudge tool, etc., and any options you set for the tool will be applied. See the section on Stroking for more information.

Brush tools work not only on image layers, but on other types of drawable objects as well: layer masks, channels, and the selection. To apply a brush tool to a layer mask or channel, simply make it the image's active drawable by clicking on it in the Layers dialog or Channels dialog. To apply a brush tool to the selection, switch to QuickMask mode. 'Painting the selection' in this way is a very powerful method for efficiently creating precise selections.

12.3.1.1 Key modifiers

- **Ctrl** : Holding down the Ctrl key has a special effect on every brush tool except the ink tool. For the Pencil, Paintbrush, Airbrush, Eraser, and Smudge tools, it switches them into 'color picker' mode, so that clicking on an image pixel causes GIMP's foreground to be set to the active layer's color at that point (or, for the Eraser, GIMP's background color). For the Clone tool, the Ctrl key switches it into a mode where clicking sets the reference point for copying. For the Convolve tool, the Ctrl key switches between blur and sharpen modes; the the Dodge/Burn tool, it switches between dodging and burning.

- **Shift**: Holding down the Shift key has the same effect on all brush tools: it places the tool into *straight line* mode. To create a straight line with any of the brush tools, first click on the starting point, *then* press the Shift key. As long as you hold it down, you will see a thin line connecting the previously clicked point with the current pointer location. If you click again, while continuing to hold down the Shift key, a straight line will be rendered. You can continue this process to create a series of connected line segments.

- Ctrl-Shift: Holding down both keys puts the tool into *constrained straight line* mode. This is similar to the effect of the Shift key alone, except that the orientation of the line is constrained to the nearest multiple of 15 degrees. Use this if you want to create perfect horizontal, vertical, or diagonal lines.

12.3.1.2 Tool Options

Figure 12.17: Tool Options shared by all brush tools

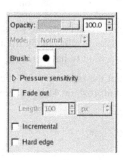

Many tool options are shared by several brush tools: these are described here. Options that apply only to one specific tool, or to a small number of tools, are described in the sections devoted to those tools.

Opacity The Opacity slider sets the transparency level for the brush operation. To understand how it works, imagine that instead of altering the active layer, the tool creates a transparent layer above the active layer and acts on that layer. Changing Opacity in the Tool Options has the same effect that changing opacity in the Layers dialog would have in the latter situation. It controls the 'strength' of all brush tools, not just those that paint on the active layer. In the case of the Eraser, this can come across as a bit confusing: it works out that the higher the 'opacity' is, the more transparency you get.

Mode The Mode dropdown list provides a selection of paint application modes; a list of modes can be found in the glossary. As with the opacity, the easiest way to understand what the Mode setting does is to imagine that the paint is actually applied to a layer above the layer you are working on, with the layer combination mode in the Layers dialog set to the selected mode. You can obtain a great variety of special effects in this way. The Mode option is only usable for tools that can be thought of as adding color to the image: the Pencil, Paintbrush, Airbrush, Ink, and Clone tools. For the other brush tools, the option appears for the sake of consistency but is always grayed out.

Brush The brush determines how much of the image is affected by the tool, and how it is affected, when you trace out a brushstroke with the pointer. GIMP allows you to use several different types of brushes, which are described in the Brushes section. The same brush choices are available for all brush tools except the Ink tool, which uses a unique type of procedurally generated brush. The colors of a brush only come into play for tools where they are meaningful: the Pencil, Paintbrush, and Airbrush tools. For the other brush tools, only the intensity distribution of a brush is relevant.

Pressure Sensitivity The Pressure Sensitivity section is only meaningful if you are using a tablet: it allows you to decide which aspects of the tool's action should be affected by how hard you press the stylus against the tablet. The possibilities are opacity, hardness, rate, size, and color. They work together: you can enable as many of them as you like. For each tool, only the ones that are meaningful are listed. Here is what they do:

Opacity The effect of this option is described above.

Hardness This option applies to brushes with fuzzy edges. If it is enabled, the harder you press, the darker the fuzzy parts of the brush will appear.

Rate This option applies to the Airbrush, Convolve tool, and Smudge tool, all of which have time-based effects. Pressing harder makes these tools act more rapidly.

Size This option applies to all of the pressure sensitive brush tools. If the option is checked, then pressing harder will increase the size of the area affected by the brush.

Color This option only applies to the painting tools: the Pencil, Paintbrush, and Airbrush; and only if you are using colors from a gradient. If these conditions are met, then pressing harder causes colors to be taken from higher in the gradient.

Fade Out This option causes each stroke to fade out over the specified distance. It is easiest to visual for painting tools, but applies to all of the brush tools. It is equivalent to gradually reducing the opacity along the trajectory of the stroke. Note that, if you are using a tablet, this option does not change the effects of brush pressure.

Incremental The Incremental checkbox activates incremental mode for the tool. If it is deactivated, the maximum effect of a single stroke is determined by the opacity, and moving the brush repeatedly over the same spot will not increase the effect beyond this limit. If Incremental is active, each additional pass with the brush will increase the effect, but the opacity can't exceed the opacity set for the tool. This option is available for all brush tools except those which have a 'rate' control, which automatically implies an incremental effect. See also Section 8.2.

Hard Edge Activating this option causes fuzzy brushes to be treated as though they were black-and-white, and inactivates sub-pixel anti-aliasing. The consequence is that all pixels affected by the tool are affected to the same degree. This is often useful if you work at a very high zoom level, and want to have precise control of every single pixel.

'Hard edge' is available for all brush tools except the painting tools (Pencil, Paintbrush, and Airbrush), where it would be redundant, because giving a hard edge to the Paintbrush or Airbrush would simply make them behave like the Pencil tool.

12.3.1.3 Further Information

Advanced users may be interested to know that brush tools actually operate at a sub-pixel level, in order to avoid producing jagged-looking results. One consequence of this is that even if you work with a hard-edged brush, such as one of the Circle brushes, pixels on the edge of the brushstroke will only be partially affected. If you need to have all-or-nothing effects (which may be necessary for getting a good selection, or for cutting and pasting, or for operating pixel-by-pixel at a high zoom level), there are two things you can do: (1) for painting, use the Pencil tool, which makes all brushes perfectly hard and disables sub-pixel anti-aliasing, or (2) for other types of brush tools, check the 'Hard edge' box in the Tool Options.

12.3.2 Bucket Fill

Figure 12.18: Toolbox Fill

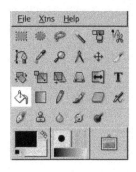

This tool fills a selection with the current foreground color. If you Shift+click and use the Bucket tool, it will use the background color instead. Depending on how the tool options are set, the Bucket Fill tool will either fill the entire selection, or only parts whose colors are similar to the point you click on. The tool options also affect the way transparency is handled.

The amount of fill depends on what Fill Threshold you have specified. The fill threshold determines how far the fill will spread (similar to the way in which the magic wand works). The fill starts at the point where you click and spreads outward until the color or alpha value becomes 'too different'.

When you fill objects in a transparent layer (such as letters in a text layer) with a different color than before, you may find that a border of the old color still surrounds the objects. This is due to a low fill-threshold in the Bucket Fill options dialog. With a low threshold, the bucket tool won't fill semi-transparent pixels, and they will stand out against the fill because they have kept their original color. If you want to fill areas that are totally transparent, you have to choose right-click|Select|Select All, and make sure that the layer's 'Keep Transparency' button (in the Layers dialog) is unchecked. If the Keep Transparency button is checked, only the opaque parts of the layer will be filled, and if you don't use the Select All command, only the opaque 'island' that you clicked on will be filled.

12.3.2.1 Activate Tool

- The Bucket Fill can be called in the following order, from the image-menu: Tools/ Paint Tools/Bucket Fill.

- The Tool can also be called by clicking the tool icon:

12.3.2.2 Key modifiers (Defaults)

Shortcut The Shift-B keys will change the active tool to Bucket Fill.

Ctrl toggles the use of BG Color Fill or FG Color Fill on the fly.

Shift toggles the use of Fill Similar Color or Fill Whole Selection on the fly.

12.3.2.3 Options

Overview The available tool options for the Fill Tool can be accessed by double clicking the Fill Tool icon.

Opacity The Opacity slider sets the transparency level for the fill. A higher opacity setting results in a more opaque fill and a lower setting results in a more transparent fill.

Mode The Mode dropdown list provides a selection of paint application modes. A list of these modes can be found in Section 8.2.

Pattern This dropdown list allows the user to select one of many fill patterns to use on the next fill operation. The manner in which the list is presented is controlled by the four buttons at the bottom of the selector.

Fill Type GIMP provides three fill types: FG Color Fill, BG Color Fill and Pattern Fill.

FG Color Fill sets the fill color to the currently selected foreground color.

BG Color Fill sets the fill color to the currently selected background color.

Pattern Fill sets the fill color to the currently selected pattern.

Affected Area

Fill similar colors This is the default setting: the tool fills the area with a color near the pixel onto you have clicked. The color similarity is defined by a brightness threshold, that you can set by a value or by a cursor position.

Fill whole selection This option makes GIMP fill a preexistent selection or the whole image. A quicker approach to do the same thing could be to click and drag the foreground, background or pattern color, leaving it onto the selection.

Finding Similar Colors Under this section you can find two options:

Fill Transparent Areas The option Fill Transparent Areas offers the possibility of filling areas with low opacity.

Sample Merged The option Sample Merged toggles the sampling from all layers. If Sample Merged is active, fills can be made on a lower layer, while the color information used for threshold checking is located further up. Simply select the lower level and ensure that a layer above is visible for color weighting.

Threshold The Threshold slider sets the level at which color weights are measured for fill boundaries. A higher setting will fill more of a multi colored image and conversely, a lower setting will fill less area.

12.3.3 Gradient Tool

Figure 12.19: The Blend tool in Toolbox.

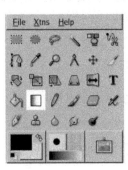

This tool fills the selected area with a gradient blend of the foreground and background colors by default, but there are many options. To make a blend, drag the cursor in the direction you want the gradient to go, and release the mouse button when you feel you have the right position and size of your blend. The softness of the blend depends on how far you drag the cursor. The shorter the drag distance, the sharper it will be.

There are an astonishing number of things you can do with this tool, and the possibilities may seem a bit overwhelming at first. The two most important options you have are the Gradient and the Shape. Clicking the Gradient button in the tool options brings up a Gradient Select window, allowing you to choose from among a variety of gradients supplied with GIMP; you can also construct and save custom gradients. Further informations about gradients can be found in Section 7.10 and Section 13.3.4.

For Shape, there are 11 options: Linear, Bilinear, Radial, Square, Conical (symmetric), Conical (asymmetric), Shapeburst (angular), Shapeburst (spherical), Shapeburst (dimpled), Spiral (clockwise), and Spiral (counterclockwise); these are described in detail below. The Shapeburst options are the most interesting: they cause the gradient to follow the shape of the selection boundary, no matter how twisty it is. Unlike the other shapes, Shapeburst gradients are not affected by the length or direction of the line you draw: for them as well as every other type of gradient you are required to click inside the selection and move the mouse, but a Shapeburst appears the same no matter where you click or how you move.

 Tip
Check out the Difference option in the Mode menu, where doing the same thing (even with full opacity) will result in fantastic swirling patterns, changing and adding every time you drag the cursor.

12.3.3.1 Activate Tool

- The Blend Tool can be called in the following order, from the image-menu: Tools/ Paint Tools/ Blend.

- The Tool can also be called by clicking the tool icon:

12.3.3.2 Key modifiers (Defaults)

Shortcut The **L** key will change the active tool to Gradient Fill.

Ctrl **Ctrl** is used to create straight lines that are constrained to 15 degree absolute angles.

12.3.3.3 Options

Figure 12.20: 'Blend' tool options

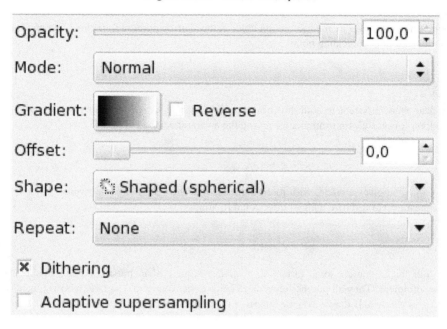

Overview The available tool options can be accessed by double clicking the Gradient Tool icon.

Opacity The Opacity slider sets the transparency level for the gradient. A higher opacity setting results in a more opaque fill and a lower setting results in a more transparent fill.

Mode The Mode dropdown list provides a selection of paint application modes. A list of these modes can be found in Section 8.2.

Gradient A variety of gradient patterns can be selected from the drop-down list. The tool causes a shading pattern that transitions from foreground to background color or introducing others colors, in the direction the user determines by drawing a line in the image. For the purposes of drawing the gradient, the Reverse checkbox reverse the gradient direction with the effect, for instance, of swapping the foreground and background colors.

Offset The Offset value permits to increase the 'slope' of the gradient. It determines how far from the clicked starting point the gradient will begin. Shapeburst forms are not affected by this option.

Figure 12.21: 'Blend' tool: Offset example

Top, Offset = 0 ; Bottom, Offset = 50%

Shape The GIMP provides 11 shapes, which can be selected from the drop-down list. Details on each of the shapes are given below.

Linear

The Lineargradient begins with the foreground color at the starting point of the drawn line and transitions linearly to the background color at the ending point.

Bi-Linear

The Bi-Linear shape proceeds in both directions from the starting point, for a distance determined by the length of the drawn line. It is useful, for example, for giving the appearance of a cylinder.

Radial

The Radial gradient gives a circle, with foreground color at the center and background color outside the circle. It gives the appearance of a sphere without directional lighting.

Square

There are four shapes that are some variant on a square: Square, Shapeburst (angular), Shapeburst (spherical), and Shapeburst (dimpled). They all put the foreground color at the center of a square, whose center is at the start of the drawn line, and whose half-diagonal is the length of the drawn line. The four options provide a variety in the manner in which the gradient is calculated; experimentation is the best means of seeing the differences.

Conical (symmetric)

The Conical(symmetrical) shape gives the sensation of looking down at the tip of a cone, which appears to be illuminated with the background color from a direction determined by the direction of the drawn line.

Conical (asymmetric)

Conical(asymmetric) is similar to Conical(symmetric) except that the "cone" appears to have a ridge where the line is drawn.

Spiral (clockwise)

The Spiral tools provide spirals whose repeat width is determined by the length of the drawn line.

Repeat There are two repeat modes: Sawtooth Wave and Triangular Wave. The Sawtooth pattern is achieved by beginning with the foreground, transitioning to the background, then starting over with the foreground. The Triangular starts with the foreground, transitions to the background, then transitions back to the foreground.

Dithering Dithering is fully explained in the Glossary

Adaptive Supersampling Adaptive Supersampling is a more sophisticated means of smoothing the "jagged" effect of a sharp transition of color along a slanted or curved line.

12.3.4 Painting Tools (Pencil, Paintbrush, Airbrush)

Figure 12.22: Painting example

Three strokes painted with the same round fuzzy brush (outline shown in upper left), using the Pencil (left), Paintbrush (middle), and Airbrush (right).

The tools in this group are GIMP's basic painting tools, and they have enough features in common to be worth discussing together in this section. Features common to all brush tools are described in the Common Features section. Features specific to an individual tool are described in the section devoted to that tool.

The Pencil is the crudest of the tools in this group: it makes hard, non-anti-aliased brushstrokes. The Paintbrush is intermediate: it is probably the most commonly used of the group. The Airbrush is the most flexible and controllable: it is the only one for which the amount of paint applied depends on the speed of brush movement. This flexibility also makes it a bit more difficult to use than the Paintbrush, however.

All of these tools share the same brushes, and the same options for choosing colors, either from the basic palette or from a gradient. All are capable of painting in a wide variety of modes.

12.3.4.1 Key modifiers

Ctrl, Ctrl Holding down the **Ctrl** key changes each of these tools to a Color Picker: clicking on any pixel of any layer sets the foreground color (as displayed in the Toolbox Color Area) to the color of the pixel.

12.3.4.2 Options

Mode The Mode dropdown list provides a selection of paint application modes. This setting appears in the Tool Options for all brush tools, but it is grayed out for all except the tools in this group, the Ink tool, and the Clone tool. A list of possible modes can be found in Section 8.2. For the most part these modes are the same as the layer combination modes available in the Layers dialog, and you can understand their effects by imagining that the paint is applied to a separate layer above the target layer, with the mode for the layer set as specified. Three of the modes are special, though:

Color Erase This mode erases the foreground color, replacing it with partial transparency. It acts like the Color to Alpha filter, applied to the area under the brushstroke. Note that this only works on layers that possess an alpha channel; otherwise, this mode is identical to Normal.

Behind This mode applies paint only to non-opaque areas of the layer: the lower the opacity, the more paint is applied. Thus, painting opaque areas has no effect; painting transparent areas has the same effect as normal mode. The result is always an increase in opacity. Of course none of this is meaningful for layers that lack an alpha channel.

Figure 12.23: Dissolve mode example

Two brushstrokes made with the Airbrush, using the same fuzzy circular brush. Left: Normal mode. Right: Dissolve mode.

Dissolve In this very useful mode, for fuzzy brushes the gray level of the brush determines not the paint density, but rather the probability of applying paint. This gives a nice way of creating rough-looking paintstrokes.

Gradient

Figure 12.24: Gradient options for painting tools.

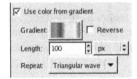

Instead of using the foreground color (as shown in the Color Area of the Toolbox), by checking the "Use color from gradient" option you can choose to paint with a gradient, giving colors that change gradually along the brush trajectory. For basic information on gradients, see the Gradients section.

You have several options to control what gradient is used and how it is laid out:

Gradient Here you see a display of the current gradient. Clicking on it brings up a Gradient Selector, which will allow you to choose a different gradient.

Reverse Normally a brushstroke starts with colors from the left side of the gradient, and progresses rightward. If "Reverse" is checked, the stroke starts with colors from the right side, and progresses leftward.

Length This option sets the distance corresponding to one complete cycle through the gradient colors. The default units are pixels, but you can choose a different unit from the adjoining Units menu.

Table 12.1: Illustration of the effects of the three gradient-repeat options, for the 'Abstract 2' gradient.

	Abstract2 Gradient
	None
	Sawtooth
	Triangular

Repeat This option determines what happens if a brushstroke extends farther than the Length specified above. There are three possibilities: "None" means that the color from the end of the gradient will be used throughout the remainder of the stroke; "Sawtooth wave" means that the gradient will be restarted from the beginning, which will often produce a color discontinuity; "Triangular wave" means that the gradient will be traversed in reverse, afterwards bouncing back and forth until the end of the brushstroke.

12.3.5   Pencil

Figure 12.25: Pencil tool

The Pencil tool is used to draw free hand lines with a hard edge. The pencil and paintbrush are similar tools. The main difference between the two tools is that although both use the same type of brush, the pencil tool will not produce fuzzy edges, even with a very fuzzy brush. It does not even do anti-aliasing.

Why would you want to work with such a crude tool? Perhaps the most important usage is when working with very small images, such as icons, where you operate at a high zoom level and need to get every pixel exactly right. With the pencil tool, you can be confident that every pixel within the brush outline will be changed in exactly the way you expect.

 Tip
If you want to draw straight lines with the Pencil (or any of several other paint tools), click at the starting point, then hold down **Shift** and click at the ending point.

12.3.5.1   Activate Tool

- The Pencil Tool can be called in the following order, from the image-menu: Tools → Paint Tools → Pencil

- The Tool can also be called by clicking the tool icon:

- or by clicking on the **N** keyboard shortcut.

12.3.5.2   Key modifiers (Defaults)

Ctrl, Ctrl This key changes the pencil to a Color Picker.

Shift, Shift This key places the pencil tool into straight line mode. Holding **Shift** while clicking Button 1 will generate a straight line. Consecutive clicks will continue drawing straight lines that originate from the end of the last line.

12.3.5.3   Options

Figure 12.26: Pencil Tool options

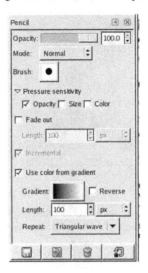

Overview The available tool options can be accessed by double clicking the Pencil Tool icon.

Opacity; Brush; Pressure Sensibility; Fade Out

 Note
See the Brush Tools Overview for a description of tool options that apply to many or all brush tools.

Mode; Color from Gradient

 Note
See the Painting Tools Overview for a description of tool options that apply to many or all painting tools.

12.3.6   Paintbrush Tool

Figure 12.27: Paintbrush

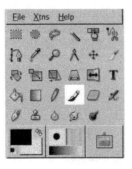

The paintbrush tool paints fuzzy brush strokes. All strokes are rendered using the current brush.

12.3.6.1 Activate Tool

- You can call the Paintbrush Tool in the following order, from the image-menu: Tools/ Paint Tools/Paintbrush .

- The Tool can also be called by clicking the tool icon:

- or by using the **P** keyboard shortcut.

12.3.6.2 Key modifiers (Defaults)

Ctrl , Ctrl This key changes the paintbrush to a Color Picker.

Shift This key places the paintbrush into straight line mode. Holding **Shift** while clicking Button 1 will generate a straight line. Consecutive clicks will continue drawing straight lines that originate from the end of the last line.

12.3.6.3 Options

Figure 12.28: Paintbrush tool options

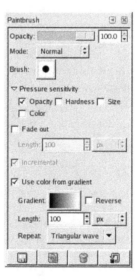

Overview The available tool options can be accessed by double clicking the Paintbrush Tool icon.

Opacity; Brush; Pressure Sensibility; Fade Out; Incremental See Brush common options.

Note
See the Brush Tools Overview for a description of tool options that apply to many or all brush tools.

Mode; Color from Gradient

Note
See the Painting Tools Overview for a description of tool options that apply to many or all painting tools.

12.3.7 Eraser

Figure 12.29: Eraser tool icon in the Toolbox

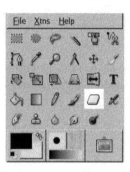

The Eraser is used to remove areas of color from the current layer or from a selection of this layer. If the Eraser is used on something that does not support transparency (a selection mask channel, a layer mask, or the Background layer if it lacks an alpha channel), then erasing will show the background color, as displayed in the Color Area of the Toolbox (in case of a mask, the selection will be modified). Otherwise, erasing will produce either partial or full transparency, depending on the settings for the tool options. You can learn more on how to add an alpha channel to a layer in Section 14.10.41.

If you need to erase some group of pixels completely, leaving no trace behind of their previous contents, you should check the "Hard edge" box in the Tool Options. Otherwise, sub-pixel brush placement will cause partial erasure at the edges of the brush-stroke, even if you use a hard-edged brush.

Tip
If you use GIMP with a tablet, you may find it convenient to treat the reverse end of the stylus as an eraser. To make this work, all you need to do is click the reverse end on the Eraser tool in the Toolbox. Because each end of the stylus is treated as a separate input device, and each input device has its own separate tool assignment, the reverse end will then continue to function as an Eraser as long as you don't select a different tool with it.

12.3.7.1 How to Activate

You can activate the Eraser tool in several ways :

• From the image menu through Tools → Paint Tools → Eraser;

• from the Toolbox by clicking on the tool icon ;

• or from the keyboard using the shortcut Shift-E.

12.3.7.2 Key modifiers

See the Section 12.3.1 for a description of key modifiers that have the same effect on all brush tools.

- **Ctrl**: For the Eraser, holding down the **Ctrl** key puts it into 'color picker' mode, so that it selects the color of any pixel it is clicked on. Unlike other brush tools, however, the Eraser sets the *background* color rather than the foreground color. This is more useful, because on drawables that don't support transparency, erasing replaces the erased areas with the current background color.

- **Alt**: For the Eraser, holding down the **Alt** key switches it into 'anti-erase' mode, as described below in the Tool Options section. Note that on some systems, the **Alt** key is trapped by the Window Manager. If this happens to you, you may be able to use Alt-Shift instead.

12.3.7.3 Tool Options

Figure 12.30: Tool Options for the Eraser tool

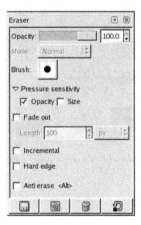

Opacity The Opacity slider, in spite of its name, determines the 'strength' of the tool. Thus, when you erase on a layer with an alpha channel, the higher the opacity you use, the more transparency you get!

Brush; Pressure sensitivity; Fade out; Incremental; Hard edge

 Note
See the Brush Tools Overview for a description of tool options that apply to many or all brush tools.

Anti Erase The Anti Erase option of the Erase tool can un-erase areas of an image, even if they are completely transparent. This feature only works when used on layers with an alpha channel. In addition to the checkbutton in the Tool Options, it can also be activated on-the-fly by holding down the **Alt** key (or, if the **Alt** key is trapped by the Window Manager, by holding down Alt-Shift).

Note

To understand how anti-erasing is possible, you should realize that erasing (or cutting, for that matter) only affects the alpha channel, not the RGB channels that contain the image data. Even if the result is completely transparent, the RGB data is still there, you simply can't see it. Anti-erasing increases the alpha value so that you can see the RGB data once again.

An annoying feature: on a layer you have created with a transparent background, using anti-erasing on non-painted areas paints with black!

Eit irriterande fenomen: Dersom du visker inn på eit lag med gjennomsiktig bakgrunn, vil viskeleret teikne med svart på område som ikkje er teikna på frå før.

12.3.8 Airbrush Tool

Figure 12.31: The Airbrush tool in Toolbox

The Airbrush tool emulates a traditional airbrush. This tool is suitable for painting soft areas of color.

12.3.8.1 Activate Tool

You can activate the Eraser tool in several ways :

- From the image-menu, through : Tools → Paint Tools → Airbrush

- By clicking on the tool icon: in the Toolbox,

- By using the **A** keyboard shortcut.

12.3.8.2 Key modifiers (Defaults)

Shortcut The **a** key, or **]** under GIMP-2.10, will change the active tool to Airbrush Tool.

Ctrl **Ctrl** changes the airbrush to a Color Picker.

Shift **Shift** places the airbrush into straight line mode. Holding **Shift** while clicking Button 1 will generate a straight line. Consecutive clicks will continue drawing straight lines that originate from the end of the last line.

12.3.8.3 Options

Figure 12.32: Airbrush options

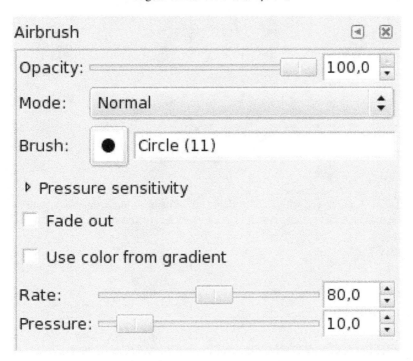

 Overview The available tool options can be accessed by double-clicking the airbrush Tool icon.

Mode; Use color from gradient

Note

See the Painting Tools Overview for a description of tool options that apply to many or all painting tools.

Rate The Rate slider adjusts the speed of color application that the airbrush paints. A higher setting will produce darker brush strokes in a shorter amount of time.

Pressure This slider controls the amount of color that the airbrush paints. A higher setting here will result in darker strokes.

12.3.9   Ink Tool

Figure 12.33: Toolbox Pen

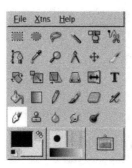

The Ink tool uses a simulation of an ink pen with a controllable nib to paint solid brush strokes with an antialiased edge. The size, shape and angle of the nib can be set to determine how the strokes will be rendered.

12.3.9.1   Activate Tool

You can find the Ink tool in several ways :

- In the image-menu through: Tools/ Paint Tools/Ink .

- By clicking on the tool icon: in Toolbox.

- By using the **K** keyboard shortcut.

12.3.9.2   Key modifiers (Defaults)

Shortcut The **k** key will change the active tool to Ink Tool.

12.3.9.3   Options

Figure 12.34: Ink Tool options

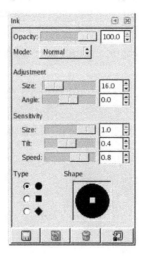

Note

See the Brush Tools Overview for a description of tool options that apply to many or all brush tools.

Overview You can find tool options by double clicking on the ink tool icon. in Toolbox.

Opacity

Note

See the Brush Tools Overview for a description of tool options that apply to many or all brush tools.

Mode **Note**

See the Painting Tools Overview for a description of tool options that apply to many or all painting tools.

Adjustment

Size Controls the apparent width of the pen's nib with values that ranges from 0 (very thin) to 20 (very thick).

Angle This controls the apparent angle of the pen's nib relative to horizontal.

Sensitivity

Size This controls the size of the nib, from minimum to maximum. Note that a size of 0 does not result in a nib of size zero, but rather a nib of minimum size.

Tilt Controls the apparent tilt of the nib relative to horizontal. This control and the Angle control described above are interrelated. Experimentation is the best means of learning how to use them.

Speed This controls the effective size of the nib as a function of drawing speed. That is, as with a physical pen, the faster you draw, the narrower the line.

Type and Shape

Type There are three nib shapes to choose from: circle, diamond, and square.

Shape The geometry of the nib type can be adjusted by holding button 1 of the mouse on the small square at the center of the Shape icon and moving it around.

12.3.10   Clone Tool

Figure 12.35: Clone tool icon in the Toolbox

The Clone tool uses the current brush to copy from an image or pattern. It has many uses: one of the most important is to repair problem areas in digital photos, by "painting over" them with pixel data from other areas. This technique takes a while to learn, but in the hands of a skilled user it is very powerful. Another important use is to draw patterned lines or curves: see Patterns for examples.

If you want to clone from an image, instead of a pattern, you must tell GIMP which image you want to copy from. You do this by holding down the Ctrl key and clicking in the desired source image. Until you have set the source in this way, you will not be able to paint with the Clone tool: the tool cursor tells you this by showing a 'forbidden' symbol.

If you clone from a pattern, the pattern is *tiled*; that is, when the point you are copying from moves past one of the edges, it jumps to the opposite edge and continues, as though the pattern were repeated side-by-side, indefinitely. When you clone from an image this does not happen: if you go beyond the edges of the source, the Clone tool stops producing any changes.

You can clone from any drawable (that is, any layer, layer mask, or channel) to any other drawable. You can even clone to or from the selection mask, by switching to QuickMask mode. If this means copying colors that the target does not support (for example, cloning from an RGB layer to an Indexed layer or a layer mask), then the colors will be converted to the closest possible approximations.

12.3.10.1   How to Activate

You can activate the Clone tool in several ways :

• From the image menu through Tools → Paint Tools → Clone.

• By clicking on the tool icon in Toolbox.

• By pressing the **c** keyboard shortcut.

12.3.10.2   Key modifiers

See the Brush Tools Overview for a description of key modifiers that have the same effect on all brush tools.

Ctrl The Ctrl key is used to select the source, if you are cloning from an image: it has no effect if you are cloning from a pattern. You can clone from any layer of any image, by clicking on the image display, with the Ctrl key held down, while the layer is active (as shown in the Layers dialog). If Alignment is set to 'Non-aligned' or 'Aligned' in Tool Options, then the point you click on becomes the origin for cloning: the image data at that point will be used when you first begin painting with the Clone tool. In source-selection mode, the cursor changes to a crosshair-symbol.

12.3.10.3 Tool Options

Figure 12.36: Tool Options for the Clone tool

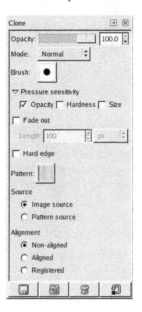

Opacity; Mode; Brush; Pressure Sensitivity, Fade out, Hard Edges

 Note
See the Brush Tools Overview for a description of tool options that apply to many or all brush tools.

Pattern Clicking on the pattern symbol brings up the Patterns dialog, which you can use to select the pattern to paint with. This option is only relevant if you are cloning from a Pattern source.

Source The choice you make here determines whether data will be copied from the pattern shown above, or from one of the images you have open. If you choose 'Image source', you must tell GIMP which layer to use as the source, by Ctrl-clicking on it, before you can paint with the tool.

Alignment The Alignment mode sets how the source position is offset from each brush stroke.

Figure 12.37: Alignement modes

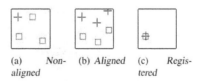

(a)   Non-
aligned   (b) Aligned   (c)   Registered

Above: schematic illustration of the three possible alignment modes. The mouse cursor is shown as a red rectangle, and the source point as a black crosshair.

Non-aligned In this mode, each brushstroke is treated separately. For each stroke, the point where you first click is copied from the source origin; there is no relationship between one brush stroke and another. In non-aligned mode, different brush strokes will usually clash if they intersect each other.

Aligned In this mode, the first click you make when painting sets the offset between the source origin and the cloned result, and all subsequent brushstrokes use the same offset. Thus, you can use as many brushstrokes as you like, and they will all mesh smoothly with one another.

If you want to change the offset, you can do this by switching to non-aligned mode, painting one stroke, then switching back to aligned mode. Subsequent strokes will use the same offset as the first stroke.

Registered This mode copies each pixel in the source to the pixel with the same offset in the target. It is most commonly useful when you want to clone from one layer to another layer within the same image. It is also useful when cloning from a pattern, if you want the left or upper edges of the pattern to line up precisely with the corresponding edges of the target layer.

12.3.10.4 Further Information

Transparency The effects of the Clone tool on transparency are a bit complicated. You cannot clone transparency: if you try to clone from a transparent source, nothing happens to the target. If you clone from a partially transparent source, the effect is weighted by the opacity of the source. So, assuming 100% opacity and a hard brush:

- Cloning translucent black onto white produces gray.
- Cloning translucent black onto black produces black.
- Cloning translucent white onto white produces white.
- Cloning translucent white onto black produces gray.

Cloning can never increase transparency, but, unless 'keep transparency' is turned on for the layer, it can reduce it. Cloning an opaque area onto a translucent area produces an opaque result; cloning a translucent area onto another translucent area causes an increase in opacity.

'Filter' brushes There are a few non-obvious ways to use the Clone tool to obtain powerful effects. One thing you can do is to create 'Filter brushes', that is, create the effect of applying a filter with a brush. To do this, duplicate the layer you want to work on, and apply the filter to the copy. Then activate the Clone tool, setting Source to 'Image source' and Alignment to 'Registered'. Ctrl-click on the filtered layer to set it as the source, and paint on the original layer: you will then in effect be painting the filtered image data onto the original layer.

History brush You can use a similar approach to imitate Photoshop's 'History brush', which allows you to selectively undo or redo changes using a brush. To do this, start by duplicating the image; then, in the original, go back to the desired state in the image's history, either by undoing or by using the Undo History dialog. (This must be done in the original, not the copy, because duplicating an image does not duplicate the Undo history.) Now activate the Clone tool, setting Source to 'Image source' and Alignment to 'Registered'. Ctrl-click on a layer from one image, and paint on the corresponding layer from the other image. Depending on how you do it, this gives you either an 'undo brush' or a 'redo brush'.

12.3.11 Convolve (Blur/Sharpen)

Figure 12.38: Convolve tool icon in the Toolbox

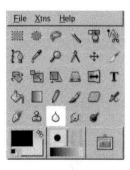

The Convolve tool uses the current brush to locally blur or sharpen your image. Blurring with it can be useful if some element of your image stands out too much, and you would like to soften it. If you want to blur a whole layer, or a large part of one, you will probably be better off using one of the Blur Filters. The direction of a brushstroke has no effect: if you want directional blurring, use the Smudge tool.

In 'Sharpen' mode, the tool works by increasing the contrast where the brush is applied. A little bit of this may be useful, but overapplication will produce noise. Some of the Enhancement Filters, particularly the Unsharp Mask, do a much cleaner job of sharpening areas of a layer.

Tip

You can create a more sophisticated sharpening brush using the Clone tool. To do this, start by duplicating the layer you want to work on, and run a sharpening filter, such as Unsharp Mask, on the copy. Then activate the Clone tool, and in its Tool Options set Source to 'Image source' and Alignment to 'Registered'. Set the Opacity to a modest value, such as 10. Then Ctrl-click on the copy to make it the source image. If you now paint on the original layer, you will mix together, where the brush is applied, the sharpened version with the unsharpened version.

Both blurring and sharpening work incrementally: moving the brush repeatedly over an area will increase the effect with each additional pass. The Rate control allows you to determine how quickly the modifications accumulate. The Opacity control, however, can be used to limit the amount of blurring that can be produced by a single brushstroke, regardless of how many passes are made with it.

12.3.11.1 How to Activate

The Convolve tool can be activated from an image menu as Tools → Paint Tools → Convolve; from the Toolbox by clicking on

the tool icon ; or from the keyboard using the shortcut **V**.

12.3.11.2 Key modifiers

See the Brush Tools Overview for a description of key modifiers that have the same effect on all brush tools.

- **Ctrl**: Holding down the Ctrl key toggles between Blur and Sharpen modes; it reverses the setting shown in the Tool Options.

12.3.11.3 Tool Options

Figure 12.39: Tool Options for the Convolve tool

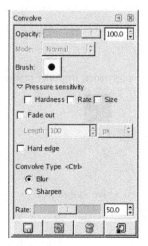

Opacity; Brush; Pressure Sensitivity; Fade Out; Hard Edges

Note
See the Brush Tools Overview for a description of tool options that apply to many or all brush tools.

Convolve Type *Blur* mode causes each pixel affected by the brush to be blended with neighboring pixels, thereby increasing the similarity of pixels inside the brushstroke area. *Sharpen* mode causes each pixel to become more different from its neighbors than it previously was: it increases contrast inside the brushstroke area. Too much Sharpen ends in an ugly flocculation aspect. Whatever setting you choose here, you can reverse it on-the-fly by holding down the Ctrl key.

I *slør-modus* blir kvar piksel som blir rørt av penselen blanda med dei nærliggande pikslane og gir såleis ei overvekt av nokså like pikslar i penselstrøket. Dette gjer at overgangen mellom fargane blir viska ut, men kan også føre til at overgangen blir mørkare.

I *skjerp-modus* blir kvar piksel litt meir ulik nabopikslane for kvart strøk. Kontrasten aukar. Held du på for lenge, kan resultatet bli uventa stygt.

Same kva innstilling du vel, kan du bytte rundt på valet ved hjelp av **Ctrl**-tasten.

Rate The Rate slider sets the strength of the convolve effect.

12.3.12 Dodge or Burn

Figure 12.40: Dodge tool

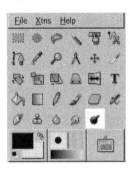

The Dodge or Burn tool uses the current brush to lighten or darken the colors in your image. The mode will determine which type of pixels are affected.

12.3.12.1 Activate Tool

• The Dodge or Burn Tool can be called in the following order, from the image-menu: Tools/ Paint Tools /DodgeBurn.

• The Tool can also be called by clicking the tool icon:

12.3.12.2 Key modifiers (Defaults)

Shortcut The key combination Ctrl-D will change the active tool to Dodge or Burn tool.

Ctrl Toggle between dodge or burn types. The type will remain switched until **Ctrl** is released.

Shift **Shift** places the Dodge or Burn tool into straight line mode. Holding Shift while clicking Button1 will Dodge or Burn in a straight line. Consecutive clicks will continue Dodge or Burn in straight lines that originate from the end of the last line.

12.3.12.3 Options

Figure 12.41: 'Dodge/Burn' tool options

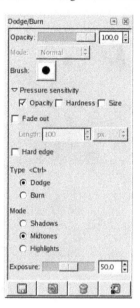

Overview The available tool options for the Dodge or Burn Tool can be accessed by double clicking the Dodge or Burn Tool icon.

Opacity; Brush; Pressure sensibility; Fade out; Hard edges

Note

See the Brush Tools Overview for a description of tool options that apply to many or all brush tools.

Type The dodge effect lightens colors.

The burn effect darkens colors.

Mode There are three modes:

- Shadows restricts the effect to darkest pixels.
- Midtones restricts the effect to pixels of average tone.
- Highlights restricts the effect to lightest pixels.

Exposure Exposure defines how much the tool effect will be strong, as a more or less exposed photograph. Default slider is 50 but can vary from 0 to 100.

12.3.13 Smudge Tool

Figure 12.42: Smudge tool

The Smudge tool uses the current brush to smudge colors on the active layer or a selection. It takes color in passing and uses it to mix it to the next colors it meets, on a distance you can set.

12.3.13.1 Activate Tool

You can find the Smudge tool in various ways :

- Through Tools → Paint Tools → Smudge. in the image menu.

- By clicking on the tool icon: in Toolbox.

- or by pressing the **S** key on keyboard.

12.3.13.2 Key modifiers (Defaults)

Shift The **Shift** key places the smudge tool into straight line mode. Holding Shift while clicking Button1 will smudge in a straight line. Consecutive clicks will continue smudging in straight lines that originate from the end of the last line.

12.3.13.3 Options

Figure 12.43: The Smudge tool in Toolbox

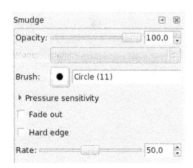

Overview The available tool options for the Smudge Tool can be accessed by double clicking the Smudge Tool icon.

Opacity; Brush; Pressure sensibility; Fade out; Hard edges

 Note

See the Brush Tools Overview for a description of tool options that apply to many or all brush tools.

Rate The rate slider sets the strength of the smudge effect.

12.4 Transform Tools

12.4.1 Common Features

Figure 12.44: An overview of the transform tools

Inside the Transformation tool dialog, you will find seven tools to modify the presentation of the image or the presentation of an element of the image, selection, layer or path. Each transform tool has an Option dialog and an Information dialog to set parameters.

12.4.1.1 Tool Options

Figure 12.45: Common options of transform tools

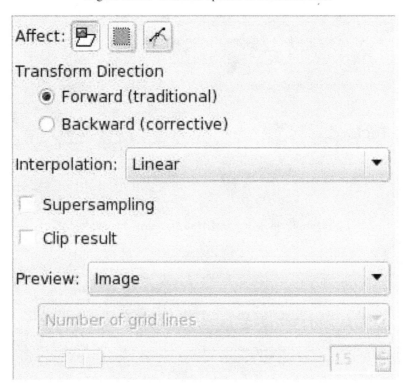

Some options are shared by several transform tools. We will describe them here. More specific options will be described with their tool.

Affect GIMP offers you three buttons which let you select which image element the transform tool will work on.

 Warning
Remind that the Affect option persists when you quit the tool.

When you ativate the first button The tool works on the active layer. If no selection exists in this layer, the whole layer will be transformed.

When you activate the second button the tool works on the selection only (the whole layer if no selection).

When you activate the third button, The tool works on the path only.

Transform Direction The Transform Direction sets which way or direction a layer is transformed. The Traditional mode will transform the image or layer as one might expect. You just use the handles to do the transformation that want to see happen on the image or layer on the grid. When you then execute the transformation the image or layer is transformed to the shape and position you put the grid into.

Corrective Rotation is primarily used to repair digital images that have some geometric errors. To do so, you just have to align the grid to show the same error as the image or layer. If you then execute the transformation the grid and the image or layer wit it are transformed 'backwards' until the grid is again in the rectangualar and straight shape it was when you started.

Interpolation The Interpolation drop-down list lets you choose the quality of the transformation. For more information about the different methods that can be employed, see the glossary entry Interpolation.

Supersampling See glossary for Supersampling

Clip Result After transformation, the image can be bigger. This option will clip the transformated image to the original image size.

Preview GIMP lets you select among four Preview possibilities :

1. Outline : Puts a frame to mark the image outline, with a handle on each corner. Movements will affect this frame only on the Preview, but the result of the transformation will concern either the content or the boundaries of the selection according to the selected Affect mode.

2. Grid : Puts a grid on the image, with four handles. Movements will affect this grid only on the Preview, but the result of the transformation will concern either the content or the boundaries of the selection according to the selected Affect mode.

3. Image : Here, the preview is a copy of the image superimposed on the image, with an outline. Movements affect this copy and the underlying image appears.

4. Grid+Image: Both turn at the same time.

Preview is only for greater convenience. Whatever your choice, result will be the same when you clic on the *Rotate* button in the Rotate Informations dialog.

Options with grid activate a drop-list with two options: Number of Grid Lines will allow control over the total number of displayed grid lines. Use the slider to set the number of grid lines. Grid Line Spacing allows control over the distance between the grid lines. Use the slider to set the distance.

Note
When rotating a path, Preview options are not valid: only Outline is active.

12.4.2 Move Tool

Figure 12.46: The Move tool in Toolbox

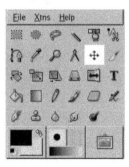

The Move Tool is used to move layers, selections or guides. It works also on texts.

12.4.2.1 Activate Tool

- The Move Tool can be called in the following order, from the image-menu: Tools → Transform Tools → Move

- The Tool can also be called by clicking the tool icon:

- or by the **M** keyboard shortcut.

- The Move tool is automatically activated when you create a guide.

Note
Holding down the **space** bar changes the active tool to Move temporarily. The Move tool remains active as long as the space bar is held down. The original tool is reactivated after releasing the space bar.

12.4.2.2 Default behaviour

By default, this tool works on the active layer and the Select a Layer or a Guide option is checked. Let's suppose that your image has more than one layer, a selection and a guide. The mouse pointer takes the shape of the familiar 4-way arrow when it passes over the image elements originating from the active layer; then, click-and-drag will move the active layer. When the mouse pointer is on an image element originating from a non-active layer or on a guide, it looks like a small hand; then, click-and-drag will move this layer or this guide.

To move a selection frame, without moving its content, Use the Ctrl-Alt key-combination. This has the same action as selecting ' Selection' in Affect.

12.4.2.3 Key modifiers (Defaults)

Alt Holding **Alt** selections can be moved without altering your image. Only the frame is moved, not its content. If Alt doesn't work try Ctrl-Alt.

Using Arrow Keys Instead of using the mouse you can use arrow keys to move the active layer by one pixel. By pressing **Shift** you move by 25 pixels.

12.4.2.4 Options

Figure 12.47: Move Tool options

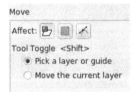

Overview The available tool options for Move can be found by double clicking the Move Tool icon.

Affect

Note

These options are described in Transform tools common options.

Keep in mind that your Affect choice persists after quitting the tool.

Tool toggle If Affect is on layer :

- Pick a layer or guide : On an image with several layers, the mouse pointer turns to a crosshair when it goes over an element belonging to the current layer. Then you can click-and-drag it. But, even if it has a small hand shape, you can also move a non-active layer by click-and-dragging a visible element of it (it becomes the active layer while moving). If a guide exists on your image, il will turn to red when the mouse pointer goes over. Then it is activated and you can move it.
- Move the current layer : Only the current layer will be moved.

If Affect is on Path :

- Pick a path : That's the default option. If your image has several layers, some of them with a path, every path will be represented in Path Dialog, and one of them will be the current path. With this option, the mouse pointer turns to a small hand when it goes over a path. Then you can move this path by click-and-dragging it (it will be the current path while moving).
- Move the current path : Only the current path will be moved. You can change the current path in the Path Dialog.

12.4.3 Crop and Resize Tool

Figure 12.48: Crop tool

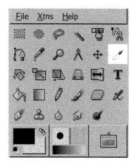

The Crop Tool is used to crop or clip an image or layer. This tool is often used to remove borders, or to eliminate unwanted areas to provide you with a more focused working area. It is also useful if you need a specific image size that does not match the original dimensions of your image.

To use the tool, click inside the image and drag out a rectangular region before releasing the mouse button. When you click, a dialog pops up showing you the dimensions of the crop region, and allowing you to perform various actions. If you want to alter the crop region, you can do so either by clicking and dragging on the corners, or by changing the values in the dialog. When you are ready, you can complete the operation either by clicking inside the crop region, or by pressing the Crop or Resize buttons on the dialog. (See below for what these mean.)

Tip

If you find that the dialog gets in your way more than it helps you, you can prevent it from appearing by holding down the **Shift** key when you first click on the image. Working this way means altering the crop region by dragging the corners, and executing the operation by clicking inside the image.

12.4.3.1   Activate Tool

- The Crop Tool can be called the following way, from the image-menu: Tools → Transform Tools → Crop and Resize.

- The Tool can also be called by clicking the tool icon:

Tip
A different and quicker way to crop selections is using the Image → Crop Image function in the Image menu.

12.4.3.2   Key modifiers (Defaults)

Shortcut The Shift-C shortcut will change the active tool to the Crop Tool.

Ctrl Holding **Ctrl** will switch the Crop Tool mode between Crop and Resize.

Shift Holding **Shift** will toggle the of Fixed Aspect ratio.

Alt Holding **Alt** will toggle the use of Allow Enlarging.

12.4.3.3   Options

Figure 12.49: 'Crop and Resize' tool options

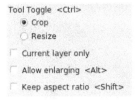

Overview The available tool options for Crop can be accessed by double clicking the Crop tool icon.

Tool Toggle The Tool Toggle for the Crop Tool alternates between Crop mode and Resize mode.

Crop Mode is the standard mode of operation for the Crop Tool. Cropping an image or layer will change a layer by eliminating everything outside the cropping area. The cropping area can be set by either dragging the tool to form a rectangle area or manually setting the origin, width, and height. Cropping areas can also be set based on an existing selection or by using the Auto Shrink button. These options are available within the Crop And Resize Information dialog which is shown when the Crop Tool is clicked on an image or layer.

If you are cropping an image (not just a layer), then Resize Mode changes the shape of the image without altering the size or shape of the layers it contains. This may leave parts of some layers extending beyond the edges of the image, where you cannot see them, but if you move the layers, you will see that the contents still exist. If you are cropping a layer, Resize Mode does the same thing as crop mode.

Note
You can also switch to Resize mode in two other ways: first, by using the Resize button on the dialog instead of the Crop button; second, by holding down the **Ctrl** key while you click inside the crop region to complete the operation.

Current Layer Only This option will make the crop or resize affect only the active layer.

Allow Enlarging This option allows the crop or resize to take place outside the image or layer boundary.

Fixed Aspect Ratio With this option, cropping will respect a fixed ratio between Width and Height.

CROP AND RESIZE INFORMATION

Origin The Origin selectors allow the manual setting of the top left corner of the cropping region. The units may also be chosen.

Width/Height The Width and Height selectors allow the manual setting of both the width and the height of the cropping area. The units may also be chosen.

From Selection This button will resize the cropping area to encompass all active selections contained within the image. If there is no selection, the cropping area is the whole image.

Auto Shrink The Auto Shrink button will attempt to locate a border from which to draw dimensions from. This option only works well with isolated objects contrasting sharply with background.

Crop and Resize buttons These two buttons act according to their function, ignoring the mode setting in tool options.

12.4.4 Rotate Tool

Figure 12.50: The Rotate tool in Toolbox

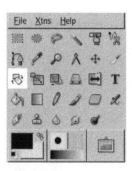

12.4.4.1 Overview

This tool is used to rotate the active layer, a selection or a path. When you click on the image or the selection with this tool, a grid or an outline is superimposed and a *Rotation Information* dialog is opened. There, you can set the rotation axis, marked with a point, and the rotation angle. You can do the same by dragging the mouse pointer on the image or the rotation point.

12.4.4.2 Activate Tool

• You can call the Rotate tool in the following order, from the image-menu: Tools → Transform Tools → Rotate

• The Tool can also be called by clicking the tool icon: in the Toolbox.

• or by using the Shift-R key combination.

12.4.4.3 Key modifiers (Defaults)

Ctrl Holding **Ctrl** will constrain the rotation angles to those only evenly divisible by 15 degrees.

12.4.4.4 Options

Figure 12.51: Rotation tool options

Overview The available tool options for the Rotate Tool can be accessed by double clicking the Rotate Tool icon.

Affect; Interpolation; Supersampling; Clip Result; Preview

 Note

These options are described in Transform tools common options.

Transform Direction The Transform Direction sets which way or direction a layer is rotated. The Traditional mode will rotate the layer as one might expect. If a layer is rotated 10 degrees to the right, then the layer will be rendered as such. This behaviour is contrary to Corrective rotation.

Corrective Rotation is primarily used to repair digital images that are not straight. If the image is 13 degrees askew then you need not try to rotate by that angle. By using Corrective Rotation you can rotate visually and line up the layer with the image. Because the transformation is reversed, or performed backwards, the image will be rotated with sufficient angle to correct the error.

Constraints 15 Degrees will constrain the rotation to angles divisible by 15 degrees.

12.4.4.5 The Rotation Information window

Figure 12.52: The Rotation Information dialog window

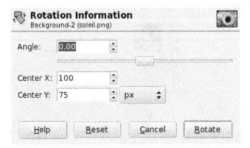

Angle Here you can set the rotation angle, from -180 to +180, i.e 360.

Center X/Y This option allows you to set the position of the rotation center, represented by a large point in the image. A click-and-drag on this point also allows you to move this center. Default unit of measurement is pixel, but you can change it by using the drop-down list.

12.4.5 Scale Tool

Figure 12.53: The Scale tool in Toolbox

12.4.5.1 Overview

The Scale Tool is used to scale layers, selections or paths (the Object).

When you click on image with the tool the Scaling Information dialog box is opened, allowing to change separately Width and Height. At the same time a Preview with a grid or an outline is superimposed on the object and handles appear on corners that you can click and drag to change these dimensions. A small circle appears at center of the Preview allowing to move this preview.

12.4.5.2 Activate Tool

- The Scale Tool can be called in the following order, from the image-menu: Tools → Transform Tools → Scale

- The Tool can also be called by clicking the tool icon:

- or by using the Shift-T key combination.

12.4.5.3 Key modifiers (Defaults)

Ctrl Holding **Ctrl** will constrain the scale height.

Alt Holding **Alt** will constrain the scalewidth. If Alt doesn't work, try **Shift+Alt**.

12.4.5.4 Options

Figure 12.54: Scale tool options

Overview The available tool options for the Scale Tool can be accessed by double clicking the Scale Tool icon in Toolbox.

Affect; Interpolation; Transform Direction; Supersampling; Clip Result; Preview

 Note

These options are described in Transform tools common options.

Constraints None: No Height/Width constraint will be imposed to scaling.

Keep Height will constrain the scale such that the height of the layer will remain constant.

Keep Width will constrain the scale such that the width of the layer will remain constant.

Keep Aspect will constrain the scale such as the Height/Width ratio of the layer will remain constant.

12.4.5.5 The Scaling Information dialog window

Figure 12.55: The Scaling Information dialog window La ventana del diálogo de información de escalado

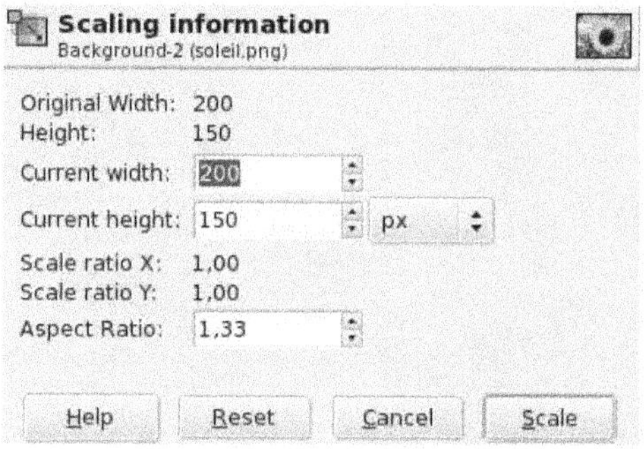

Original Width/Height Here, the width and height of the original object are displayed.

Actual Width/Height Here, you can set width and Height you want to give to the object. The default unit of measurement is pixel. You can change it by using the drop-down list.

Scale ratio X/Y The origine/actual width/height ratios are displayed here.

Aspect ratio The actual width/height ratio is displayed here.

12.4.6 Shear Tool

Figure 12.56: The Shear tool in Toolbox

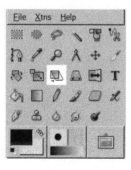

Shear tool is used to shift one part of an image, a layer, a selection or a path to a direction and the other part to the opposite direction. For instance, a horizontal shearing will shift the upper part to the right and the lower part to the left. A rectangle becomes a diamond. This is not a rotation: the image is distorted. To use this tool after selecting, click on the image or the selection: a grid is surperimposed and the Shearing Information dialog is opened. By dragging the mouse pointer on the image you distort the image, horizontally or vertically according to the the direction given to the pointer. When you are satisfied, click on the Shear button in the info dialog to validate.

12.4.6.1 Activate Tool

You can get to Shear tool in several ways :

- In the the image-menu through: Tools → Transform Tools → Shear,

- By clicking the tool icon: in Toolbox,

- or by using the Shift-S key combination.

12.4.6.2 Options

Figure 12.57: Shear tool options

Overview The available tool options for the Shear Tool can be accessed by double clicking the Shear Tool icon.

Affect; Interpolation; Transform Direction; Supersampling; Clip Result; Preview

Note

These options are described in Transform tools common options.

12.4.6.3 Shearing Information

Figure 12.58: Shearing Information window

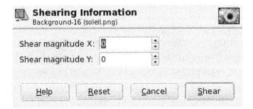

Shear magnitude X Here, you can set the horizontal shearing amplitude. A positive value producess a clock-wise tilt. A negative value gives a counter-clock-wise tilt.

Shear magnitude Y As above, in the vertical direction.

12.4.7 Perspective Tool

Figure 12.59: Perspective tool

The Perspective Tool is used to change the perspective of the active layer content, of the selection boundaries or of a path. When you click on the image, according to the Preview type you have selected, a rectangular frame or a grid pops up around the selection (or around the whole layer if there is no selection), with a handle on each of the four corners. By moving these handles by click-and-drag, you can modify the perspective. At the same time, a 'Transformation informations' pop up, which lets you valid the transformation. At the center of the element, a point lets you move the element by click-and-drag.

12.4.7.1 Activate Tool

You can get to the Perspective tool in several ways :

- In the the image-menu through: Tools/ Transform Tools/Perspective ,

- By clicking the tool icon: ![icon] in Toolbox,

- or by using the Shift-P key combination.

12.4.7.2 Options

Figure 12.60: 'Perspective' tool options

Overview The available tool options for the Perspective Tool can be accessed by double clicking the Perspective Tool icon.

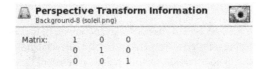

Affect; Interpolation; Transform Direction; Supersampling; Clip Result; Preview

 Note

These options are described in Transform tools common options.

12.4.7.3 The Information window for perspective transformation

Figure 12.61: The dialog window of the 'Perspective' tool

Matrix You can get a small knowledge about matrices in the Section 15.7.2.

12.4.8 Flip Tool

Figure 12.62: Flip tool

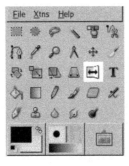

The Flip tool provides the ability to flip layers or selections either horizontally or vertically. When a selection is flipped, a new layer with a Floating Selection is created. You can use this tool to create reflexions.

12.4.8.1 Activate Tool

You can get to the Flip tool in several ways :

• In the the image-menu through: Tools/ Transform Tools/Flip ,

• By clicking the tool icon: in Toolbox,

• or by using the Shift-F key combination.

12.4.8.2 Key modifiers (Defaults)

Shortcut The Shift-F key combination will change the active tool to Flip.

Ctrl **Ctrl** lets you change the modes between horizontal and vertical flipping.

12.4.8.3 Options

Figure 12.63: 'Flip Tool' Options

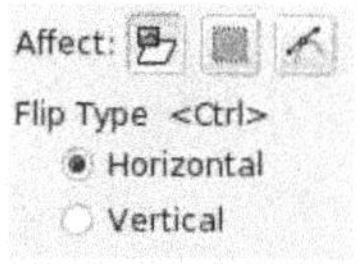

Overview The available tool options for the Flip Tool can be accessed by double clicking the Flip Tool icon.

Affect

 Note

These options are described in Transform tools common options.

Flip Type The Tool Toggle settings control flipping in either a Horizontal or Vertical direction. This toggle can also be switched using a key modifier.

12.5 Color Tools

12.5.1 Color Balance Tool

The color balance tool modifies the color balance of the active selection or layer.

12.5.1.1 Activate Tool

You can get to the Color balance tool in several ways :

- In the the image-menu through: Tools → Color Tools → Color Balance

- By clicking the tool icon:  in Toolbox, provided that you have installed color tools in Toolbox. For this, go to Tools Dialog.

12.5.1.2 Options

Figure 12.64: Color Balance options

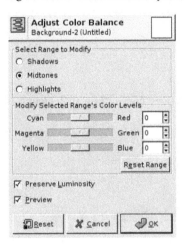

Select range to modify Selecting one of these options will restrict the range of colors which are changed with the sliders or input boxes for Shadows, Midtones and Highlights.

Modify selected range's color levels Sliders and input boxes allow to select colors weights.

Initialize range This button sets color levels of the selected range back to zero.

Preserve Luminosity This option ensures that brightness of the active layer or selection is maintained.

Preview The Preview checkbox toggles dynamic image updating. If this option is on, any change made to the RGB levels are immediately seen on the active selection or layer.

12.5.2 Hue-Saturation Tool

The Hue-Saturation tool is used to adjust hue, saturation and lightness levels on a range of color weights for the selected area or active layer.

12.5.2.1 Activate Tool

You can get to the Hue-Saturationtool in two ways :

- In the the image-menu through: Tools → Color Tools → Hue- Saturation

- By clicking the tool icon: in Toolbox, provided that you have installed color tools in Toolbox. For this, go to Tools Dialog.

12.5.2.2 Options

Figure 12.65: Hue-Saturation tool options

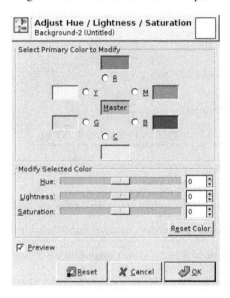

Select Primary Color to use You can choose, between six, the color to be modified. They are arranged according to the color circle. If you click on the Master button, all colors will be concerned with changes.

Modify selected color Changes appear in the small preview close to the selected color button.

- Hue : The slider and the input box allow you to select a hue in the color circle (-180, 180).
- Lightness : The slider and the input box allow you to select a value (luminosity): -100, 100.
- Saturation : The slider and the input box allow you to select a saturation: -100, 100.

The Initialize Color button deletes changes to hue, lightness and saturation of the selected color.

Preview The Preview button makes all changes dynamically so that they can be viewed straight away.

12.5.3 Colorize Tool

The Colorize tool renders the active layer or selection into a greyscale image seen through a colored glass. You can use it to give a ' Sepia' effect to your image. See *Color model* for Hue, Saturation, Luminosity.

12.5.3.1 Activate Tool

You can get to the Hue-Saturation tool in two ways :

- In the the image-menu through: Tools → Color Tools → Colori ze

- By clicking the tool icon: in Toolbox, provided that you have installed color tools in Toolbox. For this, go to Tools Dialog.

12.5.3.2   Options

Figure 12.66: Colorize options

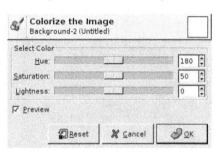

Hue The slider and the input box allows you to select a hue in the HSV color circle (0 - 360).

Saturation The slider and the input box allows you to select a saturation: 0 through 100.

Value The slider and the input box allows you to select a value (luminosity): 0 through 100.

Preview The Preview button makes all changes dynamically so that they can be viewed immediately.

12.5.4   Brightness-Contrast tool

The Brightness-Contrast tool adjusts the brightness and contrast levels for the active layer or selection. This tool is easy to use, but relatively unsophisticated. The Levels and Curve tools allow you to make the same types of adjustments, but also give you the ability to treat bright colors differently from darker colors. Generally speaking, the BC tool is great for doing a "quick and dirty" adjustment in a few seconds, but if the image is important and you want it to look as good as possible, you will use one of the other tools.

In GIMP 2.4, a new way of operating this tool has been added: by clicking the mouse inside the image, and dragging while keeping the left mouse button down. Moving the mouse vertically changes the brightness; moving horizontally changes the contrast. When you are satisfied with the result, you can either press the "OK" button on the dialog, or hit the Return key on your keyboard.

12.5.4.1   Activate Tool

You can get to the Hue-Saturation tool in two ways :

- In the the image-menu through: Tools → Color Tools → Brightness-Contrast

- By clicking the tool icon: in Toolbox, provided that you have installed color tools in Toolbox. For this, go to Tools Dialog.

12.5.4.2 Options

Figure 12.67: Brightness-Contrast options dialog

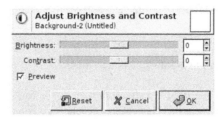

Brightness This slider sets a negative (to darken) or positive (to brighten) value for the brightness, decreasing or increasing bright tones.

Contrast This slider sets a negative (to decrease) or positive (to increase) value for the contrast.

Preview The Preview checkbox makes all changes to the brightness and contrast dynamically so that the new level settings can be viewed immediately.

12.5.5 Threshold Tool

The Threshold tool transforms the current layer or the selection into a black and white image, where white pixels represent the pixels of the image whose Value is in the threshold range, and black pixels represent pixels with Value out of the threshold range.

You can use it to enhance a black and white image (a scanned text for example) or to create selection masks.

Note
As this tool creates a black and white image, the anti-aliasing of the original image disappears. If this poses a problem, rather use the Levels tool.

12.5.5.1 Activate Tool

The Threshold Tool can be called in the following order, from the image-menu: Tools → Color Tools → Threshold,

or by clicking on the icon in Toolbox if this tool has been installed in it. You can do that through the Tool dialog.

12.5.5.2 Options

Figure 12.68: Threshold tool options

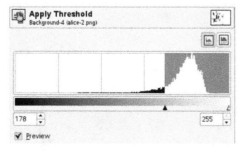

Threshold range The Threshold tool provides a visual graph, a histogram, of the intensity value of the active layer or selection. You can set the threshold range either using the input boxes or clicking button 1 and dragging on the graph. It allows you to select a part of the image with some intensity from a background with another intensity. Pixels inside the range will be white, and the others will be black. Adjust the range to get the selection you want in white on black background.

Preview The Preview toggle allows dynamic updating of the active layer or selection while changes are made to the intensity level.

12.5.5.3 Using Threshold and Quick Mask to create a selection mask

That's not always the case, but an element you want to extract from an image can stand out well against the background. In this case, you can use the Threshold tool to select this element as a whole. Grokking the GIMP described a method based on a channel mask, but now, using the Quick mask is easier.

1. First start decomposing you image into its RGB and HSV components by using the Decompose filter. A new grey-scaled image is created and the components are displayed as layers in the Layer Dialog. These layers come with a thumbnail but it is too small for an easy study. You can, of course, increase the size of this preview with the dialog menu (the small triangular button), but playing with the 'eyes ' is more simple to display the wanted layer in the decompose image. Select the layer that isolates the element the best.

Figure 12.69: The original image, the decompose image and its Layer Dialog

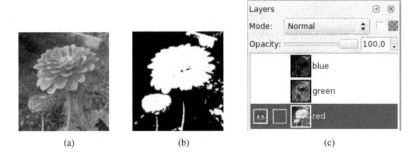

(a)   (b)   (c)

2. Call the Threshold tool from the decompose image. By moving the black cursor, fit threshold to isolate the best the element you want to extract. This will probably not be perfect: we will enhance the result with the selection mask we are going to create.

 Warning
Make sure you have selected the right layer when you call the Threshold tool: when it is opened, you can't change to another layer.

Figure 12.70: The selected layer after threshold fit

We got the best outline for our flower. There are several red objects which we must remove.

3. Make sure the image displaying the selected layer is active and copy it to the clipboard with Ctrl-C.

4. Now, make the original image active. Click on the Quick Mask button at the bottom-left corner of the image window: the image gets covered with a red (default) translucent mask. This red color does not suit well to our image with much red: go to the Channel Dialog, activate the 'Quick mask' channel and change this color with the Edit Channel Attributs. Come back to the original image. Press Ctrl-V to paste the previously copied layer.

Figure 12.71: The mask

5. Voilà. Your selection mask is ready: you can improve the selection as usually. When the selection is ready, disable the Quick mask by clicking again on its button: you will see the marching ants around the selection.

Figure 12.72: The result

(a)   (b)

We used the Zoom to work at a pixel level, the Lasso to remove large unwanted areas, the pencil (to get hard limits), black paint to remove selected areas, white paint to add selected areas, especially for stem.

12.5.6 Levels tool

The Level tool provides features similar to the Histogram tool but can also change the intensity range of the active layer or selection.

12.5.6.1 Activate Tool

You can get to the Level Tool in the image-menu through: Tools → Color Tools → Levels

You can also activate it by clicking on the icon in Toolbox if this tool has been installed there. For this, go to Tools Dialog.

12.5.6.2 Options

Figure 12.73: Level tool options

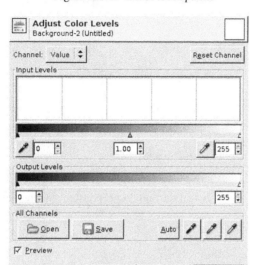

Modify Levels for Channel You can select the specific channel which will be modified by the tool: Value makes changes to the luminosity of all pixels in the image. Color channels allow to change saturation. Alpha channel works on transparency. Initialize channel cancels changes to the selected channel.

Input Levels The main area is a graphic representation of image dark, mid and light tones content (the Histogram). They are on abscissa from level 0 (black) to level 255 (white). Pixel number for a level is on ordinate axis. The curve surface represents all the pixels of the image for the selected channel. A well balanced image is an image with levels (tones) distributed all over the whole range. An image with a blue predominant color, for example, will produce a histogram shifted to the left in Green and Red channels, signified by green and red lacking on highlights.

Level ranges can be modified in three ways:

- Three triangles as sliders: one black for dark tones, one grey for midtones (often called Gamma value), one white for light tones.
- Two eyedroppers: use the left one to pick the darkest color and the right one to pick the lightest color on the image. You can use View/Info Window (Cursor tab) to find these colors.
- Three input boxes to enter values directly.

Output Levels Output Levels allows manual selection of a constrained output level range. There are also arrow-heads located here that can be used to interactively change the Output Levels.

All Channels Open: This button allows you to select a file holding level settings.

Save: Allows you to save any levels you have set to a file that can be loaded later.

Auto: Performs an automatic setting of the levels.

Three eyedroppers: These three controls determine three points on the grayscale. Any level below the "Black Point" is black; any point above the "White Point" is white. The "Gray Point", which must be between the other two, determines the middle level of Gray. All shades of gray are calculated from these three levels.

Preview The Preview button makes all changes to the levels dynamically so that the new level settings can be viewed straight away.

Histogram Scale These two options have the same action as the logarithmic and Linear buttons in the Levels dialog.

Sample Average This slider sets the 'radius' of the color-picking area. This area appears as a more or less enlarged square when you maintain the click on a pixel.

12.5.7 Curves Tool

12.5.7.1 Activate Tool

You can get to this tools in two ways :

- In the image menu through Tools → Color Tools → Curves.

- By clicking on the tool icon  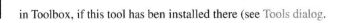 in Toolbox, if this tool has ben installed there (see Tools dialog.

12.5.7.2 Adjust Color Curves

Figure 12.74: Curves tool

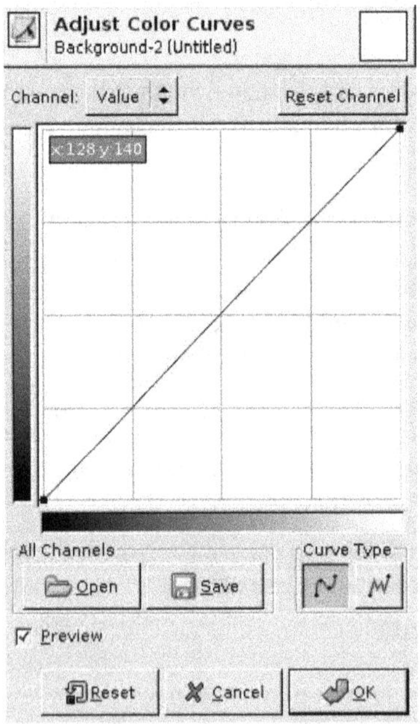

Channel There are five options: Value for luminosity and contrast; Red, Green, and Blue for saturation; and Alpha (if your image has an Alpha channel).

Reset Channel This button deletes all changes made to the selected channel and returns to default values.

Linear and Logarithmic buttons These buttons allow to choose the Linear or Logarithmic type of the histogram. You can also use the same options in Tool Options dialog.

Main Editing Area Input and Output Value Domains : The horizontal bar (x-axis) represents input values (they are value levels from 0 to 255). The vertical bar (y-axis) is only a scale for output colors of the selected channel.

The control curve is drawn on a grid and goes from bottom left corner to top right corner. Pointer x/y position is permanently displayed in top left part of the grid. If you click on the curve, a Control point is created. You can move it to bend the curve. If you click outside of the curve, a control point is also created, and the curve includes it automatically.

So, each point of the curve represents an 'x' level, corresponding to an 'y' color. If, for example, you move a curve segment to the right, i.e to highlights, you can see that these highlights are corresponding to darker output tones and that image pixels corresponding to this curve segment will go darker. With color channels, moving right will decrease saturation and can reach the complementary color.

To delete all control points (apart from both ends), click on the Initialize Channel button. To delete only one point, move it onto another point or to grid border.

All Channels Open: This button allows you to select a file holding curve settings.

Save: Allows you to save any curves you have set to a file that can be loaded later.

Curve Type Smooth: This mode constrains the curve type to a smooth line with tension. It provides a more realistic render than the following.

Free: You can draw your curve free-hand with the mouse. With curve segments scattered all over the grid, result will be surprising, but poorly repeatable.

Preview The Preview button makes all changes to the levels dynamically so that the new level settings can be viewed immediately.

TOOL OPTIONS DIALOG

Histogram Scale These two options have the same action as the logarithmic and Linear buttons in the Curves dialog.

Sample Average This slider sets the 'radius' of the color-picking area. This area appears as a more or less enlarged square when you maintain the click on a pixel.

12.5.8 Posterize Tool

This tool is designed to intelligently weigh the pixel colors of the selection or active layer and reduce the number of colors while maintaining a semblance of the original image characteristics.

12.5.8.1 Activate Tool

The Posterize Dialog can be called in the following order, from the image-menu: Tools → Color Tools → Posterize

or by double-cliking on the icon in ToolBox, if Color Tools have been added to it.

12.5.8.2 Options

Figure 12.75: Posterize tool options

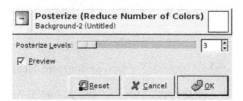

Posterize Levels This slider and the input boxes with arrow-heads allow you to set the number of levels (2-256) in each RGB channel that the tool will use to describe the active layer. The total number of colors is the combination of these levels. A level to 3 will give $2^3 = 8$ colors.

Preview The Preview checkbox makes all changes dynamically so that they can be viewed straight away.

12.6 Other

12.6.1 Path Tool

Figure 12.76: Path tool

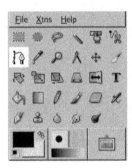

The Path tool allows to create complex selections called Bezier Curves, a bit like Lasso but with all the adaptability of vectorial curves. You can edit your curve, you can paint with your curve, or even save, import, and export the curve. You can also use paths to create geometrical figures. Paths have their own dialog box: Dialog.

12.6.1.1 Activate Tool

You can get to Path tool in several ways :

• In the image menu through Tools → Paths,

• By clicking the tool icon: in Toolbox,

• or by using the **B** keyboard shortcut.

12.6.1.2 Key modifiers (Defaults)

Note
Help messages pop up at the bottom of the image window to help you about all these keys.

Shift This key has several functions depending on context. See Options for more details.

Ctrl/Alt Three modes are available to work with the Path tool: Design,Edit and Move. **Ctrl** key toggles between Design and Edit. **Alt** (or Ctrl+Alt) key toggles between Design and Move.

12.6.1.3 Options

Figure 12.77: 'Path' tool options

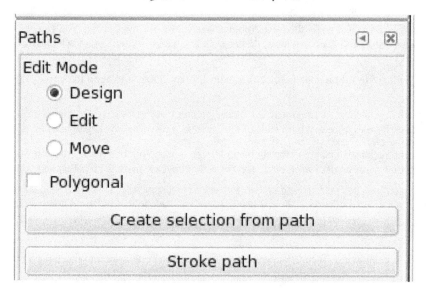

Overview The available tool options for the Path Tool can be accessed by double clicking the Path Tool icon.
As with other tools, you can delete your changes by **Ctrl-Z**.

Design Mode By default, this tool is in Design mode. You draw the path by clicking successively. You can move control points by clicking on them and dragging them. Between control points are segments.

Numbers are steps to draw a two segments straight path.

Curved segments are easily built by dragging a segment or a new node. Blue arrows indicate curve. Two little handles appear that you can drag to bend the curve.

 Tip
To quickly close the curve, press **Ctrl** key and click on the initial control point. In previous versions, clicking inside a closed path converted it into Selection. Now, you can use the *Create selection from path* button or the *Path to Selection* button in the Path Dialog.

 Tip
When you have two handles, they work symmetrically by default. Release the pressure on the mouse button to move handles individually. The **Shift** key will force the handles to be symmetrical again.

Several functions are available with this mode:

Add a new node : if the active node (a small empty circle after clicking on a node) is at the end of the path, the mouse pointer is a '+' sign and a new node is created, linked to the previous one by a segment. If the active node is on the path, the pointer is a square and you can create a new component to the path. This new component is independant from the other, but belongs to the path as you can see on the Path dialog. Pressing **Shift** forces the creation of a new component.

Move one or several nodes: On a node, the mouse pointer becomes a 4-arrows cross. You can click and drag it. You can select several nodes by **Shift** and click and move them by click and drag. Pressing Ctrl-Alt allows to move all the path, as a selection.

Modify handles: you have to Edit a node before. A handle appears. Drag it to bend the curve. Pressing **Shift** toggles to symmetric handles.

Modify segment: When you click on a segment, the mouse pointer turns to a 4-arrows cross. Drag it to bend the segment. As soon as you move, handles appear at both ends of the segment. Pressing **Shift** key toggles to symmetric handles.

Edit Mode Edit performs functions which are not available in Design mode. With this mode, you can work only on the existing path. Outside, the pointer is a small crossed circle (on the whole image if there is no path!) and you can do nothing.

Add a segment between two nodes: Click on a node at one end of the path to activate it. Pointer is like a union symbol. Click on an other node to link both nodes. This is useful when you have to link unclosed components.

Remove a segment from a path: While pressing Shift-Ctrl key combination, point to a segment. Pointer turns to -. Click to delete the segment.

Add a node to a path: point to a segment. Pointer turns to +. Click where you want to place the new control point.

Remove a node: While pressing Shift-Ctrl key combination, point to a node. Pointer turns to -. Click to delete the node.

Add a handle to a node: Point to a node. Pointer turns to small hand. Drag the node: handle appears. Pressing **Shift** toggles to symmetric handles.

Remove a handle from a node: While pressing Shift-Ctrl key combination, point to a handle. Pointer doesn't turn to the expected - and remains a hand. Click to delete the handle.

 Caution

No warning before removing a node, a segment or a handle.

Move Mode Move mode allows to move one or all components of a path. Simply click on the path and drag it.

If you have several components, only the selected one is moved. If you click and drag outside the path, all components are moved. Pressing **Shift** key toggles to move all components also.

Polygonal With this option, segments are linear only. Handles are not available and segments are not bent when moving them.

Create selection from path This button allows creation of a selection that is based on the path in its present state. This selection is marked with the usual "marching ants". Note that the path is still present: current tool is still path tool and you can modify this path without modifying the selection that has become independent. If you change tool, the path becomes invisible, but it persists in Path Dialog and you can re-activate it.

If the path is not closed, GIMP will close it with a straight line.

As the help pop-up tells, pressing **Shift** when clicking on the button will add the new selection to an eventually preexistent. Pressing the **Ctrl** will subtract the selection from the preexistent and the Shift-Ctrl key combination will intersect the two selections.

Stroke path In previous versions, you could access to this command only by the Edit sub-menu in the Image Menu. Now you can access to it also via this button. See Stroke Path and Stroke Path.

See the Pathconcept.

12.6.2 Color Picker Tool

Figure 12.78: Eye dropper

The Color Picker Tool is used to select a color on the active layer. By clicking a point on a layer, you can change the active color to that which is located under the pointer. The Sample Merge option lets you grab the color as it is in the image, resulting of the combination of all layers.

Figure 12.79: Color Picker Info Window

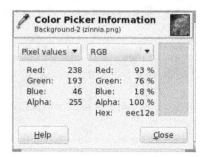

12.6.2.1 Activate Tool

You can get to this tool in several ways :

- In the image menu through Tools → Color Picker.,

- by clicking the tool icon in Toolbox,

- by pressing the **O** keyboard shortcut,

- by pressing the **Ctrl** key while using a paint tool. The Color-picker dialog is not opened during this operation and the tool remains unchanged after releasing the key.

12.6.2.2 Key modifiers (Defaults)

Shortcut The **o** key will activate the Color Picker tool.

Ctrl

Shift By pressing the **Shift** key, the Add to palette option is temporarily checked.

12.6.2.3 Options

Figure 12.80: Color Picker Options

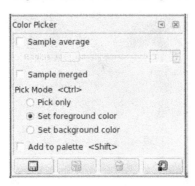

Overview The available tool options for the Color Picker can be accessed by double clicking the Color Picker tool icon.

Sample Merged The Sample Merged checkbox when enabled will take color information as a composite from all the visible layers. Further information regarding Sample Merge is available in the glossary entry, Sample Merge.

Sample Average The Radius slider adjusts the size of the square area that is used to determine an average color for the final selection. When you click the layer, the cursor will indicate the size of the square or radius visually.

Pick Mode

> **Pick Only** The color of the selected pixel will be shown in an Information Dialog, but not otherwise used.
>
> **Set Foreground Color** The Foreground color, as shown in the Toolbox Color Area, will be set to the color of the pixel you click on.
>
> **Set Background Color** The Background color, as shown in the Toolbox Color Area, will be set to the color of the pixel you click on.
>
> **Add to Palette** When this option box is checked, the picked color is sent to the active color palette. see Palette Editor

12.6.3 Magnify Tool

Figure 12.81: Zoom tool

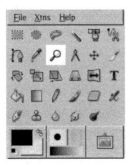

The Magnify Tool is used to change the zoom level of your working image. If you only click on the image, the zoom is applied to the whole image. But you can also click-and-drag the mouse pointer to create a zoom rectangle. Then, the action of this rectangle is better understood if the 'Allow window resizing' option is unchecked: you can see that the content of this rectangle will be enlarged or reduced so that its biggest dimension fit the corresponding dimension of the image window (if the biggest dimension of the rectangle is width, then it will fit the width of the image window).

12.6.3.1 Activate Tool

- You can get to the Magnify Tool from the image-menu through : Tools → Magnify,

- or by clicking the tool icon: 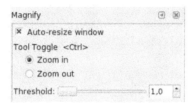 in Toolbox.

12.6.3.2 Key modifiers (Defaults)

Ctrl Holding **Ctrl** when clicking on a point of your image will change the zoom direction from zooming in to zooming out.

12.6.3.3 Options

Figure 12.82: Zoom tool options

Overview The available tool options for Magnify can be accessed by double clicking the Magnify tool icon.

Allow Window Resizing This option will allow the window containing your image to be resized if the zoom level dictates it.

Tool Toggle The two available tool toggles are used for changing the zoom direction between zooming in and zooming out.

Threshold This option sets the size that a dragged zoom rectangle must be before zooming to that rectangle actually occurs. A higher Threshold will require a larger rectangle before zooming to that rectangle happens. With a low level, a very small rectangle will push you towards a more than 2000% zoom level.

12.6.3.4 Zoom menu

Using the Magnify tool is not the only way to zoom an image. The Zoom menu provides access to several functions for changing the image magnification level. For example, you can easily choose an exact magnification level from this menu.

12.6.4 Measure Tool

Figure 12.83: Measure tool

The Measure Tool is used to gain knowledge about pixel distances in your working image. By clicking and holding the mouse button, you can determine the angle and number of pixels between the point of click and where the mouse pointer is located. The information is displayed on the status bar or can also be displayed in the Info Window.

When you pass the mouse pointer over the end point it turns to a move pointer. Then if you click you can resume the measure.

12.6.4.1 Status Bar

Informations are displayed in the status bar, at the bottom of the Image window. The status bar shows a pair of numbers. The first number is the *distance between the origine point and the mouse pointer*. Mostly the measure unit is shown as *Pixel*. The second number is the *angle* in every quadrant, from 0 to 90.

12.6.4.2 Activate Tool

- You can get to the Measure Tool from the image-menu through: Tools → Measure,

- or by clicking the tool icon: 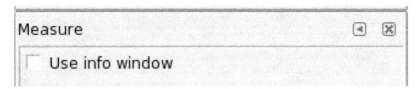 in Toolbox.

12.6.4.3 Key modifiers

Defaults Holding down the **Ctrl** key puts the tool into constrained straight line mode. The orientation of the line is constrained to the nearest multiple of 15 degrees.

Holding down the **Shift** allows to start a new measure from the pointed point without deleting the previous measure. Angle is measured from the previous line. Mouse pointer is accompanied by a '+' sign. So, you can *measure an angle*

Ctrl key pressed and click on an end point creates a horizontal guide.

Alt key and click on an end point should create a vertical guide...

Ctrl-Alt key combination and click on an end point creates a vertical and a horizontal guides.

Ctrl-Alt key combination and click on a measure line allows to move the measure.

12.6.4.4 Options

Figure 12.84: 'Measure tool options'

Measure

☐ Use info window

Overview There is only one available option for the Measure Tool.

Use Info Window This option will display an Info Window dialog that details the measure tool results. The results are more complete on the status bar.

12.6.4.5 Measuring surfaces

You can't measure surfaces directly, but you can use the Histogram that gives you the number of pixels in a selection.

12.6.5 Texttool

Figure 12.85: The Text tool in Toolbox

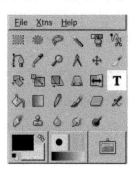

The Text tool places text into an image. When you click on an image with this tool the *Text Editor dialog* is opened where you can type your text, and a text layer is added in the Layer Dialog. In the *Text Option dialog*, you can change the font, color and size of your text, and justify it, interactively.

12.6.5.1 Activate Tool

You can get to these tool in several ways:

- In the image menu through Tools → Text,

- by clicking the tool icon in Toolbox,

- or by using the **T** keyboard shortcut.

12.6.5.2 Options

Figure 12.86: Text tool options

Overview The available tool options for the Texttool can be accessed by double clicking the texttool icon:

Font There are two ways of selecting fonts in the GIMP. The first is from the image Dialogs/Fonts menu. The second is with the Font selector in this tool. Both methods select from the installed X fonts. When you select a font it is interactively applied to your text.

Note
You can get special characters in the same way as you get them in other text editors: **AltGr** + key in Linux, **Alt** + number key pad in Windows.

Size This control sets the size of the font in any of several selectable units.

Hinting Uses the indices of adjustment to modify the characters in order to produce clear letters in small font sizes.

Force Auto-Hinter Auto Hinter tries to automatically compute information for better representation of the character font.

Antialiasing Antialiasing will render the text with much smoother edges and curves. This is achieved by slight blurring and merging of the edges. This option can radically improve the visual appearance of the rendered typeface. Caution should be exercised when using antialiasing on images that are not in RGB color space.

Color Color of the text that will be drawn next. Defaults to black. Selectable from the color picker dialog box that opens when the current color sample is clicked.

Tip
You can also click-and-drag the color from the Toolbox color area onto the text.

Justify Causes the text to be justified according to any of four rules selectable from the associated icons.

Indent Controls the indent spacing from the left margin.

Line Spacing Controls the spacing between successive lines of text. This setting is interactive: it appears at the same time in image text. The number is not the space between lines itself, but how many pixels must be added to or substracted from this space (the value can be negative).

Create Path from Text This tool creates a selection path from the selected text. Every letter is surrounded with a path component. So you can modify the shape of letters by moving path control points.

12.6.5.3 Text Editor

Figure 12.87: The Text Editor options

Overview This dialog window is opened when you click on the image with the Text Tool. It's a still basic text editor that nevertheless allows you to write on several lines. Word wrap is not possible - the text layer lengthens gradually - and you have to press the **Enter** key to move to the next line.

The text you type appears interactively in the image. If the option 'Show Layer Boundary' is checked in the View menu, this text will be surrounded with black and yellow dashes that mark the layer boundary. Now look, it's not a selection: if you want to move the text, you must click on the text itself and not inside this frame only.

You can correct the text you are writing and you can change the text font with the Font Editor.

You can move the text by using the Move Tool, but you loose the Editor then. You can re-edit this text as you will see now.

As soon as you start writing, a Text layer is created in the Layer Dialog. On an image with such a layer (the image you are working on, or a .xcf image), you can resume text editing by activating this text layer then clicking on it (double click).

To add another text to your image click on a non-text layer: a new Text Editor will appear and a new text layer will be created. To pass from a text to another one activate the corresponding text layer and click on it to activate the editor.

Load Text from File Text can be loaded from a text file by clicking the folder icon in the text editor.

Clear all Text Clicking this icon clears the editor and the associated text on the image.

From Left to Right This option causes text to be entered from left to right, as is the case with most Western languages and may Eastern languages.

From Right to Left This option allows text to be entered from right to left, as is the case with some Eastern languages, such as Arabic (illustrated in the icon).

Note

See also Text and fonts.

12.7 Color and Indicator Area

12.7.1 Color Area

Figure 12.88: Color area in the Toolbox Palette

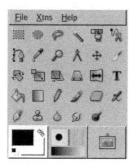

Color area This area shows GIMP's basic palette, consisting of two colors, the Foreground and Background, used for painting, filling, and many other operations. Clicking on either of the color displays brings up a Color Editor dialog, which permits you to change it.

Default colors Clicking on this small symbol resets the Foreground and Background colors to black and white, respectively.

Swap FG/BG colors Clicking on the small curved line with two arrowheads causes the Foreground and Background colors to be swapped. Pressing the **x** key has the same effect.

12.7.2 Indicator Area

Figure 12.89: Active tool indicator area

This part of the Toolbox shows the currently selected brush, pattern, and gradient. Clicking on any of them brings up a dialog that allows you to change it.

12.7.3 Active image Area

Figure 12.90: Current image in the toolbox

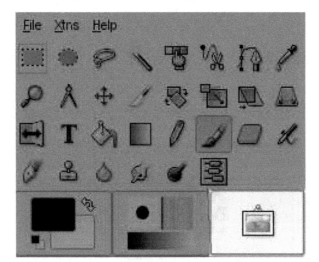

A thumbnail of the active image can be displayed in this area if the 'Display Active Image' option is checked in Preferences/-Toolbox.

Chapter 13

Dialogs

13.1   Dialog Introduction

Dialogs are the most common means of setting options and controls in the GIMP. The most important dialogs are explained in this section.

13.2   Image Structure Related Dialogs

13.2.1   Layers Dialog

Figure 13.1: Layer Dialog

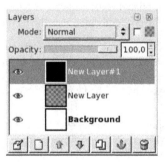

The Layers dialog is the main interface to edit, modify and manage your layers. You can think of layers as a stack of slides or clothes on your body. Using layers, you can construct an image of several conceptual parts, each of which can be manipulated without affecting any other part of the image. Layers are stacked on top of each other. The bottom layer is the background of the image, and the components in the foreground of the image come above it.

Figure 13.2: An image with layers

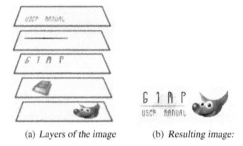

(a) *Layers of the image*   (b) *Resulting image:*

13.2.1.1   Activate Dialog

The Layer dialog can be called in many ways :

- from the toolbox-menu: File → Dialog → Layers

- from the image-menu: Dialog → Layers

- from an other dialog-menu: Add Tab → Layers

- from the (default) shortcut: Ctrl-L

13.2.1.2   Using the Layerdialog

Overview Every layer appears in the dialog in the form of a thumbnail. When an image has multiple layers as components, they appear as a list. The upper layer in the list is the first one visible, and the lowest layer the last visible, the background. Above the list one can find characteristics related individually to each layer. Under the list one can find management buttons for the layer list. A right-click in a layer thumbnail opens the Layer menu.

Layer attributes Every layer is shown in the list along with its attributes. The main attribute is the name of the layer. You can edit this by a double-click on the name or the thumbnail of the layer. In front of the thumbnail is an icon showing an eye

. By clicking on the eye, you toggle whether the layer is visible or not. (Shift-clicking on the eye causes all *other*

to be temporarily hidden.) Another icon, showing a chain   , allows you to group layers for operations on more than one layer at a time (for example with the Move tool).

> **Tip**
>
> In the case of an animation layer (GIF or MNG), the name of the layer can be used to specify certain parameters : Layer_name (delay in ms) (combination mode), for example Frame-1 (100 ms) (replace). The delay sets the time during which the layer is visible in the animation. The combination mode sets whether you combine the layer with the previous layer or replace it: the two modes are (combine) or (replace).

Layers characteristics Above the layer list, it is possible to specify some properties for the active layer. The active layer is the one highlighted in blue. The properties are : "Layer mode", "Keep transparency", and "Opacity".

Layer modes

Figure 13.3: Layer modes

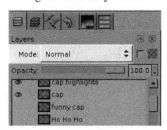

The layer mode determines how the layer interacts with the other layers. From the combo box you can access all the modes provided by GIMP. The layer modes are fully detailed in Section 8.2.

Keep transparency

Figure 13.4: Keep transparency

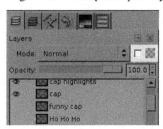

If you check this option the transparent areas of the layer will be kept, even if you have checked the Fill transparent areas option for the Bucket fill tool.

Opacity

Figure 13.5: Opacity

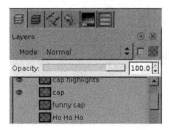

By moving the slider you give more or less opacity to the layer. With a 0 opacity value, the layer is transparent and completely invisible. Don't confuse this with a Layer Mask, which sets the transparency pixel by pixel.

Layer management Under the layer list a set of buttons allows you to perform some basic operations on the layer list.

Edit layer attributs Here you can change the name of the active layer in the list.

New layer Here you can create a new layer. A dialog is opened where you can enter the Layer name, perhaps change the default Height and Width, and choose the Layer fill type that will be the new layer's background.

Raise layer Here you can move the layer up a level in the list. Press the **Shift** key to move the layer to the top of the list.

Lower layer Here you can move the layer down a level in the list. Press the **Shift** key to move the layer to the bottom of the list.

Tip
To move a layer at the bottom of the list, it may first be necessary to add a transparency channel (also called Alpha channel) to the Background layer. To do this, right click on the Background layer and select Add Alpha channel from the menu.

 Duplicate layer Here you can create a copy of the active layer. Name of new layer is suffixed with a number.

 Anchor layer When the active layer is a temporary layer (also called floating selection) shown by this icon , this button anchors it to the previous active layer.

Delete layer Here you can delete the active layer.

More layer functions Other functions about *layer size* are available in the Layer Drop down menu you get by right clicking on the Layer Dialog. You can find them also in the Layer sub-menu of the image menu.

You will find *merging layers functions* in the Image submenu of the Image menu.

Clicking-and-dragging layers Click and hold on layer thumbnail: it enlarges and you can move it by dragging the mouse.

- So you can put this layer down *somewhere else in the layer list*.
- You can also *put the layer down into Toolbox* : a new image is created that contains this layer only.
- Finally, you can *put the layer down into another image* : this layer will be added to the layer list, above existing layers.

13.2.1.3 Layer masks

Figure 13.6: Dialog add mask

Overview A transparency mask can be added to each layer, it's called Layer mask. A layer mask has the same size and same pixel number as the layer to which it is attached. Every pixel of the mask can then be coupled with a pixel at the same location in the layer. The mask is a set of pixels in gray-tone on a value scale from 0 to 255. The pixels with a value 0 are black and give a full transparency to the coupled pixel in the layer. The pixels with a value 255 are white and give a full opacity to the coupled pixel in the layer.

To create a layer mask start with a right click on the layer to call the context menu and select Add layer mask in the menu. If the menu item is grayed first select Add Alpha channel in the same menu. A dialog appears where you can initialize the content of the mask:

- White (full opacity): the mask is white in the Layer Dialog. So, all pixels of the layer are visible in the image window since painting the mask with white makes layer pixels fully visible. You will paint with black to make layer pixels transparent.

- Black (full transparency): the mask is black in the Layer Dialog. So, the layer is fully transparent since painting the mask with black makes layer pixels transparent. Painting with white will remove the mask and make layer pixels visible.

- Layer's alpha channel: the mask is initialized according to the content of layer Alpha channel. If the layer still contains transparency it's copied in the mask.

- Transfer layer's alpha channel: Does the same thing as the previous option, except that it also resets the layer's alpha channel to full opacity.

- Selection : the mask is initialized according to pixel values found in the selection.

- Grayscale copy of layer: the mask is initialized according to pixel values of the layer.

When the mask is created it appears as a thumbnail right to the layer thumbnail. By clicking alternatively on the layer and mask thumbnail you can enable one or other. The active item is highlighted by a white border (which is not well visible around a white mask). Pressing**Alt** (or Ctrl-Alt and click on the layer mask thumbnail is equivalent to the Show Layer Mask command : the layer mask border turns to green. If you press **Ctrl** the border is red and the result is equivalent to the Disable Layer Mask command. To return to normal view redo last operation. These options are for greater convenience in your work.

Layer Mask example

Figure 13.7: A layer with layer mask

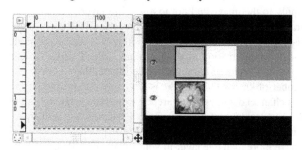

This image has a background layer with a flower and another blue one, fully opaque. A white layer mask has been added to the blue layer. In the image window, the blue layer remains visible because a white mask makes layer pixels visible.

Figure 13.8: Painting the layer mask

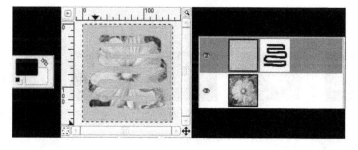

The layer mask is active. You paint with black color, which makes the layer transparent : the underlying layer becomes visible.

13.2.2 Channels Dialog

Figure 13.9: The Channel dialog

The Channels dialog is the main interface to edit, modify and manage your channels. Channels have a double usage. This is why the dialog is divided into two parts: the first part for color channels and the second part for selection masks.

Color channels: Color channels apply to the image and not to a specific layer. Basically, three primary colors are necessary to render all the wide range of natural colors. As other digital software, the GIMP uses Red, Green, and Blue as primary colors. The first and primary channels display the Red, Green, and Blue values of each pixel in your image. In front of each channel is a thumbnail displaying a grayscale representation of each channel, where white is 100% and black is 0% of the primary color. Alternatively, if your image is not a colored but a Grayscale image, there is only one primary channel called Gray. For an Indexed image with a fixed number of known colors there is also only one primary channel called Indexed. Then there is a optional channel called Alpha. This channel displays transparency values of each pixel in your image. In front of this channel is a thumbnail displaying a grayscale representation of the transparency where white is opaque and visible, and black is transparent and invisible. If you create your image without transparency then the Alpha channel is not present, but you can add it from the Layers dialog menu. Also, if you have more than one layer in your image, GIMP automatically creates an Alpha channel.

Note
GIMP doesn't support CMYK or YUV color models.

Figure 13.10: Representation of an image with channels

    (a) *Red channel*   (b) *Green channel*   (c) *Blue channel*   (d) *Alpha channel*   (e) *All Chanels*

The right image is decomposed in three color channels (red, green, and blue) and the Alpha channel for transparency. On the right image the transparency is displayed as a gray checkerboard. In the color channel white is always white because all the colors are present and black is black. The red hat is visible in the red channel but quite invisible in the other channels. This is the same for plain green and blue which are visible only in their own channels and invisible in others.

13.2.2.1 Calling the Dialog

The Channel dialog can be activated in many ways :

- from the toolbox-menu: File → Dialogs → Channels

- from the image-menu: Dialogs → Channels

- from another dialog-menu: Add Tab → Channels

13.2.2.2 Using the Channel dialog

13.2.2.2.1 Overview

The top channels are the color channels and the optional Alpha channel. They are always organized in the same order and they cannot be erased. Selection masks are described below and displayed as a list in the dialog. Every channel appears in the list in form of a thumbnail. A right-click in a channel thumbnail opens the channel menu.

13.2.2.2.2 Channel attributes

Every channel is shown in the list with its own attributes. The main attribute is the name of the channel itself. You can edit selection masks by double-clicking on their name. A double_click on the thumbnail opens a full dialog where you can also set

the visual aspect of the channel in the image window. In front of the thumbnail there is an eye icon: by clicking on it you define whether the channel is visible or not. As a result of this visibility, the view of the image changes in the image window and a white image becomes yellow if you remove the view of the blue because yellow is the complementary color for blue. If you remove the view of the Alpha channel, everything becomes transparent and nothing else than a grey checkerboard is visible.

The aspect of this virtual background can be changed in the Preferences. The chain icon enables grouping of channels for operations on multiple channels.

> **Caution**
>
> Activated channels appear highlighted (generally) in blue in the dialog. If you click on a channel in the list you toggle activation of the corresponding channel. Disabling a color channel red, blue, or green has severe consequencies. For instance if you disable the blue channel, all pixels from now on added to the image will not have blue component, and so a white pixel will have the yellow complementary color.

13.2.2.2.3 Managing channels

Under the channel list is a set of buttons allowing you to perform some basic operations on channel list.

 Edit channel attributes, only available for selection masks. Here you can change the Channel name. The other two parameters affect channel is visibility in the image window; they control Opacity and color used for the mask in the image window. A click on the color button displays the Gimp color selector and then you can change the mask color.

New channel You can create here a new channel. The displayed dialog lets you set Opacity and mask color used in the image to represent the selection. (If you use the New Channel button in Channel Menu, you can create this new channel with the options previously used by pressing the **Shift** key when clicking). This new channel is a channel mask (a selection mask) applied over the image. See Selection Mask

Raise channel, only available for selection masks : you can here put the channel up a level in the list. Press **Shift** key to move channel to top of the list.

Lower channel You can here put the channel down a level in the list. Press the **Shift** key to move the channel to bottom of the list.

Duplicate channel You can create here a copy of the active channel. Name of new channel is suffixed with a number.

Tip
You can also duplicate a color channel or the Alpha channel. It's an easy way to keep a copy of them and to use them later as a selection in an image.

Channel to selection here you can transform the channel to become a selection. By default the selection derived from a channel replaces any previous active selection. It's possible to change this by clicking on control keys.

- **Shift**: the selection derived from a channel is added to the previous active selection. The final selection is merged from both.

- **Ctrl**: the final selection is the substraction of selection derived from a channel from the previously active one.

- Shift-Ctrl: the final selection is the intersection of selection derived from a channel with the previously active one. Only common parts are kept.

 Delete channel only available for selection masks: you can here delete the active channel.

13.2.2.2.4 Channels Menu

Figure 13.11: Channels Menu

Overview You can get the channel context menu by right clicking on a channel thumbnail. This menu gives the same operations on channels as those available from dialog buttons. The only difference concerns transformation to selection operations, each of them having its own entry in the menu.

- Edit channel attributes, New channel, Raise channel, Lower channel, Duplicate channel, Delete channel: see Managing channels.

- Channel to selection: Selection derived from channel replaces any previous active selection.

- Add to selection: Selection derived from channel is added to previous active selection. Final selection is merging of both.

- Substract from selection: Final selection is substraction of selection derived from a channel from previous active selection.

- Intersect with selection: Final selection is intersection of selection derived from a channel with the previous active selection. Only common parts are kept.

13.2.2.3 Selection masks

Figure 13.12: A selection composed out of channels.

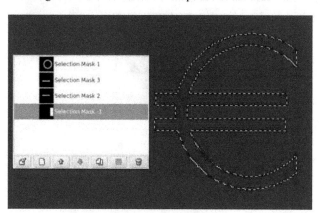

Channels can be used to save and restore your selections. Clicking on the Quick mask button on the Image window automatically creates a new channel called Qmask and saves the displayed active selection to a thumbnail in front of the channel.There are many selection tools in the GIMP like rectangular selection tool or fuzzy selection for continuous selections. Selection Masks are a graphical way to build selections into a gray level channel where white pixels are selected and black pixels are not selected. Therefore gray pixels are partially selected. You can think of them as feathering the selection, a smooth transition between selected and not selected. This is important to avoid the ugly pixelization effect when you fill the selection or when you erase its content after isolating a subject from background.

Creating Selection Masks There are several ways to initialize a selection mask. From the image window menu Select → Save to Channel if there is an active selection. From the image window the bottom-left button creates a Quick Mask; the content will be initialized with the active selection. From the channel dialog, when you click on the New channel button or from the context menu. When created, this Selection mask appears in the Channel dialog, named 'Selection mask copy' with a queuing number. You can change this by using the context menu that you get by right-clicking on the channel.

13.2.2.3.1 Using Selectionmasks

Once the channel is initialized, selected (highlighted in blue), visible (eye-icon in the dialog), and displayed as you want (color and opacity attributes), you can start to work with all the paint tools. The colors used are important. If you paint with some color other than white, grey, or black, the color Value (luminosity) will be used to define a gray (medium, light, or dark). When your mask is painted, you can transform it to a selection by clicking on the Channel to selection button or from the context menu.

You can work in selection masks not only with the paint tool but also with other tools. For instance, you can use the selection tools to fill areas uniformly with gradients or patterns. By adding many selection masks in your list you can easily compose very complex selections. One can say that a selection mask is to a selection as a layer is to an image.

 Caution

As long as a selection mask is activated you are working in the mask and not in the image. To work in the image you have to deactivate all selection masks. Don't forget also to stop displaying masks in the image by removing the eye icon. Check also that all RGB and Alpha channels are activated and displayed in the image.

13.2.2.4 Quick Mask

Figure 13.13: Dialog Quick Mask

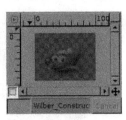

A Quick Mask is a Selection Mask intended to be used temporarily to paint a selection. Temporarily means that, unlike a normal selection mask, it will not be saved in the list after its transformation to selection. The selection tools sometimes show their limits when they have to be used for doing complex drawing selection, as progressive. In this case, using the QuickMask is a good idea which can give very good results.

13.2.2.4.1 Activate dialog

- The QuickMask can be activated in the following order, from the image-menu: Select/Toggle QuickMask.

- The QuickMask can also be activated by clicking the left-bottom button showed in red on the screenshot.

- It can also be activated by using **Shift+Q** shortcut.

13.2.2.4.2 Creating a Quick Mask

To initialize a Quick Mask, click the bottom-left button in the image window. If a selection was active in your image, then its content appears unchanged while the border is covered by a tranlucent red color. If no selection was active then all the image is covered by a tranlucent red color. At every moment you can hide the maskby clicking on the eye icon ![eye] in front of the QMask. From the channel dialog you can double click on the name or the thumbnail to edit the QMask attributes. Then you can changethe Opacity and its filling color. Once a quick mask is initialized click on it to be sure it is selected and blue highlighted in the list, and start to paint on it with any GIMP paint tool. The mask is coded in gray tones, so you must use white or gray to decrease the area limited by the mask and black to increase it. The area painted in light or dark gray will be transition areas for the selection like feathering. When your mask is ready, click again on the bottom-left button in the image window and the quick maskwill be removed from the channel list and converted to aselection. Quick mask's purpose is to paint a selection and its transitions with the paint tools without worrying about managing selection masks. It's a good way to isolate asubject in a picture because once the selection is made you only have to remove its content (or inverse if the subject is in the selection).

13.2.2.4.3 Using Quick Mask's

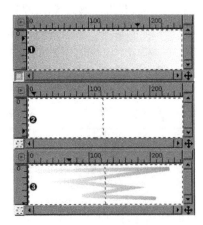

Description

 Screenshot of the image window with activated QuickMask. The QuickMask is filled with a gradient from black (left) to white (right).

Ⓞ The QuickMask is now disabled and a selection is initialised from the QuickMask, which was filled by a gradient before. You see the selection borders in the middle of the image.

Ⓞ A stroke is now added during the enabled selection. The key is, that the black color will have no opacity of the resulting stroke (right) and white color will have a full opacity of the stroke (left).

After the QuickMask Button is pressed, the command generates a temporary 8-bit (0-255) channel, on which the progressive selection work is stored. If a selection is already present the mask is initialized with the content of the selection. Once QuickMask has been activated, the image is covered by a red semi-transparent veil. This one representes the non-selected pixels. Any paint tool can be used to create the selection on the QuickMask. They should use only greyscale color, conforming the channel properties, white enabling to define the future selected place. The selection will be displayed as soon as the QuickMask will be toggled but its temporary channel will not be available anymore.

> **ⓘ Tip**
>
> To save in a channel the selection done with the Quickmask select in the image menu Select/Save to Channel

13.2.2.4.4 Usage

1. Open an image or begin a new document.

2. Activate the Quickmask using the left-bottom button in the image window. If a selection is present the mask is initialized with the content of the selection.

3. Choose a drawing tool and use it with greyscale colors on the QuickMask.

4. Deactivate the Quickmask using the left-bottom button in the image window.

13.2.3 Path Dialog

Figure 13.14: The Paths dialog

The Paths dialog is used to manage paths, allowing you to create or delete them, save them, convert them to and from selections, etc.

The Paths dialog is a dockable dialog; see the section on Dialogs and Docking for help on manipulating it. It can be activated in several ways:

13.2.3.1 Dialog call

- From the Toolbox menu: File → Dialogs → Paths.

- From the Toolbox menu: File → Dialogs → Create New Dock → Layers, Channels, and Paths. This gives you a dock containing three dialogs, with the Paths dialog one of them.

- From an image menu: Dialogs → Paths.

- From the Tab menu in any dockable dialog: Add Tab → Paths.

13.2.3.2 Using the Paths dialog

Each path belongs to one image: paths are components of images just like layers. The Paths dialog shows you a list of all paths belonging to the currently active image: switching images causes the dialog to show a different list of paths. If the Paths dialog is embedded in a "Layers, Channels, and Paths" dock, you can see the name of the active image in the Image Menu at the top of the dock. (Otherwise, you can add an Image Menu to the dock by choosing "Show Image Menu" from the Tab menu.)

If you are familiar with the Layers dialog, you have a head start, because the Paths dialog is in several ways similar. It shows a list of all paths that exist in the image, with four items for each path:

Path visibility An 'open eye' icon if the path is visible, or a blank space if it is not. "Visible" means that a trace of the path is drawn on the image display. The path is not actually shown in the image pixel data unless it has been stroked or otherwise rendered. Clicking in the eye-symbol-space toggles the visibility of the path.

chain paths A 'chain' symbol is shown to the right of the eye-symbol-space if the path is transform-locked, or a blank space if it is not. 'Transform-locked' means that it forms part of a set of elements (layers, channels, etc) that are all affected in the same way by transformations (scaling, rotation, etc) applied to any one of them. Clicking in the chain-symbol-space toggles the transform-lock status of the path.

Preview image A small preview-icon showing a sketch of the path. If you click on the icon and drag it into an image, this will create a copy of the path in that image.

 path name The name of the path, which must be unique within the image. Double-clicking on the name will allow you to edit it. If the name you create already exists, a number will be appended (e.g., "#1") to make it unique.

If the list is non-empty, at any given moment one of the members is the image's *active path*, which will be the subject of any operations you perform using the dialog menu or the buttons at the bottom: the active path is shown highlighted in the list. Clicking on any of the entries will make it the active path.

Right-clicking on any entry in the list brings up the Paths Menu. You can also access the Paths Menu from the dialog Tab menu.

Du kan klikke på alle innslaga i lista, eller gå inn på fanemenyen for å få tilgang til banemenyen.

13.2.3.3 Buttons

The buttons at the bottom of the Paths dialog all correspond to entries in the Paths menu (accessed by right-clicking on a path list entry), but some of them have extra options obtainable by holding down modifier keys while you press the button.

New Path See New Path. Holding down the **Shift** key brings up a dialog that allows you to assign a name to the new (empty) path.

Raise Path See Raise Path.

Lower Path See Lower Path.

Duplicate Path See Duplicate Path.

Path to Selection Converts the path into a selection; see Path to Selection for a full explanation. You can use modifier keys to set the way the new selection interacts with the existing selection:

Modifiers: None, *Action:* Replace existing selection
Modifiers: **Shift** , *Action:* Add to selection
Modifiers: **Ctrl** , *Action:* Subtract from selection
Modifiers: Shift-Ctrl , *Action:* Intersect with selection.

Selection to Path Holding down the **Shift** key brings up the Advanced Options dialog, which probably is only useful to GIMP developers.

Stroke Path See Stroke Path.

Delete Path Delete Path deletes the current selected path.

13.2.3.4 Paths Menu

Figure 13.15: The Paths dialog menu

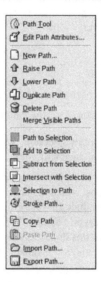

The Paths menu can be brought up by right-clicking on a path entry in the list in the Paths dialog, or by choosing the top entry ("Paths Menu") from the Paths dialog Tab menu. This menu gives you access to most of the operations that affect paths.

Path Tool Path Tool is an alternative way to activate the Path tool, used for creating and manipulating paths. It can also be activated from the Toolbox, or by using the keyboard shortcut **B** (for *Bezier*).

Edit Path Attributes Edit Path Attributes brings up a small dialog that allows you to change the name of the path. You can also do this by double-clicking on the name in the list in the Paths dialog.

New Path New Pathcreates a new path, adds it to the list in the Paths dialog, and makes it the active path for the image. It brings up a dialog that allows you to give a name to the path. The new path is created with no anchor points, so you will need to use the Path tool to give it some before you can use it for anything.

Raise Path Raise Path moves the path one slot higher in the list in the Paths dialog. The position of a path in the list has no functional significance, so this is simply a convenience to help you keep things organized.

Lower Path Lower Pathmoves the path one slot lower in the list in the Paths dialog. The position of a path in the list has no functional significance, so this is simply a convenience to help you keep things organized.

Duplicate Path "Duplicate Path" creates a copy of the active path, assigns it a unique name, adds it to the list in the Paths dialog, and makes it the active path for the image. The copy will be visible only if the original path was visible.

Note
Note that copying a visible path will make the path "disappear" from the image display: this happens because paths are drawn in XOR mode, which has the curious property that drawing an item twice "undraws" it. The paths are still there even though you don't see anything: if you move one of them, you will be able to see both.

Delete Path Delete Path deletes the current selected path.

Merge Visible Paths Merge Visible Paths takes all the paths in the image that are visible (that is, all that show "open eye" symbols in the Paths dialog), and turns them into components of a single path. This may be convenient if you want to stroke them all in the same way, etc.

Path to Selection; Add to Selection; Subtract from Selection; Intersect with Selection These commands all convert the active path into a selection, and then combine it with the existing selection in the specified ways. ("Path to Selection" discards the existing selection and replaces it with one formed from the path.) If necessary, any unclosed components of the path are closed by connecting the last anchor point to the first anchor point with a straight line. The "marching ants" for the resulting selection should closely follow the path, but don't expect the correspondence to be perfect.

Selection to Path This operation can be accessed in several ways:

- From an image menubar, as Select → To Path
- From the Paths dialog menu, as Selection to Path.
- From the Selection to Path button at the bottom of the Paths dialog.
- From the Selection to Path button in the Tool Options for the Path tool.

Selection to Path creates a new path from the image's selection. In most cases the resulting path will closely follow the "marching ants" of the selection, but the correspondence will not usually be perfect.

Converting a two-dimensional selection mask into a one-dimensional path involves some rather tricky algorithms: you can alter the way it is done using the Advanced Options, which are accessed by holding down the **Shift** key while pressing the Selection to Path button at the bottom of the Paths dialog. This brings up the Advanced Options dialog, which allows you to set 20 different options and variables, all with cryptic names. The Advanced Options are really intended for developers only, and help with them goes beyond the scope of this documentation. Generally speaking, Selection to Path will do what you expect it to, and you don't need to worry about how it is done (unless you want to).

Stroke Path This operation can be accesssed in several ways:

- From an image menubar, as Edit → Stroke Path
- From the Paths dialog menu, as Stroke Path.
- From the Stroke Path button at the bottom of the Paths dialog.
- From the Stroke Path button in the Tool Options for the Path tool.

'Stroke Path' renders the active path on the active layer of the image, permitting a wide variety of line styles and stroking options. See the section on Stroking for more information.

Copy Path Copy Path copies the active path to the Paths Clipboard, enabling you to paste it into a different image.

Tip
You can also copy and paste a path by dragging its icon from the Paths dialog into the target image's display.

Paste Path Paste Path creates a new path from the contents of the Path Clipboard, adds it to the list in the Paths dialog, and makes it the active path for the image. If no path has previously been copied into the clipboard, the menu entry will be insensitive.

Import Path "Import Path" creates a new path from an SVG file: it pops up a file chooser dialog that allows you to navigate to the file. See the Paths section for information on SVG files and how they relate to GIMP paths.

Export Path Export Path allows you to save a path to a file: it pops up a file save dialog that allows you to specify the file name and location. You can later add this path to any GIMP image using the Import Path command. The format used for saving paths is SVG: this means that vector-graphics programs such as Sodipodi or Inkscape will also be able to import the paths you save. See the Paths section for more information on SVG files and how they relate to GIMP paths.

13.2.4 Colormap Dialog

Figure 13.16: The Colormap dialog

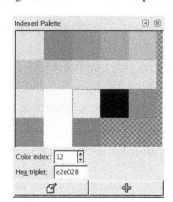

The Colormap (Indexed Palette is a better name) dialog allows you to edit the colormap of an indexed image. (If the mode of the active image is RGB or Grayscale instead of Indexed, the dialog is empty and unusable.) This is a dockable dialog; see the section on Dialogs and Docking for help on manipulating it. It can be activated in two ways:

13.2.4.1 Dialog call

- From the Toolbox menu: File → Dialogs → Colormap

- From the image menu: Dialogs → Colormap

13.2.4.2 Colormaps and Indexed Images

In an Indexed image, colors are assigned to pixels by an indirect method, using a lookup table called a *colormap*. In GIMP, the maximum number of entries in a colormap is 256. For a maximum-sized colormap, each index from 0 to 255 is assigned an arbitrary RGB color. There are no rules restricting the colors that can be assigned to an index or the order they appear in: any index can be assigned any color.

In an Indexed image, instead of being assigned a color directly (as happens in RGB and Grayscale images), each pixel is assigned an index. To determine the color that should be shown for that pixel, GIMP looks up the index in the image's colormap. Each indexed image has its own private colormap.

It is important to realize that the colors in the colormap are the *only colors available* for an indexed image (that is, unless you add new colors to the colormap). This has a major effect on many GIMP operations: for example, in a pattern fill, GIMP will usually not be able to find exactly the right colors in the colormap, so it will approximate them by using the nearest color available. [1] If the colormap is too limited or poorly chosen, this can easily produce very poor image quality.

The Colormap dialog allows you to alter the colormap for an image, either by creating new entries, or by changing the colors for the existing entries. If you change the color associated with a given index, you will see the changes reflected throughout the image, as a color shift for all pixels that are assigned that index. The entries are numbered with 0 in the upper left corner, 1 to its right, etc.

13.2.4.3 Using the Colormap dialog

Here are the operations you can perform using this dialog:

Click on a color entry This sets GIMP's foreground color to the color you click on, as shown in the Toolbox color area. As a result, this color will be used for the next painting operation you do.

Ctrl-click on a color entry This sets GIMP's background color to the color you Ctrl-click on, as shown in the Toolbox color area.

Double-click on a color entry This sets GIMP's foreground color to the color you click on, and also brings up a Color Editor that allows you to change that colormap entry to a new color.

Color index You can select a different colormap entry by typing its index here, or clicking the spinbutton to the right.

Hex triplet This area shows a hex-code representation (such as is used in HTML) for the color assigned to the currently selected colormap entry. You can edit the color here, instead of using a Color Editor, if you want to. See HexTriplet

Edit color This button (in the lower left corner of the dialog) brings up a Color Editor that allows you to change the color for the currently selected colormap entry. The effect is similar to double-clicking on the entry, except that it does not set GIMP's foreground color.

Add color This button (in the lower right corner of the dialog) allows you to add new colors to the colormap. If you click on the button, the current foreground color, as shown in the Toolbox, will be tacked on to the end of the colormap. If instead you hold down **Ctrl** and click, the background color from the Toolbox will be added. (If the colormap contains 256 entries, it is full, and trying to add more will have no effect.)

Tip
If you make a mistake, you can undo it by focusing the pointer in the image whose colormap you have changed, and then pressing **Ctrl-Z** or choosing Edit → Undo in the image menu.

Note
This dialog provides the most commonly used methods for altering the colormap for an indexed image. The color tools, such as Brightness/Contrast, Hue/Saturation, etc, do not operate on indexed images. There are a few plug-ins that do so, including the "Normalize", "Color Enhance", and "Stretch Contrast" operations, and it is possible to create others as well.

---

[1] This is sometimes referred to as Quantization, which is described in the Glossary.

13.2.5 Histogram dialog

Figure 13.17: The Histogram dialog

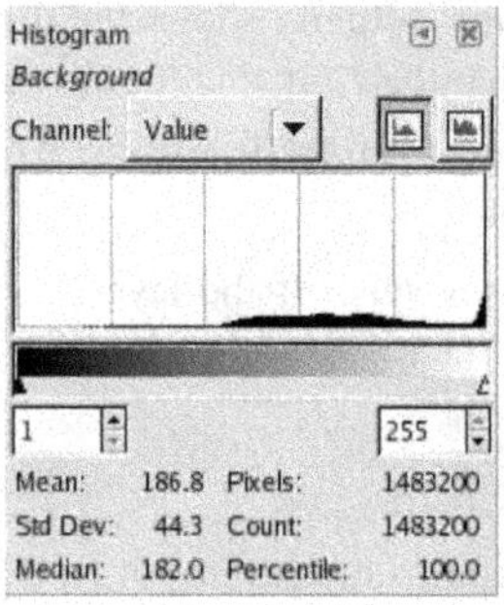

The Histogram dialog shows you information about the statistical distribution of color values in the image that is currently active. This information is often useful when you are trying to *color balance* an image. However, the Histogram dialog is purely informational: nothing you do with it will cause any change to the image. If you want to perform a histogram-based color correction, use the Levels tool.

13.2.5.1 Dialog call

This is a dockable dialog; see the section on Dialogs and Docking for help on manipulating it. It can be activated in two ways:

- From the Toolbox menu: File → Dialogs → Histogram
- From the image menu: Dialogs → Histogram

13.2.5.2 About Histograms

In GIMP, each layer of an image can be decomposed into one or more color channels: for an RGB image, into R, G, and B channels; for a grayscale image, into a single Value channel. Layers that support transparency have an additional channel, the alpha channel. Each channel supports a range of intensity levels from 0 to 255 (integer valued). Thus, a black pixel is encoded by 0 on all color channels; a white pixel by 255 on all color channels. A transparent pixel is encoded by 0 on the alpha channel; an opaque pixel by 255.

For RGB images, it is convenient to define a Value "pseudochannel". This is not a real color channel: it does not reflect any information stored directly in the image. Instead, the Value at a pixel is given by the equation $V = \max(R, G, B)$. Essentially, the Value is what you would get at that pixel if you converted the image to Grayscale mode.

For more information on channels, please consult the Section 5.1.

13.2.5.3 Using the Histogram dialog

Channel

Figure 13.18: Channel options for an RGB layer with alpha channel.

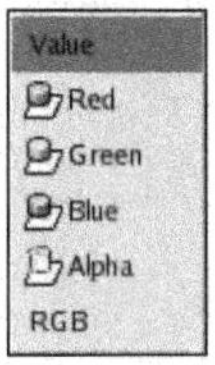

This allows you to select which channel to use. The possibilities depend on the layer type of the active layer. Here are the entries you might see, and what they mean:

Value For RGB and Grayscale images, this shows the distribution of brightness values across the layer. For a grayscale image, these are read directly from the image data. For an RGB image, they are taken from the Value pseudochannel.

For an indexed image, the "Value" channel actually shows the distribution of frequencies for each colormap index: thus, it is a "pseudocolor" histogram rather than a true color histogram.

Red, Green, Blue These only appear for layers from RGB images. They show the distribution of intensity levels for the Red, Green, or Blue channels respectively.

Alpha This shows the distribution of opacity levels. If the layer is completely opaque or completely transparent, the histogram will consist of a single bar on the left or right edge.

RGB

Figure 13.19: Combined histograms of R, G, and B channels.

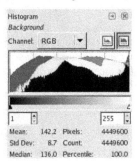

This entry, only available for RGB layers, shows the R, G, and B histograms superimposed, so that you can see all of the color distribution information in a single view.

Linear/Logarithmic buttons

Figure 13.20: The histogram shown at the top, changed to logarithmic mode.

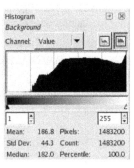

These buttons determine whether the histogram will be displayed using a linear or logarithmic Y axis. For images taken from photographs, the linear mode is most commonly useful. For images that contain substantial areas of constant color, though, a linear histogram will often be dominated by a single bar, and a logarthmic histogram will often be more useful.

Range Setting

Figure 13.21: Dialog aspect after range fixing.

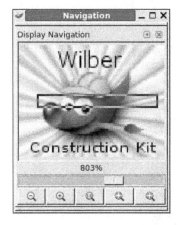

You can restrict the analysis, for the statistics shown at the bottom of the dialog, to a limited range of values if you wish. You can set the range in one of three ways:

- Click and drag the pointer across the histogram display area, from the lowest level to the highest level of the range you want.
- Click and drag the black or white triangles on the slider below the histogram.
- Use the spinbutton entries below the slider (left entry: bottom of range; right entry: top of range).

Statistics At the bottom of the dialog are shown some basic statistics describing the distribution of channel values, restricted to the selected range. These are the mean, standard deviation, and median of the selected histogram portion; the number of pixels in the image; the number whose values fall within the selected range; and the percentage whose values fall within the selected range.

13.2.6   Navigation Dialog

Figure 13.22: Navigation Dialog

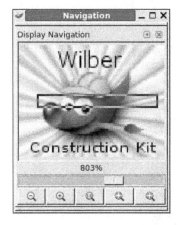

The Navigation dialog is designed to offer easy movement around the active image if the zoom is set higher than what the image window can display. If this is the case, there is an inversely colored rectangle that shows the location of the current view area in respect to the image. This rectangular outline can be dragged to change the viewing region.

13.2.6.1   Activate the dialog

The Navigation window dialog can be called in many ways :

- from the toolbox-menu: File/ Dialogs/ Navigation

- from the image-menu: Dialogs/ Navigation

- from the image-menu: View/ Navigation window, the **Shift+Ctrl+N** will call the Navigation Window.

- from another dialog-menu: Add Tab/ Navigation

You can access more quickly to it (but without the zoom functions) by clicking on the ✛ icon, at the right bottom corner of the image window.

13.2.6.2 Using the Navigation Dialog

The slider It allows easy zoom level control, more precise than with the Zoom command.

The buttons

- *Zoom Out*, *Zoom In* and *Zoom 1:1* are self explanatory.
- *Zoom Fit to Window*: After zooming, this button allows to return to the normal size.
- *Shrink Wrap*: The whole zoomed image will be displayed in an enlarged image window, if possible.

13.2.7 Undo History Dialog

Figure 13.23: The Undo History dialog

This dialog shows you a list of the actions you have most recently performed on an image, with a small sketch that attempts to illustrate the changes produced by each. You can revert the image to any point in its Undo History simply by clicking on the right entry in the list. For more information on GIMP's Undo mechanism and how it works, see the section on Undoing.

13.2.7.1 Activate the dialog

The Undo History dialog is a dockable dialog; see the section on Dialogs and Docking for help on manipulating it. It can be activated in several ways:

- From the Toolbox menu: File → Dialogs → Undo History.

- From the Toolbox menu: File → Dialogs → Create New Dock → Layers, Channels, and Paths. This gives you a dock containing four dialogs, with the Undo History dialog one of them.

- From an image menu: Edit → Undo History.

- From an image menu: Dialogs → Undo History.

- From the Tab menu in any dockable dialog: Add Tab → Undo History.

13.2.7.2 Using the Undo History dialog

The most basic thing you can do is to select a point in the Undo History by clicking on it in the list. You can go back and forth between states in this way as much as you please, without losing any information or consuming any resources. In most cases, the changes are very fast.

Det mest nærliggande er å velje eit punkt i angreloggen ved å klikke på det. Du kan trygt klikke deg framover eller bakover i lista utan å vere redd for å miste informasjon om biletet eller å bruke opp ressursane. Som oftast går forandringane svært raskt.

At the bottom of the dialog are three buttons:

Undo This button has the same effect as choosing Edit → Undo from the menu, or pressing Ctrl-Z; it reverts the image to the next state back in the undo history.

Redo This button has the same effect as choosing Edit → Redo from the menu, or pressing Ctrl-Y; it advances the image to the next state forward in the undo history.

Clear Undo History This button removes all contents from the undo history except the current state. If you press it, you are asked to confirm that you really want to do this. The only reason for doing it would be if you are very constrained for memory.

 Note

In a tab, this dialog is represented by

 Note

You can set the number of undo levels in Preferences/Environment.

13.3   Image Content Related Dialogs

13.3.1   Colors Dialog

Figure 13.24: Colors dialog

The Channel dialog lets you manage and pick up new colors. It is divided into five separate parts: GIMP, CMYK, Triangle, Watercolor and Scales. You can use the eyedropper, which is the last button of the dialog, to pick up a color anywhere on your screen.

13.3.1.1   Activate Dialog

The dialog can be called in the following ways :

- from the toolbox-menu: File → Dialogs → Colors

- from the toolbox: click on the current Foreground or Background color.

- from the image-menu: Dialogs → Colors

- from an other dialog-menu: Add Tab → Colors

13.3.1.2   Using the dialog

GIMP Selector With the GIMP Color Selector, you select a color by clicking on a one-dimensional strip located at the right edge, and then in a two-dimensional area located on the left. The one-dimensional strip can encode any of the color parameters H, S, V, R, G, or B, as determined by which of the adjoining buttons is pressed. The two-dimensional area then encodes the two complementary color parameters.

CMYK You get to this selector by clicking on the printer icon. The CMYK view gives you the possibility to manage colors from the CMYK color model.

Triangle The Triangle selector is made up of a *chromatic circle* that allows to select Hue by click-and-drag a small circle and of a *triangle* that has also a small circle to vary intuitively Saturation and Value.

Watercolor This color selector is symbolized by a brush. The function mode of this selector is a little different from that of models presented so far. The principle consists in changing the current foreground color by clicking in the rectangular palette. If the current foreground color is for example white, then it turns to reddish by clicking in the red color area. Repeated clicking strengthens the effect. With the sliding control, which is right apart from the color palette, you can set the color quantity per every mouse click. The higher the sliding control is, the more color is taken up per click.

Scales This Scales exists only in the color selector you get from the file menu of the Tool-Box or from the Dialogs menu in the image menu bar.

This selector displays a global view of R, G, B channels and H, S, V values, placed in sliders.

Color picker This color picker exists only in the color selector you get from the file menu of the Tool-Box or from the Dialogs menu in the image menu bar.

The color picker has a completely different behaviour, than the color picker tool. Instead of picking the colors from the active image, you're able to pick colors from the entire screen.

As described above, the color selection tool started from the toolbox file menu and the image menu is different from the color selection tool started in any other way. In the first tool, in the lower part of the dialog, is showed the current foreground and background colour. One of the two colors is in each case, recognizable actively from a thin grey framework, which surrounds the active color box. In order to activate a color box, you can simply click on the desired box. All the modifications you do with the color selectors, apply to the active color box.

Right up you find a symbol, consisting of two arrows, with which you can exchange the foreground and background colour. At the bottom left of the dialog, just below the foreground color block, you find a switching surface with two small, one black and the other white, partially overlapping squares. If you click on these, the front and background colour are put back to black and white respectively.

13.3.2 Brushes Dialog

Figure 13.25: The Brushes dialog

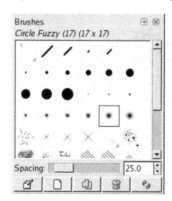

The Brushes dialog is used to select a brush, for use with painting tools: see the Brushes section for basic information on brushes and how they are used in GIMP. The dialog also gives you access to several functions for manipulating brushes. You can select a brush by clicking on it in the list: it will then be shown in the Brush/Pattern/Gradient area of the Toolbox. A few dozen basic brushes come pre-installed with GIMP, along with a few assorted bizarre ones that mainly serve to show you the range of possibilities. You can also create custom brushes using the Brush Editor, or by saving images in a special brush file format.

13.3.2.1 Activate Dialog

The Brushes dialog is a dockable dialog; see the section on Dialogs and Docking for help on manipulating it. It can be activated in several ways:

- From the Toolbox menu: File → Dialogs → Brushes.

- From the Toolbox menu: File → Dialogs → Create New Dock → Brushes, Patterns, and Gradients. This gives you a new window with several dialog docks, one of them opens the Brushes dialog.

- From the Toolbox, by clicking on the brush symbol in the Brush/Pattern/Gradient area.

- From an image menu: Dialogs → Brushes.

- From the Tab menu in any dockable dialog: Add Tab → Brushes.

- From the Tool Options dialog for any of the paint tools, by clicking on the Brush icon button, you get a popup with similar functionality that permits you to quickly choose a brush from the list; if you clic on the button present on the right bottom of the popup, you open the real brush dialog. Note that, depending on your Preferences, a brush selected with the popup may only apply to the currently active tool, not to other paint tools. See the Tool Option Preferences section for more information.

13.3.2.2   Using the brush dialog

13.3.2.2.1   Grid/List modes

In the Tab menu, you can choose between View as Grid and View as List. In Grid mode, the brush shapes are laid out in a rectangular array, making it easy to see many at once and find the one you are looking for. In List mode, the shapes are lined up in a list, with the names beside them.

Note
In the Tab menu, the option Preview Size allows you to adapt the size of brush previews to your liking.

Figure 13.26: The Brushes dialog

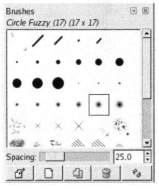

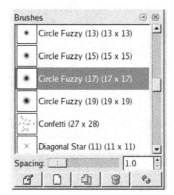

(a) *The Brushes dialog (Grid mode)*   (b) *The Brushes dialog (List view)*

Grid mode   At the top of the dialog appears the name of the currently selected brush, and its size in pixels.

In the center a grid view of all available brushes appears, with the currently selected one outlined. If you see a little "+" to the right of a brush, it means the brush is actually larger than it appears. If you see a little red triangle, it means the brush is an animated brush, also known as an "image hose". Clicking on a brush causes it to be selected as GIMP's current brush. Double-clicking activates the Brush Editor.

List mode   For the most part, the dialog works the same way in List mode as in Grid mode, with one exception:

If you *double-click* on the name of a brush, you will be able to edit it. Note, however, that you are only allowed to change the names of brushes that you have created or installed yourself, not the ones that come pre-installed with GIMP. If you try to rename a pre-installed brush, you will be able to edit the name, but as soon as you hit return or click somewhere else, the name will revert to its original value. It is a general rule that you cannot alter the resources that GIMP pre-installs for you: brushes, patterns, gradients, etc; only ones that you create yourself.

13.3.2.2.2   Buttons at the bottom

At the bottom of the dialog you find a couple of buttons:

Spacing Below the grid appears a scale entry for 'Spacing', which is the distance between consecutive brush marks when you trace out a brushstroke with the pointer.

Edit Brush This activates the Brush Editor. Pressing the button will open the Editor for any brush. It only works, however, for parametric brushes: for any other type, the Editor will show you the brush but not allow you to do anything with it.

New Brush This creates a new parametric brush, initializes it with a small fuzzy round shape, and opens the Brush Editor so that you can modify it. The new brush is automatically saved in your personal `brushes` folder.

Duplicate Brush This button is only enabled if the currently selected brush is a parametric brush. If so, the brush is duplicated, and the Brush Editor is opened so that you can modify the copy. The result is automatically saved in your personal `brushes` folder.

Delete Brush This removes all traces of the brush, both from the dialog and the folder where its file is stored, if you have permission to do so. It asks for confirmation before doing anything.

Refresh Brushes If you add brushes to your personal `brushes` folder or any other folder in your brush search path, by some means other than the Brush Editor, this button causes the list to be reloaded, so that the new entries will be available in the dialog.

The functions performed by these buttons can also be accessed from the dialog pop-up menu, activated by right-clicking anywhere in the brush grid/list, or by choosing the top item, Brushes menu, from the dialog Tab menu.

13.3.2.3   Brush Editor

Figure 13.27: The Brushes Editor dialog

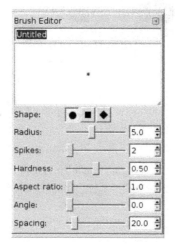

The Brush Editor allows you either to view the brush parameters of a brush supplied by GIMP, and you can't change them, or to create a custom brush from a geometrical shape, a circle, a square, a diamond. This editor has several elements:

The dialog bar: As with all dialog windows, a click on the small triangle prompts a menu allowing you to set the aspect of the Brush Editor.

The title bar: To give a name to your brush.

The preview area: Brush changes appear in real time in this preview.

Shape A circle, a square and a diamond are available. You will modify them by using the following options:

Radius Distance between brush center and edge, in the width direction. A square with a 10 pixels radius will have a 20 pixels side. A diamond with a 5 pixels radius will have a 10 pixels width.

Spikes This parameter is useful only for square and diamond. With a square, increasing spikes results in a polygon. With a diamond, you get a star.

Hardness This parameter controls the feathering of the brush border. Value = 1.00 gives a brush with a sharp border (0.00-1.00).

Aspect ratio This parameter controls the brush Width/Height ratio. A diamond with a 5 pixels radius and an Aspect Ratio = 2, will be flattened with a 10 pixels width and a 5 pixels height (1.0-20.0).

Angle This angle is the angle between the brush width direction, which is normally horizontal, and the horizontal direction, counter-clock-wise. When this value increases, the brush width turns counter-clock-wise (0 to 180).

Spacing When the brush draws a line, it actually stamps the brush icon repeatedly. If brush stamps are very close, you get the impression of a solid line: you get that with Spacing = 1. (1.00 to 200.0).

13.3.3 Patterns Dialog

Figure 13.28: The Patterns dialog

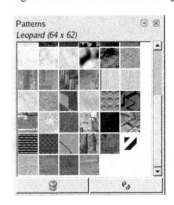

In GIMP, a *pattern* is a small image used to fill areas by placing copies of side by side. See the Patterns section for basic information on patterns and how they can be created and used.

You can use them with Bucket Fill et Clone tools and the Fill with pattern command.

The Patterns dialog is used to select a pattern, by clicking on it in a list or grid view: the selected pattern will then be shown in the Brush/Pattern/Gradient area of the Toolbox. A few dozen more or less randomly chosen patterns are supplied with GIMP, and you can easily add new patterns of your own.

13.3.3.1 Activate Dialog

The Patterns dialog is a dockable dialog; see the section on Dialogs and Docking for help on manipulating it. It can be activated in several ways:

- From the Toolbox menu: File → Dialogs → Patterns.

- From the Toolbox menu: File → Dialogs → Create New Dock → Brushes, Patterns, and Gradients. This gives you a new window with several dialog docks, one of them opens the Patterns dialog.

- From the Toolbox, by clicking on the pattern symbol in the Brush/Pattern/Gradient area.

- From an image menu: Dialogs → Patterns.

- From the Tab menu in any dockable dialog: Add Tab → Patterns.

- From the Tool Options dialog of the Clone tool and the Bucket Fill tool, by clicking on the pattern source button, you get a popup with similar functionality that permits you to quickly choose a pattern from the list; if you clic on the Bucket Fill button present on the right bottom of the popup, you open the real pattern dialog. Note that, depending on your Preferences, a pattern selected with the popup may only apply to the currently active tool, not to other paint tools. See the Tool Option Preferences section for more information.

13.3.3.2 Using the pattern dialog

Grid/List modes In the Tab menu, you can choose between View as Grid and View as List. In Grid mode, the patterns are laid out in a rectangular array, making it easy to see many at once and find the one you are looking for. In List mode, the patterns are lined up in a list, with the names beside them.

Tip
Independent of the real size of a pattern all patterns are shown the same size in the dialog. So for larger patterns this means that you see only a small portion of the pattern in the dialog at all - no matter whether you view the dialog in the list or the grid view. To see the full pattern you simply click on the pattern *and hold the mouse button for a second.*

Note
In the Tab menu, the option Preview Size allows you to adapt the size of pattern previews to your liking.

Figure 13.29: The Patterns dialog

(a) *List view*   (b) *Grid mode*

Using the Patterns dialog (Grid mode) At the top appears the name of the currently selected patterns, and its dimensions in pixels.

In the center appears a grid view of all available patterns, with the currently selected one outlined. Clicking on one of them sets it as GIMP's current pattern, and causes it to appear in the Brush/Pattern/Gradient area of the Toolbox.

Using the Patterns dialog (List view) In this view, instead of a grid, you see a list of patterns, each labeled with its name and size. Clicking on a row in the list sets that pattern as GIMP's current pattern, just as it does in the grid view.

If you *double-click* on the name of a pattern, you will be able to edit the name. Note that you are only allowed to rename patterns that you have added yourself, not the ones that are supplied with GIMP. If you edit a name that you don't have permission to change, as soon as you hit return or move to a different control, the name will revert back to its previous value.

Everything else in the List view works the same way as it does in the Grid view.

Delete Pattern Pressing this button removes the pattern from the list and causes the file representing it to be deleted from disk. Note that you cannot remove any of the patterns that are supplied with GIMP and installed in the system `patterns` directory; you can only remove patterns that you have added to folders where you have write permission.

Refresh Patterns Pressing this button causes GIMP to rescan the folders in your pattern search path, adding any newly discovered patterns to the list. This button is useful if you add new patterns to a folder, and want to make them available without having to restart GIMP.

13.3.4 Gradients Dialog

Figure 13.30: The screenshot illustrates the Gradients dialog

The Gradients dialog offers a gradient palette which is used to select a gradient -- a set of colors arranged in a linear scale -- for use with the Blend tool and numerous other operations. It also gives you access to several functions for manipulating gradients. You can select a gradient by clicking on it in the list: it will then be shown in the Brush/Pattern/Gradient area of the Toolbox. A few dozen nice gradients come pre-installed with GIMP. You can create more using the Gradient Editor. General information about gradients and how they are used in GIMP can be found in the Gradients section.

The first four gradients are particular: they reproduce the gradient between Foreground and background colors of toolbox in different ways.

13.3.4.1 Activate Dialog

The Gradients dialog is a dockable dialog; see the section on Dialogs and Docking for help on manipulating it. It can be activated in several ways:

• From the Toolbox menu: File → Dialogs → Gradients.

• From the Toolbox menu: File → Dialogs → Create New Dock → Brushes, Patterns, and Gradients. This gives you a new window with several dialog docks, one of them opens the Gradients dialog.

• From the Toolbox, by clicking on the current gradient in the Brush/Pattern/Gradient area.

• From an image menu: Dialogs → Gradients.

• From the Tab menu in any dockable dialog: Add Tab → Gradients.

• From the image by using the **Ctrl+G** shortcut.

13.3.4.2 Using the Gradients dialog

The most basic, and most commonly used, operation with the dialog is simply to click on one of the gradients in the scrollable list, in order to make it GIMP's current gradient, which will then be used by any operation that involves a gradient.

If you *double-click* on a gradient, you open the Gradient Editor where you will be able to edit its name. Note, however, that you are only allowed to change the names of gradients that you have created yourself, not the ones that come pre-installed with GIMP. If you try to rename a pre-installed gradient, you will be able to edit the name, but as soon as you hit return or click somewhere else, the name will revert to its original value. It is a general rule that you cannot alter the resources that GIMP pre-installs for you: brushes, patterns, gradients, etc; only ones that you create yourself.

Grid/List modes In the Tab menu, you can choose between View as Grid and View as List. In Grid mode, the gradients are laid out in a rectangular array. They look quite dazzling when viewed this way, but it is not very easy to pick the one you want, because of visual interference from the neighboring ones. In List mode, the more usable default, the gradients are lined up vertically, with each row showing its name.

Note
In the Tab menu, the option Preview Size allows you to adapt the size of gradient previews to your liking.

The buttons at the bottom of the dialog allow you to operate on gradients in several ways:

Edit Gradient This button activates the Gradient Editor.

New Gradient This creates a new gradient, initialized as a simple grayscale, and activates the Gradient Editor so that you can alter it. Gradients that you create are automatically saved in the gradients folder of your personal GIMP directory, from which they are automatically loaded when GIMP starts. (You can change this folder, or add new ones, using the Preferences dialog.)

Duplicate Gradient This creates a copy of the currently selected gradient. You will be able to edit the copy even if you cannot edit the original.

Delete Gradient This removes all traces of the gradient, if you have permission to do so. It asks for confirmation before doing anything.

Refresh Gradients If you add gradients to your personal gradients folder by some means other than this dialog, this button causes the list to be reloaded, so that the new entries will be available.

The functions performed by these buttons can also be accessed from the dialog pop-up menu, activated by right-clicking anywhere in the gradient list. The menu also gives you one additional function:

Save as POV-Ray... This allows you to save the gradient in the format used by the POV-Ray 3D ray-tracing program.

13.3.4.3   Gradient Editor

Figure 13.31: The gradient editor

The Gradient Editor allows you to edit the colors in a gradient. It can only be used on gradients you have created yourself (or on a copy of a system gradient), not on system gradients that come pre-installed with GIMP. This is a sophisticated tool that may take a bit of effort to understand. The concept behind it is that a gradient can be decomposed into a series of adjoining *segments*, with each segment consisting of a smooth transition from the color on the left edge to the color on the right edge. The Gradient Editor allows you to pack together any number of segments, with any colors you want for the left and right edges of each segment, and with several options for the shape of the transition from left to right.

13.3.4.3.1   How to Activate the Gradient Editor

You can activate the Gradient Editor in several ways:

- By double-clicking on the gradient stripe in the Gradient dialog.

- From the context menu you get by right clicking on the selected gradient name.

- By clicking on the Edit gradient button in the Gradient Dialog.

- From the Gradient Menu you get by clicking on the small triangle representing the Tab Menu in the Gradient Dialog.

13.3.4.3.2   Display

Name In the name area, you have the tab menu button (the small triangle) which opens a menu where you find the Gradient Editor Menu.

Gradient Display Below the name, you see the current result of your work if the Instant update option is checked; else, changes will appear only when you release the mouse button.

If you simply move the mouse pointer on this display, it works somewhat as a color-picker. Values of the pointed pixel are displayed in a rather odd way. *Position* is a number given to 3 decimal places, from 0.000 on the left to 1.000 on the right of the whole gradient. *RGB, HSV, Intensity and Opacity* are also a ratio...

If you click-n-drag on display, then only position and RGB data are displayed. But they are passed on to the Foreground color in Toolbox and to the four first gradients of the palette.

Range Selection/Control Sliders Below the gradient display, you see a set of black and white triangles lined up in row. A *segment* is the space between two consecutive *black* triangles. Inside each segment is a white triangle, which is used to 'warp' the colors in the segment, in the same way that the middle slider in the Levels tool warps the colors there. You can select a segment by clicking between the two black triangles that define it. You can select a range of segments by shift-clicking on them. The selected range always consists of a set of *consecutive* segments, so if you skip over any when shift-clicking, they will be included automatically. If 'Instant update' is checked, the display is updated immediately after any slider movement; if it is unchecked, updates only occur when you release the mouse button.

You can move sliders, segments and selections. If you simply *click-n-drag a slider*, you only move the corresponding transition. By *Click-n-drag on a segment* you can move this segment up to the next triangle. By *Shift+click-n-drag on a segment/selection*, you can move this segment/selection and compress/ dilate next segments.

Scrollbar Below the sliders is a scrollbar. This only comes into play if you zoom in using the buttons at the bottom.

Feedback Area Below the sliders is an area that initially is blank, but depending on your actions, helpful hints or feedback messages may appear here.

Buttons At the bottom of the dialog appear five buttons:

> **Save** Clicking this button causes the gradient, in its current state, to be saved in your personal `gradients` folder, so that it will automatically be loaded the next time you start GIMP.
>
> **Revert** Clicking this button undoes all of your editing. (However, at the time this is being written, this function is not yet implemented.)
>
> **Zoom Out** Clicking this button shrinks the gradient display horizontally.
>
> **Zoom In** Clicking this button expands the gradient display horizontally. You can then use the scrollbar to pan the display left or right.
>
> **Zoom All** Clicking this button resizes the display horizontally so that it fits precisely into the window.

13.3.4.3.3 Gradient Editor Menu

Figure 13.32: The Gradient Editor menu

You can access the Gradient Editor menu either by right-clicking on the gradient display, or by choosing the top item in the dialog's tab menu. The menu allows you to set the left and right edge colors for each segment, and control the transition from one color to the other.

The following commands can be found in the menu:

Left [Right] Endpoint's Color These options allow you to choose a color for the respective endpoint using a Color Editor.

Figure 13.33: The "Load Color From" submenu

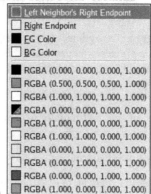

Load Left [Right] Color From

These options give you a number of alternative ways of assigning colors to the endpoints. From the submenu you can choose (assuming we're dealing with the left endpoint):

Left Neighbor's Right Endpoint This choice will cause the color of the right endpoint of the segment neighboring on the left to be assigned to the left endpoint of the selected range.

Right Endpoint This choice will cause the color of the right endpoint of the selected range to be assigned to the left endpoint.

FG/BG color These choice cause GIMP's current foreground or background color, as shown in the Toolbox, to be assigned to the endpoint.

RGBA slots At the bottom of the menu are 10 "memory slots". You can assign colors to them using the "Save" menu option described below. If you choose one of the slots, the color in it will be assigned to the endpoint.

Save Left [Right] Color To These options cause the color of the endpoint in question to be assigned to the "memory slot" selected from the submenu.

Figure 13.34: The Blending Function submenu

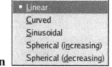

Blending Function for Segment/Selection

This option determines the course of the transition from one endpoint of the range (segment or selection) to the other, by fitting the specified type of function to the endpoints and midpoint of the range:

Linear Default option. Color varies linearly from one endpoint of the range to the other.

Curved Gradient varies more quickly on ends of the range than on its middle.

Sinusoidal The opposite of the curved type. Gradients varies more quickly on center of the range than on its ends.

Spherical (increasing) Gradient varies more quickly on the left of the range than on its right.

Spherical (decreasing) Gradient varies more quickly on the right than on the left.

Figure 13.35: The Coloring Type submenu

Coloring Type for Segment/Selection

This option gives you additional control of the type of transition from one endpoint to the other: as a line either in RGB space or in HSV space.

Flip Segment/Selection This option does a right-to-left flip of the selected range (segment or selection), flipping all colors and endpoint locations.

Replicate Segment/Selection This option splits the selected range (segment or selection) into two parts, each of which is a perfect compressed copy of the original range.

Split Segments at Midpoints This option splits each segment in the selected range in into two segments, splitting at the location of the white triangle.

Split Segments Uniformly This option is similar to the previous one, but it splits each segment halfway between the endpoints, instead of at the white triangle.

Delete Selection This option deletes all segments in the selected range, (segment or selection) replacing them with a single black triangle at the center, and enlarging the segments on both sides to fill the void.

Re-center Segment's midpoint/Selection midpoints This option moves the white triangle for each segment in the selected range to a point halfway between the neighboring black triangles.

Re-distribute Handles in Segment/Selection This option causes the black and white triangles in the selected range to be shifted so that the distances from one to the next are all equal.

Blend Endpoints' Colors This option is only available if more than one segment is selected. It causes the colors at interior endpoints in the range to be averaged, so that the transition from each segment to the next is smooth.

Blend Endpoints' Opacity This option does the same thing as the previous option, but with opacity instead of color.

Caution
There is no "undo" available within the Gradient Editor, so be careful!

13.3.5 Palettes Dialog

Figure 13.36: The Palettes dialog

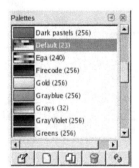

A *palette* is a set of discrete colors, in no particular order. See the Palettes section for basic information on palettes and how they can be created and used.

The Palettes dialog is used to select a palette, by clicking on it in a list or grid view. A few dozen more or less randomly chosen palettes are supplied with GIMP, and you can easily add new palettes of your own. The Palettes dialog also give you access to several operations for creating new palettes or manipulating the ones that already exist.

Note
The Palettes dialog is not the same thing as the Index Palette dialog, which is used to manipulate the colormaps of indexed images.

13.3.5.1 Activate Dialog

The Palettes dialog is a dockable dialog; see the section on Dialogs and Docking for help on manipulating it. It can be activated in several ways:

- From the Toolbox menu: File → Dialogs → Palettes.
- From an image menu: Dialogs → Palettes.
- From the Tab menu in any dockable dialog: Add Tab → Palettes.

13.3.5.2 Using the Palettes dialog

Clicking on a palette in the dialog makes it GIMP's active palette. This does not really have any significance, though. Double-clicking on a palette brings up the Palette Editor, which allows you to set GIMP's foreground or background colors by clicking on colors in the palette display.

Double-clicking on a palette *name* (in List View mode) lets you to edit the name. Note that you are only allowed to change the names of palettes that you have added yourself, not those that are supplied with GIMP. If you edit a name that you are not allowed to change, it will revert back to its previous value as soon as you hit return or move the pointer focus elsewhere.

Grid/List modes

Figure 13.37: The Palettes dialog

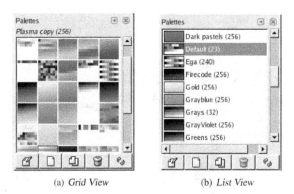

(a) *Grid View*   (b) *List View*

In the Tab menu, you can choose between View as Grid and View as List. In Grid mode, the palettes are laid out in a spectacular rectangular array, making it easy to see many at once and find the one you are looking for. In List mode (the default), the palettes are lined up in a list, with the names beside them.

Tip
In the Tab menu, the option Preview Size allows you to adapt the size of color cell previews to your liking.

Edit Palette This button brings up the Palette Editor.

New Palette See New Palette.

Duplicate Palette See Duplicate Palette.

Delete Palette See Delete Palette.

Refresh Palettes See Refresh Palettes.

13.3.5.3 Palettes Menu

Figure 13.38: The Palettes Menu

The Palettes Menu can be accessed by right-clicking in the Palettes dialog, or by choosing the top item from the dialog Tab menu.

Edit Palette 'Edit Palette' is an alternative way of activating the Palette Editor: it can also be activated by double-clicking on a palette in the Palettes dialog, or by pressing the "Edit Palette" button at the bottom of the dialog.

New Palette 'New Palette' creates a new, untitled palette, initially containing no color entries, and pops up the Palette Editor so that you can add colors to the palette. The result will automatically be saved in your personal `palettes` folder when you quit GIMP, so it will be available from the Palettes dialog in future sessions.

Import Palette

Figure 13.39: The Import Palette dialog

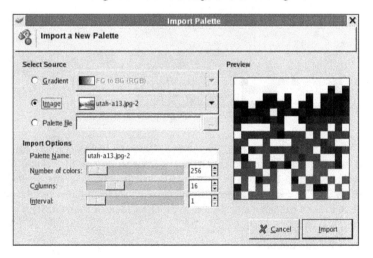

'Import Palette' allows you to create a new palette from the colors in a gradient, an image or a palette file. Choosing it brings up the "Import Palette" dialog, which gives you the following options:

Select Source You can import a palette either from any of GIMP's gradients (choosing one from the adjoining menu), or from any of the currently open images (chosen from the adjoining menu). In GIMP 2.2, you can also import a RIFF palette file (with extension `.pal`), of the type used by several Microsoft Windows applications.

Palette name You can give a name to the new palette here. If the name you choose is already used by an existing palette, a unique name will be formed by appending a number (e. g., "#1").

Number of colors Here you specify the number of colors in the palette. The default is 256, chosen for three reasons: (1) every gradient contains 256 distinct colors; (2) GIF files can use a maximum of 256 colors; (3) GIMP indexed images can contain a maximum of 256 distinct colors. You can use any number you like here, though: GIMP will try to create a palette by spacing the specified number of colors even across the color range of the gradient or image.

Columns Here you specify the number of columns for the palette. This only affects the way the palette is displayed, and has no effect on the way the palette is used.

Interval XXX I have no idea what this is.

The imported palette will be added to the Palettes dialog, and automatically saved in your personal `palettes` folder when you quit GIMP, so it will be available in future sessions.

Duplicate Palette Duplicate Palette creates a new palette by copying the palette that is currently selected, and brings up a Palette Editor so that you can alter the palette. The result will automatically be saved in your personal `palettes` folder when you quit GIMP, so it will be available from the Palettes dialog in future sessions.

Merge Palettes Currently this operation is not implemented, and the menu entry will always be insensitive.

Delete Palette Delete Palette removes the palette from the Palettes dialog, and deletes the disk file in which it is stored. Before it acts, it asks you confirm that you really want to do these things. Note that you cannot remove any of the palettes that are supplied with GIMP, only palettes you have added yourself.

Refresh Palettes Refresh Palettes rescans all of the folders in your palette search path, and adds any newly discovered palettes to the list in the Palettes dialog. This may be useful if you obtain palette files from some external source, copy them into one of your palettes folders, and want to make them available during the current session.

13.3.5.4 Palette Editor

Figure 13.40: The Palette Editor

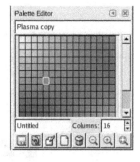

The Palette Editor is used mainly for two purposes: first, for setting GIMP's foreground or background colors (as shown in the Color Area of the Toolbox) to selected colors from the palette; second, for modifying the palette. You can activate the Palette Editor for any palette in the Palettes dialog, but you can only modify palettes that you have created yourself, not the palettes that are supplied when you install GIMP. (You can, however, duplicate any palette and then edit the newly created copy.) If you modify a palette, the results of your work will automatically be saved when you exit from GIMP.

13.3.5.4.1 How to Activate the Palette Editor

The Palette Editor is only accessible from the Palettes dialog: you can activate it by double-clicking on a palette, or by pressing the "Edit Palette" button at the bottom, or by choosing "Edit Palette" from the Palettes Menu.

The Palette Editor is a dockable dialog; see the section on Dialogs and Docking for help on manipulating it.

13.3.5.4.2 Using the Palette Editor

If you click on a color box in the palette display, GIMP's foreground color will be set to the selected color: you can see this in the Color Area of the Toolbox. If you hold down the **Ctrl** key while clicking, GIMP's background color will be set to the selected color.

Double-clicking on a color not only sets the foreground, it also brings up a color editor that allows you to modify the selected palette entry. (This only happens if the palette is one you are allowed to modify: that is, one you have added to GIMP yourself.)

Right-clicking in the palette display area brings up the Palette Editor menu. It's functions are mainly the same as those of the buttons at the bottom of the dialog.

Below the palette display area, at the left, appears a text entry area that shows the name of the selected color (or "Untitled" if it does not have one). This information has no functional significance, and is present only to serve you as a memory aid.

To the right of the name entry is a spinbutton that allows you to set the number of columns used to display the palette. This only affects the display, not how the palette works. If the value is set to 0, a default will be used.

At the bottom of the dialog are a set of buttons, which mostly match the entries in the Palette Editor menu, accessible by right-clicking in the palette display area. Here are the buttons:

Save This button causes the palette to be saved in your personal `palettes` folder. It would be saved automatically when GIMP exits in any case, but you might want to use this button if you are concerned that GIMP might crash in the meantime.

Revert This operation has not yet been implemented.

Edit Color Pops up a color editor allowing you to alter the color. If the palette is one you aren't allowed to alter, this button will be insensitive. See below

New Color from FG See below

Delete Color See below

Zoom Out See below

Zoom In See below

Zoom All See below

13.3.5.5 Palette Editor Menu

Figure 13.41: The Palette Editor Menu

The Palette Editor Menu can be accessed by right-clicking on the palette display in the Palette Editor, or by choosing the top entry from the dialog Tab menu. The operations in it can also be executed using the buttons at the bottom of the Palette Editor dialog.

Edit Color "Edit Color" brings up a color editor that allows you to modify the color of the selected palette entry. If the palette is one that you are not allowed to edit (that is, one supplied by GIMP when it is installed), then the menu entry will be insensitive.

New Color from FG; New Color from BG These commands each create a new palette entry, using either GIMP's current foreground color (as shown in the Color Area of the Toolbox), or the current background color.

Delete Color "Delete Color" removes the selected color entry from the palette. If the palette is one that you are not allowed to edit, then the menu entry will be insensitive.

Zoom Out "Zoom Out" reduces the vertical scale of the entries in the palette display.

Zoom In "Zoom In" increases the vertical scale of the entries in the palette display.

Zoom All "Zoom All" adjusts the vertical size of the entries in the palette display so that the entire palette fits into the display area.

13.3.6   Fonts Dialog

Figure 13.42: The Fonts dialog

The Fonts dialog is used for selecting fonts for the Text tool. It also allows you to refresh the list of available fonts, if you add new ones to your system while GIMP is running.

13.3.6.1   Activate Dialog

The Fonts dialog is a dockable dialog; see the section on Dialogs and Docking for help on manipulating it. It can be activated in several ways:

- From the Toolbox menu: File → Dialogs → Fonts.

- From the image menu bar: Dialogs → Fonts.

- From the Tool Options for the Text tool. If you click on the "Font" button, a Font-selector pops up. In the lower right corner is a button that, if pressed, brings up the Fonts dialog.

- From the Tab menu in any dockable dialog: Add Tab → Fonts.

13.3.6.2   Using the Fonts dialog

The most basic thing you can do is to select a font by clicking on it: this font will then be used by the Text tool. If instead of clicking and releasing, you hold down the left mouse button with the pointer positioned over the font example ("Aa"), a window showing a larger text example will pop up ("Pack my box with five dozen liquor jugs.").

Grid/List modes

Figure 13.43: The Fonts dialog

(a) *Dialog in Grid View*   (b) *Dialog in List View*

In the Tab menu for the Fonts dialog, you can choose between View as Grid and View as List. In Grid mode, the fonts are laid out in a rectangular array. In List mode, they are lined up vertically, with each row showing an example of the appearance of the font ("Aa"), followed by the name of the font.

Refresh font list Pressing the button at the bottom of the dialog causes the system font list to be rescanned. This may be useful if you add new fonts while GIMP is running, and want to make them accessible for the Text tool. You can also cause the font list to be rescanned by right-clicking in the font display, and selecting "Rescan Font List" from the menu that pops up (it is actually the only option in the menu).

 Tip
You can change the size of the font previews in the dialog using the "Preview Size" submenu of the dialog's Tab menu.

13.4   Image Management Related Dialogs

13.4.1   Buffers Dialog

Figure 13.44: The Buffers dialog

Buffers are temporary repositories for image data, created when you cut or copy part of a drawable (a layer, layer mask, etc.). You can save a document in this buffer in two ways: Edit → Buffer → Copy Named or Edit → Buffer → Cut Named A dialog pops up asking you to name a buffer to store the data in. There is no hard limit on the number of named buffers you can create, although, of course, each one consumes a share of memory.

The Buffers dialog shows you the contents of all existing named buffers, and allows you to operate on them in several ways. It also shows you, at the top, the contents of the Global Buffer, but this is merely a display: you can't do anything with it.

 Caution

Named buffers are not saved across sessions. The only way to save their contents is to paste them into images.

13.4.1.1 Activate Dialog

The Buffers dialog is a dockable dialog; see the section Section 3.2.3 for help on manipulating it. It can be activated in several ways:

- From the Toolbox menu: File → Dialogs → Buffer.
- From an image menu: Dialogs → Buffer, or Edit → Buffer → Paste Named.
- From the Tab menu in any dockable dialog: Add Tab → Buffer.

13.4.1.2 Using the Buffers dialog

Clicking on a buffer in the display area makes it the active buffer, i. e., the one that will be used for paste commands executed with the Buffers Menu or the buttons at the bottom of the dialog. Double-clicking on a buffer causes its contents to be pasted to the active image; this is a quick way of executing the 'Paste Buffer' command.

At the bottom of the dialog are four buttons. The operations they perform can also be accessed from the Buffers Menu that you get by right clicking on the active buffer.

13.4.1.2.1 Grid/List modes

Figure 13.45: The Buffers dialog (Grid View)

In the Tab menu for the Buffers dialog, you can choose between View as Grid and View as List. In Grid mode, the buffers are laid out in a rectangular array. In List mode, they are lined up vertically, with each row showing a preview of the contents of the buffer, its name, and its pixel dimensions.

 Note

You can change the size of the buffer previews in the dialog using the 'Preview Size' submenu of the dialog's Tab menu.

13.4.1.2.2 Buttons at the bottom

At the bottom of the dialog you find a couple of buttons:

Paste Buffer This command pastes the contents of the selected buffer into the active image, as a floating selection. The only difference between this and the ordinary Paste command is that it uses the selected buffer rather than the global clipboard buffer.

Paste Buffer Into This command pastes the contents of the selected buffer into the active image's selection, as a floating selection. The only difference between this and the ordinary Paste Into command is that it uses the selected buffer rather than the global clipboard buffer.

Paste Buffer as New This command creates a new single-layer image out of the contents of the selected buffer. The only difference between this and the ordinary Paste as New command is that it uses the selected buffer rather than the global clipboard buffer.

Delete Buffer This command deletes the selected named buffer, no questions asked. You cannot delete the Global Buffer.

13.4.2 Images Dialog

Figure 13.46: The Images dialog

The Images Dialog displays the list of open images on your screen; each of them is represented with a thumbnail. This dialog is useful when you have many overlapping images on your screen: thus, you can raise the wanted image to foreground.

13.4.2.1 Activate Dialog

The Images dialog is a dockable dialog; see the section on Dialogs and Docking for help on manipulating it. It can be activated in several ways:

- From the Toolbox menu: File → Dialogs → Images.

- From an image menu: Dialogs → Images.

- From the Tab menu in any dockable dialog: Add Tab → Ihmages.

13.4.2.2 Using the Images dialog

At the top of the dialog appears the name of the currently selected image, if the 'Show Image Selection' option is checked in Tab Menu. Useless if you have selected Grid mode: anyway, the name is displayed.

At center, open images appear, as a list or a grid, according to the selected mode. The current image is highlighted in list mode, outlined in grid mode. With a double click. With a simple click on an image name, you raise this image to the foreground of your screen. With a simple click you select this image so that buttons can act on it.

Three buttons at the bottom of the dialog allow you to operate on the selected image:

Grid/List modes, Previews size As in all dialogs with thumbnails, the Tab menu gives you the possibility of adapting thumbnail display to your liking. See Docking

Raise this image's display The selected image appears at the foreground of your screen.

Create a new display for this image Duplicates the image window (not the image) of the selected image.

Delete This button is not working.

13.4.3 Document History Dialog

Figure 13.47: Document History dialog

The History Dialog displays the list of the documents you have opened in previous sessions. It is more complete than the list you get with the 'Open Recent' command.

Denne dialogen opnar ei liste over dokument, dvs. bilete, du har opna tidlegare. Denne loggen er fyldigare enn den du får frå 'Sist opna filer' i verktøyskrinet.

13.4.3.1 Activate Dialog

You can access to this dialog in different ways:

- From the toolbox-menu and the image Menu bar: File → Open Recent → Document History

- From the image Menu-bar: Dialogs → Document History

13.4.3.2 Options

The scroll bar allows you to browse all images you have opened before.

The *Open the selected entry* button allows you to open the image you have selected. With "Shift" key pressed, it raises an image hidden behind others. With "Ctrl" key pressed, it opens the Open Image dialog.

The *Remove the selected entry* button allows you to remove an image from the History dialog. The image is removed from the recently open images list also. But the image itself is not deleted.

The *Recreate Preview* button updates preview in case of change. With "Shift" key pressed, it acts on all previews. With "Ctrl" key pressed, previews that can't be found out are deleted.

13.4.4   Templates Dialog

Figure 13.48: The Templates dialog

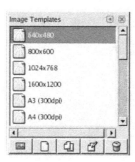

Templates are templates for an image format to be created. GIMP offers you a lot of templates and you can create your owns. When you create a New image, you can access to the list of existing templates but you can't manage them. The 'Templates' dialog allows you to manage all these templates.

13.4.4.1   Activate Dialog

The Templates dialog is a dockable dialog; see the section on Dialogs and Docking for help on manipulating it. It can be activated in two ways:

- From the Toolbox menu: File → Dialogs → Templates.
- From an image menu: Dialogs → Templates.

13.4.4.2   Using the Templates dialog

You select a template by clicking on its icon. Right clicking reveals a local menu that offers the same functions as buttons.

13.4.4.2.1   Grid/List modes

In the Tab menu for the Templates dialog, you can choose between View as Grid and View as List. In Grid mode, templates are laid out in a rectangular array of identical icons (unless you gave them a particular icon, as we will see later). Only the name of the selected template is displayed. In List mode, they are lined up vertically; icons are identical too; all names are displayed.

In this Tab menu, the Preview Size option allows you to change the size of thumbnails.

13.4.4.2.2   Buttons at the bottom

The buttons at the bottom of the dialog allow you to operate on templates in several ways:

Create a new image from the selected template Clicking on this button opens the Create a new image on the model of the selected template.

Create a new template Clicking on this button opens the New template dialog, identical to the Edit Template dialog, that we will see below.

Duplicate the selected template Clicking on this button opens the Edit Template dialog that we are going to study now.

Edit the selected template Clicking on this button opens the Edit Template dialog.

Delete the selected template No comment.

13.4.4.3 Edit Template

Figure 13.49: The Edit Template dialog

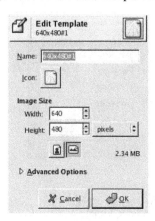

The dialog allows you to set the specifications of the selected template.

You can access to this editor by clicking on the Edit Template button in the Templates dialog.

OPTIONS

Name In this text box, you can modify the displayed template name.

Icon By clicking on this icon, you open a list of icons. You can choose one of them to illustrate the selected template name.

Image size Here you set the width and height of the new image. The default units are pixels, but you can switch to some other unit if you prefer, using the adjoining menu. If you do, note that the resulting pixel size will be determined by the X and Y resolution (which you can change in the Advanced Options), and by the setting of "Dot for Dot", which you can change in the View menu.

 Note
Please keep in mind, that every Pixel of an image is stored in the memory. If you're creating large files with a high density of pixels, GIMP will need some time for every function you're applying to the image.

Portrait/Landscape buttons These buttons toggle between Portrait and Landscape mode. Concretely, their effect is to exchange the values for Width and Height. If the X and Y resolutions are different (in Advanced Options), then these values are exchanged also. On the right, image size, image resolution and color space are displayed.

ADVANCED OPTIONS

X and Y resolution These values come into play mainly in relation to printing: they do not affect the size of the image in pixels, but they determine its size on paper when printed. They can also affect the way the image is displayed on the monitor: if 'Dot for Dot' is switched off in the View menu, then at 100% zoom, GIMP attempts to display the image on the monitor at the correct physical size, as calculated from the pixel dimensions and the resolution. The display may not be accurate, however, unless the monitor has been calibrated. This can be done either when GIMP is installed, or from the Display tab of the Preferences dialog.

Colorspace You can create the new image as either an RGB image or a grayscale image. You cannot create an indexed image directly in this way, but of course nothing prevents you from converting the image to indexed mode after it has been created.

Fill You have four choices for the solid color that will fill the new image's background layer:

- Foreground color, as shown in the Main Toolbox.
- Background color, as shown in the Main Toolbox.
- White, the more often used.
- Transparent. If this option is chosen, then the Background layer in the new image will be created with an alpha channel; otherwise not.

Comment You can write a descriptive comment here. The text will be attached to the image as a 'parasite', and will be saved along with the image by some file formats (but not all of them).

13.5 Misc dialogs

13.5.1 Tools Dialog

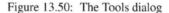

Figure 13.50: The Tools dialog

The Tools dialog is used mainly to control the appearance of the Toolbox. It allows you to customize the set of tools for which icons are shown in the Toolbox, and the order in which the icons are arranged. Probably the most common use for it is to make the Color tools available directly from the Toolbox. You can also use the Tools dialog to select a tool by clicking on its symbol, but for this purpose you might as well just use the Toolbox.

The Tools dialog is a dockable dialog; see the section on Dialogs and Docking for help on manipulating it. It can be activated in several ways:

- From the Toolbox menu: File → Dialogs → Tools.
- From an image menu: Dialogs → Tools.
- From the Tab menu in any dockable dialog: Add Tab → Tools.

13.5.1.1 Grid/List modes

In the Tab menu, you can choose between View as Grid and View as List. In Grid mode, the tools are laid out in a rectangular array. In List mode, they are lined up vertically, with each row showing the tool name, tool icon, and an 'eye' icon if the tool is currently visible in the Toolbox.

13.5.1.2 Using the Tools dialog

The most basic thing you can do is to select a tool by clicking on its icon: this has the same effect as clicking on an icon in the Toolbox. You can do this in either List or Grid mode: the other functions of the dialog are available only in List mode.

The most important function of the Tools dialog is to let you choose which tools to make visible in the Toolbox, by toggling the 'eye' icons that appear on the left side of each row in List mode. In particular, if you use the Color tools a lot, you may benefit from toggling visibility on for them here.

You can also change the order of tools in the Toolbox, by clicking on an item in the Tools dialog, in List mode, and dragging it up or down in the list. If you screw things up, you can always press the "Reset" button at the bottom of the dialog, to restore the defaults for order and visibility.

Right-clicking inside the dialog produces the Tools menu, which gives you an alternative way of toggling visibility or restoring the defaults.

13.5.2   Preferences Dialog

13.5.2.1   Introduction

Figure 13.51: List of preference pages

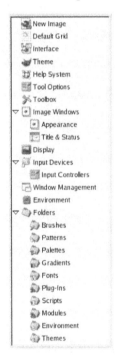

The preferences dialog can be accessed from the Toolbox menu, as File → Preferences. It lets you customize many aspects of the way GIMP works. The following sections detail the settings that you can customize, and what they affect. This information applies specifically to GIMP 2.2, but the settings for GIMP 2.0 are similar enough that you should be able to understand them based on the explanations here.

All of the Preferences information is stored in a file called gimprc in your personal GIMP directory, so if you are a 'power user' who would rather work with a text editor than a graphical interface, you can alter preferences by editing that file. If you do, and you are on a Linux system, then **man gimprc** will give you a lot of technical information about the contents of the file and what they are used for.

13.5.2.2 New Image Preferences

Figure 13.52: New Image Preferences

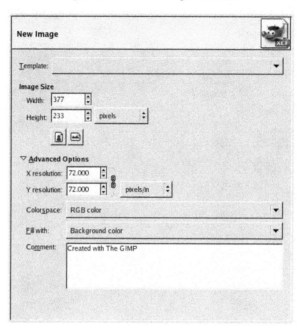

This tab lets you customize the default settings for the New Image dialog. See the New Image Dialog section for an explanation of what each of the values means.

13.5.2.3 Default Image Grid

Figure 13.53: Default Grid Preferences

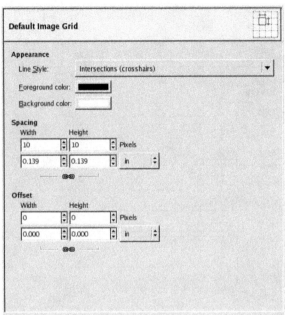

This page lets you customize the default properties of GIMP's grid, which can be toggled on or off using View → Show Grid from the image menu. The settings here match those in the Configure Image Grid dialog, which can be used to reconfigure the grid for an existing image, by choosing Image → Configure Grid from the image menu. See the Configure Grid dialog section for information on the meaning of each of the settings.

13.5.2.4 Interface

Figure 13.54: Assorted Interface Preferences

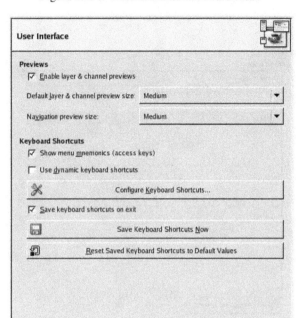

This page lets you customize layer/channel previews and keyboard shortcuts.

OPTIONS

Previews By default, GIMP shows miniature previews of the contents of layers and channels in several places, including the Layers dialog. If for some reason you would prefer to disable these, you can do it by unchecking 'Enable layer and channel previews'. If you do want previews to be shown, you can customize their sizes using the menus for 'Default layer and channel preview size' and 'Navigation preview size'.

Keyboard Shortcuts Any menu item can be activated by holding down **Alt** and pressing a sequence of keys. Normally, the key associated with each menu entry is shown as an underlined letter in the text, called *accelerator*. If for some reason you would prefer the underlines to go away (maybe because you think they're ugly and you don't use them anyway), then you can make this happen by unchecking 'Show menu mnemonics'.

GIMP can give you the ability to create keyboard shortcuts (key combinations that activate a menu entry) dynamically, by pressing the keys while the pointer hovers over the desired menu entry. However, this capability is disabled by default, because it might lead novice users to accidentally overwrite the standard keyboard shortcuts. If you want to enable it, check 'Use dynamics keyboard shortcuts' here.

Pressing the button for 'Configure Keyboard Shortcuts' brings up the Shortcut Editor, which gives you a graphical interface to select menu items and assign shortcuts to them.

If you change shortcuts, you will probably want your changes to continue to apply in future GIMP sessions. If not, uncheck 'Save keyboard shortcuts on exit'. But remember that you have done this, or you may be frustrated later. If you don't want to save shortcuts on exit every session, you can save the current settings at any time using the 'Save Keyboard Shortcuts Now' button, and they will be applied to future sessions. If you decide that you have made some bad decisions concerning shortcuts, you can reset them to their original state by pressing 'Reset Saved Keyboard Shortcuts to Default Values'.

13.5.2.5 Theme

Figure 13.55: Theme Preference

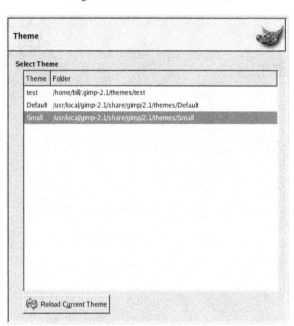

This page lets you select a theme, which determines many aspects of the appearance of the GIMP user interface, including the set of icons used, their sizes, fonts, spacing allowed in dialogs, etc. Two themes are supplied with GIMP: Default, which is probably best for most people, and Small, which may be preferable for those with small or low-resolution monitors. Clicking on a theme in the list causes it to be applied immediately, so it is easy to see the result and change your mind if you don't like it.

You can also use custom themes, either by downloading them from the net, or by copying one of the supplied themes and modifying it. Custom themes should be places in the `themes` subdirectory of your personal GIMP directory: if they are, they will appear in the list here. Each theme is actually a directory containing ASCII files that you can edit. They are pretty complicated, and the meaning of the contents goes beyond the scope of this documentation, but you should feel free to experiment: in the worst case, if you mess things up completely, you can always revert back to one of the supplied themes.

You cannot edit the supplied themes unless you have administrator permissions, and even if you do, you shouldn't: if you want to customize a theme, make a copy in your personal directory and work on it. If you make a change and would like to see the result "on the fly", you can do so by saving the edited theme file and then pressing Reload Current Theme.

13.5.2.6 Help System

Figure 13.56: Help System Preferences (Linux Screenshot)

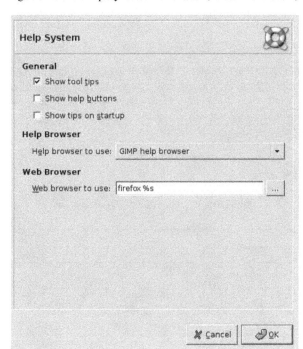

This page lets you customize the behaviour of the GIMP help system.

13.5.2.6.1 Options

GENERAL

Show tool tips Tool tips are small text bubbles that appear when the pointer hovers for a moment over some element of the interface, such as a button or icon. Sometimes they explain what the element does; sometimes they give you hints about non-obvious ways to use it. If you find them too distracting, you can disable them here by unchecking this option. We recommend that you leave them enabled unless you are a very advanced user.

Show help buttons In GIMP 2.2, this options controls whether are shown the help buttons on every tool dialog, which may be used alternatively to invoke the help system.

Show tips on startup Startup tips are helpful hints that appear each time you start GIMP. You can switch them on or off here. If you have switched them off by unchecking 'Show tip next time GIMP starts' in the tip window, you can switch them back on by checking here. Whatever you decide to do, at some point you should take the time to go through the list of tips: they are considered to be very useful, and the things they tell you are not easy to discover by experimenting. If you prefer, you can read them at any time by choosing Help → Tip of the Day in the Toolbox menu.

HELP BROWSER

Help browser to use GIMP Help is supplied in the form of HTML files, i. e., web pages. You can view them using either a special help browser that comes with GIMP, or a web browser of your choice. Here you choose which option to use. Because the help pages were carefully checked to make sure they work well with GIMP's browser, whereas other web browsers are somewhat variable in their support of features, the safer option is to use the internal browser; but really any modern web browser should be okay.

Note

Note that the help browser is not available on all platforms. If it is missing, the web-browser will be used to allow access to the help pages.

WEB BROWSER

Web browser to use If you selected 'GIMP help browser' for the Help browser, this option has no effect. If you selected 'Web browser', you can decide here which browser to use, and how to invoke it, by entering the command that will be used to run the browser. The button to the right brings up a file selector, which you can use to locate the executable file for the browser if you like, but in most cases it is probably easier to enter a command by hand.

13.5.2.7 Tool Options

Figure 13.57: Tool Options Preferences

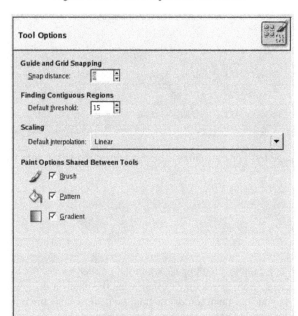

This page lets you customize several aspects of the behavior of tools.

13.5.2.7.1 Options

GUIDE AND GRID SNAPPING

Snap distance "Snapping" to guides, or to an image grid, means that when a tool is applied by clicking somewhere on the image display, if the clicked point is near enough to a guide or grid, it is shifted exactly onto the guide or grid. Snapping to guides can be toggled using View → Snap to Guides in the image menu; and if the grid is switched on, snapping to it can be toggled using View → Snap to Grid. This preference option determines how close a clicked point must be to a guide or grid in order to be snapped onto it, in pixels.

FINDING CONTIGUOUS REGIONS

Default threshold The "magic wand" tool creates selections that consist of contiguous regions, i. e., regions that are not divided by swaths of open space. This option determines how near each other two pixels need to be in order to be considered contiguous.

SCALING

Default interpolation When you scale something, each pixel in the result is calculated by interpolating several pixels in the source. This option determines the default interpolation method: it can always be changed, though, in the Tool Options dialog. There are three choices:

None is fastest, but quite crude: you should only consider using it if your machine is very seriously speed-impaired.

Linear is the default, and is good enough for most purposes.

Cubic is the best (although it can actually look worse than Linear for some types of images), but also the slowest.

PAINT OPTIONS SHARED BETWEEN TOOLS

Brush, Pattern, Gradient You can decide here whether changing the brush etc for one tool should cause the new item to be used for all tools, or whether each individual tool (pencil, paintbrush, airbrush, etc) should remember the item that was last used for it specifically.

MOVE TOOL

Change current layer or path You can decide here whether changing the current level or path when using the move tool and without pressing any key.

13.5.2.8 Toolbox

Figure 13.58: Toolbox Preferences

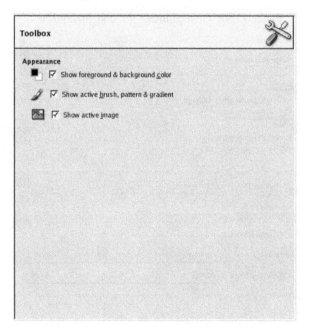

13.5.2.8.1 Options

Figure 13.59: Default Toolbox appearance

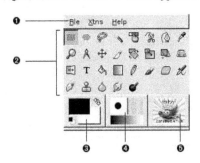

This page lets you customize the appearance of the Toolbox, by deciding whether the three "context information" areas should be shown at the bottom.

APPEARANCE

Show foreground and background color Controls whether the color area on the left (3) appears in the Toolbox.

Show active brush, pattern, and gradient Controls whether the area in the center (4), with the brush, pattern, and gradient icons, appears in the Toolbox.

Show active image Controls whether a preview of the currently active image appears on the right (5).

13.5.2.9 Image Windows

Figure 13.60: General Image Window Preference

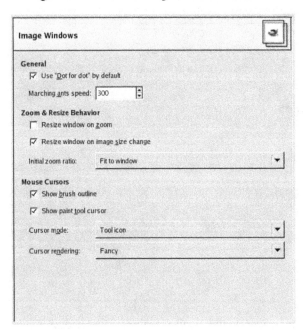

This page lets you customize several aspects of the behaviour of image windows.

13.5.2.9.1 Options

GENERAL

Use "Dot for dot" by default Using "Dot for dot" means that at 1:1 zoom, each pixel is the image is scaled to one pixel on the display. If "Dot for dot" is not used, then the displayed image size is determined by the X and Y resolution of the image. See the Scale Image section for more information.

Marching ants speed When you create a selection, the edge of it is shown as a dashed line with dashes that appear to move, marching slowly along the boundary: they are jokingly called "marching ants". The smaller the value entered here, the faster the ants march (and consequently the more distracting they are!).

ZOOM AND RESIZE BEHAVIOR

Resize window on zoom If this option is checked, then each time you zoom the image, the image window will automatically resize to follow it. Otherwise, the image window will maintain the same size when you zoom the image.

Resize window on image size change If this option is checked, then each time change the size of the image, by cropping or resizing it, the image window will automatically resize to follow. Otherwise, the image window will maintain the same size.

Initial zoom ratio You can choose either to have images, when they are first opened, scaled so that the whole image fits comfortably on your display, or else shown at 1:1 zoom. If you choose the second option, and the image is too large to fit on your display, then the image window will show only part of it (but you will be able to scroll to other parts).

MOUSE CURSORS

Show brush outline If this option is checked, then when you use a paint tool, the outline of the brush will be shown on the image as you move the pointer around. On slow systems, if the brush is very large, this could occasionally cause some lag in GIMP's ability to follow your movements: if so, switching this off might help. Otherwise, you will probably find it quite useful.

Show paint tool cursor If this is checked, a cursor will be shown. This is in addition to the brush outline, if the brush outline is being shown. The type of cursor is determined by the next option.

Cursor mode This option has no effect unless Show paint tool cursor is checked. If it is, you have three choices: Tool icon, which causes a small iconic representation of the currently active tool to be shown beside the cursor; Tool icon with crosshair, which shows the icon as well as a crosshair indicating the center of the cursor; or Crosshair only.

Cursor rendering If you choose 'Fancy' here, the cursor is drawn in grayscale. If you choose 'Black and White', it is drawn in a simpler way that may speed things up a little bit if you have speed issues.

13.5.2.10   Image Window Appearance

Figure 13.61: Image Window Appearance Defaults

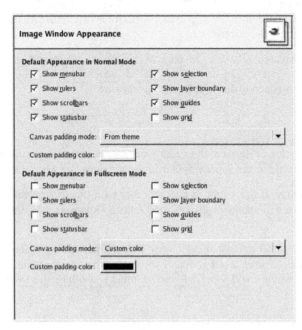

This page lets you customize the default appearance of image windows, for normal mode and for fullscreen mode. All of the settings here can be altered on an image-specific basis using entries in the View menu. See the Image Window section for information on the meaning of the entries.

The only parts that may need further explanation are the ones related to padding. 'Padding' is the color shown around the edges of the image, if it does not occupy all of the display area (shown in light gray in all the figures here). You can choose among four colors for the padding color: to use the color specified by the current theme; to use the light or dark colors specified for checks, such as represent transparent parts of the image; or to use a custom color, which can be set using the color button for 'Custom padding color'.

13.5.2.11 Image Window Title and Statusbar

Figure 13.62: Image Window Title and Statusbar formats

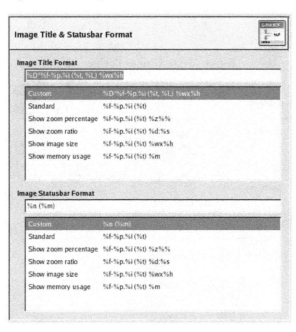

This page lets you customize the text that appears in two places: the title bar of an image, and the status bar. The title bar should appear above the image; however this depends on cooperation from the window manager, so it is not guaranteed to work in all cases. The statusbar appears underneath the image, on the right side. See the Image Window section for more information.

13.5.2.11.1 Choosing a Format

You can choose among several predesigned formats, or you can create one of your own, by writing a *format string* in the entry area. Here is how to understand a format string: anything you type is shown exactly as you type it, with the exception of *variables*, whose names all begin with "%". Here is a list of the variables you can use:

Variable: %f, *Meaning:* Bare filename of the image, or "Untitled"
Variable: %F, *Meaning:* Full path to file, or "Untitled"
Variable: %p, *Meaning:* Image id number (this is unique)
Variable: %i, *Meaning:* View number, if an image has more than one display
Variable: %t, *Meaning:* Image type (RGB, grayscale, indexed)
Variable: %z, *Meaning:* Zoom factor as a percentage
Variable: %s, *Meaning:* Source scale factor (zoom level = %d/%s)
Variable: %d, *Meaning:* Destination scale factor (zoom level = %d/%s)
Variable: %Dx, *Meaning:* Expands to x if the image is dirty, nothing otherwise
Variable: %Cx, *Meaning:* Expands to x if the image is clean, nothing otherwise
Variable: %l, *Meaning:* The number of layers
Variable: %L, *Meaning:* Number of layers (long form)
Variable: %m, *Meaning:* Memory used by the image
Variable: %n, *Meaning:* Name of the active layer/channel
Variable: %P, *Meaning:* id of the active layer/channel
Variable: %w, *Meaning:* Image width in pixels
Variable: %W, *Meaning:* Image width in real-world units
Variable: %h, *Meaning:* Image height in pixels
Variable: %H, *Meaning:* Image height in real-world units

Variable: %u, *Meaning:* Unit symbol (eg. px for Pixel)
Variable: %U, *Meaning:* Unit abbreviation
Variable: %%, *Meaning:* A literal "%" symbol

13.5.2.12 Display

Figure 13.63: Display Preferences

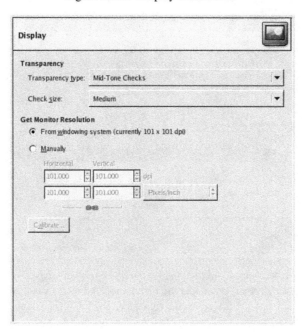

This page lets you customize the way transparent parts of an image are represented, and lets you recalibrate the resolution of your monitor.

13.5.2.12.1 Options

TRANSPARENCY

Transparency type By default, GIMP indicates transparency using a checkerboard pattern with mid-tone checks, but you can change this if you want, either to a different type of checkerboard, or to solid black, white, or gray.

Check size Here you can alter the size of the squares in the checkerboard pattern used to indicate transparency.

Figure 13.64: The Calibration dialog

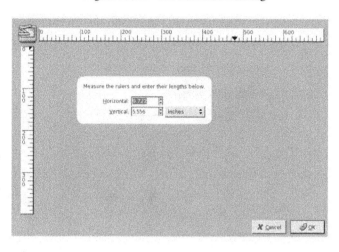

Monitor Resolution Monitor Resolution is the ratio of pixels, horizontally and vertically, to inches. You have three ways to proceed here:

- Get Resolution from windowing system. (easiest, probably inaccurate).
- Set Manually
- Push the Calibrate Button.

The Calibrate Dialog My monitor was impressively off when I tried the Calibrate Dialog. The "Calibrate Game" is fun to play. You will need a soft ruler.

13.5.2.13 Input Devices

Figure 13.65: Input devices preferences

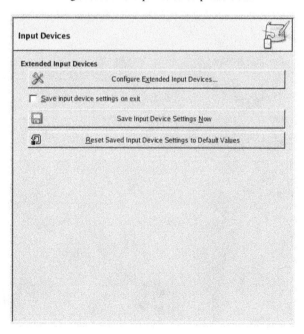

EXTENDED INPUT DEVICES

Configure Extended Input Devices This large button allows you to set the devices associated with your computer: tablet, MIDI keyboard... If you have a tablet, you will see a dialog like this:

Figure 13.66: Preferences for a tablet

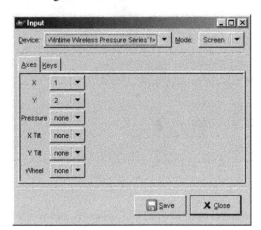

Save input device settings on exit When you check this box, GIMP remembers the tool, color, pattern and brush you were using the last time you quitted.

Save input device settings now Self explanatory.

Reset saved input device settings to default values Delete your settings and restore default settings.

13.5.2.14 Input Controllers

Figure 13.67: Input controllers preferences

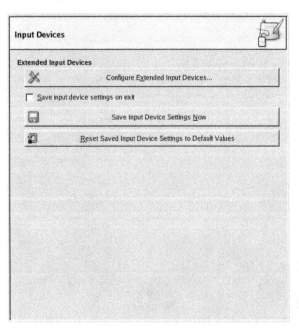

This dialog has two tabs that allow you to assign actions to the mouse wheel and to keyboard keys:

MAIN MOUSE WHEEL

General

- **Dump events from this controller**: this option must be checked if you want a print on the stdout of the events generated by the enabled controllers. If you want to see those event you should start GIMP from a terminal or making it to print the stdout to file by the shell redirection. The main use of this option is for debug.
- **Enable this controller**: this option must be checked if you want to add a new actions to the mouse wheel.

Mouse Wheel Events In this window with scroll bars you have: on the left, the possible events concerning the mouse wheel, more or less associated with control keys; on the right, the action assigned to the event when it will happen. You have also two buttons, one to Edit the selected event, the other to Cancel the action of the selected event.

Some actions are assigned to events yet. They seem to be examples, as they are not functional.

Select the action allocated to the event Afer selecting an event, if you click on the Edit button, you open the following dialog:

Figure 13.68: Select Controller Event Action

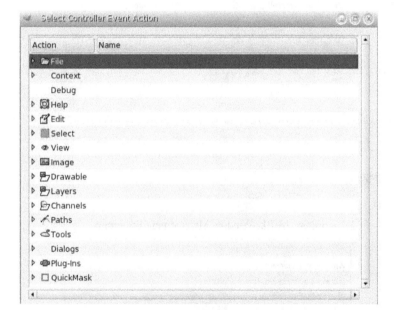

If an action exists yet for this event, the window will open on this action. Else, the window will display the sections that order actions. Click on an action to select it.

MAIN KEYBOARD

You can use this dialog in the same way as that of the mouse wheel. Events are related to the arrow keys of the keyboard, combined or not with control keys.

Figure 13.69: Main Keyboard

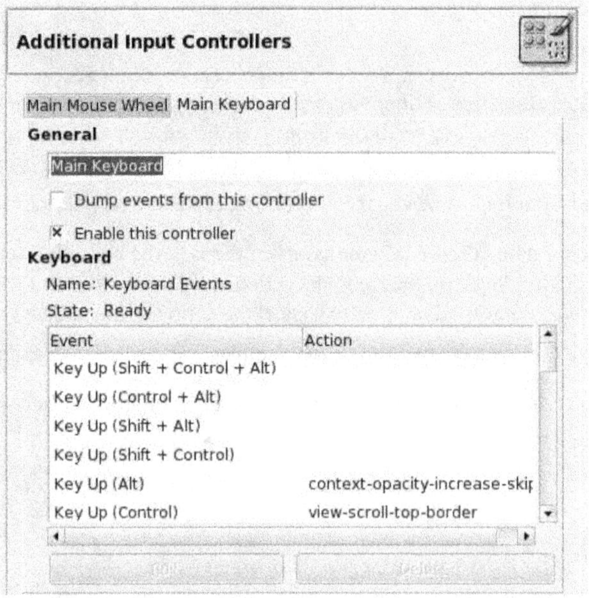

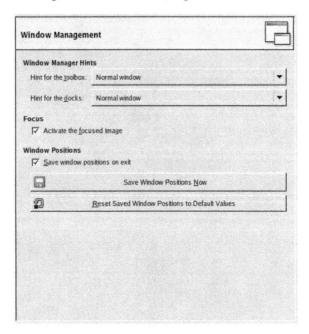

Note

You will find an example of these notions in Creating a variable size brush.

13.5.2.15 Window Managment

Figure 13.70: Window Management Preferences

This page lets you customize the way windows are handled in GIMP. You should note that GIMP does not manipulate windows directly, instead it sends requests to the window manager (i. e., to Windows if you are running in Windows; to Metacity if you are running in a standard Gnome setup in Linux; etc). Because there are many window managers, and not all of them are well behaved, it cannot be guaranteed that the functions described here will actually work as described. However, if you are using a modern, standards-compliant window manager, they ought to.

13.5.2.15.1 Options

WINDOW MANAGER HINTS

Window type hints for the toolbox and the docks The choices you make here determine how the Toolbox, and the docks that hold dialogs, will be treated. If you choose "Normal Window", they will be treated like any other windows. If you choose "Utility Window", they will be raised into visibility whenever you activate an image window, and kept in front of every image window. If you choose "Keep above", they will be kept in front of every other window at all times. Note that changes you make here will not take effect until the next time you start GIMP.

FOCUS

Activate the focused image Normally, when you focus an image window (usually indicated by a change in the color of the frame), it becomes the "active image" for GIMP, and therefore the target for any image-related actions you perform. Some people, though, prefer to set up their window managers such that any window entered by the pointer is automatically focused. If you do this, you may find that it is inconvenient for focused images to automatically become active, and may be happier if you uncheck this option.

WINDOW POSITIONS

Save window positions on exit If this option is checked, the next time you start GIMP, you will see the same set of dialog windows, in the same positions they occupied when you last exited.

Save Window Positions Now This button is only useful if "Save window positions on exit" is unchecked. It allows you to set up your windows they way you like, click the button, and then have them come up in that arrangement each time you start GIMP.

Reset Saved Window Positions to Default Values If you decide that you are unhappy with the arrangement of windows you have saved, and would rather go back to the default arrangement than spend time moving them around, you can do so by pressing this button.

13.5.2.16   Environment

Figure 13.71: Environment Preferences

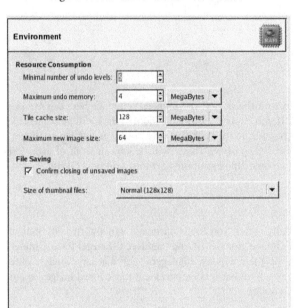

This page lets you customize the amount of system memory allocated for various purposes. It also allows you to disable the confirmation dialogs that appear when you close unsaved images, and to set the size of thumbnail files that GIMP produces.

13.5.2.16.1   Options

RESOURCE CONSUMPTION

Minimal number of undo levels GIMP allows you to undo most actions by maintaining an 'Undo History' for each image, for which a certain amount of memory is allocated. Regardless of memory usage, however, GIMP always permits some minimal number of the most recent actions to be undone: this is the number specified here. See Section 3.3 for more information about GIMP's Undo mechanism.

Maximum undo memory This is the amount of undo memory allocated for each image. If the Undo History size exceeds this, the oldest points are deleted, unless this would result in fewer points being present than the minimal number specified above.

Tile cache size This is the amount of system RAM allocated for GIMP image data. If GIMP requires more memory than this, it begins to swap to disk, which may in some circumstances cause a dramatic slowdown. You are given an opportunity to set this number when you install GIMP, but you can alter it here. See How to Set Your Tile Cache for more information.

Maximum new image size This is not a hard contraint: if you try to create a new image larger than the specified size, you are asked to confirm that you really want to do it. This is to prevent you from accidentally creating images much larger than you intend, which can either crash GIMP or cause it to respond verrrrrrrry slowwwwwwwwly.

IMAGE THUMBNAILS

Size of thumbnails This options allows you to set the size of the thumbnails shown in the File Open dialog (and also saved for possible use by other programs). The options are 'None', 'Normal (128x128)', and 'Large (256x256)'.

Maximum filesize for thumbnailing If an image file is larger than the specified maximum size, GIMP will not generate a thumbnail for it. This options allows you to prevent thumbnailing of extremely large image files from slowing GIMP to a crawl.

SAVING IMAGES

Confirm closing of unsaved images Closing an image is not undoable, so by default GIMP asks you to confirm that you really want to do it, whenever it would lead to a loss of unsaved changes. You can disable this if you find it annoying; but then of course you are responsible for remembering what you have and have not saved.

13.5.2.17 Folders

Figure 13.72: Basic Folder Preferences

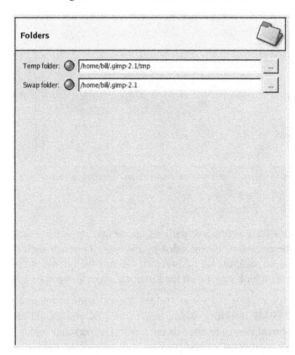

This page allows you to set the locations for two important folders used by GIMP for temporary files. The pages below it allow you to customize the locations searched for resources such as brushes etc.; see Data Folders for a description that applies to them. You can change the folders here by editing the entries, or by pressing the buttons on the right to bring up a file chooser window.

FOLDERS

Temp folder This folder is used for temporary files: files created for temporary storage of working data, and then deleted within the same GIMP session. It does not require a lot of space or high performance. By default, a subdirectory called `tmp` in your personal GIMP directory is used, but if that disk is very cramped for space, or has serious performance issues, you can change it to a different directory. The directory must exist and be writable by you, or bad things will happen.

Swap folder This is the folder used as a "memory bank" when the total size of images and data open in GIMP exceeds the available RAM. If you work with very large images, or images with many layers, or have many images open at once, GIMP can potentially require hundreds of megabytes of swap space, so available disk space and performance are definitely things to think about for this folder. By default, it is set to your personal GIMP directory, but if you have another disk with more free space, or substantially better performance, you may see a significant benefit from moving your swap folder there. The directory must exist and be writable by you.

13.5.2.18   Data Folders

Figure 13.73: Preferences: Brush Folders

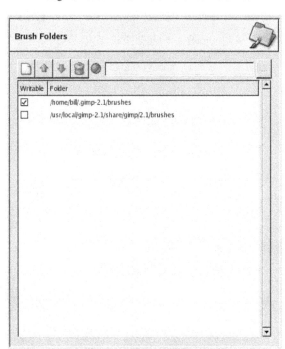

GIMP uses several types of resources – such as brushes, patterns, gradients, etc. – for which a basic set are supplied by GIMP when it is installed, and others can be created or downloaded by the user. For each such resource type, there is a Preference page that allows you to specify the *search path*: the set of directories from which items of the type in question are automatically loaded when GIMP starts. These pages all look very much the same: the page for brushes is shown to the right as an example.

By default, the search path includes two folders: a *system* folder, where items installed along with GIMP are placed, and a *personal* folder, inside your personal GIMP directory, where items added by you should be placed. The system folder should not be marked as writable, and you should not try to alter its contents. The personal folder must be marked as writable or it is useless, because there is nothing inside it except what you put there.

You can customize the search path with the buttons at the top of the dialog.

OPTIONS

Select a Folder If you click on one of the folders in the list, it is selected for whatever action comes next.

Add/Replace Folder If you type the name of a folder in the entry space, or navigate to it using the file chooser button on the right, and then click the left button, this will replace the selected folder with the one you have specified. If nothing in the list is selected, the folder you specify will be added to the list. If the light-symbol to the left of the text entry area is red instead of green, it means that the folder you have specified does not exist. GIMP will not create it for you, so you should do this immediately.

Move Up/Down If you click on the up-arrow or down-arrow buttons, the selected folder will be changed to the following or preceding one in the list. Since the folders are read in order, using those buttons change the loading precedence of the items located in those folders.

Delete Folder If you click the trash-can button, the selected folder will be deleted from the list. (The folder itself is not affected; it is merely removed from the search path.) Deleting the system folder is probably a bad idea, but nothing prevents you from doing it.

13.5.3 Device Status Dialog

Figure 13.74: The device Status Dialog

This window gathers together the current options of Toolbox, for each of your input devices: the mouse (named 'Core pointer') or either the tablet, if you have one. These options are represented by icons: foreground and background colors, brush, pattern and gradient. Excepted for colors, clicking on an icon opens the window which lets you select another option; the tool-box will be updated when changing.

In addition, you can add tabs and other dialog by click-and-drag.

The 'Record device status' button at the bottom of the window, seems to have the same action as the 'Record device status now' option in the Input Devices section in preferences.

13.5.3.1 Activate Dialog

The device status dialog is a dockable dialog; see the section Section 3.2.3 for help on manipulating it. It can be activated in several ways:

- From the Toolbox menu : File → Dialogs → Device Status

- From an image menu : Dialogs → Device Status

- From the Tab menu in any dialog : Add a Dock → Device Status

13.5.4 Error Console

The Error console offers more possibilities than the single 'GIMP Message'. This is a log of all errors occuring while GIMP is running. You can save all this log or only a selected part.

13.5.4.1 Activate Dialog

You can access to this dialog in different ways:

- You will find this command in the toolbox menu bar through File → Dialogs → Error Console,

- But also from the image menu : Dialogs → Device Status.

- Or from the Tab menu in any dialog : Add a dock → Device Status.

13.5.4.2 The 'Error Console' Dialog

Figure 13.75: 'Error Console' Dialog window

Clear errors This button lets you delete all errors in the log.

Warning
You can't 'undo' this action.

Save all errors This button lets you save the whole log. You can also select a part of the log (by click-and-dragging the mouse pointer or by using the Shift-Arrow keys key combination) and save only this selected part by pressing the **Shift** key.

A dialog window Save Error Log to File lets you choose the name and the destination directory of this file:

Figure 13.76: 'Save Error Log to file' Dialog window

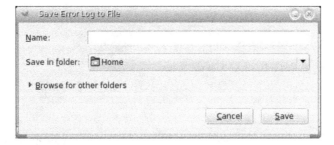

Tip
You will as well find these button actions in the dialog sub-menu by clicking on [◀] .

13.5.5 Export File

The 'Export file' is opened when you try to save a file in a format which does not support several layers or transparency.

THE FILE FORMAT DOES NOT SUPPORT ANIMATION

Portable Network Graphics (PNG)

Figure 13.77: Export PNG File Dialog

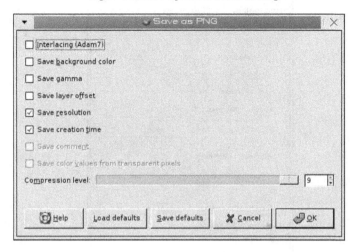

The PNG format, a lossless format, supports transparency but doesn't support animation. So, you only can Flatten image, i.e merge layers into a single one, according to the mode you have selected for the image.

JPEG File Interchange Format (JFIF, JPEG)

Figure 13.78: Export JPG File Dialog

The JPEG format, a compression format with loss, doesn't support animation nor transparency. The file will be flattened and transparency will be replaced with the background color of Toolbox.

THE FILE FORMAT SUPPORTS ANIMATION

Multiple-Image Network Graphics (MNG)

Figure 13.79: Export MNG File Dialog Diálogo exportar como MNG

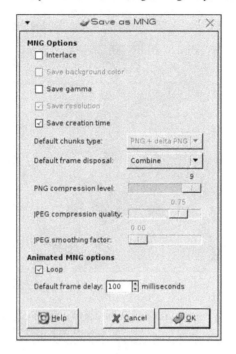

The MNG format, an animation format, supports 256 transparency levels, which, unfortunately, are not recognized by Internet Explorer 6. The dialog offers two options. Select Save as animation. The other option, Flatten Image has no sense here. and, for that matter, an image which is saved so is not recognized by GIMP.

Graphics Interchange Format (GIF)

Figure 13.80: Export GIF File Dialog

The GIF format, less sophisticated than the MNG format, supports 256 colors and 2 transparency levels only. But it will keep on being used as long as Internet Explorer doesn't support 256 transparency levels.

The dialog offers you either Flatten Image or Save as animation. See Save as GIF in Glossary.

If you have not transformed your image into a 256 colors indexed image before, this dialog will ask you choose between Convert to grayscale and Convert to indexed using default settings. Be careful: an indexed image ungoes a severe loss of colors and the added palette can give it a size bigger and a quality less than if it was saved as JPEG.

Chapter 14

Menus

14.1 Introduction to Menus

Figure 14.1: The Toolbox Menu

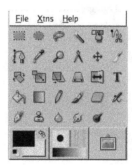

There are many places in GIMP where you can find menus. The aim of this chapter is to explain all the commands that are accessible from the menus in the Toolbox and Image windows. All the context menus and the menu entries for the other dialogs are described elsewhere in the chapters that describe the dialogs themselves.

14.1.1 Context Menus

If you right-click on certain parts of the GIMP interface, a 'context menu' opens, which leads to a variety of functions. Some places where you can access context menus are:

- Clicking on an image window displays the Image menu. This is useful when you are working in full-screen mode, without a menubar.

- Clicking on a layer in the Layers Dialog or on a channel in the Channels Dialog displays functions for the selected layer or channel.

- Right-clicking on the image menubar has the same effect as left-clicking.

- Right-clicking on the title bar displays functions which do not belong to GIMP, but to the window manager program on your computer.

14.1.2 Detachable Submenus

There is an interesting property associated with some of the menus in GIMP. These are any of the menus from the Toolbox menubar and any of their submenus, as well as the Image context menu you get by right-clicking on the image window and any of its submenus. (You can tell that a menu item leads to a submenu because there is an ▶ icon next to it.) When you bring up any of these menus, there is a dotted line at the top of it (tear-off line). By clicking on this dotted line, you detach the menu under it and it becomes a separate window.

Figure 14.2: The 'Acquire' submenu and its detached submenu

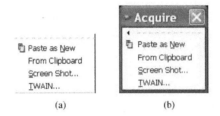

Detached submenus originating from the Toolbox are only visible when the Toolbox is active. Detached submenus originating from the Image window are actually independent. They are always visible, their functions always apply to the current image, and they persist when all of the images are closed. You can close a detached submenu by clicking on the dotted line again or closing the window from the window manager on your computer (often by clicking on an X icon in the upper right corner of the window).

14.2 Toolbox File Menu

14.2.1 The 'File' Menu of the Toolbox

Figure 14.3: Contents of the 'File' menu

The Toolbox is the heart of the GIMP. It contains the most commonly used controls, and the highest-level menus. Two of the menus, File and Help, can also be accessed from the menubars located above each image display, although their contents are somewhat different. The Toolbox is the only place to access the Xtns (Extensions) menu.

- Section 14.5.2

- Section 14.5.3

- Section 14.5.4

- Section 14.5.5

- Section 14.2.2

- Section 14.5.14

 Note
Besides the commands described here, you may also find other entries in the menu. They are not part of GIMP itself, but have been added by extensions (plug-ins). You can find information about the functionality of a Plugin by referring to its documentation.

14.2.2 Acquire

Figure 14.4: The 'Acquire' submenu of the Toolbox File menu

The Acquire submenu of the Toolbox's File menu contains a list of ways you can import images into the GIMP. This allows you to import images from sources other than a disk or the network, such a screen capture or an image from a scanner.

14.2.2.1 Activating the Submenu

- You can access this submenu from the Toolbox menubar through File → Acquire

14.2.2.2 Submenu entries

Paste as new The Paste As New command is the same as the Paste as New command of the Edit menu. Both of them open a new image and paste the contents of the clipboard in it.

 Tip
The **Print Screen** key captures the screen and puts it in the clipboard. By doing this, you can capture submenus that would otherwise disappear as soon as you click on the screen.

Screen Shot

Figure 14.5: The 'Screen Shot' window

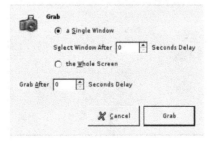

The Screen Shot command opens a dialog which has four options for grabbing the object:

Single Window a Single Window: You can select the window you want to capture.

Select Window After ... Seconds Delay Select Window After ... Seconds Delay: If you enter 0 seconds in the text box, the window is captured as soon as you click on it. If you enter a delay, you have time to modify the window before it is captured.

Whole Screen the Whole Screen: The entire screen is captured.

Grab After ... Seconds Delay Grab After ... Seconds Delay: If you enter 0 seconds in the text box, the screen is captured as soon as you click on the Grab button. If you enter a delay, you have time to modify the screen before it is captured.

Note
Before you begin the capture, make sure that the window you want to capture is not partially obscured by another one.

Image capture devices

Figure 14.6: Scanner and Webcam

The kinds of devices used to take pictures are too varied to be described here. Fortunately, their use is fairly intuitive. In the example shown, you can start a scanner or take an image with a webcam.

14.2.3 The Preferences Command

The File Preferences command displays the Preferences dialog, which lets you alter a variety of settings that affect the look, feel, and performance of the GIMP.

14.2.3.1 Activating the Command

• You can access this command in the Toolbox menu bar through File → Preferences

14.2.4 The Dialogs Sub-Menu

Figure 14.7: The Dialogs submenu of the Toolbox File menu

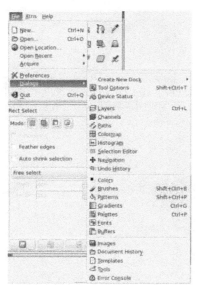

The Dialogs submenu of the Toolbox's File menu contains a list of available dialogs that you can use while you are editing an image -- patterns, palettes, brushes, etc. You can open and close dialogs as needed, or, if you want them to stay around, you can dock them. Dialogs are described in detail in Chapter 13

14.2.4.1 Accessing the Dialogs Submenu

• You can access this submenu in the Toolbox through: File → Dialogs

14.3 The 'Xtns' Menu

14.3.1 Introduction to the 'Xtns' Menu

Figure 14.8: Contents of the 'Xtns' menu

The Xtns menu gets its somewhat cryptic name from the term, 'Extensions'. Accordingly, you will find various commands for managing extensions (also known as 'plug-ins') and for accessing scripts here.

Note

Besides the commands described here, you may also find other entries in the menu. They are not part of GIMP itself, but have been added by extensions (plug-ins). You can find information about the functionality of a Plugin by referring to its documentation.

14.3.2 The Module Manager

With the Module Manager command, you can show the various extension modules which are available and control which of them should be loaded. Modules perform functions such as choosing colors and display filtering. Any changes you make to the settings with the Module Manager command will take effect the next time you start GIMP. These changes affect GIMP's functional capabilities, its size in memory and its startup time.

14.3.2.1 Activating the Command

• You can access this command from the toolbox menubar through Xtns → Module Manager

14.3.2.2 Description of the 'Module Manager' Dialog

Figure 14.9: The 'Module Manager' dialog window

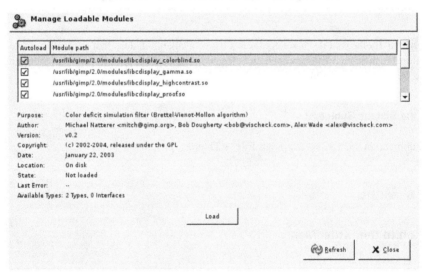

The scrolled window of the Module Manager shows the loadable modules. You can click on the boxes in the Autoload column to check or uncheck them. The directory path for each module is shown in the Module path column. Information about the selected module is displayed at the bottom of the dialog.

14.3.3 The Unit Editor

The Unit Editor command displays a dialog which shows information about the units of measurement that are currently being used by GIMP. It also allows you to create new units which can be used by GIMP in a variety of situations.

14.3.3.1 Activating the Command

• You can access this command from the toolbox menubar through Xtns → Unit Editor.

14.3.3.2 Description of the 'Unit Editor' dialog window

Figure 14.10: The 'Unit Editor' dialog window

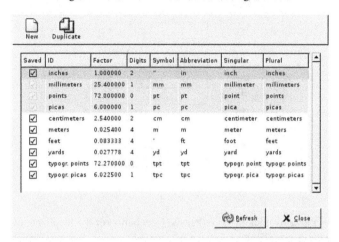

The figure above shows the 'Unit Editor' dialog window. The list shows the units of measurement which are currently defined. You can click on the New button or the Duplicate button to create a new measurement unit, as described below.

DESCRIPTION OF THE LIST ELEMENTS

- *Saved*: If this column is checked, a unit definition will be saved when GIMP exits. Some units are always kept, even if they are not marked with a check. These are highlighted in the list.

- *ID*: The string GIMP uses to identify the unit in its configuration files.

- *Factor*: How many units make up an inch.

- *Digits*: This field is a hint for numerical input fields. It specifies how many decimal digits the input field should provide to get approximately the same accuracy as an 'inch' input field with two decimal digits.

- *Symbol*: The unit's symbol if it has one (e.g. " for inches). The unit's abbreviation is used if doesn't have a symbol.

- *Abbreviation*: The unit's abbreviation (e.g. 'cm' for centimeters).

- *Singular*: The unit's singular form, which GIMP can use to display messages about the unit.

- *Plural*: The unit's plural form, which GIMP can use to display messages about the unit.

14.3.3.3 Defining New Units

Figure 14.11: The 'New Unit' dialog

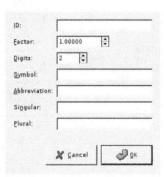

You can display the dialog shown above by clicking on either the New button or the Duplicate button on the Unit Editor dialog. The input fields on the dialog are described above.

If you click on the New button, the dialog looks as shown. If you click on the Duplicate button, the values initially displayed in the input fields of the dialog are the values of the unit you have currently selected in the Unit Editor dialog. You can then edit the values to create your new unit.

14.3.4 Plug-In Browser

The Plug-In Browser command displays a dialog window which shows all of the extensions (plug-ins) which are currently loaded in GIMP, both as a list and as a hierarchical tree structure. Since many of the filters are actually plug-ins, you will certainly see many familiar names here. Please note that you do not run the extensions from this dialog window. Use the appropriate menu entry to do that instead. For example, you can run filter plug-ins by using the Filter command on the image menubar.

14.3.4.1 Activating the Command

- You can access this command from the toolbox menubar through Xtns → Plug-in Browser

14.3.4.2 Description of the 'Plug-In Browser' dialog window

Figure 14.12: The list view of the 'Plug-In Browser' dialog window

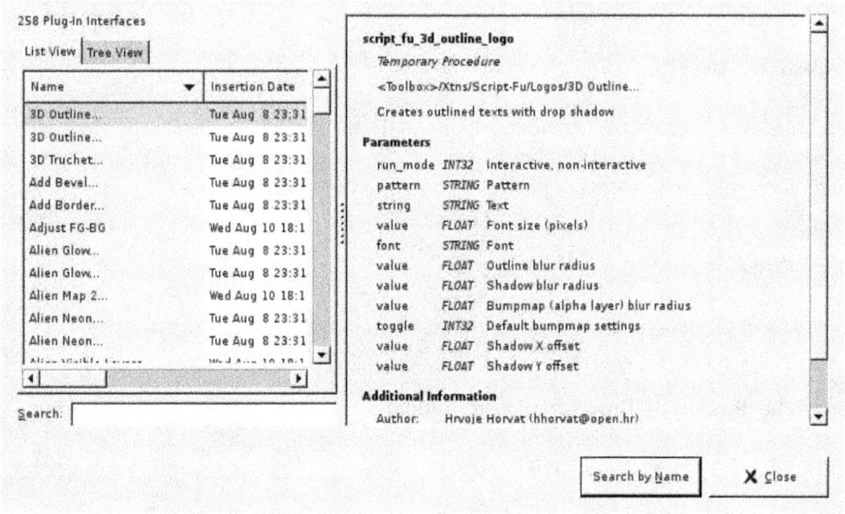

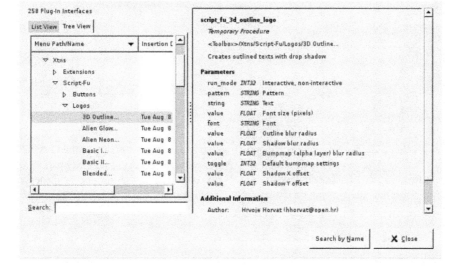

The figure above shows the list view of the Plug-In Browser. You can click on the name of a plug-in in the scrolled window to display more information about it. Select the List View by clicking on the tab at the top of the dialog.

You can search for a plug-in by name by entering part or all of the name in the Search: text box and clicking on the Search by Name button. The left part of the dialog then displays the matches found.

Figure 14.13: The tree view of the 'Plug-In Browser' dialog window

The figure above shows the tree view of the Plug-In Browser. You can click on the name of a plug-in in the scrolled window to display more information about it. You can click on the arrowheads to expand or contract parts of the tree. Select the Tree View by clicking on the tab at the top of the dialog.

You can search for a plug-in by name by entering part or all of the name in the Search: text box and clicking on the Search by Name button. The left part of the dialog then displays the matches found.

Note

Not everything in these huge dialog windows is visible at the same time. Use the scroll bars to view their content.

14.3.5 The Procedure Browser

The Procedure Browser command displays the procedures in the PDB, the Procedure Database. These procedures are functions which are called by the scripts or plug-ins. You can find a more detailed description of the PDB in the glossary. The browser is most useful for advanced users who write scripts or plug-ins.

14.3.5.1 Activating the Command

• You can access this command from the toolbox menubar through Xtns → Procedure Browser

14.3.5.2 Description of the 'Procedure Browser' dialog window

Figure 14.14: The 'Procedure Browser' dialog window

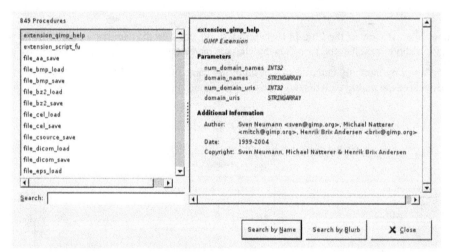

The figure above shows the Procedure Browser dialog window. If you click on an item in the scrolled list on the left, information about it is displayed on the right. You can also search for a specific procedure by name by entering part or all of the name of the procedure in the Search: text box and clicking on the Search by Name button, or search for one by its description by entering a search string in the Search: text box and clicking on the Search by Blurb button.

14.3.6   The 'Script-Fu' Submenu

Figure 14.15: The 'Script-Fu' submenu of the Xtns menu

The Script-Fu command displays a submenu which contains a large number of Script-Fu scripts and options, including the Script-Fu console. Script-Fu is a language for writing scripts, which allow you to run a series of GIMP commands automatically. These scripts create a new image : they are stand-alone scripts.

14.3.6.1   Activating the submenu

• You can access this command from the toolbox menubar through Xtns → Script-Fu

14.4   The 'Help' Menu

14.4.1   Introduction to the 'Help' Menu

Figure 14.16: Contents of the 'Help' menu

The Help menu contains commands that assist you while you are working with The GIMP.

Note

Besides the commands described here, you may also find other entries in the menu. They are not part of GIMP itself, but have been added by extensions (plug-ins). You can find information about the functionality of a Plugin by referring to its documentation.

14.4.2   Help

The Help command displays the GIMP Users Manual in a browser. You can set the browser you would like to use in the Help System section of the Preferences dialog, as described in Section 13.5.2.6. The browser may be the built-in GIMP help browser, or it may be a web browser.

 Tip

If the help does not seem to work, please verify that the 'GIMP Users Manual' is installed on your system. You can find the most recent help online [GIMP-DOCS].

14.4.2.1 Activating the Command

- You can access this command from the toolbox menubar through Help → Help,

- or by using the keyboard shortcut **F1**.

14.4.3 Context Help

The Context Help command makes the mouse pointer context-sensitive and changes its shape to a '?'. You can then click on a window, dialog or menu entry and GIMP displays help about it, if it is available. You can also access context help at any time by pressing the **F1** key while the mouse pointer is over the object you would like help about.

14.4.3.1 Activating the Command

- You can access this command from the toolbox menu through Help → Context Help

- or by using the keyboard shortcut Shift-F1.

14.4.4 Tip of the Day

The Tip of the Day command displays the Tip of the Day dialog. This dialog contains useful tips to help you gain a better understanding of some of the subtle points of using GIMP. New users will find it very valuable to pay attention to these, because they often suggest ways of doing something that are much easier or more efficient than more obvious approaches.

14.4.4.1 Activating the Command

- You can access this command in the toolbox menu through Help → Tip of the day

14.4.4.2 Description of the dialog window

Figure 14.17: 'Tip of the day' Dialog window

A new tip is displayed each time you start GIMP. You can disable this by un-checking the Show tip next time GIMP starts box on the dialog.

14.4.5 About

The About command shows the About window, which displays information about the version of The GIMP you are running and the many authors who wrote it.

14.4.5.1 Activating the About Command

- You can access this command in the toolbox menu through Help → About

14.4.5.2 Description of the dialog window

Figure 14.18: The 'About' dialog window

14.4.6 GIMP online

Figure 14.19: The 'GIMP online' submenu of the Help menu

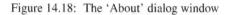

The GIMP online command displays a submenu which lists several helpful web sites that have to do with various aspects of GIMP. You can click on one of the menu items and your web browser will try to connect to the URL.

14.5 The 'File' Menu

14.5.1 File menu

Figure 14.20: The File menu of the image window

Figure 14.21: The File menu of the Toolbox

There is a File menu on both the Toolbox window and the image window. Only some of the menu items in these two menus are the same.

Note
Besides the commands described here, you may also find other entries in the menu. They are not part of GIMP itself, but have been added by extensions (plug-ins). You can find information about the functionality of a Plugin by referring to its documentation.

14.5.2 New

Using the New Image dialog, you can create a new empty image and set its properties. The image is shown in a new image window. You may have more than one image on your screen at the same time.

14.5.2.1 Activating the Command

- You can access the command from either the Toolbox menubar or the Image menubar through: File → New,

- or by using the keyboard shortcut Ctrl-N.

14.5.2.2 Basic Options

Figure 14.22: The 'New Image' dialog

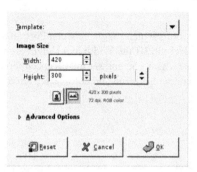

Template

Figure 14.23: The 'Create a New Image' dialog

Rather than entering all the values by hand, you can select some predefined values for your image from a menu of templates, which represent image types that are somewhat commonly useful. The templates set values for the size, resolution, comments, etc. If there is a particular image shape that you you use often and it does not appear on the list, you can create a new template, using the Templates dialog.

Image Size Here you set the Width and Height of the new image. The default units are pixels, but you can choose a different unit if you prefer, using the adjoining menu. If you do, note that the resulting pixel size is determined by the X and Y resolution (which you can change in the Advanced Options), and by setting 'Dot for Dot' in the View menu.

When you open a new image from the File menu of the Toolbox, it is created with the size defined in Preferences. If you open it from the File menu of an existing image, the size of the new image is the same as the size of the existing image.

Note
Keep in mind that every pixel of an image is stored in memory. If you create large files with a high pixel density, GIMP will need a lot of time and memory for every function you apply to the image.

Portrait/Landscape buttons There are two buttons which toggle between Portrait and Landscape mode. What they actually do is to exchange the values for Width and Height. (If the Width and Height are the same, these buttons are not activated.) If the X and Y resolutions are not the same (which you can set in Advanced Options), then these values are also exchanged. On the right of the dialog, image size, screen resolution and color space are displayed.

14.5.2.3 Advanced Options

Figure 14.24: New Image dialog (Advanced Options)

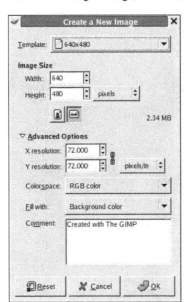

The Advanced Options are mostly of interest to more advanced GIMP users. You can display these options by clicking on the small triangle on the lower edge of the dialog window.

X and Y resolution The values in the X resolution and Y resolution fields relate mainly to printing: they do not affect the size of the image in pixels, but they may determine its physical size when it is printed. The X and Y resolution values can determine how pixels are translated into other measurement units, such as millimeters or inches.

Tip
If you want to display the image on the screen at the correct dimensions, select View → Dot for Dot Set the zoom factor to 100% to see the image at its true screen size. The calibration of the screen size is normally done when GIMP is installed, but if the image does not display at the correct size, you may have to adjust the screen parameters in the GIMP. You can do this in the Preferences dialog.

Colorspace

Figure 14.25: Colorspace menu

You can create the new image as either an RGB image or a grayscale image.

RGB color: The image is created in the Red, Green, Blue color system, which is the one used by your monitor or your television screen.

Grayscale: The image is created in black and white, with various shades of gray. Aside from your artistic interests, this type of image may be necessary for some plug-ins. Nevertheless, the GIMP allows you to change an RGB image into grayscale, if you would like.

You cannot create an indexed image directly with this menu, but of course you can always convert the image to indexed mode after it has been created. To do that, use the Image → Mode → Iindexed command.

Fill

Figure 14.26: Fill menu

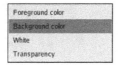

Here, you specify the background color that is used for your new image. It is certainly possible to change the background of an image later, too. You can find more information about doing that in the Layer dialog.

- Fill the image with the current Foreground color, shown in the Toolbox.
- Fill the image with the current Background color, shown in the Toolbox.
- Fill the image with White.
- Fill the image with Transparency. If you choose this option, the image is created with an alpha channel and the background is transparent. The transparent parts of the image are then displayed with a checkered pattern, to indicate the transparency.

Comment You can write a descriptive comment here. The text is attached to the image as a 'parasite', and is saved with the image by some file formats (PNG, JPEG, GIF).

 Note
With GIMP-2.2, you can't edit this comment, but you can read it back by using the Info Window.

14.5.3 Open

The Open command activates a dialog that lets you load an existing image from your hard-drive or an external medium. For alternative, and sometimes more convenient, ways of opening files, see the Files section.

14.5.3.1 Activating the Dialog

- You can access the Open dialog from the toolbox window or from an image window through: File → Open.

- You can also open the Dialog by using the keyboard shortcut Ctrl-O.

14.5.3.2 File browsing

Figure 14.27: Open Dialog

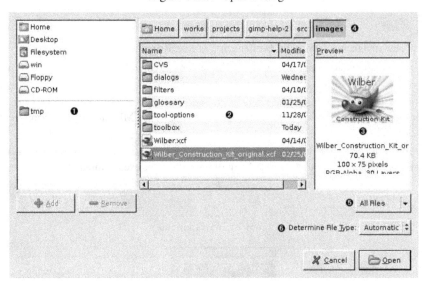

① The left panel is divided into two parts. The upper part lists your main directories and your storage devices; you cannot modify this list. The lower part lists your bookmarks; you can add or remove *bookmarks*. To add a bookmark, select a directory or a file in the middle panel and click on the Add button at the bottom of the left panel. You can also use the Add to bookmarks command in the context menu, which you get by clicking the right mouse button. You can delete a bookmark by selecting it and clicking on the Remove button.

② The middle panel displays a list of the files in the current directory. Change your current directory by double left clicking on a directory in this panel. Select a file with a single left click. You can then open the file you have selected by clicking on the Open button. Note that a double left click opens the file directly; if you have selected a file different from the current one, a message warns you before GIMP overwrites your work.

Right-clicking on the middle panel displays the Open Location dialog that allows you to type a path to a file. You can also open this dialog by typing Ctrl-L.

③ The selected image is displayed in the Preview window if it is an image created by GIMP. File size, resolution and the image's composition are displayed below the preview window.

 Tip

If your image has been modified by another program, click on the Preview window to update it.

---

④ The path of the current directory is displayed above the middle panel. You can navigate along this path by clicking on one of the buttons.

⑤ This button shows All Files by default. This means that all file types will be displayed in the middle panel, even if they are not images. You can *filter* the list for a particular file type.

⑥ The Determine File Type button has a default of Automatic. In most cases you don't need to pay any attention to this, because the GIMP can determine the file type automatically. In a few rare situations, neither the file extension nor internal information in the file are enough to tell GIMP the file type. If this happens, you can set it by selecting it from the list.

14.5.4 Open Location

The Open Location dialog lets you load an image from a network location, specified by a URI, in any of the formats that GIMP supports, or from a path to your hard disk or any drive. The default directory name is /home/<username>/ on Linux and C:\Documents and Settings\<username>\My Documents\My Images\ on Windows, which is used as the base of the relative address. You can also enter an absolute path.

Tip
When you are visiting an Internet site, you can right-click on an image and choose 'Copy link address' in the drop-down menu. Then paste it in the 'Open Location' dialog to open it in GIMP.

14.5.4.1 Activating the Command

- You can access this command from the Toolbox menubar or the image menubar through File → Open Location.

14.5.4.2 Description of the dialog window

Figure 14.28: The 'Open Location' dialog window

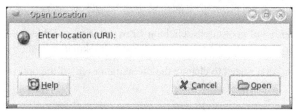

14.5.5 Open Recent

Selecting Open Recent displays a submenu with the names of the files that you have opened recently in GIMP. Simply click on a name to reopen it. You can customize the maximum number of items shown in the menu, by changing the Open Recent Menu Size value in the Interface page of the Preferences dialog. See the Document History dialog at the bottom of the Open Recent submenu, if you cannot find your image.

14.5.5.1 Activating the Command

- You can access this command from the Toolbox menubar or the image menubar through File → Open Recent,

- or by using the keyboard shortcut Ctrl-O.

14.5.6 Open as Layer

The Open Image as layer dialog is identical to the Open Image dialog. With this dialog, you can open an image file, which is added to the current image as the top layer in the stack.

14.5.6.1 Activating the Command

- You can access this command from the image menubar through File → Open as layer,

- or by using the keyboard shortcut Ctrl-Alt-O.

14.5.7 Save

The Save command saves your image to disk. If you have already saved the image, the previous image file is overwritten with the current version. If you have not already saved the image, the Save command does the same thing as the Save As command: GIMP opens the File Save dialog, so that you can choose the data format, the path and the filename of the new image file.

If the image was previously saved, it is automatically saved to the same location, using the same file name, file type, and options. To save it differently in any respect, use either Save As or Save A Copy.

If you quit without having saved your image, GIMP asks you if you really want to do so, if the 'Confirm closing of unsaved images' option is checked in the Environment page of the Preferences dialog.

14.5.7.1 Activating the Dialog

- You can access this command in the image menu bar through File → Save,

- or from the keyboard by using the shortcut Ctrl-S.

14.5.8 Save as

The Save as command displays the 'File Save' dialog. In its basic form, as shown below, this gives you a text box to assign a name to the file, and a drop-down list of bookmarks to select a directory to save it in. Normally the file format is determined by the extension you use in the file name (i.e., .jpg for a JPEG file). You can use the Select File Type option expander to pick a different file type, but you should avoid doing this unless absolutely necessary, to avoid confusion.

If the directory you want is not in the list of bookmarks, click on Browse for other folders to expand the dialog to its full form. You can find an explanation of the layout, and help on creating and using bookmarks, in the Files section.

If you saved the image previously and don't need to change the file name or any of the options, you can use the Save command instead.

14.5.8.1 Activating the Command

- You can access this command from the image menubar through File → Save as,

- or by using the keyboard shortcut Shift-Ctrl-S.

14.5.8.2 The Basic 'Save as' Dialog

There are two different forms of the Save as dialog. The simple form only lets you type in the filename and choose the directory the file should be saved in. If the folder you want is not on the list, you can type in the path to the directory, along with the filename. You can also click on the small triangle to display the full folder browser. You can also choose the image format, by selecting the file extension (e.g., .xcf or .png).

Figure 14.29: The basic 'File Save' dialog

14.5.8.3 The 'Save' Dialog with a Browser

Figure 14.30: The 'Save' Dialog (Browser)

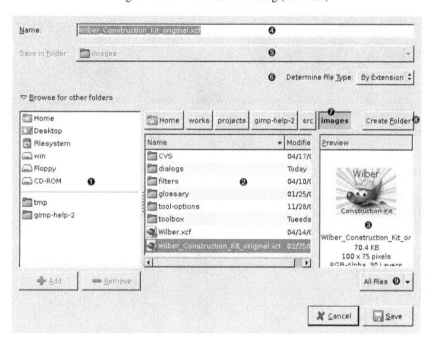

① The left panel is divided into two parts. The upper part lists your main directories and your storage devices; you cannot modify this list. The lower part lists your bookmarks; you can add or remove *bookmarks*. To add a bookmark, select a directory or a file in the middle panel and click on the Add button at the bottom of the left panel. You can also use the Add to bookmarks command in the context menu, which you get by clicking the right mouse button. You can delete a bookmark by selecting it and clicking on the Remove button.

② The middle panel displays a list of the files in the current directory. Change your current directory by double left-clicking on a directory in this panel. Select a file with a single left click. You can then save to the file you have selected by clicking on the Save button. Note that a double left click saves the file directly.

You can right click on the middle panel to access the *Show Hidden Files* command.

You can right click on the middle panel to access the *Show Hidden Files* command.

③ The selected image is displayed in the Preview window if it is an image created by GIMP. File size, resolution and the image's composition are displayed below the preview window.

If your image has been modified by another program, click on the preview to update it.

④ Enter the filename of the new image file here.

 Note
If the image has already been saved, GIMP suggests the same filename to you. If you click on *Save*, the file is overwritten.

---

⑤ This drop-down list is only available in the basic form of the dialog. It provides a list of bookmarks for selecting a directory in which to save your file.

⑥ Above the middle panel, the path of the current directory is displayed. You can navigate along this path by clicking on one of the buttons.

- If you want to save the image into a folder that doesn't yet exist, you can create it by clicking on Create Folder and following the instructions.

- This button shows All Files by default. This means that all file types will be displayed in the middle panel, even if they are not images. You can *filter* the list for a particular file type.

- At Determine File Type, you have to select the file format for saving the file. If you select By Extension, the file type is determined by the extension you add to the name, for example, '.jpg' for JPEG format.

 Note

To preserve all the components of your image when you save it — the layers, channels, etc. — use ".xcf" format, which is the GIMP's native format.

14.5.9 Save a Copy

The Save a Copy command does the same thing as the Save command, but with one important difference. It always asks for a file name and saves the image into the specified file, but it does not change the name of the active image or mark it as 'clean'. As a result, if you try to delete the image, or exit from GIMP, you are informed that the image is 'dirty' and given an opportunity to save it.

This command is useful when you want to save a copy of your image in its current state, but continue to work with the original file without interruption.

14.5.9.1 Activating the Command

- You can access this command from the image menubar through File → Save a Copy. There is no default keyboard shortcut.

14.5.10 Save as Template

The Save as Template command creates a template with the same dimensions and color space as the current image. A dialog pops up, which asks you to name the new template, then the template is saved and becomes available in the New Image dialog. If you give a name that already exists, GIMP generates a unique name by appending a number to it. You can use the Templates dialog to modify or delete templates.

14.5.10.1 Activating the Command

- You can access this command from the image menubar through File → Save as Template. There is no default keyboard shortcut.

14.5.11 Revert

The Revert command reloads the image from disk, so that it looks just like it did the last time it was saved — unless, that is, you or some application other than GIMP have modifed the image file, in which case, the new contents are loaded.

 Warning

When GIMP reverts a file, it actually closes the existing image and creates a new image. Because of this, reverting an image is not undoable, and causes the undo history of the image to be lost. GIMP tries to protect you from losing your work in this way by asking you to confirm that you really want to revert the image.

14.5.11.1 Activating the Command

- You can access this command from the image menubar through File → Revert. There is no default keyboard shortcut.

14.5.12 Print

The Print command is not really part of GIMP. It simply calls the printing interface of your operating system to set the printer options. See Print your photos.

14.5.12.1 Activating the Command

You can access this command from the image menubar through File → Print.

14.5.13 Close

The Close command closes the image and removes its window. Closing an image is not undoable: once it is closed, everything is gone, including the undo history. If the image is not 'clean' — that is, if you have changed it since the last time you saved it — you are asked to confirm that you really want to close it. Note that an image is marked as clean when it is saved to a file, even if the file format chosen does not preserve all the information in the image, so it is a good idea to think for a moment about what you are doing before closing an image. If there is the slightest possibility that you will regret it, it can't hurt to save a copy as an XCF file.

14.5.13.1 Activating the Command

- You can access this command from the image menubar through File → Close,

- or by using the keyboard shortcut Ctrl-W.

- For most systems on which the GIMP runs, you can also execute it by clicking on a 'Close' button somewhere on the image window titlebar. The location and appearance of this button are determined by the windowing system and the window manager.

Note
If you close the image window, as described above, GIMP simply closes your image. However, if you close the Toolbox window by using the 'Close' button, GIMP itself exits.

14.5.14 Quit

The Quit command causes GIMP to close all images and exit. If there are any open images which contain unsaved changes (that is, they are not marked as 'clean'), GIMP notifies you and displays a list of the unsaved images. You can then choose which images you would like to save, or you can cancel the command. Note that if you have a large number of images open, or are using a large part of the RAM on your system, it may take a little while for everything to shut down.

14.5.14.1 Activating the Command

- You can access this command from the Toolbox menubar or the image menubar through File → Quit,

- or by using the keyboard shortcut Ctrl-Q.

- For most systems on which the GIMP runs, you can also execute it by clicking on a 'Close' button somewhere on the Toolbox window's titlebar. The location and appearance of this button are determined by the windowing system and the window manager.

Note
If you close the image window, as described above, GIMP simply closes your image. However, if you close the Toolbox window by using the 'Close' button, GIMP itself exits.

14.6   The 'Edit' Menu

14.6.1   'Edit' Menu Entries

Figure 14.31: Contents of the Edit Menu

In this section, you will find help for commands in the Edit menu item.

Note
Besides the commands described here, you may also find other entries in the menu. They are not part of GIMP itself, but have been added by extensions (plug-ins). You can find information about the functionality of a Plugin by referring to its documentation.

14.6.2   Undo

If you have made drawing or editing changes to the image which you don't want to keep, the Undo command allows you to undo the last change and return the image to its previous state. Almost anything you do to an image can be undone in this way (with the exception of scripts, which deactivate this function). Further Undo operations may be performed, depending upon the number of Undo levels configured in the Environment page of the Preferences Dialog. See the section on Undoing for more information about GIMP's very sophisticated 'Undo' functions.

The operation that has been 'undone' is not lost immediately: you can get it back by using the Redo command right away. But if you perform another operation, the 'Undo' will be irretrievably lost.

14.6.2.1   Activating the Command

- You can access this command from the image menubar through Edit → Undo,

- by using the keyboard shortcut Ctrl-Z,

- or by simply clicking on the status you want in the Undo History dialog.

14.6.3 Redo

The Redo command reverses the effects of the Undo command. Each 'Undo' action can be reversed by a single 'Redo' action. You can alternate 'Undo' and 'Redo' as many times as you like. Note that you can only 'Redo' an operation if the last action you did was an 'Undo'. If you perform any operation on the image after Undoing something, then the former Redo steps are lost, and there is no way to recover them. See the Undoing section for more information.

To see the operations which you have done and undone, use the Undo History dialog.

14.6.3.1 Activating the Command

- You can access this command from the image menubar through Edit → Redo,

- by using the keyboard shortcut Ctrl-Y,

- or by simply clicking on the status you want in the Undo History dialog.

14.6.4 Undo History

The Undo History command activates the Undo History dialog, which shows you thumbnails representing the operations you have done so far on the current image. This overview makes it easier for you to undo steps or to redo them.

Use the arrows for Undo and Redo, or simply click on the thumbnail, to bring the image back to a previous state. This is especially useful when you are working on a difficult task, where you often need to undo several steps at once. It is much easier to click on step 10 than to type Ctrl-Z ten times.

The 'Clear undo History' command may be useful if you are working on a complex image and you want to free some memory.

14.6.4.1 Activating the Command

- You can access this command from the image menubar through Edit → Undo History. There is no default keyboard shortcut.

14.6.5 Cut

The Cut command deletes the contents of the image's selections, and saves them in a clipboard so that they can later be pasted using the 'Paste', 'Paste Into', or 'Paste As New' commands. If there is no selection, the entire current layer is cut. The areas whose contents are cut are left transparent, if the layer has an alpha channel, or filled with the layer's background color, otherwise.

Note
The Cut command only works on the current active layer. Any layers above or below the active layer are ignored.

14.6.5.1 Activating the Command

- You can access this command from the image menubar through Edit → Cut,

- or by using the keyboard shortcut Ctrl-X.

14.6.6 Copy

The Copy command makes a copy of the current selection and stores it in the Clipboard. The information can be recalled using the Paste, Paste Into, or Paste As New commands. If there is no selection, the entire current layer is copied. 'Copy' only works on the current active layer. Any layers above or below it are ignored.

14.6.6.1 Activating the Command

- You can access this command from the image memubar through Edit → Copy,

- or by using the keyboard shortcut Ctrl-C.

14.6.7 Copy Visible

The Copy Visible command is similar to the Copy command. However, it does not just copy the contents of the current layer; it copies the contents of the visible layers (or the selection of the visible layers), that is, the ones that are marked with an 'eye'.

 Note

Please note that the information about the layers is lost when the image data is put in the clipboard. When you later paste the clipboard contents, there is only one layer, which is the fusion of all the marked layers.

14.6.7.1 Activating the Command

- You can access this command from the image menubar through Edit → Copy Visible.

14.6.8 Paste

The Paste command puts whatever is in the Clipboard from the last 'Copy' or 'Cut' command into the current image. The pasted section becomes a 'floating selection' and is shown as a separate layer in the Layers Dialog.

If there is an existing selection on the canvas, it is used to align the pasted data. If there is already a selection, the data is pasted using the selection as a center point. If you want the selection to be used as a clipping region for the pasted data, you should use the 'Paste Into' command.

 Note

You can have only *one* floating selection at any one time. You cannot work on any other layer while there is a floating selection; you have to either anchor it or remove it.

14.6.8.1 Activating the Command

- You can access this command from the image menubar through Edit → Paste.

- or by using the keyboard shortcut Ctrl-V.

14.6.9 Paste Into

The Paste Into command acts in a similar way to the Paste command. The primary difference becomes apparent if there is a selection within the canvas. Unlike the 'Paste' command, which simply centers the pasted image data over the selection and replaces the selection with its own, 'Paste Into' clips the pasted image data by the existing selection. The new selection can be moved as usual, but it is always clipped by the original selection area.

If no selection exists, the 'Paste Into' command places the data from the Clipboard into the center of the canvas, as the 'Paste' command does.

14.6.9.1 Activating the Command

- You can access this command from the image menubar through Edit → Paste Into.

14.6.10   Paste as New

The Paste As New command creates a new image and pastes the image data from the Clipboard into it. If the data is not rectangular or square in shape, any regions that do not extend to the edge of the canvas are left transparent (an Alpha channel is automatically created). Of course, you have to Copy your selection before you use this command, so that you get an image with the same dimensions as the selection.

14.6.10.1   Activating the Command

• You can access this command from the image menubar through Edit → Paste as New.

14.6.11   Buffers

Figure 14.32: The 'Buffer' submenu of the 'Edit' menu

The commands in this submenu operate on *named buffers*. You can use the Buffers dialog to view and manage any named buffers you have created.

14.6.11.1   Activating the Submenu

• You can access this submenu from the image menubar through Edit → Buffer.

14.6.11.2   Cut Named

The Cut Named command cuts the contents of the selection from the active layer in the usual way, but instead of storing the contents in the global clipboard, it stores it in a special buffer that you name using a pop-up dialog.

ACTIVATING THE COMMAND

• You can access this command from the image menubar through Edit → Buffer → Cut,

• or by using the keyboard shortcut Shift-Ctrl-X.

14.6.11.3   Copy Named

The Copy Named command copies the contents of the selection from the active layer in the usual way, but instead of storing the contents in the global clipboard, it stores it in a special buffer that you name using a pop-up dialog.

ACTIVATING THE COMMAND

• You can access this command from the image menubar through Edit → Buffer → Copy,

• or by using the keyboard shortcut Shift-Ctrl-C.

14.6.11.4   Paste Named

The Paste Named command simply brings up the Buffers dialog. By selecting one of the listed buffers, and pressing one of the buttons at the bottom, you can either Paste Buffer, Paste Buffer Into, or Paste Buffer as New.

ACTIVATING THE COMMAND

- You can access this command from the image menubar through Edit → Buffer → Paste

- or by using the keyboard shortcut Shift-Ctrl-V.

14.6.12   Clear

The Clear command deletes everything in the current selection. If there is no current selection, the contents of the active layer are removed. If the active layer has an alpha channel, the deleted selection is made transparent. You can restore the original color to the transparent area using the Eraser tool, by setting it to Anti-Erase. If the layer does not have an alpha channel, the deleted area is filled using the current background color.

Clearing a selection does not delete the selection itself. Unlike 'Cut', 'Clear' does not place the deleted contents in the Clipboard and the contents of the clipboard are unaffected.

14.6.12.1   Activating the Command

- You can access this command from the image menubar through Edit → Clear,

- or by using the keyboard shortcut Ctrl-K.

14.6.13   Fill with FG Color

The Fill with FG Color command fills the image's selection with the solid color shown in the foreground part of the Color Area of the Toolbox. (The color is also shown to the left of the menu entry.) If some areas of the image are only partially selected (for example, as a result of feathering the selection), they are filled in proportion to how much they are selected.

Note
Please note that if the image has no selection, the whole active layer is filled.

14.6.13.1   Activating the Command

- You can access this command from the image menubar through Edit → Fill with FG Color,

- or by using the keyboard shortcut Ctrl-,.

Note
You can also fill a selection by click-and-dragging from the Toolbox foreground color.

14.6.14   Fill with BG Color

The Fill with BG Color command fills the active layer selection with the solid color shown in the Background part of the Color Area of the Toolbox. (The color is also shown to the left of the menu entry.) If some areas of the image are only partially selected (for example, as a result of feathering the selection), they are filled in proportion to how much they are selected.

Note

Please note that if the image has no selection, the whole active layer is filled.

14.6.14.1   Activating the Command

- You can access this command from the image menubar through Edit → Fill with BG Color,

- or by using the keyboard shortcut Ctrl-..

Note

You can also fill a selection by click-and-dragging from the Toolbox background color.

14.6.15   Fill with Pattern

The Fill with Pattern command fills the image's selection with the pattern shown in the Brush/Pattern/Gradient area of the Toolbox. (The pattern is also shown to the left of the menu entry.) If some areas of the image are only partially selected (for example, as a result of feathering the selection), they are filled in proportion to how much they are selected.

You can select another pattern by using the Pattern Dialog.

Note

Please note that if the image has no selection, the whole active layer is filled.

14.6.15.1   Activating the Command

- You can access this command from the image menubar through Edit → Fill with Pattern,

- or by using the keyboard shortcut Ctrl-;.

14.6.16   Stroke Selection

The Stroke Selection command strokes a selection in the image. There are two ways you can stroke the selection, either by using a paint tool or without using one. This means that the selection border, which is emphasized in the image with a dotted line, can be drawn with a stroke. There are various options which you can use to specify how this stroke should look.

Note

This command is only active if the image has an active selection.

14.6.16.1 Activating the Command

- You can access this command from the image menubar through Edit → Stroke Selection.

- You can also access it through the Selection Editor.

14.6.16.2 The 'Stroke Selection' dialog

Note
The options for stroking selections and for stroking paths are the same. You can find the documentation about the options in the dialog box in the Stroke Path section.

14.6.17 Stroke Path

The Stroke Path command strokes a path in the image. There are two ways you can stroke the path, either by using a paint tool, or without using one. There are various options which you can use to specify how this stroke should look.

Note
This command is active only if there is a path in your image.

14.6.17.1 Activating the Command

- You can access this command from the image menubar through Edit → Stroke Path.

- You can also access it by clicking on the button with the same name in the Path dialog.

14.6.17.2 Description of the Dialog Window

Figure 14.33: The 'Choose Stroke Style' dialog window

The Choose Stroke Style dialog box allows you to choose between stroking the path with the options you specify or stroking it with a paint tool. If you stroke the path with a paint tool, the current paint tool options are used to draw the stroke.

Stroke line The stroke is drawn with the current foreground color, set in the Toolbox. By clicking on the triangle next to Line Style however, the dialog expands and you can set several additional options:

Line Width You can set the width of the stroke using the text box. The default unit is pixels, but you can choose another unit with the arrow buttons.

Cap Style You can choose the shape of the ends of an unclosed path, which can be *Butt*, *Round* or *Square*.

Join Style You can choose the shape of the path corners by clicking on *Miter*, *Round* or *Bevel*.

Miter limit When two segments of a path come together, the mitering of the corner is determined by the Miter Limit. If the strokes were wide, and no mitering were done, there would be pointed ends sticking out at the corner. The Miter Limit setting determines how the gap, formed when the outer edges of the two lines are extended, will be filled. You can set it to a value between 0.0 and 100.0, by using the slider or the associated text box and its arrows.

Figure 14.34: Example of miter limit

Left: Limit=0; Right: Limit=5;Izquierda: Limit=0; Derecha: Limit=5;

Dash Pattern On the pixel level, a dashed line is drawn as a series of tiny boxes. You can modify the pattern of these boxes. The black area with thin vertical lines represents the pixels of the dash. If you click on a black pixel, you remove it from the dash. If you click on a white pixel, you add it to the dash. The gray areas indicate how the pattern will be repeated when a dashed line is drawn.

Dash Preset Instead of making your own dash pattern, you can choose one from the drop-down box. This pattern will then be displayed in the Dash pattern area, so you can get an idea of how it will look.

Anti-aliasing Curved strokes or strokes drawn at an angle may look jagged or stair-stepped. The anti-aliasing option smoothes them out.

Style You can choose whether the line is drawn in the *Solid* or the *Pattern* style. Here, Solid and Pattern are distinct from the dash pattern. If you select a Solid line with no dash pattern, an unbroken line is drawn in the foreground color set in the Toolbox. If you select a Patterned line with no dash pattern, an unbroken line is drawn with the pattern set in the Toolbox. If you select a line with a dash pattern, the color or pattern is still determined by the foreground color or pattern set in the Toolbox. That is, if you select a marbled pattern and Patterned, dashed lines, the dashes are drawn in the marbled pattern.

Stroking with a Paint Tool

Paint Tool You can select a paint tool to use to draw the stroke from the drop-down box. If you do that, the currently-selected options of the paint tool are used, rather than the settings in the dialog.

14.7 The 'Select' Menu

14.7.1 Introduction to the 'Select' Menu

Figure 14.35: The Contents of the 'Select' menu

This section explains the commands on the Select menu of the image menubar.

Note

Besides the commands described here, you may also find other entries in the menu. They are not part of GIMP itself, but have been added by extensions (plug-ins). You can find information about the functionality of a Plugin by referring to its documentation.

14.7.2 Select All

The Select All command creates a new selection which contains everything on the current layer.

14.7.2.1 Activating the Command

• You can access this command from the image menubar through Select → All,

• or by using the keyboard shortcut Ctrl-A. You can also access it with the Selection Editor.

14.7.3 None

The None command cancels all selections in the image. If there are no selections, the command doesn't do anything. Floating selections are not affected.

14.7.3.1 Activating the Command

• You can access this command from the image menubar through Select → None. In addition, you can use the Selection Editor to access it.

• You can also use the keyboard shortcut Shift-Ctrl-A.

14.7.4 Invert

The Invert command inverts the selection in the current image. That means that all of the image contents which were previously outside of the selection are now inside it, and vice versa. If there was no selection before, the command selects the entire image.

 Warning
Do not confuse this command with the Invert layer command.

14.7.4.1 Activating the Command

- You can access this command from the image menubar through Select → Invert. In addition, you can use the Selection Editor to access it.

- You can also use the keyboard shortcut Ctrl-I.

14.7.5 Float

The Float command converts a normal selection into a 'floating selection'. You can find more information about floating selections in the Glossary.

In early versions of GIMP, floating selections were used for performing operations on a limited part of an image. You can do that more easily now with layers, but you can still use this way of working with images. In addition to using the Float command, you can also create a floating selection by moving a selection using the 'Move' tool, without pressing the **Alt** key (or Shift-Alt in Linux), which automatically creates a floating selection. You can also create a temporary layer, named 'Floating Selection', with the entries on the Layer menu.

You cannot perform any operations on other layers if the image has a floating selection, so after you make the changes you want to the floating selection, you have to *anchor* it. That is, you have to attach it to a normal (non-floating) layer, usually the original layer (the one which was active previously). To anchor the floating selection, use the Anchor Layer command. You can also anchor it to an existing layer by clicking anywhere on the image outside of the floating selection, which then merges it with the background layer. You can also anchor it to a new layer by using the New Layer command.

 Tip
If you display the layer boundary by using the Show Layer Boundary command, you may have difficulty selecting a precise area of the image which you want in a layer. To avoid this problem, you can make a rectangular selection, transform it into a floating selection and anchor it to a new layer. Then simply remove the original layer.

14.7.5.1 Activating the Command

- You can access this command from the image menubar through Select → Float,

- or by using the keyboard shortcut Shift-Ctrl-L.

14.7.6 By Color

The Select By Color command is an alternate way of accessing the 'Select By Color' tool, one of the basic selection tools. You can find more information about using this tool in Select By Color.

14.7.6.1 Activating the Command

- You can access this command from the image menubar through Select → By Color,

- or by using the keyboard shortcut Shift-O.

14.7.7 From Path

The From Path command transforms the current path into a selection. If the path is not closed, the command connects the two end points with a straight line. The original path is unchanged.

14.7.7.1 Activating the Command

- You can access this command from the image menubar through Select → From Path.

- In addition, you can click on the Path to Selection button ▦ in the Path dialog to access the command.

- You can also use the keyboard shortcut Shift-V.

14.7.8 Selection Editor

The Selection Editor command displays the 'Selection Editor' dialog window. This dialog window displays the active selection in the current image and gives you easy access to the selection-related commands. It is not really intended for editing selections directly, but if you are working on a selection, it is handy to have the selection commands all together, since it is easier to click on a button than to search for commands in the command tree of the menubar. The 'Selection Editor' also offers some advanced options for the 'Select to Path' command.

14.7.8.1 Activating the Command

- You can access this command from the image menubar through Select → Selection Editor.

14.7.8.2 Description of the 'Selection Editor' dialog window

Figure 14.36: The 'Selection Editor' dialog window

The Buttons The 'Selection Editor' dialog window has several buttons which you can use to easily access selection commands:

- The Select All button.

- The Select None button.
- The Select Invert button.
- The Save to Channel button.
- The To Path button. If you hold the **Shift** key while clicking on this button, the 'Advanced Settings' dialog is displayed. Please see the next section for details about these options.
- The Stroke Selection button.

The display window In the display window, selected areas of the image are white, non-selected areas are black, and partially selected areas are in shades of gray. Clicking in this window acts like Select by Color. See the example below.

Figure 14.37: Example of clicking in the 'Selection Editor' display window

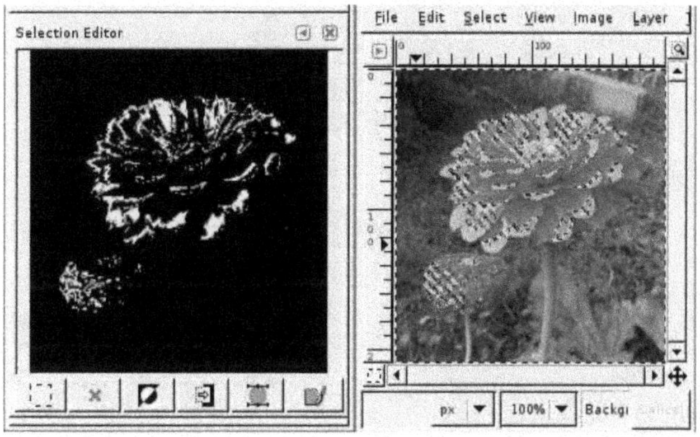

Clicking in the Selection Editor display window to Select By Color. Note that this figure could just as well show the appearance of the Selection Editor display window when Select By Color is used in the image window.

14.7.8.3 The 'Selection to Path Advanced Settings' dialog

Figure 14.38: The 'Advanced Settings' dialog window

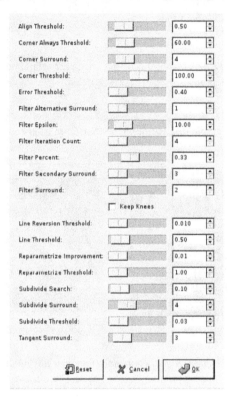

The 'Selection to Path Advanced Settings' dialog contains a number of options, most of which you can set with either a slider bar or a text box. There is also one check box. These options are mostly used by advanced users. They are:

- *Align Threshold*: If two endpoints are closer than this value, they are made to be equal.

- *Corner Always Threshold*: If the angle defined by a point and its predecessors and successors is smaller than this, it is a corner, even if it is within *Corner Surround* pixels of a point with a smaller angle.

- *Corner Surround*: Number of points to consider when determining if a point is a corner or not.

- *Corner Threshold*: If a point, its predecessors, and its successors define an angle smaller than this, it is a corner.

- *Error Threshold*: Amount of error at which a fitted spline [1] is unacceptable. If any pixel is further away than this from the fitted curve, the algorithm tries again.

---

[1] 'Spline' is a mathematical term for a function which defines a curve by using a series of control points, such as a Bézier curve.

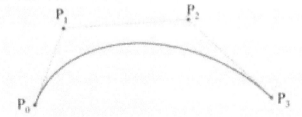

See Wikipedia for more information.

- *Filter Alternative Surround*: A second number of adjacent points to consider when filtering.

- *Filter Epsilon*: If the angles between the vectors produced by *Filter Surround* and *Filter Alternative Surround* points differ by more than this, use the one from *Filter Alternative Surround*.

- *Filter Iteration Count*: The number of times to smooth the original data points. Increasing this number dramatically, to 50 or so, can produce vastly better results. But if any points that 'should' be corners aren't found, the curve goes wild around that point.

- *Filter Percent*: To produce the new point, use the old point plus this times the neighbors.

- *Filter Secondary Surround*: Number of adjacent points to consider if *Filter Surround* points defines a straight line.

- *Filter Surround*: Number of adjacent points to consider when filtering.

- *Keep Knees*: This check box says whether or not to remove 'knee' points after finding the outline.

- *Line Reversion Threshold*: If a spline is closer to a straight line than this value, it remains a straight line, even if it would otherwise be changed back to a curve. This is weighted by the square of the curve length, to make shorter curves more likely to be reverted.

- *Line Threshold*: How many pixels (on the average) a spline can diverge from the line determined by its endpoints before it is changed to a straight line.

- *Reparametrize Improvement*: If reparameterization doesn't improve the fit by this much percent, the algorithm stops doing it.

- *Reparametrize Threshold*: Amount of error at which it is pointless to reparameterize. This happens, for example, when the algorithm is trying to fit the outline of the outside of an 'O' with a single spline. The initial fit is not good enough for the Newton-Raphson iteration to improve it. It may be that it would be better to detect the cases where the algorithm didn't find any corners.

- *Subdivide Search*: Percentage of the curve away from the worst point to look for a better place to subdivide.

- *Subdivide Surround*: Number of points to consider when deciding whether a given point is a better place to subdivide.

- *Subdivide Threshold*: How many pixels a point can diverge from a straight line and still be considered a better place to subdivide.

- *Tangent Surround*: Number of points to look at on either side of a point when computing the approximation to the tangent at that point.

14.7.9 Feather

The Feather command feathers the edges of the selection. This creates a smooth transition between the selection and its surroundings. You normally feather selection borders with the 'Feather Edges' option of the selection tools, but you may feather them again with this command.

14.7.9.1 Activating the Command

- You can access this command from the image menubar through Select → Feather.

14.7.9.2 Description of the 'Feather Selection' dialog window

Figure 14.39: The 'Feather Selection' dialog

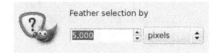

Feather selection by Enter the width of the selection border feathering. The default units are pixels, but you can also choose other units with the drop-down menu.

14.7.10 Sharpen

The Sharpen command reduces the amount of blur or fuzziness around the edge of a selection. It reverses the effect of the Feather Selection command. The new edge of the selection follows the dotted line of the edge of the old selection. Anti-aliasing is also removed.

Note

Please do not confuse this command with the Sharpen filter.

14.7.10.1 Activating the Command

• You can access this command from the image menubar through Select → Sharpen.

14.7.11 Shrink

The Shrink command reduces the size of the selected area by moving each point on the edge of the selection a certain distance further away from the nearest edge of the image (toward the center of the selection). Feathering is preserved, but the shape of the feathering may be altered at the corners or at points of sharp curvature.

14.7.11.1 Activating the Command

• You can access this command from the image menubar through Select → Shrink....

14.7.11.2 Description of the 'Shrink' dialog

Figure 14.40: The 'Shrink Selection' dialog

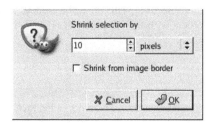

Shrink selection by Enter the amount by which to reduce the selection in the text box. The default unit is pixels, but you can choose a different unit of measurement from the drop-down menu.

Shrink from image border This option is only of interest if the selection runs along the edge of the image. If it does and this option is checked, then the selection shrinks away from the edge of the image. If this option is not checked, the selection continues to extend to the image border.

14.7.12 Grow

The Grow command increases the size of a selection in the current image. It works in a similar way to the Shrink command, which reduces the size of a selection.

14.7.12.1 Activating the Command

- You can access this command from the image menubar through Select → Grow.

14.7.12.2 Description of the 'Grow Selection' dialog

Figure 14.41: The 'Grow Selection' dialog window

Grow selection by You can enter the amount by which to increase the selection in the text box. The default unit of measurement is pixels, but you can choose a different unit by using the drop-down menu.

14.7.12.3 A Peculiarity of Rectangular Selections

When you grow a rectangular selection, the resulting selection has rounded corners. The reason for this is shown in the image below:

Figure 14.42: Why growing a rectangular selection results in rounded corners

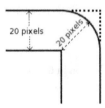

If you do not want rounded corners, you can use the Rounded Rectangle command with a 0% radius.

14.7.13 Border

Figure 14.43: Example of creating a border from a selection

(a) *An image with a selection*   (b) *After Select Border*

The Select Border command creates a new selection along the edge of an existing selection in the current image. The edge of the current selection is used as a form and the new selection is then created around it. You enter the width of the border, in pixels or some other unit, in the dialog window. Half of the new border lies inside of the selected area and half outside of it.

14.7.13.1 Activating the Command

- You can access this command from the image menubar through Select → Border.

14.7.13.2 Description of the 'Border' dialog window

Figure 14.44: The 'Border' dialog window

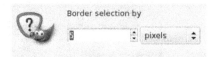

Border selection by Enter the width of the border selection in the box. The default units are pixels, but you can also choose the units with the drop-down menu.

14.7.14 Rounded Rectangle

The 'Rounded Rectangle' Script-Fu command converts an existing selection (rectangular, elliptical or other shape) into a rectangular selection with rounded corners. The corners can be curved toward the inside (concave) or toward the outside (convex). To do this, the command adds or removes circles at the corners of the selection.

14.7.14.1 Activating the Command

- You can access this command from the image menubar through Select → Rounded Rectangle.

14.7.14.2 Description of the 'Rounded Rectangle' Dialog Window Descripción de la ventana del diálogo 'Rectángulo redondeado'

Figure 14.45: The 'Rounded Rectangle' dialog

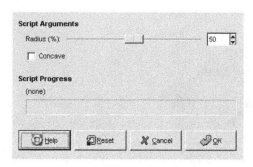

Radius (%) You can enter the radius of the rounded corner in percent by using a slider or a text field. This value is a percentage of the height or the width, whichever is less.

Concave If you check this box, the corners will be concave (curving toward the inside), rather than convex (curving toward the outside).

14.7.15 Toggle QuickMask

It has the same action as clicking on the small button in the bottom left corner of the image. See Quick Mask

14.7.15.1 Activate Dialog

- This command is found at Select → Toggle QuickMask

- Default shortcut is Shift-Q

14.7.16 Save to Channel

The Select to Channel command saves the selection as a channel. The channel can then be used as a channel selection mask. You can find more information about them in the Channel Dialog section.

14.7.16.1 Activating the Command

- You can access this command from the image menubar through Select → Save to Channel.

- You can also access it from the Selection Editor.

14.7.17 To Path

The To Path command converts a selection into a path. The image does not seem to change, but you can see the new path in the Paths Dialog. By using the Path tool in the Toolbox, you can precisely adapt the outline of the selection. You can find further information regarding paths in the Paths dialog section.

14.7.17.1 Activating the Command

- You can access this command from the image menubar through Select → To Path.

- You can also access it from the Selection Editor or from the Paths Dialog which offers you a lot of Advanced Options.

14.8 The 'View' Menu

14.8.1 Introduction to the 'View' Menu

Figure 14.46: Contents of the View menu

This section describes the View menu, which contains commands that affect the visibility or appearance of the image and various elements of the interface.

Note

Besides the commands described here, you may also find other entries in the menu. They are not part of GIMP itself, but have been added by extensions (plug-ins). You can find information about the functionality of a Plugin by referring to its documentation.

14.8.2 New View

The New View command creates a new image window for the current image, which you can set up differently from the existing display. You can create multiple views of any image, which are numbered .1, .2, etc., but only the zoom factor and other viewing options may be different. Any changes, other than viewing changes, which you make in one window also appear in the other displays which show the same image. The new views are not separate image files; they are simply different aspects of the same image. You might use multiple views, for example, if you were working on individual pixels at a high zoom factor. You could then see the effects your changes would have on the image at a normal size.

You can delete a view by closing its window. If you close the last window displaying an image, the image itself is closed. However, if you have made changes to the image which you have not yet saved, you are asked for confirmation.

14.8.2.1 Activating the Command

- You can access this command from the image menubar through View → New View.

14.8.3 Dot for Dot

The Dot for Dot command enables and disables 'Dot for Dot' mode. If it is enabled (checked) and the zoom factor is 100%, every pixel in the image is displayed as one pixel on the screen. If it is disabled, the image is displayed at its 'real' size, the size it will have when it is printed.

For Dot for Dot mode to work properly, the resolution of the image must be the same as the screen resolution in the Preferences menu.

Enabling this mode is recommended if you are working on icons and web graphics. If you are working on images intended to be printed, you should disable Dot-for-Dot mode.

14.8.3.1 Activating the Command

- You can access this command from the image menubar through View → Dot for Dot.

14.8.4 Zoom

Figure 14.47: The 'Zoom' submenu of the 'View' menu

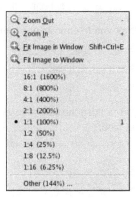

The Zoom submenu contains various commands which affect the magnification of the image in the image window (zooming). Enlarging an image (zooming in) is useful if you need to work with high precision, making pixel-level image modifications or precise selections. On the other hand, reducing an image (zooming out) is handy for getting an overall impression of the image and seeing the results of changes which affect the entire image. Please note that zooming is not undoable, since it does not affect the image data, only the way it is displayed.

Tip
Besides the entries in this submenu, there is also a zoom pull-down menu at the bottom edge of the image window (if the status bar is displayed). You can also make settings regarding zooming in the Navigation dialog. You can also use the Magnify tool which lets you zoom a particular area of the image.

14.8.4.1 Activating the Submenu

- You can access this submenu from the image menubar through View → Zoom. Note that the 'Zoom' label on the 'View' menu shows the current zoom factor, for example, Zoom (100%).

14.8.4.2 Contents of the 'Zoom' submenu

The various 'Zoom' submenu commands are described below, along with their default keyboard shortcuts, if any.

Zoom Out (Shortcut: -) Each time 'Zoom Out' is used, the zoom factor is decreased by about 30%. There is a minimum zoom level of 0.39%.

Zoom In (Shortcut: +) Each time 'Zoom In' is used, the zoom factor is increased by about 30%. The maximum possible zoom level is 25600%.

> **Note**
> The keyboard shortcut for 'Zoom In' has been somewhat controversial because this is a very common operation and on English keyboards, the **Shift** key must be pressed to use it. (This is not the case for European keyboards.) If you would like to have a different keyboard shortcut, you can create a dynamic shortcut for it; see the help section for User Interface Preferences for instructions.

Fit Image in Window (Shortcut: Shift-Ctrl-E). This command zooms the image to be as large as possible, while still keeping it completely within the window. There will usually be padding on two sides of the image, but not on all four sides.

Fit Image to Window This command zooms the image as large as possible without requiring any padding to be shown. This means that the image fits the window perfectly in one dimension, but usually extends beyond the window borders in the other dimension.

A:B (X%) With these commands, you can select one of the pre-set zoom levels. Each of the menu labels gives a ratio, as well as a percentage value. The 100% zoom level has a simple keyboard shortcut: **1**.

Other This command brings up a dialog which allows you to choose any zoom level you would like, within the range of 1:256 (0.39%) to 256:1 (25600%).

> **Tip**
> When you are working at the pixel level, you can use the New view command. This allows you to see what is happening to the image at its normal size at the same time.

14.8.5 Shrink Wrap

The Shrink Wrap command resizes the window so that it is exactly the same size as the image at the current zoom factor. If the image doesn't completely fit on the screen, the image window is enlarged so that the largest possible part of the image is shown. Please note that GIMP will do this automatically if you set the 'Resize window on zoom' and 'Resize window on image size change' options in the Image Window page of the Preferences dialog.

> **Note**
> Please note also that the behavior described here is not performed by GIMP itself, but by the 'window manager', a part of the operating system of your computer. For that reason, the functionality described may be different on your computer, or in the worst case, might not be available at all.

14.8.5.1 Activating the Command

- You can access this command from the image menubar through View → Shrink Wrap,

- or by using the keyboard shortcut Ctrl-E.

14.8.6 Full Screen

The Fullscreen command enables and disables displaying the image window on the entire screen. When it is enabled, the image window takes up the whole screen, but the image stays the same size. When you enable full-screen mode, the menubar may not be displayed, but if this happens, you can right-click on the image to access the image menu. You can set the default appearance for full-screen mode in the Preferences menu.

Note

If you use GIMP on an Apple computer, full-screen mode may not work, since Apple doesn't provide the necessary functionality. Instead, you can maximize the image window by clicking on the *Green Button*, so the image occupies most of the screen.

14.8.6.1 Activating the Command

- You can access this command from the image menubar through View → Full Screen,

- or by using the keyboard shortcut **F11**.

14.8.7 Info Window

The Info Window command displays general information about the current image, as well as information about the pixel which is currently under the mouse pointer.

14.8.7.1 Activating the Command

- You can access this command from the image menubar through View → Info window,

- or by using the keyboard shortcut Shift-Ctrl-I.

14.8.7.2 Description of the 'Info Window'

The Info Window displays basic information about the current image, including its name and a thumbnail, as well as about the pixel which is currently under the mouse pointer.

The General Tab

Figure 14.48: The 'General' tab of the 'Info Window'

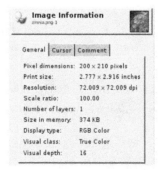

- *Pixel dimensions*: Shows the image height and width in pixels, that is, the 'physical' size of the image.

- *Print size*: Shows the size the image will have when it is printed, in the current units. This is the 'logical size' of the image. It depends upon the physical size of the image and the screen resolution.

- *Resolution*: Shows the image resolution in dots per inch (dpi).

- *Scale ratio*: Shows the zoom factor of the current image.

- *Number of layers*: Shows the number of layers in the current image.

- *Size in memory*: Shows the number of KB the image takes up in memory. This information is also displayed in the image window. The size is quite different from the size of the file on disk. That is because the displayed image is decompressed and because GIMP keeps a copy of the image in memory for Redo operations.

- *Display type*: Shows the color mode of the current image.

- *Visual class*: Shows the way the visual aspects of the screen are handled in the image, for example 'True Color'.

- *Visual depth*: Shows the color depth of the image in bits. This number can be distributed over several components of the color model. For example, an image in RGB mode has three components: R, G and B. With a visual depth of 24 bits, there are 8 bits per component, which means 256 possible color values for each of the red, green and blue channels.

The Cursor Tab

Figure 14.49: The 'Cursor' tab of the 'Info Window'

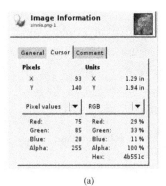

(a)

(b) *This picture shows the types of pixel data which are available with the pulldown menus in the Cursor tab.*

This tab shows color information when you move the mouse pointer over the image. It looks similar to the Color Picker tool, but it doesn't display the color.

- *Pixels*: Coordinates of the pixel you are pointing to. The origin (0,0) is in the upper left corner of the image.

- *Units*: Coordinates of the pixel you are pointing to, in the current units (such as inches or cm). The origin (0,0) is in the upper left corner of the image.

There are two pulldown menus at the bottom of the Cursor tab. Both of them contain the same choices, which makes it easier for you to compare the color values of a particular pixel using different color models. The choices on the pulldown menu are:

- *Pixel values*: This choice displays the *Red*, *Green*, *Blue* and *Alpha* values of the pixel, as numbers between 0 and 255.

- *RGB*: This choice displays the *Red*, *Green*, *Blue* and *Alpha* values of the pixel, as percentages. It also shows the hexadecimal value of the pixel's color.

- *HSV*: This choice displays the *Hue*, in degrees, as well as the *Saturation*, *Value* and *Alpha* of the pixel, as percentages.

- *CMYK*: This choice displays the *Cyan*, *Magenta*, *Yellow*, *Black* and *Alpha* values of the pixel, as percentages.

The Comment Tab

Figure 14.50: The 'Comment' tab of the 'Info Window'

This tab shows the comments which can be stored in the image, depending on the data format used.

14.8.8 Navigation Window

The Navigation Window command opens the navigation window. This allows you to easily navigate through the image, to set zoom levels and to move the visible parts of the image. You can find more information about using it in the Navigation dialog chapter.

14.8.8.1 Activating the Command

- You can access this command from the image menubar through View → Navigation Window,

- or by using the keyboard shortcut Shift-Ctrl-N.

- You can also access it more rapidly by clicking on the ✛ icon in the lower right corner of the image window.

14.8.9 Display Filters

The images you create, we hope, will be seen by many people on many different systems. The image which looks so wonderful on your screen may look somewhat different to people with sight deficiencies or on a screen with different settings from yours. Some information might not even be visible.

Display Filters allow you to view your image as if it were seen by people with a sight deficiency or on a different screen. Don't worry, the filters display the image in a different way, but they never change the image. Besides that, if you save the image that is displayed, the original image is saved. For the same reason, you can't undo the action of a filter with Ctrl-Z.

The filters available are called 'Color Deficient Vision', 'Gamma', 'Contrast' and 'Color Proof':

14.8.9.1 Activating the Command

- You can access this command from the image menubar through View → Display Filters.

14.8.9.2 Description of the 'Display Filters' Dialog

Figure 14.51: The 'Configure Color Display Filters' dialog

This dialog has two small selectboxes. The left selectbox displays the Available Filters. You can move a filter to the right selectbox by selecting it and clicking on the right arrow button. The Active Filters window on the right displays filters you have chosen and which will be applied if the adjacent box is checked. You can move filters from the right selectbox to the left selectbox by using the left arrow button. If you select a filter by clicking on its name, its options are displayed below the two selectboxes, in the Configure Selected Filter area.

14.8.9.3 Color Deficient Vision

Figure 14.52: Description of the 'Color Deficient Vision' dialog

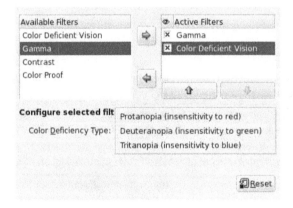

COLOR DEFICIENCY TYPE

Protanopia (insensitivity to red) Do not be afraid of this odd name. It is made up from three Greek roots: 'op' for eye, vision; 'an' for negation; 'proto' for first, the first color in the RGB Color System. So, protanopia is a visual deficiency of the color red. It's the well-known daltonism (red-green color blindness).

Protanopia is actually more complex than this; a person with this problem cannot see either red or green, although he is still sensitive to yellow and blue. In addition, he has a loss of luminance perception and the hues shift toward the short wavelengths.

Deuteranopia (insensivity to green) With deuteranopia, the person has a deficiency in green vision. Deuteranopia is actually like protanopia, because the person has a loss of red and green perception, but he has no luminance loss or hue shift.

Tritanopia (insensitivity to blue) With tritanopia, the person is deficient in blue and yellow perception, although he is still sensitive to red and green. He lacks some perception of luminance, and the hues shift toward the long wavelengths.

Examples

Figure 14.53: Example of protanopia with some text

As you can see, a red-blind person cannot see the red (255,0,0) text on a black (0,0,0) background. You have to change the text color. Daltonism occurs fairly frequently in the population.

Figure 14.54: Examples of the three types of vision deficiencies in one image

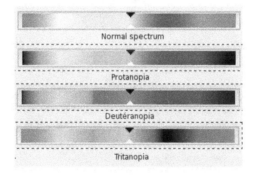

From top to bottom: normal vision, protanopia, deuteranopia, and tritanopia. It appears that the filters don't give a fair reflection of medical data. In deuteranopia, yellow is shifted toward red. In tritanopia, green is slightly represented in the blue range...

14.8.9.4 Gamma

Figure 14.55: The 'Gamma' dialog

The correspondence between electrical intensity and color brightness is not exact and it depends upon the device (the camera, the scanner, the monitor, etc.). 'Gamma' is a coefficient used to correct this correspondence. Your image must be visible in both dark and bright areas, even if it is displayed on a monitor with too much luminence or not enough. The 'Gamma' Display Filter allows you to get an idea of the appearance of your image under these conditions.

14.8.9.5 Contrast

Figure 14.56: The 'Contrast' dialog

Here, we are back in the medical domain. 'Contrast Sensitivity' is the capacity of the visual system to distinguish slight differences in contrast. Some people with cataracts (which means that the lens has opaque crystals that scatter light over the retina) or retinal disease (for instance, due to diabetes, which destroys the rods and cones) have a deficiency in sensitivity to contrast: for example, they would have difficulties distinguishing spots on a dress.

With the 'Contrast' Filter, you can see the image as if you were suffering from cataracts. You may have to increase the contrast of the image so that your grandmother can see it well. In most cases, only very low values of the Contrast Cycles parameter are of interest. Higher values create a side-effect which doesn't interest us here: if you increase the luminosity value above 255, the complementary color appears.

If you are interested in this subject, you can browse the Web for 'contrast sensitivity'.

14.8.9.6 Color Proof

The various systems for reproducing colors cannot represent the infinity of colors available. Even if there are many colors in common between the various systems and nature, some of the colors will not be the same. The 'gamut' is the color range of a system. *Color Profiles* allow you to compensate for these differences.

Before you print an image, it may be useful for you to see if you will get the result you want by applying a profile. The 'Color Proof' filter shows you how your image will look after a color profile has been applied.

Figure 14.57: The 'Color Proof' dialog El diálogo 'Color seguro'

THE 'COLOR PROOF' OPTIONS

Intent You can apply the filter you have selected in one of four ways:

> **Perceptual** The Perceptual method is the best way to reproduce photographs on ink-jet printers. The adjustment is minimal and visual relationships between colors are preserved so that they are perceived in a natural way by the human eye.

> **Relative Colorimetric** This method compares the white and black points of the source gamut with those of the destination gamut and scales the hues accordingly. It is well suited for printing photographs on ink-jet printers. It tends to darken the image, so it may be necessary to compensate the black point.

> **Saturation** This method preserves the saturation values of the original pixels. The original pixels which are outside of the range are all represented at the same saturation. This method is not very useful for photographs. It is used for documents where color punch is more important than accuracy, such as for reproducing logos. Colors which should have a continuous change are not represented very well, since there are jumps in the colors.

> **Absolute Colorimetric** This method leaves the colors of the source which are within the gamut of the destination unchanged and discards the colors outside of the gamut. There is no stretching of the colors on the white point. The accuracy of the colors is preserved, but not their relationships, and different colors may be represented in the same way.

Profile This text box and its browser button allow you to select the profile you want from a location on a storage device.

Black Point Compensation Black point compensation resamples the image to scale the hues from the black point of the original image, if the result is too different from the original.

14.8.10 Show Selection

The Show Selection command enables and disables displaying the dotted line surrounding the selection in the image window. Please note that the selection still exists, even if displaying this line is disabled.

You can set the default for displaying the selection in the Image Window Appearance dialog.

14.8.10.1 Activating the Command

- You can access this command from the image menubar through View → Show Selection,

- or by using the keyboard shortcut Ctrl-T.

14.8.11 Show Layer Boundary

The Show Layer Boundary command enables and disables displaying the yellow dotted line that surrounds a layer in the image window. The dotted line is actually only visible when the layer is smaller than the image window. When the layer is the same size as the image window, the layer boundary is obscured by the image border.

You can set the default for the layer boundary in the Image Window Appearance dialog.

14.8.11.1 Activating the Command

- You can access this command from the image menubar through View → Show Layer Boundary.

14.8.12 Show Guides

The Show Guides command enables and disables diplaying of Guides in the image window.

You can set the default for the guides in the Image Window Appearance dialog.

14.8.12.1 Activating the Command

- You can access this command from the image menubar through View → Show Guides,

- or by using the keyboard shortcut Shift-Ctrl-T.

14.8.13 Snap to Guides

The Snap to Guides command enables and disables snap to guides. When snap to guides is enabled, the guides you set (see Show Guides) almost seems magnetic; when you move a layer or selection, the guides appear to pull on it when it approaches. This is enormously useful for accurate placement of image elements.

14.8.13.1 Activating the Command

- You can access this command from the image menubar through View → Snap to Guides.

14.8.14 Show Grid

By using the Show Grid command, you can enable and disable displaying the grid. When you enable it, the grid overlays the image and makes it easier for you to line up selected image elements.

You can set the default for the grid in the Image Window Appearance dialog.

Tip
See also the Configure Grid command and the Snap to Grid command.

14.8.14.1 Activating the Command

- You can access this command from the image menubar through View → Show Grid.

14.8.15 Snap to Grid

The Snap to Grid command enables and disables snap to grid. When snap to grid is enabled, the grid you set (see Show Grid) almost seems magnetic; when you move a layer or selection, the grid points appear to pull on it when it approaches. This is enormously useful for accurate placement of image elements.

14.8.15.1 Activating the Command

- You can access this command from the image menubar through View → Snap to Grid.

14.8.16 Padding Color

Figure 14.58: Contents of the 'Padding Color' submenu

You can change the color of the canvas which surrounds the image by using the Padding Color command. The canvas is the surface the image lies on. It looks like a frame around the image in the image window. This is just a matter of personal preference, since the padding color does not have any effect on the image itself. Please note that this color is not the same as the color used by the Fill tool.

14.8.16.1 Activating the submenu

- You can access this submenu from the image menubar through View → Padding Color.

14.8.16.2 'Padding Color' Options

- *From Theme*: The color of the theme defined in Preferences Theme is used.

- *Light/Dark Check Color*: The check representing transparency, which is defined in Preferences Display is used.

- *Select Custom Color*: Opens the Color Selector window to let you choose a color to use.

- *As in Preferences*: The color selected in the Image Window Appearance is used.

14.8.17 Show Menubar

The Show Menubar command enables and disables displaying the menubar. It may be useful to disable it if you are working in full-screen mode. If the menubar is not displayed, you can right-click on the image to access the menubar entries.

You can set the default for the menubar in the Image Window Appearance dialog.

14.8.17.1 Activating the Command

- You can access this command from the image menubar through View → Show Menubar.

14.8.18 Show Rulers

The Show Rulers command enables and disables displaying the rulers. It may be useful to disable them if you are working in full-screen mode.

You can set the default for the rulers in the Image Window Appearance dialog.

14.8.18.1 Activating the Command

- You can access this command from the image menubar through View → Show Rulers,

- or by using the keyboard shortcut Shift-Ctrl-R.

14.8.19 Show Scrollbars

The Show Scrollbars command enables and disables displaying the scrollbars. It may be useful to disable them if you are working in full-screen mode.

You can set the default for the scrollbars in the Image Window Appearance dialog.

14.8.19.1 Activating the Command

- You can access this command from the image menubar through View → Show Scrollbars.

14.8.20 Show Statusbar

The Show Statusbar command enables and disables displaying the status bar. It may be useful to disable it when you are working in full-screen mode.

You can set the default for the status bar in the Image Window Appearance dialog.

14.8.20.1 Activating the Command

- You can access this command from the image menubar through View → Show Statusbar.

14.9 The 'Image' Menu

14.9.1 The 'Image' Menu of the Image Window

Figure 14.59: The Contents of the 'Image' Menu

The Image menu contains commands which use or affect the entire image in some way, not just the active layer or some other specific part of the image.

Note
Besides the commands described here, you may also find other entries in the menu. They are not part of GIMP itself, but have been added by extensions (plug-ins). You can find information about the functionality of a Plugin by referring to its documentation.

14.9.2 Duplicate

The Duplicate image command creates a new image which is an exact copy of the current one, with all of its layers, channels and paths. The GIMP Clipboard and the History are not affected.

14.9.2.1 Activating the Command

- You can access this command from the image menubar through Image → Duplicate,

- or by using the keyboard shortcut Ctrl-D.

14.9.3   Mode

Figure 14.60: The 'Mode' submenu of the 'Image' menu

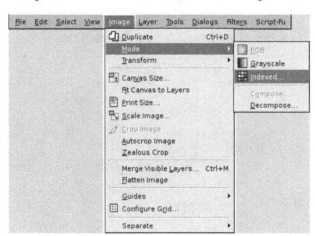

The Mode submenu contains commands which let you change the color mode of the image. There are three modes.

14.9.3.1   Activating the Submenu

• You can access this submenu from the image menubar through Image → Mode.

14.9.3.2   The Contents of the 'Mode' Submenu

• RGB

• Grayscale

• Indexed

• Compose

• Decompose

14.9.4   RGB mode

The RGB command converts your image to RGB mode. See the RGB description in the Glossary for more information. Normally, you work in this mode, which is well-adapted to the screen. It is possible to convert an RGB image to Grayscale or Indexed mode, but be careful: once you have saved the image, you can no longer retrieve the RGB colors, so you should work on a copy of your image.

14.9.4.1   Activating the command

• You can access this command from the image menu bar through Image → Mode → RGB.

14.9.5   Grayscale mode

You can use the Grayscale command to convert your image to grayscale with 256 levels of gray, from 0 (black) to 255 (white). See the glossary for more information about grayscale mode.

14.9.5.1 Activating the Command

- You can access this command from the image menubar through Image → Mode → Grayscale.

14.9.6 Indexed mode

The Indexed command converts your image to indexed mode. See indexed colors in the Glossary for more information about Indexed Color Mode.

14.9.6.1 Activating the Command

- You can access this command from the image menubar through Image → Mode → Indexed.

14.9.6.2 The 'Convert Image to Indexed Colors' dialog

The Indexed command opens the Convert Image to Indexed Colors dialog.

Figure 14.61: The 'Convert Image to Indexed Colors' dialog

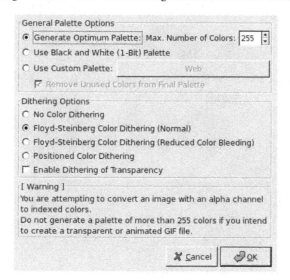

Colormap Options

- Generate optimum palette: This option generates the best possible palette with a default maximum number of 256 colors (classic GIF format). You can reduce this *Maximum Number of Colors*, although this may create unwanted effects (color banding) on smooth transitions. You may be able to lessen the unwanted effects by using dithering, however.

- Use web-optimized palette: use a palette that is optimized for the web.

- Use black and white (1-bit) palette: This option generates an image which uses only two colors, black and white.

- Use custom palette: This button lets you select a custom palette from a list. The number of colors is indicated for each palette. The 'Web' palette, with 216 colors, is the 'web-safe' palette. It was originally created by Netscape to provide colors that would look the same on both Macs and PCs, and Internet Explorer 3 could manage it. Since version 4, MSIE handles a 212 color palette. The problem of color similarity between all platforms has not been solved yet and it probably never will be. When designing a web page, you should keep two principles in mind: use light text on a dark background or dark text on a light background, and never rely on color to convey information.

  Some colors in the palette may not be used if your image does not have many colors. They will be removed from the palette if the Remove unused colors from final palette option is checked.

Dithering Options Since an indexed image contains 256 colors or less, some colors in the original image may not be available in the palette. This may result in some blotchy or solid patches in areas which should have subtle color changes. The dithering options let you correct the unwanted effects created by the Palette Options.

A dithering filter tries to approximate a color which is missing from the palette by instead using clusters of pixels of similar colors which are in the palette. When seen from a distance, these pixels give the impression of a new color. See the Glossary for more information on dithering.

Three filters (plus 'None') are available. It is not possible to predict what the result of a particular filter will be on your image, so you will have to try all of them and see which works best. The 'Positioned Color Dithering' filter is well adapted to animations.

Figure 14.62: Example: full color, with no dithering

This is an example image with a smooth transition in RGB Mode.

Figure 14.63: Example: four colors, with no dithering

The same image, after being transformed to four indexed colors, without dithering.

Figure 14.64: Example: Floyd-Steinberg (normal)

The same image, with four indexed colors and Floyd-Steinberg (normal) dithering.

Figure 14.65: Example: Floyd-Steinberg (reduced color bleeding)

The same image, with four indexed colors and Floyd-Steinberg (reduced color bleeding) dithering.

In a GIF image, transparency is encoded in 1 bit: transparent or not transparent. To give the illusion of partial transparency, you can use the Enable dithering of transparency option. However, the Semi-flatten plug-in may give you better results.

Note

You can edit the color palette of an indexed image by using the Colormap Dialog.

14.9.7 Decompose

With the Decompose command, you can decompose an image into its color components. You can find more information about using this command in the Decompose filter section.

14.9.7.1 Activating the Command

• You can access this command from the image menubar through Image → Mode → Decompose.

14.9.8 Compose

With the Compose command, you can re-compose an image that has been decomposed into its color components. You can find more information about using this command in the Compose filter section.

14.9.8.1 Activating the Command

• You can access this command from the image menubar through Image → Mode → Compose.

14.9.9 Transform

Figure 14.66: The 'Transform' submenu of the 'Image' menu

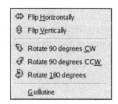

The items on the Transform submenu transform the image by flipping it, rotating it or cropping it.

14.9.9.1 Activating the Submenu

• You can access this submenu from the image menubar through Image → Transform.

14.9.9.2 The Contents of the 'Transform' Submenu

The Transform submenu has the following commands:

• Flip Horizontally; Flip Vertically

• Rotate 90 CW; Rotate 90 CCW; Rotate 180

• Guillotine

14.9.10 Flip Horizontally; Flip Vertically

You can flip the image, or turn it over like a card, by using the Flip Horizontally or Flip Vertically commands. These commands work on the whole image. To flip a selection, use the Flip Tool. To flip a layer, use the functions of the Layer → Transform menu or the Flip Tool.

14.9.10.1 Activating the Commands

- You can access the horizontal flip command from the image menubar through Image → Transform → Flip Horizontally.

- You can access the vertical flip command from the image menubar through Image → Transform → Flip Vertically.

14.9.11 Rotation

You can rotate the image 90 clockwise or counter-clockwise, or rotate it 180, by using the rotation commands on the Transform submenu of the Image menu. These commands can be used to change between Portrait and Landscape orientation. They work on the whole image. If you want to rotate the image at a different angle, rotate a selection or rotate a layer, use the Rotate Tool. You can also rotate a layer by using the Layer Transform menu.

14.9.11.1 Activating the Commands

You can access these three commands from the image menubar through

- Image → Transform → Rotate 90 degrees CW,

- Image → Transform → Rotate 90 degrees CCW and

- Image → Transform → Rotate 180.

14.9.12 Guillotine

The Guillotine command slices up the current image, based on the image's guides. It cuts the image along each guide, similar to slicing documents in an office with a guillotine (paper cutter) and creates new images out of the pieces. For further information on guides, see the glossary entry for Guides.

14.9.12.1 Activating the Command

- You can access this command from the image menubar through Image → Transform → Guillotine.

14.9.13 Canvas Size

The 'canvas' is the visible area of the image. By default the size of the canvas coincides with the size of the layers. The Canvas Size command lets you enlarge or reduce the canvas size without modifying the contents of the layers in the image. When you enlarge the canvas, you create free space around the contents of the image. When you reduce it, the visible area is cropped, however the layers still extend beyond the canvas border.

14.9.13.1 Activating the Command

- You can access this command from the image menubar through Image → Canvas Size.

14.9.13.2 Description of the 'Canvas size' dialog

Figure 14.67: The 'Canvas size' dialog

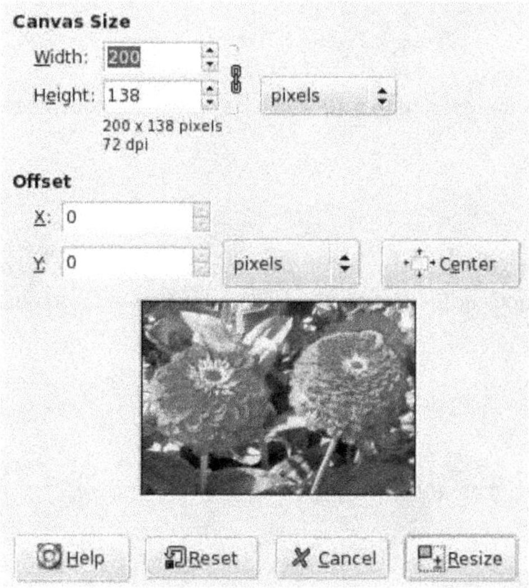

CANVAS SIZE

Width; Height You can set the Width and the Height of the canvas. The default units are pixels but you can choose different units, e.g. percent, if you want to set the new dimensions relative to the current dimensions. If the Chain to the right of the Width and Height is not broken, both Width and Height keep the same relative size to each other. That is, if you change one of the values, the other one also changes a corresponding amount. If you break the Chain by clicking on it, you can set Width and Height separately.

Whatever units you use, information about the size in pixels and the current resolution are always displayed below the *Width* and *Height* fields. You cannot change the resolution in the Canvas Size dialog; if you want to do that, use the Print Size dialog.

OFFSET

X ; Y The X and Y parameters specify the coordinates of the upper left corner of the image relative to the upper left corner of the canvas. When the canvas is smaller than the image, the X and Y values are negative. You can change these values by using the text boxes. The default units are pixels, but you can choose different units. By clicking on the arrows next to the text boxes, you can move the image one pixel at a time. You can move the image ten pixels at a time by clicking on the arrows while pressing the **Shift** key.

Center The Center button allows you to center the image on the canvas. When you click on the Center button, the offset values are automatically calculated and displayed in the text boxes.

Note

When you click on the Resize button, the canvas is resized, but the pixel information and the drawing scale of the image are unchanged.

If the layers of the image did not extend beyond the borders of the canvas before you changed its size, there are no layers on the part of the canvas that was added by resizing it. Therefore, this part of the canvas is transparent and displayed with a checkered pattern, and it is not immediately available for painting. You can either flatten the image, in which case you will get an image with a single layer that fits the canvas exactly, or you can use the Layer to Image Size command to resize only the active layer, without changing any other layers. You can also create a new layer and fill it with the background you want. By doing this, you create a digital 'passe-partout' (a kind of glass mount with a removable back for slipping in a photograph).

14.9.14   Fit Canvas to Layers

The Fit Canvas to Layers command adapts the canvas size (that is, the drawing area) to the size of the largest layer in the image, in both width and height.

14.9.14.1   Activating the command

- You can access this command from the image menubar through Image → Fit Canvas to Layers.

14.9.15   Print Size

You can use the Print Size dialog to change the *dimensions of a printed image* and its *resolution*. This command does not change the number of pixels in the image and it does not resample the image. (If you want to change the size of an image by resampling it, use the Scale Image command.)

14.9.15.1   Activating the Dialog

- You can access this dialog from the image menubar through Image → Print Size.

14.9.15.2   Options in the 'Print Size' Dialog

Figure 14.68: The 'Print Size' dialog

The output resolution determines the number of pixels used per unit length for the printed image. Do not confuse the output resolution with the printer resolution, which is expressed in dpi (dots per inch); several dots are used to print a pixel.

When the dialog is displayed, the resolution shown in the boxes is the resolution of the original image. If you increase the output resolution, the printed page will be smaller, since more pixels are used per unit of length. Conversely, and for the same reason, resizing the image modifies the resolution.

Increasing the resolution results in increasing the sharpness of the printed page. This is quite different from simply reducing the image size by scaling it, since no pixels (and no image information) are removed.

Width; Height You can set the printing Width and Height by using the text boxes. You can also choose the units for these values from the dropdown list.

As soon as you change the Width or the Height, the X and/or Y resolution values automatically change accordingly. If the two resolution values remain linked, the relationship of the width to the height of the image is also automatically maintained. If you would like to set these values independently of each other, simply click on the chain symbol to break the link.

X resolution; Y resolution You can set the resolution used to calculate the printed width and height from the physical size of the image, that is, the number of pixels in it.

Use the text boxes to change these resolution values. They can be linked to keep their relationship constant. The closed chain symbol between the two boxes indicates that the values are linked together. If you break the link by clicking on the chain symbol, you will be able to set the values independently of each other.

14.9.16 Scale Image

The Scale Image command enlarges or reduces the physical size of the image by changing the number of pixels it contains. It changes the size of the contents of the image and resizes the canvas accordingly.

It operates on the entire image. If your image has layers of different sizes, making the image smaller could shrink some of them down to nothing, since a layer cannot be less than one pixel wide or high. If this happens, you will be warned before the operation is performed.

If you only want to scale a particular layer, use the Scale Layer command.

Note

If scaling would produce an image larger than the 'Maximum new image size' set in the Environment page of the Preferences dialog (which has a default of 64Mb), you are warned and asked to confirm the operation before it is performed. You may not experience any problems if you confirm the operation, but you should be aware that very large images consume a lot of resources and extremely large images may take more resources than you have, causing GIMP to crash or not perform well.

14.9.16.1 Activating the Command

- You can access this command from the image menubar through Image → Scale image.

14.9.16.2 The 'Scale Image' Dialog

Figure 14.69: The 'Scale Image' dialog

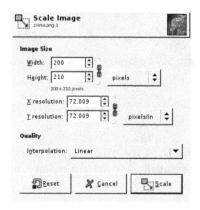

Image Size You should keep in mind that an image can be located in one of four places: in the image file, in RAM after it has been loaded, on your screen when it is displayed, or on paper after it has been printed. Scaling the image changes the number of pixels (the amount of information) the image contains, so it directly affects the amount of memory the image needs (in RAM or in a file).

However printing size also depends upon the resolution of the image, which essentially determines how many pixels there will be on each inch of paper. If you want to change the printing size without scaling the image and changing the number of pixels in it, you should use the Print Size dialog. The screen size depends not only on the number of pixels, but also on the screen resolution, the zoom factor and the setting of the Dot for Dot option.

Width; Height When you click on the Scale command, the dialog displays the dimensions of the original image in pixels. You can set the Width and the Height you want to give to your image by adding or removing pixels. If the chain icon next to the Width and Height boxes is unbroken, the Width and Height will stay in the same proportion to each other. If you break the chain by clicking on it, you can set them independently, but this will distort the image.

However, you do not have to set the dimensions in pixels. You can choose different units from the drop-down menu. If you choose percent as the units, you can set the image size relative to its original size. You can also use physical units, such as inches or millimeters. If you do that, you should set the X resolution and Y resolution fields to appropriate values, because they are used to convert between physical units and image dimensions in pixels.

If you enlarge an image beyond its original size, GIMP calculates the missing pixels by interpolation, but it does not add any new detail. The more you enlarge an image, the more blurred it becomes. The appearance of an enlarged image depends upon the interpolation method you choose. You may improve the appearance by using the Sharpen filter after you have scaled an image, but it is best to use high resolution when you scan, take digital photographs or produce digital images by other means. Raster images inherently do not scale up well.

You may need to reduce your image if you intend to use it on a web page. You have to consider that most internet users have relatively small screens which cannot completely display a large image. Many screens have a resolution of 1024x768 or even less.

Adding or removing pixels is called 'Resampling'.

X resolution; Y resolution You can set the printing resolution for the image in the X resolution and Y resolution fields. You can also change the units of measurement by using the drop-down menu.

Quality To change the image size, either some pixels have to be removed or new pixels must be added. The process you use determines the quality of the result. The Interpolation drop down list provides a selection of available methods of interpolating the color of pixels in a scaled image:

Interpolation

- None: No interpolation is used. Pixels are simply enlarged or removed, as they are when zooming. This method is low quality, but very fast.
- Linear: This method is relatively fast, but still provides fairly good results.
- Cubic: The method that produces the best results, but also the slowest method.

Note
See also the Scale tool, which lets you scale a layer, a selection or a path.

14.9.17 Crop Image

The Crop Image command crops the image to the boundary of the selection by removing any strips at the edges whose contents are all completely unselected. Areas which are partially selected (for example, by feathering) are not cropped. If there is no selection for the image, the menu entry is insensitive and grayed out.

Note
This command crops all of the image layers. To crop just the active layer, use the Crop Layer command.

14.9.17.1 Activating the command

- You can access this command on the image menu bar through Image → Crop Image.

14.9.18   Autocrop Image

The Autocrop Image command removes the borders from an image. It searches the active layer for the largest possible border area that is all the same color, and then crops this area from the image, as if you had used the Crop tool.

Caution

Note carefully that this command only uses the *active layer* of the image to find borders. If other layers have color variations extending into the border zone of the active layer, they are cropped away.

14.9.18.1   Activating the Command

- You can access this command from the image menubar through Image → Autocrop Image.

14.9.19   Zealous Crop

The Zealous Crop command crops an image using a single solid color as a guide. It crops the edges, as with the Autocrop command, but it also crops the areas in the middle of the image which have the same color (at least, in principle).

Caution

Please note that Zealous Crop crops all of the layers, although it only analyzes the active layer. This may lead to a loss of information from the other layers.

14.9.19.1   Example

Figure 14.70: 'Zealous Crop' Example

(a) *Original image*   (b) *Autocrop applied*   (c) *Zealous Crop applied*

14.9.19.2   Activating the Command

- You can access this command from the image menubar through Image → Zealous Crop.

14.9.20   Merge Visible Layers

The Merge Visible Layers command merges the layers which are visible into a single layer. Visible layers are those which are indicated on the Layers dialog with an 'eye' icon.

14.9.20.1 Activating the Command

- You can access this command from the image menubar through Image → Merge Visible Layers,

- or by using the keyboard shortcut Ctrl-M.

14.9.20.2 Description of the 'Merge Visible Layers' Dialog

Figure 14.71: The 'Merge Visible Layers' Dialog

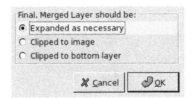

Final, Merged Layer should be: Visible layers are the layers which are marked with an 'eye' icon in the Layers dialog.

- *Expanded as necessary*: The final layer is large enough to contain all of the merged layers. Please note that a layer in GIMP can be larger than the image.
- *Clipped to image*: The final layer is the same size as the image. Remember that layers in GIMP can be larger than the image itself. Any layers in the image that are larger than the image are clipped by this option.
- *Clipped to bottom layer*: The final layer is the same size as the bottom layer. If the bottom layer is smaller than some of the visible layers, the final layer is clipped and trimmed to the size and position of the bottom layer.

14.9.21 Flatten Image

Figure 14.72: Accessing the Flatten Image menu item

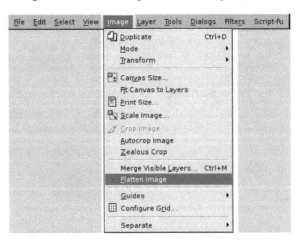

The Flatten Image command merges all of the layers of the image into a single layer with no alpha channel. After the image is flattened, it has the same appearance it had before. The difference is that all of the image contents are in a single layer without transparency. If there are any areas which are transparent through all of the layers of the original image, the background color is visible.

This operation makes significant changes to the structure of the image. It is normally only necessary when you would like to save an image in a format which does not support levels or transparency (an alpha channel).

14.9.21.1 Activating the Command

- You can access this command from the image menubar through Image → Flatten Image.

14.9.22 Guides

Figure 14.73: The 'Guides' options of the 'Image' submenu

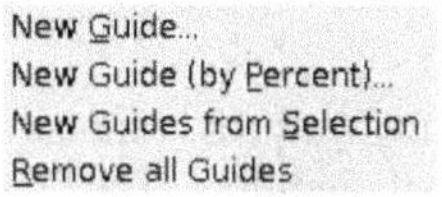

New Guide...
New Guide (by Percent)...
New Guides from Selection
Remove all Guides

The Guides submenu contains various commands for the creation and removal of guides.

14.9.22.1 Activating the Submenu

- You can access this submenu from the image menubar through Image → Guides.

14.9.22.2 The Contents of the 'Guides' Submenu Il contenuto del sottomenu 'Guide'

The Guides submenu contains the following commands:

- New Guide
- New Guide (by Percent)
- New Guides from Selection
- Remove all Guides

14.9.23 New Guide

The New Guide command adds a guide to the image. For more information about guides, see the glossary entry on Guides.

Tip
You can add guides to the image more quickly, but less accurately, by simply clicking and dragging guides from the image rulers and positioning them where you would like.

14.9.23.1 Activating the Command

- You can access this command from the image menubar through Image → Guides → New Guide

14.9.23.2 'New Guide' Options

Figure 14.74: The 'New Guide' Dialog

Direction ; Position When you select New Guide, a dialog opens, which allows you to set the Direction and Position, in pixels, of the new guide more precisely than by using click-and-drag. The Direction may be Horizontal or Vertical. The coordinate origin for the Position is the upper left corner of the image.

14.9.24 New Guide (by Percent)

The New Guide (by Percent) command adds a guide to the image. The position of the guide is specified as a percentage of the Height and Width.

Tip

You can add guides to the image more quickly by simply clicking and dragging guides from the image rulers and positioning them where you would like. Guides you draw with click-and-drag are not as precisely positioned as those you draw with this command, however.

14.9.24.1 Activating the Command

- You can access this command from the image menubar through Image → Guides → New Guide (by Percent).

14.9.24.2 'New Guide (by Percent)' Options

Figure 14.75: The 'New Guide (by Percent)' Dialog

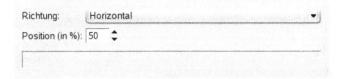

Direction You can choose the Direction of the guide, either Horizontal or Vertical, by using the drop-down list.

14.9.25 New Guides from Selection

The New Guides from Selection command adds four guide lines, one for each of the upper, lower, left and right edges of the current selection. If there is no selection in the current image, no guides are drawn.

14.9.25.1 Activating the Command

• You can access this command from the image menubar through Image → Guides → New Guides from Selection.

14.9.26 Remove all guides

The Remove all Guides command removes all guides from the image.

14.9.26.1 Activating the Command

• You can access this command from the image menubar through Image → Guides → Remove all guides.

14.9.27 Configure Grid

The Configure Grid command lets you set the properties of the grid which you can display over your image while you are working on it. The GIMP provides only Cartesian grids. You can choose the color of the grid lines, and the spacing and offsets from the origin of the image, independently for the horizontal and vertical grid lines. You can choose one of five different grid styles.

14.9.27.1 Activating the Command

• You can access this command from the image menubar through Image → Configure Grid.

14.9.27.2 Description of the 'Configure Grid' dialog

Figure 14.76: The 'Configure grid' dialog

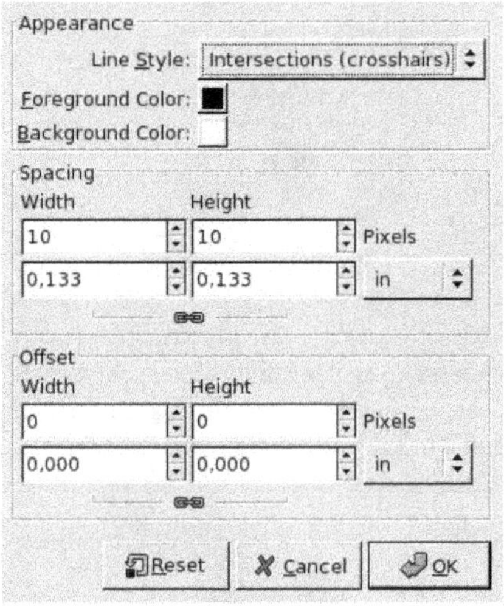

APPEARANCE

Line style

> **Intersections (dots)** This style, the least conspicuous, shows a simple dot at each intersection of the grid lines.
>
> **Intersections (crosshairs)** This style, the default, shows a plus-shaped crosshair at each intersection of the grid lines.

Dashed This style shows dashed lines in the foreground color of the grid. If the lines are too close together, the grid won't look good.

Double dashed This style shows dashed lines, where the foreground and background colors of the grid alternate.

Solid This style shows solid grid lines in the foreground color of the grid.

Foreground and Background colors Click on the color dwell to select a new color for the grid.

SPACING

Width and Height You can select the cell size of the grid and the unit of measurement.

OFFSET

Width and Height You can set the offset of the first cell. The coordinate origin is the upper left corner of the image. By default, the grid begins at the coordinate origin, (0,0).

14.10 The 'Layers' Menu

14.10.1 Introduction to the 'Layer' Menu

Figure 14.77: The Contents of the 'Layer' Menu

The items on the Layer menu allow you to work on layers. In addition to accessing the Layer menu from the Image menubar and by right-clicking on the image window, you can get to it by right-clicking on the thumbnail of a layer in the Layers dialog. You can also perform several of the operations on this menu by clicking on buttons in the Layers dialog, for example, resizing a layer, managing layer transparency and merging layers.

Note
Besides the commands described here, you may also find other entries in the menu. They are not part of GIMP itself, but have been added by extensions (plug-ins). You can find information about the functionality of a Plugin by referring to its documentation.

14.10.2 New Layer

The New Layer command adds a new, empty layer to the layer stack of the image, just above the active layer. The command displays a dialog in which you can specify the size of the new layer.

14.10.2.1 Activating the Command

- You can access this command from the image menubar through Layer → New Layer.

14.10.2.2 Description of the 'New Layer' Dialog

Figure 14.78: The 'New Layer' dialog

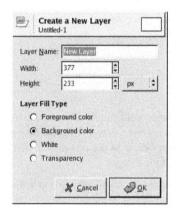

Layer Name The name of the new layer. It does not have any functional significance; it is simply a convenient way for you to remember the purpose of the layer. The default name is 'New Layer'. If a layer with the name you choose already exists, a number is automatically appended to it to make it unique (e.g., 'New Layer#1') when you click on the OK button.

Width; Height The dimensions of the new layer. When the dialog appears, the values are initialized to the dimensions of the image. You can change them by using the two text boxes. You can also change the units in the pull-down menu to the right.

Layer Fill Type There are four options for the solid color that fills the layer: the current Foreground color, the current Background color, White and Transparency.

14.10.3 Duplicate layer

The Duplicate Layer command adds a new layer to the image which is a nearly identical copy of the active layer. The name of the new layer is the same as the name of the original layer, but with ' copy' appended to it.

If you duplicate a background layer which does not have an alpha channel, the new layer is provided with one. In addition, if there are any 'parasites' attached to the active layer, they are not duplicated. (If your understanding of the word 'parasites' is limited to small, unpleasant creatures, please ignore the last sentence.)

14.10.3.1 Activating the Command

- You can access this command from the image menubar through Layer → Duplicate Layer

14.10.4 Anchor layer

When you move or paste a selection, a temporary layer, called a 'floating layer' or 'floating selection', is added to the layer stack. As long as the floating layer persists, you can work only on it. To work on the rest of the image, you must 'anchor' the floating layer to the former active layer with the Anchor layer command. If the image does not contain a floating selection, this menu entry is insensitive and grayed out.

Note

If there is an active selection tool, the mouse pointer is displayed with an anchor icon when it is outside of the selection. A left click then anchors the floating selection.

You may also click on the New layer command on the Layers dialog, which anchors the floating selection to a new layer. See Section 14.10.2.

14.10.4.1 Activating the Command

- You can access this command from the image menubar through Layer → Anchor layer,

- or by using the keyboard shortcut Ctrl-H.

14.10.5 Merge Down

The Merge Down command merges the active layer with the layer just below it in the stack, taking into account the various properties of the active layer, such as its opacity and layer mode. The resulting merged layer will be in Normal mode, and will inherit the opacity of the layer below. If the layer below is not opaque, or if it is in some mode other than Normal, then this command will generally change the appearance of the image.

The most common use of Merge Down is to construct a layer, by starting with a 'base layer' (usually opaque and in Normal mode, so that you can see what you are doing), and adding a 'modification layer' on top of it, with whatever shape, opacity, and layer mode you need. In this case, merging down the modification layer will combine the two layers into one, without changing the way the image looks.

14.10.5.1 Activating the Command

- You can access this command from the image menubar through Layer → Merge Down.

14.10.6 Delete Layer

The Delete Layer command deletes the current layer from the image.

14.10.6.1 Activating the Command

- You can access this command from the image menubar through Layer → Delete Layer.

14.10.7 Discard Text Information

This option is displayed only if a text layer is present.

Figure 14.79: Layer Text Discard command

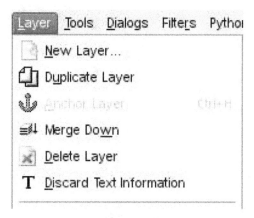

When you add text to an image, GIMP adds specific informations. This command lets you discard these informations, transforming the current text layer into a normal bitmap layer. The reason to do that is not evident.

Note that this transformation of text into bitmap is automatically performed when you apply a graphic operation to the text layer. You can get text information back by undoing the operation which modified the text.

14.10.7.1 Activating the Command

- You can access this command from the image menubar through Layer → Discard Text Information.

14.10.8 'Stack' Submenu

Figure 14.80: The 'Stack' submenu

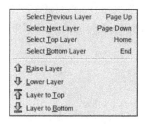

The layer stack is simply the list of layers in the Layers dialog. The Stack submenu contains operations which either select a new layer as the active layer, or change the position of the active layer in the layer stack.

14.10.8.1 Activating the Submenu

- You can access this submenu from the image menubar through Layer → Stack.

14.10.8.2 The Contents of the 'Stack' Submenu

The Stack submenu contains the following commands:

- Section 14.10.9

14.10.9   Select Previous Layer

The Select Previous Layer command selects the layer just above the active layer in the layer stack. The command highlights the layer in the Layers Dialog and makes it the new active layer. If the active layer is already at the top of the stack, this menu entry is insensitive and grayed out.

Note

Note that on a standard Windows-style English keyboard, the default shortcut **Page_Up** does not refer to the key on the numeric keypad, but to the other **Page_Up** key in the group of six keys to the left of the numeric keypad.

Tip

The keyboard shortcuts for Select Previous Layer and Select Next Layer may be very useful if you frequently pick colors from one layer to use for painting on another layer, especially when you use them with the color-picker tool, which you get by holding down the **Ctrl** key with most of the painting tools.

14.10.9.1   Activating the Command

- You can access this command from the image menubar through Layer → Stack → Select Previous Layer,

- or by using the keyboard shortcut **Page_Up**,

- or the 'Up-arrow' key,

- or simply by clicking on the layer name in the Layers Dialog.

14.10.10   Select Next Layer

The Select Next Layer command selects the layer just underneath the active layer in the layer stack. The command highlights the layer in the Layers Dialog and makes it the new active layer. If the active layer is already at the bottom of the stack, this menu entry is insensitive and grayed out.

Note

Note that on a standard Windows-style English keyboard, the default shortcut **Page_Down** does not refer to the key on the numeric keypad, but to the other **Page_Down** key in the group of six keys to the left of the numeric keypad.

14.10.10.1 Activating the Command

* You can access this command from the image menubar through Layer → Stack → Select Next Layer,

* or by using the keyboard shortcut **Page_Down**,

* or the 'Down-arrow' key,

* or simply by clicking on the layer name in Layers Dialog.

14.10.11 Select Top Layer

The Select Top Layer command makes the top layer in the stack the active layer for the image and highlights it in the Layers dialog. If the active layer is already the top layer in the stack, this menu entry is insensitive and grayed out.

Note
Note that on a standard Windows-style English keyboard, the default keyboard shortcut **Home** does not refer to the key on the numeric keypad, but to the other **Home** key in the group of six keys to the left of the numeric keypad.

14.10.11.1 Activating the Command

* You can access this command from the image menubar through Layer → Stack → Select Top Layer,

* or by using the keyboard shortcut **Home**,

* or simply by clicking on the layer name in the Layers Dialog.

14.10.12 Select Bottom Layer

With the Select Bottom Layer command, you can make the bottom layer in the stack become the active layer for the image. It is then highlighted in the Layers dialog. If the bottom layer of the stack is already the active layer, this menu entry is insensitive and grayed out.

Note
Note that on a standard Windows-style English keyboard, the default keyboard shortcut refers to the **End** key in the group of six keys to the left of the numeric keypad, not to the one in the numeric keypad.

14.10.12.1 Activating the Command

* You can access this command from the image menubar through Layer → Stack → Select Bottom Layer,

* by using the keyboard shortcut **End**,

* or simply by clicking on the name of the layer in the Layers dialog.

14.10.13 Raise Layer

The Raise Layer command raises the active layer one position in the layer stack. If the active layer is already at the top or if there is only one layer, this menu entry is insensitive and grayed out. If the active layer is at the bottom of the stack and it does not have an alpha channel, it cannot be raised until you add an alpha channel to it.

14.10.13.1 Activating the Command

- You can access this command from the image menubar through Layer → Stack → Raise Layer,

- or by clicking on the up-arrow icon at the bottom of the Layers dialog.

14.10.14 Lower Layer

The Lower layer command lowers the active layer one position in the layer stack. If the active layer is already at the bottom of the stack or if there is only one layer, this menu entry is insensitive and grayed out.

14.10.14.1 Activating the Command

- You can access this command from the image menubar through Layer → Stack → Lower Layer,

- or by clicking on the down-arrow icon at the bottom of the Layers dialog.

14.10.15 Layer to Top

The Layer to Top command raises the active layer to the top of the layer stack. If the active layer is already at the top or if there is only one layer, this menu entry is insensitive and grayed out. If the active layer is at the bottom of the stack and it does not have an alpha channel, you cannot raise it until you add an alpha channel to it.

14.10.15.1 Activating the Command

- You can access this command from the image menubar through Layer → Stack → Layer to Top,

- or by pressing the **Shift** key and clicking on the up-arrow icon at the bottom of the Layers dialog.

14.10.16 Layer to Bottom

The Layer to bottom command lowers the active layer to the bottom of the layer stack. If the active layer is already at the bottom of the stack or if there is only one layer, this menu entry is insensitive and grayed out.

14.10.16.1 Activating the Command

- You can access this command from the image menubar through Layer → Stack → Layer to Bottom,

- or by pressing the **Shift** key and clicking on the down-arrow icon at the bottom of the Layers dialog.

14.10.17 The 'Colors' Submenu

Figure 14.81: The 'Colors' submenu

The Colors submenu contains operations which alter colors within the active layer. The operations at the top of the list access the Color tools for the image. These are described in the Toolbox chapter.

 Warning
This command operates only on the layer which is *active at the time the command is called*. Even after you make another layer the active layer, the operation continues to affect the layer on which you performed the command.

14.10.17.1 Activating the submenu

- You can access this submenu from the image menubar through Layer → Colors.

14.10.17.2 Contents of the 'Colors' Submenu

In addition to the menu items relating to the color tools which are at the top of the list, the Colors submenu contains the following menu items:

- Section 14.10.18

- Section 14.10.19

- Section 14.10.21

14.10.18 Desaturate

By using the Desaturate command, you can convert all of the colors on the active layer to corresponding shades of gray. This differs from converting the image to grayscale in two respects. First, it only operates on the active layer and second, the colors on the layer are still RGB values with three components. This means that you can paint on the layer, or individual parts of it, using color at a later time.

 Note
This command only works on layers of RGB images. If the image is in Grayscale or Indexed mode, the menu entry is insensitive and grayed out.

14.10.18.1   Activating the Command

- You can access this command from the image menubar through Layer → Colors → Desaturate.

14.10.19   Invert

The Invert command inverts all the pixel colors and brightness values in the current layer, as if the image were converted into a negative. Dark areas become bright and bright areas become dark. Hues are replaced by their complementary colors. For more information about colors, see the Glossary entry about Color Model.

Note
This command only works on layers of RGB and Grayscale images. If the current image is Indexed, the menu entry is insensitive and grayed out.

Warning
Do not confuse this command with the Invert Selection command.

14.10.19.1   Activating the Command

- You can access this command from the image menubar through Layer → Colors → Invert.

14.10.19.2   Example

Figure 14.82: Applying 'Invert layer colors'

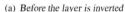

(a) *Before the layer is inverted*   (b) *After the layer is inverted*

14.10.20   Layer Color-Stretching Commands

GIMP has several automatic commands for stretching the columns of the histogram for the color channels of the active layer. By pushing bright pixels to the right and dark pixels to the left, they make bright pixels brighter and dark pixels darker, which enhances the contrast in the layer.

Some of the commands stretch the three color channels equally, so that the hues are not changed. Other commands stretch each of the color channels separately, which changes the hues.

The way the stretching is done varies with the different commands and the results look different. It is not easy to predict exactly what each command will do. If you know exactly what you are doing, you can get the same results, and even more, with the Levels tool.

Here are examples of the results of these commands, all together on one page, so you can compare them more easily. The most appropriate command depends upon your image, so you should try each of them to see which command works best on it.

El GIMP tiene varios comandos automáticos para extender las columnas del histograma para los canales de color de la capa activa. Al desplazar los píxeles claros hacia la derecha y los oscuros hacia la izquierda, hacen los píxeles claros más claros y los oscuros más oscuros, lo que realza el contraste en la capa.

Figure 14.83: The original layer and its histograms

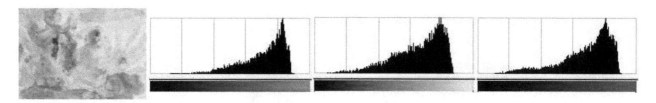

This layer doesn't have any very bright or very dark pixels, so it works well with these commands.

Figure 14.84: The 'Equalize' command

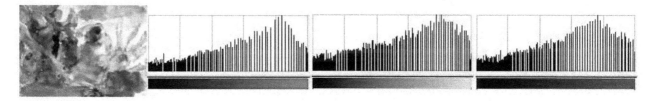

Equalize

Figure 14.85: The 'White Balance' command

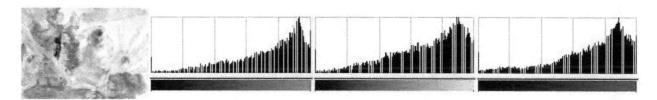

White Balance

Figure 14.86: The 'Color Enhance' command

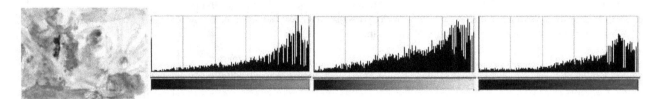

Color Enhance

Figure 14.87: The 'Normalize' command

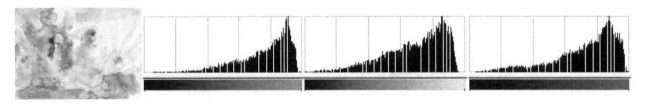

Normalize

Figure 14.88: The 'Stretch Contrast' command

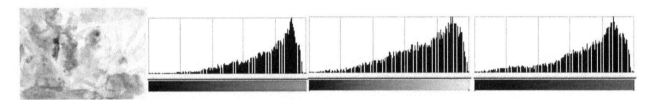

Stretch Contrast

Figure 14.89: The 'Stretch HSV' command

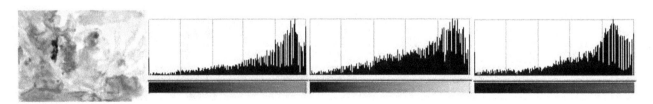

Stretch HSV

14.10.21   The 'Auto' Submenu

Figure 14.90: The 'Colors/Auto' submenu

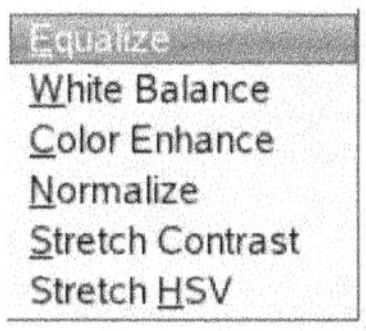

The Auto submenu contains operations which automatically adjust the distribution of colors in the active layer, without requiring any input from the user. Several of these operations are actually implemented as plugins.

14.10.21.1   Activating the submenu

• You can access this submenu from the image window through Layer → Colors → Auto.

14.10.21.2   Contents of the 'Auto' Submenu

The Auto submenu contains the following entries:

• Section 14.10.22

• Section 14.10.23

• Section 14.10.24

• Section 14.10.25

• Section 14.10.26

• Section 14.10.27

14.10.22   Equalize

The Equalize command automatically adjusts the brightness of colors across the active layer so that the histogram for the Value channel is as nearly flat as possible, that is, so that each possible brightness value appears at about the same number of pixels as every other value. You can see this in the histograms in the example below, in that pixel colors which occur frequently in the image are stretched further apart than pixel colors which occur only rarely. The results of this command can vary quite a bit. Sometimes 'Equalize' works very well to enhance the contrast in an image, bringing out details which were hard to see before. Other times, the results look very bad. It is a very powerful operation and it is worth trying to see if it will improve your image. It works on layers from RGB and Grayscale images. If the image is Indexed, the menu entry is insensitive and grayed out.

14.10.22.1   Activating the Command

• You can access this command from the image menubar through Layers → Color → Auto → Equalize.

• or by using the keyboard shortcut Shift-Page_Down.

14.10.22.2 'Equalize Layer' example

Figure 14.91: Original image

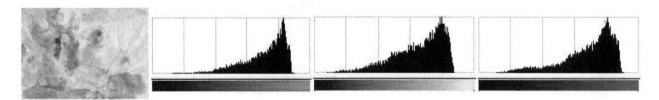

The active layer and its Red, Green, Blue histograms before Equalize.

Figure 14.92: Image after the command

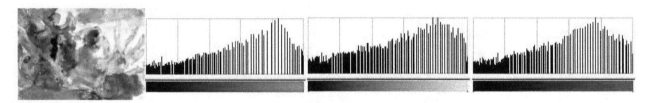

The active layer and its Red, Green, Blue histograms after treatment. Histogram stretching creates gaps between pixel columns giving it a striped look.

14.10.23 White Balance

The White Balance command automatically adjusts the colors of the active layer by stretching the Red, Green and Blue channels separately. To do this, it discards pixel colors at each end of the Red, Green and Blue histograms which are used by only 0.05% of the pixels in the image and stretches the remaining range as much as possible. The result is that pixel colors which occur very infrequently at the outer edges of the histograms (perhaps bits of dust, etc.) do not negatively influence the minimum and maximum values used for stretching the histograms, in comparison with Stretch Contrast. Like 'Stretch Contrast', however, there may be hue shifts in the resulting image.

This command suits images with poor white or black. Since it tends to create pure white (and black), it may be useful e.g. to enhance photographs.

White Balance operates on layers from RGB images. If the image is Indexed or Grayscale, the menu item is insensitive and grayed out.

14.10.23.1 Activating the Command

• You can access this command from the image menubar through Layer → Colors → Auto → White Balance.

14.10.23.2 'White Balance' example

Figure 14.93: Original image

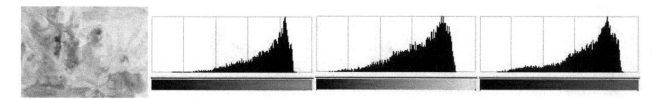

The active layer and its Red, Green and Blue histograms before White Balance.

Figure 14.94: Image after the command

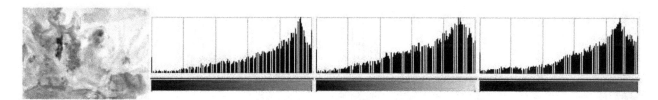

The active layer and its Red, Green and Blue histograms after White Balance. Poor white areas in the image became pure white. Histogram stretching creates gaps between the pixel columns, giving it a striped look.

14.10.24 Color Enhance

The Color Enhance command increases the saturation range of the colors in the layer, without altering brightness or hue. It does this by converting the colors to HSV space, measuring the range of saturation values across the image, then stretching this range to be as large as possible, and finally converting the colors back to RGB. It is similar to Stretch Contrast, except that it works in the HSV color space, so it preserves the hue. It works on layers from RGB and Indexed images. If the image is Grayscale, the menu entry is insensitive and grayed out.

14.10.24.1 Activating the Command

- You can access this command from the image menubar through Layer → Colors → Auto → Color Enhance.

14.10.24.2 'Color Enhance' example

Figure 14.95: 'Color Enhance' example (Original image)

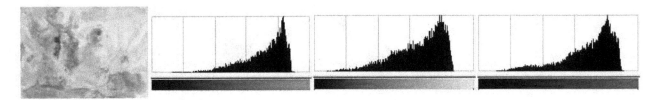

The active layer and its Red, Green and Blue histograms before Color Enhance.

Figure 14.96: 'Color Enhance' example (Image after the command)

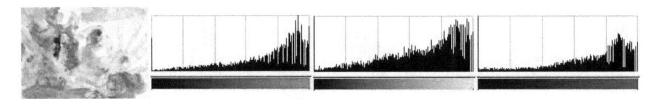

The active layer and its Red, Green and Blue histograms after Color Enhance. The result may not always be what you expect.

14.10.25 Normalize

The Normalize command scales the brightness values of the active layer so that the darkest point becomes black and the brightest point becomes as bright as possible, without altering its hue. This is often a 'magic fix' for images that are dim or washed out. 'Normalize' works on layers from RGB, Grayscale, and Indexed images.

14.10.25.1 Activating the Command

• You can access this command from the image menubar through Layer → Colors → Auto → Normalize.

14.10.25.2 'Normalize'Example

Figure 14.97: 'Normalize'Example (Original image)

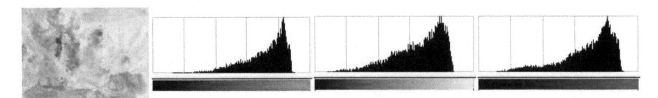

The active layer and its Red, Green and Blue histograms before Normalize.

Figure 14.98: 'Normalize' Example (Image after the command)

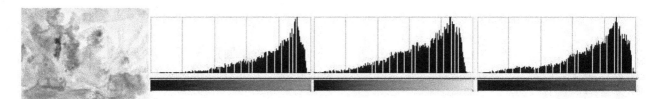

The active layer and its Red, Green and Blue histograms after Normalize. The contrast is enhanced. Histogram stretching creates gaps between the pixel columns, giving it a striped look.

14.10.26   Stretch Contrast

The Stretch Contrast command automatically stretches the histogram values in the active layer. For each channel of the active layer, it finds the minimum and maximum values and uses them to stretch the Red, Green and Blue histograms to the full contrast range. The bright colors become brighter and the dark colors become darker, which increases the contrast. This command produces a somewhat similar effect to the Normalize command, except that it works on each color channel of the layer individually. This usually leads to color shifts in the image, so it may not produce the desired result. 'Stretch Contrast' works on layers of RGB, Grayscale and Indexed images. Use 'Stretch Contrast' only if you want to remove an undesirable color tint from an image which should contain pure white and pure black.

This command is also similar to the Color Balance command, but it does not reject any of the very dark or very bright pixels, so the white might be impure.

14.10.26.1   Activating the Command

• This command can be accessed from an image menubar as Layer → Colors → Auto → Stretch Contrast.

14.10.26.2   'Stretch Contrast' Example

Figure 14.99: Original image

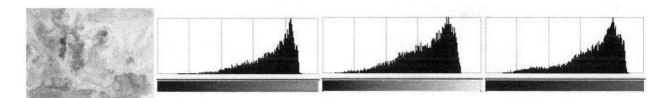

The layer and its Red, Green and Blue histograms before Stretch Contrast.

Figure 14.100: Image after the command

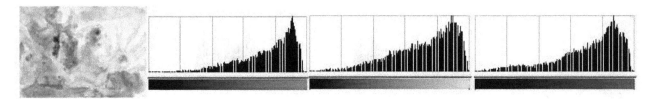

The layer and its Red and Green and Blue histograms after Stretch Contrast. The pixel columns do not reach the right end of the histogram (255) because of a few very bright pixels, unlike White Balance. Histogram stretching creates gaps between the pixel columns, giving it a striped look.

14.10.27 Stretch HSV

The Stretch HSV command does the same thing as the Stretch Contrast command, except that it works in HSV color space, rather than RGB color space, and it preserves the Hue. Thus, it independently stretches the ranges of the Hue, Saturation and Value components of the colors. Occasionally the results are good, often they are a bit odd. 'Stretch HSV' operates on layers from RGB and Indexed images. If the image is Grayscale, the menu entry is insensitive and grayed out.

14.10.27.1 Activating the Command

• You can access this command from the image menubar through Layer → Colors → Auto → Stretch HSV.

14.10.27.2 'Stretch HSV' example

Figure 14.101: Original image

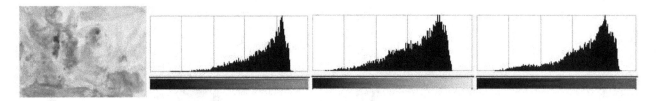

The active layer and its Red, Green and Blue histograms before Stretch HSV.

Figure 14.102: Image after the command

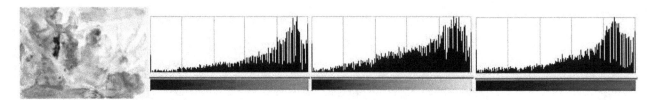

The active layer and its Red, Green and Blue histograms after Stretch HSV. Contrast, luminosity and hues are enhanced.

14.10.28   Autocrop Layer

The Autocrop Layer command automatically crops the active layer, unlike the Crop Tool, or the Crop Layer command which let you manually define the area to be cropped.

This command removes the largest possible area around the outside edge which all has the same color. It does this by scanning the layer along a horizontal line and a vertical line and cropping the layer as soon as it encounters a different color, whatever its transparency.

You can use this command to crop the layer to the dimensions of a subject that is lost in a solid background which is too large.

14.10.28.1   Activating the Command

• You can access this command from the image menubar through Layer → Autocrop Layer.

14.10.28.2   Example

Figure 14.103: Example

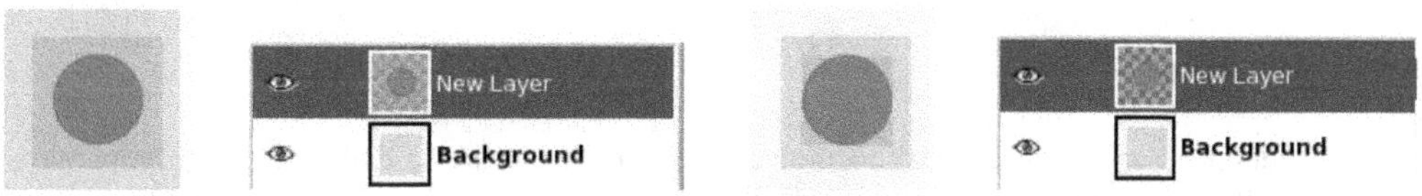

(a) *Before apply-*   (b)   (c) *After applying*   (d)
ing Autocrop Layer   *Autocrop Layer*

14.10.29   The 'Mask' Submenu

Figure 14.104: The 'Mask' submenu of the 'Layer' menu

The Mask submenu of the Layer menu contains commands which work with masks: creating a mask, applying a mask, deleting a mask or converting a mask into a selection. See the Layer Masks section for more information on layer masks and how to use them.

14.10.29.1   Activating the Submenu

• You can access this submenu from the image menubar through Layer → Mask.

14.10.29.2 The Contents of the 'Mask' Submenu

The Mask submenu contains the following commands:

- Section 14.10.30

- Section 14.10.31

- Section 14.10.32

- Section 14.10.35

- Section 14.10.33

- Section 14.10.34

- Section 14.10.36

- Section 14.10.37

- Section 14.10.38

- Section 14.10.39

14.10.30 Add Layer Mask

The Add Layer Mask command adds a layer mask to the active layer. It displays a dialog in which you can set the initial properties of the mask. If the layer already has a layer mask, or if it cannot have one because it does not have an alpha channel, the menu entry is insensitive and grayed out.

A layer mask lets you define which parts of the layer are opaque, semi-transparent or transparent. See the Layer Mask section for more information.

14.10.30.1 Activating the Command

- You can access this command from the image menubar through Layer → Mask → Add Layer Mask

- or from the pop-up menu you get by right-clicking on the active layer in the Layers Dialog.

14.10.30.2 Description of the 'Add Layer Mask' Dialog

Figure 14.105: The 'Add Layer Mask' dialog

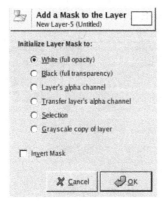

Initialize Layer Mask to This dialog allows you six choices for the initial contents of the layer mask:

White (full opacity) With this option, the layer mask will make all of the layer fully opaque. That means that you will not notice any difference in the appearance of the layer until you paint on the layer mask.

Black (full transparency) With this option, the layer mask will make all of the layer fully transparent. This is represented in the image by a checkered pattern on which you will need to paint to make any part of the layer visible.

Layer's alpha channel With this option, the contents of the alpha channel are used to fill the layer mask. The alpha channel itself is not altered, so the transparency of partially visible areas is increased.

Transfer layer's alpha channel This option does the same thing as the previous option, except that it also resets the layer's alpha channel to full opacity. The effect is to transfer the transparency information from the alpha channel to the layer mask, leaving the layer with the same appearance as before. The only difference is that the visibility of the layer is now determined by the layer mask and not by the alpha channel.

Selection This option converts the current selection into a layer mask, so that selected areas are opaque, and unselected areas are transparent. If any areas are partially selected, you can click on the QuickMask button to help you predict what the effects will be.

Grayscale copy of layer This option converts the layer itself into a layer mask. It is particularly useful when you plan to add new contents to the layer afterwards.

Invert Mask If you check the Invert Mask box at the bottom of the dialog, the resulting mask is inverted, so that transparent areas become opaque and vice versa.

When you click on the OK button, a thumbnail of the layer mask appears to the right of the thumbnail of the layer in the Layers Dialog.

14.10.31   Apply Layer Mask

The Apply Layer Mask command merges the layer mask with the current layer. The transparency information in the layer mask is transferred to the alpha channel and the layer mask is removed. If the active layer does not have a layer mask, the menu entry is insensitive and grayed out. See the Layer Masks section for more information.

14.10.31.1   Activating the Command

- You can access this command from the image menubar through Layer → Mask → Apply Layer Mask,

- or from the pop-up menu you get by right-clicking on the active layer in the Layers Dialog.

14.10.32   Delete Layer Mask

The Delete Layer Mask command deletes the active layer's layer mask, without modifying the active layer itself. If the active layer does not have a layer mask, the menu entry is insensitive and grayed out.

14.10.32.1   Activating the Command

- You can access this command from the image menubar through Layer → Mask → Delete Layer Mask,

- or from the pop-up menu you get by right-clicking on the active layer in the Layers Dialog.

14.10.33   Edit Layer Mask

When you click on the Edit Layer Mask item on the Layer Mask submenu, a check is displayed next to it, the layer mask becomes the active component of the current layer and the layer mask is displayed in the Layers Dialog with a white border. When you uncheck it, the layer itself becomes the active component and it is displayed with a white border. You can also activate the component you want more simply by clicking on it in the Layers Dialog.

14.10.33.1 Activating the Command

- You can access this command from the image menubar through Layer → Mask → Edit Layer Mask.

- You can undo this action by unchecking the menu entry in the Layer → Mask menu or by clicking on the layer component in the Layers Dialog.

14.10.34 Disable Layer Mask

As soon as you create a layer mask, it acts on the image. The Disable Layer Mask command allows you to suspend this action. When you click on the menu entry, a check is displayed next to it and the border of the layer mask's thumbnail in the Layers Dialog turns red.

14.10.34.1 Activating the Command

- You can access this command from the image menubar through Layer → Mask → Disable Layer Mask,

- or by holding down the **Ctrl** key (Ctrl-Alt on some systems) and single-clicking on the layer mask's thumbnail in the Layers Dialog.

- You can undo this action by unchecking the menu entry in the Layer → Mask menu or by **Ctrl**-clicking (or Ctrl-Alt-clicking) again on the layer mask's thumbnail.

14.10.35 Show Layer Mask

The Show Layer Mask command lets you see the layer mask better by turning the image invisible. When you click on the menu entry, a check is displayed next to it and the layer mask's thumbnail in the Layers Dialog is shown with a green border. The layer itself is not modified; you can turn it visible again later.

14.10.35.1 Activating the Command

- You can access this command from the image menubar through Layer → Mask → Show Layer Mask,

- or by holding down the **Alt** key (Ctrl-Alt on some systems) and single-clicking on the layer mask's thumbnail in the Layers Dialog.

- You can undo this action by unchecking the menu entry in the Layer → Mask submenu or by **Alt**-clicking (or Ctrl-Alt-clicking) again on the layer mask's thumbnail.

14.10.36 Mask to Selection

The Mask to Selection command converts the layer mask of the active layer into a selection, which replaces the selection that is already active in the image. White areas of the layer mask are selected, black areas are not selected, and gray areas are converted into feathered selections. The layer mask itself is not modified by this command.

14.10.36.1 Activating the Command

- You can access this command from the image menubar through Layer → Mask → Mask to Selection,

- or from the pop-up menu you get by right-clicking on the active layer in the Layers Dialog.

14.10.36.2 Illustration of 'Layer Mask to Selection'

Figure 14.106: Illustration of 'Layer Mask to Selection'

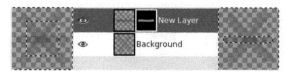

From left to right: the original image with a selection, the Layers Dialog with a layer mask created with the Layer's alpha channel option, after Mask to Selection.

14.10.37 Add Layer Mask to Selection

The Add to Selection command converts the layer mask of the active layer into a selection, which is added to the selection that is already active in the image. White areas of the layer mask are selected, black areas are not selected, and gray areas are converted into feathered selections. The layer mask itself is not modified by this command.

14.10.37.1 Activating the Command

• You can access this command from the image menubar through Layer → Mask → Add to Selection,

• or from the pop-up menu you get by right-clicking on the active layer in the Layers Dialog.

14.10.37.2 Illustration of Add Layer Mask to Selection

Figure 14.107: Illustration of Add Layer Mask to Selection

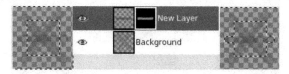

From left to right: the original image with a selection, the Layers Dialog with a layer mask created with the Layer's alpha channel option, after adding the layer mask to the selection.

14.10.38 Subtract Layer Mask from Selection

The Subtract from Selection command converts the layer mask of the active layer into a selection, which is subtracted from the selection that is already active in the image. White areas of the layer mask are selected, black areas are not selected, and gray areas are converted into feathered selections. The layer mask itself is not modified by this command.

14.10.38.1 Activating the Command

• You can access this command from the image menubar through Layer → Mask → Subtract from Selection,

• or from the pop-up menu you get by right-clicking on the active layer in the Layers Dialog.

14.10.38.2 Illustration of Subtract Layer Mask from Selection

Figure 14.108: Illustration of Subtract Layer Mask from Selection

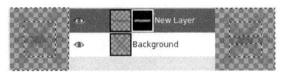

From left to right: the original image with a selection, the Layers Dialog with a layer mask created with the Layer's alpha channel option, after Subtract from Selection.

14.10.39 Intersect Layer Mask with Selection

The Intersect with Selection command converts the layer mask of the active layer into a selection. The intersection of this selection and the selection that is already active form the new selection for the image. White areas of the layer mask are selected, black areas are not selected, and gray areas are converted into feathered selections. The layer mask itself is not modified by this command.

14.10.39.1 Activating the Command

- You can access this command from the image menubar through Layer → Mask → Intersect with Selection,

- or from the pop-up menu you get by right-clicking on the active layer in the Layers Dialog.

14.10.39.2 Illustration of Intersecting the Layer Mask with the Selection

Figure 14.109: Illustration of Intersecting the Layer Mask with the Selection

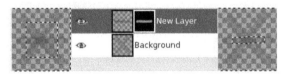

From left to right: the original image with a selection, the Layers Dialog with a layer mask created with the Layer's alpha channel option, after intersecting the layer mask with the selection.

14.10.40 The 'Transparency' Submenu of the 'Layer' menu

Figure 14.110: The 'Transparency' submenu of the 'Layer' menu

The Transparency submenu contains commands which use or affect the alpha channel of the active layer.

14.10.40.1 Activating the Submenu

- You can access this submenu from the image menubar through Layer → Transparency.

14.10.40.2 The Contents of the 'Transparency' Submenu

The Transparency submenu contains the following commands:

- Section 14.10.41
- Section 14.10.42
- Section 14.10.43
- Section 14.10.44
- Section 14.10.45
- Section 14.10.46
- Section 14.10.47
- Section 14.10.48

14.10.41 Add Alpha Channel

Add Alpha Channel: An alpha channel is automatically added into the Channel Dialog as soon as you add a second layer to your image. It represents the transparency of the image. But the background layer (or the single layer if your image has only one layer) has no Alpha channel. In this case, you can Add an Alpha channel with this command.

14.10.41.1 Activating the Command

- You can access this command from the image menubar through Layer → Transparency → Add alpha Channel.

14.10.42 Color to Alpha

You can make colors of the active layer transparent by using the Color to Alpha command. You can find a description of this command in the section about the Section 15.3.13 filter.

 Warning
This command operates only on the layer which is *active at the time the command is called*. Even after you choose another layer to be the active layer, the operation continues to affect the layer on which you performed the command.

14.10.42.1 Activating the Command

- You can access this command from the image menubar through Layer → Transparency → Color to Alpha.

14.10.43 Semi-flatten

The Semi-Flatten command is described in the Semi-flatten filter chapter. The command is useful when you need an anti-aliased image with indexed colors and transparency.

14.10.43.1 Activating the Command

- You can access this command from the image menubar through Layer → Transparency → Semi-flatten.

14.10.44 Threshold Alpha

The Threshold Alpha command converts semi-transparent areas of the active layer into completely transparent or completely opaque areas, based on a threshold you set, between 0 and 255. It only works on layers of RGB images which have an alpha channel. If the image is Grayscale or Indexed, or if the layer does not have an alpha channel, the menu entry is insensitive and grayed out. If the Keep transparency option is checked in the Layers dialog, the command displays an error message.

14.10.44.1 Activating the Command

- You can access this command from the image menubar through Layer → Transparency → Threshold Alpha.

14.10.44.2 Description of the Dialog Window

Figure 14.111: The 'Threshold Alpha' dialog

Threshold You can set the transparency value to be used as a threshold by using the slider or by entering a value between 0 and 255 in the input box. All transparency values below this threshold will become opaque and all transparency values above it will become completely transparent.

14.10.45 Alpha to Selection

The Alpha to Selection command creates a selection in the current layer from the alpha channel, which encodes transparency. Opaque areas are fully selected, transparent areas are unselected, and translucent areas are partially selected. This selection *replaces* the existing selection. The alpha channel itself is not changed.

The other commands in this group of operations are similar, except that instead of completely replacing the existing selection with the selection produced from the alpha channel, they either add the two selections, subtract the alpha selection from the existing selection, or create a selection that is the intersection of the two.

14.10.45.1 Activating the Command

- You can access this command from the image menubar through Layer → Transparency → Alpha to Selection

- or from the pop-up menu which appears when you right-click on the active layer in the Layer Dialog.

14.10.45.2 Example

Figure 14.112: Applying 'Alpha to Selection'

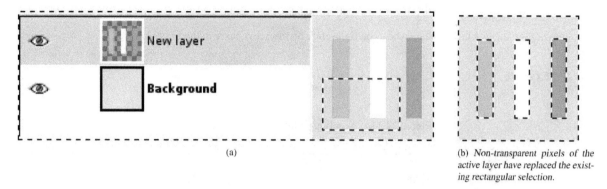

(a)

(b) *Non-transparent pixels of the active layer have replaced the existing rectangular selection.*

14.10.46 Add Alpha channel to Selection

The Add to Selection command creates a selection in the current layer from the Alpha Channel. Opaque pixels are fully selected, transparent pixels are unselected, and translucent pixels are partially selected. This selection is *added* to the existing selection. The alpha channel itself is not changed.

The other commands in this group of operations are similar, except that instead of adding to the existing selection with the selection produced from the active layer, they either completely replace the selection with a selection produced from the alpha selection, subtract the alpha selection from the existing selection, or create a selection that is the intersection of the two.

14.10.46.1 Activating the Command

• You can access this command from the image menubar through Layer → Transparency → Add to Selection.

14.10.46.2 Example

Figure 14.113: Applying 'Add to Selection'

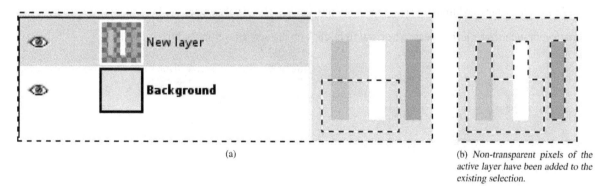

(a)

(b) *Non-transparent pixels of the active layer have been added to the existing selection.*

14.10.47 Subtract from Selection

The Subtract from Selection command creates a selection in the current layer from the Alpha Channel. Opaque pixels are fully selected, transparent pixels are unselected, and translucent pixels are partially selected.This selection is *subtracted* from the existing selection. The Alpha channel itself is not changed.

14.10.47.1 Activating the Command

- You can access this command from the image menubar through Layer → Transparency → Subtract from Selection

- or from the pop-up menu which appears when you right-click on the active layer in the Layer Dialog.

14.10.47.2 Example

Figure 14.114: Applying 'Subtract from Selection'

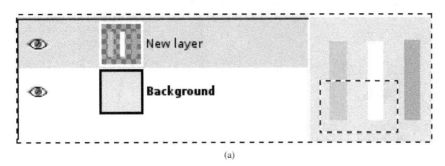

(a)

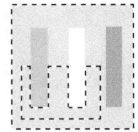

(b) *Non-transparent pixels of the active layer have been subtracted from the existing rectangular selection.*

14.10.48 Intersect Alpha channel with Selection

The Intersect with Selection command creates a selection in the current layer from the Alpha Channel. Opaque pixels are fully selected, transparent pixels are unselected, and translucent pixels are partially selected. This selection is *intersected* with the existing selection: only common parts of both selections are kept. The alpha channel itself is not changed.

14.10.48.1 Activating the Command

- You can access this command from the image menubar through Layer → Transparency → Intersect with Selection

- or from the pop-up menu which appears when you right-click on the active layer in the Layers Dialog.

14.10.48.2 Example

Figure 14.115: Applying 'Intersect with Selection'

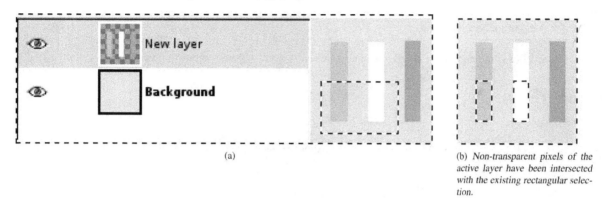

(a)

(b) *Non-transparent pixels of the active layer have been intersected with the existing rectangular selection.*

14.10.49 The 'Transform' Submenu

Figure 14.116: The 'Transform' Submenu of the 'Layer' menu

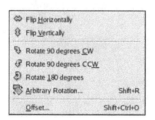

The Transform submenu of the Layer menu contains commands which flip or rotate the active layer of the image.

14.10.49.1 Activating the Submenu

• You can access this submenu from the image menubar through Layer → Transform.

14.10.49.2 The Contents of the 'Transform' Submenu

The Transform submenu contains the following commands:

• Section 14.10.50

• Section 14.10.51

• Section 14.10.52

• Section 14.10.53

• Section 14.10.54

• Section 14.10.55

• Section 14.10.56

14.10.50   Flip Horizontally

The Flip Horizontally command reverses the active layer horizontally, that is, from left to right. It leaves the dimensions of the layer and the pixel information unchanged.

14.10.50.1   Activating the Command

• You can access this command from the image menubar through Layer → Transform → Flip Horizontally.

14.10.50.2   Example

Figure 14.117: Applying 'Flip Layer Horizontally' Applicazione del comando 'rifletti il livello orizzontalmente'

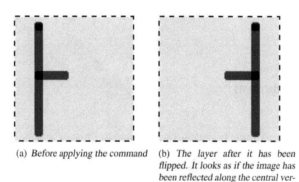

(a) *Before applying the command*   (b) *The layer after it has been flipped. It looks as if the image has been reflected along the central vertical axis of the layer.*

14.10.51   Flip Vertically

The Flip Vertically command reverses the active layer vertically, that is, from top to bottom. It leaves the dimensions of the layer and the pixel information unchanged.

14.10.51.1   Activating the Command

• You can access this command from the image menubar through Layer → Transform → Flip Vertically.

14.10.52   Rotate 90 degrees CW

The Rotate 90 degrees CW command rotates the active layer by 90 around the center of the layer, with no loss of pixel data. The shape of the layer is not altered, but the rotation may cause the layer to extend beyond the bounds of the image. This is allowed in GIMP and it does not mean that the layer is cropped. However, you will not be able to see the parts which extend beyond the boundary of the image unless you resize the image canvas or move the layer.

14.10.52.1   Activating the Command

• You can access this command from the image menubar through Layer → Transform → Rotate 90 degrees CW.

14.10.53   Rotate 90 degrees CCW

The Rotate 90 degrees CCW command rotates the active layer by 90 counter-clockwise around the center of the layer, with no loss of pixel data. The shape of the layer is not altered, but the rotation may cause the layer to extend beyond the bounds of the image. This is allowed in GIMP and it does not mean that the layer is cropped. However, you will not be able to see the parts which extend beyond the boundary of the image unless you resize the image canvas or move the layer.

14.10.53.1   Activating the Command

- You can access this command from the image menubar through Layer → Transform → Rotate 90 degrees CCW.

14.10.54   Rotate 180 degrees

The Rotate 180 degrees command rotates the active layer by 180 around the center of the layer, with no loss of pixel data. The shape of the layer is not altered, but the rotation may cause the layer to extend beyond the bounds of the image. This is allowed in GIMP and it does not mean that the layer is cropped. However, you will not be able to see the parts which extend beyond the boundary of the image unless you resize the image canvas or move the layer.

14.10.54.1   Activating the Command

- You can access this command from the image menubar through Layer → Transform → Rotate 180 degrees.

14.10.55   Arbitrary Rotation

The Arbitrary Rotation command rotates a layer by a specified angle. It is an alternate way of accessing the Rotate tool. See the section about that tool for more information.

14.10.55.1   Activating the Command

- You can access this command from the image menubar through Layer → Transform → Arbitrary Rotation,

- or by using the keyboard shortcut Shift-R.

14.10.56   Offset

The Offset command shifts the *content* of the active layer. Anything shifted outside the layer boundary is cropped. This command displays a dialog which allows you to specify how much to shift the layer and how to fill the space that is left empty by shifting it.

14.10.56.1   Activating the Command

- You can access this command from the image menubar through Layer → Transform → Offset,

- or by using the keyboard shortcut Shift-Ctrl-O.

14.10.56.2   Description of the 'Offset' dialog

Figure 14.118: The 'Offset' dialog

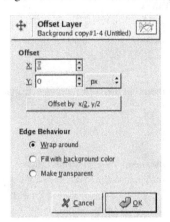

Offset

>   **X; Y** With these two values, you specify how far the contents of the layer should be shifted in the horizontal (X) and vertical (Y) directions. You can enter the offsets in the text boxes. Positive values move the layer to the right and downward. The default unit is pixels, but you can choose a different unit of measurement with the drop-down menu. A unit of '%' is sometimes useful.

>   **Offset by x/2, y/2** With this button, you can automatically set the X and Y offsets so that the contents are shifted by exactly half the width and half the height of the image.

Edge Behavior You can specify one of three ways to treat the areas left empty when the contents of the layer are shifted:

-   *Wrap around*: The empty space on one side of the layer is filled with the part of the layer which is shifted out of the other side, so none of the content is lost.

-   *Fill with background color*: The empty space is filled with the background color, which is shown in the Color Area of the Toolbox.

-   *Make transparent*: The empty space is made transparent. If the layer does not have an alpha channel, this choice is not available (grayed out).

14.10.57   Layer Boundary Size

In GIMP, a layer is not always the same size as the image it belongs to. It might be smaller or it might be larger, in which case some parts of it are hidden. The Layer Boundary Size command displays a dialog in which you can set the dimensions for the active layer. This command changes the dimensions of the layer, but it does not scale its contents.

14.10.57.1   Activating the Command

-   You can access this command from the image menubar through Layer → Layer Boundary Size.

14.10.57.2 Description of the 'Layer Boundary Size' dialog

Figure 14.119: The 'Layer Boundary Size' Dialog

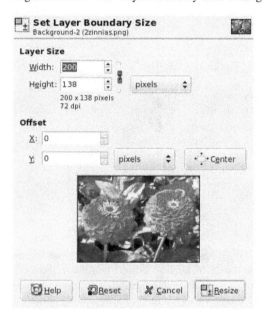

Layer Size

> **Width; Height** When the dialog is displayed, the original dimensions of the active layer are shown. You can change them by using the two text boxes. If these boxes are linked together with a chain, the width-to-height ratio is automatically maintained. If you break the chain by clicking on it, you can set the dimensions independently of each other.
>
> The default unit of measurement is pixels. You can change this by using the drop-down menu. For instance, you might use a '%' of the current size.
>
> **X Offset; Y Offset** By default, the resized layer is placed in the upper left corner of the image. Here, you can set the offset of the upper left corner of the layer relative to the same corner of the image. The default unit of measurement is pixels, but you can change it by using the drop-down menu. You can also place the layer in the center of the image by clicking on the Center button.

14.10.58 Layer to Image Size

The Layer to Image Size command resizes the layer boundaries to match the image boundaries, without moving the contents of the layer with respect to the image.

14.10.58.1 Activating the Command

• You can access this command from the image menubar through Layer → Layer to Image Size.

14.10.59 Scale Layer

The Scale Layer command resizes the layer and its contents. The image loses some of its quality by being scaled. The command displays a dialog where you can set parameters concerning the size of the layer and the image quality.

14.10.59.1 Activating the Command

- You can access this command from the image menubar through Layer → Scale Layer.

14.10.59.2 Description of the 'Scale Layer' Dialog

Figure 14.120: The 'Scale Layer' dialog

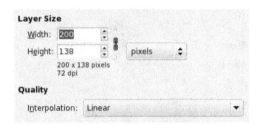

Layer Size When you enlarge a layer, GIMP has to calculate new pixels from the existing ones. This procedure is called 'interpolation'. Please note that no matter which interpolation algorithm is used, no new information is added to the image by interpolation. If there are places in the layer which have no details, you will not get any new ones by scaling it. It is much more likely that the layer will look somewhat blurred after scaling. Similarly, when you reduce a layer, the image loses some of its quality when pixels are removed.

> **Width; Height** The command displays a dialog which shows the dimensions of the original layer in pixels. You can set the new Width and Height for the layer in the two text boxes. If the adjacent chain icon is unbroken, the width and height are automatically adjusted to hold their ratio constant. If you break the chain by clicking on it, you can set them separately, but this will result in distorting the layer.
>
> However, you do not have to set the dimensions in pixels. You can choose different units from the drop-down menu. If you choose percent as units, you can set the layer size relative to its original size. You can also use physical units, like inches or millimeters. However if you do that, you should pay attention to the X/Y resolution of the image.
>
> If you enlarge a layer, the missing pixels are calculated by interpolation, but no new details are added. The more the layer is enlarged, and the more times it is enlarged, the more blurred it becomes. The exact result of the enlargement depends upon the interpolation method you choose. After scaling, you can improve the result by using the Sharpen filter, but it is much better for you to use a high resolution when scanning, taking digital photographs or producing digital images by other means. It is an inherent characteristic of raster images that they do not scale up well.

Quality To change the size of the layer, GIMP either has to add or remove pixels. The method it uses to do this has a considerable impact on the quality of the result. You can choose the method of interpolating the colors of the pixels from the Interpolation drop-down menu.

> **Interpolation**
>
> - None: No interpolation is used. Pixels are simply enlarged or removed, as they are when zooming. This method is low in quality, but very fast.
> - Linear: This method is a good compromise between speed and quality.
> - Cubic: This method takes a lot of time, but it produces the best results.

14.10.60 Crop Layer

The Crop Layer command crops only the active layer to the boundary of the selection by removing any strips at the edge whose contents are all completely unselected. Areas which are partially selected (for example, by feathering) are not cropped. If there is no selection for the image, the menu entry is insensitive and grayed out.

14.10.60.1 Activating the Command

- You can access this command from the image menubar through Layer → Crop layer.

14.10.60.2 Example

Figure 14.121: Applying 'Layer Crop'

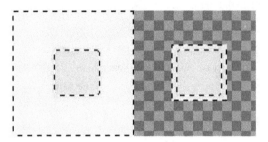

On the left: before applying the command, the layer has a selection that has feathered edges. On the right: after applying the command, the non-transparent pixels are not cropped, even if they are only partially transparent.

14.10.61 Align Visible Layers

With the Align Visible Layers command, you can very precisely position the visible layers (those marked with the 'eye' icon). This degree of precision is especially useful when you are working on animations, which typically have many small layers. Clicking on Align Visible Layers displays a dialog which allows you to choose how the layers should be aligned.

Note
In GIMP 1.2, the default base for the alignment was the top visible layer in the stack. In GIMP 2, the default alignment base is the edge of the canvas. You can still align the image on the bottom layer of the stack, even if it is invisible, by checking Use the (invisible) bottom layer as the base in the dialog.

Figure 14.122: Example image for layer alignment

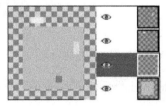

The example image contains four layers on a large (150x150 pixel) canvas. The red square is 10x10 pixels, the green rectangle is 10x20 pixels and the yellow rectangle is 20x10 pixels. The background layer (blue, 100x100 pixels) will not be affected by the command, since the Ignore lower layer option has been checked on the dialog. Note that the layers in the image seem to have a different order than their actual order in the stack because of their positions on the canvas. The yellow layer is the top layer in the image and the second one in the stack.

14.10.61.1 Activating the Command

- You can access this command from the image menubar through Layer → Align Visible layers. There is no default keyboard shortcut.

14.10.61.2   Description of the 'Layer Align' dialog

Figure 14.123: The 'Layer Align' dialog

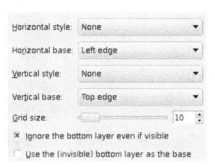

Horizontal Style; Vertical Style These options control how the layers should be moved in relationship to each other. You can choose:

- None: There will be no change in the horizontal or the vertical position, respectively.
- Collect: The visible layers will be aligned on the canvas, in the way that is determined by the Horizontal base and Vertical base options. If you select a Horizontal base of Right edge, layers may disappear from the canvas. You can recover them by enlarging the canvas. If you check the Use the (invisible) bottom layer as the base option, the layers will be aligned on the top left corner of the bottom layer.

Figure 14.124: Horizontal 'Collect' alignment (on the edge of the canvas)

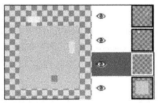

(a) *Original image with the layer stack*

(b) *The layers have been moved horizontally so that their left edges are aligned with the left edge of the canvas.*

Figure 14.125: Horizontal 'Collect' alignment (on the bottom layer)

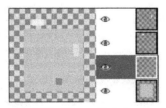

(a) *Original image with the layer stack*

(b) *The layers have been moved horizontally so that their left edges align with the left edge of the bottom layer.*

- Fill (left to right); Fill (top to bottom): The visible layers will be aligned with the canvas according to the edge you selected with Horizontal base or Vertical base, respectively. The layers are arranged regularly, so that they do not overlap each other. The top layer in the stack is placed on the leftmost (or uppermost) position in the image. The bottom layer in the stack is placed on the rightmost (or bottommost) position of the image. The other layers are placed regularly between these two positions. If the Use the (invisible) bottom layer as the base option is checked, the layers are aligned with the corresponding edge of the bottom layer.

Figure 14.126: Horizontal 'Fill' alignment (canvas)

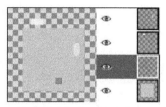 

(a) *Original image with the layer stack*

(b) *Horizontal filling alignment, Left to Right, with Use the (invisible) bottom layer as the base option not checked. The top layer in the stack, the green one, is placed all the way on the left. The bottom layer in the stack, the red one, is placed is on the right and the yellow layer is between the other two.*

Figure 14.127: Horizontal 'Fill' alignment (bottom layer)

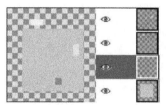 

(a) *Original image with the layer stack*

(b) *The same parameters as in the previous example, but with the lowest (blue) level as the base.*

- Fill (right to left); Fill (bottom to top): These settings work similarly to the ones described above, but the filling occurs in the opposite direction.

Figure 14.128: Vertical 'Fill' alignment (bottom layer)

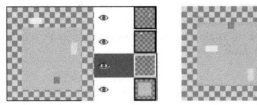

(a) *Original image with the layer stack*   (b) *Vertical Fill alignment, bottom to top, bottom layer as base*

There must be at least three visible layers in the image to use the 'Fill' options.

14.11   The 'Tools' Menu

14.11.1   Introduction to the 'Tools' Menu

Figure 14.129: Contents of the 'Tools' menu

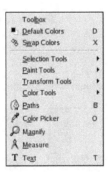

The menu entries on the Tools menu access the GIMP tools. All of the tools available in GIMP are extensively described in the Toolbox section.

14.12   The 'Filters' Menu

14.12.1   Menu 'Filters' Introduction

Figure 14.130: The 'Filters' menu

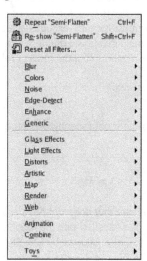

In GIMP terminology, a *filter* is a plug-in that modifies the appearance of an image, in most cases just the active layer of the image. Not all of the entries in this menu meet that definition, however; the word 'filter' is often mis-used to mean any plug-in, regardless of what it does. Indeed, some of the entries in this menu do not modify images at all.

With the exception of the top three items of the Filters menu, all of the entries are provided by plug-ins. Each plug-in decides for itself where it would like its menu entry to be placed. Therefore, the appearance of this menu can be completely different for each user. In practice, though, the appearance does not vary very much, because most plug-ins come with GIMP when it is installed, and of course they are always in the same places in the menu.

Plug-ins are not restricted to just the Filters menu: a plug-in can place entries in any menu. Indeed, a number of GIMP's basic functions (for example, Semi-flatten in the Layer menu) are implemented by plug-ins. But the Filters menu is the default place for a plug-in to place its menu entries.

For general information on plug-ins and how to use them, see the section on Plug-ins. You can find information on the filters that are provided with GIMP in the Filters chapter. For filters you install yourself, please refer to the information which came with them.

14.12.2   Repeat Last

The Repeat Last command performs the action of the most recently executed plug-in again, using the same settings as the last time it was run. It does not show a dialog or request confirmation.

 Note
Please note that this command repeats the most recently executed *plug-in*, regardless of whether it is in the Filters menu or not.

14.12.2.1 Activating the Command

- You can access this command from the image menubar through Filters → Repeat `filter`,

- or by using the keyboard shortcut Ctrl-F.

14.12.3 Re-show Last

The Re-show Last command interactively runs the most recently executed plug-in. Unlike the 'Repeat Last' command, which does not display a dialog, the 'Re-show Last' command displays a dialog window, if the plug-in has one. It is displayed with the settings you used the last time you ran the plug-in (assuming that the plug-in follows the GIMP programming conventions).

Note
Please note that this command repeats the most recently executed *plug-in*, regardless of whether it is in the Filters menu or not.

Tip
When you are using a plug-in, especially one that does not have a preview window, you may very well have to adjust the parameters several times before you are satisfied with the results. To do this most efficiently, you should memorize the shortcuts for Undo and Re-show Last: Ctrl-Z followed by Ctrl-Shift-F.

14.12.3.1 Activating the Command

- You can access this command from the image menubar through Filters → Re-show `filter`,

- or by using the keyboard shortcut Ctrl-Shift-F.

14.12.4 Reset All Filters

Normally, each time you run an interactive plug-in, its dialog is displayed with all of the settings initialized to the ones you used the last time you ran it. This may be a problem if you made a mistake setting the values and you can't remember what they were originally. One way to recover is to exit GIMP and start again, but the Reset all Filters command is a slightly less drastic solution: it resets the values for *all* plug-ins to their defaults. Because it is a dramatic step, it asks you to confirm that you really want to do it. Be careful: you cannot undo this command.

14.12.4.1 Activating the Command

- You can access this command from the image menubar through Filters → Reset all Filters.

Chapter 15

Filters

15.1 Introduction

A filter is a special kind of tool designed to take an input layer or image, apply a mathematical algorithm to it, and return the input layer or image in a modified format. GIMP uses filters to achieve a variety of effects and those effects are discussed here.

The filters are divided into several categories:

- Blur see Section 15.2.

- Colors see Section 15.3.

- Noise see Section 15.4.

- Edge-Detect see Section 15.5.

- Enhance see Section 15.6.

- Generic see Section 15.7.

- Glass Effects see Section 15.8.

- Light Effects see Section 15.9.

- Distorts see Section 15.10.

- Artistic see Section 15.11.

- Map see Section 15.12.

- Render see Section 15.13.

- Web see Section 15.16.

- Animation see Section 15.15.

- Combine see Section 15.14.

15.1.1 Preview

Most filters have a Preview where changes in the image are displayed, in real time (if the 'Preview' option is checked), before being applied to the image.

Figure 15.1: Preview submenu

Right clicking on the Preview window opens a submenu which lets you set the Style and the Size of checks representing transparency.

15.2 Blur Filters

15.2.1 Introduction

Figure 15.2: Original for demo

This is a set of filters that blur images, or parts of them, in various ways. If there is a selection, only the selected parts of an image will be blurred. There may, however, be some leakage of colors from the unblurred area into the blurred area. To help you pick the one you want, we will illustrate what each does when applied to the image shown at right. These are, of course, only examples: most of the filters have parameter settings that allow you to vary the magnitude or type of blurring.

Figure 15.3: Gaussian blur (radius 10)

The most broadly useful of these is the Gaussian blur. (Don't let the word "Gaussian" throw you: this filter makes an image blurry in the most basic way.) It has an efficient implementation that allows it to create a very blurry blur in a relatively short time.

Figure 15.4: Simple blur

If you only want to blur the image a little bit--to soften it, as it were--you might use the simple "Blur" filter. In GIMP 2.2 this runs automatically, without creating a dialog. The effect is subtle enough that you might not even notice it, but you can get a stronger effect by repeating it. In GIMP 2.0 the filter shows a dialog that allows you to set a "repeat count". If you want a strong blurring effect, this filter is too slow to be a good choice: use a Gaussian blur instead.

Figure 15.5: Selective blur

The Selective Blur filter allows you to set a threshold so that only pixels that are similar to each other are blurred together. It is often useful as a tool for reducing graininess in photos without blurring sharp edges. (In the example, note that the graininess of the background has been reduced.) The implementation is much slower than a Gaussian blur, though, so you should not use it unless you really need the selectivity.

Figure 15.6: Pixelize

The Pixelize filter produces the well-known "Abraham Lincoln" effect by turning the image into a set of large square pixels. (The Oilify filter, in the Artistic Filters group, has a similar effect, but with irregular blobs instead of perfectly square pixels.)

Note
You can find a nice explanation of the Abraham Lincoln effect at [?].

Figure 15.7: Motion blur

The Motion Blur filter blurs in a specific direction at each point, which allows you to create a sense of motion: either linear, radial, or rotational.

Finally, the Tileable Blur filter is really the same thing as a Gaussian blur, except that it wraps around the edges of an image to help you reduce edge effects when you create a pattern by tiling multiple copies of the image side by side.

Note

Tileable Blur is actually implemented by a Script-Fu script that invokes the Gaussian blur plug-in.

15.2.2 Blur

15.2.2.1 Overview

Figure 15.8: The Blur filter applied to a photograph

(a) *Original*   (b) *Blur applied*

The simple Blur filter produces an effect similar to that of an out of focus camera shot. To produce this blur effect, the filter takes the average of the present pixel value and the value of adjacent pixels and sets the present pixel to that average value.

Filter advantage is its calculation speed. It suits big images.

Filter disadvantage is that its action is hardly perceptible on big images, but very strong on small images.

15.2.2.2 Activate the filter

You can find this filter through: Filters → Blur → Blur

15.2.3 Gaussian Blur

15.2.3.1 Overview

Figure 15.9: From left to right: original, filter applied.

(a) *Original*   (b) *Blur applied*

You can find this filter in the image menu under Filters → Blur → Gaussian Blur

The IIR Gaussian Blur plug-in acts on each pixel of the active layer or selection, setting its Value to the average of all pixel Values present in a radius defined in the dialog. A higher Value will produce a higher amount of blur. The blur can be set to act in one direction more than the other by clicking the Chain Button so that it is broken, and altering the radius. GIMP supports two implementations of Gaussian Blur: IIR G.B. and RLE G.B. They both produce the same results, but each one can be faster in some cases.

15.2.3.2 Options

Figure 15.10: 'Gaussian' filter parameters settings

Blur Radius Here you can set the blur intensity. By altering the ratio of horizontal to vertical blur, you can give the effect of a motion blur. You can choose the unit with the drop list.

Blur Method IIR: IIR stands for 'Infinite Impulse Response'.This blur works best for large radius values and for images which are not computer generated.

RLE: RLE stands for run-length encoding. RLE Gaussian Blur is best used on computer-generated images or those with large areas of constant intensity.

15.2.4 Selective Gaussian Blur

15.2.4.1 Overview

Figure 15.11: The Selective Gaussian Blur filter

(a) *Original* (b) *Blur applied*

You can find this filter in the image menu under Filters → Blur → Selective Gaussian Blur

Contrary to the other blur plug-ins, the Selective Gaussian Blur plug-in doesn't act on all pixels: blur is applied only if the difference between its value and the value of the surrounding pixels is less than a defined Delta value. So, contrasts are preserved because difference is high on contrast limits. It is used to blur a background so that the foreground subject will stand out better. This add a sense of depth to the image with only a single operation.

15.2.4.2 Options

Figure 15.12: 'Selective Gaussian' filter parateters settings

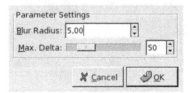

Blur Radius Here you can set the blur intensity, in pixels.

Max. Delta Here you can set the maximum difference (0-255) between the pixel value and the surrounding pixel values. Above this Delta, blur will not be applied to that pixel.

15.2.5   Motion Blur

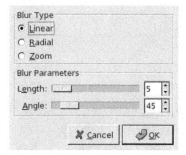

15.2.5.1   Overview

Figure 15.13: Starting example for Motion Blur filter

(a) *Original image*   (b) *Linear blur*

Figure 15.14: Using example for Motion Blur filter

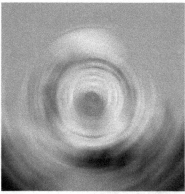

(a) *Radial blur*   (b) *Zoom blur*

You can find this filter in the image menu under Filters → Blur → Motion Blur

The Motion Blur filter creates a movement blur. The filter is capable of Linear, Radial, and Zoom movements. Each of these movements can be further adjusted, with Length, or Angle settings available.

15.2.5.2 Options

Figure 15.15: 'Motion Blur' filter options

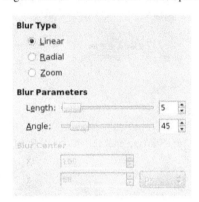

Blur Type

Linear Linear motion is a blur that travels in a single direction, horizontally, for example. In this case, Length means as Radius in other filters:it represents the blur intensity. More Length will result in more blurring. Angle describes the actual angle of the movement. Thus, a setting of 90 will produce a vertical blur, and a setting of 0 will produce a horizontal blur.

Radial Radial motion blur creates a circular blur. The Length slider is not important with this type of blur. Angle on the other hand, is the primary setting that will affect the blur. More Angle will result in more blurring in a circular direction. The Radial motion blur is similar to the effect of a spinning object. The center of the spin in this case, is the center of the image.

Zoom Zoom blurring produces a blur that radiates out from the center of the image. The center of the image remains relatively calm, whilst the outer areas become blurred toward the center. This filter option produces a perceived forward movement, into the image. Length is the main setting here, and affects the amount of speed, as it were, toward the center of the image.

Blur settings

Length Length: This slider controls the distance pixels are moved (0 - 256)

Angle Angle: (0 - 360) As seen above, Angle slider effect depends on Blur type.

Blur Center With this option, you can set the starting point of movement. Effect is different according to the Blur Type you have selected. With Radial Type for instance, you set rotation center. With Zoom Type, vanishing point. This option is greyed out with Linear type.

 Tip
You have to set the blur center coordinates. Unfortunately, you can't do that by clicking on the image. But, by moving mouse pointer on the image, you can see its coordinates in the lower left corner of the image window. Only copy them out into the input boxes.

15.2.6 Pixelise

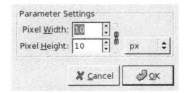

15.2.6.1 Overview

Figure 15.16: From left to right: Before and after applying Pixelise filter

(a) *Original*   (b) *Blur applied*

You can find this filter in the image menu under Filters → Blur → Pixelise

The Pixelize filter renders the image using large color blocks. It is very similar to the effect seen on television when obscuring a criminal during trial. It is used for the 'Abraham Lincoln effect': see [**?**].

15.2.6.2 Options

Figure 15.17: 'Pixelize' filter options

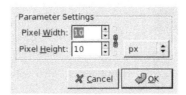

Pixel Width Here you can set the desired width of the blocks.

Pixel Height Here you can set the height of the blocks.

Chain Button If the chain is broken, you can set width and height separately. Otherwise, they are linked.

Unit Input Box Here you can select the unit of measure for height and width.

15.2.7 Tileable Blur

15.2.7.1 Overview

Figure 15.18: From left to right: original, tileable blur applied

(a) *Original*   (b) *Filter Tileable Blur applied*

You can find this filter in the image menu under Filters → Blur → Tileable Blur

This tool is used to soften tile seams in images used in tiled backgrounds. It does this by blending and blurring the boundary between images that will be next to each other after tiling.

Tip
If you want to treat only images borders, you can't apply filter to the whole image. The solution to get the wanted effect is as follows:

1. Duplicate layer(Layer → Duplicate Layer) and select it to work on it.

2. Apply 'Tileable Blur' filter with a 20 pixels radius to this layer.

3. Select all (Ctrl-A) and reduce selection (Selection → Shrink) to create a border with the wanted width.

4. Delete selection with Ctrl-K.

5. Merge layers with Layer → Merge down

15.2.7.2 Options

Figure 15.19: 'Tileable Blur' filter options

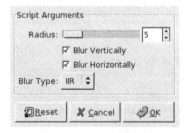

Blur Radius The bigger the radius, the more marked is the blur. By selecting Horizontal and Vertical, you can make the horizontal and vertical borders tileable.

Blur Type IIR: for photographic or scanned images.

RLE: for computer-generated images.

15.3 Color filters

15.3.1 Introduction

The Color filters group contains several filters to modify colors in an image, a layer or a selection. You can find filters to compose, decompose, uncolor colors, and many other effects.

15.3.2 Adjust FG-BG

15.3.2.1 Overview

Figure 15.20: Applying example for the 'Adjust FG-BG' filter

(a) *Original image*   (b) *Filter Adjust FG-BG applied*

You can find this filter through Filters → Colors → Map → Adjust FG-BG.

Adjust FG-BG belongs to color map filters which make connection between a color source and an image. Here, image pixels having ForeGround color will turn to black while pixels having BackGround color will turn to white. Other colors are interpolated. There will be no change if FG is black and BG is white.

Note that this filter is just a special case of the Map Color Range filter with its default colors: source colors are foreground and background color, destination colors are black and white.

 Caution

This filter does not work as expected, if the values of foreground and background color are the same for some color channel (red, green, or blue).

Even worse: the filter will happily accept your colors without displaying a warning or error message.

15.3.3 Alien Map 2

15.3.3.1 Overview

Figure 15.21: Alien Map 2 filter example

(a) *Original image* (b) *Filter applied*

You can find this filter through Filters → Colors → Map → Alien map 2.

This filter renders very modified colors by applying trigonometric functions. Alien Map 2 can work on RGB and HSV.

15.3.3.2 Options

Figure 15.22: Options for the 'Alien Map 2' filter

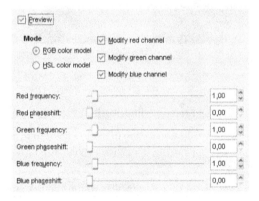

Preview This preview displays results of filter application interactively.

Mode Radio buttons RGB Color Channel and HSV Color Channel let you select the color space you want to use.

Check boxes Modify ... Channel let you select RGB/HSV Channel you want to work with.

Sliders For each channel, you can set Frequency (0-5) and Phaseshift (0-360) of sine-cosine functions, using either sliders or input boxes and their arrowheads.

Frequency around 0.3 to 0.7 provides a curve that is similar to the linear function (original image), only darker or with more contrast. As you raise the frequency level, you'll get an increasing variation in pixel transformation, meaning that the image will get more and more 'alien'.

Phase alters the value transformation. 0 and 360 degrees are the same as a sine function and 90 is the same as a cosine function. 180 inverts sine and 270 inverts cosine.

Fase alter el valor de la transformación. 0 y 360 grados son lo mismo que una función seno y 90 es lo mismo que una función coseno. 180 invierte el seno y 270 el coseno.

15.3.4 Two Colors Exchange

15.3.4.1 Overview

Figure 15.23: From left to right: Original image, after applying Color Exchange (Blue to black)

(a)   (b)

This filter is found in Filters → Colors → Map → Color Exchange.

This filter replaces a color with another one.

15.3.4.2   Options

Figure 15.24: Option of the 'Two color exchange' filter

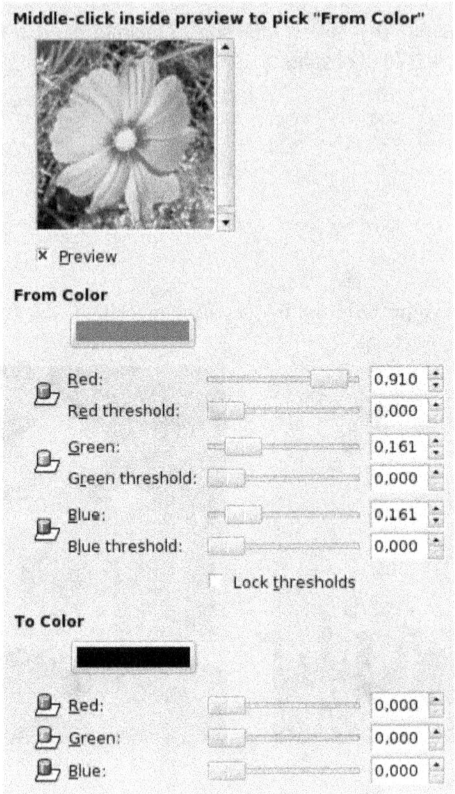

Preview In this preview, a part of the Image is displayed. A selection smaller than preview will be complete in preview. A bigger one will be cut out to be adapted to the preview.

If you middle-click inside preview , the clicked pixel color will be selected and will appear as From Color.

From color In this section, you can choose the color to be used to select pixels that will be concerned by color exchange.

Three sliders for RVB colors: If you have clicked on preview, they are automatically positioned. But you can change them. Each slider acts on color intensity. Input boxes and arrowheads work the same. Result is interactively displayed in the From swatch box.

Three sliders for thresholds, for each color. The higher the threshold, the more pixels will be concerned. Result is interactively displayed in Preview.

Lock Thresholds: This option locks threshold sliders which will act all the same.

To color Three cursors allow to select the color that pixels will have. Result is displayed in swatch box and in preview. You can also click on the color dwell to get a color selector.

15.3.5 Colormap Rotation

15.3.5.1 Overview

Figure 15.25: From left to right: Original image, after applying filter

(a) *Original image*   (b) *Filter Color Map Rotation applied*

You can find this filter through Filters → Colors → Map → Color Map Rotation.

Colormap Rotation lets you exchange one color range to another range.

15.3.5.2 Main Options

Figure 15.26: Main Options of the 'Color Map Rotation' filter

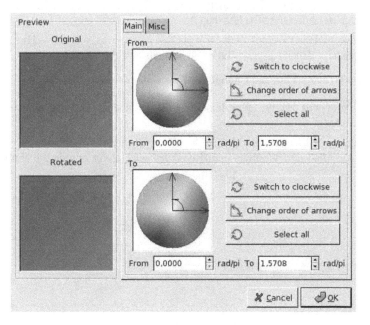

You have there two color circles, one for the 'From' color range and the other for the 'To' color range:

From The Color Circle: Two axis to define "From" range. The curved arrow in angle lets to recognise "From" axis and "To" axis of range. Click-drag these axis to change range.

Switch to Clockwise/Counterclockwise: Sets the direction the range is going.

Change Order of Arrows: Inverts From and To axis. This results in an important color change as colors in selection angle are different.

Select All selects the whole color circle.

From and To boxes display start axis and end axis positions (in rad/PI) which are limiting the selected color range. You can enter these positions manually or with help of arrow-heads.

To This section options are the same as "From" section ones.

15.3.5.3 Grey Options

Figure 15.27: Base image for Grey Options

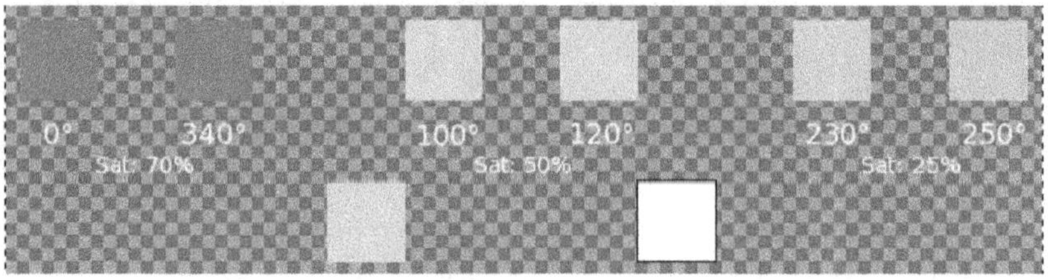

Three sectors are defined for Red, Green and Blue with different saturations. Grey and White colors are represented (0% Sat).

In this tab, you can specify how to treat gray. By default, grey is not considered as a color and is not taken in account by the rotation. Here, you can convert slightly saturated colors into grey and you can also convert grey into color.

Grey Color Circle At center of this color circle is a small "define circle". At center, it represents grey. If you increase grey threshold progressively, colors with saturation less than this threshold turn to grey.

Then, if you pan the define circle in the color circle, or if you use input boxes, you define **Hue** and **Saturation**. This color will replace all colors you have defined as grey. But result depends on Grey Mode too.

Grey Mode The radio buttons **Treat As This** and **Change As This** determine how your previous choices will be treated:

- With **Change to this**, grey will take the color defined by the define circle directly, without any rotation, whatever its position in the color circle.

- With **Treat as this**, grey will take the color defined by the define circle after rotation, according to "From" and "To" choices you made in the Main tab. With this option, you can select color only in the "From" sector, even if it is not visible in Grey tab.

Figure 15.28: Grey Mode

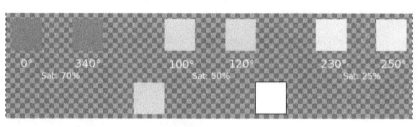

The small circle is on yellow and mode is "Change to this". Blue has changed to yellow. Note that Grey and White did so too.

Gray Threshold

Figure 15.29: Gray Threshold

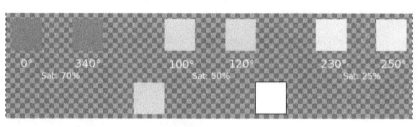

Grey-threshold is 0.25: the blue sector (sat 0.25) has turned to Grey (Note that Grey and White, that are 0% Sat., are not concerned).

You specify there how much saturation will be considered grey. By increasing progressively saturation, you will see an enlarging circle in color circle and enlarging selected areas in Preview if "Continuous update" is checked. In a black to white gradient, you can see enlarging color replacement as you increase threshold very slowly.

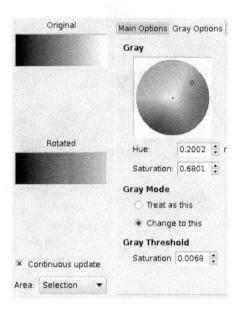

Black to White gradient, progressively filled with color, as threshold increases.

15.3.5.4 Previews

Original and Rotated The Original preview displays a thumbnail of the original image and the Rotated preview displays color changes interactively, before they are applied to the Image.

Continuous Update Continuous Update displays color changes continuously in the Rotated preview.

Area In this drop down list, you can select between

- Entire Layer: works on the whole layer (The image if there is no selection).
- Selection: displays selection only.
- Context: displays selection in image context.

15.3.5.5 Units

You can select here the angle unit used to locate colors in the Hue/Saturation circle. This choice is valid only for the current filter session: don"t click on Valid just after selecting unit, return to the wanted tab!

15.3.6 Map Color Range

15.3.6.1 Overview

Figure 15.30: Example for the Map Color Range filter

(a) *Original image*

(b) *Filter Map Color Range applied*

This filter is found in Filters → Colors → Map → Color Range Mapping.

Unlike Exchange filter, Map Color Range maps a defined color range against another defined color range. More precisely, for every image pixel the values of the color channels (red, green, blue) are separately replaced according to a mapping table. This way, the color range may be moved, stretched, compressed, and/or inverted.

 Note

This mapping does not apply to the specified source color range only. Colors outside this color range are mapped the same way by extrapolating their destination color.

15.3.6.2 Options

Figure 15.31: Options of the 'Map Color Range' filter

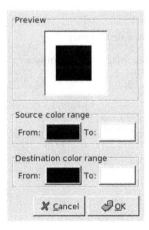

Preview Preview: This Preview displays color changes interactively, before they are applied to Image.

Color Source Range The two Color Swatch Boxes allow you to define From and To limits of source color range. Default colors are the Foreground and the Background colors of the Toolbox, but, when you click on a box, you call the Gimp Color selector which lets you select other colors.

Note that, when you select a color, you really select three separate color channels.

Caution

It's an error if for some channel both source color values are the same (you cannot map a single value to the destination range). Although the filter seems to work and will not display any warning or error message, this will lead to unexpected and probably unwanted results.

Destination Color Range The two *Color Swatch Boxes* allow you to define From and To limits of destination color range. When you click on a box, you call the Gimp's Color selector.

15.3.7 Sample Colorize

15.3.7.1 Overview

Figure 15.32: From left to right: Original image, after applying filter

| (a) *Original image* | (b) *Filter Sample Colorize applied* |

This filter is found in Filters → Colors → Map → Sample Colorize.

This filter allows you to colorize old black-and-white images by mapping a color source image or a gradient against it.

Caution

Your gray-tone image must be changed to RGB before using this filter (Image/Image>Mode>RGB).

15.3.7.2 Options

Figure 15.33: Options of the 'Sample Colorize' filter

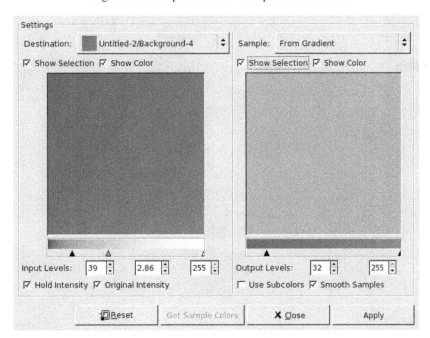

The filter window is divided into two parts: Destination on the left, Sampling on the right.

Destination, Sample By default, displayed image previews reproduce the image you invoked the filter from.

> The sample can be the whole preview, or a selection of this preview. With the drop list, you can select another sample-image among the names of images present on your screen when you called the filter. If you choose From Gradient (or From Inverse Gradient), the selected gradient in Gradient Dialog (or its inverse) will be the sample. It will be displayed into the gradient bar below the sample preview. The sampling preview is greyed out and two cursors allow you to select the gradient range that will be applied to the image or selection.

> Destination is, by default, the source image. The drop list displays the list of images present on your screen when you evoked the filter and allow you to select another destination image. If there is a selection in this image, it will be gray-scaled, else the whole preview will be gray-scaled.

Show Selection This option toggles between the whole image and the selection, if it exists.

Show Colors This option toggles between colors and gray-scale.

Get Sample Colors When you click on this button, the gradient bar below the sample preview displays colors of the sample. If your sample holds few colors, transitions may be abrupt. Check Smooth Sample Colors option to improve them.

> Use Subcolors is more difficult to understand. Let's say first that in a greyscale image there is information only for Value (luminosity, more or less light). In a RGB image, each pixel has information for the three colors and Value. So, pixels with different color may have the same Value. If this option is checked, colors will be mixed and applied to Destination pixels having that Value. If it is unchecked, then the dominating color will be applied.

Out Levels Two input boxes and two sliders act the same: they limit the color range which will be applied to destination image. You can choose this range accurately. Result appears interactively in destination preview.

In Levels Three input boxes and three sliders allow to fix importance of dark tones, mid tones and light tones. Result appears interactively in destination preview.

Apply Button When you are satisfied with the result on destination preview, click on Apply to apply results onto destination image.

Hold Intensity If this option is checked, the average light intensity of destination image will be the same as that of source image.

Original Intensity If this option is checked, the In levels intensity settings will not be taken in account: original intensity will be preserved.

15.3.8 Gradient Map

15.3.8.1 Overview

Figure 15.34: Example of gradient map

Example of Gradient Mapping. Top: Original image. Middle: a gradient. Bottom: result of applying the gradient to the original image with the Gradient Map filter.

This filter uses the current gradient, as shown in the Brush/Pattern/Gradient area of the Toolbox, to recolor the active layer or selection of the image to which the filter is applied. To use it, first choose a gradient from the Gradients Dialog. Then select the part of the image you want to alter, and activate the filter by choosing Filters → Colors → Map → Gradient Map from the image menu. The filter runs automatically, without showing any dialog or requiring any further input. It uses image color intensities (0 - 255), mapping the darkest pixels to the left end color from the gradient, and the lightest pixels to the right end color from the gradient. Intermediate values are set to the corresponding intermediate colors.

15.3.9 Border Average

15.3.9.1 Overview

You can find this filter through Filters → Colors → Border Average.

This plug-in calculates the most often used color in a specified border of the the active layer or selection, allowing a specified range to not be exact. The calculated color becomes the foreground color in the Toolbox. This filter is interesting when you have to find a Web page color background that differs as little as possible from your image border. The action of this filter is not registered in Undo History and can't be deleted with Ctrl+Z.

15.3.9.2 Options

Figure 15.35: Options of the 'Border Average Filter'

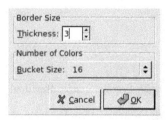

Border Size You can set there the border Thickness in pixels.

Number of Colors The Bucket Size lets you control the number of colors considered as similar and counted with the same 'bucket'. A low bucket size value (i.e. a high bucket number) gives you better precision in the calculation of the average color. Note that better precision does not necessarily mean better results (see example below).

15.3.9.3 Examples illustrating the 'Border Average' filter

Figure 15.36: Original image

Original image: colors are pure Red (255;0;0), pure Blue (0;0;255), and different but similar kinds of Green (00******;11******;00******).

Figure 15.37: 'Number of Colors' is set to 8:

The resulting color is a Red (254,2,2).

The most frequent color on the image border is pure Red (255,0,0). Since the bucket size is low, the different Green tones are not recognized as the same color. The resulting color is a nearly pure Red (254,2,2) and becomes the foreground color of the Toolbox.

Figure 15.38: 'Number of Colors' is set to 64:

The resulting color is Green (32,224,32).

Here the bucket size is high, the number of buckets low. The filter looks at only the two most significant bits of every color channel value. Now Green (0-63,192-255,0-63) is the most frequent color. The resulting color is Green (32,224,32), which is the average of all colors possibly counted by this 'bucket'.

15.3.10   Channel Mixer

15.3.10.1   Overview

Figure 15.39: From left to right: original image, after applying Channel Mixer filter

(a)   (b)

You can find this filter through Filters → Colors → Channel Mixer.

This filter combines values of the RGB channels. It works with images with or without an alpha channel. It has monochrome mode and a preview.

15.3.10.2   Options

Figure 15.40: 'Channel Mixer' filter options

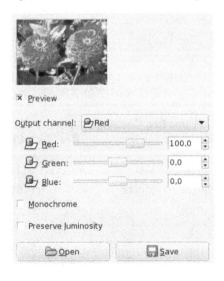

Output Channel From this menu you select the channel to mix to. Choices are Red, Green, or Blue. It is insensitive when Monochrome option is checked.

Red, Green, Blue These three sliders set the contribution of red, green or blue channel to output. Can be negative. These sliders are graduated from -200 to 200. They represent the percentage which will be attributed to the output channel. 100% corresponds to the value of the channel of the studied pixel in the image.

Monochrome This option converts the RGB image into a gray-scale RGB image. The Channel Mixer filter is often used with this aim in view, because it often provides a better result than the other ways (see Grayscale in Glossary). Makes the Output Channel menu insensitive.

Preserve Luminosity Calculations may result in too high values and an image too much clear. This option lessens luminosities while keeping a good visual ratio between them.

15.3.10.3 Buttons

Open Load settings from a file.

Save Save settings to a file.

15.3.10.4 How does Channel Mixer work?

In RGB mode In this mode, you have to select an Output Channel . This channel is the one which will be modified. In the dialog window, its default value is 100%, corresponding to the value of the channel in the original image. It can be increased or decreased. That's why slider ends are -200 and 200.

Three RGB sliders let you give a percentage to every channel. For every pixel in the image, the sum of the calculated values for every channel from these percentages will be given to the Output Channel. Here is an example:

Figure 15.41: The original image and its channels

Red square: 230, 10, 10
Green square: 10, 230, 10
Blue square: 10, 10, 230
Gray square: 225, 235, 245

RGB values of the pixels in red, green, blue, gray squares are displayed. The black rectangle is special, because black (0;0;0) is not concerned by filter (0 multiplied by any percentage always gives 0). The result can't exceed 255 nor be negative.

Figure 15.42: Output channel is red. Green Channel +50

Red square: 235, 10 10
Green square: 125, 230, 10
Blue square: 15, 10, 230
Gray square: 255, 235, 245

In the red square, the pixel values are 230;10;10. Percentages are 1;0.5;0. The claculation result is 230*1 + 10*0,5 + 10*0 =235. The same reasoning is valid for the green and the blue squares. In the gray square, which contains red color, the calculation result is above 255. It is reduced to 255. A negative value would be reduced to 0.

Figure 15.43: Output channel is red. Green Channel +50%. The Preserve Luminosity option is checked.

Red square: 156, 10 10
Green square: 83, 230, 10
Blue square: 9, 10, 230
Gray square: 228, 235, 245

The values attributed to the Red Output channel are lower, preventing a too much clear image.

In Monochrome mode When this option is checked, the image preview turns to grayscale, but the image is still a RGB image with three channels, until the filter action is validated.

Figure 15.44: Monochrome option checked. Red:100% Green: 50% Blue: 0%. Preserve Luminosity unchecked.

Red square: 235, 235, 235
Green square: 125, 125, 125
Blue square: 15, 15, 15
Gray square: 255, 255, 255

In every square, pixels have been converted into a gray level equal to the value of the Red channel in the original image (The background has been painted with pink afterwards to make white squares visible).

Here is how the Preserve Luminosity works in the monochrome mode: ' For example, suppose the sliders were Red:75%, Green:75%, Blue:0%. With Monochrome on and the Preserve Luminosity option off, the resulting picture would be at 75%+75%+0% =150%, very bright indeed. A pixel with a value of, say, R,G,B=127,100,80 would map to 127*0.75+100*0.75+80 for each channel. With the Preserve Luminosity option on, the sliders will be scaled so they always add up to 100%. In this example, that scale value is 1/(75%+75%+0%) or 0.667. So the pixel values would be about 113. The Preserve Luminosity option just assures that the scale values from the sliders always adds up to 100%. Of course, strange things happen when any of the sliders have large negative values ' (from the plug-in author himself).

Note
Which channel will you modify? : This depends on what you want to do. In principle, the Red channel suits contrast modifications well. The Green channel is well adapted to details changes and the Blue channel to noise, grain changes. You can use the Decompose filter.

Note
The 30%, 59%, 11% gives you the same gray levels as the Grayscale command in Image/Mode. This wil no longer be valid with GIMP-2.4.

15.3.11 Colorcube Analysis

15.3.11.1 Overview

Figure 15.45: From left to right: Original image, after Colorcube Analysis of the image

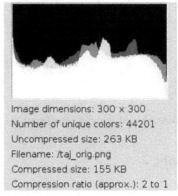

(a) *Original image*   (b) *Filter Colorcube Analysis applied*

You can find this filter through Filters → Colors → Colorcube Analysis.

It gives data about image: dimensions, file size, color number, compression ratio...

15.3.12 Colorify

15.3.12.1 Overview

Figure 15.46: From left to right: original image, after applying Colorify filter

(a) *Original image*   (b) *Filter Colorify appliedFiltro Colorear aplicado*

You can find this filter through Filters → Colors → Colorify.

It renders a greyscaled image like it is seen through colored glass.

15.3.12.2 Options

Figure 15.47: 'Colorify' filter options

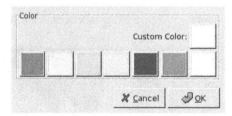

Color A color palette is available and you can select your own color by clicking on the Custom Color swatch.

15.3.13 Color to Alpha

15.3.13.1 Overview

Figure 15.48: From left to right: original image, after applying Color to Alpha filter (Blue to transparency)

(a)   (b)

You can find this filter through Filters → Colors → Color to Alpha.

The Color to Alpha filter makes transparent all pixels with a selected color. An Alpha channel is created. It will attempt to preserve anti-aliasing information by using a partially intelligent routine that replaces weak color information with weak alpha information. In this way, areas that contain an element of the selected color will maintain a blended appearance with their surrounding pixels.

15.3.13.2 Options

Color Clicking on the From color swatch provides a color selection dialog where you can select a color. If selection of a precise color is required, use the Color Picker then drag and drop the selected color from the color picker to the From color swatch. Right clicking on the color will display a menu where you can select Foreground or Background colors, White or Black.

15.3.14 Decompose

15.3.14.1 Overview

Figure 15.49: From left to right: Original image, Decomposed image (RGB decomposition).

(a) *Original image*   (b) *Filter Decompose applied*

You can find this filter through Filters → Colors → Decompose

This filter separates an image into its different components (RGB, HSV...).

15.3.14.2   Options

Figure 15.50: 'Decompose' filter options

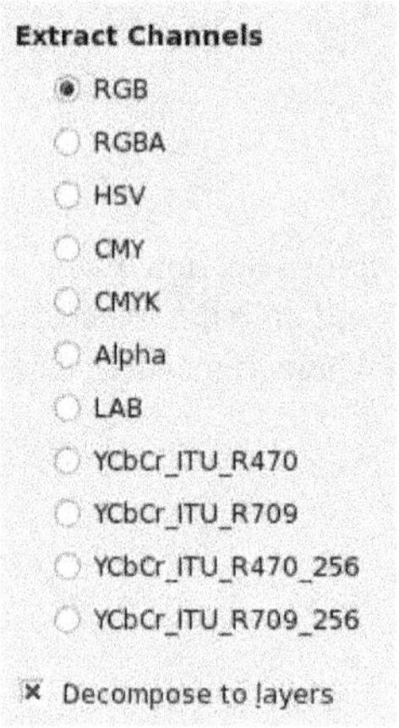

Extract Channels
- ◉ RGB
- ○ RGBA
- ○ HSV
- ○ CMY
- ○ CMYK
- ○ Alpha
- ○ LAB
- ○ YCbCr_ITU_R470
- ○ YCbCr_ITU_R709
- ○ YCbCr_ITU_R470_256
- ○ YCbCr_ITU_R709_256

☒ Decompose to layers

Decompose to Layers If this option is checked, a new grey-scaled image is created, with each layer representing one of the channels of the selected mode. If this option is not checked, every channel is represented with a specific image automatically and clearly named in the name bar.

Following options are described with 'Decompose to layers 'checked.

RGB Decomposing If the RGB radio button is clicked, a grey level image is created with three layers (Red, Green and Blue), and two channels (Grey and Alpha).

This function is interesting when using Threshold tool. You can also perform operations like cutting, pasting or moving selections in a single RBG channel. You can use an extracted grayscale as a selection or mask by saving it in a channel (right-click>Select>Save to a channel).

RGBA Decomposing If the RGBA radio button is clicked, a image is created similar at the RGB Decomposing with a additional Alpha layer filled with the transparencies values of the source image. Full transparent pixels are black and the full opaque pixels are white.

HSV Decomposing This option decomposes image into three greyscaled layers, one for Hue, one for Saturation and another for Value.

Although Hue is greyscaled, it does represent hues. In color circle, white and black are starting and arrival points and are superimposed. They represent Red color at top of circle. Grey intermediate levels are corresponding to intermediate hues on circle: dark grey to orange, mid grey to green and light grey to magenta.

Saturation and Value: White is maximum Saturation (pure color) and maximum Value (very bright). Black is minimum Saturation (white) and minimum Value (black).

CMY Decomposing This option decomposes image into three greyscaled layers, one for Yellow, one for Magenta and another for Cyan.

This option might be useful to transfer image into printing softwares with CMY capabilities.

CMYK Decomposing This option is similar at the CMY Decomposing with an additional layer for Black.

This option might be useful to transfer image into printing softwares with CMYK capabilities.

Alpha Decomposing This option extracts the image transparency stored in the Alpha channel in Channel dialog in a separate image. The full transparent pixels are Black the full opaque pixels are white. The graytones are smooth transitions of the transparency in the source image.

LAB Decomposing This option decomposes image into three greyscaled layers, layer "L" for Luminance, layer "A" for colors between green and red, layer "B" for colors between blue and yellow.

The LAB Decomposing is a color model of the Luminance-Color family. A channel is used for the Luminosity while two other channels are used for the Colors. The LAB color model is used by Photoshop.

YCbCr Decomposing In GIMP there is four YCbCr decompositions with different values. Each option decomposes image in three greyscaled layers, a layer for Luminance and two other for blueness and redness.

The YCbCr color model also called YUV is now used for digital video (initially for PAL analog video). It's based on the idea that the human eye is most sensitive to luminosity, next to colors. The YCbCr Decomposing use a transformation matrix and the different options are different values recommended by ITU (International Telecommunication Union) applied to the matrix .

15.3.15   Compose

15.3.15.1   Overview

Figure 15.51: From left to right: Decomposed image (RGB decomposition), composed image.

(a) *Original image (decomposed to RGB)*   (b) *Filter Compse applied*

You can find this filter through Filters → Colors → Compose This filter is active in Filters/Colors after using Decompose.

This filter reconstructs an image from its RGB, HSV... components.

15.3.15.2   Options

Figure 15.52: 'Compose' filter options

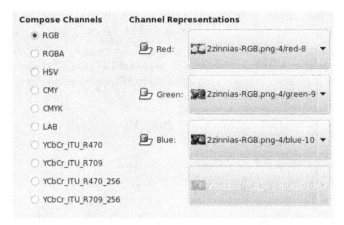

Compose Channels You can select there the color space to be used: RGB, HSV... The options are described in the following Decompose plug-in.

Channel Representation Allows you to select which channel will be affected to each image channel.

 Tip
If Compose options are different from Decompose ones, for instance an image decomposed to RGB then re-composed to LAB, you will get interesting color effects. Test it!

15.3.16   Filter Pack

15.3.16.1   Overview

Figure 15.53: From left to right: Original image, FilterPack (more Blue, more Saturation)

(a) *Original image*   (b) *Filter FilterPack applied*

This tool offers you a collection of unified filters to treat the image. Of course, same functions can be performed by particular filters, but you have here an interesting, intuitive, overview.

15.3.16.2 Starting filter Ejecutar el filtro

You can find this filter through Filters $\rightarrow$ Colors $\rightarrow$ Filter Pack.

15.3.16.3 Options

Figure 15.54: All the options for filter 'Filter Pack'

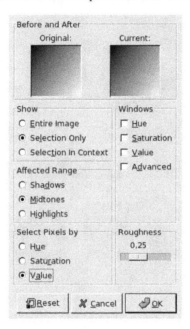

Original and Current previews Two previews display respectively before treatment and after treatment images.

Show Show sets what you want to preview:

- Entire image
- Selection only : if a selection exists (default is the whole image).
- Selection in context : the selection within the image.

Windows You can choose between:

- Hue makes one preview for each of the three primary colors and the three complementary colors of the RGB color model. By clicking successively on a color, you add to this color into the affected range, according to Roughness. To subtract color, click on the opposite color, the complementary color.

Figure 15.55: Hue option of the 'Filterpack' filter

- Saturation: Three previews for more or less saturation.

Figure 15.56: The saturation option of the 'Filterpack' filter

- Value: Three previews for more or less luminosity.

Figure 15.57: Value option of the 'Filterpack' filter

- Advanced: developed later.

Affected range Affected Range allows you to set which brightness you want to work with.

- Shadows: dark tones.
- Midtones
- Highlights: bright tones

Select pixels by Determines what HSV channel the selected range will affect. You can choose between:

- Hue
- Saturation
- Value

Roughness This slider sets how image will change when you click on a window: taking a short step or a large one (0 - 1).

Advanced Options

Figure 15.58: Advanced options of the 'Filterpack' filter

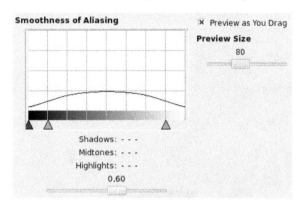

These advanced options let you work more precisely on the changes applied to the image and on the preview size.

Preview Size Something like a zoom on previews. Normal size is 80.

 Tip
In spite of Preview Size option, this size is often too small. You can compensate this by working on an enlarged selection, for instance a face on a photo. Then, you invert selection to work on the other part of the image.

Preview as You Drag FIXME

Smoothness of Aliasing This option should be called 'Importance of changes'. Here, 'aliasing' does not mean as usually in GIMP: It refers to evolution steps when you click on previews to increase or reduce the action of the filter.

The curve in this window represents the importance of the changes applied to the image. The aspect of this curve depends on the Affected range you have selected: Shadows, Midtons or Highlights. You can set the curve amplitude by using the Roughness slider in the main window of the filter.

By using the available sliders, you can set precisely set the form of this action curve.

15.3.17 Hot

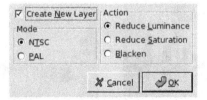

15.3.17.1 Overview

You can find this filter through Filters → Colors → Hot

It identifies and modifies pixels which might cause problem when displayed onto PAL or NTSC TV screen.

15.3.17.2 Options

Mode You have to select the TV mode: PAL or NTSC.

Action You can select:

- Reduce Luminency
- Reduce Saturation
- Blacken: this will turn hot pixels to black.

Create a new layer With this option, work will be performed on a new layer instead of the image. This will give you peace of mind!

15.3.18 Max RGB

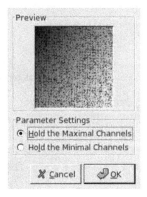

15.3.18.1 Overview

Figure 15.59: From left to right: original image, after applying MaxRGB filter

(a) *Original image*

(b) *Filter MaxRGB applied*

You can find this filter through Filters → Colors → Max RGB.

For every pixel of the image, this filter holds the channel with the maximal / minimal intensity. The result is an image with only three colors, red, green and blue, and possibly pure gray.

15.3.18.2 Options

Preview This preview displays, in real time, the resulting image after treatment by filter.

Parameter Settings Hold the maximal channels: For every pixel, the filter keeps intensity of the RGB color channel which has the maximal intensity and reduces other both to zero. For example: 220, 158, 175 max--> 220, 0, 0. If two channels have same intensity, both are held: 210, 54, 210 max--> 210, 0, 210.

Hold the minimal channels: For every pixel, the filter keeps intensity of the RGB color channel which has the minimal intensity and reduce both others to zero. For example: 220, 158, 175 min--> 0, 158, 0. If two minimal channels have same intensity, both are held: 210, 54, 54 min--> 0, 54, 54.

Grey levels are not changed since light intensity is the same in all three channels.

15.3.19 Retinex

15.3.19.1 Overview

Figure 15.60: 'Retinex' example

(a)　　　　　　　(b) *Note new details in the upper right corner.*

Retinex improves visual rendering of an image when lighting conditions are not good. While our eye can see colors correctly when light is low, cameras and video cams can't manage this well. The MSRCR (MultiScale Retinex with Color Restoration) algorithm, which is at the root of the Retinex filter, is inspired by the eye biological mechanisms to adapt itself to these conditions. Retinex stands for Retina + cortex.

Besides digital photography, Retinex algorithm is used to make the information in astronomical photos visible and detect, in medicine, poorly visible structures in X-rays or scanners.

15.3.19.2 Activate the filter

You can find this filter through Filters → Colors → Retinex.

15.3.19.3 Options

Figure 15.61: 'Retinex' filter options

These options call for notions that only mathematicians can understand. In actual practice, user has to grope about for the best setting.

Level Here is what the plug-in author writes on his site (www-prima.inrialpes.fr/pelisson/MSRCR.php): 'To characterize color variations and the lightor, we make a difference between (gaussian) filters responses at different scales. These parameters allow to specify how to allocate scale values between min scale (sigma 2.0) and max (sigma equal to the image size)'...

- Uniform: FIXME
- Low: FIXME
- High: FIXME

Scale FIXME

Scale division FIXME

Dynamic As the MSR algorithm tends to make image lighter, this slider allows you to set color saturation.

15.3.20 Semi-Flatten

15.3.20.1 Overview

You can find this filter through Filters → Colors → Semi-Flatten It is available if your image holds an Alpha channel (<Image>Layers/Transparency/Add an alpha channel). Otherwise, it is greyed out.

The Semi-flatten filter helps those in need of a solution to anti-aliasing indexed images with transparency. The GIF indexed format supports complete transparency (0 or 255 alpha value), but not semi-transparency (1 - 254): semi-transparent pixels will be transformed to no transparency or complete transparency, ruining anti-aliasing you applied to the logo you want to put onto your Web page.

Before applying the filter, it's essential that you should know the background color of your Web page. Use the color-picker to determine the exact color which pops up as the Foreground color of the Toolbox. Invert FG/BG colors so that BG color is the same as Web background color.

Semi-flatten process will combine FG color to layer (logo) color, proportionally to corresponding alpha values, and will rebuild correct anti-aliasing. Completely transparent pixels will not take the color. Very transparent pixels will take a few color and weakly transparent will take much color.

15.3.20.2 Example

Figure 15.62: Toolbox Background color (pink) and an image with feathered edges on a transparent background, at a 800% zoom level.

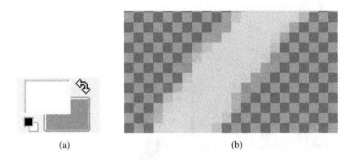

(a)   (b)

Figure 15.63: Result, in GIF format, after applying Semi-flatten filter.

Full transparency is kept. Semi-tranparent pixels are colored with pink according to their transparency (Alpha value). This image will well merge into the pink background of the new page.

15.3.21 Smooth Palette

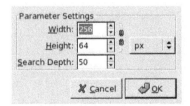

15.3.21.1 Overview

Figure 15.64: From left to right: original image, after applying Smooth Palette filter

(a) *Original image*   (b) *Filter Smooth Palette applied*

You can find this filter through Filters → Colors → Smooth Palette.

It creates a striped palette from colors in active layer or selection. The main purpose of this filter is to create color-maps to be used with the Flame filter.

15.3.21.2 Options

Parameter Settings You can set palette dimensions for Width and Height. Dimensions are linked when chain is not broken. You can also select unit.

Search Depth Increasing Search Depth (1 - 1024) will result in more shades in palette.

15.3.22 Value Invert

15.3.22.1 Overview

Figure 15.65: From left to right: original image, after applying Value Invert filter

(a) *Original image*   (b) *Filter applied*

You can find this filter through Filters → Colors → Value Invert

This filter inverts Value (luminosity) of the active layer or selection. Hue and Saturation will not be affected, although the color will sometimes be slightly different because of round-off error. If you want to invert Hue and Saturation also, use Layers → Colors → Invert.

Note that hue and saturation can be distorted quite a bit when applying twice this filter for colors with a high luminosity (for instance, HSV 102,100%, 98%, a bright green, gives HSV 96, 100%, 2% after a first application of the filter , and 96, 100%, 98% after a second application) . Thus, you should not expect to be able to apply this filter twice in a row and get back the image you started with.

Figure 15.66: Example of using this filter twice

(a) *Original image*   (b) *First application of the filter*   (c) *Second application: the image is not exactly the same as the original one.*

15.4 Noise filters

15.4.1 Introduction

Noise filters *add* noise to the active layer or to the selection. To remove small defects from an image, see the Despeckle and Selective Gaussian Blur filters.

15.4.2 Hurl

15.4.2.1 Overview

You can find this filter through Filters → Noise → Hurl.

The Hurl filter changes each affected pixel to a random color, so it produces real *random noise*. All color channels, including an alpha channel (if it is present) are randomized. All possible values are assigned with the same probability. The original values are not taken into account. All or only some pixels in an active layer or selection are affected, the percentage of affected pixels is determined by the Randomization (%) option.

15.4.2.2 Options

Figure 15.67: 'Hurl' options

Parameter Settings

Random Seed: **10** ⬍ Randomize

Randomization (%): ▭ 50 ⬍

Repeat: ▭ 1 ⬍

✗ Cancel | 🪶 OK

Random Seed Random Seed controls randomness of hurl. If the same random seed in the same situation is used, the filter produces exactly the same results. A different random seed produces different results. Random seed can be entered manually or generated randomly by pressing New Seed button.

When the Randomize option is checked, random seed cannot be entered manually, but is randomly generated each time the filter is run. If it is not checked, the filter remembers the last random seed used.

Randomization (%) The Randomization slider represents the percentage of pixels of the active layer or selection which will be hurled. The higher value, the more pixels are hurled.

Repeat The Repeat slider represents the number of times the filter will be applied. In the case of the Hurl filter it is not very useful, because the same results can be obtained faster just by using a higher Randomization (%) value.

15.4.3 Scatter RGB

15.4.3.1 Overview

Figure 15.68: Example of applying the Noisify filter

(a) *Original image*   (b) *Filter Scatter RGB applied*

You can find this filter through Filters → Noise → Scatter RGB.

The Scatter RGB filter adds a normally distributed noise to a layer or a selection. It uses the RGB color model to produce the noise (noise is added to red, green and blue values of each pixel). A normal distribution means, that only slight noise is added to the most pixels in the affected area, while less pixels are affected by more extreme values. (If you apply this filter to an image filled with a solid grey color and then look at its histogram, you will see a classic bell-shaped Gaussian curve.)

The result is very naturally looking noise.

This filter does not work with indexed images.

Resultatet ser svært naturleg ut.

Filteret verkar ikkje på indekserte bilete.

15.4.3.2 Options

Figure 15.69: 'Scatter RGB' filter options

Preview This preview displays interactively changes before they are applied to the image.

Correlated noise When checked, this radio button makes sliders R, G and B to move all together. The same relative noise will be added to all channels in each pixel, so the hue of pixels does not change much.

Independent RGB When this radio button is checked, you can move each RGB sliders separately.

Red, Blue, Green and Alfa Sliders These slidebars and adjacent input boxes allow to set noise level (0.00 - 1.00) in each channel. Alpha channel is only present, if your layer holds such a channel. In case of a grayscale image, a Grey is shown instead of color sliders.

The value set by these sliders actually determine the standard deviation of the normal distribution of applied noise. The used standard deviation is a half of the set value (where 1 is the distance between the lowest and highest possible value in a channel).

15.4.4 Pick

15.4.4.1 Overview

Figure 15.70: Example of applying the 'Pick' filter

(a) *Original image*

(b) *Filter Pick applied*

You can find this filter through Filters → Noise → Pick.

The Pick filter replaces each affected pixel by a pixel value randomly chosen from its eight neighbours and itself (from a 3×3 square the pixel is center of). All or only some pixels in an active layer or selection are affected, the percentage of affected pixels is determined by the Randomization (%) option.

15.4.4.2 Options

Figure 15.71: 'Pick' filter options

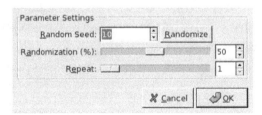

Random Seed Random Seed controls randomness of picking. If the same random seed in the same situation is used, the filter produces exactly the same results. A different random seed produces different results. Random seed can be entered manually or generated randomly by pressing New Seed button.

When the Randomize option is checked, random seed cannot be entered manually, but is randomly generated each time the filter is run. If it is not checked, the filter remembers the last random seed used.

Randomization (%) The Randomization slider represents the percentage of pixels of the active layer or selection which will be picked. The higher value, the more pixels are picked.

Repeat The Repeat slider represents the number of times the filter will be applied. Higher values result in more picking, pixel values being transfered farther away.

15.4.5 Scatter HSV

15.4.5.1 Overview

Figure 15.72: Example of applying the Pick HSV filter

(a) *Original image*   (b) *Filter Pick HSV applied*

You can find this filter through Filters → Noise → Scatter HSV.

The Scatter HSV filter creates noise in the active layer or selection by using the Hue, Saturation, Value (luminosity) color model.

15.4.5.2 Options

Figure 15.73: 'Scatter HSV' filter options

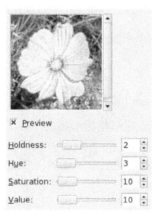

Preview This preview displays interactively changes before they are applied to the image.

Holdness This slider (1 -8) controls how much the new pixel color value is allowed to be applied compared to the existing color. A low holdness will give an important hue variation. A high holdness will give a weak variation.

Hue slider This slider changes the color of the pixels in a random pattern. It selects an increasing available color range in the HSV color circle starting from the original pixel color.

Saturation Slider This slider increases saturation of scattered pixels.

Value Slider This slider increases brightness of scattered pixels.

15.4.6 Slur

15.4.6.1 Overview

Figure 15.74: Example of applying the Slur filter

(a) *Original image* (b) *Filter Slur applied*

You can find this filter through Filters → Noise → Slur.

Slurring produces an effect resembling melting the image downwards; if a pixel is to be slurred, there is an 80% chance that it is replaced by the value of a pixel directly above it; otherwise, one of the two pixels to the left or right of the one above is used. All or only some pixels in an active layer or selection are affected, the percentage of affected pixels is determined by the Randomization (%) option.

15.4.6.2 Options

Figure 15.75: Slur filter options

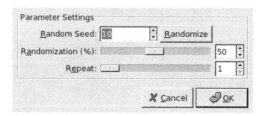

Random Seed Random Seed controls randomness of slurring. If the same random seed in the same situation is used, the filter produces exactly the same results. A different random seed produces different results. Random seed can be entered manually or generated randomly by pressing New Seed button.

When the Randomize option is checked, random seed cannot be entered manually, but is randomly generated each time the filter is run. If it is not checked, the filter remembers the last random seed used.

Randomization (%) The Randomization slider represents the percentage of pixels of the active layer or selection which will be slurred. The higher value, the more pixels are slurred, but because of the way the filter works, its effect is most noticeable if this slider is set to a medium value, somewhere around 50. Experiment with it and try for yourself!

Repeat The Repeat slider represents the number of times the filter will be applied. Higher values result in more slurring, moving the color over a longer distance.

15.4.7 Spread

15.4.7.1 Overview

Figure 15.76: Example of applying the Spread filter

(a) *Original image* (b) *Filter Spread applied*

You can find this filter through Filters → Noise → Spread.

The Spread filter swaps each pixel in the active layer or selection with another randomly chosen pixel by a user specified amount. It works on color transitions, not on plain color areas. No new color is introduced.

15.4.7.2 Options

Figure 15.77: 'Spread' filter options

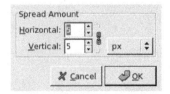

Preview This preview displays interactively changes before they are applied to the image.

Spread amount You can set the distance that pixels will be moved along Horizontal and Vertical axis. The axis can be locked by clicking the Chain icon. You can also define the Unit to be used.

15.5 Edge-Detect Filters

15.5.1 Introduction

Edge detect filters search for borders between different colors and so can detect contours of objects.

They are used to make selections and for many artistic purposes.

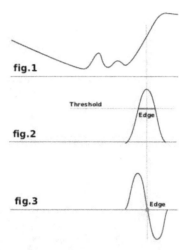

Most of them are based on gradient calculation methods and give thick border lines. Look at fig.1 which represents color intensity variations. On the left is a slow color gradient which is not a border. On the right is a quick variation which is an edge. Now, let us calculate the gradient, the variation speed, of this edge, i.e the first derivative (fig.2). We have to decide that a border is detected when gradient is more than a threshold value (the exact border is at top of the curve, but this top varies according to borders). In most cases, threshold is under top and border is thick.

The Laplacian edge detection uses the second derivative (fig.3). The top of the curve is now at zero and clearly identified. That's why Laplace filter renders a thin border, only a pixel wide. But this derivative gives several zeros corresponding to small ripples, resulting in false edges.

Some blurring before applying edge filters is often necessary: it flattens small ripples in signal and so prevents false edges.

15.5.2 Difference of Gaussians

15.5.2.1 Overview

Figure 15.78: Applying example for the Difference of Gaussians filter

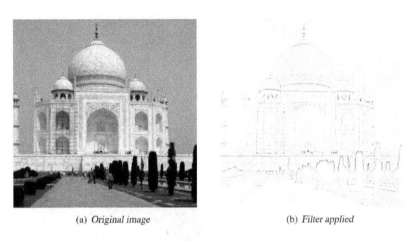

(a) *Original image*   (b) *Filter applied*

You can find this filter through Filters → Edge detect → Difference of Gaussians

This filter is new in GIMP 2.2. It does edge detection using the so-called 'Difference of Gaussians' algorithm, which works by performing two different Gaussian blurs on the image, with a different blurring radius for each, and subtracting them to yield the result. This algorithm is very widely used in artificial vision (maybe in biological vision as well!), and is pretty fast because there are very efficient methods for doing Gaussian blurs. The most important parameters are the blurring radii for the two Gaussian blurs. It is probably easiest to set them using the preview, but it may help to know that increasing the smaller radius tends to give thicker-appearing edges, and decreasing the larger radius tends to increase the 'threshold' for recognizing something as an edge. In most cases you will get nicer results if Radius 2 is smaller than Radius 1, but nothing prevents you from reversing them, and in situations where you have a light figure on the dark background, reversing them may actually improve the result.

15.5.2.2 Options

Figure 15.79: Gaussian Difference filter options

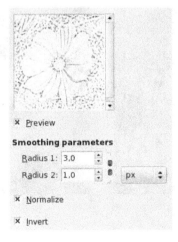

Smoothing parameters Radius 1 and Radius 2 are the blurring radii for the two Gaussian blurs. The only constraints on them is that they cannot be equal, or else the result will be a blank image. If you want to produce something that looks like a sketch, in most cases setting Radius 2 smaller than Radius 1 will give better results.

Normalize Checking this box causes the brightness range in the result to be stretched as much as possible, increasing contrast. Note that in the preview, only the part of the image that is shown is taken into account, so with Normalize checked the preview is not completely accurate. (It is accurate except in terms of global contrast, though.)

Invert Checking this box inverts the result, so that you see dark edges on a white background, giving something that looks more like a drawing.

15.5.3 Edge

15.5.3.1 Overview

You can find this filter through Filters → Edge Detect → Edge....

Figure 15.80: Applying example for the Edge filter

(a) *Original image*   (b) *After applying the filter (Sobel option)*

Figure 15.81: Applying examples for the Edge filter

(a) *After applying the filter (Prewitt option)*   (b) *After applying the filter (Gradient option)*

Figure 15.82: Applying example for the Edge filter

(a) *After applying the filter (Roberts option)*   (b)

Figure 15.83: Applying example for the Edge filter

After applying the filter (Laplace option)

15.5.3.2 Options

Figure 15.84: Edge filter options

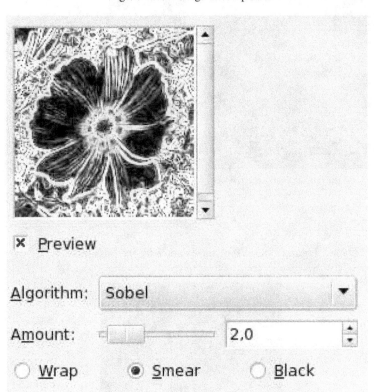

Algorithm Edge detector offers several detection methods:

- Sobel: Here, this method has no options and so is less interesting than the specific Sobel.
- Prewitt: Result doesn't look different from Sobel.
- Gradient: Edges are thiner, less contrasted and more blurred than Sobel.
- Roberts: No evident difference from Sobel.
- Differential: Edges less bright.
- Laplace: Less interesting than the specific one.

Parameter Settings Amount: a low value results in black, high-contrasted image with thin edges. A high value results in thick edges with low contrast and many colors in dark areas.

Wrap, Smear, Black: These options are not operational.

15.5.4 Laplace

15.5.4.1 Overview

Figure 15.85: Applying example for the Laplace filter

(a) *Original image*   (b) *Filter Laplace applied*

You can find this filter through Filtres → Edge detect → Laplace.

This filter detects edges in the image using Laplacian method, which produces thin, pixel wide borders.

15.5.5 Neon

15.5.5.1 Overview

Figure 15.86: Applying example for the Neon filter

(a) *Original image*   (b) *Filter Neon applied*

This filter detects edges in the active layer or selection and gives them a bright neon effect.

You will find in GIMP a script-fu also named Neon, which works in a different manner. The script-fu is an easy shortcut to construct logo-like letters outlined with a configurable neon-effect.

15.5.5.2 Activating the filter

You can find this filter through Filters → Edge Detect → Neon....

15.5.5.3 Options

Figure 15.87: Neon filter options

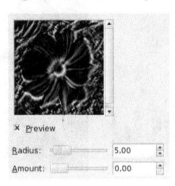

Radius This option lets you determine how wide the detected edge will be.

Amount This option lets you determine how strong the filter effect will be.

15.5.6 Sobel

15.5.6.1 Overview

Figure 15.88: Applying example of the Sobel filter

(a) *Original image*   (b) *Filter Sobel applied*

You can find this filter through Filters → Edge detect → Sobel.

Sobel's filter detects horizontal and vertical edges separately on a scaled image. Color images are turned into RGB scaled images. As with the Laplace filter, the result is a transparent image with black lines and some rest of colors.

15.5.6.2 Options

Figure 15.89: Sobel filter options

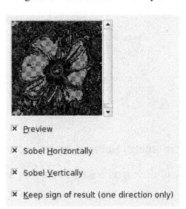

Parameters Settings

- Sobel Horizontally: Renders near horizontal edges.
- Sobel Vertically: Renders near vertical edges.
- Keep sign of result: This option works when only one direction is selected: it gives a flat relief with bumps and hollows to the image.

15.6   Enhance Filters

15.6.1   Introduction

Enhance filters are used to compensate for image imperfections. Such imperfections include dust particles, noise, interlaced frames (coming usually from a TV frame-grabber) and insufficient sharpness.

15.6.2   Deinterlace

15.6.2.1   Overview

You can find this filter through Filters → Enhance → Deinterlace.

Images captured by videocards, especially when fast movement is recorded, may look blurred and stripped, with splitted objects. This is due to how cameras work. They don't record 25 images per second, but 50, with half vertical resolution. There are two interlaced images in one frame. First line of first image is followed by first line of second image followed by second line of first image... etc. So, if there have been an important move between the two images, objects will appear splitted, shifted, stripped.

The Deinterlace filter keeps only one of both images and replaces missing lines by a gradient between previous and following lines. The resulting image, or selection, will be somewhat blurred, but can be improved by enhance filters

You can find interlaced images at Wikipedia.

15.6.2.2 Options

Figure 15.90: Deinterlace filter options

Preview When Do preview is checked, parameter setting results are interactively displayed in preview.

Mode Keep odd lines and Keep even lines: One of them may render a better result. You must try both.

15.6.2.3 Example

Figure 15.91: Simple applying example for the Deinterlace filter

(a) *Top : even lines pixels are shifted by one pixel to the right. Bottom : one line is missing. These images are zoomed to show pixels.*

(b) *Keep even fields checked. Top : odd lines have been shifted to the right, to align themselves with the even lines. Bottom: the empty line has been filled with red.*

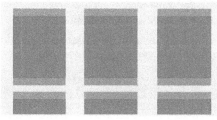

(c) *Keep odd fields checked. Top : even lines have been shifted to the left, to align themselves with the odd lines. Bottom: the empty line persists, but joins up and down through a gradient.*

15.6.3   Despeckle

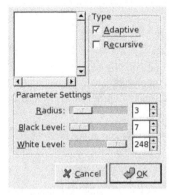

15.6.3.1   Overview

You can find this filter through Filters → Enhance → Despeckle.

It is used to remove small defects due to dust, or scratches, on a scanned image, and also moiré effect on image scanned from a magazine. You ought to select isolated defects before applying this filter, in order to avoid unwanted changes in other areas of your image.

15.6.3.2   Options

Figure 15.92: 'Despeckle' filter options

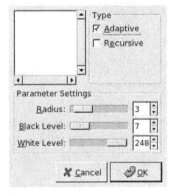

Preview Parameter setting results are interactively displayed in preview.

Type

- Adaptive: Adapts radius to image or selection content (using Histogram). If this option is checked, radius slider is not efficient. It renders a result smoother than with radius alone.
- Recursive: Repeats filter action which gets stronger.

Parameters settings

- Radius: Sets size of action window from 1 (3x3 pixels) to 20 (41x41). This window moves over the image, and the color in it is smoothed, so imperfections are removed.
- Black level: Removes pixels darker than set value (0-255).
- White level: Removes pixels whiter than set value (0-255).

15.6.4 Destripe

15.6.4.1 Overview

You can find this filter through Filters → Enhance → Destripe

It is used to remove vertical stripes caused by poor quality scanners. It works by adding a pattern that will interfere with the image, removing stripes if setting is good. This 'negative' pattern is calculated from vertical elements of the image, so don't be surprised if you see stripes on the preview of an image that has none. And if pattern 'strength'; is too high, your image will be striped.

If, after a first pass, a stripe persists, rectangular-select it and apply filter again (all other selection type may worsen the result).

15.6.4.2 Options

Figure 15.93: 'Destripe' filter options

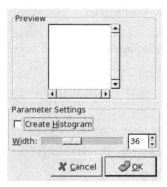

Preview Parameter setting results are interactively displayed in preview. Scroll bars allow you to move around the image.

Parameter setting

- Create histogram: This 'histogram ' is a black and white image showing the interference pattern more legibly.
- Width: Slider and input box allow to set 'strength' of filter (2-100): more than 60 is rarely necessary and may create artifacts.

Create histogram FIXME

15.6.5 NL Filter

15.6.5.1 Overview

You can find this filter through Filters → Enhance → NL Filter. NL means "Non Linear". Derived from the Unix **pnmnlfilt** program, it joins smoothing, despeckle and sharpen enhancement functions. It works on the whole image, not on the selection.

This is something of a swiss army knife filter. It has 3 distinct operating modes. In all of the modes each pixel in the image is examined and processed according to it and its surrounding pixels values. Rather than using 9 pixels in a 3x3 block, it uses an hexagonal block whose size can be set with the Radius option.

15.6.5.2 Options

Figure 15.94: 'NL Filter' options

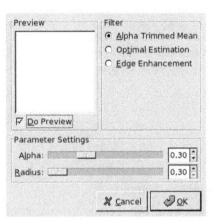

Preview When Do preview is checked, parameter setting results are interactively displayed in preview.

Parameter settings • Alpha: Meaning of this value depends on the selected option.

• Radius: Controls the strength of the filter (0.33-1.00).

15.6.5.3 Operating Modes

This filter can perform several distinct functions, depending on the value of the parameter alpha.

Alpha trimmed mean filter. (0.0 <= alpha <= 0.5) The value of the center pixel will be replaced by the mean of the 7 hexagon values, but the 7 values are sorted by size and the top and bottom *alpha* portion of the 7 are excluded from the mean. This implies that an *alpha* value of 0.0 gives the same sort of output as a normal convolution (ie. averaging or smoothing filter), where *radius* will determine the "strength" of the filter. A good value to start from for subtle filtering is *alpha* = 0.0, *radius* = 0.55. For a more blatant effect, try *alpha* 0.0 and *radius* 1.0.

An *alpha* value of 0.5 will cause the median value of the 7 hexagons to be used to replace the center pixel value. This sort of filter is good for eliminating "pop" or single pixel noise from an image without spreading the noise out or smudging features on the image. Judicious use of the *radius* parameter will fine tune the filtering. Intermediate values of *alpha* give effects somewhere between smoothing and "pop" noise reduction. For subtle filtering try starting with values of *alpha* = 0.4, *radius* = 0.6. For a more blatant effect try *alpha* = 0.5, *radius* = 1.0 .

Optimal estimation smoothing. (1.0 <= alpha <= 2.0) This type of filter applies a smoothing filter adaptively over the image. For each pixel the variance of the surrounding hexagon values is calculated, and the amount of smoothing is made inversely proportional to it. The idea is that if the variance is small then it is due to noise in the image, while if the variance is large, it is because of "wanted" image features. As usual the *radius* parameter controls the effective radius, but it probably advisable to leave the radius between 0.8 and 1.0 for the variance calculation to be meaningful. The *alpha* parameter sets the noise threshold, over which less smoothing will be done. This means that small values of *alpha* will give the most subtle filtering effect, while large values will tend to smooth all parts of the image. You could start with values like *alpha* = 1.2, *radius* = 1.0, and try increasing or decreasing the *alpha* parameter to get the desired effect. This type of filter is best for filtering out dithering noise in both bitmap and color images.

Edge enhancement. (-0.1 >= alpha >= -0.9) This is the opposite type of filter to the smoothing filter. It enhances edges. The *alpha* parameter controls the amount of edge enhancement, from subtle (-0.1) to blatant (-0.9). The *radius* parameter controls the effective radius as usual, but useful values are between 0.5 and 0.9. Try starting with values of *alpha* = 0.3 , *radius* = 0.8 .

Combination use The various operating modes can be used one after the other to get the desired result. For instance to turn a monochrome dithered image into grayscale image you could try one or two passes of the smoothing filter, followed by a pass of the optimal estimation filter, then some subtle edge enhancement. Note that using edge enhancement is only likely to be useful after one of the non-linear filters (alpha trimmed mean or optimal estimation filter), as edge enhancement is the direct opposite of smoothing.

For reducing color quantization noise in images (ie. turning .gif files back into 24 bit files) you could try a pass of the optimal estimation filter (*alpha* 1.2, *radius* 1.0), a pass of the median filter (*alpha* 0.5, *radius* 0.55), and possibly a pass of the edge enhancement filter. Several passes of the optimal estimation filter with declining *alpha* values are more effective than a single pass with a large *alpha* value. As usual, there is a tradeoff between filtering effectiveness and losing detail. Experimentation is encouraged.

15.6.6 Sharpen

15.6.6.1 Overview

You can find this filter through Filters → Enhance → Sharpen.

Most of digitized images need correction of sharpness. This is due to digitizing process that must chop a color continuum up in points with slightly different colors: elements thiner than sampling frequency will be averaged into an uniform color. So sharp borders are rendered a little blurred. The same phenomenon appears when printing color dots on paper.

The Sharpen filter accentuates edges but also any noise or blemish and it may create noise in graduated color areas like the sky or a water surface. It competes with the Unsharp Mask filter, which is more sophisticated and renders more natural results.

Figure 15.95: Applying example for the Sharpen filter

(a)   (b)

15.6.6.2   Options

Figure 15.96: 'Sharpen' filter options

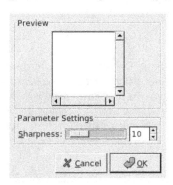

Preview   Parameter setting results are interactively displayed in preview. Scroll bars allow you to move around the image.

Parameter setting   Increase sharpness: slider and input boxes allow you to set sharpness (1-99) and you can judge result in preview. By increasing sharpness, you may increase image blemishes and also create noise in graduated color areas.

15.6.7   Unsharp Mask

15.6.7.1   Overview

Figure 15.97: Applying example for the Unsharp Mask filter

(a)	(b)

You can find this filter through Filters → Enhance → Unsharp Mask.

Out-of-focus photographs and most digitized images often need a sharpness correction. This is due to the digitizing process that must chop a color continuum up in points with slightly different colors: elements thinner than sampling frequency will be averaged into an uniform color. So sharp borders are rendered a little blurred. The same phenomenon appears when printing color dots on paper.

The Unsharp Mask filter (what an odd name!) sharpens edges of the elements without increasing noise or blemish. It is the king of the sharpen filters.

Some scanners apply a sharpen filter while scanning. It's worth disabling it so that you keep control on your image.

Tip
Some imaging devices like digital cameras or scanners offer to sharpen the created images for you. We strongly recommend you disable the sharpening in this devices and use the GIMP filters instead. This way you regain the full control over the sharpening of your images.

Tip
To prevent color distortion while sharpening, Decompose your image to HSV and work only on Value. Then Compose the image to HSV. Go to Image/Mode and click on Decompose. Make sure the Decompose to Layers box is checked. Choose HSV and click OK. You will get a new grey-level image with three layers, one for Hue, one for Saturation, and one for Value. (Close the original image so you won't get confused). Select the Value layer and apply your sharpening to it. When you are done, with that same layer selected, reverse the process. Go to Image/Mode and click on Compose. Again choose HSV and click OK. You will get back your original image except that it will have been sharpened in the Value component.

15.6.7.2 Options

Figure 15.98: 'Unsharp Mask' filter options

Preview Parameter setting results are interactively displayed in preview. Scroll bars allow you to move around the image.

Radius Radius : slider and input boxes (0.1-120) allow you to set how many pixels on either side of an edge will be affected by sharpening. High resolution images allow higher radius. It is better to always sharpen an image at its final resolution.

Amount Amount: slider and input boxes (0.00-5.00) allow you to set strength of sharpening.

Threshold Threshold : slider and input boxes (0-255) allow you to set the minimum difference in pixel values that indicates an edge where sharpen must be applied. So you can protect areas of smooth tonal transition from sharpening, and avoid creation of blemishes in face, sky or water surface.

15.6.7.3 How does an unsharp mask work?

Using an unsharp mask to sharpen an image can seem rather weird. Here is the explanation:

Think of an image with a contrast in some place. The intensity curve of the pixels on a line going through this contrast will show an abrupt increase of intensity: like a stair if contrast is perfectly sharp, like an S if there is some blur.

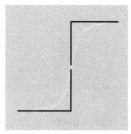

Now, we have an image with some blur we want to sharpen (black curve). We apply some more blur: the intensity variation will be more gradual (green curve).

Let us substract the blurredness intensity from the intensity of the image. We get the red curve, which is more abrupt : contrast and sharpness are increased. QED.

Unsharp mask has first been used in silver photography. The photograph fist creates a copy of the original negative by contact, on a film, placing a thin glass plate between both; that will produce a blurred copy because of light diffusion. Then he places both films, exactly corresponding, in a photo enlarger, to reproduce them on paper. The dark areas of the positive blurred film, opposed to the clear areas of the original negative will prevent light to go through and so will be subtracted from the light going through the original film.

In digital photography, with GIMP, you will go through the following steps:

1. Open your image and duplicate it Image → Duplicate

2. In the copy, duplicate the layer Layer → Duplicate layer, then drop the Filters menu down and apply Blur → Gaussian Blur to the duplicated layer with the default IIR option and radius 5.

3. In the layer dialog of the duplicated image, change Mode to 'Subtract', and in the right-clic menu, select 'Merge down'.

4. Click and drag the only layer you got into the original image, where it appears as a new layer.

5. Change the Mode in this layer dialog to 'Addition'.

Voilà. TheUnsharp Mask plug-in does the same for you.

At the beginning of the curve, you can see a dip. If blurring is important, this dip is very deep; the result of the subtraction can be negative, and a complementary color stripe will appear along the contrast, or a black halo around a star on the light background of a nebula (black eye effect).

Figure 15.99: Black eye effect

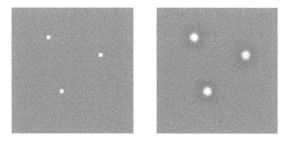

15.7 Generic Filters

15.7.1 Introduction

Generic filters are a catch-all for filters which can't be placed elsewhere. You can find:

- The Convolution Matrix filter which lets you build custom filters.

- The Dilate filter.

- The Erode filter.

15.7.2 Convolution Matrix

15.7.2.1 Overview

You can find this filter through Filters → Generic → Convolution Matrix

Here is a mathematician's domain. Most of filters are using convolution matrix. With the Convolution Matrix filter, if the fancy takes you, you can build a custom filter.

What is a convolution matrix? It's possible to get a rough idea of it without using mathematical tools that only a few ones know. Convolution is the treatment of a matrix by another one which is called 'kernel'.

The Convolution Matrix filter uses a first matrix which is the Image to be treated. The image is a bi-dimensional collection of pixels in rectangular coordinates. The used kernel depends on the effect you want.

GIMP uses 5x5 or 3x3 matrices. We will consider only 3x3 matrices, they are the most used and they are enough for all effects you want. If all border values of a kernel are set to zero, then system will consider it as a 3x3 matrix.

The filter studies successively every pixel of the image. For each of them, which we will call the 'initial pixel', it multiplies the value of this pixel and values of the 8 surrounding pixels by the kernel corresponding value. Then it adds the results, and the initial pixel is set to this final result value.

A simple example:

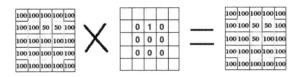

On the left is the image matrix: each pixel is marked with its value. The initial pixel has a red border. The kernel action area has a green border. In the middle is the kernel and, on the right is the convolution result.

Here is what happened: the filter read successively, from left to right and from top to bottom, all the pixels of the kernel action area. It multiplied the value of each of them by the kernel corresponding value and added results: (100*0)+(50*1)+(50*0)*(100*0)+(100) +(100*0)+(100*0)+(100*0)+(100*0)+(100*0) = 50. The initial pixel took the value 50. Previously, when the initial pixel had value=50, it took the value 100 of the above pixel (the filter doesn't work on the image but on a copy) and so disappeared into the "100" background pixels. As a graphical result, the initial pixel moved a pixel downwards.

15.7.2.2 Options

Figure 15.100: 'Convolution matrix' options

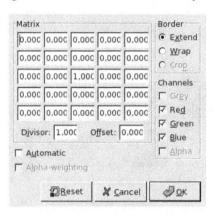

Matrix This is the 5x5 kernel matrix: you enter wanted values directly into boxes.

Divisor: The result of previous calculation will be divided by this divisor. You will hardly use 1, which lets result unchanged, and 9 or 25 according to matrix size, which gives the average of pixel values.

Offset: this value is added to the division result. This is useful if result may be negative. This offset may be negative.

Border

Source Extend, Wrap, Crop

When the initial pixel is on a border, a part of kernel is out of image. You have to decide what filter must do:

- Extend: this part of kernel is not taken into account.
- Wrap: this part of kernel will study pixels of the opposite border, so pixels disappearing from one side reappear on the other side.
- Crop: Pixels on borders are not modified, but they are cropped.

Channels You can select there one or several channels the filter will work with.

Automatic If this option is checked, The Divisor takes the result value of convolution. If this result is equal to zero (it's not possible to divide by zero), then a 128 offset is applied. If it is negative (a negative color is not possible), a 255 offset is applied (inverts result).

Alpha weighting If this option is not checked, the filter doesn't take in account transparency and this may be cause of some artefacts when blurring.

15.7.2.3 Examples

Design of kernels is based on high levels mathematics. You can find ready-made kernels on the Web. Here are a few examples:

Figure 15.101: Sharpen

(a)   (b)

Figure 15.102: Blur

(a)   (b)

Figure 15.103: Edge enhance

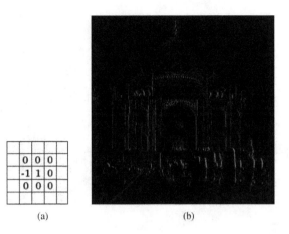

(a)　　　　　　　　　(b)

Figure 15.104: Edge detect

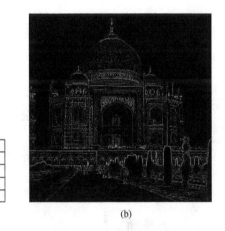

(a)　　　　　　　　　(b)

Figure 15.105: Emboss

(a)   (b)

15.7.3   Dilate

15.7.3.1   Overview

Figure 15.106: Applying example for the Dilate filter

(a) *Original image*   (b) *Filter Dilate applied*

You can find this filter through Filters → Generic → Dilate

This filter widens and enhances dark areas of the active layer or selection.

For every image pixel, it brings the pixel Value (luminosity) into line with the lowest Value (the darkest) of the 8 neighbouring pixels (3x3 matrix). So, a dark pixel is added around dark areas. An isolated pixel on a brighter background will be changed to a big 'pixel ', composed of 9 pixels, and that will create some noise in the image.

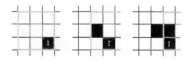

In this image, the studied pixel has a red border and the studied matrix has a green border. I hope you have understood how to go on with the process and get a 3x3 pixel block: when the 'I' pixel is inside the green border, the studied pixel turns to black.

A larger dark area will dilate by one pixel in all directions:

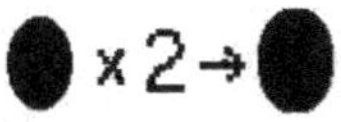

The filter was applied 3 times.

On more complex images, dark areas are widenned and enhanced the same, and somewhat pixellated. Here, the filter was applied 3 times:

Of course, if background is darker than foreground, it will cover the whole image.

15.7.3.2 Examples

Figure 15.107: Dilate text

Figure 15.108: Dilate neon effect

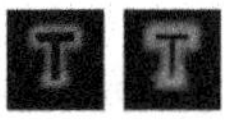

15.7.4 Erode

15.7.4.1 Overview

Figure 15.109: Erode noise

(a) *Original image*   (b) *Filter Erode noise applied*

You can find this filter through Filters → Generic → Erode

This filter widens and enhances bright areas of the active layer or selection.

For every image pixel, it brings the pixel Value (luminosity) into line with the upper Value (the brightest) of the 8 neighbouring pixels (3x3 matrix). So, a bright pixel is added around bright areas. An isolated pixel on a brighter background will be deleted. A larger bright area will dilate by one pixel in all directions.

On complex images, bright areas are widened and enhanced the same, and somewhat pixellated.

On a solid background, this filter can delete noise:

15.8   Glass Effects Filters

15.8.1   Introduction

Glass Effects filters result in an image as if it were seen through a lens or glass tiles.

15.8.2   Apply Lens

15.8.2.1   Overview

Figure 15.110: The same image, before and after applying lens effect.

(a)   (b)

You can find this filter through Filters → Glass effects → Apply Lens

After applying this filter, a part of the image is rendered as through a spherical lens.

15.8.2.2 Options

Figure 15.111: 'Apply Lens' filter options

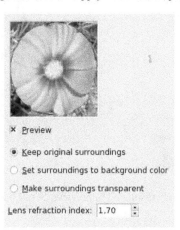

Preview Parameter setting results are interactively displayed in preview. Scroll bars allow you to move around the image.

Parameter settings • Keep original surrounding: The lens seems to be put on the image.

- Set surroundings to Background color: The part of the image outside the lens will have the Background color selected in Toolbox.
- Make Surroundings Transparent: The part of the image outside the lens will be transparent.
- Lens Refraction Index: Lens will be more or less convergent (1-100).

15.8.3 Glass Tile

15.8.3.1 Overview

Figure 15.112: The same image, before and after applying glass tile effect.

(a) *Original image*   (b) *Filter Glass Tile applied*

You can find this filter through Filters → Glass effects → Glass Tile

After applying this filter, the active layer or selection is rendered as through a glass brick wall.

15.8.3.2 Options

Figure 15.113: 'Glass Tile' filter options

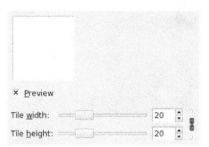

Preview Parameter setting results are interactively displayed in preview. Scroll bars allow you to move around the image.

Parameters setting • Tile width: Sets tile width (10-50 pixels).
    • Tile length: Sets tile length (10-50 pixels).

15.9 Light Effects filters

15.9.1 Introduction

Light Effects filters render several illumination effects of the image.

15.9.2 FlareFX

15.9.2.1 Overview

Figure 15.114: Example for the FlareFX filter

(a) *Original image*   (b) *Filter FlareFX applied*

You can find this filter through Filters → Light Effects → FlareFX

This filter gives the impression that sun hit the objective when taking a shot. You can locate the reflection with a reticule you can move, but you have not the possibilities that Gflare filter offers.

15.9.2.2 Options

Figure 15.115: 'FlareFX' filter options

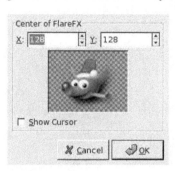

Preview Parameter setting results are interactively displayed in preview. Scroll bars allow you to move around the image.

Parameters setting • Center of FlareFX: You can set there X and Y (pixels) coordinates of glint. The coordinate origin is at upper left corner.

  • Show cursor: When this option is checked, a reticule appears in preview and you can move it with mouse pointer to locate center of flareX.

Cursor display The mouse cursor, which looks like a cross when it moves over the preview, lets you locate the filter effect even without the reticule.

15.9.3 Gflare

15.9.3.1 Overview

Figure 15.116: Example for the GFlare filter

(a) *Original image*   (b) *Filter GFlare applied*

You can find this filter through Filters → Light Effectsender → Gflare

Gflare effect reminds the effect you get when you take a photograph of a blinding light source, with a halo and radiations around the source. The Gflare image has three components: *Glow* which is the big central fireball, *Rays* and *Second Flares*

15.9.3.2 Options

The Settings tab allows you to set manually the parameters while the Selector tab let you choose presets in a list.

Preview When Auto Update Preview is checked, parameter setting results are interactively displayed in preview without modifying the image until you click on OK button.

15.9.3.3 Settings

Figure 15.117: 'GFlare' filter options (Settings)

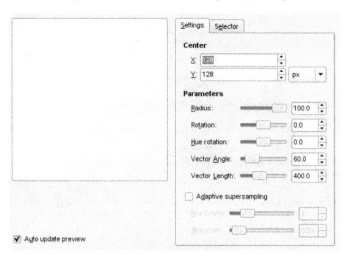

Center Center: You can set there X and Y (pixels) coordinates of glint. The coordinate origin is at the upper left corner

Parameters

- Radius: The radius of the effect. Don't be afraid to use the box with the digits instead the slider which is a bit limited.
- Rotation: Turn the effect.
- Hue Rotation: Change the tint (color) of the effect.
- Vector Angle: Turn the Second flares.
- Vector length: Vary the distance applied for the Second flares.

Adaptive Supersampling Adaptive Supersampling: Settings of the anti-aliasing following parameters like Depth and Threshold.

15.9.3.4 Selector

Figure 15.118: 'Gflare' filter options (Selector)

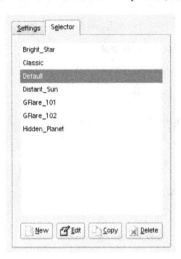

The Selector tab allows you to select a Gflare pattern, to change it and save it.

New When you click on this button, you create a new Gflare pattern. Give it a name of your choice.

Edit This button brings up the Gflare Editor (see below).

Copy This button allows you to duplicate selected Gflare pattern. You can edit the copy without altering the original.

Delete This button deletes the selected Gflare pattern.

15.9.3.5 Gflare Editor

General

Figure 15.119: 'Gflare Editor' options (General)

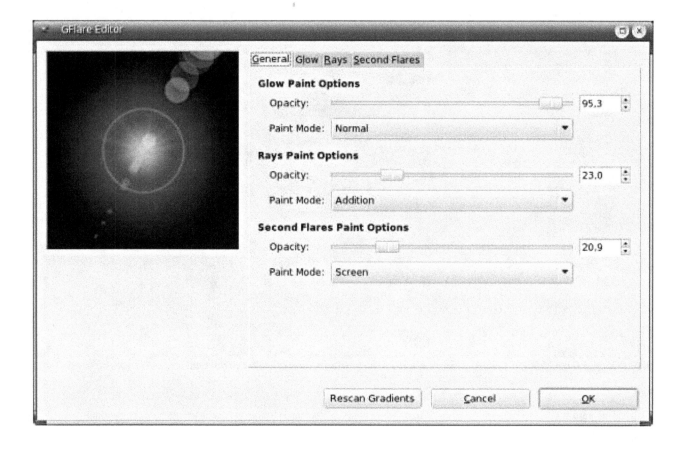

Glow Paint Options

- Opacity: Slider and input box allows you to reduce glow opacity (0-100).
- Paint Mode: You can choose between four modes:
  - *Normal*: In this mode, the glow covers the image without taking into account what is beneath.
  - *Addition*: Pixel RGB values of glow are added to RGB values of the corresponding pixels in the image. Colors get lighter and white areas may appear.
  - *Overlay*: Light/Dark areas of glow enhance corresponding light/dark areas of image.
  - *Screen*: Dark areas of image are enlightened by corresponding light areas of glow. Imagine two slides projected onto the same screen.

Rays Paint Options Options are the same as for "Glow".

Second Flare Paint Options Options are the same as for "Glow".

Glow

Figure 15.120: 'Gflare Editor' options (Glow)

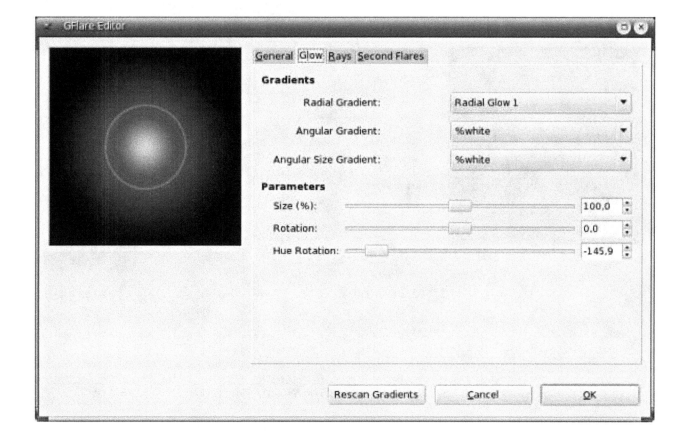

Gradients By clicking on the rectangular buttons, you can develop a long list of gradients. "%" gradients belong to the Editor.

- Radial gradient: The selected gradient is drawn radially, from center to edge.
- Angular gradient: The selected gradient develops around center, counter-clockwise, starting from three o'clock if "Rotation" parameter is set to 0. Radial and angular gradients are combined according to the Multiply mode: light areas are enhanced and colors are mixed according to CMYK color system (that of your printer).
- Angular size gradient: This is a gradient of radius size which develops angularly. Radius is controlled according to gradient Luminosity: if luminosity is zero (black), the radius is 0%. If luminosity is 100% (white), the radius is also 100%.

Parameters

- Size (%): Sets size (%) of glow (0-200).
- Rotation: Sets the origin of the angular gradient (-180 +180).
- Hue rotation: Sets glow color, according to the HSV color circle (-180 +180).

Rays

Figure 15.121: 'Gflare Editor' options (Rays)

Gradients The options are the same as for Glow.

Parameters The first three options are the same as in Glow. Two are new:

- # of spikes: This option determines the number of spikes (1-300) but also their texture.
- Spike Thickness: When spikes get wider (1-100), they look like flower petals

Second Flares

Figure 15.122: 'Gflare Editor' options (Second Flares)

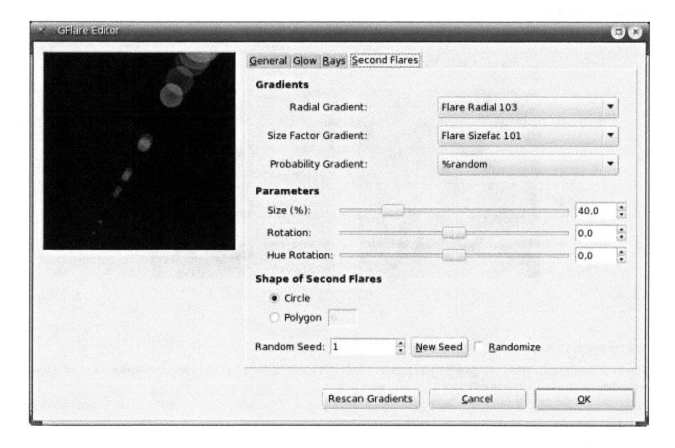

Gradients The options are the same as for Glow.

Parameters Options are the same as in Glow.

Shape of Second Flares Second flares, these satellites of the main flare, may have two shapes: *Circle* and *Polygon*. You can set the *Number* polygon sides. The option accepts 1 side (!), not 2.

Random seed and Randomize

- Random Seed: The random generator will use this value as a seed to generate random numbers. You can use the same value to repeat the same 'random' sequence several times.
- Randomize: When you click on this button, you produce a random seed that will be used by the random generator. It is each time different.

15.9.4 Lighting Effects

15.9.4.1 Overview

Figure 15.123: The same image, before and after applying Lighting filter

(a) *Original image*   (b) *Filter Light-Effects applied*

You can find this filter through Filters → Light Effectsender → Lighting Effects

This filter simulates the effect you get when you light up a wall with a spot. It doesn't produce any drop shadows and, of course, doesn't reveal any new details in dark zones.

15.9.4.2 Options

Preview When Interactive is checked, parameter setting results are interactively displayed in preview without modifying the image until you click on OK button.

If Interactive is not checked, changes are displayed in preview only when you click on the Update button. This option is useful with a slow computer.

General Options

Figure 15.124: 'Lighting' filter general options

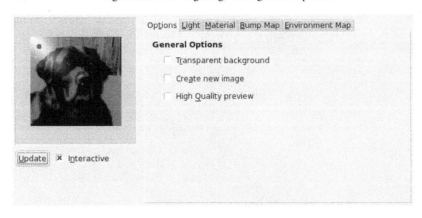

Transparent Background Transparent Background: Makes destination image transparent when bumpmap height is zero (height is zero in black areas of the bumpmapped image).

Create New Image Create New Image: Creates a new image when applying filter.

High Quality Preview High Quality Preview: For quick CPU...

Light

Figure 15.125: 'Light' Options of the Lighting filter

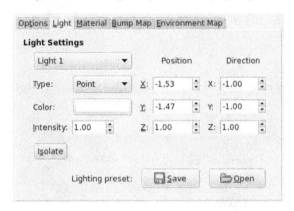

In this tab, you can set light parameters. With Light 1, 2,...6: You can create six light sources and work on each of them separately.

Light Type This filter provides several Light Types in a drop-down list:
Point: displays a blue point at center of preview. You can click and drag it to move light all over the preview.
Directional: the blue point is linked to preview center by a line which indicates the direction of light.
None: This deletes the light source (light may persist...).

Light Source Color Light Source Color: When you click on the color dwell, you bring a dialog up where you can select the light source color.

Intensity With this option, you can set light intensity.

Position Position: Determines the light point position according to three coordinates: X coordinate for horizontal position, Y for vertical position, Z for source distance (the light darkens when distance increases). Values are from -1 to +1.

Direction This option should allow you to fix the light direction in its three X, Y and Z coordinates.

Isolate With this option, you can decide whether all light sources must appear in the Preview, or only the source you are working on.

Lighting Preset You can save your settings with the Save and get them back later with the Open.

Material

Figure 15.126: 'Material' tab of the Lighting filter

These options don't concern light itself, but light reflected by objects.

Small spheres, on both ends of the input boxes, represent the action of every option, from its minimum (on the left) to its maximum (on the right). Help pop ups are more useful.

Glowing With these option, you can set the amount of original color to show where no direct light falls.

Bright With this option, you can set the intensity of original color when hit directly by a light source.

Shiny This option controls how intense the highlight will be.

Hell With this option, higher values make the highlight more focused.

Metallic When this option is checked, surfaces look metallic.

Bump Map

Figure 15.127: 'Bumpmap' options of the Lighting filter

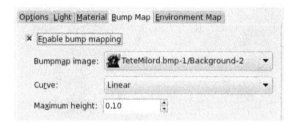

In this tab, you can set filter options that give relief to the image. See Bumpmapping.

Enable Bump Mapping With this option, bright parts of the image will appear raised and dark parts will appear depressed. The aspect depends on the light source position.

Bump Map Image Bump Map Image: You have to select there the grey-scale image that will act as a bump map.

Curve Curve: Four curve types are available: *Linear*, *Logarithmic*, *Sinusoidal* and *Spherical*. See Bump Map plug-in for explanations.

Maximum Height Maximum Height: This is the maximum height of bumps.

Environment Map

Figure 15.128: 'Environment map' options

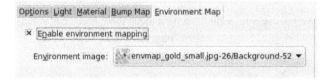

Enable Environment Mapping When you check this box, the following option is enabled:

Environment Image Environment Image: You have to select there a RGB image, present on your screen.

15.9.5 Sparkle

15.9.5.1 Overview

Figure 15.129: Applying example for the Sparkle filter

(a) *Original image*   (b) *Filter Sparkle applied*

You can find this filter in the image menu through Filters → Light Effects → Sparkle

This filter adds sparkles to your image. It uses the lightest points according to a threshold you have determined. It is difficult to foresee where sparkles will appear. But you can put white points on your image where you want sparkles to be.

15.9.5.2 Parameter Settings

Figure 15.130: 'Sparkle' filter options

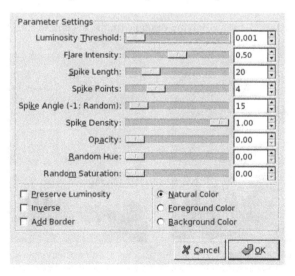

Sliders and input boxes allow you to set values.

Preview Parameter setting results are interactively displayed in preview. Scroll bars allow you to move around the image.

Luminosity Threshold The higher the threshold, the more areas are concerned by sparkling (0.0-0.1).

Flare Intensity When this value increases, the central spot and rays widen (0.0-1.0).

Spike Length This is ray length (1-100). When you reduce it, small spikes decrease first.

Spike Points Number of starting points for spikes (0-16). It's the number of big spikes. There is the same number of small spikes. When number is odd, small spikes are opposite the big ones. When number is even, big spikes are opposite another big spike.

Spike Angle This is angle of first big spike with horizontal (-1 +360). -1 determines this value at random. If a spot has several pixels within required threshold, each of them will generate a sparkle. If angle is positive, they will all be superimposed. With -1, each sparkle will have a random rotation resulting in numerous thin spikes.

Spike Density This option determines the number of sparkles on your image. It indicates the percentage (0.0-1.0) of all possible sparkles that will be preserved.

Opacity When you decrease Opacity (0.0-1.0), sparkles become more transparent and the layer beneath becomes visible. If there is no other layer, sparkle saturation decreases.

Random Hue This option should change sparkle hue at random... (0.0-1.0)

Random Saturation This option should change sparkle saturation at random... (0.0-1.0)

Preserve Luminosity Gives to all central pixels the luminosity of the brightest pixel, resulting in increasing the whole sparkle luminosity.

Inverse Instead of selecting brightest pixels in image, Sparkle will select the darkest ones, resulting in dark sparkles.

Add Border Instead of creating sparkles on brightest pixels, this option creates an image border made up of numerous sparkles.

Natural, Foreground, Background Colors You can change there the color of central pixels. This color will be added in Screen mode (Multiply if Inverse is checked). You can select between Natural color (the color of the pixel in the image), Foreground color and Background color.

15.9.6   SuperNova

15.9.6.1   Overview

Figure 15.131: Applying example for the Supernova filter

(a) *Original image*

(b) *Filter Supernova applied*

You can find this filter through Filters → Light Effectsender → Super Nova

This filter creates a big star reminding a super-nova. It works with RGB and GRAY images. Light effect decreases according to 1/r where r is the distance from star center.

15.9.6.2 Parameter Settings

Figure 15.132: 'Supernova' filter options

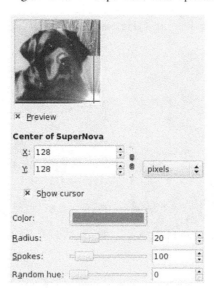

Preview Parameter setting results are interactively displayed in preview. Scroll bars allow you to move around the image.

Center of SuperNova

- You can use input boxes to set horizontal (X) and vertical (Y) coordinates of SuperNova center. You can also click and drag the SuperNova center in *preview*.

 Tip
To center Supernova precisely, select 'Percent' option in the Unit dropdown list and fix X and Y to 50%.

- Show Cursor: This option brings up a reticle in preview, centered on the SuperNova.

Color Color: When you click on the color dwell, you bring up the usual color selector.

Radius Radius: This is radius of the SuperNova center (1-100). When you increase the value, you increase the number of central white pixels according to r*r (1, 4, 9...).

Spikes Spokes: This is number of rays (1-1024). Each pixel in the nova center emit one pixel wide rays. All these rays are more or less superimposed resulting in this glittering effect you get when you move this slider.

Random Hue Random Hue: Colours rays at random. (0-360) value seems to be a range in HSV color circle.

15.10 Distort filters

15.10.1 Introduction

The distort filters transform your image in many different ways.

15.10.2 Blinds

15.10.2.1 Overview

Figure 15.133: Applying example for the Blinds filter

(a) *Original image* (b) *Filter Blinds applied*

You can find this filter through Filters → Distort → Blinds.

It generates a blind effect with horizontal or vertical battens. You can lift or close these battens, but not lift the whole blind up.

15.10.2.2 Options

Figure 15.134: 'Blinds' filter options

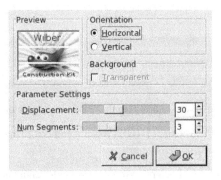

Preview All your setting changes will appear in the Preview without affecting the image until you click on OK.

Orientation Allows you to decide whether battens will be horizontal or vertical.

Background The batten color is that of the Toolbox Background. To be able to use the *Transparent* option, your image must have an Alpha channel.

Displacement Slider and input box allow to wide battens giving the impression they are closing, or to narrow them, giving the impression they are opening.

Number of segments It's the number of battens. Note that Displacement must be about 50 to have all gradations of this number.

15.10.3   Curve Bend

15.10.3.1   Overview

Figure 15.135: Applying example for the Curve Bend filter

(a) *Original image*

(b) *Filter Curve Bend applied*

You can find this filter through Filters → Distorts → Curve Bend.

This filter allows you to create a curve that will be used to distort the active layer or selection. The distortion is applied gradually from an image or selection border to the other.

15.10.3.2   Options

Figure 15.136: 'Curve bend' filter options

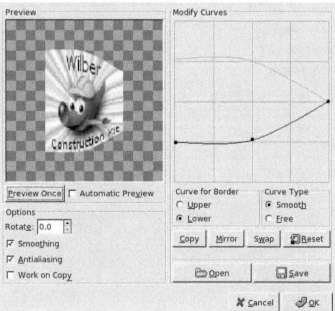

Preview The preview displays changes to image or selection without modifying the image until you press *OK*.

> **Preview Once** This button allows you to update the preview each time you need it.
>
> **Automatic Preview** With this option, preview is changed in real time. This needs much calculation and may lengthen work. It is particularly evident when using "Rotation".

Options

> **Rotate** There, you can set the application angle of filter (0-360 counter-clockwise). 0 is default setting: The curve will be applied from the upper border and/or from the lower. Set to 90, it will be applied from left border and/or from the right one.
>
> **Smoothing and Antialiasing** The distort process may create hard and stepped borders. These two options improve this aspect.
>
> **Work on Copy** This option creates a new layer called 'Curve_bend_dummy_layer_b' which becomes the active layer, allowing you to see changes to your image in normal size without modifying the original image until you press the OK button.

Modify Curve In this grid, you have a marked horizontal line, with a node at both ends, which represents by default the upper border of image. If you click on this curve, a new node appears, that you can drag to modify the curve as you want. You can create several nodes on the curve.

> You can have only two curves on the grid, one for the so named "upper" border and the other for the so named "lower" border. You can activate one of them by checking the *Upper* or *Lower* radio button.
>
> If you use the *Curve Type Free* option, the curve you draw will replace the active curve.

Curve for Border There you can select whether the active curve must be applied to the *Superior (or left)* or the *Inferior (or right)* border, according to the rotation.

Curve Type With the *Smooth*, you get automatically a well rounded curve when you drag a node.

> The *Free* option allows you to draw a curve freely. It will replace the active curve.

Buttons

> **Copy** Copy : Copy the active curve to the other border.
>
> **Mirror** Mirror : Mirror the active curve to the other border.
>
> **Swap** Swap: Swap the 'superior' and 'inferior' curves.
>
> **Reset** Reset: Reset the active curve.
>
> **Open** Open: Load the curve from a file.
>
> **Save** Save: Save the curve to a file.

15.10.4 Emboss

15.10.4.1 Overview

Figure 15.137: Applying example for the Emboss filter

(a) *Original image*   (b) *Filter Emboss applied*

You can find this filter through Filters → Distorts → Emboss.

You can use it only with RGB images. If your image is grayscale, it will be grayed out in the menu.

It stamps and carves the active layer or selection, giving it relief with bumps and hollows. Bright areas are raised and dark ones are carved. You can vary the lighting.

15.10.4.2 Options

Figure 15.138: 'Emboss' filter options

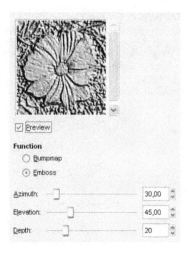

Preview All your setting changes will appear in the Preview without affecting the image until you click on OK. Don't keep *Do Preview* checked if your computer is too much slow.

Functions Bumpmap: Relief is smooth and colors are preserved.

Emboss: It turns your image to grayscale and relief is more marked, looking like metal.

Azimuth Azimuth: This is about lighting according to the points of the compass (0 - 360). If you suppose South is at the top of your image, then East (0) is on the left. Increasing value goes counter-clockwise.

Elevation Elevation: That's height from horizon (0), in principle up to zenith (90), but here up to the opposite horizon (180).

Depth Depth Seems to be the distance of the light source. Light decreases when value increases.

15.10.5 IWarp

15.10.5.1 Overview

Figure 15.139: Applying example for the IWarp filter

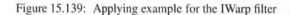

       (a) *Original image*   (b) *Filter IWarp applied*

You can find this filter through Filters → Distort → Iwarp.

This filter allows you to deform interactively some parts of the image and, thanks to its Animate option, to create the elements of a fade in/fade out animation between the original image and the deformed one, that you can play and use in a Web page.

To use it, first select a deform type then click on the Preview and drag the mouse pointer.

15.10.5.2 Settings

Settings

Figure 15.140: 'IWarp' filter options (Settings tab)

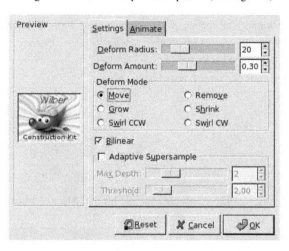

The Settings tab allows you to set parameters which will affect the preview you are working on. So, you can apply different deform modes to different parts of the preview.

Preview Here, the Preview is your work space: You click on the Preview and drag mouse pointer. The underlying part of image will be deformed according to the settings you have chosen. If your work is not convenient, press the *Reset* button.

Deform Mode

- Move: Allows you to *stretch* parts of the image.
- Remove: This remove the distortion where you drag the mouse pointer, partially or completely. This allows you to avoid pressing Reset button, working on the whole image. Be careful when working on an animation: this option will affect one frame only.
- Grow: This option inflates the pointed pattern.
- Shrink: Self explanatory.
- Swirl CCW : Create a vortex counter clockwise.
- Swirl CW : Create a vortex clockwise.

Deform Radius Defines the radius, in pixels (5-100), of the filter action circle around the pixel pointed by the mouse.

Deform Amount Sets how much out of shape your image will be put (0.0-1.0).

Bilinear This option smoothes the IWarp effect.

Adaptative Supersample This option renders a better image at the cost of increased calculation.
Max Depth: FIXME
Threshold: FIXME

Animate

Figure 15.141: 'IWarp' filter options (Animation tab)

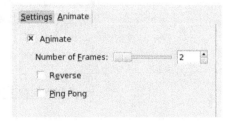

This tab allows to generate several intermediate images between the original image and the final deformation of this image. You can play this animation thanks to the plugin Playback.

Number of Frames That's the number of images in your animation (2-100). These frames are stored as layers attached to your image. Use the XCF format when saving it.

Reverse This option plays the animation backwards.

Ping-Pong When the animation ends one way, it goes backwards.

15.10.6 Mosaic

15.10.6.1 Overview

Figure 15.142: Applying example for the 'Mosaic' filter

(a) *Original image*

(b) *Filter Mosaic applied*

You can find this filter through Filters → Distorts → Mosaic.

It cuts the active layer or selection into many squares or polygons which are slightly raised and separated by joins, giving so an aspect of mosaic.

15.10.6.2 Options

Figure 15.143: Options

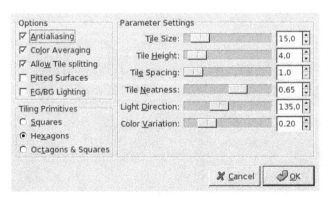

Preview All your setting changes will appear in the Preview without affecting the image until you click on OK. Note that the preview displays the whole image, even if the final result will concern a selection. Don't keep *Do Preview* checked if your computer is too much slow.

Options

>**Antialiasing** Antialiasing: This option reduces the stepped aspect that may have borders.
>
>**Color Averaging** Color Averaging When this option is unchecked, the image drawing can be recognized inside tiles. When checked, the colors inside tiles are averaged into a single color.
>
>**Allows Tile Splitting** Allows Tile Splitting: This option splits tiles in areas with many colors, and so allows a better color gradation and more details in these areas.
>
>**Pitted Surfaces** Pitted Surfaces: With this option tile surface looks pitted.
>
>**FG/BG Lighting** FG/BG Lighting: When this option is checked, tiles are lit by the foreground color of the toolbox, and shadow is colored by the background color. Joins have the background color.

Parameter setting

>**Tile Size** Tile Size: Slider and input box allow you to set the size of tile surface.
>
>**Tile Heigth** Tile Heigth: That's ledge, relief of tiles. Value is width of the lit border in pixels.
>
>**Tile Spacing** Tile Spacing: That's width of the join between tiles.
>
>**Tile Neatness** Tile Neatness: When set to 1, most of tiles have the same size. With 0 value, size is determined at random and this may lead to shape variation.
>
>**Light Direction** Light Direction: By default light comes from the upper left corner (135). You can change this direction from 0 to 360 (counter clockwise).
>
>**Color Variation** Color Variation: Each tile has only one color. So, the number of colors is reduced, compared to the original image. Here, you can increase the number of colors, a little.

Tile Primitives This options are self-undestanding:

- Squares
- Hexagons: (hexa = 6)
- Octogons and Squares: (octo = 8)

15.10.7 Page Curl

15.10.7.1 Overview

You can find this filter through Filters → Distorts → Page Curl.

It curls a corner of the current layer or selection into a kind of cornet showing the underlying layer in the cleared area. A new "Curl Layer" and a new Alpha channel are created. The part of the initial layer corresponding to this cleared area is also transparent.

15.10.7.2 Options

Figure 15.144: Options

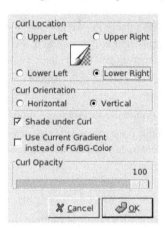

Curl Location You have there four radio buttons to select the corner you want raise. The Preview is redundant and doesn't respond to other options.

Curl Orientation *Horizontal* and *Vertical* refer to the border you want raise.

Shadow under curl This is the shadow inside the cornet.

Use current gradient instead of FG/FB-color This color refers to the outer face of the cornet.

Curl Opacity Refers to the visibility of the layer part underlying the cornet. It may be set also in the Layer Dialog.

15.10.8 Polar Coords

15.10.8.1 Overview

Figure 15.145: Example for Polar Coords filter

(a) *Original image* (b) *Polar Coords filter applied*

You can find this filter through Filters → Distorts → Polar Coords.

It gives a circular or a rectangular representation of your image with all the possible intermediates between both.

15.10.8.2 Options

Figure 15.146: 'Polar Coords' filter options

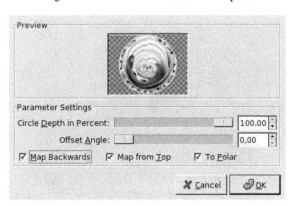

Preview The result of your settings will appear in the Preview without affecting the image until you click on OK.

Circle Depth in Percent Slider and input box allow you to set the "circularity" of the transformation, from rectangle (0%) to circle (100%).

Offset Angle This option controlles the angle the drawing will start from (0 - 359), and so turns it around the circle center.

Map Backwards When this option is checked, the drawing will start from the right instead of the left.

Map from Top If unchecked, the mapping will put the bottom row in the middle and the top row on the outside. If checked, it will be the opposite.

To Polar If unchecked, the image will be circularly mapped into a rectangle (odd effect). If checked, the image will be mapped into a circle.

15.10.8.3 Examples

Figure 15.147: With text

THE GIMP

If you have just written the text, you must Flatten the image before using the filter.

Figure 15.148: With two horizontal bars

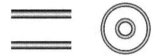

15.10.9 Ripple

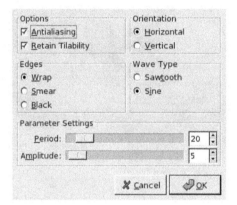

15.10.9.1 Overview

You can find this filter through Filters → Distotrts → Ripple.

It displaces the pixels of the active layer or selection to waves or ripples reminding a reflection on disturbed water.

15.10.9.2 Options

Preview The result of your settings will appear in the Preview without affecting the image until you click on OK.

Options

    Antialiasing Antialiasing: This improves the scaled look the image borders may have.

    Retain Tileability Retain Tileability: This preserves the seamless properties if your image is a tile pattern.

Orientation That's the Horizontal or Vertical direction of waves.

Edges Because ripples cause pixel displacement, some pixels may be missing on the image sides:

- With Wrap, pixels going out one side will come back on the other side, replacing so the missing pixels.
- With Smear, the adjacent pixels will spread out to replace the mixing pixels.
- With Black, the missing pixels will be replaced by black pixels.

Wave Type These options are self-explanatory

- Sawtooth
- Sine

Period The Period is related to wavelength (0-200 pixels)

Amplitude The Amplitude is related to wave height (0-200 pixels).

15.10.10 Shift

15.10.10.1 Overview

Figure 15.149: Example for the Shift filter

(a) *Original image* (b) *Filter Shift applied*

You can find this filter through Filters → Distorts → Sift.

It shifts all pixel rows, horizontally or vertically, in the current layer or selection, on a random distance and within determined limits.

15.10.10.2 Options

Figure 15.150: 'Sfift' filter options

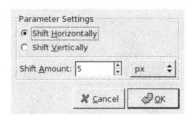

Preview The result of your settings will appear in the Preview without affecting the image until you click on OK.

These options are self-explanatory: Shift Horizontally

Shift vertically

Shift Amount

15.10.11   Newsprint

15.10.11.1   Overview

Figure 15.151: Applying example for the Newsprint filter

(a) *Original image*   (b) *Filter Newsprint applied*

You can find this filter through Filters → Distorts → Newsprint.

This filter halftones the image using a clustered-dot dither. Halftoning is the process of rendering an image with multiple levels of grey or colour (i.e. a continuous tone image) on a device with fewer tones; often a bi-level device such as a printer or typesetter.

The basic premise is to trade off resolution for greater apparent tone depth (this is known as spatial dithering).

There are many approaches to this, the simplest of which is to throw away the low-order bits of tone information; this is what the posterize filter does. Unfortunately, the results don't look too good. However, no spatial resolution is lost.

This filter uses a clustered-dot ordered dither, which reduces the resolution of the image by converting cells into spots which grow or shrink according to the intensity that cell needs to represent.

Imagine a grid super-imposed on the original image. The image is divided into cells by the grid - each cell will ultimately hold a single spot made up of multiple output pixels in order to approximate the darkness of the original image in that cell.

Obviously, a large cell size results in a heavy loss in resolution! The spots in the cells typically start off as circles, and grow to be diamond shaped. This change in shape is controlled by a spot function. By using different spot functions, the evolution in the shape of the spots as the cell goes from fully black to fully white may be controlled.

15.10.11.2 Options

Figure 15.152: 'Newsprint' filter options

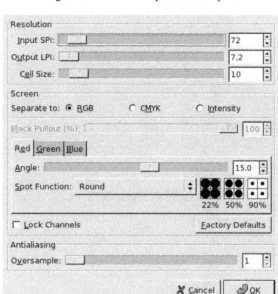

Preview All your setting changes will appear in the Preview without affecting the image until you click on OK. Note that the preview displays the whole image, even if the final result will concern a selection. Don't keep *Do Preview* checked if your computer is too much slow.

Resolution This group controls the cell size, either by setting the input and output resolutions, or directly.

> **Input SPI** Input SPI : Resolution of the original input image, in Samples Per Inch (SPI). This is automatically initialised to the input image's resolution.

> **Output LPI** Output LPI: Desired output resolution, in Lines Per Inch (LPI).

> **Cell Size** Cell Size: Resulting cell size, in pixels. Most often you will want to set this directly.

Screen

> **Separate To RGB, CMYK, Intensity** Separate To RGB, CMYK, Intensity: Select which colorspace you wish to operate in. In *RGB* mode, no colorspace conversion is performed. In *CMYK*, the image is first internally converted to CMYK, then each colour channel is separately halftoned, before finally being recombined back to an RGB image. In *Intensity* mode, the image is internally converted to grayscale, halftoned, then the result used as the alpha channel for the input image. This is good for special effects, but requires a little experimentation to achieve best results. Hint: try CMYK if you don't know which to go for initially.

> **Black Pullout (%)** Black Pullout (%) When doing RGB->CMYK conversion, how much K (black) should be used?

> **Lock Channels** Lock Channels: Make channel modifications apply to all channels.

> **Factory Defaults** Factory Defaults: Restore the default settings which should give pleasing results.

> **Angle** Angle: Cell grid angle for this channel.

> **Spot Function** Spot Function: Spot function to be used for this channel (see preview in blue cell-boxes).

Antialiasing Proper halftoning does not need antialiasing: the aim is to reduce the colour depth after all! However, since this plugin is mainly for special effects, the results are displayed on screen rather than by a black/white printer. So it is often useful to apply a little anti-aliasing to simulate ink smearing on paper. If you do want to print the resulting image then set the antialising to 1 (ie, off).

Oversample Oversample: Number of subpixels to sample to produce each output pixel. Set to 1 to disable this feature. Warning: large numbers here will lead to very long filter runtimes!

15.10.11.3 Example

Figure 15.153: Example for Newsprint

An example from plug-in author

15.10.12 Video

15.10.12.1 Overview

Figure 15.154: Applying example for the 'Video' filter

(a) *Original image*   (b) *Filter Video applied*

You can find this filter through Filters → Distorts → Sift.

Apply low dotpitch RGB simulation to the specified drawable.

15.10.12.2 Options

Figure 15.155: 'Video' filter options

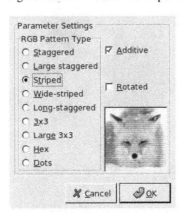

Preview This preview is unusual: Changes appear always on the same image which is not yours.

RGB Pattern Type It would be rather difficult to describe what each pattern will render. It's best to see what they render in the Preview.

Additive Set whether the function adds the result to the original image.

Rotated Rotate the result by 90.

15.10.13 Value Propagate

15.10.13.1 Overview

You can find this filter through Filters → Distorts → Value Propagate.

It works on color borders. It spreads pixels that have a Value between selected thresholds, in selected directions.

15.10.13.2 Options

Preview The result of your settings will appear in the Preview without affecting the image until you click on OK.

Propagate Mode The examples will be about the following image (zoom x8):

Figure 15.156: Original image

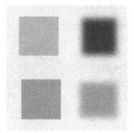

- More White: Pixels will be propagated from upper Value pixels towards lower Value pixels. So bright areas will enlarge.

Figure 15.157: More White

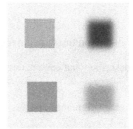

Bright pixels have been propagated to dark pixels in the four directions : top, bottom, right and left. Filter applied several times to increase effect.

- More Black: Pixels will be propagated from lower Value pixels towards upper Value pixels. So dark areas will enlarge.

Figure 15.158: More Black

Figure 15.159: To bottom only

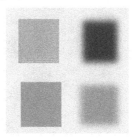

The same as above with To bottom direction only checked.

- Middle Value to Peaks: On a border between the selected thresholds, the average of both values is propagated.

Figure 15.160: Middle Value to Peaks Middelverdi til spissane

(a) *A thin border with a transitional color has been added to objets. It is not visible around objects with smoothed borders.*

(b) *Green area zoomed x800. A thin border (one pixel wide) has been added. Its value is the average between grey (90%) and green (78%) : (90 + 78) / 2 = 84.*

- Foreground to Peaks: The propagated areas will be filled with the foreground color of the toolbox.

Figure 15.161: Foreground to Peaks

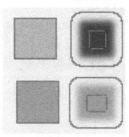

In this example, the foreground color in Toolbox is Red. A thin border, one pixel wide, red, is added around objects. With smoothed objects, this border is located at the furthest limit of smoothing. Here, another border appears inside. This is an artefact due to the small size of the object which makes the smooting area of opposite sides to overlap.

- Only Foreground: Only areas with the Toolbox Foreground color will propagate.

Figure 15.162: Only Foreground

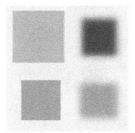

In this example, the foreground color in Toolbox is that of the green object. After applying filter several times, the green area is clearly enlarged.

- Only Background: Only areas with the Background color will propagate.
- More Opaque and More Transparent: These commands work like More White and More Black. Opaque (transparent) areas will be propagated over less opaque (transparent) areas. These commands need an image with an Alpha channel.

Figure 15.163: More opaque

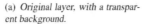

(a) *Original layer, with a transparent background.*

(b) *Filter applied several times: the green, opaque, area got increased.*

Parameters Settings

Lower / Upper Threshold Lower Threshold and Upper Threshold: These commands allow you to set the Value range that will be concerned by Propagate.

Propagating Rate Propagating Rate: That's the propagating amount. The higher it will be the more colored the propagation will be.

Propagating Direction Propagating Direction: You can select one or more directions.

15.10.14 Waves

15.10.14.1 Overview

Figure 15.164: Example for the Waves filter

(a) *Original image*   (b) *Filter Waves applied*

You can find this filter through Filters → Distorts → Waves.

With this filter you get the same effect as a stone thrown in a quiet pond, giving concentric waves.

15.10.14.2 Options

Figure 15.165: 'Waves' filter options

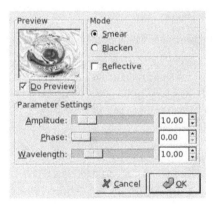

Preview All your setting changes will appear in the Preview without affecting the image until you click on OK. Don't keep *Do Preview* checked if your computer is too much slow.

Modes

- Smear: Because of the waves, areas are rendered empty on sides. The adjacent pixels will spread to fill them.
- Blacken: The empty areas will be filled by black color.

Reflective Reflective: Waves bounce on sides and interfere with the arriving ones.

Amplitude Amplitude: Varies the height of waves.

Phase Phase: This command shifts the top of waves.

Wavelength Wavelength: Varies the distance between the top of waves.

15.10.15 Whirl and Pinch

15.10.15.1 Overview

Figure 15.166: Example for the Whirl and Pinch filter

(a) *Original image*　　　　　　　　(b) *Filter applied*

You can find this filter through Filters → Distorts → Whirl and Pinch

"Whirl and Pinch" distorts your image in a concentric way.

"Whirl" distorts the image much like the little whirlpool that appears when you empty your bath.

"Pinch" can be compared to applying your image to a soft rubber surface and squeezing the edges or corners. If the Pinch amount slider is set to a negative value, it will look as if someone tried to push a round object up toward you from behind the rubber skin. If the Pinch amount is set to a positive value, it looks like someone is dragging or sucking on the surface from behind, and away from you.

Tip
The 'pinch' effect can sometimes be used to compensate for image distortion produced by telephoto or fisheye lenses ('barrel distortion').

Figure 15.167: Illustration

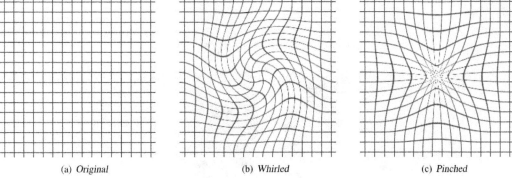

(a) *Original*   (b) *Whirled*   (c) *Pinched*

15.10.15.2 Parameter Settings

Figure 15.168: 'Whirl and Pinch' filter options

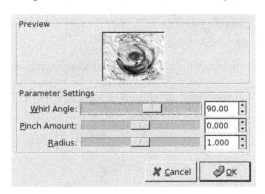

Preview Changes to parameters are immediately displayed into the *Preview*. The whirlpool is focused around the center of the current layer or selection.

Whirl Angle Whirl Angle: Clockwise or counter clockwise (-360 to +360). Controls how many degrees the affected part of the image is rotated.

Pinch Amount Pinch Amount: Whirlpool depth(-1 to +1). Determines how strongly the affected part of the image is pinched.

Radius Radius: Whirlpool width (0.0-2.0). Determines how much of the image is affected by the distortion. If you set *Radius* to 2, the entire image will be affected. If you set *Radius* to 1, half the image will be affected. If *Radius* is set to 0, nothing will be affected (think of it as the radius in a circle with 0 in the center and 1 halfway out).

15.10.16 Wind

15.10.16.1 Overview

Figure 15.169: 'Wind' filter example

(a) *Original image*   (b) *Filter Wind applied*

You can find this filter through Filters → Distorts → Wind.

The Wind filter can be used to create motion blur, but it can also be used as a general distort filter. What is characteristic about this filter is that it will render thin black or white lines. Wind will detect the edges in the image, and stretch out thin white or black lines from that edge. This is why you can create the illusion of motion, because the edges are what will be blurred in a photograph of a moving object.

15.10.16.2 Options

Figure 15.170: 'Wind' filter options

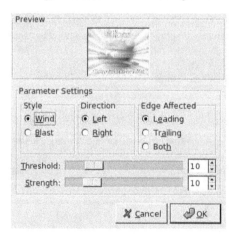

The interface is quite simple. You can set the *Strength* of the wind and a *Threshold* value. *Threshold* will restrict the effect to fewer areas of the image. *Strength* controls the amount of wind, so a high value will render a storm. You can also increase the effect by setting the *Style* to Blast, which will produce thicker lines than Wind.

You can only set the wind in two directions, either Left or Right. However, you can control which edge the wind will come from using the values Leading, Trailing or Both. Because Trailing will produce a black wind, it creates a less convincing motion blur than Leading, which will produce white wind.

The following illustrations are based on this image:

Preview All your setting changes will appear in the Preview without affecting the image until you click on OK. It reproduces a part of the image only, centred on the first modified area it encounters.

Style

- Wind: This option is the most suggestive of a moving effect. Trails are thin.
- Blast: This option tries to suggest a blast due to an explosion. Trails are thick.

Direction You can select the direction, *Left* or *Right*, from which the wind comes.

Edge Affected

- Leading: Trails will start from the front border, falling on the object itself. It suggests that a violent wind is pulling color out.

- Trailing: Trails start from the back border of the object.

- Both: Combines both effects.

Threshold Threshold: The threshold to detect borders. The higher it is, the fewer borders will be detected.

Strength Strength: Higher values increase the strength of the effect.

15.11 Artistic filters

15.11.1 Introduction

Artistic filters create artistic effects like cubism, oil painting, canvas...

15.11.2 Apply Canvas

15.11.2.1 Overview

Figure 15.171: The same image, before and after applying 'Apply Canvas' filter

(a) *Original image*　　　　　(b) *Filter Apply Canvas applied*

You can find this filter in Filters → Artistic → Apply Canvas....

This filter applies a canvas-like effect to the current layer or selection. It textures the image as if it were an artist's canvas.

15.11.2.2 Options

Figure 15.172: 'Apply Canvas' options

Preview Your changes are displayed in this preview before being applied to your image.

Direction Direction sets the starting direction of the canvas render. You can also consider that this option gives you the position of the light source which lightens the canvas.

Depth The Depth slider controls the apparent depth of the rendered canvas effect from 1 (very flat) to 50 (very deep).

15.11.3 Cartoon

15.11.3.1 Overview

Figure 15.173: The same image, before and after applying 'Cartoon' filter

(a) *Original image*

(b) *Filter Cartoon applied*

You can find this filter in Filters → Artistic → Cartoon

The Cartoon filter modifies the active layer or selection so that it looks like a cartoon drawing. Its result is similar to a black felt pen drawing subsequently shaded with color. This is achieved by darkening areas that are already distinctly darker than their neighborhood.

15.11.3.2 Options

Figure 15.174: 'Cartoon' filter options

Mask radius This parameter controls the size of areas the filter works with. Large values result in very thick black areas and much less detail in the resulting image. Small values result in more subtle pen strokes and more details preserved.

Percent black This parameter controls the amount of black color added to the image. Small values make the blend from color regions to blackened areas smoother and dark lines themselves thinner and less noticeable. Larger values make the lines thicker, darker and sharper. The maximum value makes the lines aliased. The best, most natural results are usually achieved with an intermediate value.

15.11.4 Cubism

15.11.4.1 Overview

Figure 15.175: The same image, before and after applying Cubism filter

(a) *Original image*   (b) *Filter Cubism applied*

You can find this filter in Filters → Artitic → Cubism

The Cubism plug-in modifies the image so that it appears to be constructed of small squares of semitransparent tissue paper.

Tip
If setting possibilities of this filter are not enough for you, see GIMPressionist filter which offers more options.

15.11.4.2 Options

Figure 15.176: 'Cubism' filter options

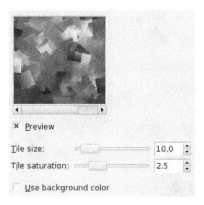

Tile Size This variable determines the size, in pixels, of the squares to be used. This is, in effect, the size of the little squares of tissue paper used in generating the new image. The slider can be used, the exact pixel size can be entered into the text box, or the arrow buttons can be used.

Tile Saturation This variable specifies how intense the color of the squares should be. This affects the opacity of the squares. A high value will render the squares very intensely and does not allow lower squares to show through. A lower value allows the lower squares to be more visible through the higher ones and causes more blending in the colors. If this is set to 0 and Use Background Color is not checked, the entire layer will be rendered black. If it is checked and the value here is zero, the background color will fill the entire layer.

Use Backgroundcolor This filter creates its tiles from all the colors of the image and paint them with a color scale which depends on the Tile Saturation. With a low Tile Saturation, this color scale lets the background color appear: default is black as you can see by setting Tile Saturation to 0. When this option is checked, the background color of the Toolbox is used. If your image has an Alpha channel, this color scale will also be transparent.

Figure 15.177: Example illustrating the action of the 'Use BackGround color' option

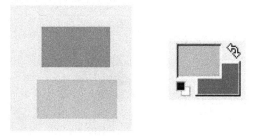

The original image and the color area of Toolbox. BG color is blue.

Figure 15.178: The option is not checked

 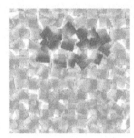

The option is not checked. On the left is no Alpha: background is black. On the right is Alpha: background is transparent black.

Figure 15.179: The option is checked

 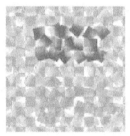

The option is checked. On the left, no Alpha: background is blue. On the right, with an Alpha channel, background is transparent blue.

 Tip
If you are using this to generate background images for web pages and the like, work with a small range of colors painted randomly on a small square. Then apply the Cubism filter with the desired settings. As a last step, try Filters/Map/Make Seamless to adjust the image so it will tile seamlessly in your background.

15.11.5 GIMPressionist

15.11.5.1 Overview

Figure 15.180: The same image, before and after applying GIMPressionist

(a) *Original image*   (b) *Filter GIMPressionist applied*

You can find this filter via the image menu under Filters → Artistic → GIMPressionist

It's the king of Artistic filters. It can do what Cubism and Apply Canvas do and much more. It gives your image the look of a painting. All is going as if your image was painted again on a paper and with a brush you'd have choosen. It works on the active layer or selection.

15.11.5.2 Parameter Settings

Preview All your setting changes will appear in the Preview without affecting the image until you click on OK. The Update button refreshes the preview window (it is not automatic, Gimpressionist has so much work to do!), and the Reset button reverts to the original image.

Presets

Figure 15.181: 'Presets' tab options

GIMPressionist has a lot of parameters. When combined, they give an astronomical number of possibilities. So, it is important, when an interesting preset has been found, to save it and also to send it to the plugin author if exceptional. Per contra, the intricacy of all these parameters makes difficult understanding and foreseeing how each one works.

- Save Current: Save current parameters. You can give a name in the input box on the left and a short description in the dialog that appear.
- Apply: Load the parameters of the selected preset in the list.
- Delete: Delete the selected preset. You can delete only the presets you have created.
- Refresh: Update the preset list.

Paper tab

Figure 15.182: 'Paper' tab options

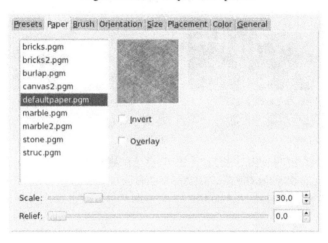

This tab concerns the texture of the canvas your image will be painted on. You have a list of textures and a Preview for the selected texture. A description is displayed on the right for every texture when selected.

Invert Inverts the paper texture: what was a hollow turns to a bump and vice-versa.

Overlay Apply the paper as it, without embossing it. It looks like if a transparent paper has been overlayed on the image.

Scale Specifies the scale of the texture (in % of the original file): controls the graininess of the texture.

Relief Specifies the amount of embossing to apply (3-150).

Brush tab

Figure 15.183: 'Brush' tab options

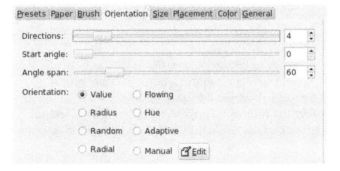

"Brush" is a general term for any material used to paint. A list of brushes is available with a Preview for the selected one.

Gamma Changes the gamma (luminosity) of the selected brush. The gamma correction brightens or darkens midtones.

Select You can also use a brush pattern you have created by selecting its image (arrow button on the Select line). This image must be on your screen before you launch the filter to be taken in account. Of course, don't use big images.

> If your image has several layers, they also will be displayed in the Select list and can be used as a brush. When selected, the layer appears in the brush preview and the normal brush is deselected.

> The Save as button allows you to save the selected brush.

Aspect ratio Specifies the brush proportions, height (0 -1) and width (0 +1).

Relief Specifies the amount of paint used for each stroke. This may evoke painting with a palette knife.

Orientation tab

Figure 15.184: 'Orientation' tab options

This tab allows to set the orientation of the brush strokes. A painter is not obliged to go over with the same paintbrush angle. To perform some effects, he can vary their orientation.

Directions With this option, you can set how many times the brush will pass through a same place, with each time a different direction, resulting in a more and more thick paint.

Start Angle Specifies the general direction of the strokes, the angle that the angle range will start from. Directions are often choosen to give some movement to the image.

Angle Span Specifies the angle, the sector, of the stroke "fan".

Orientation Specifies the direction of the brush strokes.

- Value : Let the Value (luminosity) of the region determine the direction of the stroke.
- Radius : The distance from the center of the image determines the direction of the stroke.
- Random : Select a random direction for each stroke.
- Radial : Let the direction from the center determine the direction of the stroke.
- Flowing : Not a direction question here: the strokes follow a "flowing" pattern.
- Hue : Let the hue of the region determine the direction of the stroke.
- Adaptive : The brush direction that matches the original image the closest is selected.
- Manual : The Edit button opens the Edit orientation Map dialog that allows you to set the directions manually.

Size tab

Figure 15.185: 'Size' tab options

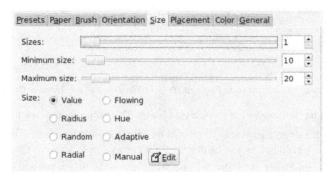

This tab allows you to set the number of brush sizes that will be used to paint, the limits of variation of these sizes and the criterion used to determine them.

Three Sliders You can specify how many brush sizes are to be used and their sizes.

- Sizes: The number of brush sizes to use.
- Minimum Size and Maximum Size : The brush sizes are between these two values. Greater the size, greater the length and width of strokes.

Sizes You have there options to specify how the size of strokes will be determined.

- Value: Let the Value (luminosity) of the region determine the size of the stroke.
- Radius : The distance from the center of the image determines the size of the stroke.
- Random : Select a random size for each stroke.
- Radial : Let the direction from the center determine the size of the stroke.
- Flowing : Not a length question here: the strokes follow a "flowing" pattern.
- Hue : Let the hue of the region determine the size of the stroke.
- Adaptive : The brush size that matches the original image the closest is selected.
- Manual : The Edit button opens the Size Map Editor. That allows you to specify the size of strokes by yourself.

Placement tab

Figure 15.186: 'Placement' tab options

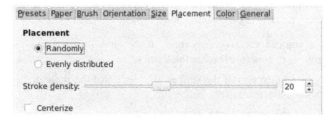

In this tab you can set how strokes will be distributed.

Placement In the preview of the Orientation Map Editor, all small arrows look like a flow around objects. Inside this flow, strokes may be placed in two different ways:

- Randomly: Places strokes ramdomly. This produces a more realistic paint.
- Evenly: Strokes are evenly distributed across the image.

Stroke Density The greater the density the closer the strokes. With a low density, the paper or background may be visible in unstroke areas.

Centerize Focus brush strokes around center.

Color tab

Figure 15.187: 'Color' tab options

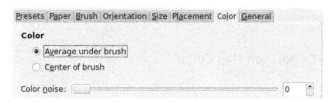

In this tab, you can set what the stroke color will be.

Color You can set the stroke color in two ways:

- Average under brush: Stroke color is computed from the the average of all pixels under the brush.
- Center of brush: Samples the color from the pixel in the center of the brush.

Color Noise This slider, and its input box, allow you to introduce noise in the stroke color, that will look less homogenous.

General tab

Figure 15.188: 'General' tab options

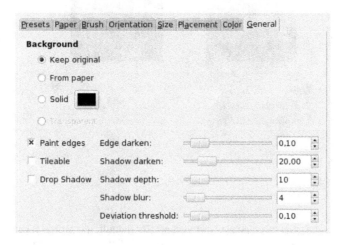

In this tab you can set what will be the background and the relief of brush strokes.

Background

- Keep Original: The original image will be used as a background.
- From Paper: Copy the texture of the selected paper as a background.

- Solid: By clicking on the color dwell you can select a solid colored background.
- Transparent: Use a transparent background. Only the painted strokes will be visible. This option is available only if your image has an Alpha channel.

Paint Edges If it is disabled, a thin border will not be painted around the outside border of the image.

Tileable If checked, the resulting image will be seamlessly tileable. The right side will match the left side and the top will match the bottom. This is interesting if your image will be repeatedly used in a Web background.

Drop Shadow Add a shadow effect to each brush stroke.

Edge Darken How much to darken the edges of each brush stroke. This increases paint relief or thickness.

Shadow Darken How much to darken the brush shadow.

How much to darken the brush shadow.

Shadow Depth How far apart from the object the drop shadow should be.

Shadow Blur How much to blur the drop shadow.

Deviation Threshold A bail-out value for adaptative selections of brush size.

15.11.6 GIMPressionist - Orientation Map Editor

15.11.6.1 Overview

The Orientation-map editor is an annexe of the GIMPressionist filter. You can get to it by clicking on the Edit button in the 'Orientation' tab. With this editor, you can set the direction that brush strokes given by filter will have.

15.11.6.2 Parameter Settings

Figure 15.189: Options of the 'Orientation-map Editor' dialog

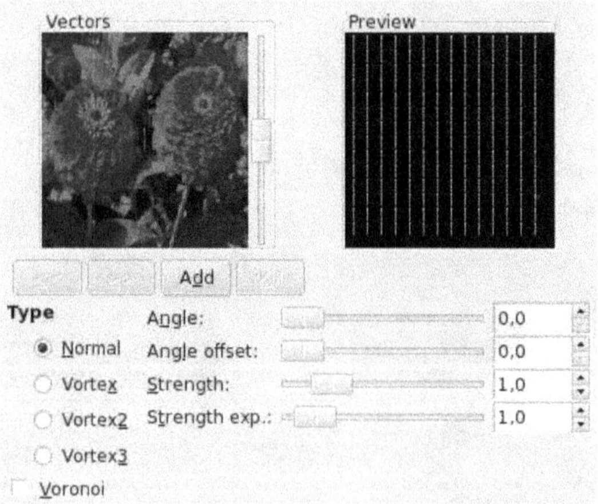

Vectors In the left windows (Vectors) you can manage your vectors. By default, a vector is at center. Vectors are red when they are active, and grey when they are not with a white point at tip. By clicking on the Add button, you add a vector at center of the window, whereas clicking with the mouse *Middle Button* puts it where you click.

Clicking with the mouse *Left Button* displaces the selected vector to the clicked point.

When clicking with the mouse *Right Button*, the selected vector points to where you have clicked.

Clicking on « and » buttons displaces focus from a vector to another.

The Delete button allows you to delete the selected vector.

Tip
With the scroll bar on the right of the Vectors panel, you can set the image brightness. This can be very useful if the image is very dark/bright and you can't see vectors well.

Preview This Preview gives you an idea of the action of the various vectors. The slider on the right border lets you change the luminosity of this preview.

Type You have there some types to arrange the brush strokes within the selected vector domain. Describing them is difficult, but you can see the result in the Preview.

Voronoi A Voronoi's diagram consists in partitioning a plane with n master points into n polygons where each polygon has only one of these n master points and where any given other point of the polygon is closer to the master point than to any other. So each polygon limit is midway between two master point. Here is an example of a Voronoi's diagram:

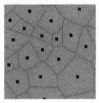

Here, when this option is checked, only the vector closest to a given point of the image influences this point.

Angle Angle: Direction of the selected vector. This slider has the same action as right-clicking (see above).

Angle Offset This slider allows you to change the angle of ALL vectors.

Strength This slider acts on the influence domain of the selected vector. This influence lowers with distance. Strength is showed with the vector length.

Strength Exp. This slider acts on the length of ALL vectors, and so changes the strength of all brush strokes.

15.11.7 GIMPressionist - Size Map Editor

15.11.7.1 Overview

The Size-map editor is an annexe of the GIMPressionist filter. You can get to it by clicking on the Edit button in the "Size" tab. With this editor, you can set the size that brush strokes given by filter will have.

15.11.7.2 Parameter Settings

Figure 15.190: 'Size-map editor options'

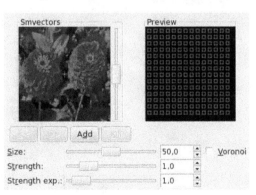

Smvectors In this window you can place your vectors. By clicking on the Add button, you add a vector at the center of the window, whereas clicking with the mouse *Middle Button* puts it where you click. Vectors are red when selected, and gray when they are not, with a white point at tip.

Clicking with the mouse *Left Button* displaces the selected vector to the clicked point.

Clicking on the mouse *Right Button*, has no evident action.

Clicking on « et » buttons displaces focus from a vector to another.

The Kill button allows you to delete the selected vector.

Tip
With the scroll bar on the right of the Vectors panel, you can set the image brightness. This can be very useful if the image is very dark/bright and you can't see vectors well.

Preview This Preview gives you an idea of the action of the different vectors. The size of squares represent the size of the brushes and their strength.

Size Change the size of the brush strokes in the selected vector domain.

Strength This slider acts on the influence domain of the selected vector. This influence lowers with distance.

Strength Exp. Change the exponent of the stroke.

Voronoi See Orientation Map Editor for an explanation.

15.11.8 Oilify

15.11.8.1 Overview

Figure 15.191: The same image, before and after applying 'Oilify' filter

(a) *Original image*   (b) *Filter Oilify applied*

This filter is found in Filters → Artistic → Oilify...

This filter makes the image look like an oil painting. The `Mask Size` controls the outcome: a high value gives the image less detail, as if you had used a larger brush.

Tip
The GIMPressionist filter can produce similar effects, but allows a much wider variety of options.

15.11.8.2 Options

Figure 15.192: 'Oilify' filter options

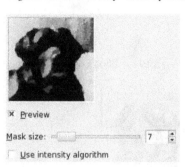

Mask Size Mask Size selects the size of the brush mask used to paint the oily render. Larger values here produce an oilier render.

Use Intensity Algorithm Use Intensity Algorithm changes the mode of operation to help preserve detail and coloring.

15.11.9 Photocopy

15.11.9.1 Overview

Figure 15.193: The same image, before and after applying Photocopy filter

(a) *Original image*   (b) *Filter Photocopy applied*

The Photocopy filter modifies the active layer or selection so that it looks like a black and white photocopy, as if toner transfered was based on the relative darkness of a particular region. This is achieved by darkening areas of the image which are measured to be darker than a neighborhood average, and setting other pixels to white.

 Tip
You may use this filter to sharpen your image. Create a copy of the active layer and use the filter on the copy. Set the Layer Mode to Multiply and adjust the opacity slider to get the best result.

15.11.9.2   Starting filter

You can find this filter from the image menu through Filters → Artistic → Photocopy.

15.11.9.3   Options

Figure 15.194: 'Photocopy' filter options

Mask radius This parameter controls the size of the pixel neighbourhood over which the average intensity is computed and then compared to each pixel in the neighborhood to decide whether or not to darken it. Large values result in very thick black areas bordering the regions of white and much less detail for black areas. Small values result in less toner overall and more details everywhere.

Sharpness With this option, you can set photocopy sharpness, from 0.0 to 1.0.

Percent black This parameter controls the amount of black color added to the image. Small values make the blend from color regions to blackened areas smoother and dark lines themselves thinner and less noticeable. Larger values make the lines thicker, darker and sharper. The maximum value makes the lines aliased. The best, most natural results are usually achieved with an intermediate value. Values vary from 0.0 to 1.0.

Percent White This parameter increases white pixels percentage.

15.11.10 Soft Glow

15.11.10.1 Overview

Figure 15.195: The same image, before and after applying SoftGlow filter

(a) *Original image*　　　　(b) *Filter SoftGlow applied*

This filter lights the image with a soft glow. Soft Glow produces this effect by making brigth areas of the image brighter.

15.11.10.2 Starting filter

You can find this filer in the Image menu: Filters → Atistic → Soft Glow.

15.11.10.3 Options

Figure 15.196: 'Soft Glow' filter options

Glow radius The glow radius parameter controls the sharpness of the effect, giving a "vaseline-on-the-lens" effect.

Brightness The brightness parameter controls the degree of intensification applied to image highlights.

Sharpness The sharpness parameter controls how defined or alternatively diffuse the glow effect should be.

15.12　Map Filters

15.12.1　Introduction

Map filters use an object named *map* to modify an image: you map the image to the object. So, you can create 3D effects by mapping your image to another previously embossed image ("Bumpmap" Filter) or to a sphere ("Map Object" filter). You can also map a part of the image elsewhere into the same image ("Illusion" and "Make Seamless" filters), bend a text along a curve ("Displace" filter)...

15.12.2　Bump Map

15.12.2.1　Overview

Figure 15.197:　From left to right: original image, bump map, bumpmapped image

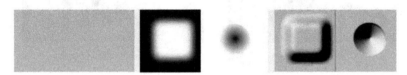

You can find this filter through Filters → Map → Bump Map.

This filter creates a 3D effect by embossing an image (the card) and then mapping it to another image. Bump height depends on pixel luminosity and you can set light direction. See Emboss for more informations about embossing. You can bump map any type of image, unlike the Emboss filter.

15.12.2.2　Options

Figure 15.198:　'Bump Map' filter options

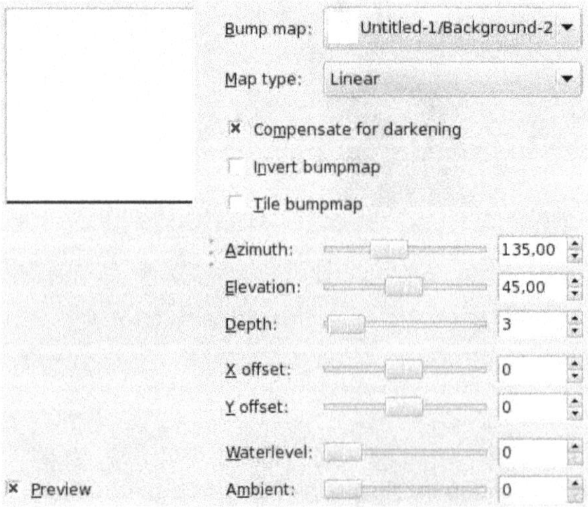

Preview　Parameter setting results are interactively displayed in preview. Scroll bars allow you to move around the image.

Bump Map This drop-down list allows you to select the image that will be used as a map for bumpmapping. This list contains images that are present on your screen when you launch the filter. Images opened after starting filter are not present in this list.

Map Type This option allows you to define the method that will be used when creating the map image:

- Linear: bump height is a direct function of luminosity.
- Sinusoidal: bump height is a sinusoidal function of luminosity.
- Spheric: bump height is a spheric function of luminosity.

Compensate for darkening Bumpmapping tends to darken image. You can compensate this darkening by checking this option.

Invert Bumpmap Bright pixels default to bumps and dark pixels to hollows. You can invert this effect by checking this option.

Tile bumpmap If you check this option, there will be no relief break if you use your image as a pattern for a web page: patterns will be placed side by side without any visible joins.

Azimut Azimut: This is about lighting according to the points of the compass (0 - 360). East (0) is on the left. Increasing value goes counter-clockwise.

Elevation Elevation: That's height from horizon (0), up to zenith (90).

Depth With this slider, you can vary bump height and hollow depth. The higher the value, the higher the difference between both. Values vary from 0 to 100.

X/Y offsets With this slider, you can adjust the map image position compared with the image, horizontally (X) and/or vertically (Y).

Sea Level If your image has transparent areas, they will be treated like dark areas and will appear as hollows after bumpmapping. With this slider, you can reduce hollows as if sea level was raising. This hollows will disappear when sea level value reaches 255. If the Invert Bumpmap option is checked, transparent areas will be treated as bright areas, and then Sea Level slider will plane bumps down.

Ambient This slider controls the intensity of ambient light. With high values, shadows will fade and relief lessen.

15.12.3 Displace

15.12.3.1 Overview

Figure 15.199: Displacement examples

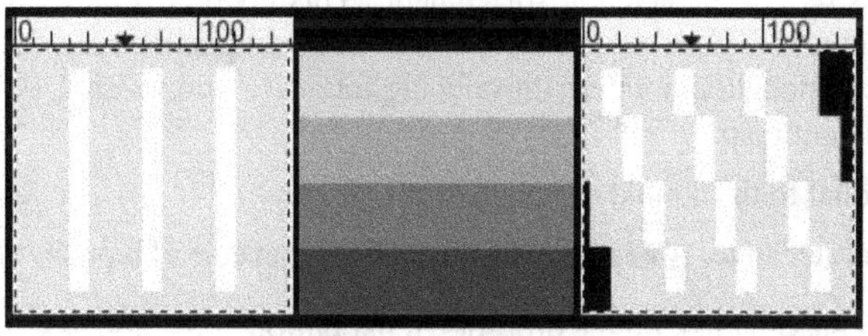

X displacement coefficient is 30 (with a negative coefficient displacement would be inverse). Vacated pixels are black. The displacement map has four grey stripes with values of 210, 160, 110, and 60, respectively. The image areas corresponding to light gray (≥ 128) were displaced 19 and 8 pixels to the left. The image areas corresponding to dark gray (≤ 127) were displaced 4 and 15 pixels to the right.

You can find this filter through Filters → Map → Displace

This filter uses a 'displace-map' to displace corresponding pixels of the image. This filter displaces the content of the specified drawable (active layer or selection) by the amounts specified in X and Y Displacement multiplied by the intensity of the corresponding pixel in the 'displace map' drawables. **Both X and Y displace maps should be gray-scale images and have the same size as the drawable** . This filter allows interesting distortion effects.

15.12.3.2 Options

Figure 15.200: Options

Preview Uncheck this option if your processor is slow.

X/Y Displacements When you select one or both options, active layer pixels corresponding to pixels in the displacement map will be displaced horizontally (X) or/and vertically (Y). Both direction and amount of displacement depend on the intensity of the corresponding pixels in the displacement map.

The map, which must be a grayscale image, has 256 gray levels (0-255). The (theoretical) average value is 127.5. The filter displaces image pixels corresponding to pixels with values less than 127.5 (0 to 127) in the map, to the right for X and downwards for Y. It moves pixels corresponding to pixels with values from 128 to 255 to the left for X and upwards for Y.

Input boxes 'X/Y Displacement' should be called *X/Y Displacement Coefficient*. What you enter in input boxes, directly or by using arrow-head buttons, is not the actual displacement. This coefficient is used in a **displacement = (intensity x coefficient)** formula which gives the pixel actual displacement according to the scaled intensity[1] of the corresponding pixel in map, modulated by the coefficient you enter. Introducing intensity into formula is important: this allows progressive displacement by using a gradient map.

This value varies in limits equal to the double of image dimensions.

This value may be positive or negative. A negative displacement is reverse of a positive one.

Selecting displacement maps When you click on the drop-down list button, a list appears where you can select a displacement map. To be present in this list, an image must respect two conditions. First, this image must be present on your screen when you call filter. Then, this image must have the same dimensions as the original image. Most often, it will be a duplicate original image, which is transformed to grey scale and modified appropriately, with a gradient. It may be possible to use RGB images, but color luminosity is used making result prevision difficult. Map may be different in horizontal and vertical directions.

---

[1] Scaled intensity = (intensity - 127.5) / 127.5; see section 'displacement calculation'.

On Edges These options allows you to set displacement behaviour on active layer or selection edges:

- Wrap: With this option, what disappears on one edge reappears on the opposite edge.
- Smear: With this option, pixels vacated by displacement are replaced with pixels stretched from the adjacent part of the image.
- Black: With this option, pixels vacated by deplacement are replaced with black.

15.12.3.3 Using gradient to bend a text

Follow following steps:

1. Start with opening your image.

2. Duplicate this image. Activate this duplicate and make it gray-scaled (<IMAGE>/Image/Mode/GrayScale). Fill it with the wanted gradient. This image will be your *Displacement map*, with the dimensions of original image.

3. Activate original image. Create a *Text Layer* with your text. Set layer to image size: right-click on the layer in layer dialog and, in the pop-menu, click on 'Layer to image size'. Note that letters in text layer lie on a transparent background; now this filter doesn't displace transparent pixels. Only letters will be displaced.

4. Activate text layer. Open Displace filter window. Set parameters particularly displacement coefficient according to the result in Preview. OK.

This method also applies to standard layers:

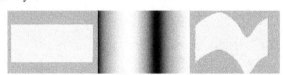

Tip
To get the wanted gradient, first draw a black to white gradient. Then use the Curves tool to modify the gradient curve.

15.12.3.4 Displacement Calculation

The following section will show you how to calculate the amount of displacement, if you are interested in these details. If you don't want to know it, you can safely omit this section.

The overview example showed the X displacement using a coefficient of 30.0: 19, 8, 4, or 15 pixels, depending on the grey level of the displacement map's color.

Why just these amounts? That's easy:

$30.0 * (I - 127.5) / 127.5 = D$ If you check these equations, you will notice that the values they give are not exactly the results we retained in the example (using non-integers, that's not surprising). So, were the results rounded to the nearest integer and then the pixels were displaced by a whole-numbered amount? No. Every pixel is displaced exactly by the calculated amount; a 'displacement by a fractional amount' is realized by interpolation. A closer look at the example image will show it:

Figure 15.201: A closer look at the displacement example

A small area zoomed in by 800 percent.

The displacement causes small (one pixel wide) areas of intermediate colors at the edges of plain color areas. E.g., the black area (zoomed in image) is caused by a displacement of -4.12, so the intermediate color is 12% black and 88% gold.

So if you select a displacement coefficient of 30.01 instead of 30.00, you will indeed get a different image, although you won't see the difference, of course.

15.12.4 Fractal Trace

15.12.4.1 Overview

This filter transforms the image with the Mandelbrot fractal: it maps the image to the fractal.

You get to this filter via the Image menu through Filters → Map → Fractal trace

15.12.4.2 Options

Figure 15.202: 'Fractal trace' filter options

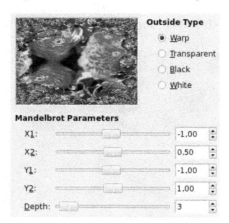

MANDELBROT PARAMETERS

X1, X2, Y1, Y2, Depth These parameters are similar to X/YMIN, X/YMAX and ITER parameters of the Fractal Explorer filter. They allow you to vary fractal spreading and detail depth.

Outside type Mapping image to fractal may reveal empty areas. You can select to fill them with Black, White, Transparency or make what disappears on one side reappear on the opposite side with Wrap option.

15.12.5 Illusion

15.12.5.1 Overview

You can find this filter through Filters → Map → Illusion.

With this filter, your image (active layer or selection) looks like a kaleidoscope. This filter duplicates your image in many copies, more or less dimmed and split, and puts them around the center of the image.

15.12.5.2 Options

Figure 15.203: 'Illusion' filter options

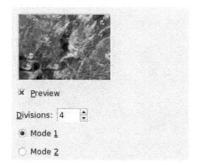

Divisions That's the number of copies you want to apply to image. This value varies from -32 to 64. Negative values invert kaleidoscope rotation.

Modes You have two arrangement modes for copies in image:

Figure 15.204: From left to right: original image, mode 1, mode 2, with Divisions=4

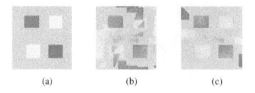

(a)   (b)   (c)

15.12.6 Make Seamless

15.12.6.1 Overview

Figure 15.205: An example of Make Seamless.

(a) *Original*   (b) *Make Seamless applied*

You can find this filter through Filters → Map → Make Seamless

This filter modifies the image for tiling by creating seamless edges. Such an image can be used as a pattern for a web-page. This filter has no option, and result may need correction.

15.12.7 Map Object

15.12.7.1 Overview

Figure 15.206: The 'Map Object' filter applied to a photograph

(a) *Original* (b) *Map Object appliedAprès application du filtre*

This filter maps a picture to an object (plane, sphere, box or cylinder).

You can find this filter through Filters → Map → Map Object.

15.12.7.2 Options

15.12.7.2.1 Preview domain

This preview has several possibilities:

Preview! Preview!: Preview is automatic for some options but you will have to press this button to update Preview after modifying many other parameters.

When mouse pointer is on Preview, it takes the form of a small hand to grab the *blue point* which marks light source origin and to displace it. This blue point may not be visible if light source has negative X and Y settings in the Light tab.

Zoom buttons Zoom buttons allow you to enlarge or to reduce image in Preview. Their action is limited, but may be useful in case of a large image.

Show Preview Wireframe Show Preview Wireframe: Puts a grid over the preview to make displacements and rotations more easy. Works well on a plan.

15.12.7.2.2 General Options tab

Figure 15.207: 'Map Object' general options tab

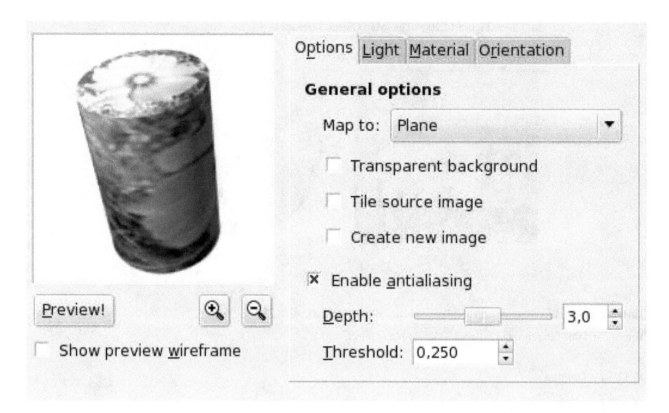

Map to This drop-down list allows you to select the object the image will be mapped on. It can be a *Plane*, a *Sphere*, a *Box* or a *Cylinder*.

Transparent background This option makes image transparent around the object. If not set, the background is filled with the current background color.

Tile source image When moving Plane object and displacing it with Orientation tab options, a part of the image turns empty. By checking the Tile source image, source image copies will fill this empty space in. This option seems not to work with the other objects.

 Note
This option works with 'Plane' only.

Create new image When this option is checked, a new image is created with the result of filter application, so preserving the original image.

Enable antialiasing Check this option to conceal this unpleasant aliasing effect on borders. When checked, this option lets appear two settings:

- Depth: Defines antialiasing quality, to the detriment of execution speed.
- Threshold: Defines antialiasing limits. Antialiasing stops when value difference between pixels becomes lower than this set value.

15.12.7.2.3 Light tab

Figure 15.208: 'Light' tab options

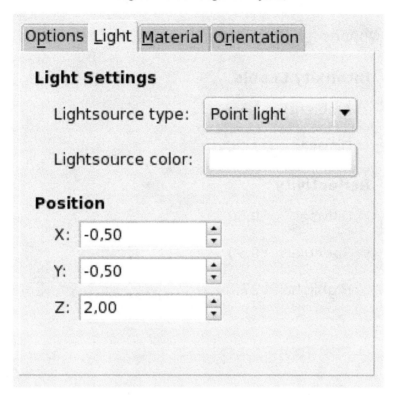

Light Settings

- Lightsource type: In this dropdown list, you can select among *Point light*, *Directionnal light* and *No light*.
- Lightsource color: Press this button to open the Color Selector dialog.

Position If 'Point light' is selected, you can control there light source *Position* (the blue point), according to X, Y and Z coordinates.

If 'Directional light' is selected, these X, Y and Z parameters controle the 'Direction vector' (effect is not evident).

15.12.7.2.4 Material tab

Figure 15.209: 'Material' tab options

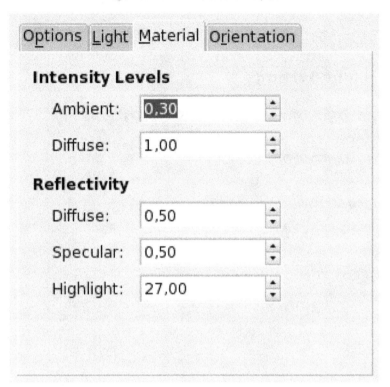

Intensity Levels

- Ambient: Amount of color to show where no light falls directly.
- Diffuse: Intensity of original color when lit by a light source.

Reflectivity

- Diffusion: Higher values make object reflect more light (looks brighter).
- Specular: Controls how intense the highlights will be.
- Highlight: Higher values make the highlights more focused.

15.12.7.2.5   Orientation tab

Figure 15.210: 'Orientation' tab options

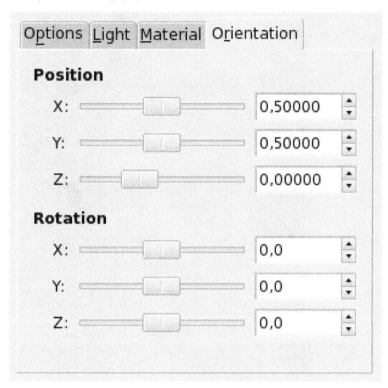

Position   These three sliders and their input boxes allows you to vary object position in image, according to the X, Y, Z coordinates of the object upper left corner.

Rotation   These three sliders make the object rotate around X, Y, Z axes respectively.

15.12.7.2.6   Box tab

This tab appears only when you select the Box object.

Figure 15.211: 'Box' tab options

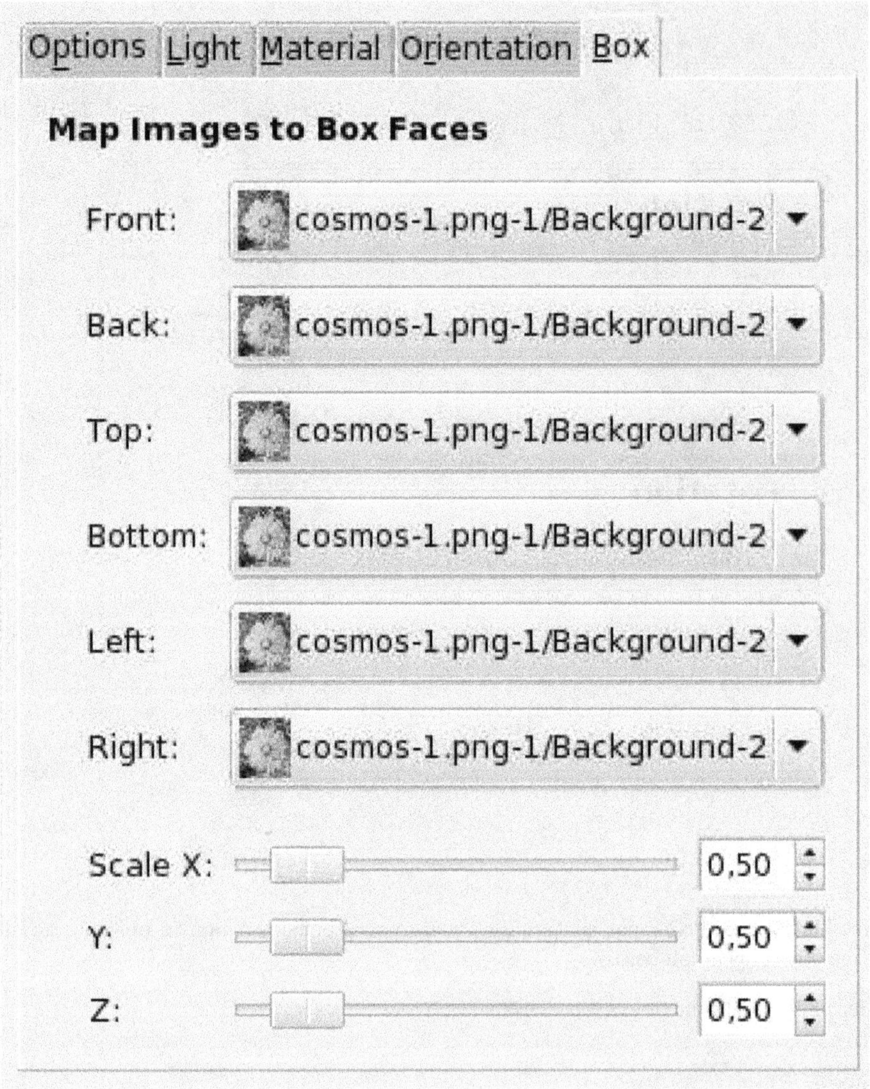

Match Images to Box Faces This function name is self explanatory: you can select an image for every face of the box. These images must be present on your screen when you call the Map Object filter.

Scale These X, Y, Z three sliders allow you to change the size of every X, Y, Z dimension of the box.

15.12.7.2.7 Cylinder tab

This tab appears only when you select the Cylinder object.

Figure 15.212: 'Cylinder' tab options

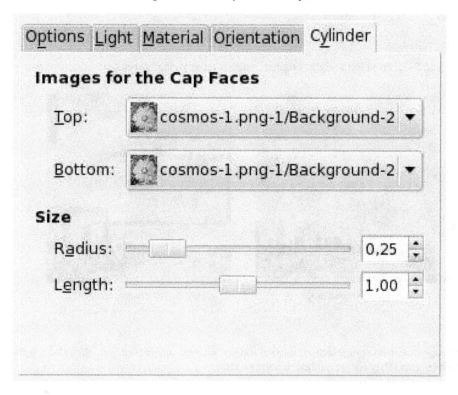

Images for the Cap Faces The name of this option is self-explanatory. Images must be present on your screen when you call the Map Object filter.

Size

- Radius : This slider and its input boxes let you control the Cylinder diameter. Unfortunately, this setting works on the image mapped onto the cylinder and resamples this image to adapt it to the new cylinder size. It would be better to have the possibility of setting size cylinder before mapping so that we could map a whole image.

- Length: Controls cylinder length...

15.12.8 Paper Tile

15.12.8.1 Overview

Figure 15.213: From left to right: original image, after applying 'Paper Tile' filter (division = 3)

(a) *Original image*

(b) *Filter Papertile applied*

This filter cuts the image (active layer or selection) into several pieces, with square form, and then slides them so that they, more or less, overlap or move apart. They can go out image borders a little.

15.12.8.2 Activate the filter

You can find this filter through Filters → Map → Paper Tile.

15.12.8.3 Options

Figure 15.214: 'Paper Tile' filter options

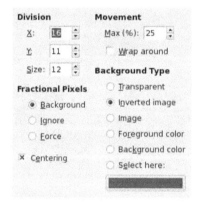

Division X, Y and Size parameters are linked, because filter starts cutting image before it displaces pieces; so, piece size and number of pieces in horizontal (X) and vertical (Y) directions must be convenient to image size.

Movement

- Max% is the maximum displacement percentage against the side size of squares.
- Wrap around : As tiles move, some can go out image borders. If this option is checked, what goes out on one side goes in on the opposite side.

Fractional Pixels Because of image cutting, original pixels can persist. There are three ways treating them:

- Background: Remaining pixels will be replaced with the background type defined in the following section.
- Ignore: Background Type option is not taken into account and remaining pixels are kept.
- Force: Remaining pixels will be cut also.

Background Type You can select the background type which will be used, if the Background radio-button is checked, among six options:

- Transparent: Background will be transparent.
- Inverted image: Background colors will be inverted (255-value in every color channel).
- Foreground Color: Remaining pixels will be replaced by the Foreground color of Toolbox.
- Background Color: Remaining pixels will be replaced by the Background color of Toolbox.
- Select here: When this radio-button is checked, clicking in the color dwell will open a Color Selector where you can select the color you want for background.

Centering If this option is checked, tiles will rather be gathered together in the center of the image.

15.12.9 Small Tiles

15.12.9.1 Overview

Figure 15.215: Example for the 'Small Tiles' filter

(a) *Original image*   (b) *Filter Small Tiles applied*

This filter reduces the image (active layer or selection) and displays it in many copies inside the original image.

15.12.9.2 Activate the filter

You can find this filter through Filters → Map → Small Tiles.

15.12.9.3 Options

Figure 15.216: 'Small Tiles' filter options

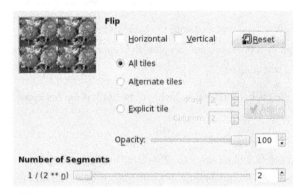

Number of Segments n**2 means 'the image into n to the power of two tiles', where 'n' is the number you set with the slider or its input box. n = 3 will make nine tiles in the image.

Opacity With this slider and its input box, you can set the opacity of the resulting image. This option is valid only if your image has an Alpha channel.

Flip You can flip tiles according to the Horizontal or/and Vertical axis by checking the corresponding option(s).

You can also decide which tiles will be flipped:

- All tiles: no comment.
- Alternate tiles: only odd tiles will be flipped.
- Explicit tile: you can define, a particular tile by using both Line and Column input boxes. This tile will be marked with a box in Preview.

15.12.10 Tile

15.12.10.1 Overview

Figure 15.217: The same image, before and after applying Tile filter

 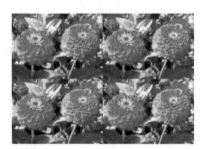

(a)   (b) *(We have reduced image size intentionally)*

You can find this filter through Filters → Map → Tile.

This filter makes several copies of the original image, in a same or reduced size, into a bigger (new) image.

15.12.10.2 Options

Figure 15.218: 'Tile' filter options

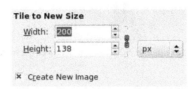

TILE TO NEW SIZE

Width/Height Input boxes and their arrow-heads allow you to enter the dimensions for the new image. Both directions are

linked by default with a chain ⛓ . You can make them independent by breaking this chain. You can choose a unit else than pixel by clicking on the drop-down list button.

The new image must be bigger than the original one . Else, you will get an image sample only. Choose sizes which are multiple of original sizes if you don't want to have truncated tiles.

Create New image It's in your interest to keep this option checked to avoid modifying your original image.

15.12.11 Warp

15.12.11.1 Overview

You can find this filter through Filters → Map → Warp. This filter has no Preview.

This filter displaces pixels of active layer or selection according to the grey levels of a *Displacement map*. Pixels are displaced according to the gradient slope in the displacement map. Pixels corresponding to solid areas are not displaced; the higher the slope, the higher the displacement.

Figure 15.219: From left to right: original image, displace map, displaced image

Solid areas of displacement map lead to no displacement. Abrupt transitions give an important displacement. A linear gradient gives a regular displacement. Displacement direction is perpendicular to gradient direction (angle = 90).

Figure 15.220: With a non-linear gradient

A non-linear gradient leads to curls.

Figure 15.221: With a complex gradient:

And a complex gradient, such as the Solid Noise filter can create, gives a swirl effect.

This filter offers the possibility of masking a part of the image to protect it against filter action.

15.12.11.2   Options

Figure 15.222: Warp filter options

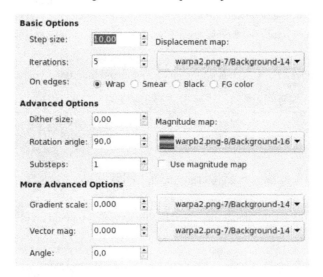

BASIC OPTIONS

Step Size 'Step' is displacement distance for every filter iteration. A 10 value is necessary to get a one pixel displacement. This value can be negative to invert displacement direction.

Iterations Iteration is the number of repetitions of effect when applying filter.

On Edges Because of displacement, a part of pixels are driven over the borders of layer or selection, and, on the opposite side, pixels places are emptying. Four following options allow you to fix this issue:

- Warp (default): What goes out on one side is going into the opposite side.
- Smear: Emptying places are filled with a spreading of the neighbouring image line.
- Black : Emptying places are filled with black color.
- FG Color : Emptying places are filled with the Foreground color of the color area in Toolbox.

Displacement Map To be listed in this drop-down list, the displacement map, which is a grey-scaled image, must be *present on your screen when you call filter and must have the same size as the original image*.

ADVANCED OPTIONS

Dither Size Once all pixels displaced, this option scatters them randomly, giving grain to the image. The higher this value (0.00-100.00), the thinner the grain.

Figure 15.223: With a 3.00 dither size:

Rotation Angle This option sets displacement angle of pixels according to the slope direction of gradient. Previous examples have been created with a vertical gradient and a 90 angle: so, pixels were displaced horizontally and nothing went out of the image borders. Here is an example with a 10 angle and 6 iterations:

Figure 15.224: With a 10 angle and 6 iterations:

Displacement is made according to a 10 angle against vertical. Pixels going out the lower border on every iteration are going into through the upper border (Wrap option checked), giving a dotted line.

Magnitude map In addition to displacement map, you can add a Magnitude Map. This map is also a grey-scaled image, with the same size as the source image and which must be present on your screen when you call filter. This map gives more or less strength to filter on some parts of the image, according to the grey levels of this magnitude map. Image areas corresponding to white parts of this map will undergo all the strength of filter. Image areas corresponding to black parts of the map will be spared by filter. Intermediate grey levels will lessen filter action on corresponding areas of the image. Use magnitude map must be checked for that.

Figure 15.225: Magnitude Map example:

From left to right: original image, displacement map, magnitude map, after applying Warp filter. You can see that the black areas of magnitude map prevent filter to take action.

MORE ADVANCED OPTIONS

The Gradient Map *The gradient map* is also a grayscaled map. Here, the displacement of pixels depends on the direction of grayscale transitions. The Gradient scale option lets you set how much the grayscale variations will influence the displacement of pixels. On every iteration, the filter works of the whole image, not only on the red object: this explains burredness.

Figure 15.226: Gradient map example

From left to right: original image, displacement map, after applying Warp filter with a Gradient Scale map. Gradient is oblique, from top left to right bottom. The part of the image corresponding to the gradient is moved obliquely, 90 rotated (Rotation Angle 90 in Advanced options).

The Vector Map

Figure 15.227: Vector map example

From left to right: original image, displacement map, after applying Warp filter with a Vector map. Gradient is vertical, from top to bottom. Vector angle is 45. The image is moved obliquely, 45 to the top left corner. The image is blurred because every iteration works on the whole image, and not only on the red bar.

With this map, the displacement depends on the angle you set in the Angle text box. 0 is upwards. Angles go counterclockwise. The Vector Magnitude determines by how many pixels the image will move on every iteration.

15.12.12   Van Gogh (LIC)

15.12.12.1   Overview

Figure 15.228: From left to right: original image, map, resulting image

Map has three strips: a solid black area, a vertical gradient area, a solid white area. One can see, on the resulting image, that image zones corresponding to solid areas of the map, are not blurred. Only the image zone corresponding to the gradient area of the map is blurred.

You can find this filter through Filters → Map → Van Gogh (LIC).

'LIC' stands for Line Integral Convolution, a mathematical method. The plug-in author uses mathematical terms to name his options... This filter is used to apply a directional blur to an image, or to create textures. It could be called 'Astigmatism' as it blurs certain directions in the image.

It uses a blur map. Unlike other maps, this filter doesn't use grey levels of this blur map. *Filter takes in account only gradient direction(s).* Image pixels corresponding to solid areas of the map are ignored.

15.12.12.2 Options

Figure 15.229: 'Van Gogh (LIC)' filter options

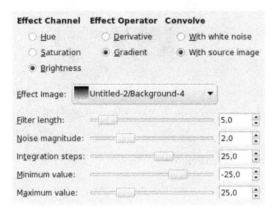

 Tip

- To create a blur, check With Source Image. Only Filter Length slider and perhaps Integration Steps slider, are useful.

- To create a texture, check With White Noise. All sliders can be useful.

Convolution You can use two types of convolution. That's the first parameter you have to set:

- With White Noise: White Noise is an acoustics name. It's a noise where all frequencies have the same amplitude. Here, this option is used to create patterns.
- With Source Image: The source image will be blurred.

Effect Image That's the map for blur or pattern direction. This map must have the same dimensions as the original image. It must be preferably a grayscale image. It must be present on your screen when you call filter so that you can choose it in the drop-list.

Figure 15.230: Blurring with vertical gradient map

With a vertical gradient map, vertical lines are blurred.

Figure 15.231: Blurring with a square gradient map

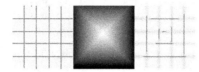

The gradient map is divided into four gradient triangles: each of them has its own gradient direction. In every area of the image corresponding to gradient triangles, only lines with the same direction as gradient are blurred.

Figure 15.232: Texture example

The With white noise option is checked. Others are default. With a vertical gradient map, texture fibres are going horizontally.

Effect Channel   By selecting Hue, Saturation or Brightness (=Value), filter will use this channel to treat image

Effect Operator   The 'Derivative' option reverses 'Gradient ' direction:

Figure 15.233: Derivative option example

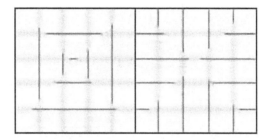

Using a square gradient map, Effect operator is on Gradient on the left, on Derivative on the right: what was sharp is blurred and conversely.

Filter Length   When applying blur, this option controls how important blur is. When creating a texture, it controls how rough texture is: low values result in smooth surface; high values in rough surface.

Figure 15.234: Action example of Filter Length on blur

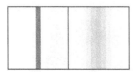

On the left: a vertical line, one pixel wide (zoom 800%). On the right: the same line, after applying a vertical blur with a Filter Length to 3. You can see that blur width is 6 pixels, 3 pixels on both sides.

Figure 15.235: Filter Length example on texture

On the left: a texture with Noise Length=3. On the right, the same texture with Noise Length=24.

Noise Magnitude   This options controls the amount and size of White Noise. Low values produce finely grained surfaces. High values produce coarse-grained textures.

Figure 15.236: Action example of Noise Magnitude on texture

Noise magnitude = 4

Integration Steps   This options controls the influence of gradient map on texture.

Figure 15.237: Action example of Integration Steps on texture

On the left: Integration Steps = 2. On the right: Integration Steps = 4.

Minimum/Maximum values   Both values determine a range controlling texture contrast: shrinked range results in high contrast and enlarged range results in low contrast.

Figure 15.238: Action example of Min/max values on texture

Minimum value = -4,0. Maximum value = 5,0.

15.13 Rendering Filters

15.13.1 Introduction

Most GIMP filters work on a layer by transforming its content, but the filters in the 'Render' group are a bit different. They create patterns from scratch, in most cases obliterating anything that was previously in the layer. Some create random or noisy patterns, others regular of fractal patterns, and one (Gfig) is a general-purpose (but rather limited) vector graphics tool.

15.13.2 Plasma

15.13.2.1 Overview

Figure 15.239: Example of a rendered plasma.

Filter Plasma applied

You can find this filter through Filters → Render → Clouds → Plasma

Plasma generates colorful clouds, which can be used for textures. You control the turbulence in the plasma cloud with the Turbulence slide.

All of the colors produced by Plasma are completely saturated. Sometimes the strong colors may be distracting, and a more interesting surface will appear when you desaturate the image using Layer/Colors/Desaturate.

 Note
An enhanced version of the Plasma plug-in, called *Plasma2*, with many more options and parameters, is available from the GIMP Plugin Registry [PLUGIN-PLASMA2].

15.13.2.2 Options

Figure 15.240: 'Plasma' filter options

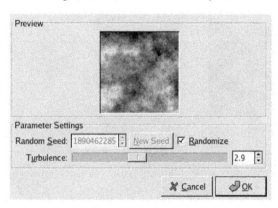

Random Seed Random Seed controls the randomization element. The Randomize check-button will set the seed using the hardware clock of the computer. There is no reason to use anything else unless you want to be able to repeat the exact same pattern of randomization on a later occasion.

Turbulence This parameter controls the complexity of the plasma. High values give a hard feeling to the cloud (like an abstract oil painting or mineral grains), low values produce a softer cloud (like steam, mist or smoke). The range is 0.1 to 7.0.

15.13.3 Solid Noise

15.13.3.1 Overview

Figure 15.241: Example of turbulent solid noise.

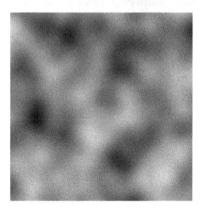

Filter Solid noise applied

You can find this filter from the image menu through Filters → Render → Clouds → Solid noise

Solid Noise is a great texture maker. Note that this noise is always gray, even if you applied it to a very colorful image (it doesn't matter what the original image looks like -- this filter completely overwrites any existing background in the layer it is applied to). This is also a good tool to create displacement maps for the Warp plug-in or for the Bump Map plug-in. With the "turbulence" setting active, the results look quite a bit like real clouds.

15.13.3.2 Options

Figure 15.242: 'Solid Noise' filter options

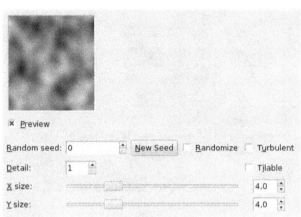

Random Seed Random Seed controls random behaviour of the filter. If the same random seed in the same situation is used, the filter produces exactly the same results. A different random seed produces different results. Random seed can be entered manually or generated randomly by pressing New Seed button.

When the Randomize option is checked, random seed cannot be entered manually, but is randomly generated each time the filter is run. If it is not checked, the filter remembers the last random seed used.

Turbulent If you check this, you'll get very interesting effects, often something that looks much like oil on water, or clouds of smoke, or living tissue, or a Rorschach blot.

Detail This controls the amount of detail in the noise texture. Higher values give a higher level of detail, and the noise seems to be made of spray or small particles, which makes it feel hard. A low value makes it more soft and cloudy.

Tileable If you check Tileable, you'll get a noise which can be used as tiles. For example, you can use it as a background in an HTML page, and the tile edges will be joined seamlessly.

X and Y Size These control the size and proportion of the noise shapes in X (horizontal) and Y (vertical) directions (range 0.1 to 16.0).

15.13.4 Flame

15.13.4.1 Overview

Figure 15.243: Example of a rendered Flame.

(a)

(b) *Filter Flame applied*

You can find this filter through Filters → Render → Nature → Flame

With the Flame filter, you can create stunning, randomly generated fractal patterns. You can't control the fractals as you can with the Ifs Compose filter, but you can steer the random generator in a certain direction, and choose from variations of a theme you like.

In the main window, you can set Rendering and Camera parameters. The first three parameters in the Render display are Brightness, Contrast and Gamma. The result of these options is visible in the Preview window, but it's generally better to stick to the default values, and correct the rendered image later with Image/Colors.

The other three parameters affect the rendering process and don't show in the preview window. Sample Density, which controls the resolution of the rendered pattern, is the most important of these. The Camera parameters allow you to zoom and offset the flame pattern, until you're happy with what you see in the preview window. Flame also offers the possibility to store and load your favorite patterns.

Warning

Unfortunately it turned out, that this filter is not working properly for large images. Even more unfortunate is, that its developer is currently not undertaking any actions with that plug-in at all, so there seems no quick fix in sight. Although we can give you the exact numbers, the plug-in worked in a quick test for a 1024x768 pixel image, but didn't do it for a 2500x2500 pixel image.

Note

This plug-in was given to GIMP by Scott Draves in 1997. He also holds the copyright for the plug-in. An descriptive page for the plug-in, provided by the author can be found in the internet [PLUGIN-FLAMES].

15.13.4.2   Options

Figure 15.244: 'Flame' filter options

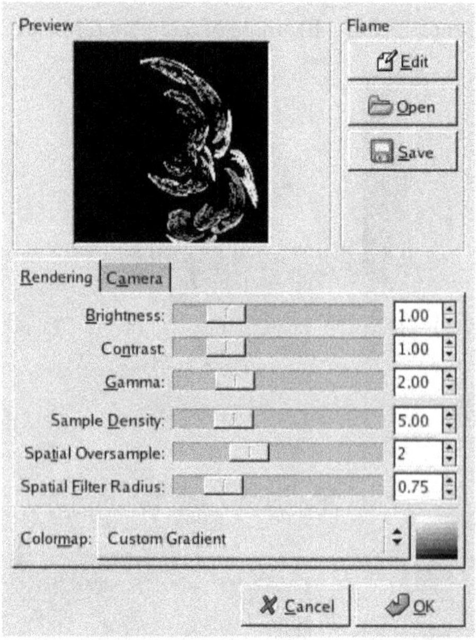

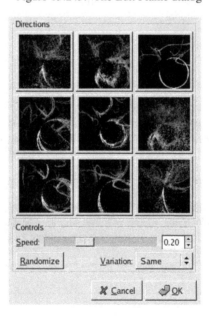

Edit

Figure 15.245: The Edit Flame dialog

Pressing this button brings up the Edit dialog. The dialog shows nine different windows. The pattern displayed in the center is the current pattern, and the eight windows surrounding it are random variations of that pattern. Clicking on the central image creates eight new variations, which can be adjusted with the Speed control. You select a variation by clicking on it, and it instantly replaces the image in the middle. To pick a certain character or theme for the variations, you can choose from nine different themes in the Variations menu. You can also use Randomize, which replaces the current pattern with a new random pattern.

Open This button brings up a file selector that allows you to open a previously saved Flame settings file.

Save This button brings up a file save dialog that allows you to save the current settings for the plug-in, so that you can recreate them later.

Rendering tab

Brightness Controls the brightness of the flame object.

Contrast Controls the contrast between brighter and dimmer parts of the flame.

Gamma Sets a gamma correction for parts with intermediate brightness.

Sample Density Controls the resolution of the rendered pattern. (Does not have any effect on the preview.) A high sample density results in soft and smooth rendering (like a spider's web), whereas low density rendering resembles spray or particle clouds.

Spatial Oversample What does this do?

Spatial Filter Radius What does this do?

Colormap This menu gives you several options to set the color blend in the flame pattern:

- The current gradient as shown in the Toolbox.
- A number of preset colormaps.
- The colors from images that are presently open in GIMP.

Camera tab

Zoom Allows you to zoom the flame in or out.

X, Y Allows you to move the flame around in the image area.

15.13.5 IFS Compose

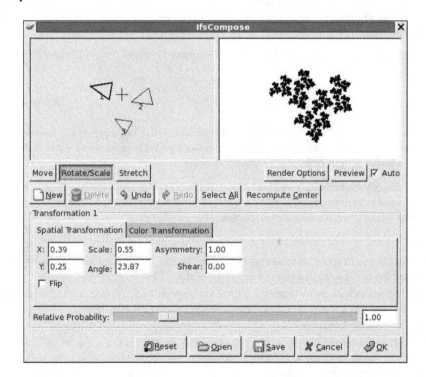

15.13.5.1 Overview

Figure 15.246: Applying example for the IFS Compose filter

Filter IFS Fractal applied

You can find this filter through Filters → Render → Nature → IFS fractal

This fractal-based plug-in is truly wonderful! With this versatile instrument, you can create amazingly naturalistic organic shapes, like leaves, flowers, branches, or even whole trees. ('IFS' stands for 'Iterated Function System '.)

The key to use this plug-in lies in making very small and precise movements in fractal space. The outcome is always hard to predict, and you have to be extremely gentle when you change the pattern. If you make a component triangle too big, or if you move it too far (even ever so slightly), the preview screen will black out, or more commonly, you'll get stuck with a big shapeless particle cloud.

A word of advice: When you have found a pattern you want to work with, make only small changes, and stick to variations of that pattern. It's all too easy to lose a good thing. Contrary to what you might believe, it's really much easier to create a leaf or a tree with IFS Compose than to make a defined geometrical pattern (where you actually know what you're doing, and end up with the pattern you had in mind).

For a brief introduction to IFS's see Foley and van Dam, et al,. *Computer Graphics, Principles and Practice*[FOLEY01].

15.13.5.2 Options

The Main Interface The plug-in interface consists of the compose area to the left, a preview screen to the right, and some tabs and option buttons at the bottom of the dialog. The Default setting (in the preview window) is three equilateral triangles. (This gives rise to a fractal pattern called the *Sierpinski Triangle*).

Toolbar Some tools are directly visible in this tool bar: Move, Rotate, Strecht, New, Delete, Undo , Redo, Select All. You can see others, if your window is not wide enough, by clicking on the drop-down list button on the right of tool bar: Recenter and Render Options where you have have several parameters:

Render Options
    Memory Enables you to speed up rendering time. This is especially useful when working with a large spot radius; just remember to use even multiples of the default value: 4096, 8192, 16384, ...
    Iterations Determines how many times the fractal will repeat itself. (A high value for Subdivide and Iterations is for obvious reasons a waste of process time unless your image is very large.)
    Subdivide Controls the level of detail.
    Spot Radius Determines the density of the 'brushstrokes' in the rendered image. A low spot radius is good for thin particle clouds or spray, while a high spot radius produces thick, solid color strokes much like watercolor painting. Be careful not to use too much spot radius -- it takes a lot of time to render.

Spatial Transformation Gives you information on the active fractal, and allows you to type a value instead of changing it manually. Changing parameters with the mouse isn't very accurate, so this is a useful option when you need to be exact.

Color transformation

Figure 15.247: 'Color transformation' tab options

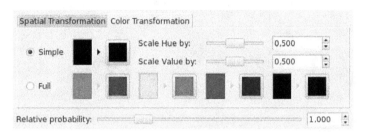

Simple color transformation Changes the color of the currently selected fractal component (default is the foreground color in the toolbox) to a color of your choice.

Full color transformation Like the Simple color transformation but this time you can manage the color transformation for each color channel and for the alpha channel (shown as a black channel).

Scale Hue/Value When you have many fractals with different colors, the colors blend into each other. So even if you set 'pure red' for a fractal, it might actually be quite blue in some places, while another 'red ' fractal might have a lot of yellow in it. Scale Hue/Value changes the color strength of the active fractal, or how influential that fractal color should be.

Relative Probability Determines influence or total impact of a certain fractal.

15.13.5.3   A Brief Tutorial

This is a rather complex plug-in, so to help you understand it, we'll guide you through an example where you'll create a leaf or branch.

Many forms of life, and especially plants, are built like mathematical fractals, i.e., a shape that reproduces or repeats itself indefinitely into the smallest detail. You can easily reproduce the shape of a leaf or a branch by using four (or more) fractals. Three fractals make up the tip and sides of the leaf, and the fourth represents the stem.

1. Before invoking the filter: Select File → New Image Add a transparent layer with Layers → Layers and Channels → New Layer Set the foreground color in the toolbox to black, and set the background to white.

2. Open IFS Compose. Start by rotating the right and bottom triangles, so that they point upward. You'll now be able to see the outline of what's going to be the tip and sides of the leaf. (If you have problems, it may help to know that the three vertices of a triangle are not equivalent.)

Figure 15.248: Tutorial Step 2

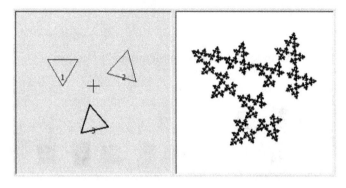

Start by rotating triangles 2 and 3, trying to keep them nearly the same size.

3. To make the leaf symmetrical, adjust the bottom triangle to point slightly to the left, and the right triangle to point slightly to the right.

4. Press New to add a component to the composition. This is going to be the stem of the leaf, so we need to make it long and thin. Press Stretch, and drag to stretch the new triangle. Don't be alarmed if this messes up the image, just use Scale to adjust the size of the overlong triangle. You'll probably also have to move and rotate the new fractal to make it look convincing.

Figure 15.249: Tutorial Step 3

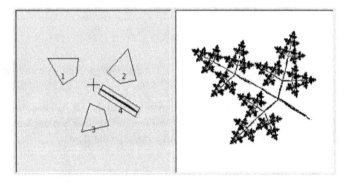

Add a fourth component, then stretch, scale, and move it as shown.

5. You still have to make it look more leaf-like. Increase the size of the top triangle, until you think it's thick and leafy enough. Adjust all fractals until you're happy with the shape. Right-click to get the popup menu, and choose Select all. Now all components are selected, and you can scale and rotate the entire leaf.

Figure 15.250: Tutorial Step 4

Enlarge component 1, arrange the other components appropriately, then select all, scale and rotate.

6. The final step is to adjust color. Click on the Color Transformation tab, and choose a different color for each fractal. To do this, check Simple and press the right color square. A color circle appears, where you can click or select to choose a color.

Figure 15.251: Tutorial Step 5

Assign a brownish color to component 4, and various shades of green to the other components.

7. Press OK to apply the image, and voilà, you've just made a perfect fractal leaf! Now that you've got the hang of it, you'll just have to experiment and make your own designs. All plant-imitating fractals (be they oak trees, ferns or straws) are more or less made in this fashion, which is leaves around a stem (or several stems). You just have to twist another way, stretch and turn a little or add a few more fractals to get a totally different plant.

15.13.6 Diffraction Patterns

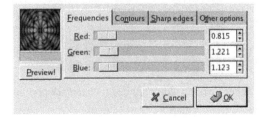

15.13.6.1 Overview

Figure 15.252: Two examples of diffraction patterns.

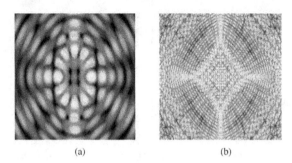

(a)   (b)

You can find this filter through Filters → Render → Patterns → Diffraction Patterns.

This filter lets you make diffraction or wave interference textures. You can change the Frequency, Contours and Sharp Edges for each of the RGB channels. You can also set Brightness, Scattering and Polarization of the texture. There is no automatic preview, so you must press the preview button to update. On a slow system, this may take a bit of time. Note that result doesn't depend on the initial image.

This is a very useful filter if you want to create intricate patterns. It's perfect for making psychedelic, batik-like textures, or for imitating patterns in stained glass (as in a church window).

It seems clear that the plugin works by simulating the physics of light striking a grating. Unfortunately, the original authors never got around to writing down the theory behind it, or explaining what the parameters mean. The best approach, then, is just to twiddle things and see what happens. Fortunately, almost anything you do seems to produce interesting results.

15.13.7 CML Explorer

15.13.7.1 Overview

Figure 15.253: Example for the 'CML Explorer' filter

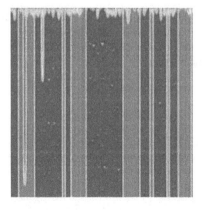

Filter CML Explorer applied with default options

This filter is the king of texture creating filters. It is extremely efficient but very complex. It uses a mathematical method named Cellular Automata. cellular_automata .

15.13.7.2 Starting filter

You can find this filter from the image menu through Filters → Render → Pattern → CML Explorer

15.13.7.3 Options

General Options

Figure 15.254: 'CML Explorer' filter options(Hue)

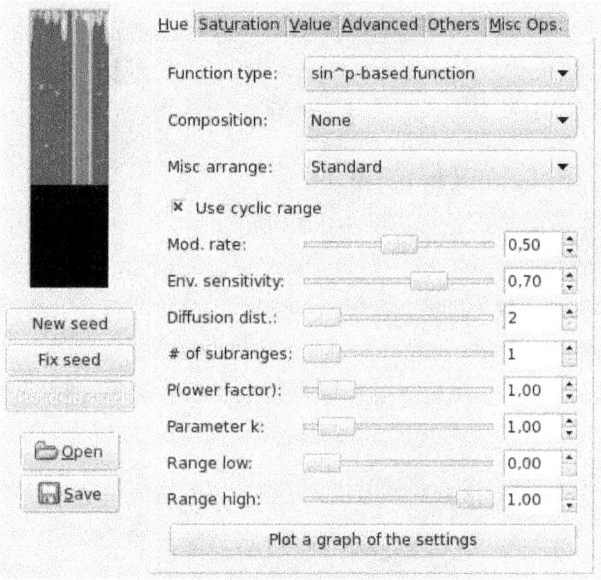

Filter options are distributed among Hue,Saturation, Value, Advanced, others and Misc.ops tabs. Some more options are available. They will be described in following section.

Preview This filter offers you a Preview where you can see the result of your settings before they are applied to the image.

New seed; Fix seed; Random seed Random plays a large part in creating patterns. With these options, you can influence the way random is generated. By clicking on the New seed button, you can force random to use a new source of random. The preview will show you the result. Fix seed lets you keep the same seed and so to reproduce the same effect with the filter. Random seed generates a random seed at random.

Open; Save With these both command buttons you can save pattern settings in a file, and to get them back later.

Hue tab This filter works in the HSV color model. In this tab, you can set options for Hue.

Function type In this drop-down list, you can select the method that will be used to treat the current layer. These methods are:

- Keep image's values: With this option, image hue values will be kept.
- Keep the first value: With this option, starting color will be standard cyan.
- Fill with k parameter, k{x(1-x)}^p, k{x(1-x)}^p stepped, kx^p, kx^p stepped, k(1-x^p), k(1-x^p) stepped: pattern look will depend on k that you will set later in options.
- Delta function, Delta function stepped: FIXME
- sin^p based Function, sin^p stepped: These options create wave-like patterns, like aurora borealis or curtain folds.

Composition Here, these options concern Hue. You can select:

None, Max(x, -), Max(x+d, -), Max(x-d, -), Min(x, -), Min(x+d, -), Min(x-d, -), Max(x+d, -), (x < 0,5), Max(x+d, -), (0,5 < x), Max(x-d, -), (x < 0,5), Max(x-d, -), (0,5 < x), Min(x+d, -), (x < 0,5), Min(x+d, -), (0,5 < x), Min(x-d, -), (x < 0,5) and Min(x-d, -), (0,5 < x).

A book could be filled with results of all these functions. Please, experiment!

Misc. Arrange This drop-down list offers you some other parameters:

Standard, Use average value, Use reverse value, With random power (0,10), With random power (0,1), with gradient power (0,1), Multiply rand. value (0,1), Multiply rand. value (0,2), Multiply gradient (0,1) and With p and random (0,1).

Also a book would be necessary to explain all possibilities of these parameters.

Use cyclic range //TODO

Mod. rate With this slider and the input box, you can set modification rate from 0.0 to 1.0. Low value results in a lined pattern.

Env. sensitivity Value is from 0.0 to 1.0

Diffusion dist. Diffusion distance: from 2 to 10.

# of subranges Number of sub-rangers: from 1 to 10.

(P)ower factor With this option you can influence the Function types using the p parameter. Value from 0.0 to 10.0.

k Parameter With this option you can influence the Function types using the k parameter. Value from 0.0 to 10.0.

Range low Set lower limit of hue that will be used for calculation. values vary from 0.0 to 1.0.

Range high Set the upper limit of hue that will be used for calculation. Variations are from 0.0 to 1.0.

Plot a graph of the settings By clicking on this large button, you can open a window that displays the graph of hue present settings.

Figure 15.255: Function graph of present settings

Saturation tab

Figure 15.256: 'CML Explorer' filter options(Saturation)

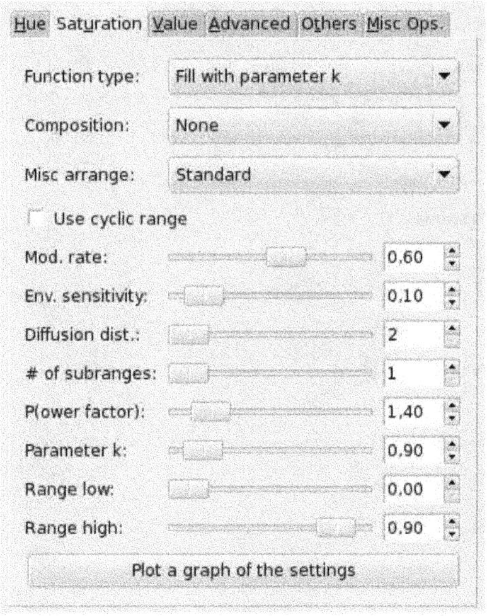

In this tab, you can set how Saturation component of the HSV color model will be used in pattern calculation. These options are similar to Hue tab options.

Value tab

Figure 15.257: 'CML Explorer' filter options (Value)

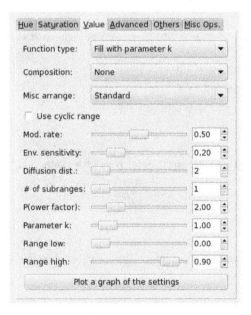

In this tab, you can set how the Value (Luminosity) component of the HSV color model will be used in pattern calculation. These options are similar to Hue tab options.

Advanced tab

Figure 15.258: 'CML Explorer' filter options (Advanced)

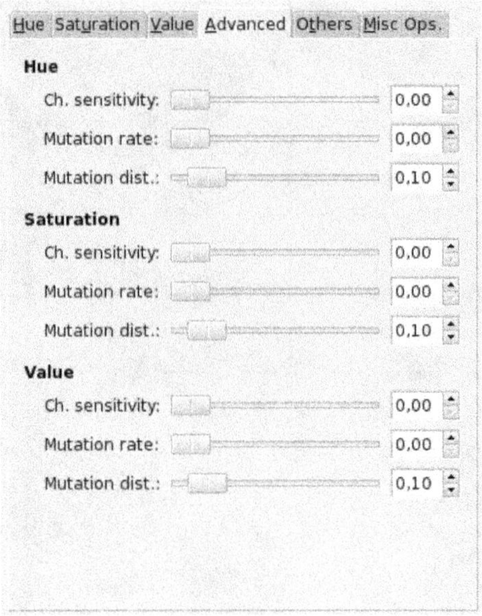

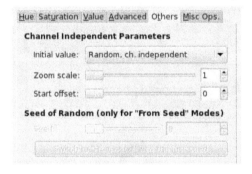

These tab settings apply to the three HSV channels.

Channel Sensitivity // TODO

Mutation rate // TODO

Mutation distance //TODO

Others tab

Figure 15.259: 'CML Explorer' filter options (Others)

In this tab, you can find various parameters about image display and random intervention.

Initial value // TODO

Zoom factor // TODO

Start offset // TODO

Seed of random // TODO

Miscellaneous options tab

Figure 15.260: 'CML Explorer' filter options (Misc.ops)

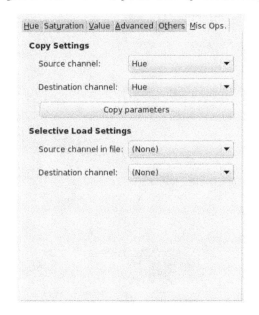

In this tab you can find various options about copy and loading.

Copy settings These options allow you to transfer information from one of the HSV channel to another one.

Selective load setting With the Open button of this filter, you can load previously loaded settings. If you don't want to load all of them, you can select a source and a destination channel here.

15.13.8 Grid

15.13.8.1 Overview

Figure 15.261: Applying example for the Grid filter

(a) *Original image*   (b) *Filter Grid applied*

You can find this filter through Filters → Render → Pattern → Grid.

It renders a Cartesian grid in the active layer, on top of the existing contents. The width, spacing, offsets, and colors of the grid lines can all be set by the user. By default, the lines are with the GIMP's foreground color. (Note: this plugin was used to create demonstration images for many of the other plugins.)

 Tip
If you set the grid line widths to 0, then only the intersections will be drawn, as plus-marks.

15.13.8.2 Options

Figure 15.262: 'Grid' filter options

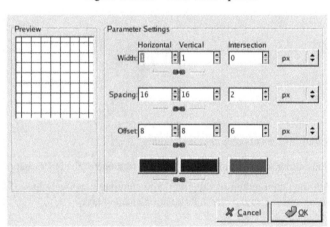

There are separate options for controlling the horizontal grid lines, vertical grid lines, and intersections. By default, the horizontal and vertical settings are locked together, so that all changes are applied symmetrically. If you want to change just one of them, click on the 'chain' symbol below it to unlock them. The results of changing the Intersection parameters are rather complex.

Besides, for some options, you can select the unit of measurement thanks to a drop-down list.

Width Sets the widths of the horizontal or vertical grid lines, or of the symbols drawn at their intersections.

Spacing Sets the distance between grid lines. The Intersection parameter clears the space between the intersection point and the end of the arms of the intersection crosses.

Offset Sets the offset for grid lines with respect to the upper left corner. For intersections, sets the length of the arms of the intersection crosses.

Color Selectors These allow you to set the colors of the grid lines and intersection marks.

15.13.9   Maze

15.13.9.1   Overview

Figure 15.263: An example of a rendered maze.

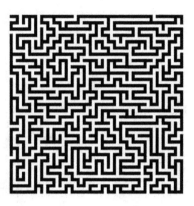

Filter Maze applied

You can find this filter in the image menu through Filters → Render → Pattern → Maze

This filter generates a random black and white maze pattern. The result completely overwrites the previous contents of the active layer. A typical example is shown below. Can you find the route from the center to the edge?

15.13.9.2   Options

Figure 15.264: 'Maze' filter options

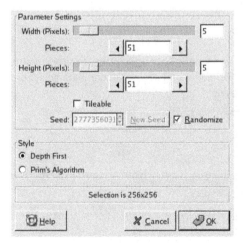

Width/Height The Width and Height sliders control how many pathways the maze should have. The lower the values for width and height, the more paths you will get. The same happens if you increase the number of pieces in the Width and Height Pieces fields. The result won't really look like a maze unless the width and height are equal.

Tileable If you want to use it in a pattern, you can make the maze tileable by checking this check-button.

Seed You can specify a seed for the random number generator, or ask the program to generate one for you. Unless you need to later reproduce exactly the same maze, you might as well have the program do it.

Algorithm You can choose between two algorithms for maze, Depth First and Prim's Algorithm. Only a computer scientist can tell the difference between them.

15.13.10 Jigsaw

15.13.10.1 Overview

You can find this filter through Filters → Render → Pattern → Jigsaw

Figure 15.265: Jigsaw filter example

(a) Original image   (b) Filter Jigsaw applied

This filter will turn your image into a jigsaw puzzle. The edges are not anti-aliased, so a little bit of smoothing often makes them look better (i. e., Gaussian blur with radius 1.0).

 Tip

If you want to be able to easily select individual puzzle-piece areas, render the jigsaw pattern on a separate layer filled with solid white, and set the layer mode to Multiply. You can then select puzzle pieces using the magic wand (fuzzy select) tool on the new jigsaw layer.

15.13.10.2 Options

Figure 15.266: 'Jigsaw' filter options

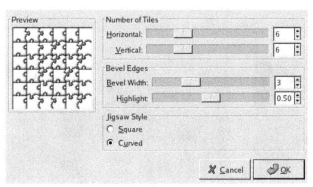

Number of Tiles How many tiles across the image is, horizontally and vertically.

Bevel Width The Bevel width slider controls the slope of the edges of the puzzle pieces (a hard wooden puzzle would require a low Bevel width value, and a soft cardboard puzzle would require a higher value).

Highlight The Highlight slider controls the strength of the highlight that will appear on the edges of each piece. You may compare it to the "glossiness" of the material the puzzle is made of. Highlight width is relative to the Bevel width. As a rule of thumb, the more pieces you add to the puzzle, the lower Bevel and Highlight values you should use, and vice versa. The default values are suitable for a 500x500 pixel image.

Jigsaw Style You can choose between two types of puzzle, Square then you get pieces made with straight lines, or Curved then you get pieces made with curves.

15.13.11 Qbist

15.13.11.1 Overview

Figure 15.267: Applying example for the Qbist filter

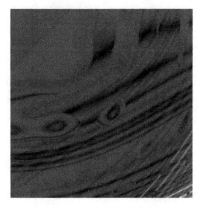

Filter Qbist applied

You can find this filter through Filters → Render → Pattern → Qbist

The Qbist filter generates random textures. A starting texture is displayed in the middle square, and different variations surround it. If you like one of the alternative textures, click on it. The chosen texture now turns up in the middle, and variations on that specific theme are displayed around it. When you have found the texture you want, click on it and then click OK. The texture will now appear on the currently active layer, completely replacing its previous contents.

Figure 15.268: Three more or less random examples of qbist renderings.

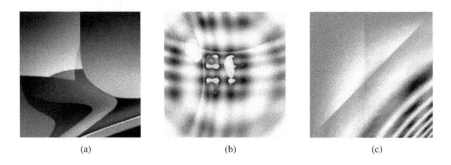

(a) (b) (c)

15.13.11.2 Options

Figure 15.269: 'Qbist' filter options

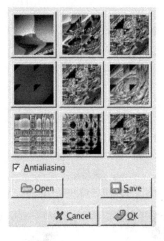

Antialiasing If you check this, it will make edges appear smooth rather than stair-step-like.

Open/Save These buttons allow you to save and reload your textures. This is quite handy because it's almost impossible to re-create a good pattern by just clicking around.

15.13.12 Checkerboard

15.13.12.1 Overview

Figure 15.270: Example for the Checkerboard filter

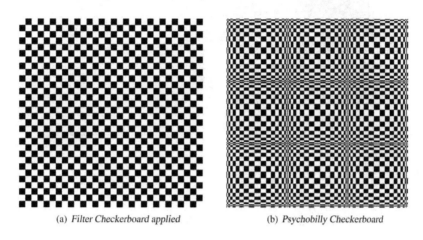

(a) *Filter Checkerboard applied*   (b) *Psychobilly Checkerboard*

This filter creates a checkerboard pattern replacing the current layer content. Colors used for pattern are current Fore- and Back ground colors of toolbox.

15.13.12.2 Starting filter

You can find this filter in the image menu through Filters → Render → Pattern → Checkerboard

15.13.12.3 Options

Figure 15.271: 'Checkerboard' filter options

Psychobilly This option gives an eiderdown look to the Checkerboard.

Size With this option, you can set checkerboard square size, in pixels, or in your chosen unit by using the drop-down list.

15.13.13   Sinus

15.13.13.1   Overview

Figure 15.272: Applying example for the Sinus filter

Filter Sinus applied

You can find this filter from the image menu through Filters → Render → Pattern → Sinus

The Sinus filter lets you make sinusoidally based textures, which look rather like watered silk or maybe plywood. This plug-in works by using two different colors that you can define in the Colors tab. These two colors then create wave patterns based on a sine function.

You can set the X and Y scales, which determine how stretched or packed the texture will be. You can also set the Complexity of the function: a high value creates more interference or repetition in the pattern. An example is shown below.

15.13.13.2 Options

Figure 15.273: 'Sinus' filter options (Settings)

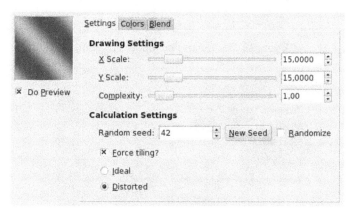

Settings tab

X and Y Scales A low X/Y value will maximize the horizontal/vertical stretch of the texture, whereas a high value will compress it.

Complexity This controls how the two colors interact with each other (the amount of interplay or repetition).

Random Seed Random Seed controls the random behaviour of the filter. If the same random seed in the same situation is used, the filter produces exactly the same results. A different random seed produces different results. Random seed can be entered manually or generated randomly by pressing the New Seed button.

When the Randomize option is checked, random seed cannot be entered manually, but is randomly generated each time the filter is run. If it is not checked, the filter remembers the last random seed used.

Force Tiling? If you check this, you'll get a pattern that can be used for tiling. For example, you can use it as a background in an HTML page, and the tile edges will be joined seamlessly.

Ideal/Distorted This option gives additional control of the interaction between the two colors. Distorted creates a more distorted interference between the two colors than Ideal.

Color settings

Figure 15.274: 'Sinus' filter options (Color)

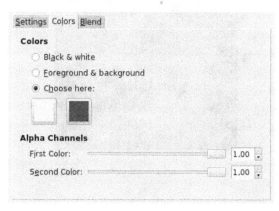

Colors Here, you set the two colors that make up your texture. You can use Black and white or the foreground/background colors in the toolbox, or you can choose a color with the color icons. The `Alpha Channels` sliders allow you to assign an opacity to each of the colors. (If the layer you are working on does not have an alpha channel, they will be grayed out.)

Blend settings

Figure 15.275: Sinus filter options (Blend)

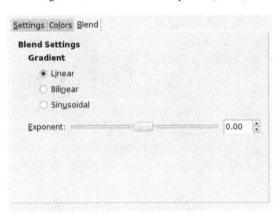

Gradient You can choose between three functions to set the shapes of the waves that are produced: Linear, Bilinear and Sinusoidal.

Exponent The Exponent controls which of the two colors is dominant, and how dominant it is. If you set the exponent to -7.5, the left color will dominate totally, and if you set it to +7.5 it will be the other way around. A zero value is neutral.

15.13.14 Fractal Explorer

15.13.14.1 Overview

Figure 15.276: The same image, before and after applying Fractal Explorer filter

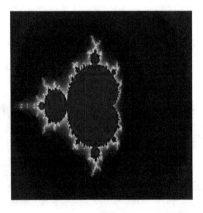

Filter Fractal Explorer applied

With this filter, you can create fractals and multicolored pictures verging to chaos. Unlike the IFS Compose filter, with which you can fix the fractal stucture precisely, this filter lets you perform fractals simply.

15.13.14.2 Starting filter

You can find this filter through Filters → Render → Nature → Fractal Explorer

15.13.14.3 Options

Figure 15.277: 'Parameters' options for Fractal Explorer filter

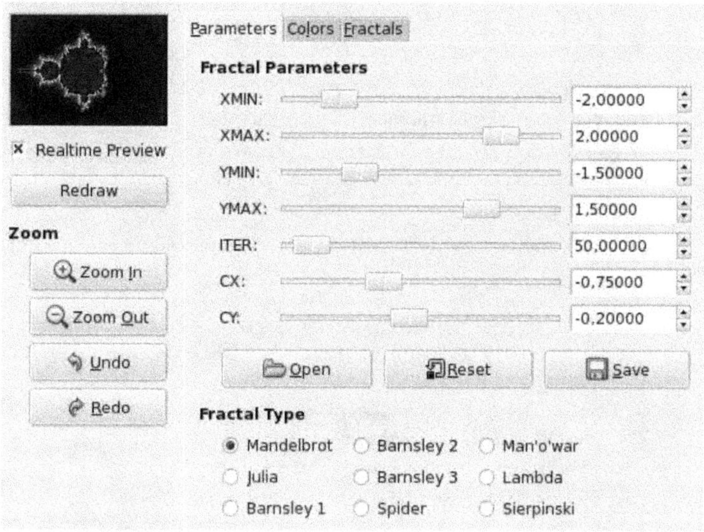

Preview domain Uncheck the Real time preview only if your computer is slow. In this case, you can update preview by clicking on the Redraw button.

By clicking-dragging mouse pointer on preview, you can draw a rectangle delimiting an area which will be zoomed.

Zoom You have there some options to zoom in or zoom out. The Undo allows you to return to previous state, before zooming. The Redo allows you to restablish the zoom you had undone, without having to re-create it with the zoom-in button.

Parameters tab This tab contains some options to set fractal calculation and select fractal type.

Fractal Parameters here, you have sliders and input boxes to set fractal spreading, repetition and aspect.

XMIN; XMAX; YMIN; YMAX You can set fractal spreading between a MINimum and a MAXimum, in the horizontal (X) and/or vertical (Y) directions. Values are from -3.0 to 3.0.

ITER With this parameter, you can set fractal iteration, repetition and so detail. Values are from 0.0 to 1000.0

CX; CY With these parameters, you can change fractal aspect, in the horizontal (X) and/or vertical (Y) directions, except for Mandelbrot and Sierpinski types.

Open; Reset; Save With these three buttons, you can save your work with all its parameters, open a previously saved fractal, or return to the initial state before all modifications.

Fractal type You can choose what fractal type will be, for instance Mandelbrot, Julia, Barnsley or Sierpinski.

Colors tab

Figure 15.278: Color tab options

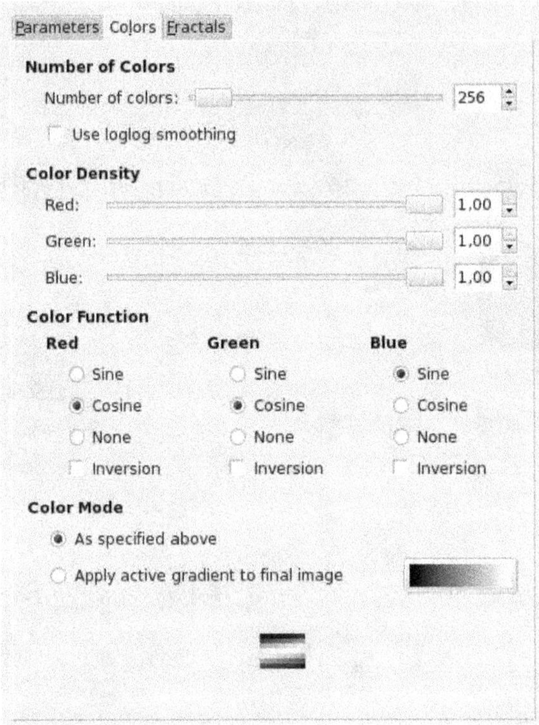

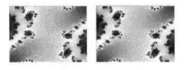

This tab contains options for fractal color setting.

Color number This slider and its input boxes allow you to set the number of colors for the fractal, between 2 and 8192. A palette of these colors is displayed at the bottom of the tab. Actually, that's a gradient between colors in fractal: you can change colors with 'Color intensity' and 'Color function' options. Fractal colors don't depend on colors of the original image (you can use a white image for fractals as well).

Use loglog-smoothing If this option is checked, the band effect is smoothed.

Figure 15.279: Loglog smoothing example

Color density These three sliders and their inputboxes let you set the color intensity in the three Red, Green and Blue color channels. Values vary from 0.0 to 1.0.

Color function For the Red, Green and Blue color channels, you can select how color will be treated:

- Sinus: Color variations will be modulated according to the sinus function.
- Cosinus: Color densities will vary according to cosinus function.
- None: Color densities will vary linearly.
- Inversion: if you check this option, function values will be inverted.

Color Mode These options allow you to set where color values must be taken from.

- As specified above: Color values will be taken from the Color density options.

- Apply active gradient to final image : used colors will be that of active gradient. You should be able to select another gradient by clicking on the gradient source button.

Fractals tab

Figure 15.280: 'Fractal tab' options

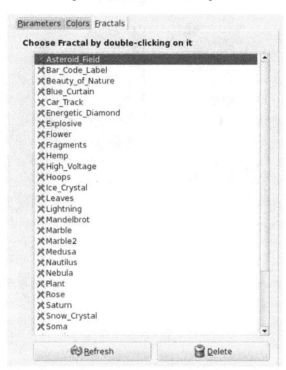

This tab contains a big list of fractals with their parameters, that you can use as a model: only click on the wanted one.

The Refresh allows you to update the list if you have saved your work, without needing to re-start Gimp. You can delete the selected fractal from the list by clicking on the Delete.

15.13.15 Gfig

15.13.15.1 Overview

Figure 15.281: The same image, before and after using Gfig

(a) *Original image*　　　　　　　　(b) *Filter Gfig applied*

This filter is a tool: You can create geometrical figures to add them to the image. It is very complex. I hope this paper will help you.

When using this filter, elements inserted in the image will be placed in a new layer. So the image will not be modified, all modifications occuring in this layer.

15.13.15.2 Starting filter

You can find this filter through Filters → Render → Gfig

15.13.15.3   Options

Figure 15.282: 'Gfig' filter options

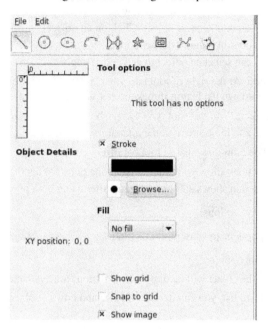

The tool bar   At the top of dialog, you can find a set of icons which represents the functions of this filter. Help pop-ups are explicit.

Functions for object drawing   On the left part of tool bar, you can find some functions for object drawing. You enable them by clicking on the corresponding icon. You can create the following objects (note that *Control points* are created at the same time as object):

- Line: With this tool, you can draw lines. Click on Preview to mark start point, then drag mouse pointer to the end point.
- Circle: With this tool, you can draw circles. Click on Preview to mark center, then drag mouse pointer to the wanted radius.
- Ellipse: With this tool, you can draw ellipses. Click on Preview to mark center, then drag mouse pointer to get the wanted size and form.
- Arc: With this tool, you can draw circle arcs. Click on Preview to set start point. Click again to set another arc point. Without releasing mouse button, drag pointer; when you release mouse button, the arc end point is placed and an arc encompassing these three points is drawn.
- Regular polygon: With this tool, you can create a regular polygon. Start with setting side number in Tool Options at the right of Preview. Then click on Preview to place center and, without releasing mouse button, drag pointer to get the wanted size and orientation.
- Star: With this tool, you can create a star. Start with setting side number (spikes) in Tool Options at the right of Preview. Then click on Preview to place center and, without releasing mouse button, drag pointer to get the wanted size and orientation.
- Spiral: With this tool, you can create a spiral. Start with setting spire number (sides) and spire orientation in Tool Options at the right of Preview. Then click on Preview to place center and, without releasing mouse button, drag pointer to get the wanted size.
- Bezier's Curve: With this tool, you can create Bezier's curves. Click on Preview to set start point and the other points: the curve will be created between these points. To end point creation press **Shift** key when creating last point.

Functions for object management In the middle of tool bar, you can find tools to manage objects:

- Move (Object): With this tool, you can move the active object. To enable an object, click on a control point created at the same time as the object.
- Move (Point): With this tool, you can click-and-drag one of the control points created at the same time as object. Each of these points moves the object in a different way.
- Copy: With this tool, you can duplicate an object. Click on an object control point and drag it to the wanted place.
- Delete: Click on an object control point to delete it.
- Select: With this tool, you can select an object to active it. Simply click on one of its control points.

Functions for object organisation At the right of tool bar, you can find tools for object superimposing (you can also get them by clicking on the drop-down list button if they are not visible). You have:

- Raise/Lower Selected Object: With this tool, you can push the selected object one level up or down.
- Raise/Lower selected object to top/bottom: self explanatory.

Functions for object display The drop-down list in tool bar offers you some more functions:

- Back/Forward: These functions allow you to jump from one object to another. Only this object is displayed.
- Show all objects: This function shows all objects again, after using both previous functions.

Preview field Preview comes with several options:

Settings In this area, you have several options to work with this filter.

Tool Options This area shows tool options.

Stroke If this option is checked, the object will be drawn. Two buttons are available, to select color and brush type.

Filling With help of this drop-down list, you can decide whether and how the object will be filled, with a color, a pattern or a gradient.

Show grid If this option is checked, a grid is applied on Preview to make object positioning easier.

Snap to Grid If this option is checked, objects will align to the grid.

Show image When this option is checked, the current image is displayed in Preview. If not checked, a white surface is shown and neither stroke color nor brush type are shown.

15.13.16 Sphere Designer

15.13.16.1 Overview

Figure 15.283: The same image, before and after the application of 'Sphere Designer' filter.

(a) *Original image*   (b) *Filter Sphere Designer applied*

This filter creates a three dimensional sphere with different textures. It replaces the original image.

15.13.16.2 Activating Sphere Designer

You can find this filter through Filters → Render → Sphere Designer.

15.13.16.3 Options

Figure 15.284: 'Sphere Designer' filter parameters

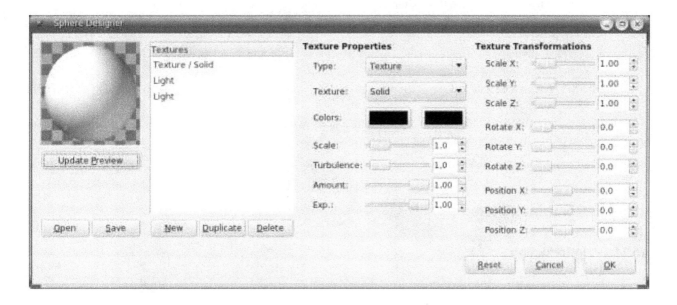

Preview All your setting changes will appear in the Preview without affecting the image until you click on OK. Note that the preview displays the whole image, even if the final result will concern a selection. Click the button *Update Preview* to see the result of the current settings.

Textures The list of textures applied to the sphere. There textures are applied in the order listed. Each item shows the type and the name of the texture.

New Creates a new texture and adds it to the end of the list. The name and the features of this new texture are the ones which are displayed in the Texture Properties area, but you can change them by operating in this area, provided that your new texture is highlighted.

Duplicate Duplicate: Copies the selected texture and adds the copy to the end of the list.

Delete Deletes the selected texture from the list.

Open/Save Allows to save current settings or load previously saved settings.

Texture properties

Type Determines the type of action on the sphere.

- Texture covers the sphere with a specific pattern.
- Bumpmap gives some relief to the texture.
- Light lets you set the parameters of the light shining on the sphere.

Texture Determines the pattern used by the texture type. If the texture applies to light then the light is distorted by this texture as if it was going through this texture before falling onto the sphere. If the texture applies to the texture itself, the texture is applied directly to the sphere. The following options are available: 'Solid', 'Checker', 'Marble', 'Lizard', 'Phong', 'Noise', 'Wood', 'Spiral' and 'Spots'.

Colors Sets the two colors to be used for a texture. By pressing the color button a color selection dialog appears.

Scale Determines the size of separate elements composing the texture. For example, for the 'Checker' texture this parameter determines the size of black and white squares. Value range is from 0 to 10.

Turbulence Determines the degree of texture distortion before applying the texture to the sphere. Value range is from 0 to 10. With values of up to 1.0 you can still make out the undistorted patterns; beyond that the texture gradually turns into noise.

Amount Determines the degree of influence the texture has on the final result. Value range is from 0 to 1. With the value of 0 the texture does not affect the result.

Exponent With the Wood texture, this options gives an aspect of venetian blind, more or less open.

Texture Transformations

Scale X/Y/Z Determines the degree of streching/compression of the texture on the sphere along the three directions. The value range is from 0 to 10.

Rotate X/Y/Z Determines the amount of a turn of the texture on the sphere around the three axes. The value range is from 0 to 360.

Position X/Y/Z Determines the position of the texture relative to the sphere. When type is Light, this parameter refers to the position of the light floodlighting the sphere.

Reset Sets all parameters to the default values.

15.14   Combine Filters

15.14.1   Introduction

The combine filters associate two or more images into a single image.

15.14.2   Depth Merge

Depth Merge is a Combine Filter which is useful to combine two different pictures or layers. You can decide which part of every image or layer will stay visible.

15.14.2.1   Overview

Every image is associated with a map which works as a mask. Simply create this map as a grayscale gradient: when applied onto the image, dark areas of the mask will show the underlying image and bright areas will mask the image.

Note

To work with this filter, images and maps must have the same size. All images to be selected must be present on screen.

You can also use this filter on an image with several layers. All layers will appear in the drop-down lists used to select images. These layers must have the same size.

15.14.2.2   Accessing this Filter

You can find this filter through Filters → Combine → Depth Merge

15.14.2.3 Options

Figure 15.285:

Source 1, Source 2 Defines the source images to use for the blending.

Depth Map Define the picture to use as transformation maps for the sources.

Overlap Creates soft transitions between images.

Offset This option shifts the merging limit, giving more or less importance to an image against the other.

Scale 1, Scale 2 Same as above for Offset, but more sensitive and applied to each map separatly. When you scale to a lower value, it will affect the map image's value, making it darker. So, black is more dominant in the merge and you will see more of the image.

15.14.2.4 Using example

Maps are grayscale gradients created with the Blend tool and modified with the Curve tool.

Figure 15.286: Source images and their maps

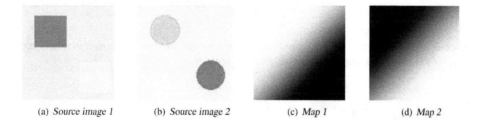

(a) *Source image 1*   (b) *Source image 2*   (c) *Map 1*   (d) *Map 2*

You can understand what's going on. Image-1 is treated by map-1: the red square is masked and the yellow square remains visible. Image-2 is treated by map-2: the red circle is masked and the green circle remains visible. In total, the green circle and the yellow square stay visible.

Figure 15.287: Results

(a) *No offset and no over-* *lap. The limit between both* *images is sharp and is sit-* *uated in the middle of the* *mask gradient.*

(b) *Offset = 0.980 : the* *limit, sharp, is shifted so* *that the image2 area is in-* *creased.*

(c) *Overlap: the limit is* *blurred.*

(d) *Scale 1 reduced to* *0.056 : as with Offset, the* *limit is shifted. Image-1* *area is increased.*

15.14.3   Film

15.14.3.1   Overview

Figure 15.288: Applying example for the Film filter

(a) *Original image*   (b) *Filter Film applied*

Film filter lets you merge several pictures into a photographic film drawing.

 Note
This filter does not invert colors, so it does not imitate negative film like the ones used to produce prints. Instead you should think of the result as an imitation of slide film or cinema film.

15.14.3.2   Accessing this Filter

You can find this filter through Filters → Combine → Film.

15.14.3.3   Options

Selection Options

Figure 15.289: 'Film' filter options (Selection)

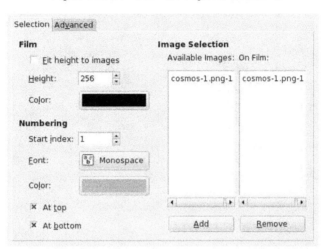

Fit Height to images Applies the height of original pictures to the resulting one.

Height This option lets you define the height of the resulting picture. If originals have different sizes, they will be scaled to this size.

Color By clicking on the color dwell you can define the color of the film (around and between pictures).

Start Index Defines the beginning number which will be used for the images.

Font Defines the font of digits.

Color By clicking on the the color dwell, you can define the font color of digits.

At Top, At Bottom Defines the position of the number.

Available Images Shows the pictures which can be used for merging. The pictures are the ones already opened in GIMP.

On Film Shows the pictures chosen to be merged.

Add This button allows the user to put an available image in the 'On film' section.

Remove This button allows to bring a picture from 'on Film ' to 'available images'. After that, the picture will not be used anymore in the resulting document.

Advanced Options

Figure 15.290: 'Film' filter options (Advanced)

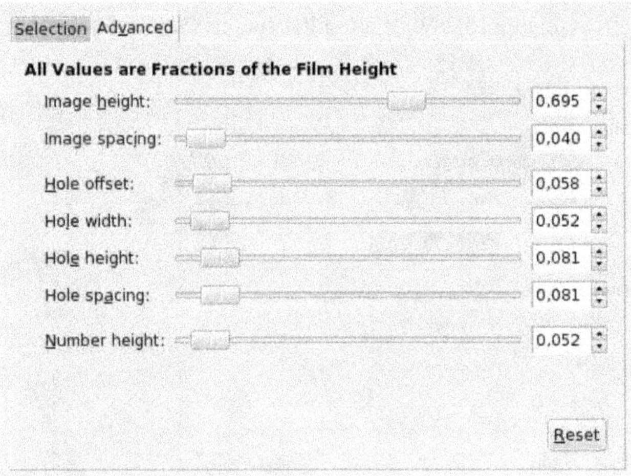

Image Height Defines the height of each pictures in the resulting image.

Image Spacing Defines the space between the pictures as they will be inserted in the future image.

Hole Offset Defines the hole position from image border.

Hole Width Defines the width of the holes in the resulting image.

Hole Height Defines the height of the holes in the resulting image.

Hole Spacing Defines the space between holes

Number Height Defines the height of the index number, proportionnaly to the height of the picture.

15.15 Animation Filters

These are animation helpers, which let you view and optimize your animations (by reducing their size). We gathered 'Optimize (Difference)' and 'Optimize (GIF)' filters together, because they are not much different.

15.15.1   Optimize

15.15.1.1   Overview

Figure 15.291: Example for the Optimize animation filters

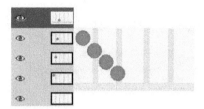

In this animation, the red ball goes downwards and past vertical bars. File size is 600 Kb.

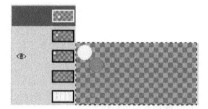

Optimize (Difference) : File size moved to 153 Kb. Layers held only the part the background which will be used to remove the trace of the red ball. The common part of layers is transparent.

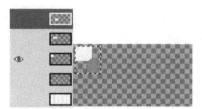

Optimize (GIF) : File size moved to 154 Kb, a bit bigger in the present example, bur layer size has been reduced. Layers held only a rectangular selection which includes the part of the background which will be used to remove the trace of the red ball. The common part of layers is transparent.

An animation can contain several layers and so its size can be important. This is annoying for a Web page. The Optimize filters let you reduce this size. Many elements are shared by all layers in an animation; so they can be saved only once instead of being saved in all layers, and what has changed in each layer can be saved only.

GIMP offers two Optimize filters: Optimize (Difference) and Optimize (GIF). Their result doesn't look very different.

15.15.1.2   Options

This Filter has no options.

15.15.2   Playback

15.15.2.1   Overview

This plug-in lets you play an animation from a multi-layers GIF, MNG or even XCF image, to test it.

15.15.2.2 Activate the filter

You can find this filter through Filters → Animation → Playback

15.15.2.3 Options

Figure 15.292: 'Playback' filter options

This dialog has :

Preview This preview of the animation automatically fits the frame size. The number of the displayed frame is shown below the preview.

Buttons Three buttons are available:

> **Play/Stop** Play/Stop to play or stop the animation.
>
> **Rewind** Rewind to re-launch the animation from start.
>
> **Step** Step to play the animation step by step.

15.16 Web Filters

Only one filter in this group for the moment: 'ImageMap'.

15.16.1 ImageMap

In Web sensitive images are frequently used to get some effects when defined areas are enabled by the pointer. Obviously the most used effect is a dynamic link to another web page when one of the sensitive areas is clicked on. This 'filter' allows you to design easily sensitive areas within an image. Web site design softwares have this as a standard function. In GIMP you can do this in a similar way.

15.16.1.1 Overview

This plug-in lets you design graphically and friendly all areas you want to delimit over your displayed image. You get the relevant part of html tags that must be merged into the right place in your page html code. You can define some actions linked to these areas too.

This is a complex tool which is not completely described here (it works about like Web page makers offering this function). However we want to describe here some of the most current handlings. If you want, you can find a more complete descriptions in Grokking the GIMP with the link [GROKKING02].

15.16.1.2   Activate the filter

From an image window, you can find this filter through Filters → Web → ImageMap

So you get this window:

Figure 15.293: Plug-in opened window

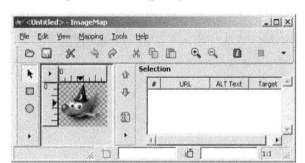

Opening example with Wilber's image

The window is a small one, but you can magnify it. The main useful areas are:

- completely on the left are vertically displayed icons, one for pointing, three for calling tools to generate various shape areas, one to edit zone properties, and finally one to erase a selected zone; you can call these functions with the Mapping menu,

- just on the right is your working area where you can draw all the shapes areas you want with the relevant tools,

- on the right is displayed an icon vertical set; its use is obvious but a help pop-up gives you some information about each function,

- finally, even on the right is a display area, as a property list of the created areas. A click on one item of the list selects automatically the corresponding shape in the working area,

15.16.1.3   Options

With the menu Edit → Preferences you can choose some web useful options within the different docks.

With the menu View you can work with a Grayscale display

With the menu Tools you can create guides and even regulary spaced rectangular areas.

Figure 15.294: ImageMap options

Example with circle and polygon areas

When you select a mapped area within the list, the corresponding shape is automatically selected in your working area; then you can modify it.

Caution

Contrary to other filters, this plug-in doesn't make an image but a text file. So you must save your work in a text format.

Tip

In the plug-in you can open the saved text file. The areas defined in your file will be loaded and overdisplayed; if the displayed image is not the original one or not with the same size, GIMP will ask you for adapting the scale.

Chapter 16

Keys and Mouse Reference

16.1 Help

Name

Help – Key reference for Help menu

Help

F1 Help

Shift+ F1 Context Help

16.2 Toolbox

Name

Toolbox – Key reference for Toolbox menu

Toolbox

TOOLS

R Rect Select

E Ellipse Select

F Free Select

Z Fuzzy Select

Shift+ O Select By Color

I Scissors

B Paths

O Color Picker

M Move

Shift+ C Crop and Resize

Shift+ R Rotate

Shift+ T Scale

Shift+ S Shear

Shift+ P Perspective

Shift+ F Flip

T Text

Shift+ B Bucket Fill

L Blend

N Pencil

P Paintbrush

Shift+ E Eraser

A Airbrush

K Ink

C Clone

V Convolve

S Smudge

Shift+ D Dodge/Burn

Note

Double click on the tool buttons opens the Tool Options dialog.

CONTEXT

X Swap Colors

D Default Colors

Note

Click on the colors to change the colors.

16.3 File

Name

File – Key reference for File menu

File

Ctrl+ N   New image

Ctrl+ O   Open image

Ctrl+ Alt+ O   Open image as new layer

Ctrl+ D   Duplicate image

Ctrl+ 1   Open recent image 01

Ctrl+ 2   Open recent image 02

Ctrl+ 3   Open recent image 03

Ctrl+ 4   Open recent image 04

Ctrl+ 5   Open recent image 05

Ctrl+ 6   Open recent image 06

Ctrl+ 7   Open recent image 07

Ctrl+ 8   Open recent image 08

Ctrl+ 9   Open recent image 09

Ctrl+ 0   Open recent image 10

Ctrl+ S   Save image

Shift+ Ctrl+ S   Save under a new name

Ctrl+ Q   Quit

16.4   Dialogs

Name

Dialogs – Key reference for Dialogs menu

Dialogs

Ctrl+ L   Layers

Shift+ Ctrl+ B   Brushes

Shift+ Ctrl+ P   Patterns

Ctrl+ G   Gradients

Shift+ Ctrl+ T   Tool-Options

Ctrl+ P   Palettes

Shift+ Ctrl+ I   Info window

Shift+ Ctrl+ N   Navigation window

Note

These open a new dialog window if it wasn't open yet, otherwise the corresponding dialog gets focus.

WITHIN A DIALOG

Alt+ F4, Ctrl+ W Close the window

Tab Jump to next widget

Shift+ Tab Jump to previous widget

Enter Set the new value

Space, Enter Activate current button or list

Ctrl+ Alt+ PgUp, Ctrl+ PgDn In a multi-tab dialog, switch tabs

Note

This accepts the new value you typed in a text field and returns focus to canvas.

WITHIN A FILE DIALOG

Shift+ L Open Location

Alt+ Up arrow Up-Folder

Alt+ Down arrow Down-Folder

Alt+ Home Home-Folder

Esc Close Dialog

16.5   View

Name

View – Key reference for View menu

View

WINDOW

F10 Main Menu

Shift+ F10, right click Drop-down Menu

F11 Toggle fullscreen

Shift+ Q Toggle quickmask

Ctrl+ W Close document window

Note

Menus can also be activated by Alt with the letter underscored in the menu name.

ZOOM

+ Zoom in

- Zoom out

1 Zoom 1:1

Ctrl+ E Shrink wrap

Shift+ Ctrl+ E Fit image in window

Shift+ mouse wheel Zoom

Note

This fits the windows to the image size.

SCROLLING (PANNING)

Ctrl+ arrows Scroll canvas

middle button drag Scroll canvas

mouse wheel Scroll canvas vertically

Ctrl+ mouse wheel Scroll canvas horizontally

Note

Scrolling by keys is accelerated, i.e. it speeds up when you press Shift+arrows, or jumps to the borders with Ctrl+arrows.

RULERS AND GUIDES

mouse drag Drag off a ruler to create guide

Ctrl+ mouse drag Drag a sample point out of the rulers

Shift+ Ctrl+ R Toggle rulers

Shift+ Ctrl+ T Toggle guides

Note

Drag off the horizontal or vertical ruler to create a new guideline. Drag a guideline onto the ruler to delete it.

16.6   Edit

Name

Edit – Key reference for Edit menu

Edit

UNDO/REDO

Ctrl+ Z   Undo

Ctrl+ Y   Redo

CLIPBOARD

Ctrl+ C   Copy selection

Ctrl+ X   Cut selection

Ctrl+ V   Paste clipboard

Ctrl+ K   Clears selection

Shift+ Ctrl+ C   Named copy selection

Shift+ Ctrl+ X   Named cut selection

Shift+ Ctrl+ V   Named paste clipboard

 Note
This places a copy of the selection to the GIMP clipboard.

FILL

Ctrl+ D   Fill with FG Color

Ctrl+ D   Fill with BG Color

Ctrl+ D   Fill with Pattern

16.7   Layers

Name

Layers – Key reference for Layers menu

Layers

PgUp, Ctrl+ Tab Select the layer above

PgDn, Shift+ Ctrl+ Tab Select the layer below

Home Select the first layer

End Select the last layer

Ctrl+ M Merge visible layers

Ctrl+ H Anchar layer

16.8 Selections

Name

Selections – Key reference for Selections menu

Selections

Ctrl+ T Toggle selections

Ctrl+ A Select all

Shift+ Ctrl+ A Select none

Ctrl+ I Invert selection

Shift+ Ctrl+ L Float selection

Shift+ V Path to selection

16.9 Plug-ins

Name

Plug-ins – Key reference for Plug-ins menu

Plug-ins

Ctrl+ F Repeat last plug-in

Shift+ Ctrl+ F Reshow last plug-in

16.10 Zoom tool

Name

Zoom tool – Key reference for Zoom tool menu

Zoom tool

click Zoom in

Shift+ click Zoom out

mouse drag Zoom into the area

Chapter 17

Glossary

A B C D F G H I J L M P Q R S T U X Y

A

Alpha

An Alpha value indicates the transparency of a pixel. The smaller the alpha value of a pixel, the more visible the colors below it. A pixel with an alpha value of 0 is completely transparent.

Within GIMP, Alpha values can be associated with the image as a whole (the Alpha Channel) and with individual layers (a Layer Mask). You can view these by using the Channels dialog and the Layers dialog, respectively.

With some image file formats, you can only specify that a pixel is completely transparent or completely opaque. Other file formats allow a variable level of transparency.

Alpha Channel   An Alpha Channel represents the transparency of the image. Imagine you can see through the image. This Alpha Channel is automatically added to the image as soon as you add a second layer. You can see it in the Channels Dialog. It gives the possibility to be transparent to layers. But this possibility is not given to the background layer : for this, you must use the 'Add an Alpha Channel' command.

You can also consider that an Alpha channel, although not visible, is added to every layer, except to the background layer. The image Alpha channel is the sum of the Alpha channels of layers.

See also Alpha channel example.

Antialiasing

Antialiasing is the process of reversing an alias, that is, reducing the 'jaggies'. Antialiasing produces smoother curves by adjusting the boundary between the background and the pixel region that is being antialiased. Generally, pixel intensities or opacities are changed so that a smoother transition to the background is achieved. With selections, the opacity of the edge of the selection is appropriately reduced.

B

Bezier curve

A spline is a curve which is defined mathematically and has a set of control points. A Bezier spline is a cubic spline which has four control points, where the first and last control points (knots or anchors) are the endpoints of the curve and the inner two control points (handles) determine the direction of the curve at the endpoints.

In the non-mathematical sense, a spline is a flexible strip of wood or metal used for drawing curves. Using this type of spline for drawing curves dates back to shipbuilding, where weights were hung on splines to bend them. The outer control points of a Bezier spline are similar to the places where the splines are fastened down and the inner control points are where weights are attached to modify the curve.

Bezier splines are only one way of mathematically representing curves. They were developed in the 1960s by Pierre Bezier, who worked for Renault.

Bezier curves are used in GIMP as component parts of Paths.

The image above shows a Bezier curve. Points P0 and P3 are points on the Path, which are created by clicking with the mouse. Points P1 and P2 are handles, which are automatically created by GIMP when you click on the line between P0 and P3 and stretch it. They change position when you stretch the curve in different ways.

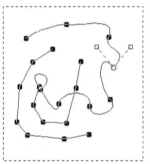

The image above shows a path which consists of two components, having both straight and curved segments, being worked on with the Path tool. Here, the open circle indicates the selected anchor and the two open squares are the two handles which are associated with this anchor from the curves on either side of it.

Bitmap

From *The Free On-line Dictionary of Computing (13 Mar 01)* :

> bitmap — A data file or structure which corresponds bit for bit with an image displayed on a screen, probably in the same format as it would be stored in the display's video memory or maybe as a device independent bitmap. A bitmap is characterised by the width and height of the image in pixels and the number of bits per pixel which determines the number of shades of grey or colours it can represent. A bitmap representing a coloured image (a 'pixmap') will usually have pixels with between one and eight bits for each of the red, green, and blue components, though other colour encodings are also used. The green component sometimes has more bits than the other two to cater for the human eye's greater discrimination in this component.

BMP

BMP is an uncompressed image file format designed by Microsoft and mainly used in Windows. Colors are typically represented in 1, 4 or 8 bits, although the format also supports more. Because it is not compressed and the files are large, it is not very well suited for use in the internet.

Bump mapping

Bump mapping is a technique for displaying extremely detailed objects without increasing the geometrical complexity of the objects. It is especially used in 3-dimensional visualization programs. The trick is to put all the necessary information into a texture, with which shadowing is shown on the surface of the object.

Bump mapping is only one (very effective) way of simulating surface irregularities which are not actually contained in the geometry of the model.

C

Channels

A Channel is a single component of a pixel's color. For a colored pixel in GIMP, these components are usually Red, Green, Blue and sometimes transparency (Alpha). For a Grayscale image, they are Gray and Alpha and for an Indexed color image, they are Indexed and Alpha.

The entire rectangular array of any one of the color components for all of the pixels in an image is also referred to as a Channel. You can see these color channels with the Channels dialog.

When the image is displayed, GIMP puts these components together to form the pixel colors for the screen, printer, or other output device. Some output devices may use different channels from Red, Green and Blue. If they do, GIMP's channels are converted into the appropriate ones for the device when the image is displayed.

Channels can be useful when you are working on an image which needs adjustment in one particular color. For example, if you want to remove 'red eye' from a photograph, you might work on the Red channel.

You can look at channels as masks which allow or restrict the output of the color that the channel represents. By using Filters on the channel information, you can create many varied and subtle effects on an image. A simple example of using a Filter on the color channels is the Channel Mixer filter.

In addition to these channels, GIMP also allows you to create other channels (or more correctly, Channel Masks), which are displayed in the lower part of the Channels dialog. You can convert a selection to a channel mask by using the Save to Channel command. You can also create a channel by right-clicking in the Channels dialog and using the New channel command. See the glossary entry on Masks for more information about Channel Masks.

Clipboard

The Clipboard is a temporary area of memory which is used to transfer data between applications or documents. It is used when you Cut, Copy or Paste data in GIMP.

The clipboard is implemented slightly differently under different operating systems. Under Linux/XFree, GIMP uses the XFree clipboard for text and the GIMP internal image clipboard for transferring images between image documents. Under other operating systems, the clipboard may work somewhat differently. See the GIMP documentation for your operating system for further information.

The basic operations provided by the clipboard are 'Cut', 'Copy', and 'Paste'. Cut means that the item is removed from the document and copied to the clipboard. Copy leaves the item in the document and copies it to the clipboard. Paste copies the contents of the clipboard to the document. The GIMP makes an intelligent decision about what to paste depending upon the target. If the target is a canvas, the Paste operation uses the image clipboard. If the target is a text entry box, the paste operation uses the text clipboard.

Color depth

Color Depth is simply the number of bits used to represent a color (bits per pixel : bpp). There are 3 channels for a pixel (for Red, Green and Blue). GIMP can supprt 8 bits per channel, referred as *eight-bit color*. So, GIMP color depth is 8 * 3 = 24, which allows 256 * 256 * 256 = 16,777,216 possible colors (8 bits allow 256 colors).

Color model

A color model is a way of describing and specifying a color. The term is often used loosely to refer to both a color space system and the color space on which it is based.

A color space is a set of colors which can be displayed or recognized by an input or output device (such as a scanner, monitor, printer, etc.). The colors of a color space are specified as values in a color space system, which is a coordinate system in which the individual colors are described by coordinate values on various axes. Because of the structure of the human eye, there are three axes in color spaces which are intended for human observers. The practical application of that is that colors are specified with three components (with a few exceptions). There are about 30 to 40 color space systems in use. Some important examples are:

- RGB
- HSV
- CMY(K)

- YUV
- YCbCr

CMY, CMYK

CMYK is a color model which has components for Cyan, Magenta, Yellow and Black. It is a subtractive color model, and that fact is important when an image is printed. It is complementary to the RGB color model.

The values of the individual colors vary between 0% and 100%, where 0% corresponds to an unprinted color, and 100% corresponds to a completely printed area of color. Colors are formed by mixing the three basic colors.

The last of these values, K (Black), doesn't contribute to the color, but merely serves to darken the other colors. The letter K is used for Black to prevent confusion, since B usually stands for Blue.

Figure 17.1: Subtractive color model

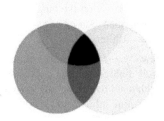

GIMP does not currently support the CMYK model. (An experimental plug-in providing rudimentary CMYK support can be found [PLUGIN-SEPARATE].)

This is the mode used in printing. These are the colors in the ink cartridges in your printer. It is the mode used in painting and in all the objects around us, where light is reflected, not emmitted. Objects absorb part of the light waves and we see only the reflected part. Note that the cones in our eyes see this reflected light in RGB mode. An object appears Red because Green and Blue have been absorbed. Since the combination of Green and Blue is Cyan, Cyan is absorbed when you add Red. Conversely, if you add Cyan, its complementary color, Red, is absorbed. This system is *subtractive*. If you add Yellow, you decrease Blue, and if you add Magenta, you decrease Green.

It would be logical to think that by mixing Cyan, Magenta and Yellow, you would subtract Red, Green and Blue, and the eye would see no light at all, that is, Black. But the question is more complex. In fact, you would see a dark brown. That is why this mode also has a Black value, and why your printer has a Black cartridge. It is less expensive that way. The printer doesn't have to mix the other three colors to create an imperfect Black, it just has to add Black.

D

Dithering

Dithering is a technique used in computer graphics to create the illusion of more colors when displaying an image which has a low color depth. In a dithered image, the missing colors are reproduced by a certain arrangement of pixels in the available colors. The human eye perceives this as a mixture of the individual colors.

The Gradient tool uses dithering. You may also choose to use dithering when you convert an image to Indexed format. If you are working on an image with indexed colors, some tools (such as the pattern fill tool) may also use dithering, if the correct color is not available in the colormap.

The Newsprint filter uses dithering as well. You can use the NL Filter (Non Linear filter) to remove unwanted dithering noise from your image.

Also note that although GIMP itself uses 24-bit colors, your system may not actually be able to display that many colors. If it doesn't, then the software in between GIMP and your system may also dither colors while displaying them.

See also the glossary entry on Floyd-Steinberg dithering, which is used in GIMP.

F

File Format

A file format or file type is the form in which computer data is stored. Since a file is stored by an operating system as a linear series of bytes, which cannot describe many kinds of real data in an obvious way, conventions have been developed for interpreting the information as representations of complex data. All of the conventions for a particular 'kind' of file constitute a file format.

Some typical file formats for saving images are JPEG, TIFF, PNG and GIF. The best file format for saving an image depends upon how the image is intended to be used. For example, if the image is intended for the internet, file size is a very important factor, and if the image is intended to be printed, high resolution and quality have greater significance. See Format types.

Feathering

GIMP uses the process of Feathering to make a smooth transition between a region and the background by softly blending the edges of the region.

In GIMP, you can feather the edges of a selection. Brushes can also have feathered edges.

Floating Selection

A floating selection (sometimes called a 'floating layer') is a type of temporary layer which is similar in function to a normal layer, except that a floating selection must be anchored before you can resume working on any other layers in the image. You can use various operations to change the image data on the floating selection. There can only be one floating selection in an image at a time.

You can anchor a floating selection in various ways. First, you can create a New layer. If you create a new layer while there is a floating selection, the floating selection is anchored to it. Second, you can anchor the floating selection to the current layer, the selection is originating from. To do this, click anywhere on the image except on the floating selection. This merges the floating selection with the current layer. You can also anchor the floating selection to the current layer by clicking on the anchor button of the Layers dialog or using the Anchor layer command (Ctrl-H).

There are also various ways to create a floating selection. The first is to convert an existing selection into a floating selection with the Float command. The 'paste' operations, Paste Named Buffer, Paste or Paste Into, also create a floating selection. In addition, the Transform tools, Flip, Shear, Scale, Rotate and Perspective, create a floating selection when they are used on a selection, rather than a layer. When the Affect mode is *Transform Layer* and a selection already exists, these tools transform the selection and create a floating selection with the result. If a selection does not exist, they transform the current layer and do not create a floating selection. (If the Affect mode is *Transform Selection*, they also do not create a floating selection.) You can also create a floating selection by clicking on a selection and dragging it.

Floating selections are a rest of the time when GIMP did not use layers. They have no practical use, but you must know what you have to do with them.

Floyd-Steinberg Dithering

Floyd-Steinberg dithering is a method of dithering which was first published in 1976 by Robert W. Floyd and Louis Steinberg. The dithering process begins in the upper left corner of the image. For each pixel, the closest available color in the palette is chosen and the difference between that color and the original color is computed in each RGB channel. Then specific fractions of these differences are dispersed among several adjacent pixels which haven't yet been visited (below and to the right of the original pixel). Because of the order of processing, the procedure can be done in a single pass over the image.

When you convert an image to Indexed mode, you can choose between two variants of Floyd-Steinberg dithering.

G

Gamma

Gamma or gamma correction is a non-linear operation which is used to encode and decode luminance or color values in video or still image systems. It is used in many types of imaging systems to straighten out a curved signal-to-light or intensity-to-signal response. For example, the light emitted by a CRT is not linear with regard to its input voltage, and the voltage from an electric camera is not linear with regard to the intensity (power) of the light in the scene. Gamma encoding helps to map the data into a perceptually linear domain, so that the limited signal range (the limited number of bits in each RGB signal) is better optimized perceptually.

Gamma is used as an exponent (power) in the correction equation. Gamma compression (where gamma < 1) is used to encode linear luminance or RGB values into color signals or digital file values, and gamma expansion (where gamma > 1) is the decoding process, and usually occurs where the current-to-voltage function for a CRT is non-linear.

For PC video, images are encoded with a gamma of about 0.45 and decoded with a gamma of 2.2. For Mac systems, images are typically encoded with a gamma of about 0.55 and decoded with a gamma of 1.8. The sRGB color space standard used for most cameras, PCs and printers does not use a simple exponential equation, but has a decoding gamma value near 2.2 over much of its range.

In GIMP, gamma is an option used in the brush tab of the GIMPressionist filter and in the Flame filter. The display filters also include a Gamma filter. Also see the Levels Tool, where you can use the middle slider to change the gamma value.

GIF

GIF™ stands for Graphics Interchange Format. It is a file format with good, lossless compression for images with low color depth (up to 256 different colors per image). Since GIF was developed, a new format called Portable Network Graphics (PNG) has been developed, which is better than GIF in all respects, with the exception of animations and some rarely-used features.

GIF was introduced by CompuServe in 1987. It became popular mostly because of its efficient, LZW compression. The size of the image files required clearly less disk space than other usual graphics formats of the time, such as PCX or MacPaint. Even large images could be transmitted in a reasonable time, even with slow modems. In addition, the open licensing policy of CompuServe made it possible for any programmer to implement the GIF format for his own applications free of charge, as long as the CompuServe copyright notice was attached to them.

Colors in GIF are stored in a color table which can hold up to 256 different entries, chosen from 16.7 million different color values. When the image format was introduced, this was not a much of a limitation, since only a few people had hardware which could display more colors than that. For typical drawings, cartoons, black-and-white photographs and similar uses, 256 colors are quite sufficient as a rule, even today. For more complex images, such as color photgraphs, however, a huge loss of quality is apparent, which is why the format is not considered to be suitable for those purposes.

One color entry in the palette can be defined to be transparent. With transparency, the GIF image can look like it is non-rectangular in shape. However, semi-transparency, as in PNG, is not possible. A pixel can only be either entirely visible or completely transparent.

The first version of GIF was 87a. In 1989, CompuServe published an expanded version, called 89a. Among other things, this made it possible to save several images in one GIF file, which is especially used for simple animation. The version number can be distinguished from the first six bytes of a GIF file. Interpreted as ASCII symbols, they are 'GIF87a' or 'GIF89a'.

GNU

The GNU project was started in 1983 by Richard Stallman with the goal of developing a completely free operating system. It is especially well-known from the GNU General Public License (GPL) and GNU/Linux, a GNU-variant with a Linux kernel.

The name came about from the naming conventions which were in practice at MIT, where Stallman worked at the time. For programs which were similar to other programs, recursive acronyms were chosen as names. Since the new system was to be based on the widespread operating system, Unix, Stallman looked for that kind of name and came up with GNU, which stands for 'GNU is not Unix'. In order to avoid confusion, the name should be pronounced with the 'G', not like 'new'. There were several reasons for making GNU Unix-compatible. For one thing, Stallman was convinced that most companies would refuse a completely new operating system, if the programs they used wouldn't run on it. In addition, the architecture of Unix made quick, easy and distributed development possible, since Unix consists of many small programs that can be developed independently of each other, for the most part. Also, many parts of a Unix system were freely available to anyone and could therefore be directly integrated into GNU, for example, the typesetting system, TeX, or the X Window System. The missing parts were newly written from the ground up.

GIMP (GNU Image Manipulation Program) is an official GNU application [WKPD-GNU].

Grayscale

Grayscale is a mode for encoding the colors of an image which contains only black, white and shades of gray.

When you create a new image, you can choose to create it in Grayscale mode (which you can colorize later, by changing it to RGB mode). You can also change an existing image to grayscale by using the Grayscale, Desaturate, Decompose, Channel Mixer, although not all formats will accept these changes. Although you can create images in Grayscale mode and convert images to it, it is not a color model, in the true sense of the word.

As explained in RGB mode, 24-bit GIMP images can have up to 256 levels of gray. If you change from Grayscale to RGB mode, your image will have an RGB structure with three color channels, but of course, it will still be gray.

Grayscale image files (8-bit) are smaller than RGB files.

Guides

Guides are lines you can temporarily display on an image while you are working on it. You can display as many guides as you would like, in either the horizontal or the vertical direction. These lines help you position a selection or a layer on the image. They do not appear when the image is printed.

To create a guide, simply click on one of the rulers in the image window and pull out a guide, while holding the mouse button pressed. The guide is then displayed as a blue, dashed line, which follows the pointer. As soon as you create a guide, the 'Move' tool is activated and the mouse pointer changes to the Move icon.

You can also create a guide with the New Guide command, which allows you to precisely place the guide on the image, the New Guide (by Percent) command, or the New Guides from Selection command.

The behavior of the guides depends upon the Affect mode of the 'Move' tool. When *Transform Layer* mode is selected, the mouse pointer turns into a small hand as soon as it gets close to a guide. Then the guide is activated and it turns red, and you can move the guide or delete it by moving it back into the ruler. If *Transform Selection* mode is selected, you can position a guide, but you cannot move it after that.

To make it easier for you to position image elements, you can 'magnetize' the guides with the Snap to Guides command. You can remove the guides with the Remove all guides command. You can enable and disable displaying the guides without removing them by using the Show Guides command.

For more information about guides, see the Grids and Guides section.

H

Hextriplet

A hex triplet is a way of encoding a color for a computer. The '#' symbol indicates that the numbers which follow it are encoded in hexadecimal. Each color is specified in two hexadecimal digits which make up a triplet (three pairs) of hexadecimal values in the form '#rrggbb', where 'rr' represents red, 'gg' represents green and 'bb' represents blue.

Histogram

In digital image processing, a histogram is a graph representing the statistical frequency of the gray values or the color values in an image. The histogram of an image tells you about the occurrence of gray values or color values, as well as the contrast range and the brightness of the image. In a color image, you can create one histogram with information about all possible colors, or three histograms for the individual color channels. The latter makes the most sense, since most procedures are based on grayscale images and therefore further processing is immediately possible.

HSV

HSV is a color model which has components for Hue (the color, such as blue or red), Saturation (how strong the color is) and Value (the brightness).

The RGB mode is very well suited to computer screens, but it doesn't let us describe what we see in everyday life; a light green, a pale pink, a dazzling red, etc. The HSV model takes these characteristics into account. HSV and RGB are not completely independent of each other. You can see that with the Color Picker tool; when you change a color in one of the color models, the other one also changes. Brave souls can read *Grokking the GIMP*, which explains their interrelationship.

- Hue: This is the color itself, which results from the combination of primary colors. All shades (except for the gray levels) are represented in a *chromatic circle*: yellow, blue, and also purple, orange, etc. The chromatic circle (or 'color wheel') values range between 0 and 360. (The term 'color' is often used instead of 'Hue'. The RGB colors are 'primary colors'.)

- Saturation : This value describes how pale the color is. A completely unsaturated color is a shade of gray. As the saturation increases, the color becomes a pastel shade. A completely saturated color is pure. Saturation values go from 0 to 100, from white to the purest color.

- Value : This value describes the luminosity, the luminous intensity. It is the amount of light emitted by a color. You can see a change of luminosity when a colored object is moved from being in the shadow to being in the sun, or when you increase the luminosity of your screen. Values go from 0 to 100. Pixel values in the three channels are also luminosities: 'Value' in the HSV color model is the maximum of these elementary values in the RGB space (scaled to 0-100).

Image Hose

An image hose in GIMP is a special type of brush which consists of several images. For example, you could have a brush with footprints, which consists of two images, one for the left footprint and one for the right. While painting with this brush, a left footprint would appear first, then a right footprint, then a left one, etc. This type of brush is very powerful.

An image hose is also sometimes called an 'image pipe' or 'animated brush'. An image hose is indicated in the Brushes dialog by a small red triangle in the lower right corner of the brush's symbol.

For information concerning creating an image hose, please see the Using Animated Brushes and Using Brushes sections.

Incremental, paint mode

Incremental mode is a paint mode where each brush stroke is drawn directly on the active layer. When it is set, each additional stroke of the brush increases the effect of the brush, up to the maximum opacity for the brush.

If incremental mode is not set, brush strokes are drawn on a canvas buffer, which is then combined with the active layer. The maximum effect of a brush is then determined by the opacity, and stroking with the brush repeatedly does not increase the effect beyond this limit.

The two images above were created using a brush with spacing set to 60 pixels. The image on the left shows non-incremental painting and the image on the right shows the difference with incremental painting.

Incremental mode is a tool option that is shared by several brush tools, except those which have a 'rate' control, which automatically implies an incremental effect. You can set it by checking the Incremental checkbox in the toolbox for the tool (Paintbrush, Pencil and Eraser).

Indexed Colors

Indexed color mode is a mode for encoding colors in an image where each pixel in the image is assigned an 8-bit color number. The color which corresponds to this number is then put in a table (the palette). Changing a color in the palette changes all the pixels which refer to this palette color. Although you can create images in *Indexed Color* mode and can transform images to it, it is, strictly speaking, not a color model.

See also the Indexed Palette section and the Convert Image to Indexed Colors command.

Interpolation

Interpolation means calculating intermediate values. When you enlarge ('digitally zoom') or otherwise transform (rotate, shear or give perspective to) a digital image, interpolation procedures are used to compute the colors of the pixels in the transformed image. GIMP offers three interpolation methods, which differ in quality and speed. In general, the better the quality, the more time the interpolation takes. The methods are:

- *None* (sometimes called 'Nearest Neighbor'): The color of each pixel is copied from its closest neighboring pixel in the original image. This often results in aliasing (the 'stair-step' effect) and a coarse image, but it is the fastest method.

- *Linear* (sometimes called 'Bilinear'): The color of each pixel is computed as the average color of the four closest pixels in the original image. This gives a satisfactory result for most images and is a good compromise between speed and quality.

- *Cubic* (sometimes called 'Bicubic'): The color of each pixel is computed as the average color of the eight closest pixels in the original image. This usually gives the best result, but it naturally takes more time.

GIMP uses interpolation when you Scale an image, Scale a layer, and when you Transform an image. You can also set the default interpolation method in the Tools Options Preferences dialog.

J

JPEG

JPEG is a file format which supports compression and works at all color depths. The image compression is adjustable, but beware: Too high a compression could severely reduce image quality, since JPEG compression is lossy.

Use JPEG to create web graphics or if you don't want your image to take up a lot of space. JPEG is a good format for photographs and for computer-generated images (CGI). It is not well suited for:

- digital line drawings (for example, screenshots or vector graphics), in which there are many neighboring pixels with the same color values, few colors and hard edges,

- Black and white images (only black and white, one bit per pixel) or

- half-toned images (newsprint).

Other formats, such as GIF, PNG or JBIG, are far better for these kinds of images.

In general, JPEG transformations are not reversible. Opening and then saving a JPEG file causes a new, lossy compression. Increasing the quality factor later will not bring back the image information which was lost.

L

L*a*b

The Lab color space (also called the L*a*b color space) is a color model developed in the beginning of the 1930s by the Commission Internationale d'Eclairage (CIE). It includes all the colors that the human eye can perceive. That contains the colors of the RGB and the CMYK color spaces, among others. In Lab, a color is indicated by three values: L, a and b. Here, the L stands for the luminance component — corresponding to the gray value — and a and b represent the red-green and blue-yellow parts of the color, respectively.

In contrast to RGB or CMYK, Lab is not dependent upon the various input and output devices. For that reason, it is used as an exchange format between devices. Lab is also the internal color model of PostScript Level II.

Layer

You can think of layers as being a stack of slides which are more or less transparent. Each layer represents an aspect of the image and the image is the sum of all of these aspects. The layer at the bottom of the stack is the background layer. The layers above it are the components of the foreground.

You can view and manage the layers of the image through the Layers dialog.

Representation of an image with layers:

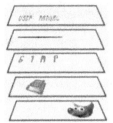

The final image:

M

Marching Ants

Marching ants is a term which describes the dotted line which surrounds a selection. The line is animated, so it looks as if little ants are running around behind each other.

You can disable the marching ants by unchecking the View → Show Selection option or by using the keyboard shortcut Ctrl-T.

Masks

A mask is like a veil put over a layer (layer mask) or all the layers of an image (selection mask). You can remove this mask by painting with white color, and you can complete it by painting with black color. When the mask is 'applied', non masked pixels will remain visible (the others will be transparent) or will be selected, according to the type of mask.

There are two types of masks:

- *Layer Mask* : Every layer can have its own mask. The layer mask represents the Alpha channel of the layer and allows you to manage its transparency. By painting on the layer mask, you can make parts of the layer opaque or transparent: painting with black makes the layer transparent, painting with white makes the layer opaque and painting with shades of gray makes the layer semi-transparent. You can use all paint tools to paint on the mask. You can also apply a filter or copy-paste. You can use the Layer mask for transition effects, volume effects, merging elements from another image, etc. See the Layer Mask section for more details.

- *Channel Mask*, also called *Selection Mask*: Channel Masks determine the transparency of a selection. By painting on a Channel Mask with white, you remove the mask and increase the selection; with black, you reduce the selection. This procedure lets you create a selection very precisely. You can also save your selections to a Channel Mask with the Save to Channel command. You can retrieve it later by using the 'Channel to selection' command from the Channel menu. Channel masks are so important in GIMP that a special type has been implemented: the Quick mask. See the Selection mask section for more details.

Moiré Effect

The moiré effect (pronounce 'Moa-ray')is an unintended pattern which appears when a regular pattern of grids or lines interferes with another regular pattern placed over it. This can happen, for example, when you are scanning an image with a periodic structure (such as a checkered shirt or a half-toned image), scanning a digital image, taking a digital photograph of a periodic pattern, or even when silkscreening.

If you discover the problem in time, the best solution is to move the original image a little bit in the scanner or to change the camera angle slightly.

If you cannot re-create the image file, GIMP offers some filters which may help you with the problem. For more information, see the Despeckle and NL Filter (Non-Linear) filters.

P

Parasite

A Parasite is additional data which may be written to an XCF file. A parasite is identified by a name, and can be thought of as an extension to the other information in an XCF file.

Parasites of an image component may be read by GIMP plug-ins. Plug-ins may also define their own parasite names, which are ignored by other plug-ins. Examples of parasites are comments, the save options for the TIFF, JPEG and PNG file formats, the gamma value the image was created with and EXIF data.

Path

A Path is a contour composed of straight lines, curves, or both. In GIMP, it is used to form the boundary of a selection, or to be *stroked* to create visible marks on an image. Unless a path is stroked, it is not visible when the image is printed and it is not saved when the image is written to a file (unless you use XCF format).

See the Paths Concepts and Using Paths sections for basic information on paths, and the Path Tool section for information on how to create and edit paths. You can manage the paths in your image with the Paths dialog.

PDB

All of the functions which GIMP and its extensions make available are registered in the Procedure Database (PDB). Developers can look up useful programming information about these functions in the PDB by using the Procedure Browser.

PDF

PDF (Portable Document Format) is a file format which was developed by Adobe to address some of the deficiencies of PostScript. Most importantly, PDF files tend to be much smaller than equivalent PostScript files. As with PostScript, GIMP's support of the PDF format is through the free Ghostscript libraries.

Pixel

A pixel is a single dot, or 'picture element', of an image. A rectangular image may be composed of thousands of pixels, each representing the color of the image at a given location. The value of a pixel typically consists of several Channels, such as the Red, Green and Blue components of its color, and sometimes its Alpha (transparency).

Plugin

Optional extensions for the GIMP. Plugins are external programs that run under the control of the main GIMP application and provide specific functions on-demand. See Section 11.1 for further information.

PostScript

Created by Adobe, PostScript is a page description language mainly used by printers and other output devices. It's also an excellent way to distribute documents. GIMP does not support PostScript directly: it depends on a powerful free software program called Ghostscript.

The great power of PostScript is its ability to represent vector graphics—lines, curves, text, paths, etc.—in a resolution-independent way. PostScript is not very efficient, though, when it comes to representing pixel-based raster graphics. For this reason, PostScript is not a good format to use for saving images that are later going to be edited using GIMP or another graphics program.

Linux distributions almost always come with Ghostscript already installed (not necessarily the most recent version). For other operating systems, you may have to install it yourself. Here are instructions for installing it on Windows:

- Go to the Ghostscript project page on Sourceforge [GHOSTSCRIPT].

- Look for the package gnu-gs or ghostscript (for non-commercial use only) and go to the download section.

- Download one of the prepared Windows distributions, such as gs650w32.exe or gs700w32.exe.

- Start the executable and follow the instructions of the installation procedure.

- Copy the executable gswin32c.exe from the bin directory of the Ghostscript installation to the Windows directory (or any other directory that is contained in the PATH). As an alternative, advanced users can set an environment variable, GS_PROG, to point to gswin32c.exe (e.g. C:\gs\gsX.YY\bin\gswin32c.exe).

Now you should be able to read PostScript files with GIMP. Please note that you must not move the Ghostscript directories once the installation is complete. The installation creates registry entries which allow Ghostscript to find its libraries. (These instructions courtesy of http://www.kirchgessner.net.)

PNG

PNG is the acronym of 'Portable Network Graphic' (pronounce 'ping'. This recent format offers many advantages and a few drawbacks: it is not lossy and gives files more heavy than the JPEG format, but it is perfect for saving your images because you can save them several times without losing data each time (it is used for this Help). It supports True Colors (several millions of colors), indexed images (256 colors like GIF), and 256 transparency levels (while GIF supports only two levels). Unfortunately, Microsoft Internet Explorer recognizes only two transparency levels).

PSD

PSD is Adobe Photoshop's native file format, and it is therefore comparable to XCF in complexity. GIMP's ability to handle PSD files is sophisticated but limited: some features of PSD files are not loaded, and only older versions of PSD are supported. Unfortunately, Adobe has now made the Photoshop Software Development Kit — which includes their file format specifications — proprietary, and only available to a limited set of developers approved by Adobe. This does not include the GIMP development team, and the lack of information makes it very difficult to maintain up-to-date support for PSD files.

PSD is Adobe Photoshop's native file format, and it is therefore comparable to XCF in complexity. GIMP's ability to handle PSD files is sophisticated but limited: some features of PSD files are not loaded, and only older versions of PSD are supported. Unfortunately, Adobe has now made the Photoshop Software Development Kit — which includes their file format specifications — proprietary, and only available to a limited set of developers approved by Adobe. This does not include the GIMP development team, and the lack of information makes it very difficult to maintain up-to-date support for PSD files.

Q

Quantization

Quantization is the process of reducing the color of a pixel into one of a number of fixed values by matching the color to the nearest color in the colormap. Actual pixel values may have far more precision than the discrete levels which can be displayed by a digital display. If the display range is too small, then abrupt changes in colors (false contours, or banding) may appear where the color intensity changes from one level to another. This is especially noticeable in Indexed images, which have 256 or fewer discrete colors.

One way to reduce quantization effects is to use Dithering. The operations in GIMP which perform dithering are the Blend tool (if you have enabled the dithering option) and the Convert to Indexed command. However, they only work on RGB images and not on Indexed images.

R

RGB

Figure 17.2: Additive color model

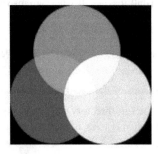

RGB is a color model which has components for Red, Green and Blue. These colors are emitted by screen elements and not reflected as they are with paint. The resulting color is a combination of the three primary RGB colors, with different degrees of lightness. If you look closely at your television screen, whose pitch is less than that of a computer screen, you can see the red, green and blue elements lit with different intensities. The RGB color model is *additive*.

GIMP uses eight bits per channel for each primary color. That means there are 256 intensities (Values) available, resulting in 256×256×256 = 16,777,216 colors.

It is not obvious why a given combination of primary colors produces a particular color. Why, for instance, does 229R+205G+229B give a shade of pink? This depends upon the human eye and brain. There is no color in nature, only a continuous spectrum of wavelengths of light. There are three kinds of cones in the retina. The same wavelength of light acting upon the three types of cones stimulates each of them differently, and the mind has learned, after several million years of evolution, how to recognize a color from these differences.

It is easy to see that no light (0R+0G+0B) produces complete darkness, black, and that full light (255R+255G+255B) produces white. Equal intensity on all color channels produces a level of gray. That is why there can only be 256 gray levels in GIMP.

Mixing two *Primary colors* in RGB mode gives a *Secondary color*, that is, a color in the CMY model. Thus combining Red and Green gives Yellow, Green and Blue give Cyan, Blue and Red give Magenta. Don't confuse secondary colors with *Complementary colors* which are directly opposite a primary color in the chromatic circle:

Le mélange des *couleurs primaires* deux à deux en mode RVB donne les *couleurs secondaires* qui sont les couleurs du mode CMJ : la combinaison du rouge et du vert donne du jaune, le vert et le bleu donnent du cyan (bleu clair), le bleu et le rouge donnent du magenta (violet). Ne pas confondre les couleurs secondaires avec les *couleurs complémentaires* qui sont diamétralement opposées aux couleurs primaires dans le cercle chromatique :

Figure 17.3: Colorcircle

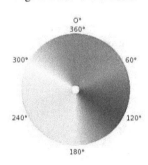

Mixing a primary color with its complementary color gives gray (a neutral color).

It is important to know what happens when you are dealing with colors in GIMP. The most important rule to remember is that decreasing the intensity of a primary color results in increasing the intensity of the complementary color (and vice versa). This is because when you decrease the value of a channel, for instance Green, you automatically increase the relative importance of the other two, here Red and Blue. The combination of these two channels gives the secondary color, Magenta, which is the complementary color of Green.

Exercise : You can check this out. Create a new image with only a white background (255R+255G+255B). Open the Tools → Color Tools → Levels dialog and select the Red channel. If necessary, check the preview box. Move the white slider to the left to decrease the Red value. You will notice that the background of your image gets closer and closer to Cyan. Now, decrease the Blue channel: only the Green will remain. For practice, go backwards, add a color and try to guess what hue will appear.

The Color Picker tool lets you find out the RGB values of a pixel and the hextriplet for the color.

S

Sample Merge

Sample Merged is an option you can set when you use the Bucket Fill tool, the Color Picker tool and various selection tools. It is useful when you are working on an image with several layers and the active layer is either semi-transparent or has a Layer Mode which is not set to Normal. When you check the Sample Merged option, the color which is used for the operation is the composite color of all the visible layers. When the Sample Merged option is not checked, the color used is the color of the active layer itself.

Saturation

This term refers to color purity. Imagine you add pigment to white paint. Saturation varies from 0 (white, fully toned down, fully diluted) to 100 (pure color).

Supersampling

Supersampling is a more sophisticated antialiasing technique, that is, a method of reducing jagged and stair-stepped edges along a slanted or curved line. Samples are taken at several locations *within* each pixel, not just at the center, and an average color is calculated. This is done by rendering the image at a much higher resolution than the one being displayed and then shrinking it to the desired size, using the extra pixels for calculation. The result is a smoother transition from one line of pixels to another along the edges of objects.

The quality of the result depends on the number of samples. Supersampling is often performed at a range of $2\times$ to $16\times$ the original size. It greatly increases the amount of time needed to draw the image and also the amount of space needed to store the image in memory.

One way to reduce the space and time requirement is to use Adaptive Supersampling. This method takes advantage of the fact that very few pixels are actually on an object boundary, so only those pixels need to be supersampled. At first, only a few samples are taken within a pixel. If the colors are very similar to each other, only those samples are used to calculate the final color. If not, more samples are used. This means that the higher number of samples is calculated only where necessary, which improves performance.

SVG

SVG stands for Scalable Vector Graphics. It a format for two-dimensional vector graphics, both static and animated. You can export GIMP paths to SVG and you can import SVG documents into GIMP from a vector graphic software. See [WKPD-SVG] for more details.

T

TGA

TGA (TARGA Image File) is a file format which supports 8, 16, 24 or 32 bits per pixel and optional RLE compression. It was originally developed by the Truevision company. 'TGA' stands for Truevision Graphics Adapter and 'TARGA' stands for Truevision Advanced Raster Graphics Adapter.

TIFF

TIFF (Tagged Image File Format) is a file format which was developed primarily for scanned raster graphics for color separation. Six different encoding routines are supported, each with one of three different image modes: black and white, grayscale and color. Uncompressed TIFF images may be 1, 4, 8 or 24 bits per pixel. TIFF images compressed using the LZW algorithm may be 6, 8 or 24 bits per pixel. Besides Postscript format, TIFF is one of the most important formats for preliminary stages of printing. It is a high quality file format, which is perfect for images you want to import to other programs like FrameMaker or CorelDRAW.

Tile

A Tile is a part of an image which GIMP currently has open. In order to avoid having to store an entire image in memory at the same time, GIMP divides it into smaller pieces. A tile is usually a square of 64 x 64 pixels, although tiles at the edges of an image may be smaller than that.

At any time, a tile may be in main memory, in the tile cache in RAM, or on disk. Tiles which are currently being worked on are in main memory. Tiles which have been used recently are in RAM. When the tile cache in RAM is full, tiles which have been used least recently are written to disk. GIMP can retrieve the tiles from RAM or disk when they are needed.

Do not confuse these tiles with those in the Tile Filter

U

URI

A Uniform Resource Identifier (URI) is a string of characters that serves to identify an abstract or a physical resource. URIs are used for the identification of resources in the Internet (such as web pages, miscellaneous files, calling up web services, and for receivers of e-mail) and they are especially used in the Worldwide Web.

URL

URLs (Uniform Resource Locators) are one type of Uniform Resource Identifiers (URIs). URLs identify a resource by its primary access mechanism (commonly http or ftp) and the location of the resource in the computer network. The name of the URI scheme is therefore generally derived from the network protocol used for it. Examples of network protocols are http, ftp and mailto.

Since URLs are the first and most common kinds of URIs, the terms are often used synonymously.

V

Value

This term often refers to the light intensity, the luminosity of a color. It varies from 0 (black) to 100 (full light).

X

XCF

XCF is a file format which is special because it is GIMP's native file format: that is, it was designed specifically to store all of the data that goes to make up a GIMP image. Because of this, XCF files may be quite complicated, and there are few programs other than GIMP that can read them.

When an image is stored as an XCF file, the file encodes nearly everything there is to know about the image: the pixel data for each of the layers, the current selection, additional channels if there are any, paths if there are any, and guides. The most important thing that is *not* saved in an XCF file is the undo history.

The pixel data in an XCF file is represented in a lossless compressed form: the image byte blocks are compressed using the lossless RLE algorithm. This means that no matter how many times you load and save an image using this format, not a single pixel or other image data is lost or modified because of this format. XCF files can become very large, however GIMP allows you to compress the files themselves, using either the gzip or bzip2 compression methods, both of which are fast, efficient, and freely available. Compressing an XCF file will often shrink it by a factor of 10 or more.

The GIMP developers have made a great effort to keep the XCF file format compatible across versions. If you create a file using GIMP 2.0, it ought to be possible to open the file in GIMP 1.2. However, some of the information in the file may not be usable: for example, GIMP 2.0 has a much more sophisticated way of handling text than GIMP 1.2, so a text layer from a GIMP 2.0 XCF file will appear as an ordinary image layer if the file is opened in GIMP 1.2.

Y

YCbCr

YCbCr is a color model which was developed for the PAL television standard as a simple modification to the YUV color model. In the meantime, it has become the CCIR-601 standard for image and video recording. For example, it is used for JPEG pictures and MPEG videos, and therefore also on DVDs, video CDs and for most other widespread digital video standards. Note that a color model is still not a color space, since it doesn't determine which colors are actually meant by 'red', 'green' and 'blue'. For a color space, there must still be a reference to a specific absolute color value.

There are color models which do not express a color by the additive basic colors, red, green and blue (RGB), but by other properties, for example, the brightness-color model. Here, the criteria are the basic brightness of the colors (from black, through gray, to white), the colors with the largest portion (red, orange, yellow, green, blue, violet, or other pure colors that lie between them) and the saturation of the colors ('gaudy' to pale). This color model is based on the ability of the eye to recognize small differences in luminosity better than small color differences, and to recognize those better than small differences in saturation. That makes gray text written on a black background easy to read, but blue text on a red background very hard to read, even with the same basic brightness. Such color models are called brightness-color models.

The YCbCr model is a slight adaptation of such a brightness-color model. An RBG color value is divided into a basic brightness, Y, and two components, Cb and Cr, where Cb is a measurement of the deviation from gray in the blue direction, or if it is less that 0.5, in the direction of yellow. Cr is the corresponding measurement for the difference in the direction of red or turquoise. This representation uses the peculiarity of the eye of being especially sensitive to green light. That is why most of the information about the proportion of green is in the basic brightness, Y, an only the deviations for the red and blue portions need to be represented. The Y values have twice the resolution of the other two values, Cb and Cr, in most practical applications, such as on DVDs.

YUV

YUV is a color model which uses two components to represent the color information, luma (the strength of the light per area) and the chrominance, or proportion of color (chroma), where the chrominance again consists of two components. The development of the YUV color model also goes back to the development of color television (PAL), where ways were sought for transmitting the color information along with the black-and-white signal, in order to achieve backwards compatibility with old black and white televisions without having to increase the available transmission bandwidth. From the YUV color model of the analog television techiques, the YCrCb color model was developed, which is used for most kinds of digital image and video compression. Erroneously, the YUV color model is also often spoken about in those fields, although the YCbCr model is actually used. This often causes confusion.

For the calculation of the luma signals, the underlying RGB data is first adjusted with the gamma value of the output device, and an R'G'B' signal is obtained. The three individual components are added together with different weights, to form the brightness information, which also functions as the VBS signal (Video Baseband Signal, the black-and-white signal) for the old black and white televisions.

Y=R+G+B

The exact calculation is more complicated, however, since some aspects of the color perception of the human eye have to be taken into account. For example, green is perceived to be lighter than red, and this is perceived to be lighter than blue. Furthermore, in some systems gamma correction of the basic color is first performed.

The chrominance signals, and the color difference signals also, contain the color information. They are formed by the difference of blue minus luma or red minus luma.

U=B-Y

V=R-Y

From the three generated components, Y, U and V, the individual color proportions of the basic color can be calculated again later:

Y + U = Y + (B - Y) = Y - Y + B = B

Y + V = Y + (R - Y) = Y - Y + R = R

Y - B - R = (R + G + B) - B - R = G

Furthermore, because of the structure of the retina of the human eye, it turns out that the brightness information is perceived at a higher resolution than the color, so that many formats based on the YUV color model compress the chrominance to save bandwidth during transmission.

Chapter 18

Bibliography

18.1 Books

[APRESS00]   Akkana Peck, *Beginning GIMP: From Novice to Professional*, Copyright © 2006 Apress Inc., Apress Inc, www.apress.com, ISBN 1-59059-587-4, http://gimpbook.com/ .

[Bunks00]   Carey Bunks, *Grokking the Gimp*, Copyright © 2000 New Riders Publishing, New Riders Publishing, www.newriders.com , ISBN 0-7357-0924-6, http://gimp-savvy.com/BOOK .

[FOLEY01]   Foley and van Dam, et al, *Computer Graphics, Principles and Practice*, Copyright © 1990 Addison Wesley, Addison Wesley, .

18.2 Online resources

[APOD01]   *Astronomy Picture of the Day (today)*, http://antwrp.gsfc.nasa.gov/apod/astropix.html .

[APOD02]   *Astronomy Picture of the Day - The Hubble Ultra Deep Field (2004 March 9)* , http://antwrp.gsfc.nasa.gov/-apod/ap040309.html .

[APOD03]   *Astronomy Picture of the Day - M51: Cosmic Whirlpool (2002 July 10)* , http://antwrp.gsfc.nasa.gov/apod/-ap020710.html .

[APOD04]   *Astronomy Picture of the Day - Saturn: Lord of the Rings (2002 February 15)* , http://antwrp.gsfc.nasa.gov/-apod/ap020215.html .

[APOD05]   *Astronomy Picture of the Day - NGC 6369: The Little Ghost Nebula (2002 November 8)* , http://antwrp.gsfc.nasa.gov/apod/ap021108.html .

[APOD06]   *Astronomy Picture of the Day - Disorder in Stephan's Quintet (2000 November 13)* , http://antwrp.gsfc.nasa.gov/apod/ap001113.html .

[APOD07]   *Astronomy Picture of the Day - The Sharpest View of the Sun (2002 November 14)* , http://antwrp.gsfc.nasa.gov/apod/ap021114.html .

[BACH04]   Michael Bach, *Face in blocks*, Copyright © 2004 Michael Bach, http://www.michaelbach.de/ot/fcs_mosaic/ .

[BUGZILLA-GIMP] *Bugzilla-GIMP*, http://bugzilla.gnome.org/browse.cgi?product=GIMP .

[DARWINORTS] *Darwin Ports Package Manager for OS X*, http://darwinports.org .

[FDL-TRANSLATION] *Inofficial translation of the GNU Free Documentation License*

[FINK]   *Fink Package Manager for OS X*, http://fink.sf.net .

[FREETYPE] *Freetype 2 home page*, http://www.freetype.org/freetype2/index.html .

[GHOSTSCRIPT] *Ghostscript project page on Sourceforge.net*, http://sourceforge.net/projects/ghostscript .

[GIMP] *GIMP - The Gnu Image Manipulation Program*, http://gimp.org .

[GIMP-DEV] *GIMP Development*, http://developer.gimp.org .

[GIMP-DEV-PLUGIN] *GIMP Plugin Development*, http://developer.gimp.org/plug-ins.html .

[GIMP-DOCS] *GIMP Documentation project page*, http://docs.gimp.org/en .

[GIMP-FONTS] *Fonts in GIMP 2.0*, http://gimp.org/unix/fonts.html .

[GIMP-REGISTRY] *GIMP-Plugin Registry*, http://registry.gimp.org .

[GIMP-WIKI01] *GIMP-Wiki - How to compile for Windows*, http://wiki.gimp.org/gimp/HowToCompileGimp/-MicrosoftWindows .

[GQVIEW] *Homepage of GQview, an image browser*, http://gqview.sourceforge.net .

[GROKKING01] *Grokking the GIMP* , http://gimp-savvy.com/BOOK/index.html .

[GROKKING02] *Grokking the GIMP (9.2 Clickable Image Maps)* , http://gimp-savvy.com/BOOK/index.html?node81.html .

[GTHUMB] *gThumb - An Image Viewer and Browser for the GNOME Desktop* , http://gthumb.sourceforge.net .

[GUNTHER04] Gunther Dale, *Making shapes in GIMP*, Copyright © 2004 Dale (Gunther), http://gug.sunsite.dk/tutorials/-gunther1 .

[INKSCAPE] *Inkscape is an Open Source vector graphics editor*, http://www.inkscape.org .

[MSKB-294714] *Microsoft Microsoft Knowledge Base Article 294714*, http://support.microsoft.com/kb/294714 .

[OPENCLIPART-GRADIENT] *Open Clipart - Gradients*, http://openclipart.org/ .

[PLUGIN-EXIF] *GIMP-Plugin Exif Browser* , http://registry.gimp.org/plugin?id=4153 ; .

[PLUGIN-FLAMES] *GIMP-Plugin Flames*, http://draves.org/gimp/flame.html ; http://flam3.com/ .

[PLUGIN-PLASMA2] *GIMP-Plugin Plasma2 at the Registry*, http://registry.gimp.org/plugin?id=501 .

[PLUGIN-REDEYE] *A plugin to quickly remove "redeye" caused by camera flash*, http://registry.gimp.org/plugin?id=4212 .

[PLUGIN-RESYNTH] *Resynthesizer is a Gimp plug-in for texture synthesis*, http://www.logarithmic.net/pfh/resynthesizer .

[PLUGIN-SEPARATE] *A plugin providing rudimentary CMYK support for The GIMP*, http://www.blackfiveservices.co.uk/-separate.shtml .

[SCRIBUS] *Scribus :: Open Source Desktop Publishing*, http://www.scribus.net/ .

[TUT01] Seth Burgess, *Tutorial: How to draw straight lines*, Copyright © 2002 Seth Burgess, http://www.gimp.org/-tutorials/Straight_Line .

[TUT02] Carol Spears, *Tutorial: GIMPLite Quickies*, Copyright © 2004 Carol Spears, http://next.gimp.org/tutorials/-Lite_Quickies/ .

[WIKIPEDIA] Wikipedia Foundation, *Wikipedia*, Copyright © 2004 Wikipedia Foundation Inc., http://www.wikipedia.com .

[WKPD-CMYK] *Wikipedia - CMYK* , http://en.wikipedia.org/wiki/CMYK .

[WKPD-EXIF] *Wikipedia - EXIF*, http://en.wikipedia.org/wiki/EXIF .

[WKPD-GAMUT] *Wikipedia - Gamut*, http://en.wikipedia.org/wiki/Gamut .

[WKPD-GNU] *Wikipedia - GNU*, http://en.wikipedia.org/wiki/GNU .

[WKPD-ICC] *Wikipedia - ICC Profile* , http://en.wikipedia.org/wiki/ICC_Profile .

[WKPD-LZW] *Wikipedia - LZW*, http://en.wikipedia.org/wiki/LZW .

[WKPD-PACKBITS] *Wikipedia - PackBits*, http://en.wikipedia.org/wiki/PackBits .

[WKPD-SVG] , http://en.wikipedia.org/wiki/SVG .

[XNVIEW] *XnView*, http://perso.orange.fr/pierre.g/xnview/enhome.html .

Appendix A

GIMP History

A.1   The Very Beginning

According to Peter Mattis and Spencer Kimball, the original creators of GIMP, in their announcement of GIMP 0.54:

The GIMP arose from the ashes of a hideously crafted CS164 (compilers) class project. The setting: early morning. We were both weary from lack of sleep and the terrible strain of programming a compiler in LISP. The limits of our patience had long been exceeded, and yet still the dam held.

And then it happened. Common LISP messily dumped core when it could not allocate the 17 MB it needed to generate a parser for a simple grammar using yacc. An unbelieving moment passed, there was one shared look of disgust, and then our project was vapor. We had to write something... *ANYTHING* ... useful. Something in C. Something that did not rely on nested lists to represent a bitmap. Thus, the GIMP was born.

Like the phoenix, glorious, new life sprung out of the burnt remnants of LISP and yacc. Ideas went flying, decisions were made, the GIMP began to take form.

An image manipulation program was the consensus. A program that would at the very least lessen the necessity of using commercial software under 'Windoze' or on the 'Macintoy'. A program that would provide the features missing from the other X painting and imaging tools. A program that would help maintain the long tradition of excellent and free UNIX applications.

Six months later, we've reached an early beta stage. We want to release now to start working on compatibility issues and cross-platform stability. Also, we feel now that the program is actually usable and would like to see other interested programmers developing plug-ins and various file format support.

A.2   The Early Days of GIMP

Version 0.54 Version 0.54 was released in February 1996, and had a major impact as the first truly professional free image manipulation program. This was the first free program that could compete with the big commercial image manipulation programs.

Version 0.54 was a beta release, but it was so stable that you could use it for daily work. However, one of the major drawbacks of 0.54 was that the toolkit (the slidebars, menus, dialog boxes, etc.) was built on Motif, a commercial toolkit. This was a big drawback for systems like 'Linux', because you had to buy Motif if you wanted to use the faster, dynamically linked GIMP. Many developers were also students running Linux, who could not afford to buy Motif.

Version 0.60 When 0.60 was released in July 1996, it had been under S and P (Spencer and Peter) development for four months. Main programming advantages were the new toolkits, GTK (GIMP Toolkit) and gdk (GIMP Drawing Kit), which eliminated the reliance on Motif. For the graphic artist, 0.60 was full of new features like: basic layers; improved painting tools (sub-pixel sampling, brush spacing); a better airbrush; paint modes; etc.

Version 0.60 was only a developer's release, and was not intended for widespread use. It served as a workbench for 0.99 and the final 1.0 version, so functions and enhancement could be tested and dropped or changed. You can look at 0.60 as the alpha version of 0.99.

Version 0.99 In February 1997, 0.99 came on the scene. Together with other developers, S and P had made several changes to GIMP and added even more features. The main difference was the new API (Application Programming Interface) and the 'PDB', which made it possible to write scripts; Script-Fus (or macros) could now automate things that you would normally do by hand. GTK/gdk had also changed and was now called GTK+. In addition, 0.99 used a new form of tile-based memory handling that made it possible to load huge images into GIMP (loading a 100 MB image into GIMP is no problem). Version 0.99 also introduced a new native GIMP file format called XCF.

The new API made it really easy to write extensions and plug-ins for GIMP. Several new plug-ins and extensions emerged to make GIMP even more useful (such as SANE, which enables scanning directly into GIMP).

In the summer of 1997, GIMP had reached version 0.99.10, and S and P had to drop most of their support since they had graduated and begun jobs. However, the other developers of GIMP continued under the orchestration of Federico Mena to make GIMP ready for prime time.

GTK+ was separated from GIMP in September 1997. GTK+ had been recognized as an excellent toolkit, and other developers began using it to build their own applications.

GIMP went into feature freeze in October 1997. This meant that no new features would be added to the GIMP core libraries and program. GUM (GIMP Users Manual) version 0.5 was also released early in October 1997. The developing work continued to make GIMP stable and ready for version 1.0.

A.3 The One to Change the World

Version 1.0 GIMP version 1.0 was released on June 5, 1998. Finally, GIMP was considered stable enough to warrant a world-wide announcement and professional use.

Version 1.2 GIMP version 1.2.0 was released on December 25, 2000. Compared to the version 1.0, it included mostly fixes and improvements of the user interface.

A.4 New in GIMP 2

Version 2.0 First, a statistic: the GIMP code base contains about 230,000 lines of C code, and most of these lines were rewritten in the evolution from 1.2 to 2.0. From the user's point of view, however, GIMP 2 is fundamentally similar to GIMP 1; the features are similar enough that GIMP 1 users won't be lost. As part of the restructuring work, the developers cleaned up the code greatly, an investment that, while not directly visible to the user, will ease maintenance and make future additions less painful. Thus, the GIMP 2 code base is significantly better organized and more maintainable than was the case for GIMP 1.2.

Basic tools The basic tools in GIMP 2 are not very different from their predecessors in GIMP 1. The 'Select Regions by Color' tool is now shown in the GIMP toolbox, but was already included in GIMP 1 as a menu option in the Select menu. The Transform tool has been divided into several specialized tools: Rotation, Scale, Shearing and Perspective. Color operations are now associated with layers in the menu Layer → Colors, but this is merely a cleanup: they were already present in the Image menu (illogically, since they are layer operations). Thus no completely new tools appear in this release, but two of the tools have been totally revamped compared to the older versions: the Text tool and the Path tool. More on this below.

The user interface for tools has also changed significantly. The 'Tool Options' dialog box was modified to not resize itself when a new tool is chosen. Most users felt that the window changing size when a new tool was selected was annoying. Now, by default the 'Tool Options' dialog is constantly open and docked under the toolbox, where it can easily be found.

Tool options The 'Tool Options' for many tools have new possibilities that weren't available in GIMP 1. Without being exhaustive, here are the most noticeable improvements.

All selection tools now have mode buttons: Replace, Add, Subtract and Intersect. In GIMP 1 the only way to change the selection mode was to use the **Ctrl** or **Shift** buttons, which could get very confusing because those buttons also had other functions. For example, pressing and holding the **Shift** key while using the Rectangle selection tool forces the rectangle to be a square. Thus, to add a square selection you would first press **Shift**, then click the mouse, then release **Shift**, then press **Shift** again, then sweep out the selection with the mouse, then release **Shift**. It can now be done more easily.

For transformation tools, buttons now control which object (layer, selection or path) is affected by the transformation. You can for example transform a rectangular selection to various quadrilateral shapes. Path transformation in particular is now easier than it was before.

'Fade out' and 'Paint Using Gradient' are now available for all drawing tools. In fact, all drawing tools now have their own individual brush, gradient and pattern settings, in contrast to GIMP 1 where there was a single global setting that applied to all drawing tools. Now you can select different brushes for the Pencil and the Paint Brush, or different patterns for the Clone and Fill tools. You can change these setting by using your mouse wheel over the relevant resource button (this is most useful for quickly and easily choosing a brush).

User Interface The most visible changes in GIMP 2 concern the user interface. GIMP now uses the GTK2+ graphical toolkit in place of GTK+. One of the nice features brought by the new libraries is dockable dialogs, and tab navigation between dialogs docked in the same window — a feature present in several popular web browsers. GIMP 1 was famous for opening dialogs anywhere on your screen; GIMP 2 can be told to use fixed boxes. Dialogs now include a little tab-customization menu, which provides maximum flexibility in organizing your workspace.

The Image window has some interesting new features. These are not necessarily activated by default, but they can be checked as options in the Preferences → Interface → Image Windows menu. 'Show Brush Outline', for example, allows you to see the outline of the brush when using drawing tools. In the 'Appearance' sub-section, you can toggle whether a menu bar is present at the top of image windows. You can set an option to work with the new fullscreen mode. Viewing options are also available from all image windows using right click to bring up the menu, then selecting 'View'. The so-called 'image' menu is also available by clicking on a little triangle in the top left corner of the drawing space. The setting you choose in the 'Preferences' dialog is used as the default value, and options you set from an image are used only for that image. (You can also toggle fullscreen mode by using the **F11** key; the **Esc** key also exits fullscreen mode).

GIMP 2 features keyboard accelerators to ease menu access. If you find that navigating through menus using your mouse is onerous, the solution may be to use the keyboard. For example, if the menu bar is present, to create a new image just hit Alt-F-N. Without the menu bar, hit Shift-F10 to open the top-left menu, and use direction keys or **F** then **N** to create the new image. Keyboard accelerators are different from shortcuts: accelerators are useful to navigate through menus, whereas shortcuts call a specific menu item directly. For example, Ctrl-N is a shortcut, and the quickest way to open a new image.

To ease access to your most commonly used menu items, the GIMP has provided dynamic shortcuts for many years. When a menu is open, you can hover over the desired menu item and hold down your shortcut combination. This feature is still present, but is deactivated by default in the GIMP 2.0, to avoid accidental re-assigning of existing shortcuts.

The GIMP also ships with a number of sets of key-bindings for its menus. If you would like to replace the default GIMP keybindings by Photoshop bindings, for example, you can move the file `menurc` in your user data directory to `oldmenurc`, rename `ps-menurc` to `menurc` and restart GIMP.

Handling Tabs and Docks The GIMP 2.0 introduces a system of tabbed dialogs to allow you to make your workspace look the way you want it to be. Almost all dialogs can be dragged to another dialog window and dropped to make a tabbed dialog set.

Furthermore, at the bottom of each dialog, there is a dockable area: drag and drop tabs here to attach dialogs beneath the bottom tab group.

Scripting 'Python-fu' is now the standard external scripting interface for GIMP 2. This means that you can now use GIMP functions in Python scripts, or conversely use Python to write GIMP plug-ins. Python is relatively easy to understand even for a beginner, especially in comparison to the Lisp-like Scheme language used for Script-Fu in GIMP 1. The Python bindings are augmented by a set of classes for common operations, so you are not forced to search through the complete GIMP Procedural Database in order to carry out basic operations. Moreover, Python has integrated development environments and a gigantic library, and runs not only on Linux but also on Microsoft Windows and Apples Mac OS X. The biggest drawback, for GIMP 2.0, is that the standard user interface offered in Python-fu does not use the complete power of the Python language. The interface is currently designed to support simple scripts, but a more sophisticated version is a goal of future development.

GIMP-Perl is no longer distributed with the standard GIMP 2 distribution, but is available as a separate package. Currently, GIMP-Perl is supported only on Unix-like operating systems. It includes both a simple scripting language, and the ability to code more polished interfaces using the Gtk2 perl module. Direct pixel manipulation is available through the use of PDL.

Script-Fu, based on 'Scheme', has the same drawbacks as before: not intuitive, hard to use and lacking a real development environment. It does, however, have one major advantage compared to Python-fu: Script-Fu scripts are directly interpreted by GIMP and do not require any additional software installation. Python-fu requires that you install a package for the Python language.

The Text Tool The big problem with the standard text tool in GIMP 1 was that text could not be modified after it was rendered. If you wanted to change anything about the text, all you could do was 'undo' and try again (if you were lucky enough to have sufficient undo history available, and then of course you would also undo any other work you had done in the meantime). In GIMP 1.2 there was also a 'dynamic text' plug-in that allowed you to create special text layers and keep them around indefinitely, in a modifiable form, but it was buggy and awkward to use. The second generation Text tool is an enhanced combination of the old Text tool and the Dynamic Text plugin. Now all options are available in the 'Tool Options': font, font size, text color, justify, antialiasing, indent, spacing. To create a new text item, click in the image and a little editor pops up. Text appears on the image while you are editing (and carriage returns are handled properly!). A new dedicated layer is created; this layer resizes dynamically to match the text you key in. You can import plain text from a file, and you can even do things like writing from right to left in Arabic. If you select a text layer, clicking on it opens the editor, and you can then modify your text.

The Path Tool The second generation Path tool has a completely new interface. The first major difference you notice is that paths are no longer required to be closed. A path can be made up of a number of disjoint curve segments. The next major difference is that now the path tool has three different modes, Design, Edit and Move.

In Design mode, you can create a path, add nodes to an existing path and modify the shape of a curve either by dragging edges of the curve or dragging the 'handles' of a node.

In Edit mode, you can add nodes in the middle of curve edges, and remove nodes or edges, as well as change the shape of the curve. You can also connect two path components.

The third mode, Move, is, as you might expect, used to move path components. If your path has several components, you can move each path component separately. To move all components at once, use the **Shift** key.

Two other path-related features are new in the GIMP 2.0. The GIMP can not only import an SVG image as a raster image, but can also keep SVG paths intact as GIMP paths. This means that the GIMP is now more able than ever to complement your favorite vector drawing tool. The other feature which has made the path tool much better is the introduction of vector-based stroking. In previous versions, stroking paths and selections was a matter of drawing a brush-stroke along the path. This mode is still available, but it is now possible to stroke a curve accurately, using the vector library libart.

Other improvements Some other improvements in brief:

- Higher-quality antialiasing in some places — most notibly in the Text tool.
- Icons and menus are skinnable. You can create your own icon set and apply it to the toolbox using the Preference → Interface menu option. A theme called 'small' is included with the standard distribution.
- An image can be saved as a template and used to create new images.
- There are four new combination modes for layers that lie one on top of another within an image: 'Hard Light', 'Soft Light', 'Grain Extract' and 'Grain Merge'.
- If there is an active selection, you can crop the image directly to the selection size using image menu Image → Crop.
- As well as being able to create guides, there's now a grid functionality in GIMP. It is complementary to the guides functionality and makes it easier to position objects so that they align perfectly.
- The Layers dialog is more coherent, in that there are no more hidden functions accessed only with right click on the miniature image of the layer that appears there. You can now handle layer operations directly from the image menu: Layer Mask, Transparency, Transformation and Layer Color operations are directly in the Layer submenu.
- Color display filters are now available from the image menu View → Display Filters. Using them, you can simulate different gamma values, different contrasts, or even color deficient vision, without altering your original image. This actually has been a feature of the GIMP developer versions for a long time, but it has never been stable enough to appear in a stable version of the GIMP before.
- The color selection dialog has a new CMYK mode, associated with the printer icon.
- Data stored in EXIF tags by digital cameras are now handled in read and write mode for JPEG files.
- MNG animations are now supported. The MNG file format can be considered as animated PNG. It has all the advantages of PNG over GIF, such as more colors, 256 levels of transparency, and perhaps most importantly, lack of patent encumbrance. The format is a web standard and all recent popular web browsers support it.
- The GIMP Animation package now does onion-skinning, a bluescreen feature was added as well as audio support.
- A channel mixer filter, previously available from the web as an add-on, appears in Filters → Colors.

Appendix B

Reporting Bugs and Requesting Enhancements

Sad to say, no version of GIMP has yet been absolutely perfect. Even sadder, it is likely that no version ever will be. In spite of all efforts to make everything work, a program as complicated as GIMP is bound to screw things up occasionally, or even crash.

But the fact that bugs are unavoidable does not mean that they should be passively accepted. If you find a bug in GIMP, the developers would like to know about it so they can at least try to fix it.

Suppose, then, that you have found a bug, or at least think you have: you try to do something, and the results are not what you expect. What should you do? How should you report it?

Tip
The procedure for making an *enhancement request*–that is, for asking the developers to add a missing feature–is nearly the same as the procedure for reporting a bug. The only thing you do differently is to mark the report as an 'enhancement' at the appropriate stage, as described below.

In common with many other free software projects, GIMP uses a bug-reporting mechanism called *Bugzilla*. This is a very powerful web-based system, capable of managing thousands of bug reports without losing track. In fact, GIMP shares its Bugzilla database with the entire Gnome project. At the time this is being written, Gnome Bugzilla contains 148632 bug reports–no, make that 148633.

B.1   Making sure it's a Bug

The first thing you should do, before reporting a bug, is to make an effort to verify that what you are seeing really *is* a bug. It is hard to give a method for doing this that applies to all situations, but reading the documentation will often be useful, and discussing the question on IRC or a mailing list may also be quite helpful. If you are seeing a *crash*, as opposed to mere misbehavior, the odds that it is a true bug are pretty high: well written software programs are not designed to crash under *any* circumstances. In any case, if you have made an conscientious effort to decide whether it is really a bug, and at the end still aren't sure, then please go ahead and report it: the worst that can happen is that you will waste a bit of time for the development team.

Note
Actually there are a few things that are known to cause GIMP to crash but have turned out to be too inconvenient to be worth fixing. One of them is asking GIMP to do something that requires vast amounts of memory, such as creating an image one million pixels on a side.

You should also make sure that you are using an up-to-date version of GIMP: reporting bugs that have already been fixed is just a waste of everybody's time. (GIMP 1 is no longer maintained, so if you use it and find bugs, either upgrade to GIMP 2 or live with them.) Particularly if you are using the development version of GIMP, make sure that you can see the bug in the latest release before filing a report.

If after due consideration you still think you have a legitimate bug report or enhancement request, the next step is to go to GIMP's bugzilla query page (http://bugzilla.gnome.org/query.cgi), and try to see whether somebody else has already reported the same thing. The query page allows you to search the bug database in a variety of ways. Unfortunately this page is a bit more complicated to use than it really ought to be, but here is basically what you should do:

Summary: Set this to 'contains any of the words/strings'.

(the adjoining entry area) Give one or more words that somebody would be likely to use in writing a one-sentence summary of a bug similar to yours. For example, if the problem is that zooming too much causes GIMP to crash, the word 'zoom' would be good.

Product: Set this to 'GIMP'

Component:, Version:, Target: Don't do anything for these.

Text information: For now, leave this alone. If your search does not turn up anything, it might be worth entering your search terms in the 'comment' area here, but this often turns out to give you either great masses of stuff or nothing.

Status: This field encodes the status of a bug report: whether it is still open, has been resolved, etc. You want to see all relevant bug reports, regardless of status, so you should hold down the mouse and sweep it across all entries. Leaving it alone will not work.

When you have set these things up, click on the 'Search' button at either the top or bottom; they both do the same thing. The result is either a list of bug reports–hopefully not too long–or a message saying 'Zarro boogs found'. If you don't find a related bug report by doing this, it may be worth trying another search with different terms. If in spite of your best efforts, you file a bug report and it ends up being resolved as 'Duplicate', don't be too upset: it has happened repeatedly to the author of this documentation, who works with GIMP Bugzilla nearly every day.

B.2 Reporting the Bug

Okay, so you have done everything you could to make sure, and you still think it's probably a bug. You should then go ahead and file a bug report. To do this, begin by going to http://bugzilla.gnome.org/enter_bug.cgi, and go down the page until you can select the component 'GIMP'.

 Note
The first time you file a bug report, you will be asked to create a Bugzilla account. The process is easy and painless, and you probably won't even get any spam as a result.

This takes you to the bug report form, which you should fill out as follows. Note that most of the information you enter can be changed later by the developers if you get it wrong, so try to get it right but don't be obsessive about it.

Summary Give a one-sentence summary that is descriptive enough so that somebody searching for similar bugs would find your bug report on the basis of the words this summary contains.

Steps to reproduce the bug Follow the directions. Be as specific as you can, and include all information that you think might possibly be relevant. The classic totally useless bug report is, 'GIMP crashes. This program sucks'. There is no hope that the developers can solve a problem if they can't tell what it is. If at all possible, give a procedure that will reliably reproduce the buggy behavior, and give it in enough detail so that a moron could follow it.

Component Set this to the part of GIMP that the bug affects. You have to pick something here, but if you aren't sure, make a guess and don't worry about it.

Severity In most cases you should either leave this as 'Normal' or set it to 'Enhancement', if it is an enhancement request rather than a malfunction. The maintainers will adjust the severity if they think it is warranted.

Priority In most cases you should leave this at 'Normal', and allow the maintainers to adjust it. Setting the priority to 'Immediate' or 'Urgent' usually just manages to annoy people.

Version Set this to the version of GIMP that you are using. Leave the Gnome version unspecified.

Operating System Set this to your OS unless you have a very good reason for thinking that the bug applies to all operating systems.

You can ignore the rest. When you have filled out all of these things, press the 'Commit' button and your bug report will be submitted. It will be assigned a number, which you may want to make note of; you will, however, be emailed any time somebody makes a comment on your bug report or otherwise alters it, so you will receive reminders in any case. You can see the current state of your bug report at any time by going to http://bugzilla.gnome.org and, at the bottom of the page, in the 'Actions:' area, entering the bug number and pressing the 'Find' button.

Sometimes it is very helpful to augment a bug report with a screenshot or some other type of data. If you need to do this, go to the web page for your bug report, click on the link 'Create a New Attachment', and follow the directions. But please don't do this unless you think the attachment is really going to be useful–and if you need to attach a screenshot, don't make it any larger than necessary. Bug reports are likely to remain on the system for years, so there is no sense in wasting memory.

B.3   What Happens to a Bug Report after you Submit it

At any time after it is submitted, a bug report has a 'Status' that describes how it is currently being handled. Here are the possible values of *Status* and what they mean:

Unconfirmed This is the initial status of a bug report, from the time it is submitted until one of the maintainers reads it and decides whether it is really a valid bug report. Sometimes the maintainers aren't sure, and in the meantime leave the status as 'Unconfirmed'. In the worst cases, a bug report can stay unconfirmed for a year or longer, but this is considered a bad thing and does not happen very often.

New This means that the bug report has been read by one of the maintainers, and is considered, for the moment at least, to be valid. It does not necessarily mean that anything is going to be done about it immediately: some bug reports, especially enhancement requests, may be perfectly valid and still go for a long time before anybody is able to deal with them. Many bugs, on the other hand, are fixed within hours of being reported.

Assigned This means that a specific person has agreed to work on the bug. It does not, this world being the kind of world that it is, mean that that person will actually *do* anything in particular, so for practical purposes this status means nearly the same thing as 'New'.

Reopened This means that the bug report was at some point considered by the maintainers to be resolved (i.e., finished), but new information came in that caused them to change their minds: most likely, a change that was intended to fix the problem did not completely work.

Needinfo This is a status you should pay particular attention to. It means that you did not supply enough information in your bug report to enable anything to be done about it. In most cases, no further action will be taken on the bug report until you supply additional information (by adding a comment). If too much time goes by without any input from you, the bug report will eventually be resolved as 'Incomplete'.

Resolved This means that the maintainers believe that they have finished dealing with the bug report. If you disagree, you can re-open it, but since you cannot force anybody to work on a bug against their will, you should have a good reason for doing so. Bugs can be resolved in a variety of ways. Here are the possible values of *Resolution* and what they mean:

> **Fixed** The bug report is considered valid, and GIMP has been changed in a way that is considered to fix it.

> **Wontfix** The maintainers agree that the bug report is valid, but it would take so much effort to fix, in relation to its importance, that it is not worth the trouble.

Duplicate This means that the same bug has already been reported by somebody else. If you see this resolution, you will also see a pointer to the earlier bug report, which will often give you a lot of useful information.

Notabug This means that the behavior described in the bug report is intentional. It may seem like a bug to you (and there may be many people who agree with you), but the program is working the way it was intended to work, and the developers don't want to change it.

NotGnome The bug report is valid, but it can't be addressed by changing GIMP. Problems in operating systems, window managers, or libaries that GIMP depends on will often be given this resolution. Sometimes the next appropriate step is to file a bug report for the software that is really at fault.

Incomplete The bug report did not contain enough information for anything to be done about it, and the reporter did not respond to requests for more information. Usually a bug report will be open for at least a month or two before it is resolved in this way.

Invalid Something is wrong with the form of the bug report: most commonly, the reporter has accidentally submitted the same bug report multiple times. (This can easily happen by mistake with some web browsers.) Bug reports that incorrectly describe how the program behaves may also be resolved as Invalid.

 Note

If you disagree with the resolution of a bug report, you are always free to add your comments to it. Any comment added to any bug report, resolved or not, causes email to be sent to the GIMP Bugzilla mailing list, so it will at least be seen by the maintainers. This does not, of course, mean that they will necessarily respond to it.

Appendix C

GNU Free Documentation License

Copyright (C) 2000,2001,2002 Free Software Foundation, Inc. 59 Temple Place, Suite 330, Boston, MA 02111-1307 USA Everyone is permitted to copy and distribute verbatim copies of this license document, but changing it is not allowed.

C.1 PREAMBLE

The purpose of this License is to make a manual, textbook, or other functional and useful document 'free' in the sense of freedom: to assure everyone the effective freedom to copy and redistribute it, with or without modifying it, either commercially or noncommercially. Secondarily, this License preserves for the author and publisher a way to get credit for their work, while not being considered responsible for modifications made by others.

This License is a kind of 'copyleft', which means that derivative works of the document must themselves be free in the same sense. It complements the GNU General Public License, which is a copyleft license designed for free software.

We have designed this License in order to use it for manuals for free software, because free software needs free documentation: a free program should come with manuals providing the same freedoms that the software does. But this License is not limited to software manuals; it can be used for any textual work, regardless of subject matter or whether it is published as a printed book. We recommend this License principally for works whose purpose is instruction or reference.

C.2 APPLICABILITY AND DEFINITIONS

This License applies to any manual or other work, in any medium, that contains a notice placed by the copyright holder saying it can be distributed under the terms of this License. Such a notice grants a world-wide, royalty-free license, unlimited in duration, to use that work under the conditions stated herein. The 'Document', below, refers to any such manual or work. Any member of the public is a licensee, and is addressed as 'you'. You accept the license if you copy, modify or distribute the work in a way requiring permission under copyright law.

A 'Modified Version' of the Document means any work containing the Document or a portion of it, either copied verbatim, or with modifications and/or translated into another language.

A 'Secondary Section' is a named appendix or a front-matter section of the Document that deals exclusively with the relationship of the publishers or authors of the Document to the Document's overall subject (or to related matters) and contains nothing that could fall directly within that overall subject. (Thus, if the Document is in part a textbook of mathematics, a Secondary Section may not explain any mathematics.) The relationship could be a matter of historical connection with the subject or with related matters, or of legal, commercial, philosophical, ethical or political position regarding them.

The 'Invariant Sections' are certain Secondary Sections whose titles are designated, as being those of Invariant Sections, in the notice that says that the Document is released under this License. If a section does not fit the above definition of Secondary then it is not allowed to be designated as Invariant. The Document may contain zero Invariant Sections. If the Document does not identify any Invariant Sections then there are none.

The 'Cover Texts' are certain short passages of text that are listed, as Front-Cover Texts or Back-Cover Texts, in the notice that says that the Document is released under this License. A Front-Cover Text may be at most 5 words, and a Back-Cover Text may be at most 25 words.

A 'Transparent' copy of the Document means a machine-readable copy, represented in a format whose specification is available to the general public, that is suitable for revising the document straightforwardly with generic text editors or (for images composed of pixels) generic paint programs or (for drawings) some widely available drawing editor, and that is suitable for input to text formatters or for automatic translation to a variety of formats suitable for input to text formatters. A copy made in an otherwise Transparent file format whose markup, or absence of markup, has been arranged to thwart or discourage subsequent modification by readers is not Transparent. An image format is not Transparent if used for any substantial amount of text. A copy that is not 'Transparent' is called 'Opaque'.

Examples of suitable formats for Transparent copies include plain ASCII without markup, Texinfo input format, LaTeX input format, SGML or XML using a publicly available DTD, and standard-conforming simple HTML, PostScript or PDF designed for human modification. Examples of transparent image formats include PNG, XCF and JPG. Opaque formats include proprietary formats that can be read and edited only by proprietary word processors, SGML or XML for which the DTD and/or processing tools are not generally available, and the machine-generated HTML, PostScript or PDF produced by some word processors for output purposes only.

The 'Title Page' means, for a printed book, the title page itself, plus such following pages as are needed to hold, legibly, the material this License requires to appear in the title page. For works in formats which do not have any title page as such, 'Title Page' means the text near the most prominent appearance of the work's title, preceding the beginning of the body of the text.

A section 'Entitled XYZ' means a named subunit of the Document whose title either is precisely XYZ or contains XYZ in parentheses following text that translates XYZ in another language. (Here XYZ stands for a specific section name mentioned below, such as 'Acknowledgements', 'Dedications', 'Endorsements', or 'History'.) To 'Preserve the Title' of such a section when you modify the Document means that it remains a section 'Entitled XYZ' according to this definition.

The Document may include Warranty Disclaimers next to the notice which states that this License applies to the Document. These Warranty Disclaimers are considered to be included by reference in this License, but only as regards disclaiming warranties: any other implication that these Warranty Disclaimers may have is void and has no effect on the meaning of this License.

C.3 VERBATIM COPYING

You may copy and distribute the Document in any medium, either commercially or noncommercially, provided that this License, the copyright notices, and the license notice saying this License applies to the Document are reproduced in all copies, and that you add no other conditions whatsoever to those of this License. You may not use technical measures to obstruct or control the reading or further copying of the copies you make or distribute. However, you may accept compensation in exchange for copies. If you distribute a large enough number of copies you must also follow the conditions in section3.

You may also lend copies, under the same conditions stated above, and you may publicly display copies.

C.4 COPYING IN QUANTITY

If you publish printed copies (or copies in media that commonly have printed covers) of the Document, numbering more than 100, and the Document's license notice requires Cover Texts, you must enclose the copies in covers that carry, clearly and legibly, all these Cover Texts: Front-Cover Texts on the front cover, and Back-Cover Texts on the back cover. Both covers must also clearly and legibly identify you as the publisher of these copies. The front cover must present the full title with all words of the title equally prominent and visible. You may add other material on the covers in addition. Copying with changes limited to the covers, as long as they preserve the title of the Document and satisfy these conditions, can be treated as verbatim copying in other respects.

If the required texts for either cover are too voluminous to fit legibly, you should put the first ones listed (as many as fit reasonably) on the actual cover, and continue the rest onto adjacent pages.

If you publish or distribute Opaque copies of the Document numbering more than 100, you must either include a machine-readable Transparent copy along with each Opaque copy, or state in or with each Opaque copy a computer-network location from which the general network-using public has access to download using public-standard network protocols a complete Transparent copy of the Document, free of added material. If you use the latter option, you must take reasonably prudent steps, when you begin distribution of Opaque copies in quantity, to ensure that this Transparent copy will remain thus accessible at the stated location until at least one year after the last time you distribute an Opaque copy (directly or through your agents or retailers) of that edition to the public.

It is requested, but not required, that you contact the authors of the Document well before redistributing any large number of copies, to give them a chance to provide you with an updated version of the Document.

C.5 MODIFICATIONS

You may copy and distribute a Modified Version of the Document under the conditions of sections 2 and 3 above, provided that you release the Modified Version under precisely this License, with the Modified Version filling the role of the Document, thus licensing distribution and modification of the Modified Version to whoever possesses a copy of it. In addition, you must do these things in the Modified Version:

A. Use in the Title Page (and on the covers, if any) a title distinct from that of the Document, and from those of previous versions (which should, if there were any, be listed in the History section of the Document). You may use the same title as a previous version if the original publisher of that version gives permission.

B. List on the Title Page, as authors, one or more persons or entities responsible for authorship of the modifications in the Modified Version, together with at least five of the principal authors of the Document (all of its principal authors, if it has fewer than five), unless they release you from this requirement.

C. State on the Title page the name of the publisher of the Modified Version, as the publisher.

D. Preserve all the copyright notices of the Document.

E. Add an appropriate copyright notice for your modifications adjacent to the other copyright notices.

F. Include, immediately after the copyright notices, a license notice giving the public permission to use the Modified Version under the terms of this License, in the form shown in the Addendum below.

G. Preserve in that license notice the full lists of Invariant Sections and required Cover Texts given in the Document's license notice.

H. Include an unaltered copy of this License.

I. Preserve the section Entitled 'History', Preserve its Title, and add to it an item stating at least the title, year, new authors, and publisher of the Modified Version as given on the Title Page. If there is no section Entitled 'History' in the Document, create one stating the title, year, authors, and publisher of the Document as given on its Title Page, then add an item describing the Modified Version as stated in the previous sentence.

J. Preserve the network location, if any, given in the Document for public access to a Transparent copy of the Document, and likewise the network locations given in the Document for previous versions it was based on. These may be placed in the 'History' section. You may omit a network location for a work that was published at least four years before the Document itself, or if the original publisher of the version it refers to gives permission.

K. For any section Entitled 'Acknowledgements' or 'Dedications', Preserve the Title of the section, and preserve in the section all the substance and tone of each of the contributor acknowledgements and/or dedications given therein.

L. Preserve all the Invariant Sections of the Document, unaltered in their text and in their titles. Section numbers or the equivalent are not considered part of the section titles.

M. Delete any section Entitled 'Endorsements'. Such a section may not be included in the Modified Version.

N. Do not retitle any existing section to be Entitled 'Endorsements' or to conflict in title with any Invariant Section.

O. Preserve any Warranty Disclaimers.

If the Modified Version includes new front-matter sections or appendices that qualify as Secondary Sections and contain no material copied from the Document, you may at your option designate some or all of these sections as invariant. To do this, add their titles to the list of Invariant Sections in the Modified Version's license notice. These titles must be distinct from any other section titles.

You may add a section Entitled 'Endorsements', provided it contains nothing but endorsements of your Modified Version by various parties—for example, statements of peer review or that the text has been approved by an organization as the authoritative definition of a standard.

You may add a passage of up to five words as a Front-Cover Text, and a passage of up to 25 words as a Back-Cover Text, to the end of the list of Cover Texts in the Modified Version. Only one passage of Front-Cover Text and one of Back-Cover Text may be added by (or through arrangements made by) any one entity. If the Document already includes a cover text for the same cover, previously added by you or by arrangement made by the same entity you are acting on behalf of, you may not add another; but you may replace the old one, on explicit permission from the previous publisher that added the old one.

The author(s) and publisher(s) of the Document do not by this License give permission to use their names for publicity for or to assert or imply endorsement of any Modified Version.

C.6 COMBINING DOCUMENTS

You may combine the Document with other documents released under this License, under the terms defined in section 4 above for modified versions, provided that you include in the combination all of the Invariant Sections of all of the original documents, unmodified, and list them all as Invariant Sections of your combined work in its license notice, and that you preserve all their Warranty Disclaimers.

The combined work need only contain one copy of this License, and multiple identical Invariant Sections may be replaced with a single copy. If there are multiple Invariant Sections with the same name but different contents, make the title of each such section unique by adding at the end of it, in parentheses, the name of the original author or publisher of that section if known, or else a unique number. Make the same adjustment to the section titles in the list of Invariant Sections in the license notice of the combined work.

In the combination, you must combine any sections Entitled 'History' in the various original documents, forming one section Entitled 'History'; likewise combine any sections Entitled 'Acknowledgements', and any sections Entitled 'Dedications'. You must delete all sections Entitled 'Endorsements'.

C.7 COLLECTIONS OF DOCUMENTS

You may make a collection consisting of the Document and other documents released under this License, and replace the individual copies of this License in the various documents with a single copy that is included in the collection, provided that you follow the rules of this License for verbatim copying of each of the documents in all other respects.

You may extract a single document from such a collection, and distribute it individually under this License, provided you insert a copy of this License into the extracted document, and follow this License in all other respects regarding verbatim copying of that document.

C.8 AGGREGATION WITH INDEPENDENT WORKS

A compilation of the Document or its derivatives with other separate and independent documents or works, in or on a volume of a storage or distribution medium, is called an 'aggregate' if the copyright resulting from the compilation is not used to limit the legal rights of the compilation's users beyond what the individual works permit. When the Document is included in an aggregate, this License does not apply to the other works in the aggregate which are not themselves derivative works of the Document.

If the Cover Text requirement of section 3 is applicable to these copies of the Document, then if the Document is less than one half of the entire aggregate, the Document's Cover Texts may be placed on covers that bracket the Document within the aggregate, or the electronic equivalent of covers if the Document is in electronic form. Otherwise they must appear on printed covers that bracket the whole aggregate.

C.9   TRANSLATION

Translation is considered a kind of modification, so you may distribute translations of the Document under the terms of section 4. Replacing Invariant Sections with translations requires special permission from their copyright holders, but you may include translations of some or all Invariant Sections in addition to the original versions of these Invariant Sections. You may include a translation of this License, and all the license notices in the Document, and any Warranty Disclaimers, provided that you also include the original English version of this License and the original versions of those notices and disclaimers. In case of a disagreement between the translation and the original version of this License or a notice or disclaimer, the original version will prevail.

If a section in the Document is Entitled 'Acknowledgements', 'Dedications', or 'History', the requirement (section 4) to Preserve its Title (section 1) will typically require changing the actual title.

C.10   TERMINATION

You may not copy, modify, sublicense, or distribute the Document except as expressly provided for under this License. Any other attempt to copy, modify, sublicense or distribute the Document is void, and will automatically terminate your rights under this License. However, parties who have received copies, or rights, from you under this License will not have their licenses terminated so long as such parties remain in full compliance.

C.11   FUTURE REVISIONS OF THIS LICENSE

The Free Software Foundation may publish new, revised versions of the GNU Free Documentation License from time to time. Such new versions will be similar in spirit to the present version, but may differ in detail to address new problems or concerns. See http://www.gnu.org/copyleft/.

Each version of the License is given a distinguishing version number. If the Document specifies that a particular numbered version of this License 'or any later version' applies to it, you have the option of following the terms and conditions either of that specified version or of any later version that has been published (not as a draft) by the Free Software Foundation. If the Document does not specify a version number of this License, you may choose any version ever published (not as a draft) by the Free Software Foundation.

C.12   ADDENDUM: How to use this License for your documents

To use this License in a document you have written, include a copy of the License in the document and put the following copyrightand license notices just after the title page:

> Copyright (c) YEAR YOUR NAME. Permission is granted to copy, distribute and/or modify this document under the terms of the GNU Free Documentation License, Version 1.2 or any later version published by the Free Software Foundation; with no Invariant Sections, no Front-Cover Texts, and no Back-Cover Texts. A copy of the license is included in the section entitled 'GNU Free Documentation License'.

If you have Invariant Sections, Front-Cover Texts and Back-Cover Texts, replace the 'with...Texts.' line with this:

> with the Invariant Sections being LIST THEIR TITLES, with the Front-Cover Texts being LIST, and with the Back-Cover Texts being LIST.

If you have Invariant Sections without Cover Texts, or some other combination of the three, merge those two alternatives to suit the situation.

If your document contains nontrivial examples of program code, we recommend releasing these examples in parallel under your choice of free software license, such as the GNU General Public License, to permit their use in free software.

Appendix D

Eeek! There is Missing Help

Sorry, but a help item is missing for the function you're looking for. You may be able to find it in the online version of the help at the GIMP docs website.

Feel free to join us and fill the gap by writing documentation for the GIMP. For more information, visit our project page on the GIMP Wiki. There is also a Mailing list available. Generally, it's a good idea to check the GIMP project page.

Appendix E

Index